LUTHER'S CORRESPONDENCE

AND OTHER

CONTEMPORARY LETTERS

Translated and Edited by
PRESERVED SMITH, Ph. D.
Fellow of Amherst College

VOLUME I
1507-1521

Wipf & Stock
PUBLISHERS
Eugene, Oregon

Wipf and Stock Publishers
199 W 8th Ave, Suite 3
Eugene, OR 97401

Luther's Correspondence and Other Contemporary Letters, Volume One
Volume 1: 1507-1521
Edited by Smith, Preserved
ISBN: 1-59752-601-0
Publication date 3/17/2006
Previously published by The Lutheran Publication Society, 1913

DEDICATED
TO
HERBERT PERCIVAL GALLINGER

"NOS TUI NON DECET IMMEMORES ET INGRATOS
ESSE PER QUEM PRIMUM COEPIT RATIONIS
LUX DE TENEBRIS SPLENDESCERE
IN CORDIBUS NOSTRIS."

PREFACE

History is now read more than ever before from the original sources. Contemporary documents give both the most vivid, and in the deepest sense, the most veracious narrative. Even when they are mistaken in point of fact, or intentionally falsified, they reveal important truths, showing what the author believed, or wanted to be believed. If they distort fact they can never belie the spirit of the times. But even objective error is far less common than might be supposed. If a man has authentic information to give, the strongest bias on his part is a matter of secondary importance. He may color facts, impute wrong motives, shade here and lighten there, but the free invention, or even suppression of important facts by strictly contemporary witnesses is almost unknown. Minor misstatements can easily be corrected; the total impression is more true to life, and therefore both more veracious and more graphic, than that which can be given by any secondary narrative, no matter how great its erudition and art.

By the great Ranke and his school the sources of history most esteemed were public documents—the treaty, the legislative act, the contract, the charter, the edict. There is now a reaction from this method. The memoir, the journal, the private letter are coming into favor again, if only as the necessary interpreters of the public act. But beyond this they are seen to convey a deeper psychological and personal meaning. The epistle, in particular, enjoys the double advantage of being written, like the public document, on the spot, and of revealing, like the memoir, the real inward attitude of an actor in the drama.

The present work aims to set before the public the history, as told by the participants and eye-witnesses themselves in all the unreserve of private correspondence, of the most momentous crisis in the annals of Europe. It is impossible here to appreciate the importance of the Reformation; I have done it, partially, elsewhere, and hope to return to it in future. Suffice it to say that the revolution which goes by this name wrought an upheaval in the political, social and religious structure of Europe and prepared the ground for our modern civilization. Every element of the movement is reflected in these letters: the return to the Bible, the revolt from ecclesiastical abuse and from papal authority, the economic and social reform, the growing nationalism and awakening subjectivism. The launching of the *Ninety-five Theses* is described and their working on the minds of men portrayed; the summons of Luther before his ecclesiastical superiors first at Heidelberg and then at Augsburg, the great debate with Eck at Leipsic, the trumpet call to spiritual emancipation in the pamphlets of 1520, the preparation of the bull of excommunication and the burning of the same, and finally, as a fitting climax, the memorable appearance of Luther before the Emperor and Diet at Worms, are all set before our eyes.

In order to present faithfully all sides of the movement I have given not only the correspondence of Luther, but the most important letters relating to him by his contemporaries. Among the writers are the Popes Leo X. and Adrian VI., the Emperors Maximilian and Charles V., and many of the Princes, Spiritual and Temporal, of Germany. Humanists and artists are among the writers: Erasmus, Hutten and Dürer. The great reformers are represented by Capito and Bucer, Œcolampadius, Zwingli and Melanchthon. Nor are the least interesting letters those of the Catholic champions, Aleander and Eck.

But the dominating personality in this work, as in the age, is Martin Luther. To many the chief value of the book will be the revelation of his inward life. His early spiritual struggles, the things by which he profited and grew, his faith, his devotion to conscience and to truth as he saw it, and his indomitable will, stand out in his unconscious autobiography. No man in history has more thoroughly represented and more completely dominated his time. And these earliest years were the most beautiful in his life; a desperate battle and a momentous victory for progress and for the right. There have been more faultless men than Luther, but there have been none who have fought harder for the good cause. Ours is an age that trusts life; that scorns a cloistered virtue, idle if stainless, but loves the warrior who rushes into the thick of the forces of evil to overthrow them, even if he is at times mistaken and now and then wrong. And in Luther we have the most active brain, the most intrepid will and the most passionate heart of his century.

It remains to say a few words about my own part in the present work. I have not included all of Luther's extant letters, but have omitted a few which were either unimportant or repetitious or which were already translated in my "Life and Letters of Martin Luther" (1911). The original of the greater part of the epistles is Latin, and may be understood to be so when not otherwise stated. Other letters from the German, English, Greek, Italian and Spanish have been included, the original language being duly stated in every case. I have not translated directly from the Italian and Spanish, but have used either the English version offered by Bergenroth and Brown in the "Calendars of State Papers," where available, or else have retranslated from the German of Kalkoff despatches relating to Luther written from the Diet of Worms. When convenient, I have, however, compared my translation with the original. Adopting Luther's own wise principle (see below, ep. no. 344), I have not tried to give a slavishly literal rendering; I trust that I have never altered the sense or the spirit of my original, but the means employed have been such as were, in my judgment and according to my powers, the best adapted to reproduce in our idiom the literary quality, flavor and effect of the document in question. The fact that in some cases, particularly in Bucer's letters, the text is uncertain and the phrasing at times ungrammatical, has given me the more justification for rather drastic treatment.

In the notes I have endeavored to give all necessary light for the comprehension of the text: explanation of allusions, corrections of mistakes, and short biographical notices of persons mentioned. The basis of my work on Luther's letters has, of course, been the edition of Enders, but with the results of thirty years' scholarship since the first volume of this was published, at my command, I have naturally been able to supplement and improve upon the work of the German editor. I have even been able to add several letters by and to Luther which escaped him.

I am proud to acknowledge the personal assistance of several distinguished scholars. The Rev. Professor Gustav Kawerau (Oberkonsistorialrat and Probst), of Berlin, has obligingly answered several questions I have put to him. Professor Gilbert Murray, LL. D., of Oxford, and Professor H. DeForrest Smith, of Amherst, have aided me in the restoration and construction of a Greek letter of Melanchthon. Professor Stanley L. Galpin, of Amherst, has interpreted for me one Spanish letter. Professor Clarence W. Eastman, of Amherst, has occasionally given me the benefit of his studies in early new high German. My wife and Miss Helen Alice Hocheimer have read large portions of the proof. In thanking these friends for such specific services, I am but expressing my obligations for the least part of what I owe them.

P. S.

AMHERST, MASSACHUSETTS, March 4, 1913.

LIST OF CORRESPONDENTS AND OF BIOGRAPHICAL NOTES

The name of Martin Luther is omitted. All other writers and receivers of letters are listed with the number of these letters opposite their names. In addition to this, the number of a letter in which a man is first mentioned is given in parentheses. On the first appearance of a man I have given a short biographical note, save in a few cases where nothing is known of him, or in cases of persons sufficiently famous not to require it.

Accolti, P. (253).
Adelmann, B. (88).
Adelmann, C., 88.
Adrian of Antwerp (37).
Adrian VI., Pope, 202, 443.
Adrian, M. (230).
Agricola, J. (150).
Agricola, R., 395.
Agrippa, H. C., 153.
Aleander, J., 318, 319, 330, 358, 359, 362, 363, 394, 396, 397, 401, 407, 416, 424, 425, 432, 437, 444, 447, 452, 453, 454, 464, 468, 473, 474, 475, 476.
Alexander, Secretary of Nassau, 423.
Alfeld, A. (254).
Alvarez, J. (192).
Amman, J. J. (338).
Amerbach, Basil, 316, 339, 384.
Amerbach, Boniface, 179, 316, 317, 332, 339, 371, 374, 384.
Amsdorf, N. v. (27), 169.
Anhalt, M. v., 193.
Anselm, T. (239).
Aquensis, P. (254).
Arcimboldi, J. A. (393).
Armstorf, P. v. (441).
Auer, J. (99).
Augsburg, Christopher v. Stadion, Bishop of (83).
Aurogallus, M. (400).
Baden, Philip, Margrave of (464).
Bamberg, George, Bishop of (328).

Bannissius, J. (393).
Basle, Christopher v. Uttenheim, Bishop of (127).
Bavaria, William, Duke of (459).
Bayer, C., 248.
Beatus Rhenanus, 57, 168, 332, 371, 374, 421, 428, 438.
Beckman, O. (27), 131.
Benedict, M. (240).
Bérauld, N., 399.
Berghes, M. de (187).
Bernhardi, B. (20).
Beroald, P. (135).
Bessler, N. (372).
Beymann, P. (219).
Biel, G. (20).
Bild, G., 81a, 103a, 247a.
Blaurer, A., 373.
Blaurer, T., 373, 398.
Bock, J. (471).
Bösschenstein, J. (103a).
Bossenstain, J. (89).
Botzheim, J. v., 398.
Bragadin, L., 238.
Brandenburg, Jerome Scultetus, Bishop of (50), 63.
Brandenburg, Joachim I., Elector of (378).
Braun, J., 1, 2.
Breisgau, John of (205).
Breitenbach, G. v. (198).
Breslau, J. v. Thurzo, Bishop of (249).
Briard, J. (245).
Briselot (187).
Bronner, J. (220).
Brück, G. (397), 434.
Brunswick-Lüneburg, Margaret v., 184.
Bucer, M., 57, 168, 219, 299, 340, 438, 441.
Bünau, G. v., 300.
Bünau, H. v., 262.
Burckhardt, F., 160.
Burckhart, P. (164).
Busch, H. v., 472.
Cæsar, J. (207).
Cajetan, Thomas de Vio, Cardinal, 73.
Calvus, F. (125).
Camerarius, J., 442.
Campeggio, L. (253), 351.
Cantiuncula, C., 153.
Capito, W. (49), 78, 94, 127, 349, 352, 375, App. III.
Caracciolo, M. (319), 464.

LIST OF CORRESPONDENTS

Carmelite, Prior at Augsburg (247a).
Carlstadt, A. (20), 64, 66, 85, 123, 159, 172.
Carondelet, J. de (362).
Carvajal, B. (253).
Catharinus, A. (414).
Collarius, J. (150).
Charles V., Emperor, 255, 342, 361, 364, 368, 381, 412, 413, 426, 430, 435, 443, 465.
Chièvres, W., 341, 357, 367.
Chiregatto, F., 298.
Christian II., King of Denmark (414), 460.
Cistein, see Ende.
Claude, Queen of France (447).
Cleen, D. v (471).
Clivanus, R., 338.
Cochlaeus, J. (464), 474.
Cologne, Hermann v. Wied, Archbishop Elector of (23).
Contarini, G., 459, 463, 466.
Cornaro, F., 456, 466.
Cowper, G., 235.
Cowper, T., 235.
Crafft, A. (259).
Cranach, L. (414).
Crautwald, V. (265).
Creutzer, M. (414).
Crotus Rubeanus, 186, 190, 251, 350.
Croy, W. de, Archbishop of Toledo (383).
Croy, W., see Chièvres.
Dandolo, M., 463.
Demuth, N. (247).
Diercx, V. (312), 314.
Dolz, J. (254).
Dolzig, J. v. (4).
Döring, C. (31).
Dorp, M. (241).
Draco, J. (281).
Dressel, M., 17.
Driedo, J. (312), 345.
Düngersheim, J. (52), 201, 264.
Dürer, A., 221.
Ebner, J. (41).
Eck, John, of Ingolstadt, 29, 61, 64, 66, 96, 101, 110, 113, 129, 139, 160, 164, 165, 195, 253, 401.
Eck, John, of Trier (452).
Egmond, N. (187).
Egranus, J. S., 52, 124.
Eichstädt, Gabriel, Bishop of (101).

Einsiedel, H. v., 310, 389.
Emser, J. (117).
Ende zum Stein, N. v. (394).
Eobanus, Hessus, H. (87), 189.
Erasmus, D. (9), 22, 87, 141, 142, 145, 149, 155, 156, 187, 188, 192, 212, 245, 257, 258, 273, 281, 285, 294, 297, 298, 311, 312, 313, 314, 331, 336, 345, 346, 351, 352, 356, 385, 399, 422, 429, 439, 477, App. III.
Erfurt, Augustinian Convent of, 3, 7.
Erfurt, University of, 211.
Eschaus, T. (240).
Faber, J., Dominican Prior of Augsburg (333).
Faber, J., Bishop of Vienna, 253, 255a.
Fach, B. F. (200).
Feige, J., 462.
Feilitzsch, F. v. (302), 306, 310, 347.
Feilitzsch, P. v. (103).
Fisher, J., 188.
Fleck, J., App. II, 1.
Fontinus, P. (178).
Franck, A. (140).
Freisingen, Philip, Bishop of (120).
Froben, J., 125.
Frosch, J. (95).
Fuchs, A. v. (186).
Fuchs, J. v. (186).
Fuchs, T. v. (186), 208.
Fug, J. (272).
Führer, J. (178).
Gambara, C. de (393).
Gattinara, M. (358), 469, 476.
Geroldseck, D. v. (127).
Geyling, J. (301).
Ghinucci, J. (73).
Giglis, S. de, Bishop of Worcester, 261.
Glapion, J. (359).
Glarean, H., 324.
Glaser, M., 154.
Göde, H. (228), App. II, 2.
Gonzaga, F. de (416), 448, 455.
Gradenigo, A., 260, 268, 423.
Gramaye, T., 334.
Greffendorf, J., 321.
Grünenberg, J. (24).
Guldennappen, W. v. (16).
Günther, F. (284).
Hauen, G., 160.
Hausmann, N., 427.

Hecker, G., 75.
Hedio, C., 308, 365.
Hegendorfinus, C., 356.
Heilingen, see Geyling.
Helt, C. (103).
Hennigk, J. (115).
Hennigk, M. (115).
Henriquez, F., 443.
Herholt, J. (151).
Herkmann, J., 433.
Hermannsgrün, L. v. (436).
Hess, John (of Breslau), (186), 197, 249, 250, 265, 267, 282, 402.
Hess, John (of Wittenberg), (200).
Hesse, Philip Landgrave of, 461.
Hildesheim, John, Bishop of (425).
Himmel, A. (39).
Hirschfeld, B. v. (449).
Hispanus, see Johannes.
Hochstraten, J., 165.
Hugwald, M. (432).
Hugwald, U. (432).
Hummelberg, M., 214, 415, 433.
Hump, H., 236.
Hutten, U. v., 189, 218, 232, 285, 291, 296, 336, 340, 354, 379, 403, 430, 450, 451, 457, 470, 472.
Hutter, C. (1).
Isolani, I., 199.
Jacobacci, D. (253).
James, an organist (161).
Jessen, F. v. (359).
Jessen, S. v. (359).
Joachim of Flora (83).
Johannes, a Spanish Augustinian (253).
Jonas, J. (140), 245, 451, 477.
Kammerer, J. (183).
Kirschberg, H. v. (404).
König, C. (230).
Kotter, J., 317.
Kunzelt, G., 270.
Lang, J., 5, 9, 10, 14, 16, 18, 20, 30, 37, 39, 43, 49, 51, 81, 87, 140, 156, 157, 158, 166, 170, 175, 197, 207, 220, 240, 259, 272, 286, 343, 411, 417, 431.
Langenmantel, C. (85), 99.
Lantschad, J., 320.
Latomus, J. (213), 370.
Lefèvre d'Étaples, J. (21).
Lehnin, Valentine, Abbot of (50).
Leiffer, G. (3), 12.

Leipsic, Theological Faculty of the University of, 105, 109.
Leipsic, University of, 118, 121, 126, 129.
Leo X, Pope, 70, 73, 74, 90, 91, 92, 137, 274, 297, 318, 319, 323, 330, 381.
Liège, Bishop of, see Marck.
Lindenau, A. v. (449).
Link, W. (3), 62, 69, 279, 372, 377, 390, 410.
Lipsius, M., 187, 212.
Lohr, A., 3, 7.
Lonicer, J. (254).
Lotther, M. (175).
Louvain, Theological Faculty of, 202.
Lupinus, P., 123.
Luther, J. (1).
Luther's sisters (344).
Mansfeld, Albert, Count of (69), 471.
Mantuan, B. (11).
Manuel, J., 255, 426, 435.
Marck, E. de la, Bishop of Liège (155).
Marck, R. de la (424).
Marlian, A., Bishop of Tui (359), 429, 439.
Martens, T. (345).
Martin, a bookseller (24).
Mascov, G., 25, 26, 36.
Mäurer, M., 315.
Maximilian, Emperor, 70.
Mayence, Albert, Archbishop Elector of (42), 44, 192, 222, 231, 323, 412, 413.
Mayence, University of, 44.
Mayr, G. (372).
Mecklenburg, Albert, Duke of (378).
Medici, Jerome de', 448, 455.
Medici, Julius de', 358, 359, 363, 393, 394, 396, 397, 407, 416, 424, 425, 432, 437, 444, 447, 452, 453, 454, 464, 468, 473, 475.
Medici, R. de', 393.
Melanchthon, P., 82, 84, 97, 102, 111, 122, 136, 138, 142, 150, 163, 167, 170, 174, 218, 232, 246, 250, 258, 267, 282, 286, 310, 329, 392, 402.
Merseburg, Adolph von Anhalt, Bishop of (64), 115.
Miltitz, C. v. (90), 112, 148, 289, 302, 307.
Minio, M., 79, 223, 224, 226.
Miritzsch, J. (117).
Moibanus (249).
Monckedamis, R. v., 370.
More, T. (49), 313.
Mosellanus, P., 157, 204.
Mühlpfort, H., 327.
Münzer, T. (262).
Murnar, T. (349), 366.

Mutian, C., 10, 13, 205, 259, 272.
Myconius, O., 244, 325, 338.
Narr, Claus (108).
Nassau, H., 341, 357.
Nathin, J. (7).
Nesen, W., 213.
Neustadt, Augustinian Convent of, 17.
Noviomagus, G., 294.
Oecolampadius, J., 163, 257.
Pace, R. (49), 446.
Palatinate, Frederic, Count of the Rhenish (441).
Palatinate, Wolfgang, Count of the Rhenish, 58.
Palencia, P. R. de la Mota, Bishop of (407).
Paltz, J. v. (7).
Pappenheim, J. v. (467).
Pappenheim, U. v. (449).
Paris, University of, 180, 334.
Pascha, Dr. (242).
Pelican, C. (254), 408.
Pelligrini, F. de, 404.
Peter (441).
Petri, A. (432).
Petzensteiner, J. (447).
Peutinger, C. (85), 333.
Pfeffinger, D. (4).
Pflug, C. v., 114.
Pflug, J. v., 204.
Philip, M., 405.
Phrygio, P. (394).
Pinder, U. (40).
Pirckheimer, W., 215, 309, 470.
Platz, L., 281.
Pomerania, Barnim, Duke of (160).
Pomerania, Bogislav, Duke of (391).
Prierias, S., 68, 72.
Probst, J. (293).
Pucci, L. (253), 362.
Rab, H., 112.
Reifenstein, W. (241).
Reinecke, J. (241).
Reinhard, M. (414), 460.
Reissenbusch, W. (304), 306.
Renée de France, Duchess of Ferrara (447).
Reuchlin, J. (5), 104, 214, 331, 403.
Reuter, K. (33).
Rhadinus, T. (316).
Riario, R., 276.

Riccius, P. (150).
Rosemund, G., 311, 312.
Rosso, A., 369.
Roth, S., 405.
Rovere, Leonard Grosso della (253).
Rozdalowsky, W., 161.
Rubeus, J. (182).
Rühel, J. (103).
Ruthall, Thomas, Bishop of Durham (446).
Sadoleto, J. (73).
Salmonius, B. (125).
Salzburg, Matthew Lang, Archbishop of (80).
Sander, M. (444).
Sasseta, A. della, 404.
Saum, C., 301.
Saxony (Albertine), George, Duke of, 90, 101, 105, 108, 109, 110, 114, 115, 118, 119, 121, 126, 128, 132, 143, 144, 147, 152, 159, 180, 209, 210, 211.
Saxony (Albertine), Henry, Duke of (414).
Saxony (Ernestine), Frederic, Elector of (22), 58, 74, 76, 86, 91, 98, 108, 120, 134, 141, 145, 146, 164, 172, 177, 195, 209, 210, 274, 276, 288, 292, 296, 302, 307, 320, 322, 341, 342, 348, 357, 361, 364, 367, 368, 380, 386, 387, 388, 409, 420, 436, 440, 445, 458.
Saxony (Ernestine), John, Duke of, 243, 288, 380, 386, 436, 449, 458.
Saxony (Ernestine), John Frederic, Duke of (378), 419.
Schart, M. (191).
Schaumburg, A. v. (256).
Schaumburg, S. v. (256), 269.
Scheurl, C., 27, 28, 29, 32, 35, 40, 41, 67, 82, 89, 107, 116, 122, 130.
Schinner, Matthew, Cardinal Bishop of Sion (393), 469.
Schleinitz, H. v. (198).
Schleinitz, John, Bishop of (117).
Schleupner, D. (230).
Schleusingen, G. (14).
Schmiedberg, H. (335).
Schneidpeck, J. (464).
Schönberg, Nicholas, Archbishop of Capua (394)
Schott, J. (233).
Schurff, J. (464).
Schwartzenburg, C. v. (474).
Schwertfäger, J. (97).
Seligmann, M., 183, 241.
Serralonga, U. de (83).
Sickingen, F. v. (218), 326.
Sieberger, W. (33).
Solms, P. v. (218).
Spain, Governors and Grandees of, 443.
Spalatin, G., 5, 6, 8, 9, 10, 15, 19, 21, 22, 23, 24, 31, 33, 34, 38, 42, 45, 46,

LIST OF CORRESPONDENTS

47, 48, 50, 53, 55, 56, 60, 71, 76, 83, 88, 89, 92, 93, 95, 100, 102, 103, 103a, 106, 117, 131, 133, 135, 136, 150, 151, 162, 167, 169, 171, 173, 181, 182, 185, 191, 194, 198, 200, 203, 206, 216, 217, 221, 225, 227, 228, 229, 230, 233, 234, 239, 242, 246, 247, 248, 252, 254, 256, 263, 266, 271, 273, 275, 277, 278, 283, 284, 287, 290, 293, 295, 299, 303, 304, 305, 322, 328, 329, 335, 344, 348, 353, 355, 360, 378, 379, 382, 387, 388, 391, 392, 400, 406, 414, 417, 421, 428, 434, 440, 441, 445, 467.
Spengler, G. (303).
Spengler, L. (303), 337.
Spenlein, G., 11.
Standish, H. (258).
Staupitz, J. v. (3), 54, 65, 77, 80, 86, 178, 237, 372, 376, 410.
Stehelin, W. (230).
Stolberg, L. v. (414).
Stolberg, W. v. (414).
Strassburg, William, Bishop of (425).
Stromer, H. (160), 162, 309.
Sturm, C. (431).
Sturz, G., 442.
Swaven, P. v. (447).
Symler, J. (60).
Tapper, R. (213).
Tartaretus, P. (57).
Taubenheim, J. v. (263), 310.
Tauler, J. (20).
Tetzel, J. (105), App. II, 3.
Teutleben, V. v., 292.
Tiepolo, N., 459.
Tischer, W. (14).
Trier, Richard v. Greiffenklau, Archbishop Elector of (120).
Trieste, Peter Bonomo, Bishop of (358).
Trutfetter, J. (30), 59.
Tucher, J. (89).
Tunstall, C., 383.
Turnhout, see Driedo.
Ulrich, J. (253).
Ulscenius, F., 375.
Urries, H. de (434).
Usingen, B. A. (12).
Vadian, J., 255a, 395, 415, App. II, 3.
Valentine (438).
Vehus, J. (464).
Velenus, W. (391).
Venatorius, T., 215.
Venice, Signory of, 79, 223, 224, 226, 260, 268, 423, 456, 466.
Vogt, James (23).
Vogt, John (16).

Volckmar, C. (116).
Volta, Gabriel della, 75, 237, 238.
Wägelin, G. (205).
Warbeck, G. (97), 449.
Warham, William (257), 418.
Watzdorf, R. v. (471).
Weissestadt (117).
Weller, A. (359).
Werthern, D. v., 119.
Wick, J. v. (278).
Wimpina, C. (31).
Wimpfeling, J. (57).
Wittenberg, University of (2), 98.
Wittiger, M. (265), 280.
Wolsey, T., 149, 261, 383, 418, 446.
Würzburg, Lawrence von Bibra, Bishop of (56).
Zasius, U. (150), 179, 196, 205.
Zeschau, W. (166).
Ziegler, N., 412, 413.
Zwingli, U., 196, 213, 244, 308, 324, 325, 365.

ABBREVIATIONS

The following abbreviations are used:

Allen—P. S. Allen: Opus Epistolarum Erasmi. Oxford. 1906ff. Vols, 1, 2, 3.

Bergenroth—Calendar of letters, despatches, and state papers, relating to the negotiations between England and Spain . . . edited by G. A. Bergenroth, P. de Gayangos and M. A. S. Hume. London. 1862ff.

Böcking—Epistolae Ulrichi Hutteni, ed. E. Böcking. Lipsiae. 1859. 2. v.

Brown—Calendar of state papers preserved in the archives of Venice, ed. R. Brown. London. 1867ff.

Burckhardt-Biedermann—Bonifacius Amerbach und die Reformation, von Th. Burckhardt-Biedermann. Basel. 1894.

Corpus Reformatorum—Volumes 1-10 contain P. Melanthonis epistolae, ed. C. G. Bretschneider, Halis. 1834-42. Volumes 94ff contain Zwinglis Briefwechsel, ed. E. Egli, G. Finsler, W. Köhler. Leipzig. 1911ff.

De Jongh—L'ancienne faculté de théologie de Louvain, par H. de Jongh. Louvain. 1911.

De Wette—Luthers Briefe, ed. W. M. L. de Wette. Berlin. 1825-8. 5 v.

De Wette-Seidemann—Luthers Briefe, Band vi., ed. W. M. L. de Wette und J. K. Seidemann. Berlin. 1856.

Enders—Luther's Briefwechsel, bearbeitet von E. L. Enders. Vols. 1-14. 1884ff. (Volumes 12ff continued by G. Kawerau.)

Erlangen—Luthers Sämtliche Werke. Erlangen edition. German works 68 volumes. Latin works 33 volumes, and, separately numbered, Opera latina varii argumenti, 7 volumes.

Gess—Akten und Briefe zur Kirchenpolitik Herzog Georgs von Sachsen. Hg. von F. Gess. Band I. Leipzig. 1905.

Grisar—Luther, von Hartmann Grisar. Freiburg in Breisgau. 1911-2. 3 v.

Kalkoff: Aleander—Die Depeschen des Nuntius Aleander von Wormser Reichstage 1521. Uebersetzt und erläutert von P. Kalkoff. 2d ed. Halle. 1898.

Kalkoff: Briefe—Depeschen und Berichte über Luther vom Wormser Reichstage 1521. Uebersetzt und erläutert von P. Kalkoff. Halle. 1898.

Köstlin-Kawerau—Martin Luther, von Julius Köstlin. Fünfte neubearbeitete Auflage, fortgesezt von G. Kawerau. Berlin. 1903. 2 v.

Krause—Der Briefwechsel des Mutianus Rufus, bearbeitet von C. Krause. Kassel. 1885.

Lutheri opera varii argumenti, see Erlangen.

Realencyclopädie—Realencyclopädie für protestantische Theologie und Kirche. 3d edition. Leipzig. 1896-1909. 22 vols.

Reichstagsakten—Deutsche Reichstagsakten unter Karl V. Hg. von. A. Kluckhohn und A. Wrede. München. 1893ff. (Volume ii. only referred to.)

Smith—The Life and Letters of Martin Luther. By Preserved Smith. Boston, New York and London. 1911.

Walch—Luthers sämmtliche Schriften, herausgegeben von J. G. Walch. Halle. 1744ff. (Volume 15, containing supplementary documents is chiefly referred to.)

Walch[2]—The same, 2d much improved edition, published by the Concordia Publishing House, St. Louis, Missouri. The letters, all in German translation, by A. F. Hoppe, are in vol. xxi, published in two parts at St. Louis, Missouri, U. S. A. 1903-4.

Weimar—Luthers Werke. Kritische Gesammtausgabe. Weimar. 1883ff. As yet have appeared volumes i-ix, x, part i, half i and parts ii and iii, ix-xvi, xvii part i, xviii-xx, xxiii-xxx, xxxii-xxxiv, xxxvi-xxxviii, xl part i, xli-xliii, xlv-xlvii, and Deutsche Bibel, volumes i-iii, and Tischreden, volume i.

LUTHER'S CORRESPONDENCE

AND

OTHER CONTEMPORARY LETTERS

1. LUTHER TO JOHN BRAUN, VICAR IN EISENACH.[1]

E. L. Enders: *Dr. Martin Luther's Briefwechsel* (Frankfurt am Main. 1884-   ) i. 1.   ERFURT, April 22, 1507.

Martin Luther was born at Eisleben, November 10, 1483. Soon afterwards his father moved to Mansfeld. 1497-8 Martin attended the school of the Brethren of the Common Life at Magdeburg. 1498-1501 he attended the school of St. George at Eisenach. 1501-5 he was at the university of Erfurt. July 17, 1505, he entered the monastery of the Augustinian Hermits at Erfurt. See Preserved Smith: *Life and Letters of Martin Luther* (Boston, 1911), chap. i. and ii.

Of John Braun nothing is known, except that he was priest of the Church of the Virgin at Eisenach, and that he was still living in 1516. Enders, i. 48. Luther had made his acquaintance during the years at Eisenach.

Greeting in Christ Jesus our Lord. I should fear, most gentle friend, to trouble your kindness by an importunate letter, did I not consider your heartfelt affection for me proved by the many benefits you have conferred upon me. Wherefore, relying on our mutual friendship, I do not hesitate to send this letter, which I am sure will find you attentive and affable.

God, glorious and holy in all his works, has designed to exalt me, wretched and unworthy sinner, and to call me into his sublime ministry, only for his mercy's sake. I ought to be thankful for the glory of such divine goodness (as much as dust may be) and to fulfil the duty laid upon me.

[1] Enders begins the letter with the word "Jhesus," which, according to Hoppe, is not found in the earlier editions. *Dr. Martin Luther's Sämmtliche Schriften.* . . . Band XXI. Die Briefe (St. Louis, 1903), p. 1.

Wherefore the fathers have set aside the Sunday Cantate [May 2] for my first mass,[1] God willing. That day I shall celebrate mass before God for the first time, the day being chosen for the convenience of my father.[2] To this I made bold to invite you, kind friend, but certainly not as though I were doing you any favor deserving the trouble of such a journey, nor that I think my poor and humble self worthy of your coming to me, but because I learned your benevolence and willingness to oblige me when I was recently with you, as I have also at other times. Dearest father, as you are in age and in care for me, master in merit and brother in religion, if private business will permit you, deign to come and help me with your gracious presence and prayers, that my sacrifice may be acceptable in God's sight. You shall have my kinsman Conrad,[3] sacristan of the St. Nicholas Church, or any one else you wish to accompany you on the way, if you are free from business yourself.

Finally I ask that you come right to the monastery and stay with us a little while (for I do not fear you will settle down here), and do not go to the inn at the cross-roads. For you ought to be a cellerer, that is, the inhabitant of a cell. Farewell in Christ Jesus our Lord.

BROTHER MARTIN LUTHER OF MANSFELD.

P. S.—Those excellent men of the Schalbe[4] Foundation cer-

[1] Primitz: Luther had been ordained priest not long before, the exact date being unknown.

[2] John (Hans) Luther, originally of Möhra, a hamlet about fifteen miles south of Eisenach. As a young man he married Margaret Ziegler, of Eisenach, and moved to the County of Mansfeld, first to the town of Mansfeld and then to Eisleben. Here he found employment in the then recently started profession of mining (cf. *Cambridge Modern History*, i. 506), in which he gradually won a small property, and attained a respected position in the town. He was bitterly opposed to Martin's entering the monastery, for on this son (his second) he relied to make a brilliant career. By this time he seems to have become reconciled, and apparently became a convinced Lutheran in later life. He died May 29, 1530.

The story first circulated by Luther's contemporary Witzel that Hans was obliged to leave Eisenach because he had committed a murder, though still repeated in some quarters, is almost certainly false. It has recently become known that there was at this time another Hans Luther at Mansfeld, a rough character to whom the anecdote may have applied. Buchwald: *Lutherkalendar*, 1910.

[3] Conrad Hutter, a relative by marriage of his mother, who came from Eisenach. O. Clemen: *Beiträge zur Reformationsgeschichte*, ii. l.

[4] This was a little Franciscan convent at the foot of the Wartburg, probably near the present Barfüsserstrasse. Frau Cotta, Luther's hostess while he at-

tainly deserve well of me, but I dare not burden them with much asking, for I am persuaded that it would not be suitable to their order and rank for me to invite them to my humble affair, and molest them with the wishes of a monk now dead to the world. Nevertheless I am in doubt whether they would be pleased or annoyed by an invitation. Wherefore kindly do not mention it, but when occasion offers, tell them how grateful I am to them.

2. LUTHER TO JOHN BRAUN IN EISENACH.

Enders, i. 4.   WITTENBERG, March 17, 1509.

Luther was called to the university of Wittenberg (founded 1502) to teach Aristotle's Ethics and Dialectic at the beginning of the winter term (circa November 1), 1508, and remained there about a year.

Brother Martin Luther sends you greeting and wishes you salvation and the Saviour himself, Jesus Christ.

Cease, master and father, even more loved than revered, cease, I pray, to wonder, as you have been doing, that I left you secretly and silently, or at least would have so left you, were there not still a tie between us, or as if the power of ingratitude, like a north wind, had chilled our love and wiped the memory of your kindness from my heart. Indeed, no! I have not acted thus, or rather I meant not to act thus, although I may have been forced to act so as unintentionally to give you occasion to think evil of me.

I went, I confess, and yet I did not go, but left my greater and better part with you still. I can only persuade you that this is so by your own faith in me. As you conceived it of your own kindness and favor only, I hope you will never suffer it to be slain or diminished without my fault, as you have never done before. So I have gone farther from you in body but come nearer to you in mind, provided you are not unwilling, which I hope you are not at all.

To come to the point, that I be not longer compelled to suspect that your friendship doubts my constancy (would that the suspicion were false!) behold how hard I have tried to

tended school at Eisenach, was a Schalbe by birth, and it may have been through her that he met the monks.

steal this time from my many and various affairs to write you, especially as messengers are scarce, and were they plentiful, could rarely be used on account of their ignorance and carelessness. My only purpose in writing is to commend myself to you, and to express my hope that you will continue to think of me as you would wish to have me think of you. Although I cannot be, and do not think I am, equal to you in any good thing, nevertheless I have a great affection for you which I cannot give you now as I have so often given it to you in the past. I know that your generous spirit expects nothing from me save the things of the spirit, that is, to have the same knowledge of the Lord, and one heart and soul as we have one faith in him.

Wonder not that I departed without saying farewell. For my departure was so sudden that it was almost unknown to my fellow monks. I wished to write you but had time and leisure for nothing except to regret that I had to break away without saying good-bye.

Now I am at Wittenberg, by God's command or permission. If you wish to know my condition, I am well, thank God, except that my studies are very severe, especially philosophy, which from the first I would willingly have changed for theology; I mean that theology which searches out the meat of the nut, and the kernel of the grain and the marrow of the bones. But God is God; man often, if not always, is at fault in his judgment. He is our God, he will sweetly govern us forever.

Please deign to accept this, which has been set down in haste and extemporally, and if you can get any messengers to me let me have a share of your letters. I shall try to do the same for you in return. Farewell in the beginning and the end, and believe me such as you wish me. Again farewell.

BROTHER MARTIN LUTHER, Augustinian.

3. LUTHER TO THE PRIOR ANDREW LOHR AND THE CONVENT OF AUGUSTINIANS AT ERFURT.

Enders, i. 7.   WITTENBERG, September 22, 1512.

Luther returned to Erfurt in the late autumn 1509, where he remained three semesters lecturing on the *Sentences* of Peter Lombard. He made a journey to Rome in the winter of 1510-11, returning to

Wittenberg to lecture on the Bible in the same year. Smith, chap. IV. The occasion of the present letter is to invite his brothers to the ceremony of taking the degree of doctor of divinity, on October 18, 1512.

Greeting in the Lord. Reverend, venerable and dear Fathers! Behold the day of St. Luke is at hand, on which, in obedience to you and to our reverend Vicar Staupitz,[1] I shall take my examination in theology in the hall of the university, as I believe you already know from the letter of our Wittenberg Prior Link.[2] I do not now accuse myself of unworthiness, lest I should seek praise and honor by my humility; God and my conscience know how worthy and how grateful I am for this public honor.

First of all I beg you for Christ's sake to commend me to God in your common prayers, for you know you are my debtors for this by the law of charity, that his well pleasing and merciful will may be with me. Then I beg that you will deign to come and be present at the celebration, if convenient, for the glory and honor of religion and especially of our chapter. I should not dare to ask you to undertake the trouble and expense of such a journey, except that the very reverend father vicar has done it, and because it would seem indecorous, unworthy and scandalous for you not to be with me on such an occasion of honor, as though you were ignorant of it or uninvited.

[1] John von Staupitz matriculated at Leipsic in 1485; in 1497 he is found as reader in theology and M. A. at the Augustinian convent at Tübingen. In 1503 he was elected Vicar of the German Province of Augustinian Hermits, and in the same year was called by Frederic the Wise to be dean of the theological faculty of the new university of Wittenberg, where he took his doctorate in divinity in 1510. Luther's relations with him were very close, and it is to him that the young monk owed his two calls to Wittenberg. Staupitz was unable to follow him in the revolt from Rome, and on August 28, 1520, laid down the office of Vicar and retired to Salzburg, securing dispensation to leave the Augustinian for the Benedictine order. Here he lived till his death by apoplexy on December 28, 1524. *Cf.* Th. Kolde: *Die deutsche Augustiner-Congregation und J. v. Staupitz* (Gotha. 1879), and in *Realencyclopädie*.

[2] Wenzel Link (January 8, 1483-March 12, 1547), of Colditz, matriculated at Leipsic 1498, and at Wittenberg 1503, where he was called to teach philosophy in 1508, and became D. D. in 1511. In 1516 he left Wittenberg for Munich. As an Augustinian he attended the general chapter at Heidelberg, April, 1518, where he was elected District Vicar to succeed Luther. In August, 1520, he was elected Vicar of the German Province to succeed Staupitz, but under the influence of the evangelic faith resigned the vicariate, became pastor of a reformed church at Altenburg and married 1523. Two years later he was called to Nuremberg, where he spent the rest of his life in useful service and in frequent communication with Luther. *Cf.* W. Reindell: *W. Link von Colditz* Band I, 1483-1522. (Marburg, 1892.) Also *Realencyclopädie*.

Moreover if the venerable reader, Father George Leiffer,[1] is able and willing to come it would please me; but if not, the Lord's will be done. Please, dear fathers, show yourself in this equal to the high opinion I justly hold you in. I shall remember and be grateful for your attention. Farewell in the Lord, my brothers, each and all of you; to him we commend ourselves in prayer.

BROTHER MARTIN LUTHER, *Augustinian*

4. LUTHER'S RECEIPT.

Enders, i. 9. (LEIPSIC), October 9, 1512.

Luther was called to Wittenberg a second time apparently in the summer of 1511, in order to take the chair of Biblical exegesis hitherto occupied by Staupitz. To fit himself for this he took, on October 18, 1512, the degree of Doctor of Divinity. The cost of the promotion was borne by the elector. Luther was obliged to walk to Leipsic (which, strange to say, was not in the elector's territory) to get the money from the government's agents, Dolzig and Pfeffinger. In the Weimar archives there is a list of the expenses of these gentlemen at the "Michaelismarkt" (fair held on St. Michael's day), October 5-16, 1512. Among the expenses is fifty gulden for Staupitz, "which Martin, Augustinian friar at Wittenberg, received against his own written receipt. These fifty gulden our most gracious Lord kindly commanded to be given to the said friar for his doctorate, which he will receive at Wittenberg shortly after this fair, in return for which Dr. [Staupitz] has undertaken that the said Martin shall during his life-time lecture on the subject assigned him at Wittenberg." H. Steinlein: *Luthers Doktorat*, Leipsic, 1912. *Sonderabdruck aus der Neuen Kirchlichen Zeitung.* Page of Errata preceding p. l. In general on the doctorate, see this work.

I, Martin, friar of the Order of Hermits at Wittenberg, acknowledge with this my own hand that I have received on account of the Prior at Wittenberg, from the honorable and trusty Degenhart Pfeffinger[2] and John von Dolzig,[3] cham-

[1] Nothing is known of Leiffer save that he was an Augustinian at Erfurt, who held the position of reader at meals. Luther wrote him on April 15, 1516 (*infra* no. 12), and mentioned him incidentally in a letter of October 15, 1516.

[2] The chamberlain, treasurer and influential councillor of Frederic the Wise. He died July 3, 1519. He is frequently spoken of by Luther as a somewhat close-fisted individual. Enders, i. 87.

[3] A treasurer and receiver of taxes (not chamberlain) who had been in Frederic's service probably before 1500. In 1517-8 he made a pilgrimage to Palestine. In 1519 he became marshal of the court. He was at Augsburg in 1530. He undertook a mission to England in 1539. Made governor of Saalfeld 1545. Died

berlains of my most gracious Lord, fifty gulden,[1] on the Saturday after St. Francis' day, anno domini 1512.

5. GEORGE SPALATIN TO JOHN LANG AT WITTENBERG.
Enders, i. 11. (End of 1513.)[2]

George Burkhardt, of Spalt (1484-January 16, 1545), always known as Spalatin, one of Luther's best friends, to whom more of his letters are addressed than to any other person, had studied at Erfurt, 1498-1502, when he went to Wittenberg. Here he first learned to know Luther. About 1513 he was made chaplain to Frederic the Wise, whose trusted confidant he was until the elector's death in 1525. In this year Spalatin married, and was appointed pastor of a church at Altenburg, where he lived the rest of his life. *Cf. Realencyclopädie*, Berbig; *Spalatin und sein Verhältnis zu Luther.*

John Lang, another good friend, matriculated at Erfurt, 1500, entered the Augustinian convent 1506, was forced to leave Erfurt on account of the quarrel of that convent with Staupitz, and so went to teach at Wittenberg 1511-16, when he returned to Erfurt, became prior of the monastery 1516, and District Vicar 1518. Left the monastery 1522, and became pastor of a church at Erfurt, where he remained till his death, 1548. He married twice, in 1522 and 1524. N. Paulus: *Usingen* 36. Förstemann & Günther: *Briefe an Erasmus* (1904), p. 378. *Realencyclopädie.*

The subject of the following letters is the Reuchlin trial. Pfefferkorn, a converted Jew, proposed to destroy all Hebrew books save the Old Testament (1509). This proposition was submitted to Reuchlin, a noted Hebrew scholar, who replied in a memorial, mentioned below, October 6, 1510, advising against this. This memorial was made the basis of a charge of heresy brought by the Dominicans of Cologne. The case was appealed to Rome, and was argued with heat in a host of pamphlets on both sides in Germany. The most famous of these, one of the world's great satires, was the *Epistolæ Obscurorum Virorum*, ridiculing the monks. The first series appeared in the autumn of 1515, and was by Crotus Rubeanus; this was followed by an enlarged edition in 1516, the additional letters being by Ulrich von Hutten, and by a new series from Hutten's pen in 1517. The best account of the affair in English is F. G. Stokes: *Epistolæ Obscurorum Virorum.* London, 1909, with Latin text, translation and full introduction.

. . . Moreover I would like to know from you whether

April 8, 1551. He was a good friend of Luther, to whose marriage he was invited. *Archiv für Reformationsgeschichte*, vi. 404.

[1] A gulden was worth fifty cents or two shillings intrinsically, but the purchasing power of money was about twenty times then what it is now.

[2] On the date see Enders, i. 12-13, and Köstlin-Kawerau, i. 752, note 1 to p. 132.

Dr. Martin has seen the memorial of our Dr. Reuchlin[1] on destroying the books of the Jews. If he has not read it, I beg nothing more at present than that he shall read it and give me his opinion on it. Although I doubt not that we all know how good and learned is Reuchlin, yet it is profitable to be on guard. . . .

6. LUTHER TO GEORGE SPALATIN.

Enders, i. 14.   WITTENBERG (January or February, 1514).

Peace be with you, Reverend Spalatin! Brother John Lang has just asked me what I think of the innocent and learned John Reuchlin and his prosecutors at Cologne, and whether he is in danger of heresy. You know that I greatly esteem and like the man, and perchance my judgment will be suspected, because, as I say, I am not free and neutral; nevertheless as you wish it I will give my opinion, namely that in all his writings there appears to me absolutely nothing dangerous.

I much wonder at the men of Cologne ferreting out such an obscure perplexity, worse tangled than the Gordian knot as they say, in a case as plain as day. Reuchlin himself has often protested his innocence, and solemnly asserts he is only proposing questions for debate, not laying down articles of faith, which alone, in my opinion, absolves him, so that had he the dregs of all known heresies in his memorial, I should believe him sound and pure of faith. For if such protests and expressions of opinion are not free from danger, we must needs fear that these inquisitors, who strain at gnats though they swallow camels, should at their own pleasure pronounce

---

[1]Luther probably did not know Reuchlin personally, but knew his works, and especially had used his *De Rudimentis Hebraecis* (1506) a grammar and dictionary in one. He mentions this in his marginal notes on Lombard's *Sentences* (1509), *Werke*, Weimar, ix. 32.

John Reuchlin (Feb. 22, 1455-June 30, 1522) of Pfortzheim, matriculated at Freiburg 1470, went soon to Paris, then, 1474, to Basle, where he took his B. A. 1475 and M. A. 1477, then returned to Paris, studied law, took LL. B. at Orleans 1479, became licentiate at Poitiers 1481, and doctor at Tübingen same year. 1482-90 he spent in Italy under patronage of Eberhard of Würtemberg. Made a noble 1492. About the same time began to study Hebrew; went to Heidelberg 1496, and under patronage of Philip Count Palatine to Rome 1498. He returned to Stuttgart 1499, where he spent twenty years, serving as Triumvir of the Swabian League 1502-13. He retired before the armies of the League to Ingolstadt, where he spent 1519-21 with Eck, after which he returned to Stuttgart. See his life by Geiger, *Realencyclopädie* and Stokes, *op. cit.* introduction.

the orthodox heretics, no matter how much the accused protested their innocence.

What shall I say? that they are trying to cast out Beelzebub but not by the finger of God. I often regret and deplore that we Christians have begun to be wise abroad and fools at home. A hundred times worse blasphemies than this exist in the very streets of Jerusalem, and the high places are filled with spiritual idols. We ought to show our excessive zeal in removing these offences which are our real, intestine enemies. Instead of which we abandon all that is really urgent and turn to foreign and external affairs, under the inspiration of the devil who intends that we should neglect our own business without helping that of others.

Pray can anything be imagined more foolish and imprudent than such zeal? Has unhappy Cologne no waste places nor turbulence in her own church, to which she could devote her knowledge, zeal and charity, that she must needs search out such cases as this in remote parts?

But what am I doing? My heart is fuller of these thoughts than my tongue can tell. I have come to the conclusion that the Jews will always curse and blaspheme God and his King Christ, as all the prophets have predicted. He who neither reads nor understands this, as yet knows no theology, in my opinion. And so I presume the men of Cologne cannot understand the Scripture, because it is necessary that such things take place to fulfill prophecy. If they are trying to stop the Jews blaspheming, they are working to prove the Bible and God liars.

But trust God to be true, even if a million men of Cologne sweat to make him false. Conversion of the Jews will be the work of God alone operating from within, and not of man working—or rather playing—from without. If these offences be taken away, worse will follow. For they are thus given over by the wrath of God to reprobation, that they may become incorrigible, as Ecclesiastes says, for every one who is incorrigible is rendered worse rather than better by correction.

Farewell in the Lord; pardon my words, and pray the Lord for my sinning soul.   Your brother,

MARTIN LUTHER.

7. LUTHER TO PRIOR ANDREW LOHR AND THE ELDERS OF THE AUGUSTINIAN CLOISTER AT ERFURT.

Enders, i. 16.   WITTENBERG, June 16, 1514.

In the early days of universities a degree meant no more than a license to teach, and for some centuries it was expected that a man should teach, for a time at any rate, at the institution where he had taken his degree, or had prepared for it. An oath to this effect was exacted at Paris until 1452 (H. Rashdall: *Universities of Europe,* i. 455f). The practice had fallen into disuse, but was apparently revived at Erfurt, which was extremely jealous of the sudden growth of Wittenberg. When Luther left Erfurt for Wittenberg and took his doctorate there, his enemies at Erfurt represented it as a breach of oath. This is his answer. *Cf.* Köstlin-Kawerau, i. 135, and Hartmann Grisar: *Luther* (Freiburg im Breisgau, 1911), i. 28ff. *Harvard Theological Review,* October, 1913.

Greeting in the Lord. Reverend Fathers, I have heard and read much evil spoken by some of you about us and especially about me, recently from the letter of Dr. John Nathin[1] as though writing for all of you, and I was so much moved by his trenchant lies and bitter, false provocations that I almost imitated the example of Dr. Paltz,[2] and poured out on him and the whole convent a vial of wrath and indignation. For which reason I sent two stupid letters to you (I know not whether they reached you) and would soon have sent a key to their meaning had not the mouth of the reviler been first stopped by the general chapter. Therefore I am obliged to consider many, or rather most of you excused. Wherefore I beg you, if any were offended or mentioned in my letters, to forgive it, and impute my action to the furious writings of Dr. Nathin. For my emotion though excessive had a just cause.

But now I hear worse: that he proclaims me perjured and infamous, I know not for what reason. Wherefore I pray if, as I fear, you are unable to stop his mouth, you at least pay

[1] Of Neukirchen, matriculated at Tübingen 1483, began lecturing on theology 1484, D. D. 1486 at Tübingen or 1493 at Erfurt, or both. Taking the same degree (*i. e.,* license to teach) at more than one university was and still is irregular in Germany; Nathin, therefore, was guilty of doing what he accused Luther of. He remained conservative, and when the cloister at Erfurt was dissolved in 1523, he seceded. Kolde: *Augustiner-Congregation,* 137, 391.

[2] John Zenser (Jenser, Genser) von Paltz, Prior of Neustadt 1475, D. D. at Erfurt 1483, superintendent of the monks' studies at Erfurt 1493, 1503, 1505-6. He died March 13, 1511. Kolde, *op. cit.,* index and 174-197; *Realencyclopädie.* His writings enjoyed much reputation. Luther's reference to him here is obscure. He was a strong defender of indulgences.

no attention to him and teach others to do the same. For I am not perjured because I took my degree elsewhere. For both universities and all of you know that I never lectured on the Bible at Erfurt, on which occasion it is customary to take an oath, nor am I aware that I ever took an oath in the whole course of my academic career. I did lecture on the *Sentences* at Erfurt, but I believe no one will affirm that I took an oath at that time. . . . I write this, excellent fathers, lest the Erfurt doctors of theology should consider me a despiser of the university to whom, as to a mother, I owe everything. . . .

But whatever men have done I am peacefully disposed towards you all, however much I may have been offended. For God has blessed me richly, unworthy as I am, and I have no cause to do ought but rejoice and love and bless even those who have deserved the contrary from me, just as I have deserved the contrary to what I receive from the Lord. Wherefore please be content, and lay aside all bitterness, if there is any, and let not my removal to Wittenberg provoke you, for thus the Lord, who is not to be resisted, willed. Farewell in the Lord.

BROTHER M. LUDER.

8. LUTHER TO SPALATIN.
Enders, ii. 287. (1514?)[1]

Greeting. I would most willingly comply with your wish, which is also mine, good Spalatin, but that you ask something which is beyond the mediocrity of my powers. I frankly confess my ignorance, for I do not know the meaning of those refrains[2] nor can I even conjecture it.

I am sure that the psalms, lxxx. and lxvii. which you

---

[1]This letter has no date in the original, and was put, for an unknown reason, by the first editor in 1519. All successors have followed him, although De Wette, Enders and the St. Louis editor all think that it properly belongs to an earlier date. The main proof of this is the signature "Luder," a form found nowhere else after September 11, 1517. Moreover a parallel passage has been found to the *Dictata super Psalterium* given by Luther 1513-6. *Werke*, Weimar ed. iii. 606; Enders, ii. 289. (There is a supplement to the *Dictata*, Weimar ix. 118, but no further parallel.) Spalatin frequently turned to Luther for exegesis of the Bible, which he had read through in 1508. On general dating *cf.* Köstlin-Kawerau, i. 754, note 2 to p. 166, and *Theologische Studien und Kritiken* 1888, p. 385.

[2]Luther was thinking of the "Selah" which occurs in Psalm LXVII and elsewhere. This was not printed in the Vulgate, but was in the original and so in the edition of Lefêvre d'Étaples which he used.

note, are the most heart-felt[1] prayers of the faithful congregation for the coming of Christ in the flesh. But you, who excel me in acumen of judgment and in wealth of learning, consider whether the author did not wish those refrains to point out that the psalms were choral,[2] like that eclogue of Virgil[3] which says, I forget how many times:

Ducite ab urbe domum, mea carmina, ducite Daphnim. . . .
You now know as much as I do. Farewell and pray for me. From the monastery.

BROTHER MARTIN LUDER, *Augustinian.*

9. GEORGE SPALATIN TO JOHN LANG AT ERFURT.

K. Krause: *Epistolae aliquot* (Einladungsschrift . . . Zerbst), 1883, p. 3. March 3 (1515).[4]

. . . Please commend me to Dr. Martin. For I think so much of him as a most learned and upright man, and, what is extremely rare, one of such acumen in judging that I wish to be entirely his friend as well as yours and of all learned men. Farewell, excellent brother, and remember me in your prayers, and also remember our Reuchlin laboring against the hatred and intolerable malignity of evil men, or rather *of cacodemons.*[5] Farewell again. I read your letter hastily. Our Erasmus[6] has returned as amiable as one stuffed with plenty.

[1] "Suspiriosissimas"; Luther certainly means something like the translation given, although the word he uses, both in classical and medieval Latin, properly means "asthmatic," "sighing."

[2] The word that Luther uses here, and two other places in the letter, "interstallares" is found neither in Harper's classical nor in Du Cange's medieval Latin dictionary. Whether he was thinking of the word "intercalares," as the first editor suggests, or not, the meaning is perfectly clear from the context.

[3] The eighth.

[4] This letter is dated by Krause and Enders (i. 13) 1514, but the true date is given by the sentence "Erasmus noster rediit quam amabilis ut qui stipatus ista copia." Erasmus returned from a five-year sojourn in England in July, 1514, and in the following December Schürer published at Strassburg a new edition of his *De Copia,* to which Erasmus prefaced a most amiable letter (*cf.* P. S. Allen: *Opus Epistolarum Erasmi,* i. p. xvii, ii. pp. 7, 17). Spalatin makes a punning reference to this work, which he doubtless sent with the letter (*ista*).

[5] Greek.

[6] Desiderius Erasmus of Rotterdam (October 28, 1466-July 12, 1536), the most noted scholar of the day, attended school at Deventer 1475-84, at Hertogenbusch 1484-6, entered the monastery of Augustinian Canons at Stein 1486, professed 1488, studied at Paris 1495-9, visited England 1499-1500, 1505-1506 and 1509-14; Italy 1506-9; lived at Louvain 1514-21, Basle 1521-8, Freiburg in Breisgau 1528-35,

For why should he not have the *horn of Amaltheia?*[1]
Yours.
SPALATIN.

10. JOHN LANG TO CONRAD MUTIANUS RUFUS.

Hekel: *Manipulus primus epistolarum.*
1698, p. 104. Enders, i. 36. (May 2, 1515.)

On May 1, 1515, Luther was elected District Vicar of his order at the Chapter held at Gotha. On that occasion he delivered a rousing sermon against the vices of the monks, the sermon probably being that printed Weimar, i. 44, against backbiting. *Cf.* Köstlin-Kawerau, i. 122. The sermon attracted the attention of Mutian, and the next day Lang sent it to him with the following letter.

Conrad Muth, usually known as Mutianus Rufus (October 15, 1471-March 30, 1526), after attending school at Deventer matriculated at Erfurt, 1486, taking the degree of M. A. in 1492. From 1495-1502 he was in Italy. He took the degree of LL.D. at Bologna. In 1503 he received a canonry at Gotha, where he spent the rest of his life in learned leisure, exercising great influence on the younger humanists and teaching that all religions are essentially the same. His letters, published by K. Krause and K. Gilbert, life in *Realencyclopädie*, and *cf.* P. S. Allen, *op. cit.*, ii. 416. He did not join the Reformation and Luther considered his death, reported to be a suicide, as a judgment of God. *Cf.* Wrampelmeyer: *Cordatus' Tagebuch*, no. 932.

You ask about that sharp orator who yesterday inveighed against the morals of those brothers who pass for little saints. He is Dr. Martin, with whom I have lived intimately at Erfurt, and who formerly helped me not a little in good studies. Our Spalatin venerates and consults him like Apollo. . . .

11. LUTHER TO GEORGE SPENLEIN AT MEMMINGEN.

Enders, i. 28. WITTENBERG, April 8, 1516.

Spenlein was an Augustinian brother, who later became evangelical pastor at Arnstadt, in which capacity Luther wrote him a letter, June 17, 1544. De Wette, v. 665.

Grace and peace to you from God the Father and the Lord

when he returned to Basle. His principal works are: *Enchiridion Militis Christiani* (1503), *Enconium Moriae* (1511), *Adagia* (1500), an edition of the Greek New Testament (March, 1516). Lives of him by A. J. Froude (1895) and E. Emerton (1899). His influence on Luther was immense. *Cf.* especially: A. Meyer: *Étude critique des rélations d'Érasme et de Luther.* Paris, 1909.
[1] Greek.

Jesus Christ. Dear Brother George:—I want you to know that I sold some of your things for two and a half gulden,[1] *i. e.*, one gulden for the coat of Brussels, half a gulden for the larger Eisenach work, and one gulden for the cowl and some other things. Some things are left, as the Eclogues of Baptista Mantuan[2] and your collections, which you must consider a loss, as hitherto we have not been able to dispose of them. We gave the two and a half gulden you owe to the reverend father vicar[3] in your name; for the other half gulden you must either try to pay it or get him to remit the debt. For I felt that the reverend father was so well inclined to you that he would not object to doing so.

Now I would like to know whether your soul, tired of her own righteousness, would learn to breathe and confide in the righteousness of Christ. For in our age the temptation to presumption besets many, especially those who try to be just and good before all men, not knowing the righteousness of God, which is most bountifully and freely given us in Christ. Thus they long seek to do right by themselves, that they may have courage to stand before God as though fortified with their own virtues and merits, which is impossible. You yourself were of this opinion, or rather error, and so was I, who still fight against the error and have not yet conquered it.

Therefore, my sweet brother, learn Christ and him crucified; learn to pray to him despairing of yourself, saying: Thou, Lord Jesus, art my righteousness, but I am thy sin; thou hast taken on thyself what thou wast not, and hast given to me what I was not. Beware of aspiring to such purity that you will not wish to seem to yourself, or to be, a sinner. For Christ only dwells in sinners. For that reason he descended from heaven, where he dwelt among the righteous, that he might dwell among sinners. Consider that kindness of his, and you will see his sweetest consolation. . . .

If you firmly believe this (and he is accursed who does not believe it) then take up your untaught and erring brothers, patiently uphold them, make their sins yours, and, if you have

---

[1] "Semitres," an unclassical translation of the German "halbdrei."
[2] A late poet (1448-1516) whose eclogues were great favorites at this time. They have recently been reëdited by W. P. Mustard. Johns Hopkins' Press, 1911.
[3] Staupitz.

any goodness, let it be theirs. Thus the apostle teaches: Receive one another even as Christ received you, for the glory of God,[1] and again: Have this mind in you which was also in Christ Jesus, who, when he was in the form of God, humbled himself, &c.[2] Thus do you, if you seem pretty good to yourself, not count it as booty, as though it were yours alone, but humble yourself, forget what you are, and be as one of them that you may carry them. . . . Do this, my brother, and the Lord be with you. Farewell in the Lord.

Your brother,

MARTIN LUTHER, *Augustinian.*

12. LUTHER TO GEORGE LEIFFER AT ERFURT.

Enders, i. 31. WITTENBERG, April 15, 1516.

Greeting in the Lord and in his Comforter. Excellent father and sweet brother in the Lord, I hear that you are tempted, shaken by the whirlwinds and disquieted by the various floods, but blessed is God the Father of mercy and God of all consolation, who has provided for you a comforter and consoler as good as any man may be, the Rev. Dr. Usingen.[3] Only let it be your care to throw away your own ideas and thoughts and make place for his words in your thoughts. I am certain from my own experience and yours, or rather from the experience of all whom I ever saw perturbed, that prudence alone is the cause of our emotion and the root of all our unquiet. For our eye is very evil, and, to speak of myself, alas! how much misery has it caused me and does it cause me yet.

The cross of Christ is distributed through the whole world, to every one certainly comes his portion. Do you therefore not cast it aside, but rather take it up as a holy relic, kept not in a golden or silver case, but in a golden, that is, gentle and

[1] Romans, xv. 7.
[2] Philippians, ii. 5, 6.
[3] Bartholomew Arnoldi of Usingen, born between 1462 and 1465, entered Erfurt 1484 and took his M. A. 1491. He taught philosophy at the University, being a follower of Aristotle in all things. He entered the Augustinian cloister about 1512, apparently under Luther's influence, and took his D. D. in 1514. He did not, however, follow Luther in the revolt, although, notwithstanding a debate in May, 1518, they remained on friendly terms until 1522 when Usingen came out strongly against the Reformation. He was obliged to leave Erfurt in 1526, going to Würzburg, where he died September 9, 1532. He was at the Diet of Augsburg, 1530. Life by N. Paulus, 1893.

loving heart. . . . Farewell, sweet father and brother, and pray for me.

BROTHER MARTIN LUTHER, *Augustinian*.

13. LUTHER TO CONRAD MUTIANUS RUFUS AT GOTHA.

Enders, i. 34.   GOTHA, May 29, 1516.

Luther was now on a journey through the various cloisters of his district. While at Gotha, he thought best to excuse himself for not calling on Mutian, whose opinion of his sermon the year before he had heard from Lang, who seems, moreover, to have introduced them.

Greeting in the Lord. The reasons, most learned and kindest Mutian, why I have neither visited you nor invited you to visit me, are first the hurry of my trip and the pressure of my business, and secondly the great opinion and true reverence I have for you. For our mutual friendship is too recent for me to dare to bring down to my mediocrity your excellence as it is in my eyes and in fact.

But now I would not leave you unsaluted, for I felt it my duty to do so, even though I feel shame for my ignorance and unrhetoric, if I may use the word. Affection for you conquered and this rustic Corydon, this barbarian Martin accustomed only to cry out among geese, salutes you, a man of the deepest and most exquisite learning. But I know, I am sure or at least I assume, that Mutian prefers the heart to the tongue and the pen, and my heart is sufficiently learned in only being your friend. Farewell, farewell, excellent father in the Lord Jesus, and be mindful of me.

BROTHER MARTIN LUTHER, *Vicar*.

P. S.—I would like you to know that Father John Lang, whom you know as a Grecian and Latinist, and, what is more, a man of sincere heart, has recently been instituted by me as prior of the convent of Erfurt. Favor him before men and pray for him to God. Farewell, in haste, as you see.

14. LUTHER TO JOHN LANG AT ERFURT.

Enders, i. 44.   WITTENBERG, June 30, 1516.

Greeting in the Lord. I wrote you from Sangershausen, excellent father, that if you have any brother of undisciplined mind you should send him there for punishment. I am writing again not to command but to request you not to deliver over, but to yield to Eisleben George Schleusingen and William Tischer until the reverend father [Staupitz] returns. For thus necessity demands; and you should say to that brother and to all that this is not done by me from violence, but because all of us, and I especially, are bound to uphold the honor of the vicariate, and especially of the reverend father Vicar....

BROTHER MARTIN, *District Vicar.*

P. S. ... A thunderstorm at Dresden so cut down the vineyards of our convent that the loss is estimated at two or three hundred gulden, besides other damage. This is my news.

15. LUTHER TO SPALATIN AT WITTENBERG.
Enders, i. 46.   WITTENBERG, August 24, 1516.

Greeting. I am going to beg a service of love and faith from you, sweetest Spalatin, that is, that you either send me a copy of Jerome's epistles[1] at once, or that, as much as you can in a short time, that you copy for me from the book of Famous Men (which I greatly desire) what that saint says about St. Bartholomew the apostle, so that I may have it before noon, for I am going to preach to the people.[2] I am much offended with the foolish lies of the Catalogue and the Golden Legend.[3]

Farewell, excellent brother.

BROTHER MARTIN LUDER, *Augustinian.*

P. S.—Don't be surprised that a theologian like myself should not have Jerome. For I am waiting for the edition[4] of Eras-

[1] I have looked through Jerome's epistles without finding anything on St. Bartholomew. Luther quotes one of them, Weimar, iv. 523.
[2] This sermon, in which Luther seriously criticizes the legend of St. Bartholomew, is printed in Weimar i. 79. For a severe opinion of the legends of the saints, in the year 1544, *cf.* Kroker: *Luthers Tischreden in der Matthesischen Sammlung.* Leipsic, 1903, no. 661.
[3] The books referred to are: Petri de Natalibus: *Catalogus sanctorum* (which was edited at Lyons, 1508) which Luther alludes to in his lectures on Romans, ed. Ficker, *Scholien,* p. 212, and Iacobi a Voragine, *Legenda aurea,* from which Luther quotes in his lectures on Psalms, Weimar, iv. 384.
[4] The edition in nine volumes which was published by Froben throughout the year 1516. Erasmus edited the first four volumes, containing the epistles; the Amerbachs, Rhenanus and others were responsible for the other works. The dedication to the whole, by Erasmus to Warham, is dated April 1, 1516. Further information is to be found in P. S. Allen: *Opus epistolarum Erasmi* (Oxonii, 1906-) ii. 210.

mus and that which I use in common with others has been taken away by John Lang.¹

16. LUTHER TO JOHN LANG AT ERFURT.

Enders, i. 48. WITTENBERG, August 30 (1516).

Greeting. Venerable father, I am sending you the oration which I delivered at our chapter at Gotha² and I trust you to fulfill my promise, namely, to send it as quickly as possible to John Braun, priest of the Holy Virgin at Eisenach, or to Wigand of Guldennappen,³ priest at Walterhausen. For I promised it to them, and I also promised to let George Leiffer, the reader, see it, and show it to his friends. Not that I think it worth reading, but I must yield to the wishes of others rather than my own.

You are certainly too much moved against John Vogt. I know nothing, nor have I heard any secrets, but I heard the prior of Magdeburg⁴ complaining about it, and just the same as he was at Eisleben, that is, desperate about sustaining the school, and several of the older brothers agreed with him. . . . Now it is your duty to receive this blow on your right cheek

---

Jerome was one of the favorite authors of this period, as the numerous editions and even translations of his letters show. If we may trust an inscription in a book in the Boston Public Library, which has been identified as Luther's hand, the reformer later owned the edition which came out at Lyons, 1518. This identification however is very doubtful. See Preserved Smith, *Life and Letters of Martin Luther*, p. 475.

¹ The text, after a lacuna, adds "and sold."
² The sermon held at Gotha, May 1, 1515; *cf. supra*, no. 10.
³ A former teacher of Luther at Eisenach. Luther later interceded for him with John Frederic, May 14, 1526.
⁴ John Vogt. An interesting notice of him from the old chronicler Berkmann of Pomerania, put by him in the year 1518, probably a mistake for 1516, is quoted by De Wette-Seidemann, vi. 530, note 3. "He invited Dr. Martin Luther, whom the Magdeburgians escorted with eighteen horsemen, and he came on July 26, at the solicitation of Dr. Vogt, with Thonamen, an old man in the Augustinian cloister, who had chosen Dr. Martin as his son. And when he could not give counsel against the wrong doctrine he was accustomed to say: 'I will complain of it to my son Martin,' for he knew what was in him. For they were both from Eisleben. Then Martin preached there about a week, and while he was there nothing was done with indulgences." Several sermons of 1516 are against indulgences, *e. g.*, Weimar i. 65, July 27, 1516, and Weimar i. 94, October 31, 1516. Vogt later became evangelical pastor at Magdeburg. Kolde: *Augustiner-Congregation*, 393. His devotion to the cause is thus amusingly portrayed in the table-talk: "When a certain Dr. Vogt wrote to him, 'My Luther, I will go with you up to the fire—but not quite into it. Only advance bravely!' he answered, 'Such martyrs Christ leads up to heaven—but not quite into it.'" *Tischreden*, Weimar i. no. 242.

and also to turn the other. For this will not be your greatest nor last temptation, but God's wisdom is preparing you for serious war, if you live. . . .

BROTHER MARTIN LUTHER.

17. LUTHER TO MICHAEL DRESSEL AND THE AUGUSTINIAN CHAPTER AT NEUSTADT.

Enders, i. 50. WITTENBERG, September 25, 1516.

Greeting in the Lord. I hear with sorrow, as I ought to hear, excellent fathers and brothers, that you live without peace and unity, and that in one house you are not of one mind, nor according to the rule do you have one heart and one soul in the Lord. This miserable and useless manner of life comes from the infirmity of your humility,—for where is humility there is peace—or from my negligence, or certainly from the fault of both of us, that we do not weep before the Lord who made us, nor pray that he would direct our ways in his sight and lead us in his justice. He errs, he errs, he errs, who would guide himself, not to say others, by his own counsel. . . .

Therefore I am forced to do absent what I would not like to do present, though I greatly wish I could now be present, but I am not able. Therefore receive my command in salutary obedience, if perchance the Lord will deign to work his peace in us. For the whole of your strife, or rather its root, is your discord with your head, the prior, which is more harmful than a quarrel between brothers. Wherefore, by the authority of my office, I command you, Brother Michael Dressel, to resign your office and seal; and by the same authority I absolve you from the duties of the priorate, in the name of the Father, and of the Son and of the Holy Ghost, Amen. And these letters shall have the same force as if I were present.

I would not have you complain that I have judged you unheard, nor would I receive your excuses. I willingly believe that you have done all with the best intentions in the world, nor can I imagine that you have purposely and maliciously fomented discord; you have done what you had grace to do. For this I thank you, and if your brothers do not thank you they will greatly displease me. . . . [Instructions for electing a new prior.] . . .

I beg that you will be diligent and faithful in the instruction of youth, as in that which is the first and main business of the convent. Farewell and pray for me and for all of us. . . .   BROTHER MARTIN LUTHER,
District Vicar of the Augustinians.

18. LUTHER TO JOHN LANG.

Enders, i. 59.   KEMBERG, October 5, 1516.

. . . It is quite clear that that nonsense you sent me about a supplication[1] to the pope against theologs has been cooked up by some rash person, for it smells of the same oven as the *Epistolae Obscurorum Virorum*. I imparted it opportunely to the faculty, which had met to license two physicians, and they were all of the same opinion in regard to it. . . .

You have rightly sought the reverend father Vicar[2] at Munich. He wrote me on September 10th from there. I do not know whether he will come to us, but I hope so. He wrote me that he was forced to remain there on account of poverty. . . .   BROTHER MARTIN LUTHER.

19. LUTHER TO GEORGE SPALATIN AT ALTENBURG.

Enders, i. 61.   (WITTENBERG, circa October 5, 1516.)

Greeting. Yesterday I received your letter and the gulden you sent me. Let it be as it must.

John Lang, prior at Erfurt, has sent me *Supplication against Theologs*. As it contains no manifest truth, it must be by the author of the *Epistolae Obscurorum Virorum* or someone who apes him. I approve his intention, not his method, because he does not forbear from reviling and contumely. In short, he was laughed to scorn by all when I recently exposed him. Take the book and read it with your accustomed moderation. Farewell.

---

[1] *Tenor supplicationis Pasquillianae,* in *Pasquillus Marranus exul* (1520), reprinted in Böcking: *Hutteni opera, supplementum,* i. 505. Further details on it in O. Clemen: *Beiträge zur Reformationsgeschichte* (1900), i. 12ff. He holds that the author of the *Tenor* was one of the Erfurt humanists.
[2] Staupitz.

20. LUTHER TO JOHN LANG AT ERFURT.

Enders, i. 54. (Middle of October, 1516.)[1]

... Therefore, take care, as your Tauler[2] commands, to persevere, keeping yourself apart and yet accessible to all men, as is befitting the son of the same God and the same church. ...

There is nothing for your schoolmen[3] to marvel at in my propositions,[4] or rather those of Bartholomew Bernhardi,[5] although my own schoolmen have expressed wonder at them. And the propositions were not composed by me, but by Bernhardi, moved thereto by the chatter of the detractors of my lectures. He did it so that, by a public discussion held, exceptionally, under my presidency, the mouths of the chatterers might be stopped or the opinions of others be heard. I offended all very much by denying that the book on true and false penitence was Augustine's.[6] It is bungling and inept, nothing if not different from Augustine's opinions and learning. I knew, indeed, that Gratian[7] and the Master of the Sentences[8] had taken a good deal from it, which was not medicine, but poison for consciences. But I offended them implacably, especially Dr. Carlstadt,[9] because, knowing this,

---

[1] This letter, without date, is placed by Enders in September, but the date here given is more likely. *Cf.* Weimar, i. 143, and St. Louis, xxi, no. 44.

[2] This is the first allusion to Tauler, the German mystic (†1361) who influenced him so much. I believe, however, that echoes of Tauler can be found in the letters of May 1, and June 22, and perhaps April 8 of this year. According to the present notice it was Lang who introduced him to this writer. Towards the end of 1516 Luther edited an anonymous tract of this school, to which he gave the name "A German Theology." *Cf.* Smith, p. 27. Köstlin-Kawerau, i. 111.

[3] Gabrielistae, followers of Gabriel Biel, the last of the great schoolmen, among whose doctrines that of the free will was prominent.

[4] These theses, defended by Bernhardi on September 25, 1516, under Luther's presidency, deny the possibility of a man's fulfilling God's commands by his free will without grace. Weimar, i. 142. Köstlin-Kawerau, i. 129-30.

[5] Of Feldkirchen in Swabia (1487-1551), student at Wittenberg and after 1518 pastor of Kemberg.

[6] Luther was quite right in denying its authenticity. He had a keen sense of style, and was also correct in exposing another work wrongly attributed to Augustine.

[7] The Decretum of Master Gratian, composed in the twelfth century at Bologna from the decrees of councils and popes, became the foundation of the Canon Law.

[8] Peter Lombard, on whose *Sentences*, the chief text book of medieval theology, also a twelfth century work, Luther had lectured 1509-11. For references to their quotations from Lombard, Enders, i. 58.

[9] Andrew Bodenstein of Carlstadt (c. 1480-1541) studied at Erfurt 1499-1503, at Cologne 1503-4, when he went to Wittenberg where he took the doctorate of

I dared to deny the authenticity of the book. Therefore, tell these wondering, or rather wonderful theologians, that they need not dispute with me what Gabriel said, or what Raphael said, or what Michael said. I know what Gabriel Biel says, and it is all very good except when he speaks of grace, charity, hope, faith and virtue; I have not time to tell in these letters how much, with his Scotus, he is a Pelagian.[1]

[Here follows a defence of one of the propositions, with some details of business.] . . .

21. LUTHER TO SPALATIN.

Enders, i. 62.   WITTENBERG, October 19, 1516.

Greeting. What displeases me in Erasmus, though a learned man, is that in interpreting the apostle[2] on the righteousness of works, or of the law, or our own righteousness, as the apostle calls it, he understands only those ceremonial and figurative observances. Moreover, he will not have the apostle speak of original sin, in Romans, chapter V, though he admits that there is such a thing. If he read Augustine's books against the Pelagians, especially the one on the Spirit and the Letter, also the one on the Deserts and the Remission of Sins, also the one against the two epistles of the Pelagians and likewise the one against Julian, almost all of which are contained in the eighth volume of his works,[3] he will see how little he

divinity 1510, became teacher and canon. 1515 visited Rome. September 1516 at Wittenberg published 151 theses attacking Aristotle and the scholastics, and asserting the doctrine of determinism. In 1518 answered Eck's attack on Luther and July, 1519, debated with Eck at Leipsic as did Luther. He was excommunicated with Luther by the bull *Exsurge Domine* of 1520. During Luther's year at the Wartburg 1521-2, Carlstadt led a series of revolutionary innovations. On the reformer's return he was discredited, withdrew to Orlamünde 1523 and was obliged to leave Saxony in 1524. After a wandering life, in which he published much on the sacrament against Luther, he was called to Basle in 1534 and lived there as professor until his death. His life in two volumes by H. Barge, 1905. *Cf.* Müller: *Luther und Carlstadt*, 1907.

[1] The Pelagians were the opponents of Augustine who maintained absolute free will against his determinism.

[2] Luther is referring to Erasmus' notes on the New Testament, which appeared with the Greek edition about March, 1516. Luther obtained the work soon after it was out, as may be seen by his lectures on Romans (Ficker: *Luthers Vorlesung über den Römerbrief*, 1908). These lasted from the summer of 1515 to the autumn of 1516, Luther's notices of Erasmus begin with the ninth chapter.

[3] Edition of Basle, 1506. The *De spiritu et litera* enjoyed a great reputation at Wittenberg, being edited by Carlstadt. *Cf.* A. Humbert: *Origines de la théologie moderne*. (Paris, 1911), p. 252ff.

follows not only Augustine's opinion, but that of Cyprian,[1] Nazianzen,[2] Rheticius,[3] Irenæus,[4] Hilary,[5] Olympius,[6] Innocent,[7] and Ambrose.[8] Perchance then he will not only understand the apostle aright, but will think Augustine deserving a higher opinion than he now does.

I have no hesitation in disagreeing with Erasmus, because in interpreting the Scriptures I consider Jerome as much inferior to Augustine as Erasmus thinks he is superior.[9] I am not betrayed into approving Augustine because I am an Augustinian, for before I read his books he had no weight with me whatever, but because I see that Jerome, as though on purpose, saw nothing but the historical sense of the Scriptures, and, strange to say, interpreted them better in his *obiter dicta,* as in his epistles, than when he set about to do it in his works.

By no means, therefore, is the righteousness of the law or of works to be understood only of ceremonies, but rather of the whole decalogue. For whatever good is done outside the faith of Christ, even if it makes Fabricii and Reguli, men who were righteous before men, yet it no more savors of justification than do apples of figs.[10] For we are not, as Aristotle thinks, made righteous by doing right, except in appearance, but (if I may so express it) when we are righteous in essence we do right. It is necessary that the character be changed before the deeds; Abel pleased before his gifts. But of this elsewhere.

I beg you to do the office of a friend and a Christian and inform Erasmus of this,[11] for as I hope his authority may be

[1] †258. His words were edited at Rome 1471, at Venice 1471, and at Paris 1512.
[2] Gregory of Nazianz, †389.
[3] Lived at the time of Constantine. None of his writings are extant; Luther knew him only from citations by Augustine.
[4] Of Lyons, †190.
[5] Of Poitiers, †367.
[6] Spanish Bishop of time of Constantine, known only from Augustine's citations.
[7] Pope Innocent I (402-17) of whose *Epistola ad Concilium Carthaginense* Luther is thinking.
[8] Bishop of Milan, †397.
[9] On Luther's opposition of Jerome and Augustine, Humbert, *op. cit.* p. 260ff.
[10] This is a reminiscence of Augustine. *Cf.* Harnack: *History of Dogma.* The well-known saying "that the virtues of the heathen were but splendid vices," often attributed to Augustine, really first occurs in Descartes' *Theodicée. Cf.* Denifle: *Luther und Lutherthum.*
[11] *Cf. infra,* no. 22.

great and famous, so I fear lest through it some will be led to defend the literal, that is the killing, sense of Scripture of which Lyra and almost all the commentators after Augustine are full. For even Lefèvre d'Étaples[1] a man otherwise, Heaven knows, spiritual and sincere, lacks this proper understanding of the Scriptures when he interprets them, although he has it abundantly in his own life and in exhorting others.

You would say that I am rash to bring such men under the rod of Aristarchus;[2] did you not know that I do it for the sake of theology and the salvation of my brothers. Farewell, my Spalatin, and pray for me. In haste, from a corner of our monastery, on the day after St. Luke's feast, 1516.

BROTHER MARTIN LUDER, *Augustinian.*

22. SPALATIN TO ERASMUS AT BRUSSELS.
P. S. Allen: *Opus epistolarum*
Erasmi (Oxford, 1906-), ii. 415. LOCHAU,[3] December 11, 1516.

On the occasion of this letter, *cf. supra,* no. 21. Erasmus received, but did not answer it, and Spalatin wrote again, in November, complaining of his silence, but received no immediate answer to this, either. *Cf.* Allen, *loc. cit.*

. . . I have recently been asked by an Augustinian priest, not less famous for the sanctity of his life than for his theological erudition, and at the same time a sincere admirer of yours, to salute you, and I thought I would do wrong not to seize the present occasion and write to you, busy as I am, the more so because we hope that the business which now[4] compels me to write will be of public interest both to contemporaries and to posterity. Therefore, although the Augustinian monk, a man, believe me, of the most candid mind and the

---

[1] James Lefèvre, of Étaples in Picardy, "the little Luther," as Michelet called him (c. 1455-1536), after studying in Italy, Germany and Paris, settled in 1507 at St. Germain-des-Pres (a church now on the Boulevard St. Germain in Paris) and devoted himself to Biblical studies. In 1509 he published a *Quintuplex Psalterium,* or Psalter in five languages, of which Luther owned and annotated a copy (his notes in Weimar, iv. 463) in 1513-16. He published the first complete translation of the Bible in French 1530. In 1521 and 1523 he was attacked by the Sorbonne for Lutheranism, and during Francis I's captivity in 1525 fled to Strassburg, but later returned and finished his life at Paris. On his doctrine of justification by faith, *cf.* Humbert, *op. cit.,* 283, and *Harvard Theological Review,* October, 1913.

[2] A proverbially captious critic of the second century B. C.

[3] A castle fifteen miles southeast of Wittenberg.

[4] *In praesentiarum,* as in text, is ungrammatical; I suggest: *in praesentarium.*

most faithful heart, has, as they say, put a saddle upon an ox,[1] yet moved by his kindness for me, I preferred, if need be, to expose my rusticity rather than to deny a favor to my friend. And if you have the goodness and wisdom to understand my letter in the spirit in which it is written, I hope that you will not only take me into the number of your clients and admirers, but that since the matter is of some importance, you will thereby greatly profit all students of the Scriptures and of that ancient, pure, uncontaminated theology, not only of our own, but of all future ages.

Having prefaced thus much, I beg you for Christ's sake to take my letter in good part, which, God is witness, I have written for no other purpose than that which I have explained to you, namely, to satisfy the wish of a very pious friend, to profit posterity and to become known to a most learned man. Far from there being any malice in my letter, all of us who have devoted ourselves to letters are your warm friends. The monuments of your genius are so highly esteemed by us that nothing is sought more eagerly in the bookstores, nor bought more quickly, nor read more diligently. My most clement prince, Duke Frederic, of Saxony,[2] Elector of the Holy Roman Empire, who is not less distinguished for wisdom and piety and learning than for fortune, has all of your books that we could find in his ducal library[3] and intends to buy whatever

---

[1] A classical proverb for assigning a task to one who is not fitted to perform it. Cicero, epp. ad Atticum, v. 15.

[2] Elector Frederic the Wise of Ernestine Saxony (1463-May 5, 1525). Became elector in 1486, and made his dominion the most powerful in the Empire. He played an important part in the election of Charles V, June, 1519. He was a patron of the arts, and founded the University of Wittenberg 1502. He was very pious, belonging to many brotherhoods and making a large collection of relics. He was the main support of Luther for eight years, 1517-25, though he never saw him except at Worms. Luther speaks of him in high terms in his lectures on Romans. *Scholia*, p. 272 (circa June, 1516).

[3] This was at Wittenberg. There is extant a list of books bought for it by Spalatin. Among those of the year 1512, are the following: *Opera Erasmi* (probably the *Lucubratiunculae*, published at Antwerp 1503, 1509 and at Tübingen 1512, is meant. *Bibliotheca Erasmiana*, i. 119), Valla's *Elegantiae* and *Annotationes in Novum Testamentum* (both edited by Erasmus), the *Psaltery* of Faber Stapulensis, the works of Augustine, Plutarch, Cicero, Nazianzen, Jerome, Ambrose, Hilary, Bonaventura, Chrisostom, Anselm, and Gerson. In 1513 were bought a *Biblia cum glossa ordinaria*, Homer's *Odyssey*, and Erasmus' *Enconium Moriae*. *Archiv für Geschichte des deutschen Buchhandels*, xviii. Leipsic, 1896. Luther had access to these books; there is one which probably belonged to Frederic annotated by Luther. It is the *Psalterium Fabri Stapulensis*, cf. Weimar, iv. 464.

else you may publish. He recently saw with admiration the works of St. Jerome so restored by your editorial care that we may say that prior to that we seemed to have nothing less than the works of Jerome.¹

But why all this? So that, most kind sir, you may believe that I am writing to you with good intentions. My friend writes me that in interpreting the apostle on the righteousness of works . . . [Here follows an almost word for word quotation from Luther's letter, *supra*, no. 21, to . . .] that some will take occasion by your example to defend the killing, that is the literal sense of Scripture, of which almost all since Augustine are full.

This, most learned sir, is what my friend thought ought to be referred to you as to the Pythian Apollo. Pray hear him, if not for my sake, for that of the whole republic of letters. Wherefore you will do what is most pleasing to us, and also most worthy of your piety, if you kindly deign to answer my good friend and me, however briefly. You will thus gratify my love for you, as my illustrious prince's zeal and reverence for you and Reuchlin and all learned men. I will never be the last in loving and revering you. Farewell, most learned man. . . .

23. LUTHER TO SPALATIN.

Enders, i. 72. WITTENBERG, December 14, 1516.

. . . I have written twice to the venerable Franciscan Father James Vogt,² the elector's confessor, first that he might give my thanks to the elector for the gift of a gown, which is of better cloth than befits a cowl had it not been a prince's gift; and, secondly, that he might make sure the affair of the sacred relics, which he commissioned our most reverend Father Vicar [Staupitz] to get in the regions of the Rhine;³ but I know not whether my letters have arrived or will arrive.

---

¹On this edition, *cf. supra*, no. 15, Frederic could read little Latin, his admiration was probably vicarious.

²Mentioned twice or thrice in these letters; he died April 15, 1522.

³Frederic was a great collector of relics, of which he had by this time more than 5000, housed in the Castle Church at Wittenberg. *Cf.* Kolde: *Augustinercongregation*, 268, 408ff; P. Kalkoff: *Ablass und Reliquienverehrung in der Schlosskirche zu Wittenberg.* Gotha, 1907. Luther had come to dislike them. *Cf.* letter to Spalatin, June 8, 1516, translated, Smith, 33f.

Wherefore will you please find out about it. The reverend Father Vicar asked for relics for the elector from the Archbishop of Cologne,[1] and the business of procuring these relics from the commissary of the archbishop was entrusted to the sub-prior of our monastery at Cologne. But after the departure of Staupitz, when the chief nun of St. Ursula[2] was required to hand over the relics, she alleged a prohibition of the Pope and said that she could not conscientiously comply without his mandate or permission. And though a writ of the licenser was shown her, yet because she doubted its authority and signature she has not yet complied. If you wish, you may tell the prince either to send thither a licenser of approved authority or else to excuse Staupitz.

As to what you write about the most illustrious prince speaking of me frequently and praising me, it does not please me at all, yet I pray that the Lord God may give glory to his humility. For I am not worthy that any man should speak of me, still less that a prince should do so and least of all that such a prince should do so. I daily see and experience that those profit me most who speak of me worst. Yet I pray you permit me to thank our prince for his favor and kindness, though I would not be praised by you or by any man, for the praise of man is vain and that of God only is true, as it is written, "not in man, but in the Lord shall my soul make her boast,"[3] and again, "glory not in your own name, but in his."[4] Not that they who praise us are to be reprehended, but that they praise man rather than God, to whom alone is laud, honor and glory. Amen.

You ask me for my opinion of your plan for translating some little works into German,[5] but it is beyond my power

---

[1] Hermann von Wied, archbishop 1505 to 1546, when the Pope deposed him for favoring the Reformation, in which he had sought the aid of Bucer and Melanchthon. Köstlin-Kawerau, ii. 561, 581.

[2] The famous church and convent at Cologne where are exhibited the bones of the eleven thousand virgins.

[3] Psalm xxxiv. 3.

[4] Psalm cv. 3.

[5] Spalatin, who later translated Melanchthon's *Loci communes* and several of Luther's things, was at this time thinking of translating some of the shorter works of Erasmus. The first thing he did translate from this author was a letter to Antony of Bergen on peace, dated March 14, 1514, under the title: *Herre Erasmus Roterodamus Epistel zu Herr Antony von Berg, Apt zu Sant Bertin, von den*

to give it. Who am I to judge what should either please or profit the public, since it lies entirely within God's grace that anything should do either? Or do you not know that sometimes the more wholesome a thing is the less it pleases? What is more wholesome than the gospel and Christ? And yet to most they seem poor and are an odor of death unto death, to very few an odor of life unto life. Perhaps you will say that you at least hope to please those who like good things. Here you have no need of my judgment; the sheep hear every call of the shepherd, and flee only from the voice of a stranger. Be assured, therefore, that whatever you do, if it is only good and the voice of Christ, will please and profit, though only a few, for sheep are few in this land of wolves.

... Do not follow your own wishes, however good and pious (for the common monk and priest err often and badly), but ask permission, or rather wait for a command to do this or anything unless you wish your work to be straw. I will add a piece of advice. If you delight in reading pure, sound theology, like that of the earliest age, and in German, read the sermons of John Tauler, the Dominican, of which I send you, as it were, the quintessence.[1] I have never read either in Latin or in our own tongue theology more wholesome or more agreeable to the gospel. Taste and see, therefore, how sweet is the Lord, as you have first tasted and seen how bitter is everything in us. Farewell, and pray for me.

BROTHER MARTIN LUTHER, *Augustinian*.

24. LUTHER TO SPALATIN.

Enders, i. 26.   WITTENBERG, December 26, 1516.[2]

manigfältigen schäden des Kriegs und was übels, nachteyls und unwesens usz den Kriegen erwechszt. Printed in quarto without place, date or name of printer. Mr. P. S. Allen (*Opus epistolarum Erasmi*, i. 551) puts this translation in 1514, but the fact that the letter would hardly circulate so briskly and the passage in the letter here translated, would indicate 1516 or 1517 as a more probable date. There is evidence in a letter from Luther to Spalatin, December 21, 1518, to show that he knew this translation.

[1] On Tauler see above no. 20. Luther owned a copy of his sermons in the edition of Augsburg 1508 and his marginal notes are printed Weimar ix. 95. The "quintessence" is the German Theology, a tract by one of Tauler's school, which Luther perhaps attributed to Tauler, and which he first edited in this year. His preface, Weimar, i. 152.

[2] This letter is put by Enders in 1515 on the ground that Luther and the Germans of his time dated the new year from Christmas. The same statement is made by Knaake (Weimar, i. 19) and by Bretschneider of Melanchthon. (*Corpus*

Greeting. Returning yesterday,[1] excellent Spalatin, I found your letters somewhat late in the day. Please answer the bookseller, Martin,[2] on my behalf, that he cannot expect to have my lectures on the Psalms. Though I would rather not have them printed at all, I am forced to. I have not yet been able to obey the command, but now, having finished lecturing

Reformatorum, i. 514.) I have compared all those letters of Luther, to 1541, in which the date is decided by the contents beyond doubt, and find that of 16, 13 assume that the New Year begins on Christmas, and 3 (1519, 1527, 1538) that it begins on January 1 or later. Luther further explains his practice in a sermon on January 1, 1531, of which the beginning is reported in the two following forms: (Weimar, xxxiv. part i. 1) "Man heist hodiernum diem das Newenjarstage, quanquam nos Christiani nostrum newen Jarstag anfangen, sicut etiam scribitur 'Anno nativitatis,' doch wollen wir diesen newen jarstag hinwegwerffen, quanquam inceptus a Romanis et hic mos mansit apud nos, sub tempore Romano sumus, Et alia multa ut Juristerei und Babstum ein gros stuck. Item secundum Romanorum horologium et dierum appelationes." And: "Man heyst diss tag des Newen jhars tag, in qua circumcisio Christi agatur. Wiewol wyr Christen begehen unsern newjars tag am Christtag, tamen illum non reiiciemus, qui a more Romano huc venit. Solden wyr all das weg werffen das von heyden her kummet, totum jus civile et Papatus reiicienda essent." However these texts have been corrupted it is plain from them that Luther knew of the beginning of the year on January 1, though at the time he speaks he thought it more Christian to begin on December 25. This would lead us to expect some variation in his practice, just as we have found to be the case. I therefore think that though the presumption is that the new year was begun on the latter date, yet the weight of evidence from the context of the letter should be decisive. The reasons why I put this letter in 1516 are the following: 1. Luther speaks of having been ordered (by whom it is not known, probably by Staupitz or possibly the elector) to print his *Dictata super Psalterium*. These lectures were not finished until 1516. In the letter to Lang of October 26, 1516, Luther says he is "collector Psalterii" (Enders, i. 67), and in this letter that the lectures "non ita collecta sunt." Luther's revision would be more likely to occupy two months than ten. 2. Luther never published the *Dictata* which first appeared in 1876, but in the spring of 1517 he did publish a commentary on the *Seven Penitential Psalms*. Köstlin-Kawerau, i. 116. I believe this was a substitute for the publication of the whole, for the time agrees exactly with what is said in this letter about being ready to publish by Lent. 3. Luther speaks of having finished lecturing on Paul. He is thinking of his lectures on Romans which probably were finished by the beginning of the winter term 1516, certainly not before, as the numerous quotations from Erasmus' Greek Testament (published March, 1516) prove. *Cf.* Ficker: *Luthers Vorlesung über den Römerbrief*, 1908. It is true that in the letter to Lang of October 26 he says that he expects to begin lecturing on Galatians on the following day, but this, though a difficulty, is not so great as would be the alternative of placing the letter in 1515. He may not have begun lecturing as soon as he expected, or it may be a simple slip.

[1] The explanation of this given in Lincke: *Luthers Reisegeschichte* (1796), p. 26, that Luther had been called to Erfurt to settle the difficulties with the faculty there mentioned in the letters of 1514, would be improbable in any circumstances, doubly so if this letter is in 1516. Luther made a good many trips on business of his order.

[2] "Martino mercatori," the second word taken by De Wette as a proper name, perhaps "Kaufmann." No such bookseller is known. There was a Martin Herbipolensis at Leipsic, and T. Martens, "the Aldus of the Netherlands," who printed at Louvain, 1512-29. Staupitz had frequent dealings with the Netherlands.

on Paul, I can give myself to this work alone. But even when it is finished, it will not be in such a form that it can be printed away from me. Moreover, the professors here wish that it should be published by our printer.[1] This cannot be done before Lent. This also pleases me (if it must be published at all), because it will thus come out in poor style; for those things which are worked up with good types and by careful and able printers do not seem to me to be worthy, but are for the most part trifles deserving the sponge. Farewell. Hastily,[2] from the monastery, the day after Christmas, noon, 1516.   BROTHER MARTIN LUDER, *Augustinian.*

25. LUTHER TO GEORGE MASCOV, PROVOST IN LEITZKAU.

Enders, i. 76.   WITTENBERG (last months of 1516).

Mascov, who later became evangelical pastor at Leitzkau, was not an Augustinian, but a Praemonstratensian whom Luther had perhaps come to know through his business relations with the town. *Cf.* letter to Lang, October 26, 1516, translated, Smith, 32f.

The date of this letter seems to be fixed by the allusion to the plague which raged in Saxony during the autumn of 1516.

Be strong in Christ, nor be troubled because hearts and bodies die. For these are signs of grace rather than of wrath. For God is most angry when he least shows it, as he says through Ezekiel, "I will be no more angry and my jealousy shall depart from thee."[3] This is to be most feared, for it is only spoken to the reprobate. At the end of my letter I beg you to pray the Lord for me, for I confess to you that my life daily approaches nearer hell, for I become worse and more miserable all the time. Farewell.

An exiled son of Adam,

MARTIN LUTHER, *Augustinian.*

26. LUTHER TO GEORGE MASCOV, PROVOST AT LEITZKAU.

Enders, i. 77.   (1516?)

Greeting. Like your order, I believe all orders are run-

---

[1] Probably John Grunenberg, who printed the Seven Penitential Psalms. Luther speaks of him elsewhere, as a poor, slow printer, but as a God-fearing man.

[2] The fact that the letter was written hastily makes it more probable that, supposing he had meant to date it 1517, he should have dated it 1516, just as we often put the date of the past year on the first days of January.

[3] xlii. 16.

ning down hill and acting slothfully so that those who are placed as their guardians may act vigilantly. If, therefore, you are not able to accomplish anything by peace and goodness, I do not advise you to fight obstinately with all your might against the majority of your monks. Give place to wrath and let the tares come up with the wheat; it is better to save the moderate in peace than to disturb all on account of many. It is better to tolerate many on account of a few than to ruin a few on account of many.

BROTHER MARTIN LUTHER.

27. CHRISTOPHER SCHEURL TO LUTHER.

Enders, i. 79.   NUREMBERG, January 2, 1517.

Scheurl (1481-1542), of Nuremberg, visited Italy 1500; LL. D., 1504; lectured on jurisprudence at Wittenberg 1507-11. Then he returned to Nuremberg and filled various high offices, e. g., being sent to represent the cities before the Emperor in Spain, 1523. He was a warm friend both of the Reformers and some of their opponents, especially John Eck, until about 1523, when he returned to the Catholic Church. In 1533 he passed through Wittenberg without seeing Luther. *Allgemeine Deutsche Biographie.*

Honored Sir,[1] and reverend Father, the Augustinian profession, your splendid virtue and great fame have so made me your subject that I greatly desire to be your friend, and to be inscribed in the catalogue of your intimates. With our common parent and vicar I conversed as much as the business of each of us permitted, and during several days and a part of the night the subject of our talk was frequently your excellence, goodness and learning. Besides Martin, we especially desired Otto Beckmann[2] and Amsdorf.[3] [The rest of the letter is chiefly concerned with Staupitz's sermon[4] on predestination.]

[1] 'Obsequia parata."
[2] Of Warburg, near Paderborn, studied at Deventer, matriculated at Leipsic 1506; B. A. 1502; entered Wittenberg 1507; M. A. 1508. He received a canonry and taught here until 1517, when he spent some weeks at Erfurt, matriculating free of cost. In 1524, having remained Catholic, he became priest at Warburg, and in 1527 was made provost of St. Giles (Aegidius) at Münster, from which city he was sent in 1530 as delegate to the Diet of Augsburg. He died in 1556. He was the author of several books. *Archiv für Reformationsgeschichte,* vii. 195ff.
[3] Nicholas von Amsdorf (December 3, 1483-May 14, 1565), Luther's most devoted follower, born at Torgau, matriculated at Leipsic 1500 and at Wittenberg 1502,

28. LUTHER TO CHRISTOPHER SCHEURL AT NUREMBERG.

Enders, i. 81.　　　　　　　　　WITTENBERG, January 27, 1517.

Greeting. Learned and kind Christopher, I received your letter, which to me was both very pleasant and very sad. Why do you frown? For what could you write more agreeable than the well merited praises of the reverend father, or rather of Christ in his vessel, our vicar? Nothing can please me more than to hear that Christ is preached, heard and received, or rather lived, felt and understood. Again, what could you write more bitter than that you desire my friendship, and than the many empty titles with which you load me? I do not wish you to be my friend, for my friendship will bring you not glory, but danger, if, at least, that proverb is true that friends have all things in common. Wherefore, if you partake of what I have by this friendship, you will find yourself richer in nothing but sin, folly and ignominy. Such are the qualities in me, which, as I have said, you called by such contrary epithets. But I know that you savor of Christ and you will say: I admire not you, but Christ in you. To which I answer: How can Christ, true righteousness, dwell with sin and folly? Nay, it is the height of arrogance to presume that you are the habitation of Christ, except that this boast is easily permitted to the apostles. Therefore I congratulate your happiness in becoming the familiar friend of our father, Staupitz, but I pray you spare your honor and do not degenerate into my friendship, even though the reverend father himself, not without peril to me, boasts of me everywhere and says: "I preach not you, but Christ in you," and I must believe it. But it is hard to believe. For this is the unhappiness of this wretched life, that the more numerous and

---

becoming M. A. in 1504 and licentiate in theology 1511. To him Luther dedicated the *Address to the German Nobility*, 1520 (Smith, 79). In 1521 he accompanied Luther to Worms. In 1524 he was called to Magdeburg. In 1534 he took a prominent part in Luther's quarrel with Erasmus, which brought him into trouble with Melanchthon and Bucer. In 1542 Luther consecrated him Evangelical Bishop of Naumburg, which position he was obliged to vacate in consequence of the Schmalkaldic war (1547). In 1552 he obtained a position at Eisenach. His last years were disturbed by quarrels with other Lutherans. *Realencyclopädie.*

[4] *De Executione aeternae predestinationis*, which Scheurl translated into German. On this work see: T. Kolde: *Augustiner-Congregation*, 280, and Humbert: *Origines de la théologie moderne*. It shows marked influence of Luther's ideas on his former teacher. Kolde, *op. cit.*, p. 296.

unanimous are the voices of our friends praising us, the more hurtful they are, as it is written:[1] "a man's enemies are those of his own household," and again, "those who praised me conspired against me."[2] For God's favor recedes as man's advances. For God will be your only friend, or will not be your friend at all. . . .

I do not write this, excellent Christopher, in scorn of your upright and kind intentions, but because I fear for myself. You do the office of a pious Christian, who ought to despise none but himself, but I must also try to be a Christian like you (if our future friendship is to be solid), that is, to despise myself. For he is not a Christian who receives a man on account of his learning, virtue, sanctity and fame (for thus the gentiles do and the little poets,[3] as they call themselves, of our age), but he who cherishes the destitute, the poor, the foolish, the sinner and the wretched. . . .

Behold your verbose friend; do you as a friend be a patient reader.

BROTHER MARTIN LUDER,
One of the Hermits of the Sect of St. Augustine.

29. CHRISTOPHER SCHEURL TO JOHN ECK AT INGOLSTADT.

Christoph Scheurls Briefbuch, hg. von Soden und Knaake, 2 v. Potsdam, 1867-72, ii. 2. NUREMBERG, January 14, 1517.

John Maier of Eck (November 13, 1486-February 10, 1543) in Swabia, matriculated at Heidelberg in 1498, at Tübingen in 1499, taking the degree of B. A. there in the same year, and M. A. in 1501. From 1502-10 he was at the university of Freiburg in Breisgau, becoming D. D. in the last named year. He published several things, among them the Chryssopassus (! *cf.* Revelations, xxi. 20). From 1510 till his death he was professor at Ingolstadt. In 1514, at the request of the banking house of Fugger in Augsburg, he maintained the justice of taking interest at 5 per cent., and debated the subject in 1515 at Bologna, and in 1517 at Vienna. He was anxious to distinguish himself, and early in 1518 attacked Erasmus for saying that the Greek of the New Testament was not as good as that of Demosthenes. About the same time Scheurl sent him Luther's *Theses*, which he answered in a work called *Obelisks*. A debate between him

---
[1] Matthew x. 36.
[2] Psalm cii. 9.
[3] The humanists frequently called themselves poets.

on one side and Luther and Carlstadt on the other was arranged at Leipsic, June and July, 1519. In March, 1520, he was at Rome, where he was largely instrumental in drawing up the bull *Exsurge Domine* against Luther. He was entrusted with the publication of it in Germany in the autumn of the same year. In 1530 he was the Catholic protagonist at the Diet of Augsburg, and after that in several religious conferences, notably that of Ratisbon, 1541. *Cf. Realencyclopädie;* Greving: *Reformationgeschichtliche Studien und Texte,* Hefte i., iv., v.; H. E. Jacobs, in *Papers of American Soc. of Ch. History,* 2d Series, ii., 1910.

. . . Among the theologians [at Wittenberg] the most eminent are Martin Luther, the Augustinian, who expounds the epistles of the Tarsan with marvellous genius, Carlstadt, Amsdorff, Feltkirchen [Bernhardi], and others. If you wish to make the acquaintance of any of them, find out if we can do anything for you.

30. LUTHER TO JOHN LANG AT ERFURT.

Enders, i. 87.   WITTENBERG, March 1, 1517.

. . . If the Psalms[1] translated and explained by me in German please no one, yet they please me exceeding well.[2] John Grünenberg, the printer, is waiting for you to finish those I sent you.

I am reading our Erasmus, and my opinion of him becomes daily worse. He pleases me, indeed, for boldly and learnedly convicting and condemning monks and priests of inveterate ignorance, but I fear that he does not sufficiently advance the cause of Christ and God's grace, in which he is much more ignorant than Lefèvre d'Étaples, for human considerations weigh with him more than divine. I judge him with reluctance, and only to warn you not to read all his works, or rather not to accept all without scrutiny. For our times are very perilous and everyone who knows Greek and Hebrew

---

[1] *Die sieben Busspsalmen,* Wittenberg, 1517. This was Luther's first publication written by himself (the very first having been the *German Theology*), printed April. Luther is perhaps sending them to Lang for revision by that friend who knew Hebrew. Reprinted, Weimar, i. 154ff.

[2] Luther probably means that they please him *because* they will please no one else, for he considered this the surest sign of divine favor. *Cf.* the letter of December 26, 1516, where he says he prefers to have them come out in poor form. Knaake (Weimar, i. 154) seems to miss this meaning when he says: "Luther hatte seine herzliche Freude an ihnen."

is not for that reason a wise Christian, seeing that Jerome, with his five languages, did not equal Augustine with his one, although Erasmus thinks him so superior. But the opinion of him who attributes something to man's will is far different from the opinion of him who knows nothing but grace.[1] I much prefer to conceal this opinion for fear of confirming the enemies of Erasmus; the Lord will perchance give him understanding in his own time. Farewell and salute the professors and Leiffer, and inquire whether Trutfetter[2] has deigned to answer anything.[3]

BROTHER MARTIN LUTHER, *Augustinian Vicar.*

31. LUTHER TO SPALATIN.

Enders, i. 89. (WITTENBERG, Spring of 1517.)

Greeting. As you wish, excellent Sir, I am sending you the Latin tract on predestination,[4] and if you wish it in German, I send you also Scheurl's translation, which is more ornate than the original. Of all the books, I have kept only *The Imitation of Christ's Death*[5] for myself, the others I have given away. Therefore use my copy and I will see if I can get some more. The third book,[6] the little Adam, is unlike

---

[1] It is interesting to see that the subject of the great debate between Erasmus and Luther, 1524-5, was thus early clearly defined.

[2] Jodocus Trutfetter (c. 1460-c. December 1, 1519) of Eisenach, matriculated at Erfurt 1476, became M. A. 1484, bachelor of divinity 1489 and D. D. 1504. He taught logic on which he published a number of books of the "modern," *i. e.*, Occamist school. In 1507 he was called to teach at Wittenberg, where he was elected Rector at once, and on May 1, 1508, Dean of the theological faculty. After a violent quarrel with some of his colleagues, he returned to Erfurt in the summer of 1510, where he remained as professor the rest of his life. Life by G. Plitt, 1876.

[3] This refers to a letter of Luther to Lang, February 8 (translated Smith, 26) in which the writer enclosed some propositions criticizing the prevalent logic and especially Aristotle, which he desired to have communicated to Trutfetter and Usingen.

[4] This is the sermon of Staupitz, *Libellus de executione aeternae praedestinationis*, mentioned by Scheurl, January 2, 1517. Scheurl translated it, and edited both the German, January 20, and the Latin, February 6. *Cf.* Humbert, *op. cit.*, 318ff.

[5] Staupitz' *Ein buchlin von der nachfolgung des willigen sterbens Christi.* Leipzig, 1515.

[6] Luther means his edition of the *German Theology* of 1516, of which the title was: *Eyn geystlich edles Buchleynn, von rechter underscheyd und vorstand. Was der alt unn new mensche sey. Was Adams und was gottis kind sey. Unn wie Adam ynn uns sterben unnd Chrystus ersteen sall. Cf.* Weimar, i. 153.

anything that has ever come into my hands (I lie not) and most theological. I send it, but I shall be sorry I have done so if you read it carelessly. Behold most learned Erasmus and Jerome so much praised by him! I do not know whether they could compose such a book, but I know they have not done so.

I no longer have the Psalms, but the printer.[1] Truly, I am sorry that you want them so much, for they are not published for choice minds, but for the simplest, of whom I have to bear with many. Therefore they are not provided with learned apparatus and are without parallel passages in Scripture, and, though very verbose, strange to say, insufficiently explained. For their subject is foreign to men, or rather they are incapable of understanding it. So it is not for your mind to eat predigested food like this. You already have enough in the works just mentioned, or if they are not enough, I beg you trust yourself to me this once, and with all your power lay hold on the book of Tauler's sermons, of which I spoke to you before. You can easily get it from Christian Döring,[2] a most theological man. From this book you will see how the learning of our age is iron, or rather earthen, be it Greek, Latin or Hebrew, compared to the learning of this true piety. Farewell.

My opinion of Wimpina's book on predestination[3] is the same as Carlstadt's, namely, that he has labored in vain as far as the subject goes. You can easily form an opinion of the labored elegance of his style. Even if the theses he tries to prove were true, he should not draw the conclusions which he does from it.

[1] *The Seven Penitential Psalms.*
[2] A goldsmith who was also a printer and bookseller, mentioned often by Luther as a friend. He died circa 1534.
[3] *De divina providentia.* Frankfort a. O. March 1, 1516. Conrad Koch, known as Wimpina (c. 1460-May 17, 1531), matriculated at Leipzig 1479, B. A. 1481, M. A. 1486, doctor theol. 1503. At this time, or perhaps earlier, he visited Rome. He was involved in a quarrel with Pollich, first rector of Wittenberg. In 1506 he was called by the elector of Brandenburg to be dean of the new university of Frankfort-on-the-Odor, where he spent the rest of his life. In 1517 he had a controversy with Egranus which will be noticed below. On January 20, 1518, John Tetzel, the indulgence preacher, took Luther's *Theses* to Frankfort and with Wimpina's help composed a reply. In 1523 he wrote the *Anacephalaeosis* (printed 1528) against Luther and in 1530 was at the Diet of Augsburg. Life by J. Negwer, 1909.

32. CHRISTOPHER SCHEURL TO LUTHER.

Enders, i. 92. NUREMBERG, April 1, 1517.

Honored Sir:—I told my friend, John Eck,[1] about your virtue, which makes him desirous of knowing you. He does not write, but sends you the book of his disputation.[2] I doubt not that you will answer him and discharge my obligation, as you think it base to be conquered in love or overcome in kindness. Please write him cordially, for I think him worthy of your friendship. The reverend father[3] speaks of you often and hopes you are well. I desire to commend myself to your prayers. Beckmann will explain what the Emperor[4] is doing. Farewell.

DR. C. S.

33. LUTHER TO SPALATIN.

Enders, i. 94. WITTENBERG, April 3, 1517.

Good men have told me, excellent Sir, that you were the trustee for the estate of the late Dr. Reuter,[5] to distribute clothing to the poor. I have, therefore, been requested to ask you for something for this youth Wolfgang,[6] whom we are maintaining here from charity; he is an honest and promising boy. . . .

34. LUTHER TO SPALATIN.

Enders, i. 95. (WITTENBERG, April 9, 1517.)

Greeting. I thank you, dear Spalatin, for your splendid inclination towards me. For I look at the mind only, which is to be preferred to all gifts. You ask me to tell you what you ought to read these days; I advise Augustine on the grace of the New Testament to Honoratus, in which he also

---

[1] *Cf. supra*, no. 29.
[2] *Disputatio Joan. Eckii Theologi Viennae Pannoniae habita.* Augsburg February 1, 1517. On taking interest.
[3] Staupitz.
[4] This refers to the endeavors of Maximilian to get his grandson Charles elected king of the Romans.
[5] Kilian Reuter of Mellerstadt, M. A. of Cologne, matriculated at Wittenberg 1505, died 1516.
[6] Wolfgang Sieberger of Munich, matriculated 1515, in 1517 was taken into the Black Cloister where he became a sort of a servant. After all the monks had left but Luther, he remained as his faithful servant for many years. See Kroker: *Catharina von Bora* (Leipzig, 1906), p. 186.

treats Psalm, xxii., so suitable for this season, or else Hilary's *Explanation of the Psalms,* or else Cyprian's not inept sermons, or Augustine on John, beginning with chapter xiii., which narrates the events of Easter week. I shall try, if I am able, to-morrow to teach how Christ may be seen in every man.[1] Farewell.

MARTIN LUTHER.

35. LUTHER TO CHRISTOPHER SCHEURL AT NUREMBERG.
Enders, i. 96. WITTENBERG, May 6, 1517.

Greeting. Dear Sir, I thank you for your gifts of Staupitz's works, but I am sorry that the reverend father distributed my foolish trifles[2] among you. For they were not written for Nurembergers, that is, for delicate, discerning souls, but for Saxons, rude people as you know, who need their Christian doctrine chewed and predigested for them with all possible care. But even if I wished it, I would not be able to write anything tolerable to Latin ears, less than ever now that I have chosen to devote myself to the service of the dull crowd. Wherefore I pray you keep my book from the inspection of the learned as much as you can.

I have written a friendly and careful letter to our Eck as you asked me, but I do not know whether it has reached him.

I am sending you these declarations, which they call *Theses,* and through you to Father Wenzel Link, and to any others who may care for this sort of tidbit. If I mistake not, you have here not the *Paradoxes* of Cicero,[3] but those of our Carlstadt,[4] or rather of St. Augustine, which are as much more wonderful and worthy than those of Cicero, as Augustine or rather Christ is more worthy than Cicero. For these *Paradoxes* convict of carelessness or ignorance all those to whom they seem more paradox than orthodox, not to say those who, having not read, or not understood, Paul and Augustine, rashly judge them heterodox,[5] blinding themselves

[1] Two sermons *De passione Christi,* Weimar, i. 335.
[2] *I. e.,* the *Seven Penitential Psalms.*
[3] Ciceronis *Paradoxa ad M. Brutum.*
[4] On Carlstadt's *Theses, cf. supra,* p. 42, note.
[5] Cacodoxa.

and others. They are paradoxes to men of mediocre ability, who had not thought of them, but they are good doctrine and fair doctrine to the wise, and to me the best of doctrine.[1] Blessed be God who again commands light to shine in the darkness. . . .

BROTHER MARTIN LUDER, *Augustinian*.

36. LUTHER TO GEORGE MASCOV, PROVOST IN LEITZKAU.
Enders, i. 98. WITTENBERG, May 17, 1517.

Greeting. I sympathize, Reverend Father; I pity the fall of your brother and ours; he yesterday, we to-day, or rather he yesterday, we yesterday, to-day and always are sons of Adam and, therefore, do the works of Adam. Yet we must not despair of God's powerful hand. It is difficult for me to judge and counsel you what to do with him, especially as I do not know your rules. If they do not punish such a transgression with death or life-long imprisonment, it seems to me that he should be made to suffer the full penalty. For it is not you who punish him thus, but justice and the law of which you are not the judge, but the officer. Let not the thought that you are an equal or greater sinner move you. It is enough to confess this to God. It is edifying to think that we must almost always correct those who are better than ourselves, teach those who are more learned, help the worthier, that the saying of the Lord[2] may be established, that the princes of the nations rule over them as their inferiors, but the princes of the faithful serve them as their superiors; for, he says, whosoever is greatest amongst you let him be your servant. Therefore keep your heart humble and gentle to this man, but show the power of a strong hand, since the power is not yours, but God's, but the humility ought not to be God's, but yours. Who knows whether he was permitted to make the stench of his sin public because he could not cure it in secret, but only by public shame. God is wonderful in all his ways above the sons of men. He cures many of sin by sin, as poison is counteracted by poison. Where-

---

[1] "Sunt igitur paradoxa modestis, et qui non ea cognoverint, sed eudoxa et calodoxa scientibus, mihi vero aristodoxa."
[2] Luke xxii. 25.

fore be not afraid; it is the Lord who does this. Praise and love him and pray him for this poor man and for me more devoutly. Farewell.

BROTHER MARTIN LUTHER, *Augustinian*.

37. LUTHER TO JOHN LANG AT ERFURT.

Enders, i. 101.   WITTENBERG, July 16, 1517.

I am preparing six or seven candidates for the master's examination, of whom one, Adrian,[1] is preparing theses to shame Aristotle, for whom I want to make as many enemies and as quickly as I can. . . .

38. LUTHER TO SPALATIN AT WITTENBERG.

Enders, i. 105.   (WITTENBERG, end of August, 1517.)

Greeting. Do you and the confessor,[2] with his friend, come about nine o'clock.[3] If Christopher Scheurl, as ambassador,[4] is with you, let him come, too; otherwise, I have asked Beckmann to invite him. Farewell. Try to get some wine for us, for you know you are coming from the castle to the cloister, not from the cloister to the castle.

BROTHER MARTIN LUTHER.

39. LUTHER TO JOHN LANG AT ERFURT.

Enders, i. 106.   WITTENBERG, September 4, 1517.

Greeting. I have sent to you by Beckmann[5] my *Theses against Scholastic Theology*,[6] and my sermons on the Ten Commandments,[7] but I did not have time to write then, as his departure was announced to me suddenly. But I am

---

[1] Adrian of Antwerp, mentioned in the letter of October, 1516, who died a martyr to the evangelic faith in 1531. On the theses *cf. infra*, no. 39.

[2] James Vogt. He and Spalatin were both attending the elector at the castle.

[3] Ten in the morning was the usual hour for the principal meal, supper being about five p. m. It must be remembered Luther and his contemporaries rose at four or five in the morning.

[4] It is not known what Scheurl's business at Wittenberg was. He had previously taught jurisprudence there.

[5] Who was now going to study at Erfurt

[6] This was the disputation under Luther's presidency by Francis Günther of Nordhausen on his promotion to the first theological degree (baccalaureus ad Biblia), held on the very day this letter was written. Printed, Weimar, i. 221.

[7] The *Decem Praecepta Wittenbergensi praelicata populo*, sermons delivered from the summer of 1516 to Lent 1517, but not printed until 1518. Weimar, i. 394.

waiting with the greatest eagerness and anxiety to know what you think of these paradoxes. Truly I fear that they will seem not only paradox, but heterodox, to your teachers, which can be only orthodox to us. Please let me know this as soon as possible, and assure my truly reverend masters in the theological faculty and in the other departments, that I am most ready to come and defend the theses publicly, either in the university or in the monastery, so that they may not think I am whispering in a corner, if, indeed, they esteem our university so meanly as to think it a corner.

I am sending you the Ten Commandments in both Latin and German,[1] so that if you wish you may preach them to the people, for it is that I did according to the gospel precept as I understand it. . . . Farewell.

BROTHER MARTIN LUDER.

P. S.—Please send back as soon as possible my lectures on Galatians,[2] for the copy belongs to Brother Augustine Himmel,[3] of Cologne.

40. LUTHER TO CHRISTOPHER SCHEURL AT NUREMBERG.
Enders, i. 108.   WITTENBERG, September 11, 1517.

Greeting. Sweet Christopher, even if this letter has no occasion worthy of a man so great as you, yet I thought I had sufficient reason to write only in our friendship, not regarding the titles with which you are worthily adorned, but only your pure, upright, kind and recent affection for me. For, if ever silence is a fault, it is silence between friends, for a little nonsense now and then fosters and even perfects friendship as much as gravity does. . . . Wherefore I preferred to write nonsense, rather than not to write at all. And

---

[1] Luther's text is known only in Latin; when a German version appeared at Basle in 1520 it was made by Sebastian Münster.

[2] These were the lectures on Galatians begun October 27, 1516 (cf. supra, p. 49), but not printed until 1519, and then in a revised form. A copy of the original lectures by an unknown student is still in existence. Köstlin-Kawerau, i. 107, note 2. According to this the lectures were finished March 17, 1517.

[3] Born at Emmerich am Rhein, matriculated at Wittenberg 1516, returned 1521 to Cologne, where his lectures were forbidden, then to Wittenberg again. He was at Luther's recommendation made pastor first of Neustadt-am-Odor and then of Colditz 1529. He succeeded Spalatin (1545) at Altenburg and died there 1553. Enders, vi. 142.

how, ye gods, could that Brother Martin, falsely called a theologian, write anything but nonsense, since he has been reared amidst the hissing and frying of syllogisms, and has had no time to cultivate his pen? . . .

Of the valuable[1] books of Staupitz, which you sent me by Ulrich Pinder,[2] I sold part; part I gave to good friends of the reverend author, and as you bade, I devoted the money to the poor; that is, I spent it on my brothers and myself, for I know none poorer. Please send me, if possible, some more books with the same command, worth a gulden, which I will repay you. For some persons still want the books.

I am sending my propositions,[3] which will seem paradoxes, if not heterodox, to many, which you may show to our learned and ingenious Eck, so that I may hear and see what he has to say about them. . . .

BROTHER MARTIN LUDER,
Augustinian of Wittenberg.

41. CHRISTOPHER SCHEURL TO LUTHER.

Enders, i. 111. NUREMBERG, September 30, 1517.

Greeting in Jesus Christ. You have certainly done well, reverend and learned Father, to write and excuse your silence, for it is known to many that I am an Augustinian who think it base to be conquered in love. Our special friend, Wenzel Link, a good and learned man, bears witness to this. . . . Among others, the most conspicuous for learning and sanctity is Jerome Ebner, the honey and darling of Nuremberg, a duumvir,[4] and of all men the kindest and most upright. He is most devoted to your eminence, at table he hears and speaks of you, he has, reads and admires your *Decalogue, Propositions*[5] and other publications.[6] . . . I will send you fifteen

---

[1] "Ferme pro 2 aureis," worth about two gulden, or one dollar, the purchasing power of money at that time being nearly twenty times what it is now.

[2] Of Nuremberg, matriculated at Wittenberg 1511, studied law, and became professor of it in 1525. The next year he was sent on an embassy by the elector to the Emperor in Spain.

[3] On scholastic philosophy, *cf.* last letter.

[4] Nuremberg, a free city, was ruled by two officers called in German "Losunger." Ebner (January 5, 1477-August 26, 1532), became second Losunger 1515, first Losunger and judge of the Empire 1524.

[5] See last letter.

[6] The *German Theology* or the *Seven Penitential Psalms*.

copies of Staupitz's tract as soon as I can and for a gift. I will send your *Propositions on Scholastic Theology* to Eck, and would like to send them to the theologians of Cologne and Heidelberg, for I know several of them. Farewell.

42. LUTHER TO SPALATIN.

Enders, i. 121. (Early in November, 1517.)

Greeting. I have determined, dear Spalatin, never to communicate the *Dialogue*[1] to anyone. My only reason is that it is so merry, so learned, so ingenious (that is, so Erasmian), that it makes the reader laugh and joke at the vices and miseries of Christ's church, for which rather every Christian ought to pray and weep. But as you ask for it, here it is, read it and use it and then return it.

I do not wish my *Theses*[2] to come into the hands of the illustrious elector or of any of the courtiers before they are received by those who believe that they are branded by them, lest perchance it be thought that I had published them at the instigation of the elector[3] against the Bishop of Magdeburg,[4]

[1] F. A. F. *Poetae Regii libellus de obitu Julii P. M.* 1513. Reprinted in Böcking: *Hutteni opera* (1859-66), iv. 421, and in Jortin's *Life of Erasmus* (1758-60), ii. 600-622. Translated in Froude's *Erasmus*. The authorship is much disputed. Knaake (Weimar vi. 393) and Pastor: *History of the Popes*, English translation by Antrobus, vi. 438, note, attribute it to Faustus Andrelinus Forliviensis; Jortin, *loc. cit.*, and Nichols: *Epistles of Erasmus* (1901-4), ii. 446-9, give it to Erasmus, on the ground of a letter from More to Erasmus; so does Allen: *Opus epistolarum Erasmi*, Ep. 502. But *cf*. More's statement, Jortin ii. 686. Luther at one time thought of translating the dialogue, but gave it up fearing he could not do it justice. Kroker: *Luthers Tischreden* (1903) no. 45. *Cf. infra*, February 20, 1519, no. 130.

[2] The famous Ninety-five Theses on Indulgences. Reprinted Weimar, i. 233, and in *Luthers Werke in Auswahl*, ed. O. Clemen, 1912, i. 1. They were first printed in October and sent around to various Church dignitaries, including Albert of Mayence. On October 31 Luther posted them on the door of the Castle Church. *Cf.* Smith, *op. cit.*, 40ff.

[3] Albert was a rival of Frederic in other matters besides collecting relics, of which Luther speaks in his lectures on Romans, *Scholia*, 305. Luther several times defends himself against the charge here mentioned, *e. g.*, in his *Wider Hans Wurst*, 1542.

[4] Albert (June 20, 1490-September 24, 1545), was the second son of the Elector John Cicero of Brandenburg and Margaret, a daughter of William of Saxony. Destined to the Church, his family influence early secured him advancement. In 1513 he became Archbishop of Magdeburg and Administrator of Halberstadt, and on March 9, 1514, was elected Archbishop and Elector of Mayence and Primate of Germany. For papal confirmation in these illegal pluralities he had to pay enormous sums, for raising which Pope Leo X, in August, 1515, granted an indulgence sale for eight years. Luther, who had already preached against indulgences several times, on October 31, 1517, posted the famous *Ninety-five*

as I already hear some persons dream. But now, we can even swear that they were published without the knowledge of Frederic. More at another time, for now I am very busy. Farewell.   BROTHER MARTIN ELEUTHERIUS,[1]
Augustinian of Wittenberg.

P. S.—You wrote me that the elector had promised me a gown; I would like to know to whom he gave the commission.

43. LUTHER TO JOHN LANG AT ERFURT.

Enders, i. 124.   WITTENBERG, November 11, 1517.

Greeting in Christ. Behold I am sending you some more paradoxes,[2] reverend Father in Christ. Even if your theologians are offended, and say, as they all continually do, that I am rash, proud and hasty in condemning the opinions of others, I answer through you by this letter. I am much pleased with their ripe moderation and long-suffering sobriety, if only they would show it now instead of blaming me for levity and hasty rashness. But I am surprised that they do not look at their Aristotle with the same eyes, or if they look at him, how it is that they do not see that Aristotle in every sentence and clause is nothing but Momus, the very Momus of Momuses.[3] If that heathen, in spite of his cutting bold-

Theses against them (Weimar, i. 229) and sent them with a letter to Albert (*cf.* Smith, p. 40ff). The prelate did not answer the letter, but began a process against Luther which was soon dropped in view of the process at Rome. In 1518 Albert was made cardinal. At this time he posed as a patron of art and learning, and, from entirely worldly motives, took a mediating stand in the Lutheran affair throughout 1520 and at the Diet of Worms, 1521. In 1525 he had thoughts of becoming Lutheran in order to turn his bishoprics into temporal estates, as his cousin Albert of Prussia had done, but he decided against this course. In 1530, at Augsburg, he again mediated between the hostile parties. The Reformation gradually encroached on his dominions and he became more consistently opposed to it. See *Realencyclopädie,* Boehmer: *Luther im Lichte der neueren Forschung* (Leipzig, 2d ed., 1910), p. 66ff, and Preserved Smith, chap. v.

[1] From the Greek ἐλεύθερος meaning free. The custom of turning their names into Latin or Greek was very prevalent among the humanists. It has often been noticed that Luther adopted this name immediately after publishing his Theses on Indulgences, though he later dropped it. Hutten adopted a similar name in his *Eleutherii Byzeni in sequens enconium triumphanti Capnioni decantatum* . . . *Praefatio.* (Capnio was Reuchlin. Erasmus also wrote an apotheosis of Reuchlin, 1522.) This is put by Böcking (*Hutteni opera,* i. 236) in 1518. So Hess writes to Lang (*ibid.* 240, 1518?), "Huttenus noster factus est Eleutherius."

[2] The *Ninety-five Theses.*

[3] According to Erasmus' adage, which Luther well knew, Momus was the god of fault-finding, born of Night and Sleep.

ness, so pleases them and is so much read and cited, why should I a Christian so displease them by giving them a taste of something like their gentle Aristotle? Does a drop of vice displease in me, when a whole sea of it pleases in Aristotle?

Then I wonder that they do not hate and condemn themselves. For what are those schoolmen of yours except critics, Aristarchuses[1] and dumb Momuses? They may judge the opinions of all, only to me is it forbidden. Finally I ask, if my judgment displeases them and they so praise moderation, why do they still judge me and exercise moderation in waiting for the end? . . .

Thus you see that I do not esteem those ghosts of Momuses more than the ghosts they are, nor am I moved by what they think or do not think. . . . I only beg from you and your theologians, that, apart from the faults of the author, you would let me know what you really think of my theses, and show me whatever errors may be in them. . . .

I do not wish that they should expect from me the same humility—that is hypocrisy—that they once thought I ought to show towards their advice and decrees, for I do not wish that what I produce should be by the operation and advice of man, but by that of God. For if the work is of God who will forbid it? If it is not of God who will bring it to pass? . . .

BROTHER MARTIN ELEUTHERIUS,

or rather the servant and captive, Augustinian of Wittenberg.

44. RECTOR AND COUNCILLORS OF THE UNIVERSITY OF MAYENCE TO ALBERT, ARCHBISHOP AND ELECTOR OF MAYENCE.

Ed. Herrmann, *Zeitschrift für*
    Kirchengeschichte, xxiiii. 266.   MAYENCE, December 17, 1517.

Albert on December 1 sent Luther's *Ninety-five Theses* to the University of Mayence with a request for an opinion, and received the following answer:

Most reverend Father in Christ, most illustrious and gracious Prince and Lord! We promise our devoted obedience. We have received with due humility the theses posted at the famous university of Wittenberg by a professor of the order

[1] Another proverbially severe critic.

of St. Augustine, which were sent us by your Reverence. We have read them and among other things we find that they limit and restrict the power of the Pope and the Apostolic See, in which they contradict the general opinions of many blessed and venerable doctors. Wherefore we offer your Reverence the following humble opinion: [Here follows a restatement of the same objection with citations from the Canon Law to prove it.] . . .

45. LUTHER TO SPALATIN.

Enders, i. 131. WITTENBERG, December 20, 1517.

[Luther answers a question about the women who visited Christ's grave.] . . .

I hear that Conrad Wimpina is doing something or other against the preacher of Zwickau[1] on the same question, forsooth he confutes the history of St. Anna and restores those three Marys. He seems to me to have been hardly able to confute him, though I would not take the legend away contentiously on account of the people, but rather let it cool down and cease, especially since an error like that, born of piety, is not to be so severely condemned as that which leads men to worship the saints for money. Farewell.

BROTHER MARTIN ELEUTHERIUS, *Augustinian.*

46. LUTHER TO SPALATIN.

Enders, i. 135. WITTENBERG, December 31, 1517.

Greeting. You ask me, excellent Spalatin, what I would think of publishing some theses asserting that the worship of the saints for temporal goods is superstitious. It was never my idea, Spalatin, to call the veneration of the saints superstitious, even when they are invoked for the most worldly causes. For this is what our neighbors the Beghards[2] of Bohemia think. At least it is better to pray God through his saints for anything whatever, seeing that every gift is of God, than to seek it, as some do, from the devil through magicians

---

[1] John Sylvius Egranus wrote against the legend that St. Anna, the mother of the Virgin, had married three husbands, Joachim, Cleophas and Salome [!] and had borne a daughter named Mary to each of them. Wimpina answered this attack, defending the legend. *Cf.* Kawerau, article Wimpina in *Realencyclopädie.* On Egranus, *cf. infra*, no. 52.

[2] The extreme Hussites.

and wizards. But I would say that it is superstitious, or rather impious and perverse, to pray God and the saints for temporal goods exclusively, and not rather for the goods of the soul and salvation and the will of God, as though forgetful or doubtful of his words: "Seek ye first the kingdom of God and all these things shall be added unto you." Indeed Christ teaches us to despise our vile bodies and their needs. If it is lawful to seek such things, it is only permitted to those who are of imperfect faith and live rather under Moses than under Christ. Wherefore such worship of the saints is a thing to be tolerated only on account of the weak, not to be extolled as a thing worthy of a Christian life. Think a moment, whether any saint is famous among the people for giving chastity, patience, humility, faith, hope, charity and other spiritual goods. These things are not sought, nor have we any saints who, for the sake of such things, have crowds of worshippers, churches and special services. St. Lawrence is worshipped for fire, Sebastian for the plague, Martin and even that unknown St. Roch on account of poverty, St. Anna with her son-in-law and the blessed Virgin for many things, St. Valentine for epilepsy, Job for the French itch; and thus Scholastica, Barbara, Catharine, Apollonia, in short, all famous saints are famous for some temporal goods, and so famous that they are preferred to the apostles, though they would be little esteemed if no one needed temporal goods nor cared for them.[1] Why should we not invoke St. Paul to bring our minds out of the ignorance of Christ, just as we do St. Christopher, for I know not what nocturnal folly? Such worshippers I say, if they are weak, are to be tolerated, and gradually instructed to know better, condemn corporal and seek spiritual blessings, so that we may not always be children under Moses, but may at last

---

[1] This whole passage is clearly an echo of Erasmus' *Enchiridion militis Christiani*, published first 1503, and often. Reprinted, *Erasmi opera* (Lugduno Batavorum, 1703), v. 26. There are several passages in Luther's sermons parallel to it, *e. g.*, Weimar, i. 130-1 (February 2, 1517); iv. 639-41 (December 4, 1517?); and strongest of all, i. 420. In this passage Luther says that the worship of the saints has gone so far that it would be better that their names were not known and their feasts abolished. The sermons of which this is one were first given from the summer of 1516 to Lent 1517, but were not published until July, 1518, when they were more or less retouched. I am inclined to agree with Barge (*Historischer Zeitschrift*, ic. 271) that passages like the one just quoted were probably put in at the later date.

lay hold on Christ a little. If the worshippers are of better faith they are to be convinced that they seek unworthy things. It is a mistake to foster the worship of the saints by the fears of evil and desire for temporal goods. But this is not to be taught to all at all times, but only to the little ones and to the weak; the other should be taught to ask for just the contrary things, punishments, diseases, scourges, crosses and divers torments, as he says:[1] "Examine me, O Lord, and prove me; try my reins and my heart." . . . Thus the Lord's prayer teaches us to seek for spiritual gifts in the first three petitions, and for the things of God, and afterward for our own. . . .

BROTHER MARTIN ELEUTHERIUS, *Augustinian.*

47. LUTHER TO SPALATIN AT WITTENBERG.[2]

Enders, i. 140.   WITTENBERG, January 18, 1518.

Greeting. Hitherto, excellent Spalatin, you have asked me things that were within my power or at least within my daring, to answer, but now that you ask to be directed in those studies which pertain to knowledge of the Scriptures you demand something beyond my abilities, especially as I have hitherto been able to find no guide for myself in this matter. Different men think differently, even the most learned and most gifted. You have Erasmus who plainly asserts that Jerome is the great, almost the only, theologian in the Church.[3] If I oppose Augustine to him I will seem an unjust and partial judge, partly because I am an Augustinian and partly on account of the long established judgment of Erasmus, since he has said that it is most impudent to compare Augustine and Jerome. Other men think differently. Among such judges of such things I feel unable to decide anything on account of the mediocrity of my learning and talents. But among those who

[1] Psalm xxvi. 2.
[2] Luther says he answers Spalatin's letter on the day it was written, which would imply that Spalatin must at least be very near Wittenberg.
[3] Luther expressed similar thoughts in his letter of October 19, 1516. The expressions in the present letter seem to indicate that he had read the introductions to the edition of Jerome which appeared in 1516 (P. S. Allen, epp. 326, 396). *Cf.* Luther to Spalatin, August 24, 1516. It is noticeable that the direct comparison of Augustine and Jerome, which I have not found elsewhere in Erasmus, was clearly defined in the letter of the humanist to Eck, May 15, 1518 (Allen, ep. 844), first published in August, 1518. There is a good deal about Jerome and Augustine in the *Apology* mentioned below.

either hate or slothfully neglect good letters (that is, among all men) I always praise and defend Erasmus as much as I can, and am very careful not to ventilate my disagreement with him, lest perchance I should thus confirm them in their hatred of him. Yet there are many things in Erasmus which seem to me far from the knowledge of Christ, if I may speak as a theologian rather than a grammarian; otherwise there is no man more learned or ingenious than he, not even Jerome whom he so much extolls. But if you communicate this opinion to others you will violate the laws of friendship. I warn you in prudence. There are many, you know, who search out every occasion of defending sound learning. What I tell you is therefore a secret. Indeed you should not believe it until you have proved it by reading. If you extort from me the result of my studies I will conceal nothing from you, as my dearest friend, but only on condition that you will not follow me except in using your own judgment.

In the first place it is most certain that the Bible cannot be mastered by study or talent. Therefore you should first begin by praying that not for your glory, but for his, the Lord may be mercifully pleased to give you some comprehension of his words. . . . You must completely despair of your own industry and ability and rely solely on the influx of the Spirit. *Experto crede.* Then having achieved this humble despair, read the Bible from the beginning to the end, that first you may get the simple story in your mind (as I believe you have already done) in which Jerome's epistles and commentaries will be of great help. But for the understanding of Christ and the grace of God, this is for the hidden knowledge of the spirit, Augustine and Ambrose seem to me far better guides, especially as Jerome seems to Origenize, that is, allegorize, too much. This I say saving Erasmus' judgment, as you asked for my opinion, not for his.

You may begin, if you like my course of study, reading Augustine's *The Spirit and the Letter*, which now our Carlstadt, a man of incomparable zeal, has edited and thoroughly well annotated. . . . Finally I am sending you the *Apology*[1] of

---

[1] *Apologia contra Fabrum Stapulensem*, Antwerp, Martens (1517). Lefèvre d'Étaples, in his edition of Hebrews (1512) had proposed reading "Thou hast

Erasmus, but I am very sorry that such a war should have arisen between two such princes of letters. Erasmus, indeed, conquers and speaks the better, even if a little bitterly, though in some things he acts as if he wished to keep his friendship with Lefèvre. Farewell, dear Spalatin.

BROTHER MARTIN ELEUTHERIUS.

48. LUTHER TO GEORGE SPALATIN.

Enders, i. 152.   WITTENBERG, February 15, 1518.

Greeting. What you request, or rather command, excellent Spalatin, I now do, namely, send through you my thanks to the most illustrious elector for the splendid and princely gift of game donated by him to our students newly promoted to the degree of master. I told them all it was from the elector. And personally I am wonderfully pleased by the kindness of the clement and generous prince, for even a man loveth a cheerful giver.

You again subjoin two little questions. First, as to what should be the attitude of mind of one who is about to sacrifice[1] or to do other pious works. I answer briefly: You should be at once despairing and confident in doing any work, despairing on account of yourself and your work, confident as regards God and his mercy. . . . To speak plainly, whenever you would sacrifice or do a good work, know positively and firmly believe that this work of yours will not please God at all, no matter how good, great and difficult, but that it will be worthy of reprobation. Wherefore judge yourself first, accuse yourself and your work and confess before God. . . . Therefore when you are thus desperate, and have humbly confessed before God, you must without hesitation assume that he will be merciful. For he sins no less who doubts God's mercy than he who trusts in his own efforts. . . .

Secondly, you ask me how much indulgences are worth. The

---

made him a little lower than God" instead of "than the angels." Erasmus by rejecting this interpretation in his New Testament, had drawn down the animadversions of the French scholar in the second edition of Paul's Epistles, Paris, 1517, and it is to this that his *Apology* is directed. Luther got the work very promptly, as it only appeared late in 1517. *Cf. Bibliotheca Erasmiana, Admonitio*, etc. (Gand, 1900), p. 89ff.

[1] The Roman Catholics regard the mass as a sacrifice offered by the priest to God, and as a good work.

matter is still in doubt, and my *Theses* overwhelmed with abuse. Yet I may say two things, the first to you and my friends only, until the matter shall be decided publicly. Indulgences now seem to me to be nothing but a snare for souls, and are worth absolutely nothing except to those who slumber and idle in the way of Christ. Even if our Carlstadt does not share this opinion, yet I am certain that there is nothing in them. For the sake of exposing this fraud, for the love of truth I entered this dangerous labyrinth of disputation, and aroused against myself six hundred Minotaurs, not to say Radamanthotaurs and Aeacotaurs.[1]

Secondly I may say, what is not in doubt and what even my adversaries and the whole Church are forced to confess, that alms and helping our neighbor is incomparably better than buying indulgences. Therefore take heed to buy no indulgences as long as you find paupers and needy neighbors to whom you may give what you may wish to spend for pardons. . . . God willing, you will see more of this when I publish the proofs of my *Theses*. For I am compelled to do this by those men more ignorant than ignorance itself, who proclaim me a heretic in all their speeches, and are so furious that they even try to make the University of Wittenberg infamous and heretical on account of me. I labor much more to restrain myself, and not to despise them, though by thus doing I sin against Christ, than to triumph over them. . . . I am particularly sorry to have to inform you that those brawlers and others with them have constructed another engine against me, by spreading the rumor that all that I do is at the hest of our prince on account of his hatred to the Archbishop of Magdeburg.[2] . . .

49. LUTHER TO JOHN LANG AT ERFURT.

Enders, i. 157. WITTENBERG, February 19 (1518).

Greeting. Wolfgang Capito[3] writes, reverend Father, that

---

[1] Theseus slew the Bull of Minos (Minotaur) in the Labyrinth of Crete. Minos, Radamanthus and Aeacus were the three judges of the infernal regions; Luther means that he had excited all the monsters of hell against himself.

[2] *I. e.*, Albert of Mayence. Luther mentions this charge elsewhere.

[3] Wolfgang Fabritius Köpfel of Hagenau (1478?-1541), studied at Freiburg and Ingolstadt, where he took his doctorate in divinity by 1512. In 1513 he went to Basle, where he became cathedral preacher and professor of theology in the

Erasmus's *Adages*[1] are being reprinted in an enlarged edition, besides the *Querela Pacis*,[2] *The Dialogues of Lucian*,[3] the *Utopia*[4] of More[5] (mentioned by Richard Pace),[6] More's *Epigrams*, the *Institutiones Hebraicae*[7] of Capito himself, and that work on account of which I am now writing, Erasmus's *Apology against Lefèvre d'Étaples*.[8] I mention these books that you may know what to recommend to your book-dealers who are going to set out to the Frankfort Fair. I much desire More's *Utopia* and Capito's *Hebraic Institutions*, but especially the *Apology*, unless it is the same[9] that we have had here for some time. . . .

50. LUTHER TO GEORGE SPALATIN.

Enders, i. 177. (WITTENBERG, middle of March, 1518.)

The dating of this letter is a puzzle. Enders dates "end of March or beginning of April," and this is defended by O. Clemen: *Luthers Werke in Auswahl*, 1912, i. p. 10, because the letter assumes that the *Sermon on Indulgence and Grace* had already been published; as this

University. In 1520 he entered the service of Archbishop Albert of Mayence. Three years later he declared for the Reformation and went to Strassburg, at which place, in company with Bucer, he occupied a leading position for the rest of his life, taking part in the Synod of Bern in 1532, and in the Wittenberg Concord of 1536. His religious views were already advanced in 1512, from which time on for several years he was an ardent admirer of Erasmus. *Cf.* Baum: *Capito und Butzer* (1860), P. Kalkoff: *Capito im Dienste Albrechts von Mainz* (1907) and *Realencyclopädie*. This letter to Luther is lost; Luther answered it, *cf. infra*, September 4, 1518, no. 78.

[1] The *Adagia*, first printed in 1500, were repeatedly revised and enlarged; the edition here referred to being that of Froben, 1518. *Bibliotheca Erasmiana*, i. 2.

[2] First issued 1516, reprinted by Froben, December, 1517; *op. cit.*, 166.

[3] *Luciani Saturnalia et complures dialogi Erasmo interprete*, printed at the end of the *Querela Pacis* of 1517.

[4] This famous work, first published at Louvain, 1516, was reprinted with More's *Epigrams* by Froben in March, 1518.

[5] Thomas More (1477-1535), later Chancellor of Henry VIII. He was consistently opposed to the Reformation, taking an active part in the controversy between his king and Luther. Lives by Brigett and Hutten and by Sidney Lee in *Dictionary of National Biography*.

[6] Pace (1482?-1536), studied in Italy, where he met Erasmus (1507-8), and then entered the diplomatic service. He was sent on a mission to Switzerland in October, 1515. While at Constance he composed his *De Fructu qui ex doctrina percipitur*, Basle, Froben, October, 1517. Leaving Constance in October, 1517, he is found in England in January, 1518 (*Letters and Papers of Henry VIII*, ii. index), on the trip very probably passing through Erfurt (Enders, *loc. cit.*). His reference to More's *Utopia* may have been at this time orally or in his *De Fructu*. He was employed by Henry VIII to negotiate for the imperial election in 1519, and by Wolsey in the endeavor to get the papacy in 1521 and 1523. *Dictionary of National Biography*.

[7] Basle, Froben, 1518.

[8] *Apologia adv. Fabrum Stapulensem*, Antwerp, 1517; Basle, 1518.

[9] It was the same; *cf. supra*, no. 47.

sermon contains allusions to the theses of Tetzel-Wimpina, defended at Frankfort on the Oder on January 20th, which Clemen thinks arrived in Wittenberg not earlier than March 17th, the sermon and consequently the letter must be some time after that date. I think it possible, however, that the Tetzel-Wimpina theses may have come to Luther's hands before they were offered for sale at Wittenberg and seized by the students, on which see next letter.

P. Kalkoff, on the other hand, puts the letter early in March because he believes that the visit of the Abbot of Lehnin, which Luther says took place "yesterday," came soon after March 5. *Zeitschrift für Kirchengeschichte*, xxxii. 411, note. As Kalkoff, however, admits that the *Sermon on Indulgence and Grace* was published during the last week in March, he must interpret the passage referring to that sermon differently from my understanding of it. The matter is further complicated by a letter to Spalatin, March 25th (*infra*, no. 53), assuming that the visit here recorded has already been made. Perhaps "middle of March," making the sermon as early and the visit of the abbot as late as possible, best satisfies all requirements.

Greeting. Having received power of remission and absolution in all cases save a few, you should be thankful to him who gave you this power.[1] I am glad about the power of judging cases, but as to the remission of penalties, that is indulgences, you know what I think of them, though even here I say nothing positively. My opinion is the same about the weekly fasts[2] in the city of Rome, since they are nothing but indulgences. For I think the prayers said or works done to acquire indulgences worth more than the pardons themselves. . . .

Yesterday the Lord Abbot of Lehnin[3] was with me on behalf of the reverend Bishop of Brandenburg,[4] from whom he brought me a letter. He also expressed to me the hope and request of the said bishop that I should defer for a little while the publication of my *Resolutions*[5] and of all other lucubra-

---

[1] It is well known that certain sins were reserved for absolution by the Pope, who occasionally delegated this power to others.

[2] "Stationes." Cf. *Realencyclopädie*,³ v. 771.

[3] The Abbot Valentine, whose family name is unknown, of Lehnin, about fifteen miles northeast of Wittenberg, was made abbot 1509, and died 1542. He took considerable part against the Reformation, in the employ of Elector Joachim I of Brandenburg. *Zeitschrift für Kirchengeschichte*, xxxii. 410, note.

[4] Jerome Scultetus, son of a village judge (Schultheis, hence his name) of Gramschitz in the duchy of Glogau, was made Bishop of Brandenburg in 1507, and of Havelberg also in 1520. He died 1522.

[5] *Resolutiones disputationum*, a defence of the *Theses*, Weimar, i. 525. As Wittenberg was in the diocese of Brandenberg, Luther submitted this work to his spiritual superior before publishing it.

tions I might have on hand. Moreover he was very sorry that I had published a *Sermon on Indulgences*[1] in the vernacular, and he begged that no more copies be printed or sold. I was overcome with confusion to think that so great a bishop had sent so great an abbot so humbly to me for the sake of this only; I replied: "I am satisfied; I prefer to obey rather than to work miracles even if I could," and other things to excuse my zeal. For although the bishop thought there was no error in my work, but that all my propositions were catholic, and although he himself would condemn the "indiscreet" proclamations of indulgences, yet for fear of scandal, he judged it better to be silent and patient a little while. Farewell in the Lord.

BROTHER MARTIN ELEUTHERIUS, *Augustinian.*

51. LUTHER TO JOHN LANG AT ERFURT.

Enders, i. 168. WITTENBERG, March 21, 1518.

Greeting. Reverend Father, I sent you some sheets of Carlstadt's edition of Augustine's *The Spirit and the Letter*, as I did to some others, but I forget to whom I sent which ones. . . .

The false preachers of indulgences are thundering against me in wonderful style from the pulpit, and as they cannot think of enough monsters with which to compare me, they add threats, and one man promises the people that I shall certainly be burned within a fortnight and another within a month. They publish *Theses* against me, so that I fear that some day they will burst with the greatness of their wrath. Everybody advises me not to go to Heidelberg[2] lest perchance what they cannot accomplish against me by force they will do by guile. But I shall fulfill my vow of obedience and go thither on foot, and I shall pass through Erfurt, but do not wait for me as I can hardly leave here before April 13.[3] Our elector, with great kindness, as he is inclined to favor our theology, unasked

---

[1] *I. e.*, the *Sermon von Ablass und Gnade*, which Luther had expressed the intention of publishing in a letter to Scheurl of March 5, translated in my *Luther*, p. 43f. The "Sermon" was really a series of German theses on indulgences. Weimar, i. 243.

[2] A general chapter of the Saxon Province of Augustinians was to be held at Heidelberg in April and May. Gabriel della Volta, General of the order, had instructed Staupitz to force Luther to recant at this meeting. Smith, p. 46.

[3] In fact Luther left on Sunday, April 11.

took me and Carlstadt completely in his protection, and will not suffer them to drag me to Rome, which greatly vexes my enemies who know it.

If rumor has perhaps told you anything about the burning of Tetzel's *Theses*[1] lest anyone should add anything to the truth, as is usually the case, let me tell you the whole story. The students are remarkably tired of sophistical and antiquated studies and are truly desirous of the Holy Bible; for this reason, and perchance also because they favored my opinion, when they heard of the arrival of a man sent from Halle by Tetzel, the author of the *Theses*, they threatened the man for daring to bring such things here; then some students bought copies of the *Theses* and some simply seized them, and, having given notice to all who wished to be present at the spectacle to come to the market place at two o'clock, they burned them without the knowledge of the elector, the town council, or the rector of the university or of any of us. Certainly we were all displeased by this grave injury done to the man by our students. I am not guilty, but I fear that the whole thing will be imputed to me. They make a great story out of it, and are not unjustly indignant. I know not what will come of it except that my position will be made still more perilous. Everyone says that Dr. Conrad Wimpina is the author of those *Theses*, and I think it is certainly so. I send one rescued from the flames to show you how mad they have become against me. . . .

52. LUTHER TO JOHN SYLVIUS EGRANUS AT ZWICKAU.

Enders, i. 172. WITTENBERG, March 24, 1518.

John Wildenhauer (Sylvius) of Eger in Bohemia (†June 11, 1535) matriculated at Leipsic 1500, B. A. 1501, M. A. 1507. He was preacher at Zwickau 1516-1521, when a quarrel with Thomas Münzer forced him to leave. For two years he preached at Joachimsthal, and then resumed a wandering life. At first a warm friend of Luther he afterwards became alienated. Allen, iii. 409. *Allgemeine deutsche*

---

[1] Luther's *Theses* cut into Tetzel's profits and forced him to stop selling indulgences. Hoping to combat them on their own ground, he went to the University of Frankfort-on-the-Oder, and with the help of Conrad Wimpina composed a set of counter theses, recently reprinted by W. Kohler: *Luthers 95 Thesen samt seinen Resolutionen, sowie die Gegenschriften von Wimpina-Tetzel, Eck und Prierias, und die Antworten Luthers darauf.* Leipzig, 1903.

Biographie. Life by O. Clemen in *Mitteilungen des Altertumsvereins für Zwickau,* vi., vii. (1899, 1902). *Cf.* also G. Buchwald: *Ungedruckte Predigten des J. S. Egranus* (at Zwickau 1519-22). Leipsic, 1911. *Cf. supra,* no. 46.

Greeting. I have seen the theses of Dr. Düngersheim of Ochsenfurt,[1] apparently directed against you, though without mentioning your name. Be strong and constant, dear Egranus, as you ought. If these things were of the world, the world would love its own. Whatever is in the world must necessarily perish in the world, that the spirit be glorified. If you are wise, congratulate me, as I do you.

A man of signal and talented learning and of learned talent, has recently written a book called *Obelisks* against my *Theses.* I mean John Eck, doctor of theology, chancellor of the University of Ingolstadt, canon of Eichstätt, and now, at length, preacher at Augsburg, a man already famous and widely known by his books. What cuts me most is that we had recently formed a great friendship. Did I not already know the machinations of Satan, I should be astonished at the fury with which Eck has broken that sweet amity without warning and with no letter to bid me farewell.

In his *Obelisks* he calls me a fanatic Hussite, heretical, seditious, insolent and rash, not to speak of such slight abuse as that I am dreaming, clumsy, unlearned, and that I despise the Pope. In short, the book is nothing but the foulest abuse, expressly mentioning my name and directed against my *Theses.* It is nothing less than the malice and envy of a maniac. I would have swallowed this sop for Cerberus,[2] but my friends compelled me to answer it. Blessed be the Lord Jesus, and may he alone be glorified while we are confounded for our

---

[1] Jerome Düngersheim (1465-1540), of Ochsenfurt on the Main, matriculated at Leipsic 1484, was B. A. in 1485, M. A. 1489. Ordained priest 1495, and took a degree in theology at Cologne in 1496, after which he lectured at Leipsic. 1501 he became priest at Zwickau, in 1504 went to Italy. 1505 returned to lecture at Leipsic. He wrote several works. Wrote to Erasmus about his New Testament, March 18, 1517 (Allen, *op. cit.,* ep. 554). Life in the *Allgemeine Deutsche Biographie.* The theses referred to here were directed against some propositions made by Egranus in the Zwickau pulpit. Egranus answered them in an article published within two weeks after this letter was written, for which Luther wrote an introduction. Weimar, i. 315. On Düngersheim's relations with Luther, *infra,* 192.

[2] As Burke would have said: "This honeyed opiate compounded of treason and murder."

sins. Rejoice, brother, rejoice, and be not terrified by these whirling leaves, nor stop teaching as you have begun, but rather be like the palm tree which grows better when weights are hung on it.

The more they rage, the more cause I give them. I leave the doctrine they barked at yesterday for one they will bark at more fiercely to-morrow. . . . I wrote to Dr. Düngersheim of Ochsenfurt that your assertions did not seem to me errors, but truths, and that his propositions appeared to me for the most part erroneous, and I dared say with confidence that you would defend both your "errors" and mine. But if he offered arguments from the schoolmen, I said that he knew he would only waste his words.

I vow there is hardly any theologian or scholastic, especially at Leipsic, who understands one chapter of the Bible, or even one chapter of Aristotle's philosophy, which I hope to prove triumphantly if they give me a chance. Conning over the words of the Gospel is not understanding it. Wherefore flee not before the face of ignorance, and forget this clamor of doctors, universities and professors, for they are specters, not men, but apparitions, which you would not fear if you could see them clearly. The Lord teach and comfort you. Farewell in him.

MARTIN LUTHER, *Augustinian.*

53. LUTHER TO SPALATIN.

Enders, i. 179. (WITTENBERG, c. March 25, 1518.)

This letter is placed by Enders "shortly before Easter, April 4, 1518." The more exact date given by Kalkoff, in *Zeitschrift für Kirchengenschichte,* xxxii. 411.

Greeting. Briefly, I will do all you write. For the reverend lord bishop[1] has answered and freed me from my promise. Only I do not know whether I can preach on these three following days, but I will see; if not, my colleague Amsdorf will supply my place.

BROTHER MARTIN ELEUTHERIUS.

[1] *I. e.,* of Brandenburg. This refers to his prohibition to Luther to print his Resolutions, on which *cf. supra,* no. 50. Luther apparently sent them to the press at once; *cf.* O. Clemen, in his edition of *Luthers Werke,* i. 15.

54. LUTHER TO JOHN STAUPITZ.

Enders, i. 175. WITTENBERG, March 31, 1518.

Greeting. Dear Father in the Lord, I am so busy that I must write briefly. First, I know perfectly well that my name is in bad odor with many, so much have even good men found fault with me for condemning rosaries, tonsures, chanting psalms and other prayers, in short, all "good works." St. Paul had the same experience with those who said that he said: "Let us do evil that good may come."[1] Truly I have followed the theology of Tauler and of that book[2] which you recently gave to Christian Döring to print; I teach that men should trust in nothing save in Jesus Christ only, not in their own prayers, or merits, or works, for we are not saved by our own exertions, but by the mercy of God. From these words my opponents suck the poison which you see they scatter around. But as I did not begin for the sake of fame, I shall not stop for infamy. God will see to it. My adversaries excite hatred against me from the scholastic doctors, because I prefer the Fathers and the Bible to them; they are almost insane with their zeal. I read the scholastics with judgment, not, as they do, with closed eyes. Thus the apostle commanded: "Prove all things; hold to that which is good."[3] I neither reject all that they say nor approve all. Thus those babblers make the whole of a part, a fire of a spark and an elephant of a fly. But with God's help I care nothing for their scarecrows. They are words; they will remain words. If Duns Scotus, Gabriel Biel and others had the right to dissent from Aquinas, and if the Thomists have the right to contradict everybody, so that there are as many sects among the schoolmen as there are heads, or as hairs on each head, why should they not allow me the same right against them as they use against each other? If God is operating, no one can stop him. If he withholds his aid, no one can help the cause. Farewell and pray for me and for the truth of God wherever it may be.

BROTHER MARTIN ELEUTHERIUS, *Augustinian.*

[1] Romans iii. 8.
[2] Namely, Staupitz's own book, "Von der Liebe Gottes."
[3] 1 Thessalonians, v. 12.

55. LUTHER TO GEORGE SPALATIN.
Enders, i. 183.　　　　　　　　　　　　Coburg, April 15, 1518.

On April 11th, Luther set out to attend the General Chapter of the Augustinians at Heidelberg, whither he had been summoned by Staupitz at the request of the General Volta, in hopes of making him recant. He did not do so, but resigned his office of District Vicar, to which his friend Lang was elected. *Cf. supra*, no. 51, and Smith, p. 46.

Greeting. Dear Spalatin, I expect you have heard from our friend Pfeffinger[1] all that we said to each other when I met him at Judenpach. Among other things I was glad to have a chance to make a rich man a little poorer. For you know how pleased I am, whenever I can do it conveniently, to be a burden to the rich, especially when they are my friends. I took care that he should provide supper even for my two strange companions, which cost him ten grosschen apiece. Even now, if possible, I would make the elector's steward[2] at Coburg pay for us; if he will not do so, still we shall live at the elector's expense. I have not yet seen the man, nor do I know whether I am to see him. For when we arrived in the evening very tired, we sent him the letters by a messenger. But he went late to the castle nor has he returned yet. I do not know why he did it; perhaps he is too busy to take care of us. Urban himself, our messenger, remembers perfectly that he was ordered to go to Würzburg with us. But whether he comes or not with God's favor we shall continue our journey to-morrow.

Everything else is all right, by God's grace, except that I confess that I sinned in coming on foot. Since my contrition for this sin is perfect, and full penance has been imposed for it, I do not need an indulgence for it. I am terribly fatigued, but can find no vehicles free, and thus I am abundantly, much, greatly and sufficiently contrite and penitent. . . .

　　　　　　　　　　Brother Martin Eleutherius.

56. LUTHER TO GEORGE SPALATIN.
Enders, i. 185.　　　　　　　　　　　　Wurzburg, April 19, 1518.

Greeting. We arrived finally at Würzburg yesterday [Sun-

[1] He was probably sent by the elector to make sure that Luther would be perfectly safe in going to Heidelberg.
[2] Perhaps Paul Bader whom Luther learned to know when in 1530 he spent six months at the castle of Feste Coburg.

day], dear Spalatin, and the same evening presented the letters of our illustrious elector. . . . The reverend lord bishop himself,[1] when he had received the letters, summoned me, and having talked with me face to face, expressed the wish to send a messenger at his own expense to accompany me to Heidelberg, but as I found several of my order here, especially our Erfurt Prior John Lang, I thanked the clement bishop, but said I thought it was not necessary to send the messenger for my sake. I wish we could all get conveyances, since I am very tired walking. I only asked that he would deign to provide me with a letter as a passport (as it is called). I have just received this, and will set out in a wagon. . . . Farewell. From our monastery at Würzburg.

BROTHER MARTIN LUTHER, *Augustinian.*

57. MARTIN BUCER TO BEATUS RHENANUS AT BASLE.

Briefwechsel des Beatus Rhenanus, gesammelt und herausgegeben von A. Horawitz und K. Hartfelder, Leipzig, 1886, p. 106ff.

HEIDELBERG, May 1, 1518.

Martin Bucer was born at Schlettstadt, 1491, and entered the Dominican order there in 1506. After his transfer to Heidelberg, he took much interest in the humanists, and especially Erasmus. He met Luther at the time this letter was written, and from then on was his devoted follower. In 1521 he left the cloister and became chaplain to the Elector Palatine, at Landstuhl, coming into close relations with Hutten and Sickingen at the time of the Diet of Worms. From 1523-49 he was the leading Reformer of Strassburg, making it his particular aim to reconcile the Lutheran and Zwinglian branches of the Protestant Church, in which he attained partial success in the Wittenberg Concord, 1536. In 1549 he was called to England, where he taught a year at Cambridge, dying in 1551. See J. W. Baum: *Capito und Butzer,* Eberfeld, 1860; Harvey: *Bucer in England,* 1907. Many of Bucer's letters have been published in M. Lenz: *Briefwechsel des Landgrafen Philipp von Hessen mit Butzer,* 1880ff, 3 vols., and in T. Schiess: *Briefwechsel der Blaurer,* 1908ff.

Beatus Bild, of Rheinau (1485-May 20, 1547), matriculated at Paris, 1503, B. A. 1504, M. A. 1505. He then began working as proofreader for Henry Estienne; in 1507 returned to Schlettstadt, and in 1508 to Strassburg. From 1511 to 1526 he worked at Basle, publishing and editing books for Froben. From 1526 to his death he lived at Schlett-

[1] Lawrence von Bibra, Bishop 1495-February 6, 1519, was a warm admirer of Luther. On one occasion, shortly before his death, he advised the elector not to let Luther be taken away from Wittenberg.

stadt. His historical work was large and good (E. Fueter: *Geschichte der neueren Historiographie* (1911) 190-2), and he was also a friend and assistant of Erasmus, whose religious views he shared. His letters published, *op. cit. supra*, with life by his friend John Sturm. *Cf.* P. S. Allen, *Opus epistolarum Erasmi*, ii. 60.

I have read your attack on our theologians, and I should have been sorry had it been vain. Wherefore, lest you should seem to yourself to have triumphed, after we Heidelbergers had deserted the cause (for it fared otherwise with our elder Wimpfeling,[1] although he defended us nobly), I will oppose to you a certain theologian, not, indeed, one of our number, but one who has been heard by us in the last few days,[2] one who has got so far away[3] from the bonds of the sophists and the trifling of Aristotle, one who is so devoted to the Bible, and is so suspicious of antiquated theologians of our school (for their eloquence forces us to call them theologians and rhetoricians, too), that he appears to be diametrically opposed to our teachers. Jerome, Augustine and authors of that stamp are as familiar to him as Scotus[4] or Tartaretus[5] could be to us. He is Martin Luther, that abuser of indulgences, on which we have hitherto relied too much. At the general chapter of his order celebrated here, according to the custom, he presided over a debate, and propounded some paradoxes, which not only went farther than most could follow him, but appeared to some heretical. But, good

[1] James Wimpfeling of Schlettstadt (1450-November 15, 1528), matriculated at Freiburg, 1464, B. A. 1466, then to Erfurt. In 1469 he went to Heidelberg, where he studied and taught philosophy, becoming Rector in 1481. From 1484-98 he was at Spires, while there writing in favor of the Immaculate Conception. The next three years he spent at Strassburg, where he wrote a history of Germany. Then he taught at Freiburg and Heidelberg until 1510, when he returned to Strassburg for five years. From 1515 till his death he lived at Schlettstadt, taking some part in opposing Luther. Life by J. Knepper.

[2] The Disputation took place April 25.

[3] I frankly confess I am unable to restore the certainly corrupt text of this passage, of which I believe I am giving the sense. For "volvere iussit" I have thought of putting "vulgatis sit," but this would hardly do. Bucer's hand is extremely difficult to read, which causes some of the text of his letters to be uncertain. No help towards reconstructing this passage is given by the extremely free translation of the letter from the MS. in Baum's *Capito und Butzer*, p. 96.

[4] Duns Scotus, the famous opponent of Aquinas (1274-1308).

[5] Peter Tartaretus (Tataretus) one of the most eminent of the later Scotists, taught at Paris 1490. Edited commentaries on Aristotle 1494, *Expositio in Summulas Petri Hispani*, first ed. without date, then 1501 and 1503, commentary on Scotus' *Quodlibetica* 1519, and on Scotus' commentary on the *Sentences* 1520. Wetzer und Weltes: *Kirchenlexicon, s. v.*

Heavens! what real authentic theologian would these men approve, whose touchstone in approving or condemning doctrines is Aristotle, or rather the pestilent poison disseminated by his corrupters? Why should I not say this frankly of the foolish trifling with which they drench and foul the divine food of our minds, the holy oracles and their most holy interpreters, and thus make men forget the noble artificer of celestial splendor? But I repress my most just wrath against them lest they should make too much of sportive beginnings.

To return to Martin Luther: although our chief men refuted him with all their might, their wiles were not able to make him move an inch from his propositions. His sweetness in answering is remarkable, his patience in listening is incomparable, in his explanations you would recognize the acumen of Paul, not of Scotus; his answers, so brief, so wise, and drawn from the Holy Scriptures, easily made all his hearers his admirers.

On the next day I had a familiar and friendly conference with the man alone, and a supper rich with doctrine rather than with dainties. He lucidly explained whatever I might ask. He agrees with Erasmus in all things, but with this difference in his favor, that what Erasmus only insinuates he teaches openly and freely. Would that I had time to write you more of this. He has brought it about that at Wittenberg the ordinary textbooks have all been abolished, while the Greeks, and Jerome, Augustine and Paul are publicly taught.

But you see there is no room to write more. I enclose his paradoxes and their explanations, as far as I was able to take them down during the disputation or was taught them by him afterwards. I expect you will be much pleased to see them; if not, take them in the spirit in which they were sent. . . .

[Among the Theses for the Heidelberg Disputation enclosed by Bucer, are the following:]

I. The law of God, that most wholesome instruction unto life, is not able to justify a man, but rather hinders this.

III. It is probable that the works of men which seem to be specious and good are really mortal sins.

XIII. Since the fall, free will is a mere name; when the will does what is in its power it sins mortally.

58. WOLFGANG, COUNT PALATINE OF THE RHINE, TO FREDERIC, ELECTOR OF SAXONY.

Luthers Sämtliche Schriften, hg. von J. G. Walch, Halle, 1745, xv., 517, German.   HEIDELBERG, May 1, 1518.

Wolfgang (1494-1558), brother of the Elector Palatine Lewis V, educated for the Church, matriculated at Wittenberg in March, 1515, and in the following summer was made Rector of the University.

My kind service and love to you, highborn Prince, kind, dear Lord and Cousin: We have received and carefully read your Grace's letter requesting us to help according to our power Dr. Martin Luther, Augustinian, lecturer at Wittenberg, in case he should need it. We give your Grace kindly to know that we, as a member of the said university, at your Grace's request, are anxious to help the said doctor in all that is in our power, should he desire anything, but that he has shown us nothing in which he needed our help, as you will doubtless learn from himself. He has acquitted himself so well here with his disputation, that he has won no small praise for your Grace's university, and was greatly lauded by many learned persons. This we would not withhold from your Grace, for we are always ready to serve you.

WOLFGANG,
by God's grace Count Palatine of the Rhine and Duke of Bavaria.

59. LUTHER TO JODOCUS TRUTFETTER AT ERFURT.

Enders, i. 187.   ERFURT, May 9, 1518.

On the return journey from Heidelberg, Luther passed through Erfurt, where he tried to see his old professors, who were now his opponents, Usingen and Trutfetter. His first attempt was unsuccessful, whereupon he wrote this letter to Trutfetter, fully explaining his position in regard to indulgences and other matters; later he got an interview, but effected only a temporary reconciliation. The most interesting passage in the letter, showing how far he had already progressed in his programme for a general reformation of the Church, is the following:

To explain myself further, I simply believe that it is impossible to reform the Church unless the Canon Law, scholastic theology, philosophy and logic, as they are now taught, are thoroughly rooted out and other studies put in their stead. I am so fixed in this opinion that I daily ask the Lord, as far as now may be, that the pure study of the Bible and the Fathers may be restored. You think I am no logician; perhaps I am not, but I know that I fear no one's logic when I defend this opinion. . . .

60. LUTHER TO GEORGE SPALATIN.

Enders, i. 191.   WITTENBERG, May 18, 1518.

Greeting. Dear Spalatin, with Christ's favor I have returned home, arriving at Wittenberg on Saturday, May 15th. I, who had gone out on foot, returned in a wagon, for my superiors forced me to ride with the Nurembergers almost to Würzburg, thence with the brothers of Erfurt and from Erfurt with those of Eisleben, who took me at their own expense with their own horses to Wittenberg. I was well all the way. The food and drink agreed with me remarkably, so that some think I look stronger and fatter now.

[At Heidelberg] the most illustrious Count Palatine Wolfgang and James Symler[1] and Hazius,[2] Master of the court, received me. The count invited us, *i. e.*, Staupitz, our Lang, now District Vicar, and myself to a meal, at which we had a very pleasant conversation. We saw the ornaments of the castle chapel, and then wandered around that royal and noble castle, surveying the armor and almost everything it contains. Symler could not sufficiently commend the letter given by the Elector of Saxony in my behalf, saying, in his dialect: "By God, you have a fine passport."[3] We lacked nothing which kindness could supply.

The doctors heard my disputation gladly, and answered me with such moderation that I was much obliged to them. For, although my theology seemed strange to them, yet they skirmished with it subtly and politely, except one, who was

---

[1] A friend of Wimpfeling, who had been tutor to Count Wolfgang and had also accompanied him to Wittenberg.
[2] Otherwise unknown.
[3] Dicens sua Neccharena lingua: ihr habt by Godd einen kystlichte Credenz. (Heidelberg is on the Neckar.)

the fifth and younger doctor, who moved the laughter of the whole audience by saying: "If the peasants heard this they would stone you to death."

To Erfurt my theology is poison;[1] Dr. Trutfetter especially condemns all my propositions; he wrote me a letter accusing me of ignorance even of dialectic, to say nothing of theology. I would have disputed publicly with them had not the festival of the cross prevented. I had a conference with Trutfetter face to face and at least made him understand that he could not prove his own position nor refute mine; rather that their opinion was like that beast which is said to eat itself. But in vain is a story told to a deaf man; they obstinately stuck to their own little ideas, though they confess that these ideas are supported by no other authority than natural reason, which we consider the same as dark chaos, for we preach no other light than Christ Jesus, the true and only light. I talked with Dr. Usingen, who was my companion in the wagon, more than with all the others, trying to persuade him, but I know not what success I had, for I left him pensive and dazed. This is what comes of growing old in wrong opinions. But the minds of all the youths are tremendously different from theirs, and I have great hope that, as Christ rejected by the Jews went over to the Gentiles, so this true theology of his, rejected by those opinionated old men, will pass over to the younger generation. . . .

BROTHER MARTIN ELEUTHERIUS, *Augustinian.*

61. LUTHER TO JOHN ECK AT INGOLSTADT.

Enders, v. 1.   WITTENBERG, May 19, 1518.

Certain *Obelisks*[2] have come to me by which you have tried to refute my *Theses* on indulgences; this is a witness of the friendship which you offered me unasked, and also of your spirit of evangelic charity according to which we are bidden to warn a brother before we accuse him. How could I, a

---

[1]Here and elsewhere in the letter Luther uses a proverb which he found in Erasmus' *Adages;* as these are the first quotations from that work I have noticed in his letters it is probable that he had recently bought the new edition which he had spoken of in his letter to Lang in February, *supra,* no. 49.

[2]Eck gave this name (literally small daggers with which notes are marked) to his attack on Luther's *Theses.* Luther received it from his friend Link not long before March 24. *Cf.* Preserved Smith, 58f.

simple man, believe or suspect that you who were so smooth-tongued before my face would attack me behind my back? Thus you have fulfilled the saying of Scripture: "Which speak peace to their neighbors, but mischief is in their hearts."[1] I know that you will not admit that you have done this, but you did what you could;[2] see what your conscience tells you. I am astonished that you have the effrontery alone to judge my opinions before you know and understand them. This rashness of yours is sufficient proof that you think yourself the only theologian alive, and so unique that not only do you prefer your own opinion to all others, but even think that what you condemn, though you do not understand it, is to be condemned because it does not please Eck. Pray let God live and reign over us.

But to cut the matter short, as you are so furious against me, I have sent some *Asterisks* against your *Obelisks,* that you may see and recognize your ignorance and rashness; I consult your reputation by not publishing them, but by sending them to you privately so as not to render evil for evil as you did to me. I wrote them only for him from whom I received your *Obelisks,* and sent them to him to give you. Had I wished to publish anything against you I should have written more carefully and calmly, though also more strongly. If your confidence in your foolish *Obelisks* is still unshaken, pray write me; I will meet you with equal confidence. Perchance it will then happen that I shall not spare you, although God knows that I should prefer to convert you; if anything in me displeases you, write me privately about it, as you ought to know a theologian is bound to do. For what harlot, if provoked, could not have vomited forth the same curses and reviling against me that you have done, and yet so far from repenting you boast of it and think that you have done right. You have your choice; I will remain your friend if you wish, or I will gladly meet your attack, for as far as I can see, you know nothing in theology except the husks of scholasticism. You will find out how much you can do against

[1] Psalm xxviii. 3.
[2] According to Enders the writing of the only extant copy of this letter is very hard to read; I therefore venture to alter the reading of this sentence to the following: "Scio te nolle id a *te* fieri, sed fecisti *ut* potuisti."

me when you begin to prefer war to peace and fury to friendship.

May the Lord give to you and to me good sense and may he vouchsafe what is good to both of us. Behold, though attacked, I lay aside my arms, not because I fear *you*, but God; after this it will not be my fault if I am compelled to defend myself publicly. But enough. Farewell.

62. LUTHER TO WENZEL LINK AT NUREMBERG.

Enders, i. 215. (WITTENBERG, May 19, 1518.)

This letter, the preface to Luther's *Asterisks*, is dated in Enders, August 10, 1518. This is a late guess, as the *Asterisks* were not printed until 1545, when the date was added. Knaake (Weimar, i. 279f) dates this letter March 23, 1518, and this is followed by the St. Louis Walch edition. Clemen, in *Zeitschrift für Kirchengeschichte*, xxvii. 100, argues for an intermediate date. In my judgment, the true date is given by comparing this letter with that of Luther to Eck, of the same date, no. 61.

It seemed good to me to go over the *Obelisks* concocted by our friend Eck against my *Theses,* which you sent me, one by one, and to add *Asterisks* to those of my propositions, which are a little obscure. If you wish, you may communicate them to Eck,[1] clear as they now are, that he also may understand how rash it was to attack others' work, especially when he did not understand it, and particularly how treacherous and unjust it was to provoke so bitterly an unsuspecting friend, and one who assumes that everything will be taken for the best by his friend. But the Scripture is true: "All men are liars."[2] We are men and will remain men. . . .

63. LUTHER TO JEROME SCULTETUS, BISHOP OF BRANDENBURG.

Enders, i. 147. WITTENBERG, May 22, 1518.

After writing his *Resolutions* in defence of his *Theses,* Luther submitted them to his superior, the Bishop of Brandenburg. *Cf. supra,* no. 50. On the assumption that he sent this letter with them, the date affixed to the letter has been disregarded, and the missive put

---

[1] Link showed the *Asterisks* to Pirckheimer, but begged him not to show them to anyone else. W. Reindell: *W. Linck,* p. 257.
[2] Psalm cxvi. 11.

back to February 13th by Enders, and to February 6th by Knaake in the Weimar edition, i. 523, and Köstlin-Kawerau, 169. Kalkoff has shown, however (*Zeitschrift für Kirchengeschichte,* xxxii, 411), that the first letter sent with the *Resolutions* has been lost and that the one here translated is a second letter, intended by the author as an introduction to that work, which he was now at liberty to publish. *Cf. supra,* no. 53. He later changed this plan and substituted dedications to Staupitz and Leo X.

Luther speaks in his *Tischreden,* ed. Förstemann und Bindseil, ii. 367 and iii. 315, of the reception accorded his epistle as follows: "The Bishop of Brandenburg answered my letter, saying that I should not go on with the thing, for if I once began I would get plenty to do, as the matter touched the Church. There spoke the devil incarnate in this bishop!" Kalkoff, *loc. cit.,* 409, note, thinks this answer was given when the bishop visited Wittenberg, in February, 1519.

Recently, excellent Bishop, new and unheard of dogmas about indulgences have begun to be proclaimed throughout our regions so that many learned as well as unlearned men are both surprised and moved. Thus it happened that I was asked by many strangers as well as by many friends, both by letters and orally, what I thought of their novel, not to say licentious, doctrines. I put them off for a while, but finally their complaints became so bitter as to endanger the reverence for the Pope.

What was I to do? I had no power to decide anything, and I feared to cross the indulgence sellers, for I only wished that they might seem to preach the truth, and yet their opponents proved so clearly that they only taught false, vain doctrines, that I confess they completely convinced me. That, therefore, I might satisfy both, the best plan seemed to be neither to approve nor to disapprove, but to hold a debate on the subject until the Holy Church should decide what to believe. Thus I posted topics for debate, and invited the public, and urged my learned friends privately, to give me their written opinions on the subject, for it seemed to me that my propositions were contradicted by neither the Bible nor the Fathers nor the Canon Law, but only by a few canonists who spoke without authority, and by a few scholastics, who expressed their opinions without giving proof. For it seemed to me most absurd that things should be preached in the Church for which we could not give a reason to heretics who might ask it, and thus we would make Christ and his Church a scorn and a mockery.

Moreover, it is established that we owe no allegiance to the scholastics and canonists, when they only give their own opinions, for if it is commonly said to be base for a lawyer to speak without authority, it is surely baser for a theologian to do so, and by authority I mean not Aristotle (for they give his authority far too readily), but the Bible, the Canons and the Fathers. Furthermore, I thought that it became my profession and office to call in question such matters which are both very doubtful and if false very dangerous, for during centuries no Christian has doubted that the schools have the right to debate even the most sacred and awful matters. . . .

Since, therefore, no one has responded to my universal challenge, and since I see that my propositions for debate have flown farther than I would have wished, and were accepted everywhere not as inquiries, but as assertions, I have been compelled against my hope and intention to expose my lack of eloquence and my ignorance, and to publish my propositions with their proofs, thinking it better to jeopard my reputation than to let the propositions fly about in a form which might lead people to think they were positive assertions. For I doubt some of them, am ignorant about others and deny some, while not positively asserting any, but submitting all to the Holy Church.

And since, reverend Prelate, you are by Christ's mercy the bishop of this place, and since you not only warmly love good and learned men, as many are said to do, but even venerate and cherish them to such a degree that you almost risk your pontifical dignity (far be this from flattery, for I praise not you, but Christ's gifts in you!)—it was most right that I should offer my work especially to you, whose duty it is to inspect and judge what is done here, and to lay at your feet whatever I do.

Wherefore deign, most clement Bishop, to take these foolish trifles of mine, that all may know that I assert nothing rashly, and that I not only allow, but even beg your Reverence to strike out whatever you wish, or even to burn the whole; it is of no consequence to me. . . .

64. JOHN ECK TO ANDREW CARLSTADT.

J. G. Olearius: *Scrinium Antiquarium*,
Halle, 1671, p. 30. INGOLSTADT, May 28, 1518.

Most famous Carlstadt, I have heard that you and your Wittenbergers are moved against Eck, because I wrote something privately for my bishop[1] against the opinion of our common friend Martin Luther, thinking that this trifling effort of mine would never be subjected to the criticism of learned men. I suspect, though I do not know, how it slipped out of the hands of my bishop and was laid before you. Had I known this would have happened, I should not have written ex tempore without consulting any books, just as my thought suggested, nor should I have composed it in so hasty and careless style. But as you know, we are all freer in writing private letters than when publishing. Wherefore I am much surprised that you are so incensed against your most devoted Eck. They say that you charge Eck with fawning on the bishop. You do not know how incapable is Eck of such a thing. All who know Eck freely confess that he is a man who cannot be insincere. Nor, could I have flattered, would I have done so, especially that bishop with whom, I believe, from some accidental cause, indulgences have very little weight. People also say that you are planning a single combat with Eck. I can hardly believe that. If it is true, I wonder why you do not gird yourself against your neighbors of Frankfort on the Odor, and against the inquisitor, who intimates that Luther has erred a hundred times, or rather that he is wild, mad and insane, and have expressed this opinion in published writings. Truly, if I may presume upon my recently formed friendship, I shall consider it a friendly act if you will let whatever you meditate against innocent Eck fall into oblivion. For it was not my intention to hurt Luther. If you think meanly of Eck's friendship, and propose to disregard it, I neither can nor desire to impose a rule on you; but you will do better to inform Eck as soon as possible if you wish to publish anything. When I learn that

---

[1]Adolph of Anhalt, Bishop of Merseburg 1514-26. He was a brother of Ernest of Anhalt (*infra*, November 4, 1519, no. 193) and of Louis of Anhalt, the begging prince whom Luther saw at Magdeburg in 1497. Smith, p. 4.

I have erred I will willingly confess my error without shame. But if I see you excited and bitter against me, I will try, with the counsel of good teachers and of friends, to defend myself, as much as truth urges, in those studies which are most regarded throughout Christendom. But I prefer to avoid this business. It will be yours to consider this, and after due consideration to advance. Farewell, Carlstadt, whom I truly wish to fare well.

65. LUTHER TO JOHN STAUPITZ.

Enders, i. 196.   WITTENBERG, May 30, 1518.

This letter is one preface to Luther's *Resolutions,* a defence of the *Theses,* reprinted Weimar, i. 522. Another prefatory letter was to Leo X., translated, Smith, pp. 44ff.

I remember, reverend Father, among those happy and wholesome stories of yours, by which the Lord used wonderfully to console me, that you often mentioned the word "penitence,"[1] whereupon, distressed by our consciences and by those torturers who with endless and intolerable precept taught nothing but what they called a method of confession, we received you as a messenger from Heaven, for penitence is not genuine save when it begins from the love of justice and of God, and this which they consider the end and consummation of repentance is rather its commencement.

Your words on this subject pierced me like the sharp arrows of the mighty,[2] so that I began to see what the Scriptures had to say about penitence, and behold the happy result: the texts all supported and favored your doctrine, in so much that, while there had formerly been no word in almost all the Bible more bitter to me than "penitence" (although I zealously simulated it before God and tried to express an assumed and forced love), now no word sounds sweeter or more pleasant to me than that. For thus do the commands of God become sweet when we understand that they are not to be read in books only, but in the wounds of the sweetest Saviour.

[1] "Poenitentia" means both "penance" and "repentance," it was apparently taken in the former sense by the "torturers" and in the latter by Staupitz. Preserved Smith, *op. cit.,* p. 40.
[2] Psalm cxx. 4.

After this[1] it happened by the favor of the learned men who taught me Hebrew and Greek that I learned that the Greek word is μετάνοια from μετά and νοῦν, i. e., from "afterwards" and "mind," so that penitence or μετάνοια is "coming to one's right mind, afterwards,"[2] that is, comprehension of your own evil, after you had accepted loss and found out your error. This is impossible without a change in your affections. All this agrees so well with Paul's theology, that, in my opinion, at least, nothing is more characteristically Pauline.

Then I progressed and saw that μετάνοια meant not only "afterwards" and "mind," but also "change" and "mind," so that μετάνοια means change of mind and affection. . . .

Sticking fast to this conclusion, I dared to think that they were wrong who attributed so much to works of repentance that they have left us nothing of it but formal penances and elaborate confession. They were seduced by the Latin, for "poenitentiam agere"[3] means rather a work than a change of affection and in no wise agrees with the Greek.

When I was glowing with this thought, behold indulgences and remissions of sins began to be trumpeted abroad with tremendous clangor, but these trumpets animated no one to real struggle. In short, the doctrine of true repentance was neglected, and only the cheapest part of it, that called penance, was magnified. . . . As I was not able to oppose the fury of these preachers, I determined modestly to take issue with them and to call their theories in doubt, relying as I did on the opinion of all the doctors and of the whole Church, who all say that it is better to perform the penance than to buy it, that is an indulgence. . . . This is the reason why I, reverend

---

[1] Luther has just been speaking of his first acquaintance with Staupitz during the dark years in the Erfurt cloister, 1505-10; it was at this time that he began to study Hebrew, on which perhaps he got some help from a Jew while he was at Rome, December, 1510, cf. Smith, op. cit., p. 26f. Grisar: *Luther*, i. 27. Greek he first began to learn from his friend Lang during the years 1513-16, but he is apparently referring to the study of the New Testament in Greek edited by Erasmus in March, 1516. In this letter he follows Erasmus' note to Matthew iii. 2.

[2] "Resipiscentia," Erasmus translates μετανοεῖτε "Resipiscite."

[3] These words in the Vulgate might mean either "Repent ye" or "Do penance," and were usually taken in the latter sense by Luther's contemporaries. E. g., see Thomas More, *Confutation of Tyndale* (1532) in *Works* (1557), p. 418. Cf. supra, note 1.

Father, who always love retirement, have unhappily been forced into the public view. . . .

I ask, therefore, that you will receive this poor book of mine, and forward it with what expedition you can to the excellent Pope Leo X. I ask this not to involve you in my danger (for I prefer to take all the risk myself), but that I may have at Rome if not a champion, at least an answer to all my opponents.

66. ANDREW CARLSTADT TO JOHN ECK AT INGOLSTADT.

J. G. Olearius: *Scrinium antiquarium.* Halle. 1671, p. 32.

WITTENBERG, June 11, 1518.

Greeting. Most learned Eck, I am in receipt of your elegant letter. I answer briefly to let you know that I am greatly displeased with the taunts with which you have assailed my most learned friend, Martin Luther. For you have accused the man of the worst and greatest crimes, *lèse majesté*, heresy and schism. You have publicly called him a seditious Hussite. You deny that you published this opinion? Well, your own Scotus says that whatever is written is *ipso facto* published, and you certainly wrote it. You not only gave us a chance to reply, but you forced us to do so. Wherefore it happened that I published a challenge, or rather an apology, against some of your conclusions. This was printed and is sold here at Wittenberg. I weep for the wound your humanity received in forcing on us the necessity of fighting you. If things done could be undone, I should prefer to conquer your accusations with patience rather than with battle. The reason why I chose you particularly for an adversary, instead of that unlearned inquisitor or someone like him, was not envy or anger, but was your elegance, industry and acumen, and especially your own salvation and that of the people. For I hope that you will come over to our opinion; I believe that from Saul you will be made Paul. For I would not have a wild ass or a balking ass, but a noble lion [Leo] or an eloquent Mark. I thought it would not hurt me to strive by imitating your arts to become more elegant. Please pardon me if I have hurt you. But consider whether you ought to hurt me already wounded; think whether you will thereby become the hostile disturber of a man or of the Holy Word. I have determined rather to endure war and tyrannical siege than a perverse peace at the price of disparaging the divine writings and of my own perdition. I will stick to this, whatever may happen to myself. But if you let me I should prefer to enjoy your friendship. Indeed, I love you heartily. May I perish if I desire you to perish or any evil to befall you. It is my particular study by what means God's Word, unfortunately for our unhappy skulking in a corner, may daily become sweeter and better known, that is, as well known as possible. Long live our Luther who gives us a chance to extract the kernel of the law of God. Long live Eck, as his friend. But if he be an enemy, let him at least be a sincere lover of the truth. This is all I have leisure to write at this time. . . .

67. LUTHER TO CHRISTOPHER SCHEURL AT NUREMBERG.

Enders, i. 208.   WITTENBERG, June 15, 1518.

Greeting. What you ask in behalf of our Eck, dearest Christopher, would have been superfluous from such a friend, had there been nothing to complicate the situation and had he himself written before you did. But my suspicion that Eck's mind is alienated from me is confirmed by the fact that after he called me such dreadful names, even though only in private, he wrote me no letter and sent me no message. And now, since our Carlstadt's theses[1] have been published, though without my knowledge or consent, I am not quite sure what both of us ought to do. I know that we love the man's nature and admire his learning; I am, moreover, certain and bear witness to it, that what I did, at least, was done rather in sorrow than in anger or envy. As for myself, I have written him the enclosed letter,[2] which you see is friendly and full of good will towards him. I am quite reconciled to him, not

---

[1] While Luther was at Heidelberg Carlstadt published some theses on free will and the authority of Scripture directed against Eck, who replied with some counter-theses. On this, and on the "dreadful names" Eck called Luther, see Smith, *op. cit.*, 58f.

[2] Luther probably meant a letter, now lost, sent with that of Carlstadt, no. 66.

only for your sake, but because of his own candid confession that it would displease him, if not me, to have anything [untoward] happen by reason of someone else's guilt or malice. Therefore you have my authority to do what you want in this matter, and so does Eck. I only charge your kindness to see that he does not reply too sharply to our Carlstadt, considering, as he ought, that the first fault was his in stirring up a quarrel with friends. Since I sent my *Asterisks* to him privately, I believe he will be under no necessity of answering them unless he wants to. But if he prefers to answer, I am ready for him, though I should prefer peace. Act therefore so that we may know that you grieve with us that this temptation has been sent by the devil, and also that you rejoice with us that with Christ's aid it has been overcome and quieted. Farewell. I wrote you before, but I see you have not yet received the letter.

BROTHER MARTIN LUTHER, *Augustinian.*

68. SILVESTER PRIERIAS TO LUTHER.

Enders, i. 163. (ROME, June, 1518.)

This letter is dated by Enders "Erste Monate, 1518," but as the *Dialogue,* to which it is the preface, appeared in June (F. Lauchert: *Die Italienischen lit. Gegner Luthers,* 9), it may be dated in that month, and is dated by the St. Louis edition, xxi. no. 81, "Zweite Hälfte Juni, 1518."

Silvester Mazzolini, of Prierio, in Piedmont (1456-1523), entered the Dominican order at the age of 15, and was made priest eight years later. He taught at Bologna and Padua. In 1508, he was elected Vicar of the Lombard Province of his Order, and for the three following years was a member of the inquisition at Brescia. He wrote a good deal on scholastic topics. In 1514, he was called by Leo X. to teach at Rome, and in the following year was made Master of the Sacred Palace; or official theological adviser to the Pope, in which capacity he took an active part against Reuchlin. Luther's *Theses* were sent to the Pope by Albert of Mayence, reaching Rome before the end of 1517. Prierias was asked to give an opinion on them, which he did with great thoroughness, and which he published, of his own accord, under the title of *Dialogus de postestate Papae,* in June, 1518. Luther answered, and the controversy continued. Life of Prierias, by F. Michalski, 1892. *Cf.* Lauchert, *op. cit.,* 7ff, and *Realencyclopädie.*

It has been long, Martin, since I have ceased writing, chiefly because my powers are exhausted by old age, but the challenge you vociferate to all athletes, as though you were another Dares,[1] has impelled me again to approach the wrestling ring to defend the truth and the Apostolic See.

Since I could not see the grounds of the notice which, it is said, you have published, and although you have brought no proof to your propositions, and some of them may bear both a true and a false sense, I did not wish at first to contend with you save by supporting and defending the opposite sense of your false propositions, so that you may tell us on what grounds you rely. Wherefore, having run through and balanced your opinions, I have prepared the way for our future contest by a *Dialogue*, in which we, who are to contend, are the interlocutors. Let us invoke God's blessing! Farewell and learn better!

69. LUTHER TO WENZEL LINK AT NUREMBERG.

Enders, i. 210.   WITTENBERG, July 10, 1518.

The date of this letter is a puzzle. It is not known in MS.; the earliest edition by Aurifaber, followed by De Wette, dates "die 12 Fratrum," which would be September 1. Enders believes that "XII" was put by mistake for "VII" and dates accordingly "day of the seven brothers," *i. e.,* July 10. As Luther always used Arabic numerals this mistake could hardly have been made by him, but may have been introduced by Aurifaber. But the letter speaks of Luther's leaving Wittenberg; if this refers to the projected trip to Augsburg, as Enders thinks, the letter could hardly have been written before September 1, as Luther certainly did not know he was summoned thither until that date. Smith, *op. cit.,* p. 47. If it refers to the summons to Rome, the letter could not have been written as early as July 10, for Luther first received the summons to Rome in August. Smith, *loc. cit.,* and Enders, i. 214ff. But I believe the reference is to a projected journey to Dresden, which Luther actually undertook late in July, *cf. infra,* no. 117, and about which the Count of Mansfeld would be more likely to be informed than about the citation to Rome. For the earlier date also speak two facts: first, that the *Resolutions* were not yet very far along in the press, although they were finished on August 28 (*infra,* no. 76), and that the "recent" sermon on the ban was one of the causes of the citation to Augsburg, which was determined upon on August 23.

Greeting. I would have sent my *Resolutions*, reverend

[1] Virgil: *Aeneid,* v. 369ff.

Father, but for the slowness of our printer. I myself am much put out at this delay. Only eighteen of the *Resolutions* are as yet printed, which I now try to send. That trifle which I lately published against my Timon[1] has been recently republished. I was unwilling to republish it myself, in which I followed the advice of my friends, although even so I did not satisfy them. Others attribute it to my impatience, although I meant it rather in sport than in anger. . . .

Our vicar, John Lang, who was here to-day, says that Count Albert,[2] of Mansfeld, has written him a letter warning him by no means to let me leave Wittenberg. Snares have been laid by I know not what great men,[3] either to kill me or to baptize me unto death. I am simply, as Jeremiah says,[4] that man of strife and contention who daily irritate the Pharisees with what they consider new doctrines. But as I am certain that I teach only the purest doctrine, I have long foreseen that it would be a stumbling block to the most holy Jews and foolishness to the wisest Greeks.[5] But I know that I am a debtor to Jesus Christ, who, perhaps, is saying to me: "I will show him how much he must suffer for my name's sake."[6] For if he does not say this why does he make me so bold in defending his Word, or why does he not teach me to say something else? His holy will be done.[7] The more they threaten the bolder I am; my wife and children are provided for, my fields, houses and whole substance are in order, my name and fame are torn to bits; all that is left me is my weak and broken body, of which if they deprive me they will shorten my life by an hour or two, but truly

---

[1] The Athenian cynic to whom Luther compares Tetzel. The "trifle" was *Ein Freiheit des Sermons*.

[2] Born 1480, younger son of Ernst I. See Grössler: *Graf Albrecht VII von Mansfeld. Zeitschrift des Harz-Vereins*, xviii. 365. As a native of his dominions Luther felt particularly loyal to him. From 1521 to 1545 he wrote him a number of letters, and it was at his request that in 1545 and 1546 he journeyed to the county of Mansfeld to settle a dispute between Albert and his brother Gebhard. Smith, *op. cit.*, 417ff.

[3] On Luther's unpleasant experiences at Dresden, whither he was planning to go, and whither he soon went, *cf. infra*, no. 117. Duke George had already begun to be unfriendly to him, though he could not have meant to put him to death.

[4] Jeremiah, xv. 10.

[5] 1 Corinthians, i. 23.

[6] Acts of the Apostles, ix. 16.

[7] Reading "fiat" for "fuit." *Cf.* Enders, ii. 536.

will not take away my soul. I sing with John Reuchlin: Who is poor fears nothing, for he has nothing to lose, but he sits in hope, for he hopes to get something. . . .

I recently delivered a sermon on the ban,[1] in which, incidentally, I taxed the tyranny and ignorance of the common herd of sordid officials, commissaries and vicars. All my hearers exclaimed in surprise they had never heard such a sermon before. Then, in addition to whatever evil is awaiting me, we expect that a new fire has been kindled, but this is the sign that the word of truth is being opposed. I wanted to have a public debate on the matter, but rumor anticipated it and stirred up some officials, so that they induced my Bishop of Brandenburg to send a messenger to put off such a debate, which I have done and still do, especially as my friends advise it. See what a monster I am, since even my attempts are intolerable.

Dr. Trutfetter has sent me a letter full of zeal (for by this name we must dignify the man's fierce passion), a letter much more bitter than the one you heard read in my presence at the Chapter,[2] and one which says just what he said to me at Erfurt. These men are goaded to madness, because they are told to be fools in Christ, and because they are judged to have erred by the whole world and the authority of so many ages. I don't care a fig for those fools and their threats, provided only that Christ be a propitious God to me, to whom I am prepared to yield the defence of the Word. I have written at length because I like to chat with you. Farewell.

BROTHER MARTIN LUTHER.

70. THE EMPEROR MAXIMILIAN TO POPE LEO X AT ROME.
M. Lutheri Opera latina varii argumenti, ed. H. Schmidt. Erlangen, 1865, ii. 349. AUGSBURG, August 5, 1518.

Most blessed Father and most revered Lord! We have recently heard that a certain Augustinian Friar, Martin Luther by name, has published certain theses on indulgences

---

[1] *Sermo de virtute excommunicationis* (Weimar i. 634ff), printed by Luther in August. According to Köstlin-Kawerau, i. 194, Luther delivered the sermon on May 16th, but this seems too early.
[2] *I. e.*, at the General Chapter at Heidelberg, April and May. On Luther's interview with Trutfetter at Erfurt on the way home, *cf. supra*, no. 59 and 60.

to be discussed in the scholastic way, and that in these theses he has taught much on this subject and concerning the power of papal excommunication, part of which appears injurious and heretical, as has been noted by the Master of your sacred palace. This has displeased us the more because, as we are informed, the said friar obstinately adheres to his doctrine, and is said to have found several defenders of his errors among the great.

And as suspicious assertions and dangerous dogmas can be judged by no one better, more rightly and more truly than by your Holiness, who alone is able and ought to silence the authors of vain questions, sophisms and wordy quarrels, than which nothing more pestilent can happen to Christianity, for these men consider only how to magnify what they have taught, so your Holiness can maintain the sincere and solid doctrine approved by the consensus of the more learned opinion of the present age and of those who formerly died piously in Christ.

There is an ancient decree of the Pontifical College on the licensing of teachers, in which there is no provision whatever against sophistry, save in case the decretals are called in question, and whether it is right to teach that, the study of which has been disapproved by many and great authors.

Since, therefore, the authority of the Popes is disregarded, and doubtful, or rather erroneous opinions are alone received, it is bound to occur that those little fanciful and blind teachers should be led astray. And it is due to them that not only are many of the more solid doctors of the Church not only neglected, but even corrupted and mutilated.

We do not mention that these authors hatch many more heresies than were ever condemned. We do not mention that both Reuchlin's trial and the present most dangerous dispute about indulgences and papal censures have been brought forth by these pernicious authors. If the authority of your Holiness and of the most reverend fathers does not put an end to such doctrines, soon their authors will not only impose on the unlearned multitude, but will win the favor of princes,[1]

---

[1] Perhaps a special allusion to the Elector Frederic of whom Maximilian was jealous. He was now holding the Imperial Diet at Augsburg. He probably

to their mutual destruction. If we shut our eyes and leave them the field open and free, it will happen, as they chiefly desire, that the whole world will be forced to look on their follies instead of on the best and most holy doctors.

Of our singular reverence for the Apostolic See, we have signified this to your Holiness, so that simple Christianity may not be injured and scandalized by these rash disputes and captious arguments. Whatever may be righteously decided upon in this our Empire, we will make all our subjects obey for the praise and honor of God Almighty and the salvation of Christians.

71. LUTHER TO SPALATIN AT AUGSBURG.[1]

Enders, i. 213.   WITTENBERG, August 8, 1518.

Greeting. I now need your help more than ever, dear Spalatin, or rather the honor of our whole university needs it. I mean that I want you to use your influence with the elector and Pfeffinger to get the elector and his Imperial Majesty[2] to request the Pope to allow my case to be tried in Germany,[3] as I have written the elector. For you see how subtly and maliciously those murderous Dominicans[4] are acting for my destruction. I would have written on the same account to Pfeffinger, to request his influence in obtaining this favor for me from Emperor and elector, but I had to write in great haste. They have given me but a short time, as you see by the Citation, that Lernaean swamp full of hydras and other monsters. Therefore be diligent, if you love me and

---

wrote this letter at the instigation of the Papal Legate, Cajetan. Luther's enemies had taken notes of his *Sermon on the Ban* (*cf. supra*, no. 69), which they had reduced to a series of propositions, and sent to Cajetan. *Cf.* Smith, 47f.

[1]The Emperor Maximilian held an Imperial Diet at Augsburg in the summer of 1518. Spalatin was present in attendance on the Elector Frederic.

[2]Maximilian I. (Emperor from 1493 till his death, January 12, 1519), in this case acted as Luther wished, getting the case transferred to Augsburg, not from the desire to help the Saxon, but apparently because he felt he could deal with him more summarily so. Smith, *op. cit.*, p. 48. *Supra*, no. 70.

[3]Finding that Luther had not recanted at Heidelberg, the Curia summoned him to Rome to recant within sixty days, which summons, together with Prierias' *Dialogue* (*supra*, no. 68), Luther had just received. Smith, p. 47.

[4]"Praedicatores." It would be possible to translate this "preachers of indulgences," but it is more likely that Luther meant the "order of preachers," as the Dominicans were called, for they had, indeed, been particularly active against him. Tetzel, Eck and Prierias were all Dominicans. Smith, *ibid*.

hate iniquity, to get the advice and aid of the elector at once, and when you have got it, communicate it to me, and still more to our reverend father vicar Staupitz, who is perchance now with you at Augsburg, or soon will be. For he is in Salzburg, having promised to be at Nuremberg on August 15. Finally, I pray you, be not moved or sad for me; with the trial the Lord will also make a way of escape.

I am answering the sylvan and wild *Dialogue* of Sylvester Prierias,[1] all of which you will have as soon as it is ready. The same sweet man is both my enemy and my judge, as you will see by the Citation. Farewell. As I have much to write I cannot say more to you now.

BROTHER MARTIN ELEUTHERIUS, *Augustinian.*

72. LUTHER TO SYLVESTER PRIERIAS AT ROME.
Enders, i. 216.   (WITTENBERG, about August 10, 1518.)

That supercilious *Dialogue* of yours, very reverend Father, written in the usual style of an Italian and a Thomist, has reached me. You boast in it that you, an old man, done with fighting, are impelled anew by my words to the combat, but nevertheless, you say you will get the victory over me in the unequal contest, as Entellus did over Dares,[2] but by this alone you show that you are vainglorious Dares rather than Entellus, because you boast before you are safe and ask for praise before victory.[3] Pray do what you can; the Lord's will be done. . . .

Behold, reverend Father, I am sending your treatise back quickly, because your refutation seems trifling; therefore, I have answered it ex tempore with whatever came uppermost in my mind. If, after that, you wish to hit back, be careful to bring your Aquinas better armed into the arena, lest perchance you be not treated as gently again as you are in this encounter. I have forborne to render evil for evil.

Farewell!

73. POPE LEO X TO CARDINAL CAJETAN AT AUGSBURG.
Luthers Werke (Weimar), ii. 23.   ROME, August 23, 1518.

By this breve the Pope transfers jurisdiction in Luther's case to

[1] On him and the Dialogue, *cf. supra*, no. 68, and *infra*, no. 72.
[2] Virgil: *Aeneid,* v. 369ff.   [3] Erasmus: *Adages.*

Cajetan. A copy of it was secured by the Elector Frederic's agents at Augsburg and forwarded to Luther, whom it reached at Nuremberg late in October. *Infra*, no. 93, October 31. Luther incorporated it in his *Acta Augustana*, and thus it has reached posterity. Ranke and others have doubted its genuineness, but on insufficient grounds. *Cf.* Weimar, *loc. cit.*, p. 22, and *Realencyclopädie, s. v.* Sadoleto.

Giacomo de Vio, of Gaeta (thence known as Cajetan and usually as Thomas, the name he assumed on becoming a monk; February 20, 1469-9 or 10 August, 1534), became a Dominican 1484, studied at Naples, Bologna and Padua; 1500 called to Rome as Procurator of his Order; 1507 began to teach at the University, and the next year was elected General of his Order. He was active against the schismatics at the Council of Pisa 1511-2. Made Cardinal by Leo, July 1, 1517, and Bishop of Palermo 1518. In December, 1517, he published a work on indulgences, which seems to refer to Luther's Theses (*Zeitschrift für Kirchengeschichte*, xxxii., 201). In 1518 he was sent as legate to the Diet of Augsburg, and here saw Luther, *Infra*, no. 85. In 1519 he was made Bishop of Gaeta, and in 1523 legate to Hungary. From 1524, to the sack of Rome, 1527, he lived in that city as councillor of Clement VII, and again from 1530-4. Life, by A. Cossio (1902), *Realencyclopädie*, Lauchert, *op. cit.*, 133ff; *Zeitschrift für Kirchengeschichte*, xxiii. 240ff.

Beloved Son, greeting and the apostolic blessing! After it had come to our ears that a certain Martin Luther, reprobate Augustinian, had asserted some heresies and some things different from those held by the Roman Church, and in addition to this, of his own rashness and obstinacy, forgetting the duty of obedience and not consulting the mistress of the faith, the Roman Church, had dared to publish some slanderous books in divers parts of Germany, we, desirous of paternally correcting his rashness, ordered our venerable brother Jerome,[1] Bishop of Ascoli, General Auditor of the Curia, to cite the said Martin to appear personally before him to be examined under certain penalties and to answer for his faith. The said Auditor Jerome, as we have heard, issued this citation to the said Martin.

But recently it has come to our notice that the said Martin, abusing our clemency and become bolder thereby, adding

[1] Jerome Ghinucci, of Siena, secretary of Julius II., by whom he was made Bishop of Ascoli. By Leo X. he was made Auditor, *i. e.*, Supreme Justice of the Papal Curia, and sent at one time as nuncio to England. In 1538 he was made cardinal, and died July 3, 1541. *Dizionario de Erudizione* (Venice, 1844), *s. v.*

evil to evil and obstinately persisting in his heresy, has published some other propositions and slanderous books, containing other heresies and errors. This disturbed our mind not a little. Wherefore, agreeably to our pastoral duty, desiring to prevent such a pest from growing strong and infecting the minds of the simple, we, by these presents, direct you (in whose circumspection we confide much in the Lord, on account of your singular learning, your experience and your sincere devotion to this holy see of which you are an honorable member) not to delay on receipt of this letter, but, since the affair has become notorious and inexcusable and has lasted long, to force and compel the said Martin, now declared to be a heretic by the said auditor, to appear personally before you. To accomplish this, call on the assistance of our most beloved son in Christ, Maximilian, Emperor Elect of the Romans, and of the other German princes, cities, corporations and powers, both ecclesiastical and secular; and when you have Martin in your power, keep him under a safe guard until you hear further from us, as shall be determined by us and the apostolic see.

If he shall come to you of his own accord, craving pardon for his rashness, and showing signs of hearty repentance, we give you power of kindly receiving him into the communion of holy mother Church, who never closes her bosom to him who returns. But if, indeed, persevering in his contumacy, and despising the secular arm, he will not come into your power, then in like manner we give you power of declaring in a public edict like those which were formerly written on the praetor's bill-board,[1] to be posted in all parts of Germany, that he and his adherents and followers are heretics, excommunicated, anathematized and cursed, and are to be avoided by all the faithful as such. And in order that this plague may be the more quickly and easily exterminated, you may admonish and require, by our authority and under pain of excommunication and other penalties mentioned below, all and singular prelates and other ecclesiastical persons, as well sec-

---

[1] The Album praetorium was the place where the praetor used to publish his edicts. Ducange, *s. v.* The phrase simply means, therefore, notices to be posted up in public.

ular as regular of all orders, including the mendicants, and all dukes, marquises, counts, barons, cities, corporations and magistrates (except the aforesaid Maximilian Emperor Elect) that, as they desire to be considered Christians, they should seize all his adherents and followers and give them into your charge.

And if (which we deprecate and cannot believe) the said princes, cities, corporations and magistrates, or any of them, should receive Martin or his adherents and followers in any way, or should give the said Martin aid, counsel or favor, openly or secretly, directly or indirectly, for any cause whatever, we subject the cities, towns and domains of these princes, communities, corporations and magistrates to the interdict[1] as well as all the cities, towns and places to which the said Martin may happen to come, as long as he remains there and for three days afterwards. And we also command all and singular princes, cities, corporations and magistrates aforesaid, to obey all your requisitions and commands, without exception, contradiction or reply, and that they abstain from giving counsel, aid, favor and comfort to the aforesaid. The penalty of disobedience, in addition to that mentioned above, shall be for the clergy deprivation of their churches, monasteries and feudal benefices forever, and for laymen, except the aforesaid Emperor, the penalties of infamy, inability to do any legitimate act, deprivation of religious burial and forfeiture of the fiefs held from us or from the apostolic see, together with whatever secular penalties may be hereby incurred. And by these presents we give you power of rewarding the obedient with a plenary indulgence or grace according to your judgment, notwithstanding previous privileges granted and confirmed by the apostolic authority to churches, monasteries and persons, even if it be expressly provided therein that they cannot be excommunicated. . . .

Given at Rome, at St. Peter's, under the fisherman's ring, in the sixth year of our pontificate.

J. SADOLETUS.[2]

[1] *I. e.*, prohibition of all religious rites except baptism and extreme unction. This threat, aimed chiefly at the Elector Frederic, was not carried out for political reasons.

[2] Jacopo Sadoleto, 1477-1547, was a well-trained theologian, employed as papal

74. POPE LEO X. TO THE ELECTOR FREDERIC OF SAXONY.
Lutheri Opera varii argumenti (Erlangen, 1865), ii. 352.

ROME, August 23, 1518.

Beloved Son, greeting and the apostolic blessing! . . . It has come to our ears from all quarters that a certain son of iniquity, Friar Martin Luther, of the German Congregation of Augustinian Hermits, forgetting his cloth and profession, which consists in humility and obedience, sinfully vaunts himself in the Church of God, and, as though relying on your protection, fears the authority or rebuke of no one. Although we know this is false, yet we thought good to write to your Lordship, exhorting you in the Lord, that for the name and fame of a good Catholic Prince such as you are, you should retain the splendor of your glory and race unsoiled by these calumnies. Not only that we wish you to avoid doing wrong, as you do, for as yet we judge that you have done none, but we desire you to escape the suspicion of doing wrong, in which Luther's rashness would involve you.

As we are certain from the report of most learned and religious men, and especially of our beloved son, the Master of our Sacred Palace, that Luther has dared to assert and publicly to affirm many impious and heretical things, we have ordered him to be summoned to make answer, and we have charged our beloved son, Cardinal Cajetan, Legate of the Holy See, a man versed in all theology and philosophy, to do with Luther as seems best.

As this affair concerns the purity of the faith of God and the Catholic Church, and as it is the proper office of the Apostolic See, the mistress of faith, to take cognizance who think rightly and who wrongly, we again exhort your Lordship, for the sake of God's honor and ours and your own, please to

secretary on account of his elegant Latinity. He was born in Modena, studied at Ferrara, went to Rome 1502, where he took orders and entered the service of Cardinal Oliviero Caraffa. Leo X. immediately on his accession to the papal throne named Sadoleto and Bembo secretaries of breves. He was made Bishop of Carpentras 1517, where he lived during the pontificate of Adrian VI., and again after the sack of Rome, 1527. In 1536 he was made cardinal and member of the Commission for Reform appointed by Paul III. He wrote commentaries on the Bible and other works, including some against Luther. F. Lauchert: *Die Italienischen Gegner Luthers*, 385ff. I have not seen: S. Ritter: *Un umanista teologo, Jacopo Sadoleto*, Roma, 1912.

give help that this Martin Luther may be delivered into the power and judgment of the Holy See, as the said legate will request of you. . . .

Given at St. Peter's, under the fisherman's ring, in the sixth year of our pontificate.

JAMES SADOLETUS.

75. GABRIEL DELLA VOLTA, GENERAL OF THE AUGUSTINIAN HERMITS, TO GERARD HECKER, PROVINCIAL OF SAXONY.

Zeitschrift für Kirchengeschichte, ii. 476.

CORI (near Rome), August 25, 1518.

Gabriel della Volta of Venice (Venetus) was nominated General of the Augustinians by Leo X. at the beginning of 1518. He at first declined, but was persuaded by a letter of February 3, 1518 (*P. Bembi Epistolarum libri, xvi.* Lugduni, 1538, no. 18), chiefly because Leo thought him the best man to deal with Luther. In this letter the Pope begged him to "quiet that man, for newly kindled flames are easily quenched, but a great fire is hard to put out." Accordingly, at the General Chapter at Venice, in June, 1519, Gabriel was elected General. He had already endeavored to get Staupitz to deal with Luther (Smith, p. 46) and failing in this turned to Hecker. Kolde: *Augustiner-Congregation,* index.

Hecker, since 1480 Augustinian at Lippstadt, lecturer at Bologna, 1488. In 1502 he came to Erfurt, where he was Luther's teacher. He was thrice Provincial of Thuringia and Saxony. In 1521 he came out for the Reformation, going to Osnabrück, where he lived until his death, in 1536. Kolde, *loc. cit.,* 474; Enders, vii. 83.

You can hardly estimate into what a mass of evils a certain Brother Martin Luther of our order and of the Congregation[1] of the Vicar, has brought us and our profession.[2] Thinking himself wise, he has become the most foolish of all who were ever in our order. We had previously heard from the Reverend Auditor[3] of the Apostolic Chamber, and as has now been communicated to us by our Supreme Lord Leo X., Luther has come to such a degree not only of noxiousness, but also of most damnable heresy, that he has not feared to lecture and dispute openly against the Holy Roman Church and the

---

[1] The German Augustinians were divided into two bodies, the Congregation of Observants, of which Staupitz was vicar, and the Conventuals, under Hecker.
[2] "Religio" in the usual monastic sense.
[3] Jerome Ghinucci.

Supreme Most Blessed Pontiff, and publicly to preach his false doctrine and many other propositions suitable not to a monk and a Christian as he is, but to a schismatic heretic and to one whose name, perhaps, has been erased from the book of life. Now we have warned this rebel to his profession and this enemy of the cross of Christ to desist from his cursed doings, and we have cited him to Rome, either to correct or to show reason for all that he has said against Our Supreme Lord[1] and the Holy Roman Church. But as he was blind enough in his heresy to dare to lift up his face against heaven, and to rage and rebel against Our Supreme Lord, thus he did not fear to show his rebellious contumacy against his vow and us. Now his iniquity has multiplied and his sin has grown to such a degree that by the command of the Supreme Pontiff Our Lord, we ought to apply opportune remedies to this contagious pestilence, and, lest he should infect and ruin others, to proceed against him as a rebel to his vow and a heretic towards the Holy Roman Church. And as we cannot be everywhere, we rely on your well-tried virtue, moderation and probity. Therefore we command you under pain of losing all your promotions, dignities and offices, when you receive this letter, to proceed to capture the said Brother Martin Luther, have him bound in chains, fetters and handcuffs, and detained under strict guard in prison at the instance of our Supreme Lord Leo X. And as he belongs to that Congregation which thinks itself free from your[2] government, that he may have no way of escape, we give you in this matter all our authority, and we inform you that our Supreme Lord, the Pope, has delegated to you plenary apostolic authority to imprison, bind and detain this man, notwithstanding anything done to the contrary, all of which, in as far as concerns this business, his Holiness expressly waives. Furthermore, he grants you power of putting the interdict on all places, and of excommunicating all persons by the apostolic authority, as you will see further in the apostolic breve, and of doing all things which seem to you needful for imprisoning this scoundrel; all of this in the name

[1] Usual designation of the Pope.
[2] Reading "vestra" for "nostra." The Observants never denied the supremacy of the General, but they did refuse obedience to the Conventuals headed by Hecker.

of the Father, and of the Son, and of the Holy Ghost. Amen. We command all those under us, of whatever Province, Congregation, title, dignity or office,[1] to help and advise you in this matter, and not only this, but on their duty of obedience and under pain of excommunication, for which, though unwillingly, in this letter we give such persons the triple warning commanded by the Canon Law, that they should obey and serve you as they would ourself. Know that in this matter you will not only do a great favor to us and to our profession, but will also put under a great obligation our Supreme Lord Leo X., who of his own accord offers to pay you amply for it. Know also that if you accomplish this, no one in the order will in future be dearer to us than you; by this one service you will win for yourself more benefits, honors and dignities than you could in all the rest of your life. Proceed, therefore; look to God, the inspirer of holy works, that men may recognize in you a man whose mind and heart are fit to do great deeds. The whole order will praise you for this, and we shall always be in your debt. Hereafter, our profession will always consider you as the renewer of the honor of our order and the zealous supporter of the Holy Roman Church. The thing is too important to admit delay; therefore we command you to spare no labor, to refuse no expense to get this heretic into the hands of the Supreme Pontiff. We also command you to write to us as often and as fully and as quickly as possible, whenever you have any news in this business. You will be paid to the uttermost farthing. Farewell.

76. LUTHER TO SPALATIN AT AUGSBURG.

Enders, i. 218.   WITTENBERG, August 28, 1518.

This letter, dated "sabbatho octavae Assumptionis D. Mariae," or "Saturday week after the Assumption of Mary" (August 15), is put by Enders on August 21. The wording is doubtful, but the letter seems, from other reasons, to have been written a week later, *i. e.*, August 28. *Cf. Zeitschrift für Kirchengeschichte*, xvii. 167, note 2, and *Luthers Werke*, ed. Clemen, i. 15.

Greeting. The messenger I sent to the Illustrious Elector

---

[1] This was intended particularly for Staupitz, who sympathized with Luther, and had failed to make him recant at the General Chapter held at Heidelberg in May, although he had been instructed to do so by Volta.

Frederic has not returned, therefore I am still waiting to know what the Lord will do in my cause through you. But I have heard that the Very Reverend Cardinal Cajetan has been particularly commanded by the Pope to do everything possible to alienate the minds of the Emperor and princes from me. So much does conscience make such popes cowards, or rather so intolerable is the power of truth to works which are done in darkness!

But as you know, Spalatin, I fear nothing. For even if their sycophancy and power should succeed in making me hateful unto all, yet my heart and conscience would tell me that all things which I have and which they attack, I have from God, to whom willingly and of my own accord I refer them and to whom I offer them. If he takes them away, let them be taken away, if he preserves them, let them be preserved, and may his name be holy and blessed forever. Amen.

I do not see in what way I can escape all their censures unless the elector helps me. On the other hand, I would much prefer to be always under their censures than to make the elector incur odium for my sake. Therefore, as I formerly offered myself, believe that I am still ready to be offered up, and convince of this any other whom you may think fit. I will never be a heretic; I may err in debate, but I wish to decide nothing. Yet I would not be captive to the doctrines of men. . . .

I send my *Resolutions*, very badly printed on account of my rather long absence.[1] Prierias' *Dialogue*[2] with my answer are being printed at Leipsic. . . .

BROTHER MARTIN ELEUTHERIUS, *Augustinian.*

77. LUTHER TO JOHN STAUPITZ.

Enders, i. 222. (WITTENBERG), September 1, 1518.

Greeting. Doubt not, reverend Father, that in future I shall be free in examining and treating the Word of God. For neither does that citation to Rome, nor do their threats

---

[1] Luther had recently been to Dresden, on which, *cf. infra.* no. 117, having preached there on July 25. But he is here probably referring to his trip to Heidelberg, April 11-May 15.
[2] Luther himself printed Prierias' *Dialogue*, with his answer. Reprinted Weimar, i. 644. *Cf. supra*, nos. 68, 72.

move me; you know that I suffer things infinitely worse,[1] which would make me consider these temporal and passing thunderbolts trifles, were it not that I sincerely desire to cherish the power of the Church. If I am excommunicated by men my only fear is of offending you, whose judgment in these matters I think is right, faithful and given with God's authority. . . .

My opponents strive, I see, to prevent Christ's kingdom of truth coming, and do all in their power to prevent truth being heard and preached in their own kingdom. I desire to be a part of this kingdom, at least with a veracious tongue and a pure heart confessing the truth, even if my life does not correspond. And I learn that the people are sighing for the voice of their shepherd Christ, and that the youth burns with great zeal towards the Holy Scriptures. . . .

Brother Martin Luther.

78. WOLFGANG FABRICIUS CAPITO TO LUTHER.

Enders, i. 228.   Basle, September 4, 1518.

Greeting. Your last kind letter[2] I answered from Strassburg, telling you of Erasmus' opinion of you, that is, how honorably and frankly he admires your *Theses*,[3] Since then I have seen your *Sermon on Penitence* and that on *Indulgences and Grace*, each of which declares open war against the customs of this age. I was seized with anxiety for the safety of my friend, who exposes a naked side to dense throngs of enemies, though, indeed, he seems well armed with the weapons of truth. But I much fear that you will be attacked by far different weapons, and that there is danger lest force be resorted to. Wherefore, if you will give ear to a faithful counsellor, I warn you, as one who knows, that you will play the part of Sertorius.[4] Believe me, you will accomplish more obliquely than by a direct assault in full force. You see they occupy a fortress defended at all points. They sleep, as it were, on their arms, sheltered behind a triple rampart, the authority of the Pope, that is, of the universal Church, the

---

[1] Luther refers to his spiritual temptations.
[2] *Cf. supra*, no. 49.
[3] *Cf. infra*, no. 87.
[4] Sertorius was a Spanish rebel who maintained himself for a time, but was finally assassinated.

power of kings, and the obstinate agreement of the universities. Forsooth you will hardly ever easily break this thick and triple cord of the cacodemon. There is need of an Alexander, to cut it, like the Gordian knot, with his sword; to loose it by genius or reason is hard. Simple but pious men stand at the beck and call of the fictitious Church. The wiser heads fear her tyranny. And especially we theologians, who sell the greatest of all things, the holy knowledge of Christ, give up Christ for our pride, and, inveighing against all the stains on religion, under the pretext of piety take care to lose nothing by it. Wherefore, lest your splendid attempt should turn out vain, I pray you use a little artifice, by which you may fix your hook in the reader before he suspects that a hook has been baited for him.

Thus the apostles urged nothing suddenly, nothing openly, but always preserved decorum and courtesy. With what strategy does Paul approach in the Epistle to the Romans! What does he not do to keep their favor? He simulates one thing and dissimulates another, he winds in and out, he displays his rich burden from afar, again he conceals it, in short, he weighs his words so that he may never arouse hatred or disgust.

The Acts of the Apostles are full of examples of his method. Thus in a tumult St. Paul answers like a turncoat: he does not say, "I do not speak against the law," but "Of the resurrection I am called in question,"[1] thus with wonderful prudence diverting attention from the observance of the law. Thus great things are safely accomplished by oblique methods. Thus I wish that you might always keep some window open by which you might escape when you are harassed in debate.

Recently I received Prierias' foolish pamphlet against your *Theses*. If you answer him I hope it will be prudently and according to the true example of Christ in the gospel. Speak expressly of religion in its inception and growth, of the customs of the ancients, the reason of old error, and the various decrees of the popes and councils, so that your argument gain credence as though drawn from the fountain of truth. You can more frequently discredit single abuses by ridicule

[1] Acts, xxiii. 6.

than by attacking them seriously. Carefully abstain from abusing the Pope, but rather give all the blame to Prierias, as an impudent flatterer who only for the sake of his belly places an unworthy burden on the pontifical dignity. . . .

But behold how my friendship has made me forget myself in telling you what to do. Pray forgive my solicitude. You have more than one champion, Carlstadt, Spalatin, Egranus and Melanchthon, a wonderful aggregation of genius. If you rely on their counsels, you will never publish anything weak or ridiculous. . . .

Erasmus greatly approves of Egranus' book,[1] with its nervous, rapid and clear argument. He wished that it might be republished at Basle,[2] although he would have been angry had it been printed here first. John Eck has written against Carlstadt. Do what you can you will not debate before an impartial tribunal, but at least consider us safe. I am writing a free answer to Eck, in a private letter. . . . Farewell.

YOURS, WHOM YOU KNOW.

79. MARCO MINIO TO THE SIGNORY OF VENICE.

R. Brown: *Calendar of State Papers . . . in . . . Venice.* London, 1869, ii. 1069.   ROME, September 4, 1518.

Minio was the agent of the Venetian Government at Rome, 1518-9. His letter, as given by me after Mr. Brown, is abbreviated.

To-day in the consistory the Pope announced his intention of sending the Rose[3] to the Elector of Saxony, as that prince was a good Christian and one of the chief princes of Germany. The Pope did this to try, through the medium of the Elector of Saxony, to allay the heresy, as they style it, of a certain Dominican [!] friar, who was preaching in those parts against the apostolic see, condemning the forms observed by the Church of Rome, alleging moreover that the indulgences daily conceded were of no value, and many other doctrines.

---

[1] His *Apologetica Responsio,* for which Luther wrote a preface. *Cf.* Enders, i. 181. Weimar, i. 316.

[2] As was done, Enders, *ibid.*

[3] The anointed golden rose, a much prized token sent by the Pope to faithful princes. *Cf.* Smith, *op. cit.,* 54. Rodocanachi: *Rome au temps de Jules II. et de Léon X.,* p. 294f.

80. STAUPITZ TO LUTHER.

Enders, i. 234. SALZBURG, September 14, 1518.

Possess your soul in patience for salvation. I have enough to write to fill a book, but will express myself briefly. It seems to me that the world is exasperated against truth; with so great hatred was Christ once crucified, and to-day I see nothing waiting for you but the cross. Unless I mistake, the opinion prevails that no one should examine the Scripture without leave of the Pope in order to find for himself, which Christ certainly commands us to do. You have few defenders, and would that they were not hiding for fear of enemies. I should like you to leave Wittenberg and come to me, that we may live and die together. This would also please the archbishop.[1] Here I finish. It is expedient thus to be, that abandoned we may follow abandoned Christ. Farewell, and a good journey to you. Your brother,

JOHN STAUPITZ.

81. LUTHER TO JOHN LANG AT ERFURT.

Enders, i. 236. (WITTENBERG), September 16, 1518.

... The most learned and perfect Grecian Philip Melanchthon[2] is teaching Greek here. He is a mere boy in years, but one of us in various knowledge, including that of almost all books. He is not only master of Greek and Latin, but of all the learning to which they are the keys, and he also knows some Hebrew.

The most illustrious elector has written me that he has brought it about that the Legate Cajetan has written to Rome to ask that my case be referred to a German tribunal[3] and that I may expect that it will be. So I hope that I will not be censured. But I displease many, most, almost all. ...

[1]Matthew Lang (1468-1540), of Augsburg, who had become a trusted councillor of Maximilian, became Bishop of Gurk 1505, Cardinal 1511, Coadjutor of Salzburg 1514 and Archbishop of that see 1519, Bishop of Albano 1535. He was a warm friend of Staupitz. To his judgment it was at one time proposed to refer the Lutheran affair. Smith, *op. cit.*, pp. 55, 107. He was, however, always a bitter opponent of the Reformation, persecuting its adherents, including Erasmus, and distinguishing himself by his cruelty in suppressing the Peasants' Revolt of 1525. Belford Bax: *Peasants' War*, p. 187ff. In general *Realencyclopädie*.
[2]On him see letter no. 82.
[3]*Cf. supra*, no. 76, and *infra*, no. 83.

81a. GUY BILD TO LUTHER.

Zeitschrift des historischen Vereins für Schwaben und Neuburg. 1893.
Vol. xx, p. 219.   Augsburg, September 21, 1518.

Bild was born at Höchstädt 1481, studied at Ingolstadt, came to Augsburg 1500, where he took a position as parish clerk at St. Ulrich. In 1503 in consequence of a severe illness he became a monk at that convent. He died in the last half of 1529. A sketch of his life and some of his letters, *op. cit. supra*, 173ff. In 1518 Bernard Adelmann gave Bild some of Luther's works. At the Diet of Augsburg in the same year, he had an interview with Spalatin on the subject of Luther. When the Wittenberger came to Augsburg in October, however, Bild did not go to see him.

Reverend Father in Christ [I wish you] Jesus the protector of the just.[1] A few days ago I received the theses inscribed with your name, and have now been able to acquire a fuller knowledge of the author. For it happened that that noble man, George Spalatin, who is not only imbued with the rudiments of all sciences, but is decked with a garland of all the virtues, and is a dear and faithful friend of yours, having some business with me on behalf of his elector,[2] told me during the conversation, at my request, what he could of your worth, person and piety. As he knew my favorable opinion of your Reverence, he talked freely about you; indeed, you were the alpha and omega of his discourse. Also the Reverend Father Prior of the Convent of Ramsau,[3] once your disciple as he said, fairly made me dance with joy,[4] by instructing me more fully about your exemplary life (I speak without base adulation) and thus he so inflamed my mind that I am no less bound to your Reverence than was Jonathan to his faithful David. Our common friend George Spalatin will more clearly reveal to you what I think of your Reverence's doctrines, learning, instruction and defence. Wherefore, reverend Father, I humbly beg and deserve pardon of you for wishing to approach your Reverence with my inelegantly written letter. For I was assured of your mercy not only by words, but because I

---

[1] Instead of the usual greeting: "Salutem," meaning: "(I wish you) health."
[2] This was to order twelve sundials from Bild, who was an expert in making them.
[3] Martin Glaser, on whom, *cf. infra*, no. 154. He had been introduced to Bild by Spalatin in a letter dated September 2.
[4] "Accumulavit gaudiis tripudia"; one may suspect a corrupt text.

was not ignorant that you constantly, by good deeds, preached the kingdom of God and salvation of souls. Wherefore I decided, relying on the offices of a friend, to send you this note in order that (though I ask it foolishly) I may be inscribed in the register of your friends, even as the least of them, so that aided by your prayers before God Almighty I may rejoice to have merited the kind friendship of such a man. Farewell, and be commended to God and to all the saints.

GUY BILD OF HOCHSTADT.

82. PHILIP MELANCHTHON TO CHRISTOPHER SCHEURL AT NUREMBERG.

Corpus Reformatorum, i. 48.   WITTENBERG, September 24, 1518.

Philip Melanchthon (Schwartzerd) (1497-1560), Luther's ablest lieutenant, a grand-nephew of Reuchlin, born at Bretten near Pforzheim. He matriculated at Heidelberg 1509, and was B.A. in 1511. Thence he went to Tübingen, where he took his M.A. in 1514. By 1516 he had already attracted the attention of Erasmus, and at the recommendation of Reuchlin was called in 1518 to Wittenberg. His inaugural address, *De corrigendis studiis,* was warmly received. From this time on he became Luther's warmest friend and chief aid. After Luther's death his position approached more nearly the Catholic than many Protestants liked, and he thus caused a schism in the evangelic fold. Lives of him by G. Ellinger and in *Realencyclopädie,* and in English by Richard (1898). His works in *Corpus Reformatorum,* vols. 1-28, to which several supplements have been added.

. . . I have begun to teach Greek and Hebrew to the Saxons, which undertaking I hope God will favor. I have also determined to publish as soon as possible some sacred writings of the Greeks, Hebrews and Romans with commentaries. Wherefore I pray you either for the love of these studies, or for the honor of the Elector Frederic or of our university to order at my expense, from the booksellers of Coburg, a Greek Bible, for we have the Hebrew Bible extremely well printed here. You will understand how much this will redound to the credit of the elector, the university and your own name, and I would be the first to declare it, did you not already have a witness in Luther, that honored, good and learned leader of true Christian piety. . . .

83. LUTHER TO GEORGE SPALATIN.

Enders, i. 239.   Early morning, AUGSBURG, October 10, 1518.

Greeting. Dear Spalatin, I arrived at Augsburg[1] on October 7. I arrived tired, for having contracted some grave stomach trouble, I almost fainted by the wayside, but I have recovered. This is the third day since I arrived, nor have I yet seen the very reverend lord legate, though on the very first day I sent Dr. Wenzel Link and another to announce me. Meantime a safe-conduct is being secured for me by my friends from the imperial councillors. They are all very cordial to me for the sake of the illustrious elector. But although the very reverend cardinal legate himself promises to treat me with all clemency, yet my friends will not allow me to rely on his word alone, so prudent and careful are they. For they know that he is inwardly enraged at me, no matter what he may outwardly pretend, and I myself clearly learned this elsewhere.

But to-day, at any rate, I shall approach him, and seek to see him and to have my first interview, though whether it will so turn out I do not know. Some think my cause will be affected by the absence of the Cardinal of Gurk,[2] some say the same of the absence of the Emperor, who is not far away, but is daily expected to return. The Bishop of Augsburg[3] is also absent from the city. Yesterday, I dined with Conrad Peutinger,[4] a doctor [of law], a citizen and a man, as you know well, extremely zealous in my cause; nor are the other councillors behind. I know not whether the most reverend legate fears me or whether he is preparing some treachery. Yesterday he sent to me the ambassador of Montferrat,[5]

---

[1] Luther's summons to Rome was changed to one to appear at Augsburg before Cardinal Cajetan. This was in accordance with his own wishes, and with the policy of Cajetan. Smith, *op. cit.*, 48-54, *supra*, nos. 76 and 81.

[2] Matthew Lang.

[3] Christopher von Stadion (Bishop 1517-43), later a great friend of Erasmus.

[4] Peutinger (1465-1547), of Augsburg, studied in Italy, in 1497, was appointed town clerk of his native city, in the service of which he discharged various missions, and was made imperial councillor by Maximilian. His passion was the study of antiquities, on which he produced several works. He was a friend of Erasmus and of the Reformation. *Allgemeine Deutsche Biographie*.

[5] Urban da Serralonga, who had been ambassador at the elector's court from Count William IX, of Montferrat, attached himself to Cajetan after William's death in 1517. On his interview with Luther, Smith, *op. cit.*, 48f.

to sound me on my position before the interview with himself. All think that the man came to me suborned and instructed by the legate, for he plead with me long, advancing arguments for sanity (as he called it), saying that I should simply agree with the legate, return to the Church, recant what I had said ill. He gave me the example of the Abbot Joachim of Flora[1] who, by acting as he [Serralonga] advised me to do, deserved to be considered no heretic, although he had uttered heresy. Then the suave gentleman dissuaded me from defending my opinions, asking if I wished to make it a tournament. In short, he is an Italian and an Italian he will remain. I said that if I could be shown that I had said anything contrary to the doctrine of the Holy Roman Church, I would soon be my own judge and recant. Our chief difficulty was that he cherished the opinions of Aquinas beyond what he can find authority for in the decrees of the Church. I will not yield to him on this point until the Church repeals her former decree on which I rely. "Dear, dear," said he, "so you wish to have a tournament?" Then he went on to make some insane propositions, as, for example, he openly confessed that it was right to preach lies, if they were profitable and filled the chest. He denied that the power of the Pope should be treated in debate, but that it should be so exalted that the Pope might by his sole authority abrogate everything, including articles of faith, and especially that point we were now disputing on. He also made other propositions which I will tell you when I see you. But I dismissed this Sinon,[2] who too openly showed his Greek art, and he went away. Thus I hang between hope and fear, for this clumsy go-between did not give me the least confidence. . . .

The very reverend Vicar John Staupitz writes that he will certainly come when he hears that I have arrived. . . .

We know that the Pope has sent the Rose[3] to our most illustrious elector, a favor they give to great men with lively

---

[1]Joachim of Flora (1145-1202) started an eschatological movement in Italy which made a great commotion when his works were published by some of his followers after his death under the name of "The Eternal Gospel" (1254).

[2]The Greek who persuaded the Trojans to admit the wooden horse into their city. Virgil, *Aeneid,* ii. 79ff.

[3]*Cf. supra,* no. 79.

hope of reward, and that he promises him all good will. In short, the Roman Church, if I may say so, is insatiable for gold, and increases her appetite by eating. Farewell forever, and thank the elector for me and commend me to him.

BROTHER MARTIN LUTHER, *Augustinian*.

84. LUTHER TO PHILIP MELANCHTHON AT WITTENBERG.
Enders, i. 244. AUGSBURG, October 11, 1518.

. . . Play the man, as you do, and teach the youth the things that are right. If it please the Lord I am going to be sacrificed for you and for them. I prefer to perish, and, what is my greatest sorrow, to lose your sweetest society forever rather than to recant what has been well said, and thus became the occasion for the ruin of the noblest studies.

With these enemies of literature and of learning, men as foolish as they are bitter, Italy is cast into the palpable darkness of Egypt.[1] They are completely ignorant of Christ and of the things which are Christ's, yet we have them as lords and masters of our faith and morals. Thus is the wrath of God fulfilled against us, as he says:[2] "I will give children to be their princes and effeminate men shall rule over them." Farewell, my Philip, and avert the wrath of God with pure prayers. BROTHER MARTIN LUTHER.

85. LUTHER TO ANDREW CARLSTADT AT WITTENBERG.
Enders, i. 249. De Wette, i. 159. German.[3]

AUGSBURG, October 14, 1518.

I wish you happiness and salvation, Honored Doctor. I must write briefly for time and business press me. At another time I will write you and other people more. For three days my affair has been in a hard case, so hard, indeed, that I had no hope of coming to you again and saw nothing ahead of me more certain than excommunication.

---

[1] "Tenebras palpabiles" from Exodus, x. 21, "tenebrae tam densae ut palpari queant," in our version, "darkness which may be felt." I have kept Luther's phrase exactly, as it is found in Milton, *Paradise Lost*, xii. 188.

[2] Isaiah, iii. 4, following the Vulgate translation.

[3] This letter was originally written in Latin, but only the German translation has survived.

For all the while the legate would not allow me to debate publicly nor privately with him alone, meantime boasting that he will not be my judge, but will act as a father towards me in everything. None the less, he will hear nothing from me except, "I recant, I revoke, I confess that I erred," which I would not say.

Our chief difficulty was over two articles. 1. That I said indulgence was not the treasury of the merits of our Lord and Saviour Christ. 2. That a man going to the sacrament must believe, etc.[1]

Against these propositions the Legate brought forward the decretal *Unigenitus*,[2] relying on which he became extremely presumptuous as though I were wholly refuted and wished thereupon to force me to a recantation. He alleged for his side the common, though insane, opinion of the schoolmen on the power and effect of the sacrament, and also the uncertainty of the recipient of the sacrament.[3]

Since the legate wished to act by force alone, I have today, through the intercession of several persons, obtained permission to send in my answer in writing, in which the aforesaid decretal *Unigenitus* is dealt with and turned against the legate and his purpose, as I hope, by divine counsel. It shamed the legate, who let all else go and during my absence desired to speak alone with the reverend father vicar Dr. Staupitz. When the vicar came to him he was right friendly. But we don't trust the Italian further than we can see, for, perhaps, he is acting treacherously.

But I have drawn up an appeal, as well drafted and grounded as possible, and suited to the occasion. It is also my intention, if the legate tries to use force against me, to publish my answer on the aforesaid two points, so that the whole world may see his foolishness. For truly from his opinion various senseless and heretical positions may be de-

---

[1] *I. e.*, Luther asserted that the efficacy of the sacrament was dependent on the faith of the recipient, whereas the Catholic doctrine was that it acted automatically, "ex opere operato."

[2] *Canon Law*, lib. 5, tit. 9, cap. 6. Reprinted in B. J. Kidd: *Documents of the Continental Reformation*, p. 1.

[3] *I. e.*, Cajetan said that according to Luther's doctrine a man would never know whether he had sufficient faith and therefore whether the sacrament did him any good or not.

rived. Perchance he is a fine Thomist, but a puzzle-headed, obscure, senseless theologian and Christian, as well fitted to deal with and judge this business as an ass to play the harp.

Therefore my cause stands in so much the more danger, because it has such judges who are not only bitter enemies, but are unable to understand it. But the Lord lives and rules here as elsewhere, to whom I commend myself and all mine, and I doubt not that some God-fearing people will help me with their prayers, for it seems to me that prayer is said for me.

But whether I come to you again safe and sound, or whether under the ban I go to another place, be brave and hold fast to Christ and exalt him.

Christopher Langenmantel[1] is so faithful to me that I am ashamed of his great care for me. I have the favor and support of all men except the crowd who hold with the cardinal, although the cardinal himself always calls me his dear son, and said to Staupitz that I had no better friend than he. But, as I said above, I think he does it for the sake of honor. I know that I would be the most agreeable and dearest of all, if only I would say this one word: "Revoco," that is, "I recant." But I won't make myself a heretic by contradicting the opinion which made me a Christian. I will die first by fire, or be exiled and cursed.

Be of good cheer, dear sir, and show this letter to our theologians, Amsdorf, Melanchthon, Otto Beckmann and the rest, so that you may all pray for me as I do for you. For your business is being done here, namely, the faith of the Lord Christ and the grace of God.

86. JOHN VON STAUPITZ TO THE ELECTOR FREDERIC OF SAXONY.

Zeitschrift für historische Theologie. Leipsic. 1837. VII. Jahrgang. Heft II., p. 122. German. T. Kolde: *Die Augustiner-Congregation,* 443.　　　　　　　　　　AUGSBURG, October 15, 1518.

Serene, highborn Prince, my most gracious Lord! . . . The legate from Rome acts as (alas!) they all do there: he

[1] A canon of Freising and an Imperial Councillor, who had matriculated at Ingolstadt 1500, at Tübingen 1506. About 1510 he became treasurer of Cardinal Matthew Lang.

gives fair words, but all empty and vain. For his whole soul is intent on making Luther recant, not considering that Luther offers to stay still and debate publicly at Augsburg, and to give an answer and reason for this debate; yes, for every word in it. But the unjust judge does not want him to debate, but to recant. Nevertheless, Dr. Luther has in writing so answered his fundamental argument, that the cardinal is straightened therein, and no longer trusts his own argument, but seeks here and there, this and that, how he may extirpate innocent blood and force recantation. God will be the just judge and protector of the truth.

He says also that there is in the land a letter[1] of the General against Luther. Dr. Peutinger has heard that it is also against me, with the purpose of throwing us in prison and using force against us. God be our guard! Finally I fear our professor must appeal and expect force. God help him! His enemies have become his judges; and those who sue him give judgment against him. Herewith I commend myself to your Grace and your Grace to the eternal God. I know nothing as yet certain to write. But if the affair shall take a more favorable turn I will write in haste to your Grace.

Your Grace's humble, obedient chaplain,

DR. JOHN VON STAUPITZ.

87. ERASMUS TO JOHN LANG AT ERFURT.

Allen, iii. 408. LOUVAIN, October 17 (1518).

Please believe, most candid of theologians, that if you vanquish me in writing letters, I at least do not yield to you in love. For Hess,[2] that man of all accomplishments, stumbled upon me first ill and then very busy. I love Staupitz,[3] the

[1] *Supra*, no. 75.
[2] Helius Eobanus Hessus (1488-October 4, 1540), properly Koch, matriculated at Erfurt in 1504 and the next years published poems on the plague and on a student brawl, of which extracts are reprinted by Preserved Smith, *op. cit.*, 442ff. Although a hard drinker, in 1517 he became professor of Latin at Erfurt. Late in 1518 he went to Louvain to see Erasmus, of which he published an account in his *H. Eobani Hessi a profectione ad D. Erasmum hodoeporicon* . . . Erfurt, 1519, a rare book, of which a copy is at Harvard. He took with him letters from Lang and others, one of which Erasmus is here answering. In 1526 he went to teach at Nuremberg, in 1533 returned to Erfurt, and in 1536 was called to the University of Marburg, where he spent his remaining years. *Allgemeine deutsche Biographie*.
[3] This is Erasmus' first allusion to Staupitz. It is possible that he met him at

truly great, and for long I have despised those little sycophants. What else should I do? Ought I give them an account of my conscience? It is sufficient for me that all the most prominent and best bishops like me; if I saw any way of life which would please Christ better I would forthwith adopt it. For love neither of fame nor of money nor of pleasure nor of life rules my mind. I will put your little gift among *my treasures,*[1] and among the more precious ones. Egranus has learnedly answered concerning Cleopas.[2] I hear that Eleutherius is approved by all good men, but it is said that his writings are unequal. I think his *Theses*[3] will please all, except a few about purgatory, which they don't want taken from them, seeing that they make *their living from it.*[4] I have seen Prierias's bungling answer.[5] I see that *the monarchy of the Roman high priest*[6] (as that see now is) is the plague of Christendom, though it is praised through thick and thin by shameless preachers. Yet I hardly know whether it is expedient to touch this open sore, for that is the duty of princes. But I fear they conspire with the pontiff for part of the spoils. I wonder what has come over Eck[7] to begin a battle against Eleutherius. But what, cursed love of fame, wilt thou not force mortal breasts to do?[8] I have inscribed my Suetonius to the illustrious elector[9] who sent me a medal. Farewell, excellent sir, and commend me to Christ in all your prayers.   ERASMUS OF ROTTERDAM.

88. CONRAD ADELMANN, CANON OF AUGSBURG TO SPALATIN.

Walch, xv. 732. German.   AUGSBURG, October 18, 1518.

Conrad Adelmann (1462-1547), studied at Heidelberg 1475, Basle Bologna in 1507-8, but more likely that Mutian or some common friend had made them acquainted since Erasmus' return to Germany in 1514.

[1] These words in italics are Greek in the original.
[2] On this, *supra,* no. 45.
[3] Erasmus first spoke of them on March 5, 1518. Allen, iii. 239, 241. *Cf. supra,* no. 78.
[4] Greek. *Cf. Adagia,* iii. 6, 31.
[5] It was sent by Luther to Lang (Enders, i. 236), and by him presumably to Erasmus.
[6] Greek.
[7] On the battle of Eck and Luther, *supra,* nos. 61 and 62.
[8] Virgil: *Aeneid,* iii. 56-7.
[9] *Cf.* Allen, *op. cit.,* ii. 578ff.

1476, Ferrar 1471 and Tübingen 1476. In 1502 he was made Canon of Augsburg. He was at first strongly for Luther, then returned to the Catholic Church. His brother Bernhard (1457-1523) studied at Heidelberg, Ferrara and Tübingen. He was made canon of the cathedrals at both Eichstätt and Augsburg, between which he divided his time. He was a bitter personal enemy of Eck, and sided with Luther against him. For this Eck had him excommunicated in 1520. Bernhard submitted and was absolved, but still favored Luther until his death. Life by F. X. Thurnhofer. 1900.

My dear Spalatin! Your letter was welcome to my brother and myself, as coming from a good friend, but far more welcome to us was the opportunity of seeing and speaking to dear Dr. Martin Luther, so well endowed with both virtue and learning. We often visited him, as one we heartily love, and showed him our good will.

You will pardon me for saying that he was not well guarded when he left you, and was not provided with what he most needed. But among others the imperial councillors gave him safe-conduct, of which you should have thought first. When he had obtained the safe-conduct he appeared with more courage and confidence before the legate. You will learn from Luther himself, when, please God, he arrives home, what happened before the legate, so I won't bother you with it, for it would be a long song to sing here. But I will not conceal from you that Dr. Luther acquitted himself before the legate as beseems a Christian man. First he offered to leave everything to our Holy Father the Pope, to support what pleased his Holiness and to root out what did not. Secondly, he said that he had debated questions before the universities, according to their custom, and if they desired he would debate further. And if any one came with good reasons and arguments from Scripture he would abandon his opinion and embrace a better one. Further, that if the Christian Church desired to take exception to a single saying of his he would at once submit to her. It was not his intention and never had been to write or say anything against the holy see or against the honor or dignity of the Pope.

If, dear Spalatin, this seems to you to be Luther's opinion, it will become you to use your influence with our most Gracious Lord Elector Frederic, to get him to write or send an embassy to his Holiness, requesting him to receive this sheep commended to him, gently and favorably according to the example of our Redeemer, and that he would let Luther fulfill his offers. For Pope Leo, as I have heard from several people, is gentle and merciful when he is not influenced by his courtiers; wherefore I think he might well take Dr. Martin into favor again. . . .

89. CHRISTOPHER SCHEURL TO SPALATIN.

Christoph Scheurls Briefbuch, hg. von F. von Soden und J. K. F. Knaake. Potsdam, 1872, ii. 53.   NUREMBERG, October 21, 1518.

Hail, Spalatin. I excuse myself for not going on with our Luther[1] on account of my duties to the town council, and because your instructions were doubtful on this point. You will learn from Luther's own letters what was done about him. The favor of all for him is wonderful. When he applies to us we will do all in our power to restore him safe to Saxon soil, and will omit no service we can do him. To-day Vicar Staupitz arrives, whom I consult, for yesterday Wenzel Link returned. I will write you what we may decide to do about Luther's affair after we have taken counsel. In the meantime, at your order in the presence and with the consent of John Bossenstain,[2] the Augustinian prior, I paid Luther four gold gulden; lest it should embarrass him, I took care to have some coins struck with the image of the elector. Farewell, and with your holy fame pray for me and take care of my son, John Tucher.[3] Again, farewell.

C. S., DR.

90. POPE LEO X TO DUKE GEORGE OF SAXONY.

F. Gess: *Akten und Briefe zur Kirchenpolitik Herzog Georgs von Sachsen,* Leipsic, 1905, i. p. 45.   CIVITAVECCHIA, October 24, 1518.

George the Bearded, son of Albert the Brave of Saxony, born 1471, well educated, especially in theology. Duke of Albertine Saxony 1500-April 17, 1539. From the time when he heard the Leipsic debate

---

[1] Luther left Augsburg October 20, arriving at Nuremberg apparently on the 21st. Here he was entertained by Pirckheimer.

[2] On whom I can find nothing else. He was not the Hebrew professor John Böschenstein mentioned occasionally by Luther.

[3] Otherwise unknown.

(1519) to his death, he was Luther's most determined opponent. Life in *Realencyclopädie,* and *cf.* Smith, *op. cit.,* index.

Beloved Son, salutation and the apostolic blessing! Not without pain we have learned from many letters and from rumor what has been done among the faithful people of your part of Germany, which was always considered a Catholic province, and one most devoted and obedient to the apostolic see. We have heard that Martin Luther, a son of perdition, at the suggestion of that cruel enemy of our salvation, the devil, has not blushed to say evil of us and of the said see, in preaching, or rather in cursing. Now as this not only savors of heresy, but is worthy of severe punishment, and should not longer be borne by your devotion and obedience to us, desiring to extirpate this tare and coccle from the fertile field of the Lord by your aid, fearing lest, should we wink at it, it would put forth deeper roots among the too credulous people, we have charged Charles von Miltitz,[1] our notary, secret chamberlain and nuncio in the Lord, and a cleric of the Church of Meissen, to do so. For the wickedness of the thing demands it, and we hope it can be rightly and swiftly done. We have enjoined the said Charles to expound to you our paternal love, hoping that he can rely on the help of your highness; and we charge you for the sake of all the faithful and of the Catholic Church, and the unity and dignity of our see, that, considering the gravity of the present scandal and the rash and damnable error and boldness of the said Martin, you should favor the said Charles and help him to execute his commission. You will thus please God, whose cause you defend, and will also win praise from us and the said see.

91. POPE LEO X. TO ELECTOR FREDERIC OF SAXONY.
Walch, xv. 812. (Spalatin's German translation of the Latin original.)
CIVITAVECCHIA, October 24, 1518.

Beloved Son, noble Sir. Greeting, etc. We are the more willing to send you, through our beloved son, our notary and chamberlain, Charles von Miltitz, your Grace's loyal subject,

[1] A Saxon noble (1490-November 20, 1529), matriculated at Cologne as jurist 1508, at Bologna 1510, in Rome 1513-8. Made chamberlain to the Pope 1514. In 1518 he was sent to negotiate with Luther, but without success. Later he

the holy golden Rose, blessed with our hands, and nobly consecrated on the fourth Sunday of last Lent, our noblest gift, a thing of secret meaning and a splendid decoration for the noble House of Saxony this year. The said Charles will show your Grace what we have commanded him to undertake against the dire foes of the Christian man and against the crime and presumptuous error of a friar Martin Luther.

Noble Sir and beloved Son. It seems to us more necessary every day to take thought for a crusade against the Turk's unholy wrath. . . . But while we were considering how to bring this to pass, and were bending all our forces to this end, Satan reveals this son of perdition or of damnation, Martin Luther, of the order of St. Augustine, who has dared in your territories to preach to the Christian flock against us and the holy Roman see. This not only savors of open heresy, but merits heavy punishment, of which, as it is well known both to us and to you, we shall say nothing more. It becomes us not to tolerate this any longer, both because of our honor and that of the papal see, and because the credulous people may be hereby led to evil doctrine with great scandal. In order, therefore, that this infected, scrofulous sheep may not grow strong in the healthy sheepfold of the Lord, and in order that the boldness of this wicked Martin may stop, and not send his root too deep and firm to be rooted out of the field of the Lord given to our charge, and as we know and have no doubt that this troubles your conscience not a little, for the reputation and honor of yourself and of your famous ancestors, who were always the hottest opponents of heresy, we have commanded the said Charles, our nuncio and chamberlain, in another letter and breve, to take cognizance of this affair and to act against the said Martin and against his followers, who support his scandalous opinions. This is further explained in our letter of credence. We remind your Lordship, and admonish you paternally, to act according to your reason and the virtue of a Christian prince, on which not a little depends, for the sake of your noble reputation, to

became canon of Mayence and Meissen. L. von Pastor: *History of the Popes* (English translation), vol. viii. H. A. Creutzberg: *Karl von Miltitz,* 1907. P. Kalkoff: *Die Miltitziade,* 1911.

favor and support the said Charles in whatever he may ask of you in our name not less than you would ourself. . . .

92. POPE LEO X. TO GEORGE SPALATIN.

Lutheri opera latina varii argumenti, ed. H. Schmidt. Erlangen, 1865, ii. 448.   CIVITAVECCHIA, October 24, 1518.

Here this letter is dated January 1, 1519, but according to Walch, xv. 106, the true date is October 24, and this is so probable that I have followed it. Similar letters were sent to Degenhardt Pfeffinger and other powerful men, and to the Wittenberg Town Council.

Beloved Son, greeting and the apostolic blessing! Considering the merits of the beloved and noble Frederic Elector of Saxony, and the favor which, following the custom of his famous ancestors, he has shown to us and the apostolic see, and which he may show in greater measure hereafter, we have decided, with much affection and paternal love, to send him the most sacred golden rose, annually consecrated with mysterious rites on the fourth Sunday of Lent, and sent to some powerful Christian king or prince. We send it by our beloved son, Charles von Miltitz, our chamberlain and servant. We want you to know some things which concern the dignity and authority of us and of the aforesaid see.

For we know how much favor, and deservedly, you have with the said elector, and how highly he considers your wholesome and prudent counsel. Wherefore we exhort you in the Lord, and paternally charge you on your duty and devotion to us and to the said see, that you consider how great an honor and gift we are sending the said elector, and that you also consider how detestable is the overbearing boldness of that only son of Satan, Friar Martin Luther. Consider also that he savors of notorious heresy, and can blacken the name and fame of the great elector and his ancestors. Take counsel then with our nuncio Miltitz, and try to persuade the said elector to consult our dignity and that of our see, and his own honor. Let him crush the rashness of the said Luther, for his erroneous doctrines, now, alas! widely sown among the credulous people, can only be extirpated by your aid and counsel. Your devotion to God, our Saviour, whose cause is now at stake, will be a special favor to us, whose chief care is to weed out the tares and coccle from the field of the Lord. You will always find us grateful and propitious to you, as you will learn more fully from Miltitz.

Given under the fisherman's ring, in the seventh year of our pontificate. EVANGELISTA.[1]

93. LUTHER TO GEORGE SPALATIN.

Enders, i. 272. WITTENBERG, October 31, 1518.

Greeting. Dear Spalatin, I have come to-day to Wittenberg safe, by God's grace, but know not how long I shall remain so, for my case is in such a state that I both fear and hope. I appealed from the Pope badly informed to the Pope to be better informed, and thus I departed, having left behind a brother to present the appeal to the cardinal in the presence of a notary and witnesses. Meantime I shall prepare another appeal to a future council, following the precedent of the Parisians[2] in case the Pope from the plentitude of his power, or rather tyranny, refuses my first appeal. I am so full of joy and peace that I wonder that many strong men regard my trial as severe.

Certainly the cardinal legate showed great benevolence and clemency to me, as he promised the illustrious elector, but we did not understand him. He offered to do all paternally, most paternally, and doubtless would have acted accordingly, had I only wished to recant. For our whole difficulty was that I would not, and he *would*, nor do I think he had instructions to do anything but condemn me; therefore, I was obliged to appeal.

I shall publish my answer[3] to his arguments, together with my *Appeal* and a theological commentary on the Apostolic—or diabolic—Breve,[4] of which you often wrote me formerly, and of which you recently sent a copy, delivered to me, with other letters of instruction, at Nuremberg on my return

---

[1] One of the papal secretaries, not certainly to be identified, perhaps Evangelista Maddaleni de Capodiferro, a poet and historian, and (1514) a municipal officer of Rome. *Cf.* E. Rodocanachi: *Rome au temps de Jules II et de Leon X.* Paris, 1912, pp. 228, 283, 323.

[2] On March 27, 1518, the University of Paris had appealed to a future council. Luther followed their form of appeal to protect himself.

[3] The *Acta Augustana*, Weimar, ii. 6ff. Smith, 53.

[4] The papal Breve to Cajetan of August 23, 1518, *supra*, no. 73.

journey. It is incredible that such a monster should come from a pope, especially from Leo X. Therefore, whoever the rascal was who, under the name of Leo X., proposed to terrify me with this decretal, shall know that I also recognize folly when I see it. But if it *did* come from the curia I will teach them their impudent rashness and wicked ignorance.

Personally, the cardinal greatly pleased me. I suspect the Romans begin to be afraid and to distrust their own strength, and thus cunningly seek a way out. I will tell you more another time, I hope, face to face. Commend me to the elector and give him my thanks. . . .

94. WOLFGANG CAPITO TO CANDID THEOLOGIANS.

Herminjard: *Correspondance des Réformateurs des pays de la langue française.* (1866ff), i. 61.   (BASLE, October, 1518).

This is the Preface to the first edition of Luther's *Works*, printed at Basle, October, 1518, by Froben. The anonymous preface was written by Capito. See Baum: *Capito und Butzer*, p. 32. It is reprinted by Herminjard from the subsequent edition, *sine loco*, 1520, and conjecturally dated by him "Wittenberg?, March, 1520."

Here you have the theological works of the Reverend Father Martin Luther, whom many consider a Daniel sent at length in mercy by Christ to correct abuses and restore the evangelic and Pauline divinity to theologians who have forgotten the ancient commentaries and occupy themselves with the merest logical and verbal trifles. And would that he might arouse all theologians from their lethargy, and get them to leave their somnolent summaries[1] of divinity and choose the gospel rather than Aristotle, Paul rather than Scotus, or even Jerome, Augustine, Ambrose, Cyprian, Athanasius, Hilary, Basil, Chrysostom, Theophylact rather than Lyra, Aquinas, Scotus and the rest of the schoolmen. May they no longer drag Christ to the earth, as Thomas Aquinas always does, but may they instruct the earth in the doctrine of Christ. May they cease saying one thing in their farcical universities, another at home, another before the people and something else to their friends; and may they cease calling

[1] A pun, "omissis somniis, summis dictum oportuit."

good men who refuse to fool with them heretics as they now do for small cause or for no cause at all. . . .

95. LUTHER TO GEORGE SPALATIN AT ALTENBURG.
Enders, i. 279. (WITTENBERG), November 13, 1518.

Greeting. Dear Spalatin, we tried to get some citizen to offer Father John Frosch[1] his doctor's banquet,[2] but we fear our efforts are vain. And so, not to turn away a worthy man without honor, we have turned to our monastery, where, depending on the elector's promise, we will, at our own inconvenience, give him his banquet. For, indeed, we are poor, and there are many of us, so that we cannot do it by ourselves. Wherefore I beg you to ask the elector to provide us with game for November 18, or rather the 17th. If this cannot be, make it next week, Monday [November 22]. And send me an answer by this messenger as quickly as possible what is to be done, so that we may not make vain preparations. Farewell in Christ.

BROTHER MARTIN LUTHER, *Augustinian*.

96. LUTHER TO JOHN ECK AT INGOLSTADT.
Enders, i. 280. (WITTENBERG), November 15, 1518.

On the debate planned with Eck, *cf. supra*, no. 61, and Smith, *op. cit.*, pp. 58ff.

Greeting. My dear John Eck, Dr. Carlstadt is pleased with what we agreed at Augsburg, namely, that you should meet at Leipsic or Erfurt and debate honorably for the discovery of the truth, that there may be an end of contention and of writing books. He begs, therefore, that you will fix the day for the meeting, and the place, one of the two mentioned. He would have fixed them himself, but thought he ought to defer to you because you live farther away and are perhaps busier than he. Therefore act so that I may not have per-

---

[1] Of Bamberg, had studied at Erfurt 1504, taken his baccalaureate of theologie at Toulouse and his licentiate at Wittenberg 1516. He was with Luther at Augsburg, from which he returned to obtain the doctorate as here related. Later he became evangelical preacher at Augsburg, keeping up a desultory correspondence with Luther. Enders, i. 275, v. 401.

[2] The taking of the doctorate was always the occasion of a festive meal known as the *Doktorschmaus*. Luther's diploma to him, dated November 22, 1518, printed in *Theologische Studien und Kritiken*, 1913, p. 120.

suaded Carlstadt in vain, or rather so that our adversaries may vainly hope that theologians will always fight among themselves and never agree. Farewell. Hastily amidst divers occupations.   Yours,   MARTIN LUTHER.

97. LUTHER TO PHILIP MELANCHTHON AT WITTENBERG.
Enders, i. 301.   (WITTENBERG, November 22, 1518.)

To Philip Melanchthon Schwarzerd, Grecian, Latin, Hebrew, German, never Barbarian, Greeting. May the Muse and Apollo forgive you for despising me and the new doctor[1] to-day. Now, though it is not particularly my affair, I have forgiven it, but unless you instantly appear before Dr. Carlstadt and Licentiate Amsdorf, and especially the Rector,[2] not even your Greek will excuse you, not to mention "that little brother Martin," as Cajetan calls me. The new doctor believes (as he says in joke) that he is despised as a Barbarian by a Greek. Take care what you do, for I have most certainly promised that you would come at once. You will do me a favor if you come alone, yet I greatly wish that you would also bring with you Guy Warbeck[3] and John Schwertfäger.[4] For this evening I shall be the host to my most intimate and dearest friends. Induce them to come by your advice, and by my command, if "that little brother" can command. Farewell.   Your little brother,
MARTIN *Eleutherius*.[5]

98. THE RECTOR,[6] PROFESSORS AND DOCTORS OF THE UNIVERSITY OF WITTENBERG TO THE ELECTOR FREDERIC OF SAXONY.
Lutheri opera varii argumenti (Erlangen, 1865), ii. 426.
WITTENBERG, November 23, 1518.

Most illustrious and clement Prince, that venerable man,

[1] John Frosch. The diploma, dated November 22, given him by Luther, reprinted *Theologische Studien und Kritiken*, 1913, p. 120.
[2] Bartholomew Bernhardi, of Feldkirchen.
[3] Matriculated at Wittenberg in 1514, five years later became canon of St. George's Church at Altenburg, and in the same year accompanied the Elector to the Imperial Election at Frankfort, where he made himself useful by his knowledge of French. He died in 1534. His daughter married Luther's son Paul.
[4] Of Meissen, matriculated at Wittenberg 1507, in 1521 became professor of law, died 1524.
[5] This word written in Greek letters.   [6] John Frosch.

Brother Martin Luther, M. A., D. D., a noble and most famous member of our university, has related to us what the Very Reverend Legate Cardinal Cajetan has written to your Highness; namely, that he urges you to send the said Luther to Rome or to exile him from your territories, on account of certain propositions debated by him and long ago offered to the Supreme Pontiff. Luther adds that he offered to debate publicly or to give a private answer in writing, and that he prayed that his errors might be pointed out to him in writing, with the reasons and authorities from the Scripture and the holy Fathers added, so that by their light he might perceive his errors, but that none of these requests was granted, but he was simply ordered to retract what he had said wrongly. Nor was the care of the faithful shepherd shown to him, for the shepherd is bound to give a reason to everyone asking it, and is even commanded to teach willing and unwilling alike, in season and out of season.

Therefore Luther has asked and obtained that we should intercede with your Highness, and should beg that your most illustrious Highness should deign to write to the legate or even to the Pope and graciously to intervene, requesting that the articles and points of his errors should be shown him in writing, and that reasons and authorities should be given, so that he may know that he has erred and thus recant, not being forced to condemn opinions before he knows whether they should be condemned. It was the ancient custom of the Church, as the examples of the Fathers show, to urge the correction of error by reason and authority and not to condemn by mere assertion the sayings of anyone. . . .

99. LUTHER TO CHRISTOPHER LANGENMANTEL AT AUGSBURG.

Enders, i. 305. WITTENBERG, November 25, 1518.

Greeting. Excellent Christopher, I arrived safely and happily at home by God's grace. The offices of extraordinary humanity and kindness with which you overwhelmed my unworthy self, have made your name and fame a pleasant and sweet savor to us. For I commended your fidelity and that of Dr. Auer[1] as it deserved, not for the purpose of glorifying you, but of giving an example of such fidelity to others. Moreover, the Lord Jesus, who made you think of, will and do such things, will recognize and approve his own works in you. Truly pure faith and sincere friendship is a rare bird.

Recently the lord legate wrote[2] our elector accusing me of leaving by fraud, and complaining that I had armed myself with a safe-conduct and had appealed. He condemns everything I did, especially that I did not recant my cursed propositions, particularly those on indulgences, and blaming me for not sparing the Pope's Holiness, in saying that he abused the Scripture. Finally he advises the elector to send me to Rome, or to banish me, lest he should stain his glory for the sake of "one little brother." Thus also did the Jews act against Christ before Pilate, wishing him to believe them before they brought forward definite charges. Thus does Cajetan shout: "May your most illustrious lordship believe me; I speak from certain knowledge, not from mere opinion. I will preserve the rule of Jesus Christ, which I know is being violated thus, for Luther seeks nothing but to violate the truth." That golden rose which rumor said was being sent to the elector is nowhere, nor has the elector heard anything of it. I see that the Romans are determined to condemn me. I, on the other hand, am determined not to yield. So I await their censures. The Lord will be my counsellor and helper. If they kill me they will cease pursuing a dead flea.[3] I answered the letter of the lord legate of which the elector sent me a copy, and I desired him to enclose my answer in his reply to the legate. My *Acta Augustana*[4] is now being edited, for the elector dissuaded me from publishing it before. You will learn the rest from the recently promoted Father Prior John Frosch. You will recognize the signs agreed upon.[5] I hope my faithful protector,

[1] John Auer, an Augsburg Councillor, who helped Luther draw up his Appeal.
[2] His letter, October 25, 1518, Enders, i. 268. The elector sent it to Luther, who drew up a reply on November 19, 1518, Enders, i. 283, which the elector sent to Cajetan with a note of his own, December 8, 1518, Enders, i. 310.
[3] *Cf.* 1 Samuel xxiv. 14.
[4] The account of the doings at Augsburg, Weimar, ii. 6ff.
[5] *Signa supersunt cognoscenda.* An obscure sentence, apparently referring to

Doctor John Auer, is strong in the Lord, and I desire to be remembered to him. Dr. Carlstadt, Amsdorf, Otto Beckmann and all your friends heartily salute you.

Farewell in the Lord, may he keep you in eternity as he does in this world. Greet from me the truly noble John Schenk.

BROTHER MARTIN LUTHER, *Augustinian*.

100. LUTHER TO GEORGE SPALATIN AT ALTENBURG.

Enders, i. 307. WITTENBERG, December 2, 1518.

Greeting. Had not your letters come yesterday, dear Spalatin, I should already have left,[1] and I am yet prepared for either alternative. The solicitude of our friends for me is remarkable, and greater than I myself can bear. Some urge me to give myself into the elector's custody, for him to keep somewhere, in which case he could write the legate that I was being kept bound in a safe place pending my examination. I leave this plan to your wisdom, I am in the hands of God and of my friends.

One may surely believe that the elector favors me and the university, as I recently heard from one who I know would not lie to me. In the court of the Bishop of Brandenburg they lately discussed what favor and whose support I had. Someone said: "Erasmus, Capito and other learned men favor him." "No," replied the bishop, "these men are nothing to the Pope; it is the University of Wittenberg and the Elector of Saxony that really count." So I know it is commonly believed that the elector is with me, which displeases them. I only wish they were as much afraid of the university. Truly the suspicion cast upon the elector will compel me to withdraw, if necessary, although the elector may excuse himself in his writings by saying that as a layman he is unable to judge of such matters, especially as he sees that a university approved by the Church does not contradict me. But these are incidentals. If I stay here I shall not have much freedom of

---

some message sent in cipher. Hoppe translates: "Es bleibt noch übrig, die Aufzeichnungen kennen zu lernen" which he confesses is "etwas dunkel." *Luthers Werke*, St. Louis, xxi. A, 119f.

[1] After Cajetan's request to the elector to give Luther up or to banish him, there was some talk of doing so, and also of hiding him in a castle, as was done later (1521-2) in the Wartburg. *Cf.* Smith, *op. cit.*, p. 53.

writing and speaking; if I go I will pour out everything and offer my life for Christ. Farewell.

BROTHER MARTIN LUTHER.

101. JOHN ECK TO DUKE GEORGE OF SAXONY.
Gess, i. 47. INGOLSTADT, December 4, 1518.

Your Grace doubtless knows that recently Dr. Martin Luther, of Wittenberg, published some theses on papal indulgences and other main articles of the Christian faith. And when they came into my hands, at the request of my gracious Lord Gabriel, Bishop of Eichstädt[1] and Chancellor of the University of Ingolstadt, I wrote out an opinion explaining why I did not consider some of them Christian. But when my writing came into the hands of the said Dr. Luther, Dr. Andrew Bodenstein, of Carlstadt, at Wittenberg, attacked me in writing and undertook to defend Luther's propositions and doctrine. It then became necessary for me to defend my doctrine according to the truth and the holy faith, and I did so with more moderation than the said Carlstadt deserved of me. But I made the express proviso that, should he abide by his error (as I consider it), I would challenge him to a debate before the Pope, or the learned men of the university of Rome or Paris or Cologne, hoping humbly and kindly that thereby all offence and hatred that might have come from our polemics be avoided. And when the said Carlstadt, to my surprise, refused to debate at any of these places, I offered to meet him at some other university, and he proposed Erfurt or Leipsic. Wherefore, as I do not fear to debate before any learned men, I beg your Grace for permission to debate at Leipsic. . . .

102. MELANCHTHON TO GEORGE SPALATIN.
Corpus Reformatorum, i. 56. Böcking, Supp. ii. 789.
WITTENBERG (Early in December, 1518).[2]

. . . I enclose Luther's *Appeal to a General Council,* nor

---
[1] Bishop, 1496-1535.
[2] The date is given by the reference to Luther's *Appeal to a Council,* which he drew up on November 28, and which was printed by December 11. Köstlin-Kawerau, i. 218.

is there any reason why you should fear much from the rage of the Romanists. This sort of people think that they are not ruling unless they are acting like tyrants, although Heaven knows that ruling in a Christian people ought to mean no more than doing as the father of a household would.[1] But ambition and avarice bring forth all things. Luther clears himself so entirely that they cannot pretend that he is guilty of a new crime. For what he does has been done before and not blamed by the Romanists. May God Almighty preserve his people. Farewell. YOUR PHILIP.

103. LUTHER TO GEORGE SPALATIN.

Enders, i. 313. (WITTENBERG), December 9, 1518.

Greeting. What your letter, Spalatin, forbade me to do, is already done. My *Acta Augustana* is already published, written with the freedom of much truth, albeit not with the whole truth, for I see that in this as in all things I am obliged to hurry.

I heard yesterday from Nuremberg that Charles von Miltitz is on the way, having three papal breves. They write me that a trustworthy man has seen the breves and that they order him to capture me and deliver me to the Pope. That doctor of Eisleben,[2] who, with Philip von Feilitzsch[3] stood by me before the legate at Augsburg, has warned me through our prior[4] to take care; he said that on a journey he had heard a certain courtier asserting that he had promised to deliver me to the Pope. I hear other things also, and whether they are true or are invented to frighten me I do not think they are to be despised. Therefore, lest they should kill me unex-

---

[1] Quid debebat in christiano populo non esse aliud imperare quam τὸ οἰκονομεῖν.

[2] John Rühel, a fellow-townsman of Luther, who became councillor and then chancellor of Mansfeld. Luther became quite intimate with him in 1525, during which year he wrote him several letters, as well as some in subsequent years as late as 1539.

[3] One of the elector's councillors, who appears in Luther's letters last in December, 1522.

[4] Conrad Helt of Nuremberg, in which city he joined the Augustinians at an early age. Matriculated at Wittenberg 1512, became B. A. 1514 and M. A. 1516. In 1518 he was elected prior, in which position he was rather lax. He followed Luther until February, 1522, when he left Wittenberg. After short stays at Nuremberg and Nordhausen, he became prior of the Augustinian convent at Heidelberg, which position he held until his death, August 24, 1548. *Archiv für Reformationsgeschichte*, vii. 264ff.

pectedly or crush me with their censures, I am waiting in all readiness for the plan of God. I have even appealed to a future council. The more they rage and seek my life the less am I afraid. Sometime I shall be freer against these Roman hydras. What you have heard about my saying farewell to the people of Wittenberg is false; I said this: "I am an uncertain and unsettled preacher, as you have found out. How often have I left you suddenly without bidding you good-bye? If the same thing should ever happen again, in case I do not come back, I wish to say farewell to you." Then I warned them not to be afraid of the furious papal censures against me, and that they should not blame the Pope or any mortal for them, or wish anyone evil, but should commit the affair to God, and the like. I lecture and teach as before. Farewell.
BROTHER MARTIN ELEUTHERIUS.

103a. GEORGE SPALATIN TO GUY BILD AT AUGSBURG.
Zeitschrift des historischen Vereins für Schwaben und Neuburg. 1893. xx. 220. ALTENBURG, December 10, 1518.

... I am sorry you did not see our Dr. Martin Luther when he appeared before the very reverend legate at Augsburg, for as far as I can guess you did not meet him. If you ask how he is, for all I know he is well, and, as I who write have found out, of too lofty and strong a mind to be turned by any blast of furious fortune from doing what he has proposed and from the path he has set for himself. For the sake of Christ and the truth he shuns no misfortune, he flees no calamity, he fears no evil. His mind seems strengthened to a perpetual pursuit of the gospel truth, or rather to propagate the word of the Lord before so many Pharaohs. Now farewell and pray for Dr. Luther and me, for we favor you. In haste, GEORGE SPALATIN.

[1] P. S.—That most holy, true and German theology, not fouled by the dregs of metaphysics and dialectics, not polluted by human traditions, not burdened with old wives' tales, but

---

[1] As this is printed it is not quite certain whether this is a postscript to the above letter, or an extract from another letter. At any rate, it must have been written near the same time.

such as the primitive theologians knew, praised and extolled to heaven, this theology, I say, is taught (praise be to God!) in the university of my elector at Wittenberg with such success that those learned doctors of theology, Martin Luther and Carlstadt have full lecture-rooms and disciples not only eager to learn, but already proficient, who do not fear even the greatest of the sophists. Philip Melanchthon teaches Greek there to about four hundred pupils. There are also not a few scholars of Dr. John Bösschenstein,[1] who teaches Hebrew. In short, the best studies are so successfully taught at Wittenberg that you would call it another Athens.

104. LUTHER TO JOHN REUCHLIN.

Enders, i. 320.   WITTENBERG, December 14, 1518.

The Lord be with you, valiant man! Most learned humanist, I thank God that by his mercy you have at length stopped the mouth of those speaking iniquity. For you were indeed the instrument of divine wisdom, although unconscious of it yourself, yet most welcome to all lovers of sound theology. How differently has God shaped your course from what you thought! I am one of those who longed to be with you, but had no opportunity. Yet was I always with you in prayer and fervent hope. But what was then denied to me as your ally, has been granted to me as your successor [in persecution]. For the teeth of these behemoth lay hold on me, if by any means they can avenge on me the shame that they have received from you. I, too, fight them, though with far inferior resources of genius and learning than you displayed in both fighting and overcoming them, yet with a no less steadfast mind. They avoid meeting my arguments, they refuse to reply to me, but attack me murderously by mere force and violence. Truly Christ lives, and I, who have nothing, can lose nothing. For by your valor the horns of these bulls have been broken in pieces. The Lord worked through you, that the king of the sophists may learn to be more slow and cautious in opposing sound theology, and Germany may

---

[1] Bösschenstein (1472-1532) came from Ingolstadt to Wittenberg as the first professor of Hebrew. He left early in 1519 under unpleasant circumstances. Enders, i. 243, ii. 12f.

breathe again after so many hundred years during which the teaching of the Scriptures lay dormant or rather extinct.

. . . .

But am I not bold to speak to you so familiarly without any laudatory preface? My hearty love for you has impelled me to write, for I feel [although I have not met you] familiar with you, partly because I think so much of you, and partly by meditation on your books. Another reason for writing is that our admirable Philip Melanchthon, who has almost every virtue known to man, and is my dear, intimate friend, has urged me to write boldly, assuring me that you would not take my awkwardness ill, but would thank me. But do not blame him, if you must blame anyone, as I wish you to regard this letter solely as a witness to my affection for you, which is nothing if not frank.

Farewell and rejoice in the Lord, my truly venerable teacher!

105. THE DEAN AND DOCTORS OF THE THEOLOGICAL FACULTY OF THE UNIVERSITY OF LEIPSIC TO DUKE GEORGE.

Gess, i. 49. LEIPSIC, December 16, 1518.

We send your Grace certain letters of Dr. Eck. We surmise that he is trying to get from your Grace that which he spoke about in his letters to our faculty. And that your Grace may briefly comprehend the affair we give your Grace to understand what happened last summer about the day of St. John [June 24], when there was a dispute about papal graces and indulgences between the Reverend Dr. Martin Luther, of Wittenberg, and John Tetzel,[1] then of Frankfort [on the Oder], as your Grace doubtless remembers. Then Lord

[1] John Tetzel, born about 1465 at Pirna, studied at Leipsic, where he took his B. A. in 1487, shortly after which he became a Dominican. Visited Rome in 1497. As a member of the convent at Glogau he was made inquisitor for Poland 1509. In 1516 he was preacher of indulgences for Arcimboldi, and the following year for Albert of Mayence. It was his preaching that was attacked by Luther in the *Ninety-five Theses*. Tetzel defended himself by drawing up counter *Theses* with the help of Conrad Wimpina, which he defended at Frankfort on the Oder, January 20, 1518. But his business was ruined and his character assailed. In 1518 he withdrew to Leipsic, where he lived until his death of chagrin in August, 1519. In his last days Luther wrote him a letter, now lost, "not to be troubled, for the affair did not begin with him, but the child had another father." N. Paulus: *Die Deutschen Dominikaner im Kampfe gegen Luther*. 1903, 1ff.

Albert, Archbishop and Cardinal of Magdeburg and Mayence, sent an honorable embassy to us to inquire which side in this dispute was nearer the truth and what our opinion on the said difference was. But considering that certain imperial counsellors at that time refused to give an opinion we did the same, and sent his electoral grace our memorial testifying our good will and to the following effect: Whereas both sides have brought much scandal among the people and we fear that more will arise, and as each side is convinced that it is in the right, our opinion would not make them lay aside theirs, but would only impel them to assail each other with injury and scandal. Moreover, as the affair concerns the Holy Father at Rome, it is not fitting that we should meddle with it. But we advised that his electoral grace should assemble a synod and have the thing heard and decided by them. Otherwise, we feared an increase in scandal. In the meantime John Eck, as he informs us, gave his opinion on the same question to the bishop of Eichstätt and thereby fell into a dispute with Dr. Carlstadt, of Wittenberg. And when he offered to dispute at Rome, Paris or Cologne, Dr. Carlstadt declined. And though we were long ago requested by Dr. Luther in behalf of Dr. Carlstadt, as well as by Dr. Eck, to interfere in this affair, we have thought it best for sundry reasons to refuse both parties. For we feared that others, even laymen, might be drawn into the quarrel and that the Elector Frederic might lay it up against this university and that thereby there might arise a quarrel between him and your Grace. Wherefore we recommend Eck to commit the chief points of Dr. Martin Luther's propositions to some bishops for decision, or to a select board drawn from certain universities, for thus, by a written or oral disputation between select commissioners the thing might be ended. . . .

106. LUTHER TO GEORGE SPALATIN.

Enders, i. 332. (WITTENBERG), December 21, 1518.

Greeting. Dear Spalatin, if I rightly understand you, you ask whether an expedition against the Turks can be defended and commanded by me on Biblical grounds. Even supposing the war should be undertaken for pious reasons rather than for gain, I confess that I cannot promise what you ask, but rather the opposite. Recently at the request of a friend I published a sermon on this subject, which has fallen into the hands of the heroes of Brandenburg, on whose account I suspected the request was made to me. In this I argued that no such war should be undertaken.[1] I am still of the same opinion until I shall be refuted with better reasons. Erasmus expresses the same opinion in many places, as you know better than I.[2] It seems to me if we must have any Turkish war we ought to begin with ourselves. In vain we wage carnal wars without, while at home we are conquered by spiritual battles.

Moreover, neither in the Old nor in the New Testament was any war ever waged by human might, save with an unhappy and disgraceful issue; if it were successful it was because of aid from heaven as I could amply substantiate. Now that the Roman curia is more tyrannical than any Turk, fighting with such portentous deeds against Christ and against his Church, and now that the clergy is sunk in the depths of avarice, ambition and luxury, and now that the face of the Church is everywhere most wretched, there is no hope of a successful war or of victory. As far as I can see, God fights against us; first, we must conquer him with tears, pure prayers, holy life and pure faith. But of this elsewhere.

I remain at Wittenberg, awaiting without doubt the proof of Roman wretchedness, although I hope the very fear of conscience will prevent them acting with precipitate fury. I will consult lawyers about drawing up my Appeal.[3]

Except for one scrap, I have completely forgotten the sermon I gave at Weimar,[4] for which you ask. I am only sure that I preached the gospel against hypocrites and self-righteous men, as I always do. I know there is one such in that court, whom you will know even if I do not name him.

[1] Luther later changed his opinion on this subject, writing in favor of the Turkish war in 1527. *Cf.* Smith, *op. cit.*, 226f.
[2] Spalatin had translated Erasmus' letter on peace to Antony of Bergen, March 14, 1514. *Cf. supra*, December 14, 1516, no. 23, and Allen: *Opus Epistolarum Erasmi*, i. 551.
[3] *I. e.*, to the Council. Luther consulted Scheurl about the proper form of the appeal; Scheurl wrote him at length on the subject, December 20. Enders, i. 325.
[4] On the journey to Augsburg Luther preached at Weimar, September 29.

Nothing is more harmful to magistrates and nobles than that sort of men, who, though they never learned anything, teach all things, even the religion of the angels. I wish to do my best to oppose their ideas. . . .

BROTHER MARTIN LUTHER, *Augustinian*.

107. CHRISTOPHER SCHEURL TO LUTHER.
Enders, i. 335. (NUREMBERG, December 22, 1518.)

My friend Charles says that he has been soliciting the rose[1] for three years, and demanded this province of right, and that he is not a legate, but a simple commissioner, with instructions to act on the legate's[2] advice. At Augsburg he dispatched more than forty breves to the powers of Germany, in which he asks aid against a helpless man. Those who give assistance are blessed, those who resist are damned forever. He says that he will not use these powers, but will do what he can to please the elector, and that he comes as a private man; not a judge, but a friend, only to find out what the elector decides, what Martin thinks and to win the favor of all. He says he will inform the legate and the Pope that the apostolic see has never had a harder, more anxious or more delicate affair than this. He says you must do something, at the very least correct the violence of your letter to the cardinal, for he took your departure and that of Staupitz very hard, since you did not say good-bye to him, as though wishing to mock him. I excused you, and he confessed that you could not have returned to him except in good will. He denies that the cardinal is staying in Germany for the sake of this affair, but says that he is waiting for the assembly of the princes next Easter, at Worms or Frankfort. The Emperor has promised to come to Augsburg on January 6, and in my opinion the legate will also follow from Lintz. Miltitz says that you ought to come, too,[3] and if you do, everything will be discussed kindly and that you will have nothing to fear. In these circumstances we must not fear the [papal]

---
[1] *I. e.*, the anointed golden rose sent by the Pope to the Elector Frederic.
[2] Cajetan.
[3] A meeting between Miltitz, Spalatin and Luther was arranged at Altenburg, January 4-5 (or 5-6), on which *cf.* Smith, p. 54ff.

thunders, nor rashly believe everything, but must act with great moderation, and strive hard that you get a hearing in Germany, and that your university and town councillors should recommend you, and promise that you will be a true son of the Church, and will do whatever you ought and can with God's approval. I do not despair, for God will give his grace, which is never lacking to those who fear him. Again farewell.

108. ELECTOR FREDERIC TO DUKE GEORGE OF SAXONY.

Gess, i. 51.   ALTENBURG, December 29, 1518.

... I have with me a papal ambassador, Charles von Miltitz, who is not satisfied with Dr. Luther and has great power to proceed against him. And it well might happen that he would refuse to give me the golden rose unless I banished the monk and said that he was a heretic. But I fancy I can do as Clauss Narr[1] says, go on drinking my wine and being a heretic all my days. . . .

109. DUKE GEORGE TO THE DEAN AND DOCTORS OF THE THEOLOGICAL FACULTY OF LEIPSIC.

De Wette-Seidemann, vi. 658. Gess, i. 52.   December 30, 1518.

Honorable, learned, dear and trusty Gentlemen! We have received your letter and one from our dear and trusty Dr. John Eck of Ingolstadt, in which he begged that he might hold a public debate with Dr. Andrew Carlstadt of Wittenberg, before you. And we have read the reasons why you refused this, and we consider that if instead you would do all you could to further it, and would give these doctors of other universities a place to debate in, you would win no little fame, praise and honor thereby. And if you did this you would not therefore be compelled to give any assent or recognition to the debate, but at need could recommend the decision to the papal commissaries or other proper authorities who stand ready to take the responsibility. Moreover you should

---

[1] The court fool. "Drinking wine" was proverbial for not letting anything trouble one. So Luther, in one of the *Eight Sermons in Lent*, "The Word, while I slept and drank beer with Melanchthon and Amsdorf, has broken the Papacy more than any king or emperor ever did." Weimar xiii. p. 18f.

not be anxious lest any uproar or unpleasantness might arise from the propositions, but when and if it should arise we can then deal with it. . . .

110. DUKE GEORGE OF SAXONY TO JOHN ECK.

De Wette-Seidemann, vi. 658. Gess, i. 53.   December 31, 1518.

Dear and trusty Sir! We have received your request to hold your debate with Dr. Carlstadt at Leipsic, and have graciously noted the same, being pleased that you have chosen our university. We trust to you that this debate may not be dangerous, but only for the sake of elucidating the truth. We have therefore given order to our university to grant your request. . . .

111. PHILIP MELANCHTHON TO LUTHER.

Enders, i. 336. Greek.   (WITTENBERG), January, 1519.

This poem, in iambic trimeter, was the dedication of Melanchthon's *Elegantissima quaedam opuscula*, Haganau, January, 1519, and, like most dedications, was probably written shortly before the work went to press. As printed the text is so corrupt—some of the words being impossible and some of the lines not scanning—as to have puzzled not only myself, but such distinguished Greek scholars as Prof. Harry de Forrest Smith, of Amherst, U. S. A., and Prof. Gilbert Murray, of Oxford, England. With the obliging help of these gentlemen, I have radically restored and construed the text according to its apparent meaning. I think the poem is worth giving as testimony to the reverence, almost idolatry, in which Luther was thus early held by his followers.

Holy Nazarite of Israel, offerer of peace-making sacrifices,[1] elect servant of uncorrupted truth, protector of souls, ruler of pious desires, divinely inspired messenger of wisdom and of motherless justice, happy priest of the divine word and of the life-giving spirit, spreading abroad the sweet smelling balsam of the anointed Church,[2] faithful and sleepless shepherd of the temple of all-merciful God, driving out the Arabian wolf and the sophist Belial, thou champion of truth, smite with the wonder-working staff of Moses the doting brains of the enemies of the Word, even the superstitious magicians; cauterize the

---

[1] *I. e.*, as priest offering the sacrifice of the mass.
[2] Or, "of the eucharist of the Church."

unclean tongues with the juniper coals of the Word;[1] fight steadfastly and unceasingly follow light-bearing Jesus; guard the blessed lot of the faithful.

112. HERMANN RAB TO CHARLES VON MILTITZ.

Tentzel-Cyprian: *Historischer Bericht vom Anfang und vom ersten Fortgang der Reformation Lutheri* (Leipsic, 1718), ii. 106. Quoted by N. Paulus: *Die deutschen Dominikaner im Kampfe gegen Luther* (Freiburg i. B., 1903), p. 10.[2] Walch, xv. 863.

LEIPSIC, January 3, 1519.

Hermann Rab, of Bamberg, matriculated at Leipsic 1486, soon after which he joined the Dominican order there, where he knew Tetzel. In 1511 he became Vicar and in 1516 a member of the theological faculty. He visited Rome in 1518 and again in 1519. He took a fairly active part against Luther. He died in 1534. *Cf.* Paulus, *op. cit.,* pp. 9ff.

May the Lord forgive Martin Luther, who was and is very anxious to involve us who are innocent in his affair, in order to draw his own head out of the noose. Everyone who has read or heard the *Appeal*[3] and other writings of the said Martin, knows how he attacks and has attacked the Reverend Father John Tetzel, although the latter has defended and does not cease to defend the authority of the Pope, even to his own disadvantage, as his sermons prove and as all who have heard him bear witness. In fact, I cannot find anyone who has done and suffered so much for the glory of the apostolic see. If only our Holy Father knew this! I doubt not that he would fittingly recognize his services. All the street corners echo with the slanders and lies brought together to crush him. Wherefore I recommend him to your Grace, as a true friend and lord, and to the protection of the papal see, for which he fights and suffers danger of imprisonment. Had your Grace only heard the sermon which he preached on January 1,[4] you would know how he felt and feels towards the papal see. Wherefore, I recommend him again to your Lordship.

[1] *Cf.* Isaiah vi. 5-7.
[2] I know this only in the quotations of Paulus and Walch which are in German; the original was presumably Latin.
[3] *Supra,* no. 102.
[4] Tetzel, who had been made extremely unpopular by Luther's attack on indulgences, had now taken refuge in the Dominican cloister at Leipsic. Paulus,

113. LUTHER TO JOHN ECK AT INGOLSTADT.

Enders, v. 4.   LEIPSIC, January 7, 1519.

After the meeting with Miltitz at Altenburg (on which *cf. supra*, no. 107), Luther and Melanchthon went to Leipsic for a few days to see friends and make arrangements for the coming debate with Eck.

My dear Eck, we did our best to get the Leipsic faculty to grant us the favor of which you write,[1] but they simply refused, alleging that it was none of their business to get mixed up in this affair, but that jurisdiction belonged to the bishops. The dean of the faculty of theology answered my letter in such a way that I fear our debate will come to nothing unless you have some other plan.

I am, however, waiting with great eagerness to see you show, as you promise, that in my *Resolutions* not even the foundations are valid. You wonder that I have preferred Tauler alone ("I know not who he is," you say) to Aquinas, Bonaventura and Alexander of Hales. It seems ridiculous to you that, when I have rejected so many men, I should demand that this one should be received by you, although he is unknown to the Church. Before you make an end of this dreamer, please deign to read him through, lest you, trained in habits of inveterate trifling, should prove to be one of those tremendously wise men who call the Church the Pope, the bishops and the teachers of the universities, and should say that whatever they do not know is unknown to the Church. Yet I wonder who told you that Tauler was unknown to the Church. I suppose you are the Church and know all things. Be careful not to take immaturely considered premises for granted, nor to judge from them. Wherefore if you wish to admonish me, pray avoid bitterness and pay careful attention to the individual propositions. Consider that I was not ignorant that he was unknown to your Church when I said that he was not to be had in the universities and did not write in Latin. Then I gave my reason for preferring him to the

---

op. cit., p. 5. Very likely Rab wrote at his instigation, but the intervention did no good as Miltitz came to Leipsic in the middle of January and, according to the tradition, censured him so severely that he died of chagrin on the following August 11.

[1] *I. e.*, privilege of debating. *Cf. supra*, no. 109 and 110.

schoolmen, namely, that I learned more from him alone than from all the others. Very prudent of you to pass over these words of mine! I am at a loss to know why you should threaten so dire a castigation for my ignorance, accusing me of never having read nor understood what you wrote, when you say of my authority: "I know not who he is." Beware of this ignorance; first, read the man, lest you should be found a foolish judge, condemning what you do not know. And not to demand what is beyond your power, I do not desire that you should gather together all your schoolmen in order to find one sermon like one of his; I do not exact this, for I know that you could not do it. I only urge you to strain every nerve of your mind and scholastic learning to see whether you can rightly understand a single one of his sermons. After that we will believe you, that he is a dreamer, and you alone wide awake or at least sleeping with open eyes. I write thus, Eck, to spare you the trouble of admonishing me vainly, in hopes that you will put up something which I shall not be able to tear down and which will not need to be changed, something, that is, worthy of your genius and study, so that neither of us may lose our time. Farewell in the Lord, my dear Eck.

114. CAESAR PFLUG[1] TO DUKE GEORGE OF SAXONY.

Gess, i. 53.   LEIPSIC, January 10, 1519.

. . . The theologians at Leipsic are extremely sorry to allow the disputation between Martin Luther and the professor of Ingolstadt, and beg that your Grace will be present at it in person. . . .

115. ADOLPH, BISHOP OF MERSEBURG, TO GEORGE, DUKE OF SAXONY.

Gess, i. 54.   MERSEBURG, January 11, 1519.

We doubt not that your Grace well knows that many scandalous writings and sayings about indulgences have recently gone about, causing much offence among the common people and much danger to souls. Also, we have recently heard from

---

[1] A trusted councillor of Duke George, and father of the celebrated bishop of Naumberg, Julius Pflug. According to a saying in the table talk (Bindseil: *Colloquia*, i. 151) he cared little for religion.

his Holiness at Rome that he will not suffer such matters to be disputed, inasmuch as they are not doubtful or disputable.[1] But we are informed by the worthy and learned dean of Meissen and his brother[2] that Dr. John Eck, of Ingolstadt, has begged of the University of Leipsic the opportunity to dispute on indulgences, as your Grace doubtless knows. But we think, as the Pope expressly forbids the same, that we are straightly bound by our oath to hinder in our diocese all that might offend or disparage the honor of the Roman see. Wherefore we have written and warned the dean of the university. . . .

116. LUTHER TO CHRISTOPHER SCHEURL AT NUREMBERG.
Enders, i. 348. (WITTENBERG), January 13, 1519.

Greeting. Though I steal this hour from myself and my business, yet I write so that I may not seem ungrateful for all your letters and never to answer them. Wherefore I thank you heartily for your sincere and friendly advice and trouble. I would willingly make an end of this disturbance if only my adversaries would do the same. For as far as I see, they propose to end the affair not with gentleness, but with mere force and clamor. So it happens that they arouse ever greater trouble and labor in vain. For I know well that nothing is ever quieted by force. I know the affair will find its end in goodness.

It seemed highly unworthy in me to answer Prierias' trifles, if indeed they are his, for they are childish and womanish complaints of his own pain, nothing less.

I had a most friendly interview with Miltitz and agreed: first, that silence should be imposed on both sides, and secondly, that the Pope should delegate some German bishop to pick out the errors which I should recant. But unless God intervenes, nothing will come of this agreement, especially if they press me with that new decretal,[3] which I have not seen as yet, but

---

[1] This refers to the bull on indulgences of November 9, 1518. Kidd, *op. cit.*, p. 39.
[2] John Hennigk was dean of Meissen from 1506-27. His brother Matthew was a professor of theology at Leipsic in 1521.
[3] *I. e.*, the bull *Cum postquam*, November 9, 1518. Kidd, *op. cit.*, p. 39. *Cf.* last letter.

which I have heard rests only on the plenary power [of the Pope], without the authority of the Bible or the Canon Law, which certainly I would not allow even to the oldest decretal. Who knows what God proposes to bring forth from these monsters. As much as in me is I neither fear nor desire to protract the affair. There are many things which may move this Roman slough, things which I will press home if they will let me. But if God does not wish them to let me, his will be done. I heartily desire to have the Ebners[1] as patrons, and I thank them for the box[2] they sent me. I hope that your Nurembergers[3] will answer to your hopes, since they are under the best teachers and attend the choicest lectures. Farewell in the Lord, and throw your care and mine on him, lest you be too anxious for me.

BROTHER MARTIN LUTHER, Augustinian.

117. LUTHER TO GEORGE SPALATIN AT ALTENBURG.
Enders, i. 349.   (WITTENBERG), January 14 (1519).

Greeting. Dear Spalatin, do not be surprised that some people say I was conquered at a banquet in Dresden,[4] for they have long been saying just what they pleased. While there with our John Lang and our Dresden prior,[5] I was compelled rather than invited by Jerome Emser[6] to attend an evening

---

[1] Jerome Ebner and his family.

[2] What the box was I do not know. The word "casula" usually means "hut," but can hardly do so in this context.

[3] *I. e.*, two Nuremberg boys studying at Wittenberg, by name Conrad Volckmar and John Tucher.

[4] Luther went to Dresden in July, 1518, preaching there before Duke George of Saxony on July 25. The fullest account of this trip is in Grisar: *Luther*, i. 300ff.

[5] Melchior Miritsch of Dresden matriculated at Wittenberg 1507. Prior at Cologne 1512, later Prior at Dresden and for a short time in the Netherlands. In 1522 he was Prior of Magdeburg, and is spoken of occasionally in Luther's letters as a follower of his until 1532. Enders, ii. 473.

[6] Jerome Emser (1477 or 1478-November 8, 1527) matriculated at Tübingen 1493, but migrated to Basle, where he took his B. A. 1498 and M. A. 1499. He was then for some time in the service of Cardinal Raimond Peraudi. In 1504 he lectured at Erfurt, Luther being one of his students, but moved to Leipsic, where, in 1505, he was made lecturer in theology, and was later employed on various commissions by Duke George. From 1519 to 1527 he had a bitter controversy with Luther, and in 1524 with Zwingli. In 1527 he produced a German translation of the Bible to correct the errors of Luther's. See biographies by P. Mosen (1890) and G. Kawerau (1898). *Corpus Reformatorum*, xc. 230ff. *Zwingliana*, 1911, col. 428. His controversial works with Luther of 1521, published by L. Enders, 2 vols., 1890, 1892.

drinking party. Thinking at first that I was among friends, I soon found out that I was in a trap. There was present one little Leipsic professor,[1] a little Thomist, who thought he knew everything. Though full of hatred he spoke kindly, but later when a dispute arose inveighed against me bitterly and loudly. All the while there stood outside, without my knowing it, a Dominican preacher,[2] listening to all I said. Later I heard that he said he was so much annoyed by what I said that he could hardly restrain himself from coming in and spitting in my face and calling me foul names. It tortured the man to hear me refute Aquinas for that little professor. He is the man who boasts even to-day that I was on that occasion so confused that I could not answer either in German or in Latin. For because we argued as usual in mixed German and Latin,[3] he confidently asserted that I did not know the learned tongue. For the rest, our dispute was on the silly trifles of Aristotle and Aquinas; I showed him that neither Aquinas nor any of his followers understood one chapter of Aristotle. At last, when he got boastful, I asked him to gather together all the forces of his Thomistic erudition and explain to me what it was to fulfil the commands of God, "for," said I, "I know that no Thomist knows that." This man of the primary school,[4] conscious of his ignorance, cried: "Give him some food, for that is the payment for schoolmasters." What else could he say, since he did not know the answer? We all laughed at his silly reply, and left the table.

Afterwards the Dresden prior wrote me how they boasted and how in Duke George's court they called me unlearned, proud, and I know not how many other bad names, also how

---

[1] His name was Weissestadt. *Cf.* Bindseil: *Colloquia,* i. 152. *Zeitschrift für Kirchengeschichte,* xxxiii. 36.

[2] *Terminarius, i. e.,* a brother who was appointed to preach in the district assigned to the convent in which to collect alms. Du Cange, *s. v.* Kalkoff's translation "Almosensammler" (*Zeitschrift für Kirchengeschichte,* xxxiii. 37) is a little vague. This person collected what Luther said, together with other things he had uttered in his sermon and some things from his writings, and sent them promptly to Rome, where they produced a great effect. Indeed, this probably had great weight in inducing Leo to change Luther's summons to Rome to a citation to Augsburg, where it was thought he could be more expeditiously dealt with. Kalkoff, *loc. cit.*

[3] The table talk shows that this was indeed Luther's usual custom. *Cf.* Preserved Smith: *Luther's Table Talk* (1907), p. 90ff.

[4] *Homo ex trivio,* Enders would translate "man of the street," following the

they twisted my sermon given in the castle. I treated the pious history of the three virgins, and later they said in the court that I had traduced the virgins. In short, I found them a generation of vipers, wishing to do everything and able to do nothing, and considering it a spot on their glory if they leave a single word of mine unblamed. Despising these scare-crows, I wrote back to the prior to keep quiet and let me have my Cain and Judas. But Emser earnestly excused himself at the time, and lately, also, meeting me at Leipsic,[1] he swore that he had not set any ambush for me; I told him I scorned such futile fury. If they are so learned, they have ink and paper, let them publish something to show the splendor of their magnificent erudition. My sermon was on July 25, the day of St. James the Greater, on the text:[2] "Ye know not what ye ask." I animadverted on men's foolish prayers to God, and taught what a Christian ought to ask for.

I wonder what has happened to the Bishop of Meissen.[3] I suspect that he is finding out the truth of the proverb in Ecclesiasticus: "Honors change the character,"[4] to which we commonly add "rarely for the better." I never saw him, but I know he was formerly a great friend of Staupitz. Do not be surprised, Spalatin, to hear evil said of me. I rejoice to hear it; were I not cursed by men I would not believe that what I did was of God. Christ must be a sign[5] of contradiction, set up for the fall of many, not of the gentiles, but of Israel and of the elect. . . .

I confidently despise that man of little scruples who thinks I have become anathema. For as I do not fear those decretals, mere traditions of men (which my opponents fear, though they despise God without end), I shall boldly make war against them sometime. The wrath of the decretals does not bind nor hurt when the mercy of Christ protects. Would that this were

---

rare classical usage. I believe the reference here is to the medieval "trivium" or primary course of studies.

[1] *I. e.*, January 7, or thereabouts, *cf.* last letter.
[2] Matthew, xx. 20ff.
[3] John VII. of Schleinitz, bishop since October 16, 1518. Letters and documents about his visitation in Electoral Saxony 1521-22 are published by K. Pallas in *Archiv für Reformationsgeschichte*, v. 217ff.
[4] "Honores mutant mores—raro in meliores."
[5] Luke, ii. 34.

the greatest and only occasion for him who does God's work to fear. . . . MARTIN ELEUTHERIUS.

P. S.—I do not think it worth while to answer Prierias, for we are agreed that one of the *Obscure Men*[1] has impersonated him, mocking the man by putting folly in his mouth to tempt me to answer him.

118. RECTOR[2] AND DOCTORS OF THE UNIVERSITY OF LEIPSIC TO DUKE GEORGE.

Gess, i. 55. LEIPSIC, January 15, 1519.

We would have your Grace know that Dr. John Eck has asked for a convenient time and place to hold his debate with Dr. Carlstadt. . . . Wherefore we forward his prayer to your Grace and ask that you will write us what you think on the matter. We will labor diligently in this for the profit of the university, not considering the earnest and written protest of Lord Adolph, Bishop of Merseburg. . . .

119. GEORGE, DUKE OF SAXONY, TO DIETRICH VON WERTHERN, FOR REPRESENTATION TO ADOLPH, BISHOP OF MERSEBURG.

Gess, i. 58. (Before January 17, 1519).

A letter from Duke George to Adolph, much to the same purpose as this, dated January 17, is given in translation in B. J. Kidd: *Documents of the Continental Reformation*, p. 46. (Wrongly dated there June 17; *cf. ibid.*, p. viii.)

Dietrich von Werthern (1468-September 4, 1536) studied at Erfurt 1479, and at Bologna 1486, where he got his doctorate in law in 1495. In 1498 he went to Prussia, where he became Chancellor of the Teutonic Order. Later he entered the service of Duke George, whose trusted councillor he was until his death. He was a strong Catholic and particularly bitter against Luther. *Allgemeine deutsche Biographie.*

Dr. Eck has desired of us that he might debate after the scholastic manner before the theological faculty of Leipsic with Dr. Carlstadt, and has prayed that we should arrange with the said faculty for a time and place, and that we should

[1] *I. e.*, one of the authors of that great satire against the theologians, the *Epistolae Obscurorum Virorum*.

[2] The Rector for the winter semester was John Lange of Löwenburg. G. Erler: *Die Matriket der Universität Leipsic*, 1895.

be present in person to hear the debate. We have no objection to the same, thinking that it will redound to the honor and glory of the university to have such able men dispute before it. And we represented to the said faculty that they should not object to the same, considering that they were in no wise committed to the subject of the debate, but could take what stand they chose in it, and moreover, as they were doctors and teachers of the Holy Scripture, that it was their duty to bring to light what is true and what is false. But the dean of Meissen has informed me that it is not considered well that the disputation should take place, which I think he did at the instigation of the faculty. For they are so small minded that they fear they will get into trouble through this debate, or perchance, as they themselves confess, they are not able to converse with such learned men. . . . But we think that they should earn their bread by discharging the duty of theologians, namely, bringing the truth to light. . . . For otherwise I should have to tell the truth to Dr. Eck, namely, that I found my theologians so unlearned that they were afraid to dispute with such learned men. . . .

120. LUTHER TO THE ELECTOR FREDERIC OF SAXONY.

Enders, i. 368. De Wette, i. 575. German.

WITTENBERG (circa January 19, 1519).

Serene, high-born Prince, gracious Lord! Humbly to serve your Grace I hereby give you my opinion, the articles and means[1] pointed out by your Grace to settle the hard business between myself and the papal indulgence.

First, I am ready in all humility to honor the Roman Church, and to prefer nothing to her, either in heaven or on earth, save God alone and his Word; wherefore, I will willingly recant any article proved to me to be erroneous. For it is impossible to recant everything indiscriminately.

Secondly, I am not only willing, but eager, never to preach or teach again. For I have neither pleasure nor love in doing so, and get neither wealth nor honor by doing it. For I also know well that the treatment of God's Word is intolerable

[1] These were articles proposed by Miltitz to the elector.

to the world. But I have been and still am submissive to God's command and will in this matter.

Thirdly, to have an impartial judge in the matter is all my desire, and in my favor. And as such a judge, I would name the reverend father in God, the Archbishop of Trier,[1] or the Archbishop of Salzburg,[2] or the serene Lord Bishop Philip of Freisingen and Naumburg.[3]

Fourthly, it has long moved me to think that in Pope Julius' time, nine cardinals with all their followers were unable to accomplish anything, and that also the Emperor and kings were often humiliated by him;[4] on the other hand, I have been strengthened, because I am absolutely positive that the Roman Church will not and may not suffer the inept and noxious preaching which I pointed out in my *Theses;* she cannot bear it nor uphold it, nor allow the poor people of Christ to be deceived by the specious indulgence.

It is small wonder that in these last, bad times, one or two men should be crushed, when we consider that in the time of the heretic Arius, when the Church was new and pure, all bishops were driven from their churches, and the heretics, with the support of the Empire throughout all the world, persecuted the solitary St. Athanasius. So, if God in those blessed times so tried the Church, I shall not be much surprised if a poor man like myself be suppressed. But the truth remains and will remain forever.

Fifthly, the new decretal[5] just issued at Rome on indulgences, seems to me very extraordinary. In the first place, it says nothing new. Secondly, it repeats in a dark and difficult form what the other decretals said. Thirdly, it does not repeal the other papal laws on which I founded my argument, and thus leaves the matter in contradiction. Fourthly (and

[1]Richard von Greiffenklau, Archbishop Elector, 1511-1531, who played an important part at Worms. *Cf. infra,* April and May, 1521.
[2]Matthew Lang.
[3]Philip, Count Palatine of the Rhine, Bishop 1517-1541.
[4]Miltitz had written the elector to tell Luther to consider that in the time of the late Pope Julius II., "nine cardinals, the Emperor, the kings of France, England, Scotland, Burgundy, and the whole of Italy were against the Pope, and began a council, notwithstanding which the Pope has deposed the said cardinals and burned their statues, and that the Holy Church had thus always triumphed." Enders, i. 369.
[5]*Cum postquam,* November 9, 1518. Kidd, *op. cit.,* 39.

this is the most important point), it does not, as all other decretals do, cite any word of the Bible, the Fathers or the Canon Law, or give any reason, but consists of mere words, which have nothing to do with my request to be heard.

And as the Church is under obligation to give a reason for her doctrine, as St. Peter commands,[1] and as it is frequently forbidden to receive anything not proved, as St. Paul says,[2] I cannot recognize the said decretal as an established and sufficient doctrine of the Church, and must rather hearken to God's commands and prohibitions. But though I will not adore this decretal, yet I will not wholly reject it. . . .

Your Grace's humble servant, DR. MARTIN LUTHER.

121. DUKE GEORGE OF SAXONY TO THE UNIVERSITY OF LEIPSIC.

Gess, i. 63. DRESDEN, January 19, 1519.

We have read your letter [January 15] and as Dr. Eck has made the same request to us, we consider that honor, glory and profit will come to the university and to all of you from this debate. And as our uncle and friend, the Bishop of Merseburg, objects to this debate, we have written him a letter, which we hope will make him change his opinion, and we are glad to hear that you are all united in favor of the debate now. . . .

122. MELANCHTHON TO CHRISTOPHER SCHEURL AT NUREMBERG.

Corpus reformatorum, i. 60. (WITTENBERG), January 20, 1519.

. . . Our Martin, thank God, is yet alive. Do not desert the man, for he is sure that those men are the scourges, rather than the rulers of the Church,[3] and mighty only to oppose justice.[4]

123. LUTHER TO PETER LUPINUS AND ANDREW CARLSTADT.

Enders, ii. 136. De Wette, i. 329. Weimar, ii. 445.

(WITTENBERG, January (?), 1519.)

Peter Wolf (Lupinus), of Radhem, matriculated at Wittenberg in

---
[1] 1 Peter, iii. 15.
[2] 1 Thessalonians, v. 21.
[3] Hos Ecclesiae οἰκοπλῆτας, desierunt enim οἰκονόμοι esse.
[4] A Hebrew word interpreted in the note.

1502, and later became professor of philosophy and theology there. He was a friend and follower of Luther until his death, May 1, 1521.

This letter is the preface to Luther's *Commentary on Galatians,* which appeared in print early in September, 1519. This letter, however, was certainly composed considerably earlier. Luther speaks of Erasmus' *Paraphrase to Galatians,* published August, 1519, as not yet out. Moreover, the absence of all allusion to the debate with Eck, which began to play a considerable part in his thoughts as early as February, leads us to place this letter about January. The *Commentary* is reprinted Weimar, ii. 476ff.

Most learned Sirs, I have recently been chatting about indulgences, trifling words, as I thought, about trifling matters, but now, as I have found out, serious words about the most serious of all matters. For, foolish and erring, I measured sins and errors by the divine commands and the holy gospel of Christ, but those friends of mine, in their glorious wisdom, measured every kind of work by the power of the Pope and the privileges of the Roman Church. This is the reason why we think so differently, and why I have raised such a storm against myself among those most Christian and religious professors of theology. What I always feared has happened to me, namely, that I should be variously judged; to some I seem impious, to others quarrelsome, to others vainglorious, to every man something different. This is the common lot of men who (as is commonly said) build in public and write for the public. I have found almost as many teachers as readers, and that gratis, under whose auspicious guidance I had to learn, under penalty of becoming an obstinate heretic, that no man could sin more gravely than he who doubts the opinions of men and opposes their zeal for disputing, even if by not doing so he meantime denies Christ and Christ's faith and childish matters of that sort.

When I was at Augsburg I had, as you know, a paternal and kind instructor in this matter. And the most illustrious rule of these most illustrious men has brought it to pass that there now obtains a new and admirable Christian liberty, by which men may do what they like with impunity, provided they do not sin against the only law that is left, namely, the power of the Pope and the privileges of the Roman Church. Hence, it is holy to connive at and consent unto all the crimes and corruptions which now, under the innocent and sacred name of Pope and Church, flood every land without end; it is even pious to praise them for the highest virtues, but it is sacrilegious to murmur against them. So great is the wrath of Almighty God, and so much has our impious ingratitude deserved that the tyranny of hell has been borne so long. We see that it has long made men groan in vain, and has made the holy and terrible name of Christ, in which we are justified, glorified and sanctified, become a cloak for foul, dirty, horrible monsters of avarice, tyranny, lust and impiety. It has forced the name of Christ into the service of vice, and, what is the last of evils, has crushed the name of Christ by itself, has laid waste the Church in the name of the Church, and has altogether mocked, deceived and damned us by the very instruments of salvation.

Wherefore, while they are occupied with these **great matters**, while they bite, while they cut themselves with knives[1] before their Baal, while they sacrifice to the Lindian god,[2] while they boast of their *Extravangantes*[3] and of those faithful witnesses of Roman learning, their declaratory decretals, I determined to betake myself to the least of things, that is, to the sacred writings, and among them to those of Paul the Apostle, who, by his own testimony, was the least of writers. For he was not yet the chief of the apostles, or pontifex maximus, but he proclaims himself the least[4] of the apostles, not worthy to be called an apostle. So far is he from boasting that he is most holy of all; he even says that he was of the tribe of Benjamin,[5] the son of Joseph,[6] who was called the least of all his brethren, and that everything might be "least," he judges[7] that he knows nothing save Christ, and him crucified, that is, the least and last of all things. For he was well aware that it was not for an ignorant, unlearned

[1] 1 Kings, xviii. 28.
[2] According to Erasmus' *Adages*, s. v., this proverb is used of those who begin a holy cause with a bad omen. Hercules stole two oxen from a peasant of Lindus, and the latter cursed him with so little effect that it only made Hercules laugh.
[3] Part of the Canon Law. Luther has especially in mind the decretal *Cum postquam* of November 9, 1518.
[4] 1 Corinthians, xv. 9.
[5] Philippians, iii. 5.
[6] Genesis, xlii. 34.
[7] 1 Corinthians, ii. 2.

apostle, but only for thrice great theologians, to treat of those greatest and chief of all things, the power of the Roman Church and her decretals.

I hope that this work of mine will have better fortune, because it treats affairs of no consequence, the power of Christ, by which he is strong in us even against the gates of hell, and the privileges of the celestial Church, which knows neither mighty Rome nor holy Jerusalem, nor any other place, nor seeks Christ here or there, but worships the Father in spirit and in truth.[1] Why should these great men be moved or irritated by these trifles, since they are outside of their province? Wherefore I appear before the public the more safely because I abstain from speaking of what irritates them, and treat little matters suitable to my mediocrity. But if anything is left of that old commotion over important matters, I leave it to them, because I am one poor, weak man, and while they stand idle all the day, I am very busy. Wherefore, it is unnecessary for both parties to this quarrel to be hurt by it, it is sufficient evil that one party grieve and be sad.

Speaking seriously, excellent sirs, I honor the Roman Pontiff and his decrees. None is above him, without exception, save the prince of this vicar of Christ, namely, Jesus himself, Lord of us and of all men. I prefer his word to the words of his vicar, and have no doubt that we should judge all the words and deeds of the vicar by *his* word. For I desire him to be subject to this universal rule of the apostle: "Prove all things, hold to that which is good."[2] I will suffer none to withdraw his neck from this yoke, whether in the name of the mother or of the mistress of all churches. I have the more reason for this position as in our time we see some councils rejected and others accepted,[3] theology treated as a matter of mere opinion, the sense of law depend on the arbitrary opinion of one man, and in short, everything so confounded that almost nothing certain is left to us. But it is

---

[1] John, iv. 20ff.
[2] 1 Thessalonians, v. 21.
[3] The authority of the Council of Basle was formally repudiated by the Lateran Council of 1512, a measure later confirmed by Leo X.'s bull *Pastor aeternus*, in *Septim. Decret.* lb. 3, tit. 7, c. 1. Luther had quoted this already in the *Acta Augustana* (October, 1518), and in a letter of November 19, 1518. Enders, i. 283.

clearer than day that many decretals are repugnant to the gospel, so that we are simply forced to fly for refuge to that solid rock of Scripture, and not to believe anything, no matter what, that speaks, commands or does anything without this authority. . . .

But to return to myself and to you, excellent Sirs; I refer to you, or, to use Paul's word,[1] I lay before you this study of mine on Paul's epistle, a small thing, not so much a commentary as a witness of my faith in Christ, unless, perhaps, I shall have run in vain[2] and not have seized Paul's meaning. In this point, because it is a mighty matter from God, I desire to learn even from a boy. Certainly I should have preferred to have waited for the commentaries long since promised us by Erasmus,[3] that theologian too great even to envy. But while he procrastinates (may God grant it be not forever), this fate which you see, compels me to publish. I know I am a child and unlearned, but yet, if I dare say it, zealous for piety and Christian learning, and in this more learned than those who have made the divine commands simply ridiculous by the impious addition of human laws. I have only aimed to make Paul clearer to those who read my work, so that they may surpass me. If I have failed, I shall have willingly lost my labor, for at least I shall have tried to incite others to study Pauline theology, for which no good man will blame me. Farewell.

124. LUTHER TO JOHN SYLVIUS EGRANUS AT ZWICKAU.
Enders, i. 407. (WITTENBERG), February 2, 1519.

Greeting. Learn briefly, Egranus, my present situation. Charles von Miltitz was sent to our elector armed with more than seventy papal breves, all drawn up with the purpose of having me sent alive and bound to that murderous Jerusalem,[4] Rome. But on the way he was smitten to the earth by the Lord, that is, he was frightened by the numbers of those who favor me, for everywhere he carefully inquired what men

---
[1] Galatians, ii. 2.
[2] 1 Corinthians, ix. 26.
[3] Erasmus' *Paraphrase to Galatians*, published by Froben, Basle, August, 1519. *Bibliotheca Erasmiana*, i. 143.
[4] "Jerusalem that killest the prophets," Matthew, xxiii. 37.

thought of me and changed his violence into an easily assumed benevolence, pleading with me at great length to recant for the honor of the Roman Church. I answered him[1] to this intent: Let the method of recantation be prescribed, and the reason of my error given, and let it be such a reason as to appeal both to the learned and to the people, lest a recantation on suspicious grounds should excite more hatred against Rome.

We finally agreed to leave the matter to the arbitration of either the Bishop of Salzburg or the Bishop of Trier, and thus we separated amicably, with a kiss (a Judas kiss!) and tears—I pretended that I did not know they were crocodile tears. Thus far we got; I know not what they will do at Rome.

Miltitz says that no affair has arisen for a hundred years that has caused more trouble to that most idle crowd of cardinals and of Romanizing Romanists, and that they would rather give ten thousand ducats[2] than let the thing go on as it has begun. I rejoice and commend everything to God.

I wrote you before, advising you not to leave Zwickau, for you can get plenty of leisure and books to study Greek there. You owe more to God, that is, to the people of God, than to yourself and culture. I desire to know what you dislike in the doctrine of faith which seems so plain and open to me. For I do not separate justifying faith from love; rather we believe on him who pleases us, and he in whom we believe is loved. Grace makes the Word pleasant to us, and makes us believe it, which is the same as loving it. All the propositions recently put forward about faith, hope and charity do not please me, for those who discuss them seem to me to understand none of them.

I saw our friend Eck at Augsburg and tried to get him to meet our Carlstadt at Leipsic to decide their dispute, and after some demur he agreed. What does the man do then? He takes my *Theses,* rips them up, and says not a word about him with whom he is disputing. You might think it a carnival mask.[3] I am forced to engage the man at close quarters to

---

[1] On the meeting with Miltitz at Altenburg early in January, Smith, 54ff.
[2] A ducat was $2.50 or ten shillings.
[3] At carnival time in Germany (just before Lent, *i. e.,* about the time Luther

defend my opinions of indulgences. The boastful little beast is most unfortunate. He promises a fight after Easter. Some say he is suborned by the Dominicans. The Lord's will be done. I would have sent a copy of his paper, but I only have one sent me from Nuremberg. I send Carlstadt's booklet on the *Justification of the Wicked*[1] and the conclusion of his edition of Augustine's *De spiritu et litera*,[2] hoping that you have the first part. Farewell in Christ and pray for me.

MARTIN LUTHER.

125. JOHN FROBEN TO MARTIN LUTHER.
Enders, i. 420. BASLE, February 14, 1519.

John Froben (c. 1460-1527), of Hammelburg in Franconia, studied at Basle, where he printed his first book, a Bible, 1491. In 1500 he made a partnership with John Amorbach. In 1514 he formed a connection with Erasmus for the purpose of bringing out the Greek Testament and Jerome's works, both of which appeared in 1516. After this his relations with Erasmus were close until his death. Life in *Allgemeine deutsche Biographie*. This letter, which is of great interest as showing how early Luther's books attained an international reputation, arrived at Wittenberg on March 12th.

Blasius Salmonius,[3] a printer of Leipsic, gave me some of your books, which he had bought at the last Frankfort Fair,[4] which, as they were approved by all the learned, I immediately reprinted.[5] We have sent six hundred copies to France[6] and Spain;[7] they are sold at Paris, and are even read and ap-

was writing this) masks or pantomimes were played by mummers. They are known as "Fastnachtspiele."

[1]*Epitome A. Carolstadii De impii justificatione.* Leipsic, 1519.

[2]*Cf. supra*, no. 51 and A. Humbert: *Les Origines de la théologie moderne*, p. 329.

[3]Otherwise unknown.

[4]The great book-mart of Germany. *Cf.* J. W. Thompson: *The Frankfort Book Fair: the Francofordiense Emporium of Henri Estienne.* Chicago. Caxton Club, 1911.

[5]In the days before copyright books were free for all. In this case the learned did not include Erasmus, who protested earnestly against the publication of Luther's works. *Cf. infra*, no. 149. Froben's volume contained *The Ninety-five Theses*, the *Resolutions*, the *Answer to Prierias*, and the sermons on *Penitence* and on the *Eucharist.* Also Carlstadt's *Theses* of May, 1518. De Jongh: *L'ancienne Faculté de Théologie à Louvain*, p. 206. *Cf. supra*, no. 94.

[6]So Glarean writes to Zwingli on November 1, 1520, from Paris, that no books are bought more quickly than Luther's. *Corpus Reformatorum*, xciv. 362. Thus also Lefèvre d'Étaples learned to know Luther, to whom he sent a greeting on April 9, 1519. Herminjard: *Correspondance des réformateurs*, i. 45

[7]An early indication of the spread of Lutheranism and probably of Lutheran

proved by the doctors of the Sorbonne,[1] as certain of our friends have assured us; for some of the most learned say that they have hitherto missed among those who treat Scripture the same freedom that you show.

Francis Calvus,[2] also a bookseller of Pavia, a most learned man, one devoted to the Muses, has taken a good part of your books to Italy to distribute them among all the cities. Nor does he do it so much for gain as to aid piety. He has promised to send epigrams written in your honor by all the learned in Italy, so much does he like your constancy and skill. . . .

We have exported your books to Brabant and England.[3] We only printed three hundred copies of your *Reply to Prierias*. . . . We have sold out all your books except ten copies, and never remember to have sold any more quickly. We expect to bring out the second edition of Erasmus' New Testament much enlarged, within ten days. Farewell, reverend Father

126. RECTOR, PROFESSORS AND DOCTORS OF THE UNIVERSITY OF LEIPSIC, TO DUKE GEORGE OF SAXONY.

Gess, i. 69. LEIPSIC, February 15, 1519.

At your Grace's written command, we have granted permission to the honorable and learned doctors, John Eck and Andrew Carlstadt, to debate. Thereupon the said Dr. Eck reduced to writing his conclusions on Dr. Martin Luther's propositions concerning grace, in order to give public notice of the debate with Dr. Carlstadt at your Grace's university.

---

books in Spanish dominions is the condemnation of a Lutheran at Majorca in 1523. H. C. Lea: *History of the Spanish Inquisition* (1907), iii. 413. *Cf. infra,* April, 1521, no. 443.

[1] *Cf.* Tschudi to Rhenanus, May 17, 1519. Herminjard, i. 47. On April 15, 1521, Luther's works were formally condemned by the Sorbonne. *Cf.* Smith, *op. cit.*, 453.

[2] Calvus is often mentioned in Erasmus' letters. On the sale of Luther's works in Venice, Pavia, and Bologna, *cf.* Pastor, *History of the Popes* (English translation by Kerr), x. 306. Also Benrath: *Reformation in Venedig,* p. 2, where for 1518 read 1519. Also *Realencyclopädie,* ix. 524. On Calvus, Förstemann-Gunther, *s. v.*

[3] *Cf. Oxford Historical Collectanea,* i. 81ff. Daybook of John Dorne, bookseller of Oxford, for 1520. Among Luther's works the following were then sold: *Opera,* 2 copies; *Leipsic Debate,* 1; *Commentary on Galatians,* 1; *De potestate Papae,* 6 or 7; *Resolutions* (for Leipsic debate), 1; *Response to Prierias,* 1.

Straightway Dr. Luther,[1] compelled by this to mix in the debate, thinking to defend and uphold Dr. Carlstadt, publishes a letter in which he announces, contrary to your Grace's written command and the decision of the whole honorable university, that the said debate is at an end, and, nevertheless, without greeting your Grace or the university, he publicly and in writing announces that *he* will debate at your Grace's university. And as the said Dr. Martin touches the legal rights of the Pope's Holiness, the said debate would be thereby hindered, and everyone would be deceived by having the truth thus abandoned. Wherefore we beg that your Grace will see to it that Dr. Luther should not announce debates without your Grace's or the university's consent.

127. WOLFGANG FABRICIUS CAPITO TO LUTHER.

Enders, i. 424. BASLE, February 18, 1519.

Switzerland and the Rhine country as far as the ocean, is solid for Luther, and his friends in these regions are both powerful and learned. Recently, when it was rumored that you were in danger,[2] Cardinal Matthew Schinner, the Count of Geroldseck,[3] and a certain learned and much honored bishop,[4] and not a few of our other friends,[5] promised you not only financial support, but a refuge, in which you might either hide or live openly. When it was noised abroad that you were laboring in great difficulty, some men tried to send you a large sum of money through me and they certainly would have done so. But this evening we received golden news, that Luther lives and will live always. Then we saw a copy of the letter of the illustrious and truly princely elector to Cardinal Cajetan, by which we know that you do not need our aid.[6] But if we can do anything we certainly will. We

---

[1]On this *cf*. Smith, *op. cit.*, p. 59.

[2]*I. e.*, of being sent to Rome, when Luther was thinking of leaving Wittenberg, *supra*, no. 100.

[3]Diebolt III von Geroldseck of Swabia, administrator of the cloister of Einsiedeln, a dear friend of Zwingli, with whom he died at the battle of Kappel, October 11, 1531.

[4]Christopher von Uttenheim, Bishop of Basle 1502-1526, when he resigned, dying the next year.

[5]Including Zwingli, thinks Kalkoff. *Corpus Reformatorum*, xciv. 403, note 1. But Zwingli had as yet shown small interest in Luther.

[6]December 8, 1518, refusing to give Luther up. Enders, i. 310.

have printed your collected works, as you will learn from Froben's gift, and within six weeks after the Frankfort Fair sent them to Italy, France, Spain and England, in this consulting the public welfare, which we think is advanced by having the truth spread abroad as widely as possible. Nature by means of truth allures even an enemy to love her. Forgive me for recently telling you of Erasmus' opinion,[1] which was bringing owls to Athens.[2]

128. LUTHER TO DUKE GEORGE OF SAXONY.

Enders, i. 428. De Wette-Seidemann, vi. 10. German.

WITTENBERG, February 19, 1519.

My humble poor prayers and lowly service to your Grace. Serene, high-born Prince, gracious Lord! The worthy Dr. Eck writes that he has applied to your Grace to permit and graciously to favor a debate against the worthy Dr. Carlstadt in your Grace's university at Leipsic. But although Dr. Eck proclaims that he will debate against Dr. Carlstadt, yet he hardly notices his articles, but falls with all his might on my position. Therefore, it would become me to meet this presumptuous giant[3] and defend my position or let myself be better instructed. Wherefore it is my humble petition to your Grace, for the love of the truth kindly to allow such a debate. For now the worthy gentlemen of the university have written that what I formerly heard they had promised to Dr. Eck has been refused by them, for they lay it up against me that I let my propositions for debate be published before I asked permission of your Grace; this was because I had confidence that your Grace would not forbid me, but would be ready, as Dr. Eck has boasted you promised him. I pray you graciously forgive me, and may God mercifully spare and uphold you. Amen.

Your Grace's obedient chaplain,
DR. MARTIN LUTHER, *Augustinian.*

[1]*Cf. supra*, no. 78.
[2]*I. e.*, "coals to Newcastle."
[3]"Denn unüorwarntenn ryssen. zcu empfaeü." I follow Hoppe's modernization: "Den unverwarnten Riesen zu empfahen" (St. Louis Walch, xxi. A. p. 148). I have also thought that "ryssen" might stand for "Reise," *i. e.*, "undertake this unexpected journey."

129. JOHN ECK TO THE UNIVERSITY OF LEIPSIC.
Gess, i. 73. INGOLSTADT, February 19, 1519.

I was somewhat troubled when I heard that you did not care to bear the burden of hearing and judging us, although I received your letter late, that is on February 4. But now I am made more cheerful, since I have learned that you have changed your opinions, for which I render you immortal thanks. Concerning the time of the debate I should like it to begin on June 27, for reasons given in another letter to your university, for I shall be obliged for urgent reasons to be away from our University of Ingolstadt then anyway. . . . I am writing to Luther to be present, for there is just as much reason for his presence as for that of Carlstadt, for in my poor opinion, both of them are equally in error. We shall find out by this debate. . . .

130. LUTHER TO CHRISTOPHER SCHEURL AT NUREMBERG.
Enders, i. 432. WITTENBERG, February 20, 1519.

Greeting. I blame myself, excellent doctor, for so rarely writing in answer to your numerous greetings. But again I excuse myself in that I am laboring with such a monstrous mass of business. That learned *Dialogue of Julius and Peter*[1] pleased me much, for it contains much fruit if read carefully. I regret that it is not known at Rome. I almost dared to translate it;[2] not that the author is the first to reveal the horrors of the Roman curia, but he confirms what has, alas! long been known. Would that the Roman prelates might be warned of their tyranny and impious rashness even by trifles of this sort, which they see are spread abroad through the world.

Eck, who has hitherto fairly dissimulated his rage against me, now reveals it. See what sort of man he is. But the God of gods knows what catastrophe he is planning for this tragedy. In this neither will Eck act for his own ends, nor I

[1] *Cf. supra,* no. 42.
[2] According to the table talk Luther tried to do so but gave it up fearing he could not do the style justice. In the same saying he attributes the authorship rightly to Erasmus. E. Kroker: *Luthers Tischreden in der Matthesischen Sammlung,* 1903, no. 45.

for mine, for I think God's counsel is directing it all. I have often said that what I have hitherto done has been mere play, but that now I will act in earnest against the Pope and Roman arrogance. . . .

BROTHER MARTIN LUTHER, *Augustinian*.

131. OTTO BECKMANN TO SPALATIN.

Kolde: *Analecta*, 6. (ERFURT?), February 24, 1519.

. . . I hardly know what to promise about our Eleutherius. I wrote you before that almost everyone here approves what should not be approved for the sake of seeming Lutheran, even when they least agree with Luther, as, for example, on the power of the Pope, which can neither be assailed nor diminished by our barking. The common crowd like to hear evil of ecclesiastics, especially in our time when, for our sins, the clergy has become a byword in society. It is said that recently while preaching in the church of St. Peter, he raved I know not what folly about the throne of the Pope and the power of the keys, all of which was diligently written down by enemies. You would do well to write to Amsdorf to admonish Martin not to speak so angrily without cause in public about the Pope and the other prelates. Some portent is brewing; but may Christ grant that it come not among us. We must go another road. The Church cannot be reformed by our contrivance, if it has to be reformed at all. I write from my heart, knowing that you cherish the honor of the university. Yours,

OTTO BECKMANN.

NOTE.—At this point Enders (i. 442) inserts a letter from Luther to Leo X., dated "(Altenburg), March 3, 1519," and it is taken into the St. Louis edition (xxi. no. 155), dated February. It was really composed in January, at Luther's interview with Miltitz, but as it did not satisfy the latter it was never sent, and is therefore not included in my translation. Köstlin-Kawerau, i. 224.

132. DUKE GEORGE OF SAXONY TO LUTHER AT WITTENBERG.

Enders, i. 445. DRESDEN, March 4, 1519.

Worthy, learned, dear and pious Sir! We have received

your letter¹ about the debate allowed by us to be held at our University of Leipsic, between Drs. Eck and Carlstadt, and containing your excuses, all of which we have noted. Since Dr. Eck wrote us that he had agreed on the debate with Dr. Carlstadt and prayed for permission to hold it at Leipsic, we did not wish to refuse him. If now you agree among yourselves to debate, and then make a further request to us, we will then, as beseems us, consider your petition and give you a prudent and gracious answer. This in answer to your letter.

133. LUTHER TO GEORGE SPALATIN AT ALTENBURG.
Enders, i. 446. (WITTENBERG), March 5, 1519.

Greeting. Dear Spalatin, you have twice urged me to make mention of faith and works and of obedience to the Roman Church in my German apology.² I think that I have done so, although it was published before your warnings came. It was never my intention to secede from the apostolic Roman see; indeed, I am content that the Pope should be called, or even should be, the lord of all. What business is it of mine? For I know that we must honor and tolerate even the Turk because of his power, and because I know, as Peter says,³ that there is no power save what is ordained of God. But I act for my faith in Christ, that they may not treat his Word as they please, and contaminate it. Let the Roman decretals leave me the pure gospel and take away all else, I will not move a hair. What more can I or ought I do? Moreover, most willingly shall I abide by the agreement,⁴ for I hope this debate will be a debate for the learned only, and my instruction will be sufficient for the laity. Farewell.

You desire to know who were the men who requested the elector to change the course of studies.⁵ They were the

---
¹February 19, *supra*, no. 128.
²*Unterricht auf etliche Artikel*, Weimar, ii. 66. This was a paper drawn up at the request of Miltitz, *cf.* Smith, 56f. Perhaps Spalatin had been influenced by the letter of Beckmann, *supra*, no. 131.
³*Cf.* 1 Peter, ii. 13, though Luther probably meant Paul's Epistle to the Romans, xiii. 1.
⁴*I. e.*, with Miltitz to keep silence, *cf.* Smith, 55f.
⁵For some time Luther and his friends had been desirous of reforming the curriculum by curtailing the lectures on Aristotle's *Physics* and on Aquinas's

rector,[1] Carlstadt, Armsdorf and I. The protest does not please many, though they have poor reason for objecting to it, for they consider not the profit of the students, but the salaries of the professors. Conversing with one of them recently, I said if the salaries were given for the sake of supporting the professors, the university was changed into an eleemosynary institution. Let the needy be supported in some other way; here we must consider proper studies alone. They are blind and without judgment. I hope the most illustrious elector will take good counsel in this matter.

BROTHER MARTIN LUTHER.

134. LUTHER TO THE ELECTOR FREDERIC OF SAXONY.
Enders, i. 448. De Wette, i. 236. German.

WITTENBERG, March 13, 1519.

My poor, humble prayer is ever for your Grace! Most serene, high-born Prince, most gracious Lord! Your Grace's chaplain, Spalatin, has sent to me certain points concerning me, forwarded to your Grace by the Honorable Charles von Miltitz, commissary of the Pope's Holiness, demanding, namely, that I should henceforth keep silence and not begin anything new, as we agreed at Altenburg. Now God knows that I am anxious and would be happy to have the game end thus, as far as in me lies; and I have kept myself so strictly to the agreement that I have let Silvester Prierias' *Answer*[2] go, although it gave me much cause to reply, and has given my opponents much reason to mock me; yet have I kept silence contrary to the advice of my friends. However, Miltitz knows well that our agreement was that I should keep silence on condition that my enemies did the same. But now Dr. Eck has without warning attacked me, in such manner that he seems to seek not my shame only, but the dishonor also of your Grace's University of Wittenberg. Many respectable people think that he was bribed to do so. It did not become me to pass over his fickle, treacherous attack and

(Aristotle's?) *Logic*, devoting the salaries paid for these courses partly to increasing Melanchthon's pay and partly to hiring a professor to lecture on Ovid's *Metamorphoses*. *Cf.* De Wette-Seidemann, vi. 13.

[1] Bartholomew Bernhardi of Feldkirch.

[2] *Replica F. Sylvestri Prieriatis*, 1518, on which *cf.* Lauchert, *op. cit.*, 18ff.

leave the truth to be mocked. Thus they would gag me, and open everyone else's mouth; thus your Grace can imagine that in this case any man, who otherwise perhaps would not dare to look at me, might fall upon me. Now with all my heart I am disposed obediently to follow your Grace's true counsel, and always keep still, provided they will do the same, for I have much to do, and do not seek my own pleasure. But if they won't keep silence, I humbly pray your Grace not to take it ill that my conscience will not suffer me to abandon the truth. And although my position touches the Pope's Holiness, yet was I obliged, in the course of the debate, to take the opposite side [to Dr. Eck's], always reserving my humble obedience to the Holy Roman See. God grant your Grace salvation. Amen.

Your Grace's humble chaplain,
DR. MARTIN LUTHER, *Augustinian.*

135. LUTHER TO GEORGE SPALATIN.

Enders, i. 448. WITTENBERG, March 13, 1519.

It will be beyond Melanchthon's power, dear Spalatin, to give so many extra lectures, when he already has more than enough to do. Even if you think he should lecture alternate days, yet he will have none the less anxiety. Moreover, Aristotle's *Physicis* are completely useless to every age; the whole book is an argument about nothing, and, moreover, a begging of the question. His *Rhetoric* is of no use either, unless one wishes to become an expert in rhetoric, which is much as though one exercised his mind studying dung or other stuff. God's wrath has decreed that for so many ages the human race should occupy itself with these follies, and without even understanding them. I know the book inside out, for I twice have expounded it to my brothers, having rejected the usual commentaries.[1] In short, we have decided to allow these lectures to continue only for a short time, since even an oration of Beroald[2] would be more profitable, as

[1] Luther lectured on Aristotle's *Ethics* and *Physics* during his first year at Wittenberg, 1508-9. His dislike of the Stagirite began about this time. *Cf.* note to Augustine, Weimar, ix. 27.
[2] Philip Beroald, 1453-1505, lectured on eloquence at Parma, Milan and Paris.

Aristotle has not even an understanding of natural phenomena. Of like quality are his books on *Metaphysics* and the *Soul*. It is unworthy of the mind to wallow in such a slough of folly; if he must be read to fulfil the requirements, he had better be read without comprehension than with.

I send the letter[1] of Eck, as boastful as if he were victor at the Olympian games.

John Froben sent me my works printed by him. If you wish to see them I will send them.[2]

I am too busy to translate my *Exposition of the Lord's Prayer*[3] into Latin. I daily expound to children and the simple the Ten Commandments[4] and the Lord's Prayer, besides which I preach and am now getting out Paul's Epistle to the Galatians.[5] Moreover, there are orations and lectures to be given on special occasions, so I have not time enough, much less, time to spare. I am planning a sermon on the *Meditation of Christ's Holy Passion*,[6] but know not whether I shall have leisure to write it, but I will try.

I am studying the decrees of the Popes[7] for my debate, and (I speak it in your ear), I know not whether the Pope is Antichrist[8] himself or his apostle, so terribly is Christ, that is, the truth, corrupted and crucified by him in the decretals. I am terribly distressed that the people of Christ should be thus deceived by the semblance of laws and of the Christian name. Sometime I will make you a copy of my notes on the Canon Law, that you too may see what it is to make laws regardless of Scripture, simply from ambition and tyranny,

---

[1] Of February 19, Enders, i. 428.
[2] *Supra*, no. 125.
[3] *Auslegung deutsch des Vaterunsers für die einfältigen Laien*, Weimar, ii. 74.
[4] *Decem Praecepta populo Wittembergensi praedicata*. This was the beginning of Luther's Catechism (1529). *Cf.* Weimar, xxx. part i, introduction.
[5] *Commentary on Galatians*, published by Luther at this time, Weimar, ii. 436.
[6] *Sermon von der Betrachtung des heiligen Leidens Christi*, Weimar, ii. 131.
[7] I. e., the Canon Law, for the Leipsic Debate. *Cf.* Smith, *op. cit.*, 60ff.
[8] The idea of Antichrist, taken from the Apocalypse, had become quite common by this time, and had been applied to the Pope at least since John Huss's *De Ecclesia* (circa 1400). Luther did not know this work till a year later, but he probably did know a *Buch von des Endtechrists Leben und Regierung*, Erfurt, 1516. He later worked the idea out in detail in his *Responsio ad Ambrosium Catharinum*, Weimar, vii. 777f. (1521). *Cf.* H. Preuss: *Die Vorstellungen vom Antichrist im späteren Mittelalter, bei Luther und im konfessionellen Polemik*, Leipsic, 1906. H. Grisar, *op. cit.*, ii. 113ff.

not to mention the other works of the Roman curia, which are like those of Antichrist. Daily there arises in me a greater and greater aid and defence for the sacred books.

Our Erasmus has published a work on the method[1] of studying the Bible, which Froben sent me. Please return the letters of Froben, Eck and the others. . . .

BROTHER MARTIN LUTHER, *Augustinian*.

[P. S.][2]—I send a letter to the most illustrious elector on the matter[3] which you wrote about, and I ask you to thank him for me for his most kind care. I am very sorry and unwilling that his Grace should be troubled by his anxiety for me. I have answered Eck nothing except three words, namely, that it was his fault, not mine, that he is branded as a sophist throughout the world. I do not wish to treat with the man at length; he is wholly faithless, and has openly broken the laws of friendship.

136. MELANCHTHON TO SPALATIN.

Corpus Reformatorum, i. 74.   WITTENBERG, March 13, 1519.

Hail, most learned George. Luther has promised to send the letter of Eck[4] when he had finished Paul,[5] in which he is

---

[1] *Ratio seu compendium verae theologiae per Erasmum Roterodamum.* Basle, Froben, 1519.

[2] This postscript Enders, ii. 221, as the second postscript to a letter of Luther to Spalatin dated by Enders early in November, 1519 (the correct date is October, *cf. infra*, no. 185). Enders informs us, however, that this postscript is on a separate sheet, and may not belong to this letter at all. That it cannot belong to the letter is shown by the words about Eck. Luther says that he has answered him only three words, which would not apply to the eleven-page letter of October, 1519 (Enders, ii. 214, De Wette, i. 353), and adds "he has openly broken the laws of friendship," a phrase he would certainly not use of the avowed enmity of the Leipsic debate. That the postscript *may* belong to this letter of March 13, is shown by the fact that the originals of both are in the Anhalt Ges.-Archiv, and that extant MS. copies of both are found in the same codex. That the postscript *must* belong to this letter of March 13, is shown by comparing the passage on Eck, "Eccio nihil respondi, nisi tria verba, scilicet eum sophistam per orbem non mea, sed sua culpa famari . . . totus infidus est, et aperte rupit amicitiae jura," with Luther's letter to Eck of February 18, 1519 (Enders, v. 6): "Doleo, mi Ecci, inveniri tandem simulatam tuam in me amicitiam tam manifestis argumentis. . . . Proinde quod nugator et sophista nunc per orbem vocitaris, tuae intemeritati imputabis, non mihi." These words are absolutely inapplicable to the letter of October, 1519, to Eck. Also note the allusion to the letter to the elector.

[3] *Cf.* last letter.

[4] February 19, 1519. Enders, i. 429.

[5] *In epistolam Pauli ad Galatas M. Lutheri commentarius*, Leipsic, Lotther, 1519. Weimar, ii. 436ff.

now wholly occupied. He intends to write a meditation on the passion of the Lord.[1] Yesterday we received letters and books from Basle.[2] Every good man thinks well of our cause. Froben has sent a little book of Erasmus, the *Method of Theology*[3] in which that celebrated man seems to touch on many things, which have been touched by Luther, and he seems to be freer in his treatment of them because he has a companion in this sacred and true knowledge. . . .

137. POPE LEO X. TO LUTHER AT WITTENBERG.

Enders, i. 491.   VILLA MAGLIANA,[4] March 29, 1519.

Beloved Son, greeting and the apostolic blessing! We were highly pleased to learn from the letter[5] written by our beloved son and nuncio, Charles von Miltitz, to our beloved son, the noble Frederic, Elector of Saxony, that what had been incorrectly written or said by you, was not done with the plan and purpose of attacking us or the apostolic see or the Holy Roman Church, but because you were provoked by a certain monk commissioned by our beloved son Albert, Cardinal Archbishop of Mayence, to publish certain indulgences. We learn that it was while attacking him that you went further than you would have wished, and exceeded the bounds of decorum and truth, and that when you had sufficiently considered what you had said, you were heartily grieved, and were prepared to revoke everything in writing, and to notify the princes and others to whom your works had come, of your error, and in future to abstain from similar expressions. We also learn that you would have revoked everything before our legate, had you not feared that he would have favored the monk whom you consider the cause of your error, and have too severely reprimanded you.

We, therefore, considering that the spirit indeed is willing, but the flesh weak, and that many things are said in the heat of anger which must later be corrected by saner counsel,

---

[1] Reprinted, Weimar, ii. 131ff.
[2] *I. e.*, from Froben. *Cf.* his letter to Luther, February 14, 1519.
[3] *Ratio seu compendium verae theologiae.* Basle, Froben, January, 1519.
[4] Leo's hunting lodge on the Tiber, ten miles from Rome.
[5] This letter is lost. Evidently Miltitz had written over-sanguinely of his success with Luther. Smith, *op. cit.,* 56.

thank Almighty God who has deigned to enlighten your heart and to vouchsafe that Christians who rely on your authority and learning may not be led into grave and pernicious errors in those things which concern the salvation of their souls. Wherefore we, who are the vicegerent on earth of him who desireth not the death of a sinner, but that he shall turn from his wickedness and live,[1] with paternal love accept your excuses, and because of the benevolence with which we regard all learned men, especially those learned in divinity, desire to hear and see you personally, so that you may be able safely and freely to make before us, the vicar of Christ, that recantation which you feared to make before our legate. Wherefore on receipt of this letter prepare for a journey and come straight to us. We hope, moreover, that you will lay aside hatred and reconcile your mind to us, that you will be filled with no passion, but with the Holy Spirit alone, and armed with charity, so that you will care for those things which make for the glory of Almighty God, that we may thus rejoice in you as an obedient child and that you may be happy to find in us a kind and merciful father.

Given under the fisherman's ring, in the seventh year of our pontificate.   J. SADOLETO.

138. MELANCHTHON TO STUDENTS OF THEOLOGY.

Preface to Luther's *Operationes in Psalmos*.[2] *Corpus Reformatorum*, i. 70.   WITTENBERG, March, 1519.

[He congratulates them on the brilliant scholarship of the day, adorned by the names of Erasmus, Reuchlin, Capito, Oecolampadius and Carlstadt.] . . . Martin Luther has illustrated the sacred songs with a commentary, which we desire especially to commend to the student, because, while many things have been written on David, few have grasped his real character. But how much this commentary excels may be proved by anyone who will diligently compare it with the very best of the old ones. Meanwhile, readers, it is your part to make the most of Luther's faithful labor and to strive to bring pure minds to the study of it, having laid aside all

---

[1] Ezekiel, xxxiii. 11.   [2] Reprinted, Weimar, vol. v.

human prejudices; in short, to read Christ's book under Christ's guidance. Farewell.

139. LUTHER TO JOHN ECK AT INGOLSTADT.
Enders, v. 7.   WITTENBERG, April 5, 1519.

I am writing again, Eck, for this reason. The most illustrious Duke George of Saxony has answered[1] me that he would like to reply to my petition to debate with you at Leipsic, provided only that he were certain that you and I agreed on this point, for your letters to him had spoken of Carlstadt, but not of me. Since Carlstadt is properly disgusted with your wily tricks, so that perchance he will not deign to meet you, and because you also having learned to dread the man's power, have yet deceived the duke, declining battle with one and challenging another, it is your duty to inform either the duke or me what you want to do, so that we may not let him longer be in suspense. Therefore, take care to send me a letter[2] as quickly as possible, that I may seek full permission to debate, for I already have the consent of the University in writing. Farewell, and try to be a theologian instead of a sophist.

140. LUTHER TO JOHN LANG AT ERFURT.
Enders, ii. 9.   WITTENBERG, April 13, 1519.

Greeting. I rejoice and congratulate you, reverend Father, on being one of those who bear the cross of Christ. Be a brave man; thus do we go, or rather thus are we carried to the skies.[3] We thank you for your gifts. You know why I did not come to your ceremony.[4] You should not condemn my silence so much as the condition of the road, which is such that we rarely or never have anyone going from hence to Erfurt. . . .

Eck has signified that our debate will take place on June 27; it will take place between him and me as you see by the enclosed paper. For Carlstadt will not debate with him on

---
[1] *Supra*, no 132.
[2] Eck apparently did not answer this letter. *Cf. infra*, no. 143.
[3] Sic itur, imo vehitur ad astra. *Cf.* Ovid, *Metam.*, ix., 272, xv. 846.
[4] A promotion of doctors at Erfurt on February 24.

these points, partly because they are mine, partly because that wily sophist drags in the Pope. This would either put Carlstadt in danger of offending the Pope (intolerable to one who holds a prebend),[1] or else by scaring him in this way would crush him without a real fight or a real victory. But they will debate on other things, not on the power of the Pope or on indulgences. For these impious men, who themselves foully transgress the commandments of God, consider such things as the papal power and indulgences the only thing against which a Christian man can sin. All fear that I shall be worsted on my twelfth proposition.[2] But although I do not expect to catch that crafty, loud-mouthed, arrogant sophist, yet with Christ's help I will defend my own position. For this will give me a chance to expose publicly the folly of these clumsy, impious *Decretals*[3] by which we Christians have been terrified in vain, for, stuffed with lies as they are, they are recommended by the name of the Roman Church. Christ will expose these bugbears, and as Job says: "He will pull aside the covering of his countenance, and will enter into the midst of his mouth."[4]

The Leipsic theologians and the Bishop of Merseburg have done their best, and are still trying to prevent the debate. They would almost have moved their duke, but finally, strengthened by a word from our elector, he acted authoritatively. My university has answered and consented. The duke writes that he will let us debate as soon as I convince him that Eck wants to debate with me, and I am now taking measures to do so. For the duke thinks only Carlstadt has a dispute with Eck.

Meantime, the theologians are reviling me, especially that bull, ox and ass,[5] not the ox that knoweth his owner, but

[1] Carlstadt held a benefice of the Pope. *Cf.* Smith, *op. cit.*, p. 59.
[2] Asserting that the supremacy of the Roman Church dated only four centuries back. *Cf.* Smith, p. 59.
[3] The Canon Law, which already excited Luther's indignation to a high degree. *Cf.* Smith, 61f.
[4] Job, xli. 4, according to the Vulgate translation, which differs entirely from ours. In our version the verse is no. 13.
[5] This allusion is referred by Enders to Jerome Dungersheim von Ochsenfurt, who wrote Luther several letters, the first of which is dated by Enders January 18, 1519, i. 355. In reality this letter should be dated October 7, 1519 (Knaake in *Theologische Studien und Kritiken*, 1900, p. 269). Luther is evidently speaking

one which eats chaff. They shout at the people of Leipsic not to adhere to new heresies. Thus perhaps they will arouse the people by hatred of us and fear of the Pope to exclude us. It is said that when Tetzel heard that the debate was going to come off, he said: "That's the devil."[1] ...

Cajetan has again written about me to our elector, such folly or insanity that I am glad his Italian ignorance will be exposed to the laity. ...

I am sending Carlstadt's *Wagon*,[2] by which he depicts the folly[3] of theologians, and against which they are raging at Leipsic. Andrew Franck[4] writes me that one man publicly in the pulpit tears his hands, and another inquires of youths in confession whether they laugh at the *Wagon* or have Luther's works, and that they fine those who confess to these faults. See their darkness, their insanity, and they are theologians!

I expect that you have received the first of my lectures on the Psalms.[5] I send another copy by which you can correct yours. ...

I am publishing my commentary on Galatians at Leipsic.[6] If two of my sermons, a Latin one on *Double Justice*[7] and a German one on marriage,[8] come into your hands, please help me. They were published without my knowledge, both taken down and printed, to my shame, with great inaccuracy. I also send my exposition of the Lord's prayer.[9] Melanchthon tells you the rest. I believe you have seen Erasmus' new

---

of some one who is inciting the people against him, perhaps Tetzel (*cf. supra*, no. 112) or Emser, *cf. supra*, no. 117.

[1] "Das walt der Teufel," a usual German oath.

[2] In 1517, at Augsburg, John von Leonrodt published a woodcut representing two wagons, one carrying people to heaven, the other to hell. Carlstadt republished it in 1519 with an explanation that the second wagon was full of schoolmen.

[3] "Moria," perhaps in allusion to Erasmus' famous *Enconium Moriae*, of which, however, Luther does not speak elsewhere until many years later.

[4] Andrew Franck, of Camenz, professor of Leipsic, at this time favorable to the reformers, against whom he turned about 1520. He died 1546.

[5] The *Operationes in Psalmos*, Weimar, vol. V. Melanchthon had sent Lang a copy on April 3. *Corpus Reformatorum*, i. 76.

[6] Weimar, ii. 436. The first edition was by Melchior Lotther of Leipsic.

[7] *Sermo de duplici justitia*, Weimar, 143. First published in February or March, 1519, by Stöckel of Leipsic.

[8] *Ein Sermon von dem ehelichen Stand*, Weimar, ii. 162. Published by Stöckel from a sermon delivered January 16, 1519.

[9] *Auslegung deutsch des Vaterunsers*, Weimar, ii. 74.

Method of Theology; I am sorry it came to an end so soon.[1] . . .

Melancthon and I have written to Erasmus.[2]

Now I have told you all you wanted to know. The reverend father Vicar Staupitz has forgotten me, for he writes nothing. . . .

In closing let me admonish you again about Hebrew, in the study of which let us assist the best youths, and those who are the best theologians and the ones who are most eager for sound learning. Farewell with your cross,[3] if Christ will. BROTHER MARTIN LUTHER, *Augustinian.*

P. S.—Especially remember me to our Jonas,[4] and tell him I like him. . . .

141. DESIDERIUS ERASMUS TO THE ELECTOR FREDERIC OF SAXONY.

Allen, iii. 527.   ANTWERP, April 14, 1519.

Most illustrious Prince, although I never happened to see or speak to your illustrious Highness face to face, which I count not the least of my misfortunes, yet moved by the report of all, who with one accord acclaim your splendid talents as worthy even of supreme rule[5] and moved by the praises of those who say that your mind is bent on promoting the cause of sound learning, and is especially propitious to me, I ventured to dedicate to you my edition of the *Lives of the Caesars,*[6] desiring and seeking nothing else from your

---

[1] *Cf. supra,* no. 136. What Luther means by the last phrase is not certain, whether the book was soon out of print, or too short.

[2] Luther's letter, Enders, i. 488, March 28. Smith, 200.

[3] For "crus" I read "crux," see beginning of letter. Otherwise the sense would be, "Farewell, and may your leg get better."

[4] Jodocus Koch (1493-1555), at Erfurt 1506, M. A. 1510, priest 1514 or 1515, LL. D. 1518. In 1519 he went to Louvain to see Erasmus. In April, 1521, he followed Luther from Erfurt to Worms, receiving there a call to teach at Wittenberg, where he spent the next twenty-one years, taking a prominent part in the Reformation. In 1542 he went to Halle. He was with Luther at Eisleben at Luther's death in February, 1546. After the Schmalkaldic war (1547), he was forced to leave Halle, and wandered around to various places. He was three times married. Letters published by G. Kawerau. Life in *Realencyclopädie.* Always known as Justus Jonas.

[5] After the death of the Emperor Maximilian (January 12, 1519), Frederic was a prominent candidate for the position.

[6] Erasmus dedicated his edition of the *Historiae Augustae Scriptores* to the Elector Frederic and Duke George of Saxony. It was first printed by Froben in

Highness than to make the study of the best disciplines more pleasing to you, and to show that I could repay the free favor of so great a prince with mutual love.

The reason why I did not send you the volume from Basle, where it was printed, was the long distance, for you were then at Wittenberg, and the lack of a safe messenger. Later it seemed superfluous to send a book which was published everywhere.[1] In the meantime, I may be permitted to send this letter to inquire, as it were, whether my zeal were pleasing or otherwise. If my boldness chanced to be unfortunate, I will take care that whatever mistake has been perpetrated here shall be mended elsewhere. Nor do I doubt that your singular and well-known clemency will easily pardon that fault in one whose mind was certainly zealous and anxious to please, and who, however much he may have lacked judgment, certainly had the desire to please your Highness.

But if what we dared to do was fortunate, we ask no other reward than that you should continue to favor the cultivation of good literature, which has now begun to flourish everywhere throughout our Germany, and to defend this part of your fame, which, perhaps, will bring no less glory to our country or to her princes than war has hitherto done. This felicity will come to us if benignant princes shall cherish the best writers and the most promising youths, and if their authority shall continue by force of arms to protect us against those enemies of the Muses and that tyranny of inveterate ignorance. For what do the adversaries of sound learning not attempt? What wiles, what spies, what fraud will they not use? What traps will they not set? What engines will they not set up? What poisoned darts will they not shoot at us? What a conspiracy, what an alliance they have formed to confound learning! Not having learned as boys, they are ashamed to do so as old men, and yet they could learn with less pains than they take to destroy learning. How well agreed are they who never agree save to destroy! How much genius they show for this who are too stupid to learn anything

June, 1518, but Erasmus' dedication is dated a year earlier, June 5, 1517. Allen: *Opus epistolarum Erasmi*, ii. p. 578.

[1] According to the *Bibliotheca Erasmiana*, ii. 31, it was first republished in 1521.

better! How vigilant they are in this respect, though they sleep over all else!

Recently some works by Martin Luther have been published, and at the same time rumor says that the man was beyond measure oppressed by the authority of the very reverend Cardinal Cajetan, who is now legate of the Roman Pontiff in Swabia. How glad were these men, how did they exult and rejoice when they thought that this gave them the desired opportunity of hurting learning! For the Greek proverb has it, that the wicked lack nothing but opportunity, for this gives them the chance to do the evil they always desire. Immediately their sermons to the people, their universities, their councils, their repasts, rang with the words "heresy" and "antichrist." And to make their course of action more odious, these crafty men, especially when addressing women or the unlearned, would speak of Greek and Hebrew, of eloquence and polite literature, as though Luther relied on them for protection, or as though from these fountains flowed heresies. This more than brazen impudence displeased all good men, especially as it furnished an excuse for war to some men who consider themselves the champions of theology and the pillars of Christianity. Behold how purposely and blindly indulgent we are to our own vices; we think it an atrocious slander, a crime near to heresy, if anyone calls a pettifogging theologian (of whom there are not a few) a vain babbler. But we forgive ourselves when before a numerous assembly we call any man we are angry with a heretic and an antichrist!

As Luther is absolutely unknown to me, no one will suspect me of favoring him as a friend. It is not mine to defend his works, nor to disapprove them, for I have not read them, save a bit here and there. No one who knows the man does not approve his life, since he is as far as possible from suspicion of avarice or ambition, and blameless morals even among heathen find favor. It is not becoming to the gentle character of theologians, immediately without reading a book, to rage so savagely against the name and fame of a good man, and that in the presence of the unlearned multitude, especially as he only proposes his opinions for debate and submits them to the judgment of all, whether fitted to judge or not. No one has admonished him, no one has taught him, no one has refuted him; yet they bawl out that he is a heretic, and with tumultuous clamors incite the people to stone him. You would say that they thirsted for human blood rather than for the salvation of souls. The more hateful to Christian ears is the name of heresy, the less rashly ought we to charge anyone with it. Every error is not heresy, nor is he forthwith a heretic who may displease this man or that. Nor are those who make such splendid pretences always acting in the interest of the faith. Rather the greater number are acting in their own interests, and for their own gain or power, when with a hasty wish to wound they condemn in another what they condone in themselves.

In short, since there are so many old and new writers, in the books of none of whom there is not some dangerous error, why should we quietly and placidly read most of them, and fiercely rage against one or two? If we defend the truth alone, should we not be equally offended by what is untrue wherever it is found? It is a most holy thing to defend the purity of religious faith, but it is a most rascally thing under color of defending the faith to serve our own passions. If they desire all that is received in the universities to be held as an oracle, why are there such differences between this school and that? Why do the scholastic doctors fight and fence with each other? Nay, why in the Sorbonne itself does one doctor differ from another? You will find very few who agree, unless in conspiracy. Moreover, these men will often be found condemning in recent books what they do not condemn in Augustine or Gerson, as though truth depended on the author. They read what they like so that they find some excuse, however far-fetched, for everything; they slander everything in what they don't like.

The best part of Christianity is a life worthy of Christ. When this is found we ought not easily to suspect heresy. But now they invent what they call new criteria; *i. e.,* they lay down new laws by which they teach that what they don't like is heresy. Whoever accuses another of heresy, ought himself to show a character worthy of a Christian, charity in admonishing, gentleness in correcting, fairness in judging, mercy in condemning. As none of us is free from error, why should we be so hard on other men's slips? Why should we prefer rather to conquer a man than to heal him, to crush him rather than to teach him? Even he who alone is free from all error does not break the bruised reed nor quench the smoking flax.[1] Augustine did not wish the Donatists, who were worse than heretics, to be compelled, but to be taught, and he protected from the sword of the magistrate the necks of those who sought to assassinate him. But we, whose special business it is to instruct, prefer to use force, for it is easier.

I write this more freely, most illustrious Duke, because I have no concern in Luther's cause. As it is your Highness's duty to protect Christianity, you should exercise caution not to let an innocent man, under the protection of your justice, be sacrificed to the impiety of others on the pretext of piety. Pope Leo desires the same, for he has nothing more at heart than that innocence may be safe. He loves to be called father, nor does he love those who under his name act tyrannically. Nor does anyone better obey Leo's wishes than he who follows justice. What they think of Luther at Rome I know not. Certainly I see that here his books are eagerly read by the best men, though I have not yet had time to peruse them. Farewell. May Christ, most good and great, long keep your Highness for us safe and prosperous.

Your Highness's most devoted
ERASMUS.

142. ERASMUS TO MELANCHTHON AT WITTENBERG.
Allen, iii. 539. *Corpus reformatorum*, i. 77.   LOUVAIN, April 22, 1519.

. . . Everyone here approves Luther's life; there are various opinions of his doctrine. I myself have not yet read his books. Some of his criticisms and proposals are certainly right, but would that he expressed them with as much felicity as freedom. I have written about him to the illustrious Elector Frederic,[2] at the same time taking occasion to ask him how he liked my dedication to him of the *Lives of the Caesars*. . . .

[1] Isaiah, xlii. 3.
[2] *Supra*, no. 141.

143. LUTHER TO DUKE GEORGE OF SAXONY.

Enders, ii. 17. De Wette-Seidemann, vi. 15. German.

WITTENBERG, April 28, 1519.

My poor prayer and endeavor be always at your Grace's humble service. High-born, serene Prince, gracious Lord! I have received your Grace's letter and kind answer, and have communicated your Grace's opinion to Dr. Eck, and have hitherto awaited his reply. Inasmuch as the said Dr. Eck has published a paper in which he not only challenges both of us, Carlstadt and me, but taunts us bitterly and perhaps already sings a song of triumph over us, which, as I perceive, concerns your Grace, therefore, it is now as formerly my humble prayer to your Grace, kindly to permit us to hold our debate. And as the affair has brought me danger to my life and much enmity, I pray your Grace for God's sake to give me a safe-conduct. For I must not venture to tempt God by despising human help, for which I requite your Grace with my humble prayer before God.

Your Grace's humble chaplain,

MARTIN LUTHER, *Augustinian at Wittenberg.*

144. DUKE GEORGE OF SAXONY TO MARTIN LUTHER.

Enders, ii. 27. German. DRESDEN, May 7, 1519.

Worthy, learned, dear and pious Sir! We have received your second letter and noted the contents. Considering that if you wish to debate with Dr. Eck, you must have his consent thereto, we previously announced to you that you should agree with him, and that when you and he together request a place for the said debate, we would give you a definite answer. We still remain of this opinion, but did not wish to let your letter lie unanswered.

145. THE ELECTOR FREDERIC OF SAXONY TO ERASMUS.

Lutheri Opera latina varii argumenti. Erlangen. ii. 460.
Allen, iii. 577. GRIMMA, May 14, 1519.

Although we did not doubt, most learned Erasmus, that you would ascertain from our letter recently sent to you by Justus Jonas, that we were always most grateful for your affection for us, and especially for the dedication of Suetonius and the other histories, yet we have decided to answer your letter written to us from Antwerp April 14. It was a most learned and elegant letter, and put in a stronger light what we knew before of your theological erudition and your pious love. There is, as you write, a strange conspiracy of the haters of sound learning who are fit for nothing but to injure the good, pious and well instructed.

We rejoice that the Lutheran cause is not condemned by the learned, and that Dr. Luther's works are eagerly read by the best men, especially as the majority of good and learned men, as well in our dominions as elsewhere, with one accord praise the man's life and character as much as his learning. That we have allowed him to stay in our Saxony, is not so much on account of the man as of the cause, for we have no intention of allowing punishment to fall on those worthy of rewards. Nor, with the help of God Almighty, shall we ever suffer by our fault any innocent man to be given a prey to those who seek their own ends.

Moreover, with God's help, we shall henceforth cherish good letters and right studies as well as their cultivators, no less than in the past. Our special gratitude to you has impelled us to write this to you. Farewell, most learned Erasmus.

146. LUTHER TO THE ELECTOR FREDERIC OF SAXONY.

Enders, ii. 35. De Wette, i. 283. German. (WITTENBERG, May, 1519.)

Most serene Prince, most gracious Lord! We are obliged to build a room,[1] and have humbly requested permission of the town council of Wittenberg to allow us to build out of the walls on the graves, but they give us no answer. Wherefore we pray your Grace kindly to give us leave for this necessary addition, and expect a gracious answer, as, before God, we deserve.

Also I pray your Grace to buy me at this Leipsic fair a white and a black cowl. Your Grace owes me the black cowl, and I humbly beg the white one. For two or three years

---

[1] The Black Cloister was built right against the city wall, outside of which was the monks' cemetery. Enders and Grisar (*Luther*, i. 323f.) conjecture that this "room" was a privy, for they were usually built on the walls to carry the sewage outside the city.

ago your Grace promised me one which I never got.[1] For although Pfeffinger spoke me fair, yet either because of business or because, as people say of him, he is slow to spend money, he put off getting it. So I was obliged to get myself another, which has lasted to the present and thus saved your Grace's promise. In this need I humbly pray your Grace if the Psalter[2] deserves a black cowl, to let the Apostle[3] earn a white one, and pray do not let Pfeffinger neglect it.

Your Grace's humble, obedient chaplain,

DR. MARTIN, *Augustinian at Wittenberg.*

147. LUTHER TO DUKE GEORGE OF SAXONY.

Enders, ii. 52. De Wette-Seidemann, vi. 16. German.

WITTENBERG, May 16, 1519.

My poor humble prayers for your Grace. Gracious, highborn Prince and Lord! I humbly pray your Grace for God's sake not to take it ill that I write to your Grace again. Your Grace's last letter compels me to write, for it greatly troubles and horrifies me. For I fear that I have done something to displease your Grace, and to deserve your displeasure. This was unintentional and I greatly regret it.

For your Grace granted permission to Dr. Eck to debate with Carlstadt on the simple request, or agreement, of the latter, but you will not grant the same permission to me on Dr. Eck's public letter in which he openly challenges me to debate, and this in a printed paper, which clearly proves that he forces me to debate with him at Leipsic as I previously wrote your Grace. And as, according to your Grace's first letter, I wrote Dr. Eck to request your permission I do not know what more to do, and can only think that I am in disgrace. Now, my gracious Lord, I know that the world stood before me and will stand after me, whether I debate or not. I have not forced it on Dr. Eck, but he on me. Wherefore I pray your Grace for God's sake to signify to me what I ought to do. For I am perfectly willing to give it up. For I can-

---

[1] Luther wrote to the elector on this subject in November, 1517. Letter translated in Smith, *op. cit.*, p. 34.

[2] *The Operationes in Psalmos*, dedicated to the elector, March 27, 1519. Weimar, vol. v.

[3] *The Commentary on Galatians.*

not compel Dr. Eck to write to your Grace on my behalf. But I will write him again and request him to do so. Will your Grace please forgive me, and may God protect you.

Your Grace's humble chaplain,

DR. MARTIN LUTHER, *Augustinian of Wittenberg.*

148. LUTHER TO CHARLES VON MILTITZ AT COBLENZ.
Enders, i. 53.   WITTENBERG, May 17, 1519.

Greeting. Dear Sir, I received your Excellency's letter[1] advising me that it would be to my advantage forthwith to repair to Coblenz. Please listen to me patiently. In the first place, when we came together at Altenburg, my presence did not seem to myself necessary; for as my books, in which I most clearly opened my mind to all, were published, I thought it sufficient if, after weighing my opinions, articles should be determined on for me to revoke, and reasons should be assigned for the recantation, so that it might appear efficacious and praiseworthy, for otherwise men would say that it had been extorted from me by force and the last state should be worse than the first. I am of this opinion still.

But even if I ought to come, you yourself can see how foolish those who have charge of this affair think me, since you write that the mandate has not yet come from Rome, and that the archbishop[2] does not summon me in virtue of such a mandate. I am not sure that the mandate will arrive, especially in this crisis in the Empire,[3] nor am I sure, should it come, that the archbishop would receive it. How can I, therefore, trust myself to such a doubtful and perilous situation, or how can so poor a man as I get the necessary money? I have already spent so much in this matter that I have wearied my patrons and am ashamed to ask for more, not to mention the fact that during the interregnum no one can give a safe-conduct, particularly to a man with as many enemies as I have.

Furthermore, the great debate, which the most reverend

[1]Dated Coblenz, May 3. Enders, ii. 18. Luther wrote Spalatin, May 16, that he considered Miltitz's proposals ridiculous. Enders, ii. 46.

[2]*I. e.,* the Archbishop of Trier, in whose jurisdiction Coblenz was. On referring Luther's cause to him *cf. supra,* no. 120.

[3]The Emperor Maximilian had died on January 12, and a new election was about to be held.

lord cardinal[1] refused to allow me to hold at Augsburg, is coming off at Leipsic. For I am challenged by John Eck, and should I decline, in so just a cause, to meet him, with how much shame should I brand not only myself and all my friends, but our most illustrious elector and our whole order and my university. In this debate the whole case will be examined by many learned men impartially, with good arguments on both sides, which could not be the case before either the archbishop or the cardinal. So that it is better that your proposal should wait on the debate than that the debate be hindered. . . .

But come! Even if all these difficulties were met, yet would I not wish to have the cause tried by the cardinal. I do not want him present, for he is not worthy of it. He tried to harass me from the Christian faith at Augsburg, wherefore I doubt whether he is a Catholic Christian himself. If I had time I would write to the Pope and cardinals and expose him, unless he should retract all his rank errors. I regret that the legates of the Apostolic See are men who try to destroy Christ.

Thus, Sir, I think that I have justly excused myself from coming. I might add that a certain spy, armed with many letters, has been here, seeking first you and then me, and he excited a lively suspicion that he was preparing some violence against me;[2] finally he was obliged to flee, lest he should be ducked in the Elbe, as he almost was and would have been had not we prevented it, for men thought that he was your agent, especially after we heard that you were lingering in Germany, though you promised us to go straight to Rome. So it happened that although I exonerated you from this charge, yet I saw that there were snares all around for me to fear. . . .

If what you write is true about having to come after me with papal letters, may God grant that you come safely. I am very busy, serving many men, and am not able to lose time and wander abroad without causing loss to many. Farewell, excellent Sir.

BROTHER MARTIN LUTHER, *Augustinian.*

[1] Cajetan, of course, is meant.
[2] This was probably the man of whom Luther spoke as coming to visit him with sinister intent. *Cf.* Smith, p. 68.

149. ERASMUS TO THOMAS WOLSEY, CARDINAL ARCHBISHOP OF YORK.

Allen, iii. 587.   ANTWERP, May 18 (1519).

Thomas Wolsey (1471-1530), the famous statesman and cardinal. His life by M. Creighton. On the part he took against Luther, *cf.* Preserved Smith: "Luther and Henry VIII." *English Historical Review*, no. c. Erasmus had known him for a long while. *Cf.* Allen, *op. cit.*, i. p. 284, etc.

. . . They accuse me of writing every hateful book that comes out. You might say that it was the very essence of calumny to confound, as they do, the cause of sound learning with that of Reuchlin and Luther, when really they have nothing to do with each other. . . . Luther is absolutely unknown to me, nor have I had time to read more than a page or two of his books, not because I have not wanted to, but because my other occupations have not given me leisure. And yet they say that he has been helped by me! If he has written well I deserve no credit, if otherwise no blame, since of his writings not a jot is mine. Anyone who wishes to investigate the matter will find this absolutely true. The man's life is approved by the unanimous consent of all, and the fact that his character is so upright that even enemies find nothing to slander in it, must considerably prejudice us in his favor. So that even if I had abundant leisure to read the writings of such a man, I would not have the presumption to judge them, although even boys nowadays rashly pronounce this erroneous and that heretical. Moreover, I have sometimes been opposed to Luther for fear that he might make hateful the cause of sound learning, which I am unwilling to have more burdened than it is; nor has it escaped me that it would be an invidious task to tear down that from which priests and monks reap their best harvest.

First there appeared quite a number of theses on indulgences; two pamphlets, on confession and on penitence, followed hard upon them; when I heard that some printers[1]

---

[1] Froben; Erasmus repeats several times that he tried to prevent him printing Luther's works. He did not succeed however, for Froben brought out a volume of Luther's works in October, 1518. This included one of the pamphlets mentioned above, *Sermo de penitentia* (Weimar, i. 317), but not, I think, the other, *Instructio pro confessione peccatorum* (Weimar, i. 257). *Cf. supra*, no. 125.

were going to publish them, I tried hard to dissuade them lest they might thereby hurt sound learning. Even those who wish Luther well will agree to this. Then followed a whole swarm of tracts; no one ever saw me reading them or even heard me express an opinion, favorable or otherwise, about them. For I am not so rash as to approve what I have not read, nor such a sycophant as to condemn what I do not know, even if this is now the regular custom of those who are least fitted of all to pronounce judgment. . . .

150. MELANCHTHON TO GEORGE SPALATIN.
Corpus Reformatorum, i. 80. WITTENBERG, May 21, 1519.

Hail, Spalatin, my dearest friend in the Lord. I fear lest you will not have time to read my trifles. You will greatly thank a man careful not to speak a little too much. We are reading Erasmus' letter.[1] Glory be to God who has given the elector such a herald for his virtues, and Luther such a rare, and, as the lawyers say, eloquent supporter.[2] It will be your duty to commend us to Erasmus.

Yesterday there was with us a certain Hebrew scholar,[3] moderately learned, who studied the grammar at Heidelberg and taught it afterwards and now expects to lecture at Leipsic, but will come to us if the excellent elector wishes. I conferred with Luther about him and we both thought him moderately good and likely to improve with practice. . . .

Riccius[4] has attacked Eck, who blandly boasts that he has fought against Zasius[5] the lawyer, Luther the theologian and Riccius the philosopher, so that he may seem to be a Hercules,

---

[1] *I. e.,* to the Elector Frederic, *cf. supra,* no. 141.

[2] "Suffragatorem pedarium"; the *pedarii* were senators who could speak but not vote.

[3] John Cellarius, of Kunstadt, a supporter of Eck, who later turned Zwinglian, and still later Lutheran. Died at Frankfort a. M., 1542. Enders, ii. 58.

[4] Paul Riccius, who wrote in April, 1519, *Naturalia et prophetica de anima coeli adversus Eckium.* He is spoken of in the *Tischreden* (Weimar, i. no. 205) as having been at the Diet of Ratisbon, 1532.

[5] Ulrich Zäsi of Constance (1461-November 24, 1535), matriculated at Tübingen 1481, after some years returned as bishop's notary to Constance, in 1491 went to Freiburg in Breisgau as town clerk. He studied law, taking his doctorate in 1500, lectured on poetry till 1506, when he obtained the professorship of jurisprudence, which he held till the end of his life. His writings on the subject are numerous. Allen, *op. cit.,* ii. 9. He was at first favorable to Luther, then drew back. His epistles said to have been published by Riegger, 1774.

equal not to two, but to three other men. Behold, this Christian moderation and how the popes, theologians, princes and people stand silently gaping at it! This is the fury of the Lord. I am wretched whenever I think of it. I beseech you, Spalatin, for aid. Luther, the soldier of the Lord, has brought this on himself. Stand fast and watch with us. I write this earnestly and in sadness thinking over the crimes of the theologians. . . . Agricola[1] and I have begun to take down Luther's lectures for you, and I hope we shall all have a good book from them, for the subject now begins to glow. All your friends salute you.

YOUR PHILIP.

I hoped that the printer would have finished the sermon on marriage,[2] but his laziness is too much for me.

151. LUTHER TO GEORGE SPALATIN.
Enders, ii. 56. (WITTENBERG), May 22, 1519.

Greeting. Erasmus' letter[3] greatly pleased me and my friends. Only I should have preferred not to have my praises sung by so great a man. I know myself, at least this side of myself.

Before you leave,[4] please tell us what the elector proposes to do about the professor of Hebrew. . . .[5] The number of students is growing[6] and their quality is good. One of the last to come was a Nuremberg licentiate in theology, a man of mature age, preacher in the church of St. Sebald.[7] Our

---

[1] John Agricola of Eisleben (1494-1566), at Wittenberg 1516, M. A. 1518, in which year he published from his own notes Luther's homilies on the Lord's prayer. He married 1520, and taught at Wittenberg and Eisleben. He was present at the Diets of 1526, 1529, 1530. He had a violent quarrel with Luther and Melanchthon, on account of which he moved to Berlin about 1540. He took an important part in the Interim, 1548. Life by G. Kawerau, 1881. *Cf.* Smith, 282ff.

[2] Luther's *Sermon von dem ehelichen Stand*, preached January 16, 1519. Weimar, ii. 162.

[3] To the Elector Frederic. *Supra*, no. 141. It was published in 1519 by Melchior Lotther of Leipsic. As this printer did some of Luther's work at this time, we may conjecture that Erasmus' epistle was published by Luther's friends.

[4] For Frankfort on the Main, where the elector was going to take part in the imperial election.

[5] On this *cf.* last letter.

[6] The number rose from 232 in 1517 to 458 in 1519 and 579 in 1520.

[7] John Herholt, who matriculated May 26, 1519. Luther had met him at Nuremberg in the autumn of 1518. Enders, i. 317.

city is almost giving out of lodging houses. More at another time. Farewell.

BROTHER MARTIN LUTHER, *Augustinian*.

152. DUKE GEORGE OF SAXONY TO LUTHER.
Enders, i. 59. German. DRESDEN, May 23, 1519.

Worthy, dear and pious Sir! We have received your letter, in which you speak again of the debate, and noted the contents. We are not aware of having conceived any displeasure for you, though indeed it is true that all sorts of things have come to our ears, on which we should not be sorry to speak to you, but we will let them wait until some time when you come to us.[1]

We are much surprised that, after you had heard that no good would come of a debate on these matters, and that the doctors of the theological faculty of Leipsic had refused to allow it, you should be so determined to hold the debate. It is true that Dr. Carlstadt did not ask us for permission, but we were informed by Dr. Eck that he had agreed to debate with Carlstadt. If the same happens in this case, and if you agree with one another, and if you then write us how you stand, we will, as stated in our last letter, then give you a definite answer. This in reply to your letter.

153. CLAUDIUS CANTIUNCULA TO HENRY CORNELIUS AGRIPPA OF NETTISHEIM.
H. C. Agrippae ab Nettesheym. . . . Operum Pars Posterior. Lugduni. Per Beringos Fratres, *s. a.,* p. 748. (BASLE), May 23, 1519.

Cantiuncula (Chansonette), of Metz, a distinguished lawyer, met Agrippa at this city in 1518 while he was still very young. In 1517 he went to Basle to study, becoming Dr. juris and professor there in 1519. Later (1533), he became one of Ferdinand's financial officers, a position he held until his death in 1549. Cf. *Claude Chansonette et ses lettres inedits.* Bruxelles. 1878. Förstemann-Günther: *Briefe an Erasmus,* p. 318. A. Prost: *Corneille Agrippa,* Paris, 1881, pp. 307, 316, 345, 354f. *Corpus Reformatorum,* xciv. 363.

Henry Cornelius Agrippa, of Nettesheim (1486-1535), born at Cologne, studied at Paris, was in Italy 1511-18, in Metz 1518-20, then at Cologne, Geneva, Freiburg, Lyons and Paris, and the Netherlands.

---
[1] When Luther came to Leipsic in July the duke had a private interview with him, on which *cf.* Smith, p. 67.

He was chiefly noted for his skill in the occult arts, but wrote a work *De Vanitate Scientium*, showing an enlightened skepticism. At this time (1519), he sympathized strongly with Luther (Prost, *op. cit.*, i. 393), later became an Erasmian. Life by Prost.

Agrippa, in a letter from Metz, apparently written early in May (*Opera*, p. 744), had asked for Luther's works.

. . . Believe me, dear Agrippa, I have scoured the whole of Basle without finding Luther's works, as they were all sold long ago. They say they will soon be printed again at Strassburg. Neither could I find the legal work you asked for. But I am giving you Erasmus' *Method of Theology*, a work, unless, Henry, I mistake, likely to please you. I also send Luther's and Eck's *Theses* to be debated this year, and some trifles about the Emperor.

154. LUTHER TO MARTIN GLASER, AUGUSTINIAN PRIOR AT RAMSAU.

Enders, ii. 62. (WITTENBERG), May 30, 1519.

Martin Glaser, of Nuremberg, matriculated at Wittenberg 1506. Then he became prior of the Augustinian Convent at Ramsau in the Bishopric of Freisingen, near Munich. Later he joined the Augustinian cloister at Nuremberg, but at its dissolution in 1524, he became evangelical pastor at Kraftshof, nearby, and married. In 1530 he was transferred to Hilpoltstein. Enders, vii. 145, viii. 273. *Cf. supra*, 81a.

Venerable Father, you are quite rightly surprised and even indignant that I have hitherto written you nothing. Though I have plenty of excuses, yet I prefer to confess my fault. I hope you will be indulgent to a poor man like me in the affair of your horse,[1] on account of the intercession of the Venerable Father Staupitz. Doubtless you gave it to God, not to me. I hope we may see you here again, as I am glad to learn from Staupitz is likely to be the case. I believe that you know about my coming debate at Leipsic and all my other doings. I am lecturing on the Psalter again, and the students are enthusiastic. The town is full of students. Rome burns to destroy me, but I coolly laugh at her. I am told that a paper Luther was publicly burned and cursed on the Campo

---
[1]Perhaps a horse borrowed by Luther on leaving Augsburg for Manheim, October 20, 1518.

di Fiore.¹ I am ready for their rage. My commentary on Galatians is being printed; you will soon see it.

I am well and calm, and less poor than formerly. Our friend Helt² is a fine ruler and organizer—of the kitchen, for he cares chiefly for the belly; perhaps he will care more for his head later.

I read what you wrote about that Franciscan babbler, but I am used to such hatred. The whole world is reeling, body and mind alike. God knows the future. We prophesy death and war. God have mercy on us. Farewell in him and pray for poor me.   BROTHER MARTIN LUTHER, *Augustinian*.

155. DESIDERIUS ERASMUS TO LUTHER AT WITTENBERG.
Enders, ii. 64. Allen, iii. 605.   LOUVAIN, May 30, 1519.

This letter was published at Leipsic in June, 1519, and at Augsburg. It almost immediately got Erasmus into trouble. In the first place the Bishop of Liège was indignant at the reference to himself as a favorer of Luther, a matter at once inquired into by the theologians of Louvain. (*Infra*, no. 370. P. Kalkoff: *Die depeschen des Nuntius Aleander*, p. 220). The rumor even stimulated the process against Luther at Rome. (L. v. Pastor: *History of the Popes*, English translation, v. 398.) Accordingly, when Erasmus himself published the letter in the *Farrago* of 1519 for "episcopus Leodiensis," he substituted "eximius quidam," which he claimed was what he originally wrote (*Bibliotheca Erasmiana. Colloquia*, i. 65). But this did not end the author's troubles. The letter was found by Hochstraten, the inquisitor, and made by him the base of an accusation of favoring heresy. (*Infra*, nos. 187, 188.) To clear himself, Erasmus wrote to the Archbishop of Mayence. *Infra*, no. 192.

Dearest brother in Christ, your epistle,³ showing the keenness of your mind and breathing a Christian spirit, was most pleasant to me.

I cannot tell you what a commotion your books are raising⁴ here. Nor can these men by any means be disabused of the

[1] We know nothing of Luther's being burned in effigy at Rome; his writings were publicly burned there on the Piazza Navona about June 7, 1521. Enders places this in 1520, as does Rodocanachi: *Rome au temps de Jules II. et de Leon X.*, 1912, p. 162. On the true date *cf.* L. Pastor: *History of the Popes*, English translation by R. Kerr, viii. 37.
[2] He was at this time prior at Wittenberg.
[3] March 28, 1519. Translated, Smith, *op. cit.*, 200f.
[4] This is the true translation of "tragoedias excitare," though as J. H. Lupton remarks, with demure sarcasm, "it has become the fashion" to translate these words, "make a tragedy."

suspicion that your works are written with my aid, and that I am, as they call it, the standard-bearer of your party. They think they thus have a good chance to suppress sound learning, which they hate mortally as if it offended the majesty of theology. . . . I have testified that you are entirely unknown to me, that I have not read your books and neither approve nor disapprove anything. I only warned them not to vociferate against your books without reading them, and not to excite the hatred of the people against them, but to refer them to the judgment of those whose opinion would have most weight. . . .

In England there are men who think well of your writings, and they the very greatest. So do some here, among them the Bishop of Liège.[1] I try to keep neutral, so as to help the revival of learning as much as I can. And it seems to me that more is accomplished by this civil modesty than by impetuosity. Thus Christ brought the world under his sway. . . . It is more expedient to attack those who abuse the authority of the Pope than the Pope himself; and similarly of kings. . . . Wherefore, we must take care not to speak arrogantly or factiously. . . . I have looked over your *Commentaries on the Psalms*,[2] which pleased me very much.

156. ERASMUS TO JOHN LANG AT ERFURT.

Allen, iii. 609. LOUVAIN, May 30 (1519).

Reverend Father, do not judge my affection for you by the paucity of the letters I write, for I am so overwhelmed with letters that I hardly have time to read them. I greatly like your Christian soul, inflexible for Christian truth. I hope that Christ will favor your plans, and those of men like you. Here hitherto the papists, united to do their utmost, have

---

[1]Eberhard de la Marck, Prince Bishop of Liège 1506-1538, a member of one of the most powerful families in Europe. He was made cardinal in August, 1521. Notwithstanding Erasmus' information, he always appears to have been hostile to the new movement. Luther called him in 1535 "a most pestilent organ of the devil." Enders, x. 203.

[2]*Operationes in Psalmos*, 1519-1521. The first five Psalms published separately, March 27, 1519. Weimar, v.; Kostlin-Kawerau: *Martin Luther* (Berlin, 1903), i. p. 275. In October, 1518, Froben had published a volume of Luther's pamphlets which he sent to Erasmus. Enders, i. pp. 420-22. Hollonius to Erasmus, December 5, 1518. Allen, iii. 445.

raged furiously, but some are milder and I hope that the others will sometime be ashamed of their madness. All good men love Luther's boldness. I doubt not that his prudence will prevent faction and discord. I think we should mainly try to instill Christ into men's minds, rather than fight with professing Christians, from whom no glory or victory will be obtained until the tyranny of the Roman See and that of its satellites, Dominicans, Carmelites and Franciscans, I mean only the bad ones, is abolished. I do not see how that can be tried without serious disturbance. Farewell, excellent Father, to whose kindness I am aware that I owe much.

ERASMUS OF ROTTERDAM.

157. MOSELLANUS TO JOHN LANG AT ERFURT.

Kolde: *Analecta*, 8. LEIPSIC, May 30, 1519.

Peter Schad, or Schade (c. 1493-April 19, 1524) of Bruttig on the Moselle (hence Mosellanus), matriculated at Cologne 1512, taught at Freiburg 1513-4, in April, 1515, settled at Leipsic, and became professor at the University in 1517. *Cf.* Allen, *op cit.*, ii. 517. Mosellanus was a supporter of Luther at the Leipsic debate, at which he presided.

Our Martin[1] has been again cited to Coblenz by Charles von Miltitz without the authority of our bishop and to the great indignation of Frederic. May Luther make it turn out badly for the sophists. But their plans are vain, for the elector will not expose an innocent man to this ambush, but will have the whole thing judged by the Elector of Trier, and in his own time will avenge this rascal deserter from his native Germany. You will soon see the letter of Erasmus commending innocent Martin to the hero Frederic. It cannot be had now. As far as I see, the debate will not be affected by the guile of these men, for I have hitherto heard nothing about moving it. . . .

158. LUTHER TO JOHN LANG AT ERFURT.

Enders, ii. 69. WITTENBERG, June 6, 1519.

Greeting. We have heard of the death of Dr. Trutfetter.[2] May God receive his soul, and forgive him all his sins and us all ours. I send what you see, not having anything else.

[1] On this, Smith, *op. cit.*, 95.
[2] A premature rumor; Trutfetter was ill and died about December 1.

I am now publishing my proof of my thirteenth proposition,[1] on account of the hatred which is trying to prevent my appearance at Leipsic to defend it. Although I wrote three letters, I could get no certain answer from Duke George. Rab of Leipsic has again gone to Rome for my sake, taking more lies there and bringing more rash folly back. Yet will I go to Leipsic to offer to debate. It is all settled about Carlstadt.

Another trial, greater than these, has come to me, by all of which the Lord teaches me what a thing is man, although I thought I knew it pretty well before. If you come I will tell you more about it. . . . Farewell and pray for me, a great sinner. I need absolutely nothing but God's mercy. Thus their hatred is frustrated, for they know I do not need other things.

Greet the Fathers Nathin and Usingen for me and all the others. You will soon see my proof of my thirteenth proposition about the primacy of the Pope, which I hope is irrefutable. BROTHER MARTIN LUTHER, *Augustinian.*

159. DUKE GEORGE'S SAFE-CONDUCT FOR CARLSTADT AND HIS COMPANIONS.

Gess, i. 86. WEISSENFELS, June 10, 1519.

At the desire of Dr. Carlstadt, we, George, Duke of Saxony, grant to him and to those[2] whom he may bring with him, for the debate to take place at Leipsic with Dr. Eck, as long as he may be with us and until he returns to his own home, free and safe conduct.

160. JOHN ECK TO GEORGE HAUEN AND FRANCIS BURCKHARDT AT INGOLSTADT.

Walch, xv. 1456. German translation of Latin original.

LEIPSIC, July 1, 1519.

Hauen (1484-August 23, 1536), a priest, taught Latin at Passau 1513, then went to Ingolstadt, where he became professor of Canon Law, and in 1519 Prorector and in 1523 Rector.

---

[1] *Resolutio Lutheriana super propositione decima tertia de potestate papae.* Weimar, ii. 180. This was the proposition stating that the papal power arose but four centuries previously, quoted as the twelfth proposition above, the number having been changed by the interpolation of one thesis. *Cf.,* no. 140. Smith, 61, 66.

[2] Luther's name was omitted as a snub to him. In accordance with this permission, Carlstadt, Luther, Melanchthon and other Wittenbergers set out for

Burckhardt is otherwise unknown to me, save that he was also a professor of law at Ingolstadt, and possibly a relative of Peter Burckhardt, on whom *cf.* no. 164.

Greeting. Our friendship demands that I should give you news of myself. At first the strong, heating beer was bad for me. From Pfreimd to Gera I didn't have a single good drink. At Leipsic also the beer was bad for me, so I stopped drinking it for six days, and feel better. . . .

Luther and Carlstadt entered in great state, with two hundred Wittenberg students, four doctors, three licentiates, many professors and many Lutherans, Lang of Erfurt the Vicar, impudent Egranus, the preacher of Görlitz,[1] the pastor of Annaberg, Bohemians and Hussites sent from Prague, and many heretics who give out that Luther is an able defender of the truth, not inferior to John Huss. . . .

So far of Carlstadt, now of the other monster, Luther. [On the margin Eck wrote: "I have done Luther a good mischief, of which I will tell you orally."] At his arrival I heard that he did not want to debate, and I moved everything to get him to. We met in the presence of the ducal commissioners and of the university; I left everything to them; they wanted Luther to debate on the same conditions as Carlstadt, but he said much about instructions from his prince. I said to him I did not want the elector as judge, though I did not exclude him; that he might choose a university and if Germany were too small, he might take one abroad, in France or Spain. But he would not have any judge, and was therefore not admitted to debate, for, according to the ducal instructions, no one should debate who did not allow a judge. I desired at that time that the commissioners and university should give me a testimony of this, although many of them are Lutherans. Dr. Auerbach,[2] the physician of the Archbishop of

Leipsic, where they arrived June 24. Carlstadt and Eck debated June 27-July 3, and again July 15 and 16. Luther and Eck debated July 4-14. The best account of the sojourn at Leipsic and the debate there is found in a letter of Luther to Spalatin, dated (Wittenberg), July 20, 1519, translated in Smith, *op. cit.*, pp. 64-68. Other accounts are given below.

[1] The Reformation was started at Görlitz in 1522 by the pastor Francis Rothbart; I cannot say whether he is the one here meant.

[2] H. Stromer von Auerbach (1482-November 26, 1542), famous as the first host of "Auerbach's Keller" celebrated in Faust, matriculated at Leipsic 1497, M. A. 1502, taught philosophy, Rector of the University 1508. Then he studied medicine,

Mayence and the doctor of the Counts of Mansfeld and many others urged Luther on, as he would lose everyone's favor if he would not allow any judge in the world. . . . Finally, we agreed to decide on a judge at the end of the debate, and in the meantime that it should [not] be allowed to have the debate printed. . . . The Wittenbergers are full of gall, rage and poison, and arouse odium against me. The Town Council received so many threats from them, though none of them were definite, that on the same night they put a guard of thirty-four armed men in the next houses, so that if there was any disturbance its authors might get what they deserved.

People still put their hopes on Luther, but none whatever on Carlstadt. Luther was not allowed to preach at Leipsic, but the Duke of Pomerania,[1] who is Rector of Wittenberg, at the suggestion of the monk, got him to preach on the gospel for the day in the castle, which he did. The whole sermon, delivered on June 29, was Bohemian. On the next morning, Sunday, at the desire of citizens and doctors, I preached and rebutted his hair-splitting errors. . . .

161. WENZEL ROZD'ALOWSKY TO LUTHER.

Enders, ii. 78.   PRAGUE, July 17, 1519.

On July 16, John Poduska, a Hussite priest, who had already embraced Luther's doctrine, wrote him a letter of encouragement. On the following day his assistant, Rozd'alowsky, provost of the Emperor Charles's Collegium at Prague, wrote the letter here translated. Both Poduska and Rozd'alowsky died of the plague in 1520. The letters reached Luther on October 3, after having been apparently opened and read by some Catholics, who reported the contents to Emser, who on August 13 forwarded this information to Zack, a Catholic official at Prague. Luther later came into close touch with the Bohemian Brethren, many of whom followed him.

Dear Martin Luther, I have read your works through and

becoming M. D. in 1511, and in 1516 was made professor of pathology. In 1519 he married and in 1524 became dean of the medical faculty. He was a friend of Erasmus and Reuchlin, and special physician to Albert of Mayence. G. Wustmann: *Der Wirt von Auerbachs Keller*, 1902. O. Clemen in *Neues Archiv für sächsische Geschichte*, xxiv. 1903.

[1] Duke Barnim XI. of Pomerania (1501-1573), began to reign in conjunction with his elder brother George in October, 1523. He studied at Wittenberg in 1515, soon after which he was made honorary Rector of the institution. He was a warm friend of the Reformation, which was organized in his dominions by Bugenhagen in 1534. *Allgemeine deutsche Biographie*.

through, and daily discuss with my friends who you are, what you are doing, what you are trying to do, or rather what Christ's spirit is doing through you in the Church. And behold, while we were talking of these things, a certain organist named James, who loves you much, came upon us and told us all that is now being done between you and Eck and your other enemies. I cannot tell you, Father, how pleased, happy and delighted we were when he told us of the glorious victory you had won over your adversaries and especially over Eck's scholastic and Aristotelian rather than Christian theology. His narrative gave much praise both to you and to the most illustrious Elector Frederic, to you, because you proved yourself worthy of admiration, to him because he appreciates those virtues of which you seem daily to give the greatest proofs, and by which your enemies are cast down and your friends rejoiced. For are they not better than gold?

Wherefore I congratulate your Reverence, and I thank the God of heaven, who has deigned not only to keep you safe amidst so many perils and so many enemies, but also to give you a glorious victory in your just battle. Moreover this same James told us that you greatly desired the books of John Huss,[1] the apostle of the Bohemians, that you might learn what sort of man he was and how great, not from rumor nor from the ill-advised Council of Constance, but from the true mirror of his mind, that is, his books. So I am sending your Reverence his book on the Church,[2] and I am sending it the more boldly because I have read certain propositions which you are now defending against old and new errors at Leipsic, which are also proved in this book. It is a small gift and one which might at first seem ridiculous, but, perhaps, it will not be wholly unacceptable to you, especially if it comes in answer to your wishes and prayers, and also because this was the one book on account of which the author,

[1] Almost as Rozdalowsky was writing this Luther was declaring in his debate at Leipsic that "among the articles of John Huss there are many which are most Christian and evangelic, which the universal Church is not able to condemn." O. Seitz: *Leipziger Disputation*, p. 87.

[2] As Enders could find no edition of this from a Hussite press prior to this time he concludes that the book was in manuscript. It was printed by Hutten in Germany in August, 1520. It made a tremendous impression on Luther. *Cf. infra*, no. 239, and Smith, 71f.

during his life-time, was exposed to the contumely of all the higher clergy, and for which he was hated, mocked, cursed and called a heretic by them, and for which, in short, he was at last, though an innocent man and a splendid preacher of the divine word, burned so unjustly by the Council of Constance.

But enough of him now. If necessary and if you order it, I will gladly send you the record of his trial with other things. I will only add that I am sure that what John Huss formerly was in Bohemia, that are you, Martin Luther, in Saxony. What then do you need? Watch and be strong in the Lord, and beware of men. Do not quail if you hear yourself called a heretic and excommunicated, remembering what Christ and the apostles suffered and what all men who wish to live piously in Christ suffer even to-day.

Farewell, Martin, and love me though unknown to you, for be sure that you are loved by me.

162. HENRY STROMER OF AUERBACH TO GEORGE SPALATIN.

G. Wustmann: *Der Wirt von Auerbachs Keller. Dr. H. Stromer von Auerbach.* Leipsic, 1902, p. 90.   LEIPSIC, July 19, 1519.

. . . At Leipsic in the castle I attended the theological debate of Eck, Carlstadt and Luther. Eck, the loud theologian, and Carlstadt disputed on free will. Martin Luther, a man famous for eloquence, divinity and holiness of life, disputed with Eck on the power of the Pope, on purgatory, indulgences and the power of priests to loose and to bind, whether they all have it or not, and on some other obscure theological points. It is extraordinary how much holy theological learning was modestly distilled by Martin. He seems to me a man worthy of immortality. He uttered nothing but what was sound and wholesome, omitting all heathen learning and content only with the majestic gospel and writings of the apostles. Some, infected either with unbecoming legality or with malice, reviled him; he was like a harmless sheep among wolves, and the more hostile they were to him the greater and more holy was his learning. Did I not know that you were already favorable to him, I would write you to commend him to the elector, but there is no need of spurring one running of his own accord. . . .

163. MELANCHTHON TO JOHN OECOLAMPADIUS AT AUGSBURG.

Corpus Reformatorum, i. 87.   WITTENBERG, July 21, 1519.

John Hussgen (Hausschein-Oecolampadius; 1482-1531), a friend of Zwingli and leader in the Swiss Reformation. He studied at Heilbronn and Bologna, and in 1499 took up theology at Heidelberg, winning his M.A. in 1503. In 1513 he matriculated at Tübingen, where he studied Greek with Melanchthon. 1515-8 he was at Basle helping Erasmus edit the New Testament. From 1518 to 1520 he was at Augsburg; in 1520 he entered a monastery to escape the religious controversy, but in 1522 emerged and became the Evangelical pastor of Basle. He took a prominent part in the Marburg Colloquy of 1529. *Realencyclopädie.*

. . . And to begin at the beginning, Eck last year published some notes called *Obelisks* on Luther's *Theses on Indulgences,* and he wrote too bitterly for me to quote anything from them. Carlstadt picked out some of Eck's propositions in *his Theses,* which are published. Eck answered in an *Apology,* which was somewhat milder than the *Obelisks.* Carlstadt confuted the *Apology* in a pamphlet; it was a tedious accusation expressed at length. Omitting details, it was determined to dispute on the chief point. The day was set. Eck, Carlstadt and Luther came together at Leipsic. The subject of the debate was digested in a few propositions to make it more definite. I think you will agree that it is proper in a debate to have notaries take down the speeches and to have their reports published so that each may judge the merits of the debaters. But Eck first told the judges appointed by Duke George of Saxony, that Maecenas of humane letters, that he did not agree to this plan, for he thought that the nature of the debate precluded its being reported, for that the force of the debaters was increased by speaking *ex tempore* and would be decreased by the delay of writing, that while minds were stimulated by rapidity they would be enervated by delay. But it seems to me that this is just what is to be desired. . . . You know how Nazianzen advises this, and how Erasmus does. [Follows a description of the debate between Carlstadt and Eck on free will.]

Then Martin descended into the arena, for up to this time it was uncertain whether he would debate, because he was not able to appoint judges in such a delicate matter saving his right to appeal. However when this was settled he began to debate on the power of the Pope and on whether it could be considered as existing *jure divino.* For he frankly confessed its existence *de facto,* and only disputed the divine right. As the dispute waxed somewhat sharp, five days were spent on this point. Eck spoke bitterly and discourteously and tried every means to excite odium against Luther among the people. Eck's first argument was that the Church could not be without a head, since it was a corporate body, and therefore that the Pope was, *jure divino,* head of the Church. Then Martin said that Christ was the head of the Church, which, being spiritual, needed no other, as is said in Colossians, i. [verse 18]. Eck replied by citing several passages from Jerome and Cyprian, which he thought proved the divine right. But now certain passages in those writers whom he cited as sure supporters, were quoted as showing that they were doubtful. He boasted the authority of Bernard's epistle to Eugenius, as if it were Achilles in his magic armour, although there are certain things in that very book which support Luther's position. Moreover, who is so stupid as not to see what small authority Bernard could have had in this matter? From the gospel Eck quoted the text, "Thou art Peter, and upon this rock I will found my Church." Luther interpreted that as a confession of faith; said that Peter represented the Church and that the rock on which Christ founded the Church was himself; and he proved this by the order of the words. Again that text: "Feed my sheep," was said to Peter, alone and privately, as Luther alleged, after the like authority had been given to all the apostles, in the words, "Receive the Holy Spirit, and whose sins ye loose on earth shall be loosed unto them in heaven, etc." With these words, he said, Christ showed what it was to feed the sheep and what sort of man he wished the shepherd to be. Against this Eck urged the authority of the Council of Constance, where Luther's proposition had been condemned as one of Huss's articles and where it was said that it was necessary to salvation to believe the Roman pontiff was universal. He advanced several reasons to show that a council could not err. Luther prudently replied that all the condemned articles should not be considered heretical, and he added more on the authority of a council, which it would be tiresome to report here. Plainly, however, a council cannot found articles of faith. The audience did not care for this proposition, because it seemed as if Luther were resisting the power of councils, whereas he really desires nothing more devoutly than their authority. He was therefore accused of heresy, Hussite opinions and crimes of that nature. Eck conceded that the authority of all apostles was equal, but that it did not follow that all bishops were equal. . . .

After this they debated on the power of the Pope over souls in purgatory, and Eck took a new tack and began to prove from the text in Maccabees that purgatory[1] existed. Luther, following Jerome, denied that Maccabees was authoritative. . . .

In Luther, now long familiarly known to me, I admire a lively talent, learning and eloquence, and cannot help loving his sincere and entirely Christian mind. Greet our common friends. You know the Greek proverb, that there is much vain boasting in war. Wherefore do not believe all that is told you about the result of this debate. Farewell.

164. JOHN ECK TO ELECTOR FREDERIC OF SAXONY.
Enders, ii. 90. German.   Leipsic, July 22, 1519.

Serene, high-born Elector! My humble, ready service to your Grace, together with my poor prayers to God for you. Most gracious Lord! I humbly pray your Grace not to take it ill nor with displeasure that I have allowed myself to debate with your Grace's professors from Wittenberg, for I did not do it to hurt your Grace's university, but, on the contrary, am much inclined to serve your Grace, as one who

---

[1] Maccabees xii. 43-6, reads in the Vulgate: "Et facta collatione, duodecim millia drachmas argenti misit Jerosolymam offerri pro peccatis mortuorum sacrificium, bene et religiose de resurrectione cogitans, (nisi enim eos, qui ceciderant, resurrecturos speraret, superfluum videretur, et vanum orare pro mortuis,) et quia considerabat, quod hi, qui cum pietate dormitionem acceperant, optimam haberent repositam gratiam. Sancta ergo, et salubris est cogitatio pro defunctis exorare, ut a peccatis solvantur." On Luther's opinion of Maccabees, *infra*, no. 194.

is renowned before other princes of the Empire *for cherishing letters and learned men.*[1] But only for the sake of the truth of the holy faith have I debated, and because Dr. Carlstadt compelled me to by printing and publishing certain Conclusions with many words of contempt and reviling against me, although he had no cause to insult people thus. As to Dr. Luther, whom I pity because of the *singular excesses*[1] into which his fair *genius*[1] has fallen in taking up this matter, I was compelled to answer him because of his publication of a great deal of stuff from which, in my poor opinion, much error and scandal will arise. Your Grace may judge that he does not to this day in the least moderate his views, in that on a certain matter he denies and repudiates the opinion of the holy fathers Augustine, Ambrose, Jerome, Gregory, Leo, Cyprian, Chrysostom and Bernard. It sounds evil for a Christian to presume to say that of his own wisdom he understands the sense of Holy Scripture better than the holy Fathers. It is also hard to hear him say, as he did in the debate, that many articles of John Huss and the Bohemians, condemned by the holy Council of Constance, are *most Christian* and *evangelic.*[1] It is easy to imagine what joy the heretics conceive on hearing such things. He also says that St. Peter did not have the *primacy*[1] over the other apostles from Christ, and many other things. As a Christian prince your Grace may judge whether these and similar things may be allowed in Christianity. In my poor opinion they cannot be; wherefore, solely for the sake of the truth, I will withstand them where I can.

Neither Dr. Luther nor anyone else can say that he has received a pennyworth of his doctrine from our Holy Father, the Pope, or from the great heads of the Church. Yet I, although a poor parson, came here at my own expense to meet your Grace's professors, and am still ready, if Dr. Luther thinks he has not yet debated enough, to go with him to Cologne, Louvain or Paris. For I know just what they will do. For when they proposed to me the University of Leipsic, they would have had it thought that they had refused to debate there, but that I compassed it with the prince and

[1] The words in italics are Latin.

the university. Most gracious Lord, I do not mean to reproach Dr. Luther with all this, nor do I write to injure him, but only to excuse myself to your Grace, who would otherwise hear untruths to my dishonor; and I also give your Grace *occasion*[1] to consider what you owe to Christ, the Christian religion, the land and the people. Long ago I desired to excuse myself to your Grace, and came to your Grace's court at Augsburg[2] six times, and I know not for what reason I was not allowed to come before your Grace.

Although your Grace's professors departed with sundry threats to write much, I debated in such wise that it would be unnecessary to write anything. For we made an agreement to keep still[3] until judgment shall have been given by the universities selected as umpires. Wherefore I left them free choice of all the universities which are in good repute in the whole of Christendom, to take which ones they liked. Well, let them write; I don't care much, only I wish they wrote with the seriousness demanded by the subject, and not so frivolously, impertinently and abusively, especially as I am sure your Grace has no pleasure in such words. What is written by theologians should be in such language that anyone who reads it may understand that a theologian has written it with the purpose of seeking the truth, and not like a groom who is only able to revile people. . . .

Your Grace's obedient chaplain,
DR. JOHN VON ECK.

P. S.—Most gracious Lord, it has just occurred to me that in debating with Dr. Luther *on the power of the Pope*,[1] I took away the whole foundation of his argument. For his position is not novel, many mistaken persons have held it before. But if from mere suspicion he has conceived the opinion that some of your Grace's subjects have given me his recently printed book[4] (as they have told Caesar Pflug that they think Dr. Peter Burckhart[5] has done so), let me say that it is false

[1] Latin.
[2] During the Diet of 1518; Luther saw Eck at Augsburg in October. *Cf.* *supra*, no. 96.
[3] Before the debate all parties agreed not to publish the arguments until the judges had decided. Enders, ii. 71.
[4] *Resolutio . . . de Potestate Papae*, Weimar, ii. 180.
[5] Since September, 1518, professor of medicine at Wittenberg. In the sum-

and that they do Dr. Burckhart and the others wrong, for he has never mentioned the matter to me and I have not yet seen the book, unless, as I thought, he read from it at the debate. But I know well enough from similar writings what it contains. Your Grace would do a praiseworthy act to burn it on a bonfire.

165. JOHN ECK TO JAMES HOCHSTRATEN AT COLOGNE.
Lutheri Opera varii argumenti (Erlangen, 1866), iii. 476.

LEIPSIC, July 24, 1519.

James Hochstraten (Hoogstraaten) studied at Louvain, where he took his M. A. in 1485. He became a Dominican, was made prior and eventually chief inquisitor for many years. He was the leading prosecutor of Reuchlin for heresy. He took an active part against Erasmus (*infra*, no. 187) and Luther, who wrote against him, very briefly, in 1519. Weimar, ii. 384. He wrote against Luther *Epitome de Fide et Operibus* in 1525. He died in 1527. N. Paulus: *Die deutschen Dominikaner*, p. 87ff.

I would not have you ignorant, Reverend Father, how I have hitherto withstood those rash men of Wittenberg who despise all the doctors of the last four hundred years, no matter how holy and wise, and who disseminate many false and erroneous ideas among the people, seducing and infecting them chiefly by means of works printed in German.

Recently we disputed at Leipsic, before an audience of learned men, who had come together from all parts, where (praise, honor and glory be to God), their reputation, even with the vulgar, was much diminished, and was completely destroyed with most learned men. You should have heard their rash assertions, how blind they were and bold to commit crimes.

Luther denies that Peter was the prince of the apostles; he denies that obedience is owed to the Church by divine law, but only by human agreement, that is, by agreement of the Emperor. He denies that the Church was built on Peter.[1] When I cited on this point Augustine, Jerome, Ambrose, Greg-

---

mer of 1521 he went to Ingolstadt, where he died in the spring of 1526. He became a strong opponent of Luther. He had studied medicine at Ferrara, and taught it at Ingolstadt after 1497. *Zeitschrift für Kirchengeschichte*, xviii. 77.

[1] Matthew xvi. 18.

ory, Cyprian, Chrysostom, Leo, Bernard and Theophilus, he repudiated them all without blushing, and said that he alone would oppose all of them, relying only on the text that Christ was the foundation of the Church, and that other foundation no man can lay.[1] I did away with this by citing Revelation xii.[2] about the twelve foundations. Luther also defended the Greeks and schismatics, saying that they would be saved even if they are not under the obedience of the Pope.

Of the articles of the Bohemians, he says that some of those condemned by the Council of Constance are most Christian and evangelic; by which rash error he frightened many, and alienated those who had previously supported him.

Among other things I said to him: If the primacy of the Pope is merely a matter of human law and of the agreement of the faithful, where does he (Luther) get the dress he wears? where does he get the power of preaching and of hearing the confessions of his parishioners, etc.? He answered that he wished there were no mendicant orders, and many other scandalous and absurd things, as that a council, consisting of men, could err, and that purgatory was not proved by the Bible, as you may see by reading our debate, which was taken down by faithful notaries. . . .

There were many of them; besides the two doctors, there was their Vicar Lang, two licentiates in theology,[3] a nephew[4] of Reuchlin who assumes a good deal, three doctors of law, several professors, who aided him privately and publicly even in the course of the debate. But I alone, with nothing but right on my side, withstood them.

To brothers of your order I committed the care of copying the debate and sending it to you as soon as possible. Wherefore I pray you by him whom I serve, zealously to defend the faith as you long ago undertook to do. I do not wish you to involve yourself or make either your person or your order odious, but please aid me with your advice and learning. The Wittenbergers hesitated to debate; in fact, they

[1] 1 Corinthians, iii. 11.
[2] Rather, xxi. 14.
[3] A number of professors and two hundred students accompanied Luther to Leipsic; *cf. supra,* no. 160.
[4] Melanchthon.

sought excuses. Luther was at first unwilling to take as judge any university in the world. The most Christian Duke George of Saxony would not allow any dispute on articles of faith unless it should be referred for judgment to the masters of our faith. Luther was therefore forced and spurred on by his followers, for had he not debated and admitted some judge, they would all have receded from him. When I then offered him his choice of all the universities, he chose Paris and Erfurt.

As I know that your university has close relations with Paris, I beg you earnestly, for the sake of Christ's faith, to write to your friends there, or even, if it seem good, to the whole university, that when the excellent Duke George shall write them and send the debate with a request for judgment they may not decline, but should undertake it like champions, as we have both agreed to them as judges, and I think the matter is so plain that it will not need long discussion. . . .

On the day of St. Peter,[1] in the absence of the duke, Luther delivered at court a sermon full of Hussite errors. Straightway on the day[2] of the Visitation of the Virgin and the day after, I preached against his errors to a larger audience than I have ever had, and I stirred up in the people disgust for Lutheran errors, and I will do the same to-morrow when I bid Leipsic good-bye. . . .

166. LUTHER TO JOHN LANG AT ERFURT.

Enders, ii. 97. (WITTENBERG), July 26, 1519.

Greeting. Reverend Father, I found the Vicar General[3] at Grimma, together with Wenzel Link, making a round of visits to the convents under their charge. You did well to abstain from visiting them. For he said it was his business now. I fear that the prior[4] there will give up his place. We are daily expecting the advent of his reverence[3] from Dres-

---
[1]June 29. On this *cf.* Smith, *op. cit.*, 67.
[2]July 2.
[3]Staupitz. Luther met him as he was returning from the Leipsic debate. Luther apparently left Leipsic while Carlstadt was still debating, on July 15 or 16. He was at Wittenberg on July 20. He does not now describe the debate more fully as Lang was present.
[4]Wolfgang Zeschau, spoken of by Luther, November 5, 1518. Enders, i. 276, later Master of the Hospice of St. John at Grimma.

den or Herzberg. He told me to notify you and all others
that I could of his arrival; please do the same. Eck is singing a song of triumph everywhere. He has been taken by
Duke George[1] to Annaberg, perhaps to resuscitate indulgences
there. More presently. Farewell.

      BROTHER MARTIN LUTHER, *Augustinian.*

167. MELANCHTHON TO SPALATIN.

Corpus Reformatorum, i. 103.   July 29, 1519.

. . . Here you have Luther's *Resolution*[2] written, as you
think, bitterly, but as I think, prudently. You see how he
repels hatred and transfers it all into this fire-brand and
author of the whole war. But I hope he will write more on
the other propositions and dedicate it to you. . . .

168. MARTIN BUCER TO BEATUS RHENANUS.

A. Horawitz & K. Hartfelder: *Briefwechsel des Beatus Rhenanus.*
1886, p. 165.   HEIDELBERG, July 30, 1519.

. . . Behold, dear Beatus, how vigilant are these wicked
men, and how they conspire to murder, not Luther or others,
but Truth herself. I have read Erasmus' epistle[3] to Elector
Frederic of Saxony, deploring this. It was written from
Antwerp, and made me suspect that he was so sick of the
quarrels with the professors of Louvain that he had left that
university. Certainly they are unworthy of so divine a genius.
Smitten with grief on this account, I wished to write it to
you, my only defence, hoping that you might have something
happier to write back. We have little hope left here. One
day when I was presiding at some stupid debates (for there
is a great dearth of learned men here), I made some propositions differing from their rules, and barely escaped stoning.
My chief offence was that I defended the proposition that
charity was commanded to our neighbor. Next to that was a
proposition on divorce, which was debated fiercely.

---

[1] Duke George went to Annaberg to the consecration of a church on July 24,
Eck following him next day. An indulgence was proclaimed on this occasion.
[2] *Resolutio Lutheriana super Propositione sua Tertia decima de Potestate Papae.*
Leipsic, 1519. Weimar, ii. 180.
[3] *Supra,* no. 141.

Not only Louvain[1] and Cologne, but Oxford[2] and Cambridge have declared war on Luther, their purpose being to ruin Christian philosophy[3] and crush polite learning. The leaders are said to be Cajetan and Adrian, both cardinals.[4] For the delegates of Louvain and Cologne agreed with Cajetan at Coblenz that he should keep the sale of indulgences as his department and leave the rest to them. They were going to cavil at this, but he, much more courteous than they, yielded to them, for it was his opinion that it would be sufficient to brand as error that which they attacked as the crime of heresy. For I have learned from a trustworthy friend, in whom Cajetan confided, that there was almost no page in a book of Luther's on which they had not written "heresy, heresy," several times. They showed the book thus disfigured to the cardinal, led perhaps by their own prejudice to hope that he would endorse their judgment at once. But when he had examined the book and their dirty notes, he said: "We must not strike out too much. There is a very slight difference between some things which you have called heresies and the orthodox view. They are errors, not heresies. Let James[5] be an example to you." . . .

169. NICHOLAS VON AMSDORF TO SPALATIN.

Walch, xv. 1404. German.   WITTENBERG, August 1, 1519.

Greeting. It would be long and prolix to relate the order and procedure of the Leipsic debate; much more prolix and tedious to describe the same. For as often as I think of the said debate, I am moved and kindled, not, as God knows, for the love I bear Dr. Luther but for that I bear the truth. I doubt not that truth is certain, unchangeable and eternal, though hated by all gross fellows. Even before this time I

[1] *Cf.* de Jongh: *L'ancienne Faculté de théologie à Louvain*, p. 206ff. Luther's works arrived in the Netherlands at latest early in 1519, and their sale was immediately forbidden by the University of Louvain, which, at the same time, despatched a messenger to get the opinion of the University of Cologne on Luther. The condemnation of him by Cologne followed on August 30.
[2] I can find no other reference so early as this to any action of the English universities against Luther. It was abundantly true later.
[3] "Philosophia Christi" was the name adopted by Erasmus for his system.
[4] Paliatus; this is evidently the meaning, though not given in Du Cange.
[5] Probably Hochstraten, or James, iii. 1, iv. 11, v. 20. On this whole affair, *cf.* De Jongh, *op. cit.*

knew that what Eck and his supporters brought forth was falsehood.

This is not remarkable, for Eck is entirely unversed in the Holy Scriptures. And, what is more, he does not even know as much sophistry[1] as a man who wants to be thought so great a debater ought, for he boasts and claims to be a father and patron of sophistry. For I have smelled about a little, and understand the affair rightly (although I have neither reason nor discrimination), namely, that Eck speaks all that is in his mind and memory without reason, judgment or discrimination, although he can utter the words he has learned with great pomp and proper gesture. He does not seek the truth, but only to show off his memory and to defend the teachers of his school. . .

That you may believe that what I say is true, hear a text of the Bible which, with the counsel of the inept and unlearned sophists of Leipsic, Eck cited and brought forward to defend papal indulgence. It stands in Isaiah lxi. 1: "The spirit of the Lord is upon me; therefore the Lord has anointed me to preach good tidings unto the meek; he hath sent me to bind up the broken-hearted, to proclaim to the captives indulgence,"[2] that is, forgiveness of sins. See, my dear Spalatin, this one word (indulgence), which these famous sophists of Leipsic found in the large Concordance to the Bible, wrote for Eck with chalk upon a blackboard and sent to him the following day to support papal indulgences which have recently been invented for the sake of gain. For the prophet[3] does not speak of the forgiveness of sins by indulgence, but of our Lord and Saviour becoming a man. Just look at the unhappy, stupid sophists. But I am not surprised, for they know nothing. But I am surprised that Eck took the said text into the debate and uttered it before so remarkable an assembly, and dictated it to the notaries.

It is true, however, that Eck surpassed Dr. Carlstadt by far in memory and delivery, so that I was sorry that the thing had been begun, not because Eck won the victory, but because, had

---
[1] Amsdorf means scholastic learning, but the effect is comic.
[2] "Indulgentiam" in the Vulgate; "liberty" in our authorized version.
[3] After all, which was the more unhistorical error, that of Eck or that of Amsdorf?

the speeches not been taken down in writing, our champions would have come off with great shame. For Eck argues and turns around in the Italian manner with nine or ten arguments by which he does not seek to establish the truth, but only his own honor, just as all sophists, that is, all schoolmen, do. . . . But the audience consider him the victor who shouts the loudest and has the last word, and for these reasons the men of Leipsic honor Eck as the victor. . . .

I do not consider Eck equal to Luther either in doctrine or art, either in delivery or in memory; I would as soon compare stones or mere filth to the purest gold. . . .

170. MELANCHTHON TO JOHN LANG AT ERFURT.

Corpus Reformatorum, i. 106.   WITTENBERG, August 11, 1519.

. . . Eck reviled us with fierce and uncivil calumnies, either to indulge his own temper or because he thought himself insulted and thus revenged himself. . . . After our departure he disseminated a large number of false slanders about Luther among the princes. What can you do to him? I love and cling to the pious zeal and learning of Luther as much as I do to any human thing. . . .

171. LUTHER TO GEORGE SPALATIN.

Enders, ii. 124.   (WITTENBERG, before August 18, 1519.)

Greeting. Please let me know, Spalatin, if possible, what you wanted done about the foundation for commemorating the Passion.[1] I am not much in favor of binding a man to certain stated services, unless it is a man who is profited by such a rule.

We all beg you to send us a copy[2] of the Leipsic debate by this messenger. We have a reason for wanting it, which you will learn in due time. As we ask you we have no doubt that you will comply. Farewell and pray for me, a very busy

---

[1] The Elector, at the suggestion of his confessor, James Vogt, in 1519, endowed a foundation for two priests and eight acolites to sing Psalms on certain days in the Wittenberg Castle Church.

[2] This was a manuscript copy of the minutes of the debate, which had been sent by Melanchthon to Spalatin on August 11.

sinner. May the Lord preserve our elector[1] for us. Amen.

BROTHER MARTIN LUTHER, *Augustinian.*

172. LUTHER AND CARLSTADT TO THE ELECTOR FREDERIC.

Enders, ii. 126. De Wette, i. 307. German.

WITTENBERG, August 18, 1519.

Most serene, high-born Prince, most gracious Lord! Our humble, obedient service and prayers for your Grace. Most gracious Prince and Lord! We have received your Grace's note with Dr. Eck's letter[2] and noted the contents. Dr. Eck says he does not intend to slander us before your Grace, and yet labors with his sophistry and habitual loose talk to get your Grace, only on the strength of his letter and hasty judgment, to drive us out of the land. We are not surprised that he considers your Grace such a person as he dares address such a letter to. For we learn every day more clearly that Dr. Eck is and remains Dr. Eck, do what he will.

May your Grace not take it ill that we have not given you an account of this debate before. For we esteem it an unfortunate affair, carried on with mere hate and envy, wherefore we did not wish to be the first of whom people could say (as Dr. Eck unnecessarily fears that they will) that we desired with our glory to shame others. But as we are forced by Dr. Eck's letter, we pray that your Grace will hear the affair with kindly patience, although we are sorry to inflict so long and unprofitable a story on your Grace. But the affair will speak for itself, and show whether Dr. Eck, with all his boasting and protestation, is inclined to serve or to hurt your Grace's university.

In the first place, Dr. Eck complains that I, Andrew Carlstadt, published certain theses against him, with sarcasms and contemptuous words, although he does not think that I have any right to insult people. I reply: Dr. Eck can esteem me as he likes, but it would have mightily become him, had he, along with his complaint, told how he attacked Dr. Luther,

[1]The elector was ill in 1519. To console him Luther wrote the *Tesseradecas.* Smith, *op. cit.,* p. 78.
[2]*Supra,* no. 164.

to revile and shame us and your Grace's university. His words would have been too much even for a bad woman, for in his poisonous *Obelisks,* he reviled him as a *Hussite, a heretic, a rebel, a shameless brawler, a new prophet,*[1] and everything else he pleased, more than twenty times as much as I, who was too moderate against his misconduct, ever called him for the vindication of our honor.

For I think Dr. Eck has much less right, not only to revile such a man, but to slander all of us, to the shame of your Grace's university, and so criminally to libel us without any ground or reason. And if the goad pricks Dr. Eck too hard, the said *Obelisks* are at hand, and we will publish them, which hitherto, to spare his honor, we have refrained from doing. We have deserved his great ingratitude by not paying him back in kind. And if necessary, we will also collect on paper all the ugly, sharp, disagreeable words and gestures with which he made the debate a simple obstacle to the truth. . . .

May God reward him for pitying me, Martin Luther. I would only like to hear what are the *"singular excesses,"* for which he so mercifully punishes me. But I can have nothing to do with him on articles of faith, except perhaps in that of penitence; as for my *opinion on indulgences, purgatory and the power of the Pope,* I confess that, "according to his poor opinion" (as he truly says), I have made much scandal and offence, not for the common people, but for the Pharisees and scribes, for whom also Christ and all the apostles made offence. Truly, I cannot stop doing this even now, whether it wins the "good opinion" of Dr. Eck or not.

He blames me shamelessly for denying the authority of all the holy fathers at once, Augustine, Ambrose, Jerome, Gregory, Leo, Chrysostom, etc., and for arrogating to myself alone the understanding of Scripture. Thus it is fitting that a doctor of divinity should speak out roundly and forcibly before a prince. Your Grace may note how much inclined Dr. Eck is to serve us, in daring cheerfully to write such things about us. Had he said that I had contradicted some fathers, he would have had a show of reason, but his own clear con-

[1] Here and elsewhere in this letter the words printed in italics are Latin in the original.

science knows that it is not true that I contradicted them all. Let me tell your Grace the exact truth: I did, indeed, set one doctor, with the text of the Bible, against another, whom Dr. Eck cited alone, naked and without the Bible, and I will not cease doing this my life long. That is what Dr. Eck calls contradicting all the holy Fathers, and says that it sounds badly in the new Eckian Christianity. . . .

For I have said that when I had a clear text I would stand by it even if the exegesis of the teachers was contrary to the sense. St. Augustine often does this and teaches us to do it. For, as the lawyers say, we should put more faith in one man who has the Bible for him, than in the Pope and a whole council without the Bible. From this, my dear friends, Dr. Eck and the men of Leipsic conclude roundly that I have repudiated all teachers. What can one do with such false tongues and hearts? In like manner he has thrown up at me the Council of Constance, and accuses me of contradicting it. I will answer this charge in due time, and show his false heart to the world. . . .

[The rest of this letter is a long argument of ten pages on the power of the Pope and other points which came up in the debate with Eck.]

173. LUTHER TO SPALATIN.

Enders, ii. 129.   WITTENBERG, August 18, 1519.

Greeting. Behold, Spalatin, we are sending letters to the illustrious elector, our patron, in answer to the calumnies of Eck. We should be pleased if the illustrious elector will deign to send them to Eck; but if not, God's will be done. For the reverend Vicar Staupitz has made us doubtful whether the elector would have wished us to answer Eck in this style, and not rather with the Latin propositions[1] on which we are now working; wherefore we are sending both. But if the German letter is to be sent, we desire that anything in it be changed, which either the elector or you think should be changed. I have looked for Eck's letter among my papers without finding it; I will seek more diligently.

[1] *Resolutiones Lutherianae super propositionibus suis*, Weimar, ii. 391. *Cf.* Enders, ii. 102.

Eck (whom now, without sin, we may judge and accuse) is ever playing the part of neither a good man nor a gentleman. He gave the Bishop of Brandenburg a memorial on the articles which the brothers of Jüterbogk have falsely cooked up against me.[1] The man is impudent and shameless, ready to assert or deny anything for a little puff of glory. His only aim is by right or wrong to hurt Wittenberg. I am opposing him, and with God's help will expose the sycophant and his lies to the public.

Meantime the Bishop of Brandenburg, without hearing the other side, is spreading abroad Eck's falsehoods, and by his name giving them, in the eyes of many, authority, thus hurting me, and showing fairly the animus he has always had towards me. I fear that I can hardly do anything without involving him, and betraying how like his ignorance and rashness is to that of Eck. The Franciscans are working with them; we are the only ones whose press is too slow to publish our answer quickly.

According to your wish I have begun publicly to apply myself to the foundation for commemorating Christ's Passion,[2] and the more I think of it the less I find to please me. The Church is already overburdened with ceremonies, so that almost all the serious concerns of Christian piety have degenerated into superstition. This means to have an easy faith in external works and complacently to leave out the real spiritual essence. Wherefore I am not yet prepared to say how I can make this foundation at once seemly without and fruitful within. It is difficult to combine both, since the gospel has placed the most excellent piety in fraternal love and mutual good-will. I will write more later. Farewell, and commend me to my patron the elector.

MARTIN LUTHER, *Augustinian.*

[1]Francis Günther became preacher at Jüterbogk and in Passion Week, 1519, delivered a series of sermons containing various propositions considered heretical by the Franciscans of that village. These friars published a broadside entitled *Articuli per Fratres Minores de observantia propositi . . . Episcopo Brandenburgensi contra Lutheranos,* which came into Luther's hands in May and was answered by him on May 15. Enders, ii. 36. When the Elector Joachim of Brandenburg visited Leipsic in the summer of 1519, he requested Eck's opinion on these charges, which was given in a memorial handed to the Bishop of Brandenburg.

[2]*Cf. supra,* no. 171.

174. PHILIP MELANCHTHON TO THE READER.
Corpus Reformatorum, i. 120.   WITTENBERG (c. August), 1519.

This is one of the prefaces, written under the pseudonym of Otho Germanus, to Luther's *Commentary on Galatians,* which appeared early in September.

. . . It seems, therefore, that we have very little true theology left. But if any one calls attention to this he is dubbed a heretic and schismatic for his pains. Thus it happened to Luther, a man respected for his manner of life and uncommonly learned in sacred letters. When he was forced to propose certain theses for scholastic debate in order to resist those who, under the pretext of religion abused the Scripture for their own desires, and when in doing so he had differed from theologians of indulgences and of Aristotle, first he was cited to Rome under the grave suspicion of heresy. Then, on account of the difficulty of the journey and moved by the prayers of friends, he was allowed to go to Augsburg instead; but when he had gone there he was tried by various arts and sent away so that he does not yet know why he went there. But, at least, it is certain that a man who deserved well of Christendom on account of his serious and fruitful treatment of the Scriptures (as his numerous auditors can bear witness), was treated as a madman by certain coxcombs. If he speaks of this and complains of it in the following epistle,[1] it may not be pleasant, but it will be necessary. Moreover, while he was thus defamed and his life imperilled, he composed, among other profitable works, this commentary on the epistle of Paul to the Galatians. And being unable to polish it on account of his preoccupations with his enemies, he disdained to call it a regular commentary, and it was published by his friends against his will.[2] . . .

175. LUTHER TO JOHN LANG AT ERFURT.
Enders, ii. 138.   (WITTENBERG), September 3, 1519.

Greeting. Reverend Father, I wonder why your Erfurt

[1] Luther's dedicatory epistle to Lupinus and Carlstadt, January, 1519, is meant. *Supra,* no. 123.
[2] *The Commentary on Galatians* is, in fact, the most polished of Luther's commentaries, the style having been probably revised by Melanchthon. *Cf.* Ellinger: *Philip Melanchthon,* 100.

professors are so slow.¹ I await their judgment, although I expect that they will be too prudent to mix in these foreign and hateful causes. Meanwhile, we have anticipated their sentence; we judge each other and are judged by each other;² ignorant and learned alike, we all write poems.³

Eck impetuously scatters letters⁴ around and distributes triumphal crowns. Leipsic alone brings forth simple Herodoti, critics, Aristarchi,⁵ Momi,⁶ and that kind of frogs without number. Leipsic, who was always dumb, has only on account of the debate begun to bark louder than many Scyllas. She is driven by wretched envy to try to establish the victory of our opponents by mere clamor. Truth will conquer.

I would send my little lectures on the Psaltery, but because you do not write whether you want them, or how many of them you have, I suppose you do not care for them. This man⁷ sells my last *Resolutions* against Eck. Lotther,⁸ at Leipsic, is printing for me an apology⁹ against him, in which I refute the thirteen articles charged against me by the Franciscans of Jüterbok, and hatefully proved by Eck to be heretical; on my part I charge them with twenty-four articles, and the quarrel is getting warm.

They tell me my Commentary on Galatians is finished to-day.

Our illustrious elector is tempted by Miltitz with the golden rose.¹⁰ Miltitz boasted in Dresden, "Dr. Luther is in my

---

¹*I. e.*, in giving judgment on the Leipsic debate.
²This refers to Melanchthon's letter to Oecolampadius of July 21 (*supra*, 163), and to Eck's reply.
³*Scribimus indocti doctique poemata passim, cf.* Juvenal, vii. 53.
⁴*Cf. supra*, Eck to Elector Frederic, no. 164.
⁵A proverbially bitter critic.
⁶According to Erasmus' *Adages, s. v.*, Momus was the child of Night and Sleep, who did nothing but find fault.
⁷*I. e.*, the bearer of the letter.
⁸Of Aue in Saxony, first found at Leipsic about 1500, as a printer. From 1518 he printed a number of Luther's things, and toward the end of 1519, with types bought of Froben, and with his younger brother Michael (for Melchior and Michael Lotther were apparently not old Melchior's sons, as Enders thinks, ii. 29), he started a press at Wittenberg. In 1525, on account of slanders about him, he returned to Leipsic, where he died in 1542. Enders, *loc. cit.,* and v. 24.
⁹*Contra malignum Eccii judicium*, Weimar, ii. 621.
¹⁰On the golden rose *cf. supra*, January 1, 1519. Miltitz got the rose from the Fuggers at Augsburg and took it to Altenburg, where, in the absence of the elector, who lay sick at Lochau, he gave it, on September 25, to one of his officers.

hands,"[1] but by God's grace he accomplishes nothing. Farewell and pray for me, a very busy brother.

BROTHER MARTIN LUTHER.

176. LUTHER TO GEORGE SPALATIN.

Enders, ii. 156. WITTENBERG, September 22, 1519.

Greeting. At length, Spalatin, my *Tesseradecas*[2] is coming to you, late, indeed, but even thus hardly having weathered the storms of all my other occupations. If you care to, you may translate it and offer it to our most illustrious elector with a prefatory letter. For I have begun to consider it too minute a thing for a double epistolary dedication to the elector, like a two-handed loving-cup.[3]

I am also sending my "foolish Galatians,"[4] preserved in the brine of wit.[5] Lotther, of Leipsic, sent them to be given to you, as you see. My work against Buck Emser is not yet done.[6] . . .

The bearer of this letter begs me to write to the elector for him for license to exercise the baker's craft at Wittenberg. For I hear that the bakers have forbidden him to do so because he is son of a man who was once a bathman; so exclusive is the nobility of tradesmen. Lest I should annoy the elector, I ask you to make this petition to him, in my name if you wish.

But, dear me, I almost forgot to say that I would like to see my copy of the *Tesseradecas* again after it has served its time. For I am wont to console myself with these trifles, nor do I always have before me the considerations which I there set down, if only for the reason that by thinking of them they become ever richer. Farewell and commend me to the elector.

MARTIN LUTHER, *Augustinian*.

[1] Miltitz's words in German.
[2] Weimar, vi. 99. *Cf.* Smith, *op. cit.*, 78.
[3] A pun; "ampulla" means both a cup with two handles and bombast.
[4] *Cf.* Galatians, iii. 1.
[5] "Multo sale conditos"; I use "wit" in the old-fashioned sense of general intellectual keenness. From the stylistic standpoint, the Galatians was the most carefully prepared of all Luther's commentaries.
[6] *Contra Aegocerotem Emserum*, one of the sequels of the Leipsic debate. Weimar, ii. 655.

177. LUTHER TO THE ELECTOR FREDERIC OF SAXONY.

Enders, ii. 181. De Wette, i. 339. German.

WITTENBERG, October 1, 1519.

Most serene, high-born Prince, most gracious Lord! I humbly give your Grace to know that Charles von Miltitz has written me to appoint a day to meet him at Liebenwerda, as your Grace may see by his enclosed letter. As I am better aware of Miltitz's pretence than perhaps he thinks, I did not wish to do this without your Grace's knowledge, but have appointed him Sunday week, October 9, not having been able to find an earlier date. I humbly beg, if it please your Grace, to send him my letter with your Grace's messenger. I commend myself obediently to your Grace. May God long and blessedly maintain you. Amen.

Your Grace's obedient chaplain,
DR. MARTIN LUTHER, *Augustinian.*

178. LUTHER TO JOHN STAUPITZ.

Enders, ii. 182. (WITTENBERG), October 3, 1519.

Greeting. I send two copies of "foolish Galatians,"[1] reverend Father. I do not care for what I have written, as I see the epistle could have been expounded so much more fully and clearly; but who can do all things at once or many things at the same time? I trust the work may prove clearer than previous ones written by others, even if it does not satisfy me. My commentary on the Psalms is in press, but is delayed by the slow printer.

Our elector, now restored to health, remains at Lochau. Charles von Miltitz has appointed next Sunday to meet me at Liebenwerda; he has the consent of the elector and his letter was honeyed, but I know him for a fox. I know not what will happen at this interview. He has at length brought the golden rose to Altenburg, having tried to bring it to Wittenberg with great pomp. The elector was absent when he arrived. . . .

I have just received letters[2] from two utraquist priests of

---

[1] *Cf.* Galatians, iii. 1.
[2] *Supra,* no. 161. The Hussites had gathered at the Leipsic debate. Luther read the book of Huss early in 1520, it was the *De Ecclesia.* For its great influence on him, *cf.* Smith, *op. cit.,* 71f.

Prague, learned in the Scriptures, together with a book of John Huss, which I have not yet read. They exhort me to constancy and patience and say that I teach pure theology. The letters were Erasmian in both contents and style. They came to me through the court, having been forwarded by Spalatin. Everyone knows of them.

You have seen Melanchthon's *Theses*,[1] somewhat bold, to be sure, but most true. His answers are miracles. If Christ deign, Melanchthon will make many Luthers and a most powerful enemy of scholastic theology, for he knows both their folly and Christ's rock; therefore shall he be mighty. Amen.

Letters have come from France reporting that Erasmus said: "I fear Luther will perish for his righteousness," and of Eck that his name lacks one letter and he should be called "Jeck," which is the Dutch for fool.[2] Thus Christ beats down vainglory, so that him whom Leipsic adores as Eck, all learned men (they say) simply detest as "Jeck."

My Bishop of Brandenburg has brought forth a monster; a fine fellow he is, like Moab, boasting more than he can do. It is reported that he said he would not lie down in peace, until he had burned Luther, "just like this stick," at the same time throwing one on the fire. Thus have Eck's windy words inflated this poor bladder.

So much for others, now about myself. What will you? You are leaving me. I have been sad for you to-day, as a weaned child for his mother. I pray you praise the Lord even in a sinner like me. I hate my wretched life; I fear death; I am empty of faith and full of qualities which, Christ knows, I should much prefer to do without, were it not to serve him thereby.

The Franciscans are holding a chapter here and having such a merry dispute about the stigmata of St. Francis and the glory of his order, that we, who formerly respected both,

---

[1] Denying transubstantiation, *ed.* K. and W. Krafft: *Briefe und Documente*, p. 6.

[2] The same pun was made by Glarean writing from Paris to Zwingli, November, 1520. *Zwinglis Werke* (1904ff), vii. 362. Also by Zwingli, 1524, *ibid*, iii. 81. Jeck is the same as the rare English word, geck (fool) used by Shakespeare: *Cymbeline*, act v., scene iv., line 67. *Cf.* also O. Schade: *Satiren und Pasquille* (1858), i. 48.

now begin to doubt both. For they bring up points which seem more false than true, and the same fate overtakes them in their excessive praise of their founder as has happened to the Dominicans who too greatly lauded St. Thomas Aquinas. Hatred of this fellow Luther leads them into this dispute, and they disseminate rumors that I have preached against the stigmata. Thinking that this gives them a weapon ready to their hand they hope soon to take action against me. I am happy to see that they all love to attack me so that they even invent doctrines and attribute them to me in order to overthrow them, but I regret that they needlessly bring ridicule upon their whole order. It was a man of Erfurt who started this debate, indeed, a colleague of our friend Lang in the university. To-morrow Peter Fontinus[1] will debate, who intends to stab me and all our little dabblers and sciolists by the theory that we ought to have the same insane day-dreams as the ancient fathers. We shall see great feats from these little Franciscan prestidigitators. What needless tragedies such ignoramuses start! I say "needless," because their baccalaureate James,[2] who to-day spoke for the whole company, excelled them all and both of our professors, too, because he was moderate and stated his theses in good form. He is of Zwickau, educated at Wittenberg, equally good and talented. Christ humbles the proud and exalts the lowly.

Last night I had a dream about you; I dreamed that you were leaving me while I wept bitterly, but you waved to me and told me to cease weeping, for you would come back to me, which, indeed, has happened this very day. But now farewell, and pray for me in my wretchedness.

BROTHER MARTIN LUTHER.

179. BONIFACE AMERBACH TO ULRICH ZASIUS AT FREIBURG.

T. Burckhardt-Biedermann: *Bonifacius Amerbach und die Reformation*. Basle, 1894, p. 137.   BASLE, October 3 (1519).

Boniface Amerbach (October 11, 1495-April 5, 1562), son of the

---

[1] Of Borna, hostile to the Reformation until 1525, when he married and became a pastor at Wohlau.

[2] James Führer of Zwickau, took his bachelor's degree at Wittenberg October 2, 1518.

Basle printer, matriculated there 1509, M. A. 1513. He then studied law with Zasius at Freiburg, and with Alciati at Avignon May, 1520-1524, with an interval of May, 1521-May, 1522, at Basle. He took his doctor's degree at Avignon 1525, after which he spent his life teaching and practising law at Basle. He was one of Erasmus' best friends, and his executor. Allen, *op. cit.*, ii. 237.

. . . Martin edits commentaries on Galatians at Wittenberg. It is said that he will soon publish commentaries on the Psalter. We already have in our native tongue his commentary on the Seven Penitential Psalms and his sermon on confession. The speeches of the Leipsic debate are being printed at Leipsic so that Eck, who as an unconquered Thraso, boasts of I know not what triumph, may no longer be able to claim the victory as he does. Indeed, he had the egregious folly to tell Capito he found Martin's lungs full of heresy. How sweet it is to live, especially now, when all sciences and especially theology, on which our salvation depends, have left trifling and are brought back to their sister, light. I send you Luther's pamphlet on the power of the Pope. You will enjoy reading it, I know, for it is Christian and cannot be assailed by the Pope's flatterers with reason, but only with scurrility, for this stiff-necked throng does what cannot be done by reason by reviling and papal thunder. . . .

180. DUKE GEORGE OF SAXONY TO THE UNIVERSITY OF PARIS.

Gess, i. 100. DRESDEN, October 4, 1519.

Greeting. The Rector and Professors of our University of Leipsic are sending you the acute debate of John Eck of Ingolstadt and Martin Luther of Wittenberg, professors of theology, which was held on some matters of theology and the Bible a few days ago with our permission at the University of Leipsic, and which was taken down from the mouths of the debaters by notaries public. Both sides agreed to refer judgment to the canonists and theologians of your ancient university, excluding the Augustinians and Dominicans, and we also desire this for the sake of the public peace and the pure doctrine. . . .

181. LUTHER TO SPALATIN.

Enders, ii. 187.

(LIEBENWERDA, October 9, or WITTENBERG, October 10, 1519.)

First, he[1] bade me give his greetings to our most illustrious elector. Secondly, he told me to give his greeting to you. Thirdly, he asked whether I would stand by the agreement we made at Altenburg to have the Archbishop of Trier as judge. I said I would. This was the last act of our farce. At the end he said that by this conversation he had executed the papal commission, and that, as he was soon going to Rome, he did not wish to leave without having spoken with me about his commission.

MARTIN LUTHER.

P. S.—Instead of a chorus[2] we had a comic dialogue on the power of the Pope, in which we agreed that the Pope did not have by divine right that power which he certainly did have, but that yet he had a sort of commission from the other apostles; and when I asked what other kind of power there could be for the other apostles, he said that it was the same, save that the world had been given to Peter in a different sense. "Ah, we shall soon agree on this matter,"[3] he concluded.

182. LUTHER TO GEORGE SPALATIN.

Enders, ii. 192. (WITTENBERG), October 13, 1519.

Greeting. I never said a word, dear Spalatin, nor even thought of going with Miltitz to Trier. I am surprised at the man's impudence or forgetfulness. When I was hardly brought to come to him at Liebenwerda, is it likely that I should promise to make so much longer a journey in his company? . . . I believe that because he has been frustrated in his hope he thus trifles without conscience, or else that he simply romances according to his custom. A certain doctor, a provost of Kollerburg in Pomerania, who dined here yesterday, told us that Miltitz was such a man. The doctor, who had just come from Rome, went with us to dinner with our

---

[1] I. e., Miltitz, with whom Luther had a meeting at Liebenwerda on October 9, *supra*, no. 177.
[2] Luther evidently thought of the chorus as a sort of entr'acte.
[3] Miltitz's words in German.

Rector, the Duke of Pomerania, and told us that in Rome people thought very little of Miltitz. They say he so boasted of his relationship by marriage with the Dukes of Saxony, that he was always called by the Italians after his relative, the Duke of Saxony. The provost told other vain, ridiculous things about Miltitz, concluding that the man was to be pitied, for as he always had been mocked he always would be. . . .

Please excuse my sudden departure. I did it because I know the name of monks is in bad repute in courts,[1] and also because I did not wish to offend that man of whom I spoke to you, who, I thought, regarded me as an uncongenial guest at table. You know that for the sake of one man we ought to refrain even from lawful acts.[2] You also see how sharply the men of Leipsic observe me. If that man had secretly written to his friends at Leipsic that I had been gay and frivolous, and had played at dice with our baker, would not they have seized this chance to compare my life with the Word, which my teaching makes odious to them, and would not they have thus caused me to become a hindrance to the gospel of Christ?[3] What would they not write, who through Rubeus[4] have blabbed that at Leipsic I carried in my hand a bunch of flowers,[5] for the sake of their odor and beauty? Had they dared they would have said that I wore the flowers on my head. I neither can nor wish to prevent all such stories; I will give place, as far as I can, to weakness and envy. Wherefore I did not hurry away in scorn, but for fear of offending.

A cruel pestilence is raging in Switzerland, having taken off sixteen thousand men, not counting women and children. The provost above mentioned told us this. . . . Vicar Staupitz came safe and sound to Nuremberg on September 24, and thence went to Munich.

[1] "Propter aulas et ollas," literally "by courts and pots," a derogatory way of speaking of courts chiefly recommended by the pun.
[2] *Cf.* 1 Corinthians, viii. 13.
[3] *Cf.* 1 Corinthians, ix. 12.
[4] John Rubeus, a Franconian studying at Leipsic, had published an account of the debate favorable to Eck. For the title of his work, and Montanus's answer to it, *cf.* Enders, ii. 157.
[5] Luther was very fond of flowers, and is usually said to have carried a bouquet of them at the Leipsic debate. *Cf.* Smith, p. 365. But does he not seem to deny this in the passage here translated?

Now I begin to wish and to ask that our answer to the elector be sent to Eck.[1] He has written to the Pope, glorifying himself, and telling how he left us two conquered and prostrate at Leipsic. The man is boasting, boastful, boastified and boastiferous. He even dared to ask the Pope to reimburse him for his expense in this matter. The above mentioned provost told us this. Farewell, in great haste.

BROTHER MARTIN LUTHER.

183. LUTHER TO MARTIN SELIGMANN AT THALMANSFELD.

Enders, ii. 195.   WITTENBERG, October 14, 1519.

Seligmann born at Heilbronn, sympathized with the Reformation, and for a while was a follower of Münzer. He died in 1548. He was in 1519 in a little village near Mansfeld, and wrote to ask Luther if it were permissible to flee from a plague-stricken town.

Greeting. I have received your letter with the questions, excellent Sir, and I greatly approve what you say about fraternal charity and bearing the scourge of God strongly. Would that all Christians were such as those you here describe. But what shall we do if they are not all equal to all things?[2] Ought we not to bear with and support the weak, as Romans xv. teaches?[3] What you say about the duty of bearing one another's burdens[4] seems to me rather to pertain to those against whom you quoted it. For those who flee death are weak, rather than those who await it. Moreover, famine and war are doubtless plagues sent by God as much as is pestilence, as is said frequently by the Prophets. . . .

Wherefore, in my opinion, all men should be exhorted to bear the hand of the Lord with fortitude, but they should not be forced to do so, or called sinners if they do not, or, if they are called sinners, yet they ought to be borne as weaker brethren. Did not Christ bear with the apostles when, fearing death, they woke him up,[5] and did he not bear with the infirmity of Peter,[6] although he reproached him for fearing

---
[1] *Supra*, no. 172. It had already been sent to Eck on October 12. Enders ii. 191.
[2] Adapted from Virgil's "non omnia possumus omnes."
[3] Romans, xv. 1 and xiv. 1.
[4] Galatians, vi. 1.
[5] Matthew, viii. 25f.
[6] Matthew, xiv. 21.

to walk on the sea? If the pestilence and all other scourges of God are to be borne passively, it follows that we have no right to pray the saints of God for bodily health. Then let us remove all physicians and apothecaries, since we are not allowed to seek through them an escape from or remedy of the scourge of God, although even infirmity is a scourge of God. But the divine goodness provides such things for the weak in faith.

But the perfect, who spontaneously seek death, have no need of these things. For when the Church prays to be delivered from the plague, lightning and tempest, she does not pray, as it were, for the weak, in trying to avert the scourges of wrath. It would be an evil prayer, were it not allowable to flee from, repel and shun, as far as possible, the scourge of God. But when a man, of fraternal love, perseveres in these as in other ills, his virtue is perfect and very praiseworthy, and when necessary, is even commanded, as love to one's neighbor. And it is necessary when there is no one else to go to those who are dying of the pestilence, or to serve the sick. For I am sure that the priest who has the cure of souls may not flee or appoint a substitute.

On this matter read the learned epistle of Augustine to Honoratus, which is found in the eleventh part of his legend written by Possidonius, towards the end.[1] He teaches that the shepherd must be with the sheep of Christ, and lay down his life for them,[2] as one whom it behooves to be perfect. Wherefore let us who are strong bear the infirmities of the weak,[3] and let us give them permission to flee and save their bodies, even if we do not praise them for it. Take it in good part that I write briefly. Commend me to Jonas Kammerer,[4] and please all pray for me, a sinner. I also desire to be well in body,[5] and I despise the barkings of my enemies. Farewell in Christ.   BROTHER MARTIN LUTHER.

[1] Possidonius, *De vita Augustini*, chap. xxx.
[2] John, x. 12.
[3] Romans, xv. 1.
[4] Pastor of the Church of St. George at Thalmansfeld.
[5] Enders refers the words "carnem meam quoque valere cupio" to Luther's family, who lived at Eisleben, not a great distance from Thalmansfeld, but it is surely far more natural to refer them to the bodily health of which Luther has just been speaking at length in this letter.

184. LUTHER TO MARGARET, DUCHESS OF BRUNSWICK.
Enders, ii. 217. De Wette, i. 386. German.

(WITTENBERG, middle of October, 1519.)

Margaret, a daughter of Count Conrad of Rietberg, married on November 16, 1483, Duke Frederic of Brunswick-Lüneburg, who died March 5, 1495. Luther had never seen her. *Infra,* no. 185.

In dating this letter, the dedication to Luther's *Sermons on the Sacraments,* which in Enders is assigned simply to October, with a question mark, I follow the St. Louis edition, vol. xxi., no. 226. The first sermons appeared early in November, and the dedication must have been written earlier. See further *Luthers Werke,* ed. Clemen, i. 174.

High-born Princess, gracious Lady, certain of my friends,[1] priests and gentlemen, have besought me to dedicate some spiritual and Christian writing to your Grace, as a grateful recognition of your gracious favor and pleasure in my unworthy self, and to show my humble service. My own sense of obligation often urged me to do the same, but the difficulty was that I had very little material ready with which I might satisfy my desire and discharge my debt, especially as I am certain that Christ, the master of all of us, has long since anticipated me. But finally I have allowed myself for the sake of your Grace's pious love of the Scripture, which has often been told me, to publish certain sermons[2] dedicated to your Grace, on the holy, precious and comfortable sacraments of penance, baptism and of Christ's body. For I considered that many consciences are troubled and pained, and I have found people here who do not know the holy and full grace of the sacraments nor how to use them; but alas! presume to seek peace rather in their own works than in the holy sacrament of God's grace. For doctrines of men have hidden and taken from us the holy sacraments. I pray that your Grace will recognize my small service and not take my presumption ill. For I am always humbly ready to serve your Grace, whom I now and then commend to God. Amen.

[1] Particularly Otto Beckmann, *infra,* no. 185.
[2] *Sermone von der Busse der Taube, und dem Leichnam Christi.* Weimar, ii. 713ff. On Luther's sacramental system. Smith, *op. cit.,* 89f., *infra,* no. 206.

185. LUTHER TO SPALATIN.

Enders, ii. 220.   WITTENBERG (middle of October), 1519.

On the second postscript to this letter, which belongs to Luther's letter to Spalatin, March 13, 1519, *cf. supra,* no. 135.

Enders dates this letter as late as early in November, 1519, because of the second postscript, without which, he says, the date might be the end of October. But the postscript not belonging to this letter, the allusions to Miltitz and the dedication to the Duchess of Brunswick, indicate the middle of October. The St. Louis edition dates October 15. Vol. xxi., no. 225.

Greeting. Dear George, I have been asked by several people for nothing more often or more earnestly, than for that which you write the most illustrious elector asks of me.[1] Of all that I do there is nothing I would do more willingly than that, because by this means alone I believe I could succor the priests and monks, so that they might cut off and reject those dirty fables of sermon-writers, which rather proscribe than describe Christ, and that they might have something by which they might publish the pure theology of Christ among the people, and expel those errors which flood the land like a deluge. Would that the great prelates would care for this matter, for it is their duty.

The more I wish to succeed in this matter the less I fear I shall do so, for I am too busy to attend to this, or if I do it I shall have to limit my public lecturing and preaching, which will be difficult. But I will try and arrange it; if it please God, it will proceed, and I only desire to serve him in this. Farewell and commend me to the elector. Stromer's excellent advice pleases me.

I think no answer should be sent to Charles von Miltitz. The thing was done as I wrote and said, and I cannot speak otherwise unless I wish to lie. If he played the riddler with me, who attended only to his plain meaning, it was not my fault.   BROTHER MARTIN LUTHER, *Augustinian.*

P. S.—You will be surprised that I may dedicate my sermons to the duchess; I am surprised, too, for I never saw her, but I have been besieged by the prayers of our Otto Beckmann to gratify so highly praised a woman.

---

[1] *I. e.*, to write *Postilla*, or homilies on the gospel and epistle for Sundays and feast days.

186. CROTUS RUBEANUS TO LUTHER.
Enders, ii. 204.   BOLOGNA, October 16, 1519.

John Jäger of Dornheim (Crotus Rubeanus, 1480-c. 1539), matriculated at Erfurt, 1498, B. A. 1500, M. A. 1507. In 1510 he went with Hutten to Fulda. In 1515 he published the first series of the *Epistolae Obscurorum Virorum*. From 1517-20 he was at Bologna, 1524-31 with Albert of Brandenburg (Duke of Prussia) at Königsberg, from that time on a canon at Halle. Until 1531 he was an enthusiastic admirer of Luther, more from patriotic than religious reasons, but after this he broke with the Reformer. Life in *Allgemeine deutsche Biographie* and *cf.* G. Stokes: *Epistolae Obscurorum Virorum*, Introduction, pp. lx.ff, and W. Reindell: *Luther, Crotus und Hutten.* Marburg, 1890. The bearer of the letter was John Hess of Nuremberg. Luther received it early in December.

Greeting. Two things, reverend and beloved Martin, have kept my love for you strong: first, our intimacy while in youth we were studying at Erfurt, an intimacy which time and similarity of character made the foundation of a close friendship; and secondly, because we have in you a splendid defender of true piety, which you protect with the shield of Scripture while others, in the main, try to destroy it. Wherefore it has come to pass that I who have been so long absent chat with you, clasp your hand and dream of you more often than those whom you have near you. I make our friend Hess[1] witness of this, who is my ambassador to you as well as his own.

Martin, I am moved by your controversy with the Dominicans, who, with many others, conspire against your life. And had you not been sent by Heaven to this corrupt age, and had not a celestial hand guarded you as a teacher of Christian doctrine, we should long ago have delivered your funeral oration, so great is the fury of those who prefer their doctrine to that of *Christ;*[2] so great is Roman avarice that it would find a thousand ways of poison and treason, if there

---

[1] John Hess of Nuremberg (1490-January 5, 1547), studied at Leipsic 1506-10, then at Wittenberg till 1513. He then became secretary of John Turzo, Bishop of Breslau. In 1517 he was in Italy, in 1519 back at Wittenberg. Then he went to Breslau, which he reformed. He had a good deal to do with Caspar Schwenckfeld. In 1522 he went to Oels, in 1523 to Nuremberg, and then back to Breslau, where he remained the rest of his life. Biography by Köstlin in *Zeitschrift für Geschichte und Altertums Schlesiens*, vi. 97ff, 181ff, xii. 410ff.
[2] Greek.

were any gain therein. While I was still in Germany,[1] your Punic war was not yet heard of; a year afterwards, when James Fuchs,[2] a sincere admirer of yours, came to St. Peter's on a vow, he brought us the first news of the captured arms. The first thing from the literary battle which came into our hands was the *Dialogue* of Prierias, that acute theologian, whose scurrilous wit was so felicitous that it might even have broken your "iron nose."[3] After that, Andrew Fuchs,[4] dean of Bamberg, sent us your *Resolutions* and your *Acta Augustana*. We read them eagerly and passed them on to many learned men at Rome in order to suppress the false rumors about you circulated by evil men. We had to do this secretly, that they might come into the hands of the readers without our names being mentioned, lest we should prepare for ourselves in those places where the power of the priests is formidable, a misfortune by our imprudence, for at Rome those who have your books are esteemed heretics, and those who import the books do it at the peril of their lives. Rome is intolerant, proud and always fearful lest the truth should free some of those over whom she tyrannizes. When your cause was known the most prudent theologians discussed it with their heart for you, but dissenting from you with their lips, not so much because they feared the power of the Pope as because they feared that detracting from his authority would disturb the peace of Christendom. Let them answer for the righteousness of this opinion; for my part I believe that Christianity does not need fraud, and that he who says what he does not believe in his heart is not the disciple of Christ who taught us that our words should be Yea, yea, and Nay, nay.[5] And if the more recent theologians, who are as firm as brass walls for Aristotle's decrees, had not acted on this principle, we should not have come to the present state of affairs, when we are forced to obey rather the will of the Pope than the commands of Christ, nor would you, in this

[1] Crotus was last in Germany in 1517.
[2] James von Fuchs, a nobleman and canon at Bamberg and Würzburg. After 1523 he renounced his priestly character and married, dying in 1539.
[3] A quotation from the *Dialogue*.
[4] A brother of the former, also canon of Bamberg.
[5] Matthew, v. 37.

controversy, have been so harassed by the Pope's authority, nor would Rome have yet changed the Catholic faith into another. For now the head of that faith, though a mere man, allows divine honors to be paid to him, despising the example of him, who, though he was God, emptied himself, taking on the form of a servant.[1] It is commonly said at Rome, even by those who seem to have sense, that it is impossible that anything which pleases the Pope should not be most Christian, even if it goes counter to a hundred Pauls and the whole Bible. For they say he is Christ's vicar and is guided by the Holy Spirit, and they bandy about some texts of Scripture badly understood, by which they try to stop the mouths of their opponents at the beginning of the argument.

What good, therefore, will your controversy do us? What fruit will the Scriptures bear us, when we disregard all other authority? None, forsooth, unless princes and bishops deem it more holy to defend the Word of God than to pour out a mighty quantity of gold for all their pallia, indulgences, bulls, trifles and nonsense, to enable the holy fathers to support their harlots and male prostitutes. As, in conversation with a certain Dominican master, I was once blaming the immoderate license of Rome, by which the people of Christendom were oppressed and their morals polluted, he replied that it was all done by divine Providence, and that we should not question the will of God. I answered: "If crimes can be defended under the plea of Providence, it would be much more holy to cut them down by the authority of Scripture, the sword of the spirit, which is the Word of God.[2] For we know the will of God only from the testimony of Scripture, which has issued from the mouth of the Most High."[3]

I tell you this, Martin, that you may understand how little it avails at Rome to say, "Thy testimonies, Lord, are wonderful, therefore doth my soul keep them."[4] For they have got to such a degree of impiety that the words "good Christian"

[1] Philippians, ii. 6f.
[2] Ephesians, vi. 17.
[3] *Cf.* Calvin's saying that the Bible flowed "ex ipsissimo Dei ore." The "Protestant principle" of the supreme authority of the Bible was thus early gaining ground.
[4] Psalm, cxix. 129.

or "theologian" are epithets of extreme contempt, but it is esteemed great good fortune to obtain the title of chamberlain or butler to the Pope. The Pope holds the first place of honor, Christ the last. When the High Priest goes forth, as many cardinals, protonotaries, bishops, legates, provosts and attorneys follow him as hungry birds gather around carrion. But Christ's eucharist follows on an ass in the last company made up of unchaste women and prostituted boys. I was recently at Rome with our Hess; saw the ancient monuments and the seat of pestilence; I was glad I saw it, and yet sorry. There certain persons, who thought themselves clever, attacked me on the subject of indulgences and the power of the Pope, as though I either could or wished to dispute about them, especially at Rome. . . .

Wherefore, Martin, you do not conquer—although armed with the armor of Scripture and with the sword of the Holy Spirit you seek the life of the enemy—for the judgment of victory is with the Roman See, not with the Scripture, for, witness your friend Prierias, the very Bible gets its authority from the Pope. But your appeal to a general council saves you from this difficulty. The appeal itself is drawn up so carefully, according to divine and human laws, that it deserves praise even from enemies. Yet it excites extraordinary anger from the Florentine faction,[1] which fears, if it loses the power of giving indulgences for the dead, that afterwards similar arguments may deprive it of the power of issuing pallia, reservations, bulls, privileges, and of its wide jurisdiction and other things to which have been given the name of ecclesiastical liberty, though they are really but nets for catching the money of poor wretches. Germany will be blind as long as she remains in her error, and as long as scholars do not declaim and write against the bad morals with which Rome infects us. Let them admonish the simple people of the Roman guile, and that we, who have so often been despoiled under the guise of religion for pallia, for confirmations, for fighting the Turk, now suffer a greater wrong in

---

[1] *I. e.*, the papal faction, Leo X. being a Florentine. It excited all the more wrath because there was even among Catholics a large party which maintained that a council was superior to the Pope. *Cf.* Smith, *loc. cit.*, p. 97.

being forced to receive cardinals in the midst of Germany; for the event will soon show what this new step of the Florentines means.

Whenever you, Martin, are mentioned, I am wont to call you the *pater patriae,* worthy of a golden statue and of annual feasts, for having first dared to deliver the people of the Lord from noxious opinions and to assert true piety. Go on as you have begun, leave an example to posterity; for what you do is not without the inspiration of the gods. Divine Providence intended this when, as you were returning from your parents, a thunderbolt from heaven prostrated you like another Paul on the ground before the town of Erfurt and forced you from our company, sad at your departure, into the walls of the Augustinian fold.[1] After this time, even though I rarely saw you, yet my mind was always with you, as you may have learned from the letter I sent you last year at Augsburg, if you got it,[2] at which time I earnestly commended you to Thomas Fuchs,[3] a knight esteemed by the Emperor. You are now weary and have suffered much in body and reputation, but arduous deeds are not done without hard labor, and when your evil days come to an end, you will remember them with pleasure and will say: "I went through fire and through water and am saved."[4] Then Germany will turn her face towards you, and will hear with admiration the Word of God from you. But by your kindness I pray you, do not hereafter descend into the arena of public debate, especially against rash men. Do you not know what boys say: "Strive not with words against the wordy man"? Debate within your monastery, with the pen, quietly; that argument is held most exact, which is set down on paper, but

---

[1] This passage is most interesting as being the earliest distinct account of the storm and "vision" which, on July 2, 1505, decided Luther to enter the monastery. *Cf.* the accounts by Jonas, 1538, in Scheel: *Documente zu Luthers Entwickelung,* p. 30, and by Luther, 1539, in H. E. Bindseil: *Lutheri Colloquia,* iii. 187. Also Smith, *op. cit.,* p. 9. *American Journal of Psychology,* xxiv. (1913), 360ff.

[2] Not extant, spoken of by Luther in a letter of November 25, 1518.

[3] A brother of James and Andrew, a knight of Schneeberg, Imperial captain at Ratisbon, an office obtained after a controversy between that city and the Emperor Maximilian in 1512. *Cf. infra,* no. 208. After 1523 Fuchs took a neutral attitude towards the Reformation.

[4] Psalm lvi. 12.

that which is bandied to and fro orally lacks judgment and often leads the mind of the debater from the truth, not to mention that it is base for a theologian to descend to strife. When we first heard of your debate we were sorry for it, for Bologna and Vienna well know Eck's character.[1] But the epistles of Lang and Melanchthon inform us that the debate resulted favorably to us.

Farewell and love me. I will not cease to love you. As much as I safely can I will defend your honor here. Pardon my haste; I preferred to write you at length and without care, rather than to compose a short letter with elegance. I have hardly had a chance to reread it.

CROTUS RUBEANUS.

187. ERASMUS TO MARTIN LIPSIUS OF BRUSSELS.

Sitzungsberichte der phil.-hist. Classe der kaiserlichen Akademie der Wissenschaften. Wien. 1882, c. 689.

(LOUVAIN, middle of October, 1519.)

Horawitz, who published this letter, dated it 1520, but the true date is given by comparison with that of October 17 to Fisher (no. 188), in a part of which not translated Erasmus speaks of Hochstraten's visit, and still more definitely by the minutes of the theological faculty of Louvain (printed by de Jongh, *op. cit.*, p. 43), in which it is stated that Hochstraten on October 12 handed to Louvain the condemnation of Luther by Cologne.

Martin Lipsius, born at Brussels, spent his life as an Augustinian canon at Louvain. He died 1555. He was a great-uncle of the more famous Justus Lipsius. His correspondence has been published by Horawitz, *loc. cit.* Life in *Biographie Nationale de Belgique*.

Hochstraten is at Louvain. He found my epistle[2] to Luther, and thinks it sufficient to convict me of favoring Luther, though I myself am publishing[3] it to show how little Luther and I have in common. If I favor him, what is there monstrous in that? Hochstraten influenced the courtiers, especially the Lord[4] of Bergen, but there were some who rightly under-

---

[1] Eck had previously debated at both Bologna and Vienna.
[2] No. 155.
[3] In the *Farrago nova* of October, 1519.
[4] Maximilian des Berghes, Lord of Zevenberghen, one of the numerous grandsons of John Labeo, the warrior of Philip the Good. He becomes prominent as a diplomat at the time of the election of Charles. Scant notices of him in A. Walther: *Die Anfänge Karls V.*, 1911.

stood the affair. Yet I suspect that Briselot[1] the suffragan bishop of Cambray and Hochstratten have conspired with Egmond,[2] not so much against me as against Luther. . . .

188. ERASMUS TO JOHN FISHER, BISHOP OF ROCHESTER.
Erasmi opera (1703), iii. 511.   LOUVAIN, October 17, 1519.

John Fisher (1459?-1535), made Bishop of Rochester 1504. For many years connected with Cambridge University. In May, 1520, he preached against Luther, and in 1523 wrote two books against him. Cf. *English Historical Review*, c. 657, 659. Fisher was put to death by Henry for refusing to recognize the king as head of the Church. Life by Bridgett, and in *Dictionary of National Biography*.

. . . [The first part of this letter is on various enemies of Erasmus, and on the death of Colet.] . . . The Elector Frederic of Saxony has written to me twice[3] in answer to my one epistle. Luther is protected by him alone. He writes that he has given himself to the cause rather than to the person of Luther, and that he does not propose that in his dominions innocence should be oppressed by the malice of those who seek their own profit and not that of Jesus Christ. . . . [Follows a high eulogy of Frederic for declining the imperial crown which he might have had.]

189. ULRICH VON HUTTEN TO EOBAN HESS AT ERFURT.
E. Böcking: *Hutteni opera* (Leipsic, 1859-66), i. 313.

STECKELBERG, October 26, 1519.

Ulrich von Hutten (April 21, 1488-August or September, 1523), had been forced by his father to enter the Benedictine monastery of Fulda in 1499, but escaped six years later, and wandered to various universities in wretched health and dire poverty for eight years. In 1513 his brilliant defence of his cousin, John von Hutten, who had been murdered by Duke Ulrich of Würtemberg, made him prominent. He visited Italy 1515-7. In 1516 he published the second series of the *Epistolae Obscurorum Virorum* in defence of Reuchlin. He embraced Luther's cause with fervor, chiefly for patriotic reasons. His plan

---
[1] John Briselot (†September 11, 1520), studied at Paris, D. D. 1502. He was a Carmelite, Suffragan Bishop of Cambray, and in his last years confessor of Prince Charles of Spain. Allen, iii. 4.

[2] Nicholas Baechem of Egmond in Holland, studied at Louvain, then taught. Doctor of theology 1505, became a Carmelite in 1507 at Malines. In 1510 he returned to Louvain, where, except for the year 1517 at Brussels, he spent the rest of his life until his death on August 24, 1526. He was dean of the faculty 1520 and 1524, and inquisitor from 1521-6. He was the most decided enemy of Erasmus and Luther. De Jongh, 152ff.

[3] No. 145. The second letter is not extant. For Erasmus' letter, cf. *supra*, no. 141.

was discredited by the fall of Sickingen, in May, 1523; and he died a lonely and broken exile. Life by David Friedrich Strauss, 4th ed., 1895 (English translation).

Some days ago, when I told you what I was writing, I asked to be informed what you were doing and whether you dared aught for the glory of the fatherland and the freedom of this nation to be redeemed from the Roman tyrants. Pray try something, and meantime let me know what it is, that I may refresh myself with hope. I dare not admit Luther as an ally in this attempt, on account of Elector Albert, who is persuaded rashly that the affair pertains to him, though I think otherwise and regret that this chance of signally avenging the fatherland has been taken from me. Even if I do nothing else meanwhile, I will do that, and perchance more directly because by my own motion. Besides, Luther has in Melanchthon an author able to polish his works. . . .

190. CROTUS RUBEANUS TO LUTHER.

Enders, ii. 211.   BOLOGNA, October 31, 1519.

Greeting. At Rome Eck is celebrated as the victor of Leipsic. So much is one's own testimony worth, when people are already prejudiced in one's favor. I told them not to be too hasty with their judgment, lest Rome should again suffer that which she lately suffered with shame, when she awarded the Empire with certainty to the French King, although our princes elected Charles.[1] But let her have her own opinion as long as it is clear that all her decrees are not just. But it is folly both to decree the victory and to be in doubt about it. Eck sent a letter[2] to Rome, seen by very few besides the Pope and two theologians. While it was being secretly read, a certain physician who is my friend overheard it, and what he was able to retain in memory he communicated to me with fraternal faith. I report it to you, Martin, in the same confidential manner, asking you not to give it out lest it harm the physician. The epistle was divided into many headings, explaining the order of the debate at Leipsic, and telling the Pope what he ought to do. The bishops for

[1] On June 28, 1519, the electors chose Charles of Spain Emperor, the defeated candidate being Francis I. of France, supported by Leo X.
[2] Lost.

drawing up your condemnation are appointed, with a certain number of other persons necessary for giving judgment; the method in which those whose opinions go counter to the Church are treated is shown, and some precedents are given. You are held up to hatred first on account of the Bohemian heresy and your approval of Hussite dogmas; then poets and cultivators of polite literature are accused, my friend Hutten being mentioned by name, some of whose songs on Florentine fraud are cited.[1] As an additional proof of the immediate peril of the Church, the new and daily increasing study of Latin and Greek is cited. Then the Pope is diligently admonished in this dangerous state of affairs to lose no time, but to force the University of Paris and ours at Erfurt to pronounce sentence; for if he delays, it is said that he will soon lose Thuringia, Meissen and the Mark,[2] and soon after that, other regions in which the people are embracing with all their heart your "heresy" as Eck calls it. The physician did not remember the rest, and I can't tell you what I don't know, but you can guess that it was something like what went before. As it is no small matter, keep it deep in your mind, but keep it quiet so as not to endanger me and the physician. When next spring I come again into Germany, I can show my contempt for the false apostles who devour us and smite us on the face; but here I must dissemble. As a reward for his debate, Eck asked to be appointed chief inquisitor over three dioceses, but now he has changed his mind and asks for the parish of Ingolstadt, and in the aforementioned letter he takes the Pope severely to task for not quashing someone else's claim on the parish in favor of himself who has suffered so much for the Church. Salute Carlstadt. In haste. . . .

191. LUTHER TO SPALATIN.

Enders, ii. 218.   (WITTENBERG), November 1, 1519.

Greeting. Please thank Mark Schart,[3] dear Spalatin, for

[1] *Epigrammata Hutteni ad Crot. Rub. de statu Romano ex urbe missa.* Hutteni Opera, ed. Böcking, iii. 278.
[2] The Duchy of Meissen, around the city of that name, was the core of Duke George's dominion of Albertine Saxony; the Mark is Brandenburg. These districts remained Catholic for twenty and sixteen years respectively after the date of this letter.
[3] A noble retainer of Frederic the Wise, who granted him fiefs in 1496 in

the ten gulden, and send him some of these books.¹ Truly on the same day on which I became rich, the need of certain men to whom I was obliged to lend something made me poorer than ever.

I am ashamed that among the people of Christ there is so little charity left that those who have less than twenty gulden are obliged to succor each other. I think that the money was given to me because the Lord wished to help them through me, but it was not enough. Wherefore, after consulting you, I will even apply to the clement elector to relieve poverty. By God's grace I ask nothing for myself.

Furious Eck has published a defence against my letter to you.² I am answering him, having this week completed six sheets and given them to the press. It is remarkable how the man rages, stuffed with lies as he is. When he attacks me hardest and most cleverly he imprudently forgets his hypocrisy, on which account alone, passing over other things, I have laid hold on him to force him still further to betray himself and his Leipsic supporters. I will soon send a copy of my book. . . .

Farewell in the Lord.   MARTIN LUTHER.

192. ERASMUS TO ALBERT, CARDINAL ARCHBISHOP ELECTOR OF MAYENCE.

Erasmi opera, iii. 513.   LOUVAIN, November 1, 1519.

. . . In the first place, I must preface that I never had anything to do with the cause either of Reuchlin or of Luther. I never cared for the Cabala and Talmud, whatever they may be. I was highly displeased by the violent collisions between Reuchlin and the party of James Hochstraten. Luther is as unknown to me as any one can be, nor have I yet had time to read his works, except that I have glanced at them hastily. If he has written well I deserve no praise; if otherwise, there

---

return for services. Later he became the tutor of Frederic's natural sons, Frederic and Sebastian von Jessen, with whom he lived in Jessen until his death on March 21, 1529. *Archiv für Reformationsgeschichte*, vi. p. 66, and viii. p. 33. Schart several times gave Luther money, *cf.* Enders, iii. 74.

¹There is extant a copy of Luther's *Sermon on Preparation for Death*, with his own inscription, "To my dear friend Mark Schart."

²On August 15 Luther dedicated to Spalatin his *Resolutiones super propositionibus suis*, Enders, ii. 102. Eck replied on September 2. Luther's answer, De Wette, i. 353. Enders, ii. 214.

is no reason to charge it to me. But I see that good men are little offended with his writings; not, I think, that they approve everything, but that they read him in the same way that we read Cyprian, Jerome and even Peter Lombard, winking at many things. I was sorry that Luther's books were published, and when some of them began to come out I did my best to prevent it, principally because I feared they might cause a tumult. Luther has written me a right Christian letter, at least to my way of thinking, and I answered, incidentally warning him not to write anything seditious nor insolent to the Roman pontiff, nor anything too proud or angry, but to preach the evangelic doctrine with sincere mind and all gentleness. I did it courteously so as to have more effect. I added that this was the way in which he could best conciliate the opinion of men; which some have interpreted to mean that I favor him, although none of them ever warned him, but only I. I am neither the accuser, nor the defender nor the judge of Luther; I dare not judge his spirit, for that is most difficult, especially to give an unfavorable judgment.[1] But if I did favor him as a good man, as all, even his enemies, confess that he is, or as a prisoner on trial, which even sworn judges are allowed to do, or as one oppressed, as humanity would dictate, or as one overwhelmed by those who use him as a pretext to crush sound learning, why should I be loaded with so much odium? At least I do not interfere with the cause. Finally I think it is Christian so to favor Luther that if he is innocent he may not be condemned by wicked faction, and if he is in error he may be rather cured than destroyed. This is most agreeable to the example of Christ, who, according to the prophet, does not quench the smoking flax nor break the bruised reed.[2] I should prefer that that heart which seems to strike forth some splendid sparks of gospel truth should not be crushed, but corrected and called back to preach the glory of Christ. Now the theologians whom I know neither warn nor teach Luther, but only traduce him with wild clamors before the people, or attack him with violent abuse, having nothing at their tongue's end but the

---

[1] "Praesertim in partem pejorem," or, "especially the worst side of a man."
[2] Isaiah, xlii. 3.

words heresy, heretics, heresiarchs, schism and antichrist. It cannot be denied that these epithets are odiously applied to him before the people by those who have not read his books. It has been found that some have expressly condemned what they have not understood. One of their charges is this: Luther has written that we are not bound to confess mortal sins, except those which are known,[1] meaning those which are known to us when we confess. But someone interpreted his meaning to be that we need not confess any sins except what were *publicly* known, and he made a tremendous ado about this thing he did not understand.

It has been found that things are condemned in Luther's books as heretical which are considered orthodox and edifying in Bernard and Augustine. I warned them from the beginning to keep from clamor and to treat the affair in writings and discussions. First, I said, that should not be publicly condemned, which has not been read, weighed, and, if I may say it, understood. Secondly, it was unbecoming for theologians to do anything by clamor, for their judgment ought to be mature; thirdly, they should take heed how they ran wild against a man whose life was approved by all. Finally, I said, perhaps it was not safe to ventilate these matters before a promiscuous multitude, among whom there were many who did not like to confess their sins at all. If they should hear that there were theologians who considered it unnecessary they might easily get a wrong idea. Although I only told them what every decent man must think, they immediately conceived the suspicion that Luther's books were largely mine, written by me at Louvain, although I never wrote a tittle of them, nor were they published with my knowledge or consent. Yet, on account of this false suspicion, without the least warning they stir up commotions here which are the fiercest I have ever seen in my life. Moreover, though it is becoming for theologians to teach, I now see many who try

---

[1] In the *Sermo de Poenitentia* (1518, Weimar, i. 322), Luther says: "Do not take upon yourself to confess all daily sins, nor even all mortal sins, for no one can know all mortal sins, and formerly men only confessed public and known mortal sins." This was condemned by the bull *Exsurge Domine*, article 8, in 1520. When Erasmus wrote, it was on the point of being condemned also by the theologians of Louvain. (November 7.)

to do nothing but compel, destroy and crush, although Augustine, even against the Donatists, who were not only heretics, but savage robbers, does not approve those who only compel without teaching. The men who should be the gentlest of all seem to thirst for nothing but human blood; they only pant for Luther's capture and death. But this is to be hangmen rather than theologians. If they wish to prove that they are great divines, let them convert the Jews, or those hostile to Christ; let them amend the morals of Christians, than which nothing is more corrupt even among the Turks.

How can it be right that he should be haled to punishment who first proposed questions for debate, theses which have always been debated in theological schools? Why should he be chastized who wishes to be instructed, who submits himself to the judgment of the Roman see and to that of the universities? It should not seem strange that he does not care to entrust himself to the hands of those who would rather see him dead than right. Let us examine the origin of this evil. The world is loaded down with human laws, with the opinions and dogmas of the schools, with the tyranny of the mendicant friars, who, though they are the retinue of the Roman see, have become so powerful and numerous that they are formidable even to the Pope and to kings. When the Pope does what they want he is more than God; when he acts against them he has no more authority than a dream. I do not condemn all, but there are some of this order who snare the consciences of men for their own profit and tyranny. And with brazen forehead they have now begun to omit Christ from their discourses and to preach nothing but their own new and impudent dogmas. They speak of indulgences so that even laymen cannot bear their words. By such means the vigor of the gospel is gradually vanishing, and it will come to pass that if things keep on going from bad to worse, finally even that spark of Christianity from which charity might be kindled will be extinguished, and the whole of religion will be reduced to more than Jewish ceremonialism. Good men, even theologians who are not monks, deplore this, and even monks confess it in their private conversations. These things, I believe, have moved Luther to dare to oppose their intolerable impudence. For what else can be the motive of one who desires neither advancement nor money? I do not now discuss the articles with which they have charged Luther, I only speak of the cause of his action. Luther dared to doubt indulgences, but others had too impudently asserted their power. He dared to speak imprudently of the power of the Pope, but others before him had written too immoderately about it on the other side, especially these three Dominicans, Alvarus,[1] Prierias and Cardinal Cajetan. Luther dared to despise the laws of Aquinas, but the Dominicans almost preferred them to the gospel. He dared to raise some scruples about confession, but the monks had long abused it to snare the consciences of men. He dared partly to neglect the scholastic canons, but they had honored them too much, and, moreover, differed about them among themselves, and these canons moreover, they were continually changing, repealing old laws and passing new ones. It tortured pious minds to hear in the universities not a word of the gospel, and to learn that the ancient and approved Fathers of the Church were considered superseded, and that even in divine service not a word of Christ was spoken, but a great deal of the power of the Pope and of the opinions of modern doctors. Their whole speech was nothing but open avarice, ambition, flattery and guile. I think it is their fault if Luther has written too intemperately.

Whoever loves the gospel loves the Pope, who is the first preacher of the gospel, just as the other bishops are. All bishops are vicegerents of Christ, but he the chief. We should believe that he cares for nothing more than the glory of Christ, whose minister he is. Those who in adulation attribute more to him than he himself recognizes or than is expedient for the Christian flock, deserve ill of him. And yet some of the authors of these tragedies are not zealous for the power of the Pope, but use it only for their own gain and arbitrary

---

[1] John Alvarez (1488-1557), a Dominican, taught at Salamanca. Nominated bishop by Charles V., but declined. Forced by Adrian VI. to take the See of Cordova. Created Cardinal 1538. Zealous against heresy. *Dizinario di Erudizione*, ed. G. Moroni, Venice, 1840ff. What he wrote against Luther I cannot find. He is mentioned as a despicable theologian by Crotus Rubeanus in a letter to Hutten, Rome, July 1, 1519. *Hutteni opera*, i. 277.

power. We have, I believe, a pious Pope, but one who does not know all that is going on behind these tumults, and even if he knew it could not prevent it all, as Virgil says: "The charioteer is carried along by the horses, nor does the car obey the reins." His piety will be helped by those who exhort him to do what is worthy of Christ. It is no secret that they incite his Holiness against Luther, or rather against all who dare to mutter against their doctrines. But great princes should rather consider what is the permanent will of the Pope than the duty they owe to a command wrongly extorted from him. . . .

They take it very ill that sound learning and the tongues should flourish, and the old, worm-eaten, dust-covered authors should revive to recall the world to its former state. These men fear for their own failings; they cannot bear to seem ignorant of anything, and they are afraid that something may wound their dignity. They kept the sore spot covered for a while, but at last pain has conquered their pretence and they have had to show it. They, especially the Dominicans and Carmelites, whom I prefer to consider fools rather than knaves, did their best even before Luther's books appeared. But when Luther did begin to publish they took his works as a convenient excuse to attack Greek and sound learning, Reuchlin, Luther and even me, confounding us all and not separating the good from the bad. In the first place, what on earth has the degree of a man's learning to do with his piety? And then what have I to do with Reuchlin and Luther? But they mixed all things together so as to render all cultivators of sound learning invidious alike. One can see how little candor they displayed when they themselves confessed that there was no author, ancient or modern, in whom some errors were not found. But they don't notice the many errors of Alvarus, or Cajetan, or Prierias, because they are Dominicans. They only clamor against Reuchlin because he knows Hebrew and Greek, and against Luther because they think him more learned than themselves. But Luther wrote much rather imprudent than impious. . . .

Formerly a heretic was one who erred from the gospel truth. . . . now whoever displeases them is a heretic. It is heresy to know Greek, to write a polished style, to do whatever they do not. . . .[1]

193. LUTHER TO THE PRINCESS MARGARET OF ANHALT.

Mitteilungen des Vereins für Anhaltische Geschichte und Altertumskunde, x. 137 (1904). WITTENBERG, November 4, 1519.

Margaret of Anhalt-Dessau, née Duchess of Münsterberg, married Ernest of Anhalt in 1494. He died in 1516. She is not to be confounded with Margaret of Anhalt-Cöthen, née von Schwarzburg (Enders, xi. 327), or Margaret, wife of John of Anhalt, by birth of the house of Brandenburg (Enders, xi. 256). She was a friend of Wenzel Link, who early in 1514 dedicated to her a tract on marriage, and on January 22, 1515, wrote asking her to send him some venison for a banquet he was to give. Dessau, where she lived, was only twenty-five miles from Wittenberg, and Luther must often have passed through it on the road to Erfurt. W. Reindell: *W. Linck aus Colditz,* 1892, p. 253. She was the mother of Luther's friends, George, Joachim and John. Witty and pious, she was at first inclined to the Reformation, but turned away before her death on June 28, 1530. F. Westphal: *Fürst Georg von Anhalt,* 1907.

My humble prayers for your Grace. High-born, gracious Princess! It is long since I have been with your Grace, and although I could give good reason and excuse for this, yet will I not do so, for my heart and mind have never been away from your Grace, and I have always been inclined to come to you. For the same reason I have not written to you nor conferred with you. It is the fault of my pride that I do not willingly blame myself to anyone. But that your Grace may see my humble devotion, I have charged this relative of mine to offer your Grace my humble prayers and give you these sermons.[2] I am sorry that I have nothing better; also they are so many who give me a bad name, that I hardly dare publish my own stuff, but must let them burst forth and hold myself in, and endure it as well as I can. But if I get a little peace and time I will return again, hoping to do your Grace's pleasure thereby. God keep your Grace. But

---

[1]This letter was entrusted for delivery to Ulrich von Hutten. *Cf. infra,* January 26, 1520, no. 220.

[2]These sermons may have been that on *Preparation for Death,* Weimar, ii. 685, and the one on *Penance* dedicated to Margaret of Brunswick, middle of October, *supra,* no. 184.

if on account of my bad name my presence would displease your Grace or any of your court, please do not conceal it from me, for I know well that my wind will not blow from Leipsic or Merseburg. Herewith I commend myself to your Grace.   Your Grace's chaplain,

DR. MARTIN LUTHER, *Augustinian.*

194. LUTHER TO SPALATIN.

Enders, ii. 224.   WITTENBERG, November 7, 1519.

Greeting. I am girt up for the labor of explaining the Epistles and Gospels,[1] and am very busy, dear Spalatin. But I send what I can. . . .

I know nothing nor have I ever heard anything of the authority of Ecclesiastes[2] on purgatory. But the farthing mentioned in Matthew,[3] with which Eck attacked me at Leipsic, is as applicable to purgatory as to anything else. What will not anything signify to those who take it apart from its context rather than rightly consider it? But even by the text itself Eck is evidently refuted by the adverb "till," which in biblical use does not signify a definite time, as they think, as, for example, in Matthew, ii.[4] "and knew her not till she had brought forth a son." See Erasmus[5] and Jerome. Secondly, because Christ speaks of a man who would not agree with his adversary, that is, who did not obey Christ's command, and thus, as they themselves confess, sinned mortally. Wherefore that prison is hell, from which no one is freed, for even Eck and his friends send only into purgatory those who have done all and have agreed with their adversary. Therefore the text is only valid against them, unless they agree that those who die in hatred, wrath and dissension with their enemies only go to purgatory, which I hope even they

---

[1]The so-called *Church Postilla*, or sermons on the Gospel and Epistle for Sundays and feast days, which first appeared in March, 1521. *Cf. supra*, no. 185.
[2]Ecclesiastes, iv. 14, cited by Eck; *supra*, no. 163.
[3]Matthew, v. 26, cited by Eck, "Thou shalt by no means come out thence, till thou hast paid the uttermost farthing."
[4]Rather Matthew, i. 25. Luther always cites by chapters alone, because the division into verses was not made until after his time.
[5]*Cf.* Erasmus' note on the New Testament (*Opera*, 1703, vi. p. 11). William Tyndale, in his translation of the New Testament, says that the words did not imply that "St. Joseph knew Our Lady" even after she had borne Jesus.

will not have the brazen impudence to assert. Any boy can see that Christ speaks of such men. The passage of the apostle to the Corinthians[1] was taken from Eck, as it were by force, though he babbled about its being very clear for him. Paul's words clearly mean that the day of the Lord shall prove everyone's works, which day, he says, shall be revealed by fire. Whence even an insane person can see that Paul's words speak of the last judgment, in which the world will be dissolved by heat; and that only by force or a figure of speech (for which there is no evidence) can they be applied to purgatory. Christ's words in John,[2] about purging the Branch, have been applied to purgatory by a certain Vincent,[3] than whom no one ever twists the sense of Scripture more. If the word "purge" always connotes the idea of purgatory, why don't they apply it to the text of Luke, ii.[4] "When the days of her purification [purgationis] were fulfilled." What can they understand who consider Vincent's words articles of faith? The text in Maccabees[5] is left, and is quite plain. But that book does not make articles of faith, nor do the Fathers consider it an authority; the second book especially is several times rejected by Jerome. In short, although I know that our Church believes in purgatory, I do not know that all Christians do. It is certain that no one is a heretic for not believing in purgatory, nor is it an article of faith, since the Greeks who do not believe it are never considered heretics, except by these new abnormally keen heresy hunters. And at the council of Basle the Greeks gave a splendid account of their faith. Farewell and pray for me.

MARTIN LUTHER, *Augustinian.*

195. JOHN ECK TO THE ELECTOR FREDERIC OF SAXONY.

Enders, ii. 226.   German.   INGOLSTADT, November 8, 1519.

This prolix letter of nearly thirty pages is mainly a detailed theological argument in answer to Luther's letter, *supra,* no. 172. I

---

[1] 1 Corinthians, iii. 15, "If any man's work shall be burned, he shall suffer loss; but he himself shall be saved; yet so as by fire."
[2] John, xv. 2.
[3] Vincent of Beauvais, died 1264, treats of purgatory in his *Speculum morale.*
[4] Luke, ii. 22.
[5] 2 Maccabees, xii. 46, quoted *supra,* no. 163.

translate only two passages, the first, Enders, lines 122-137, expressing the Catholic doctrine of the interpretation of Scripture and the second, lines 710-729, containing some personalities.

And as every Christian knows that the Holy Scripture is prized and honored before all else, I have written that no one should interpret Scripture according to his own reason, but should follow the doctrine of the Fathers. Then here comes Luther and calls it my own prating and sets up this as his goal, "that if he has a clear text he will abide by it even if the exegesis of the doctors is against it." May your Grace note the impertinence that is concealed in his cowl! That is the same principle which led all heretics astray, namely, their own self-conceit, so that they won't follow anyone else, but think that they understand better than all the holy doctors. If the text is clear he will abide by it. Is the text clear then? How, pray, did the sainted doctors not understand it? How is it then, if one thinks he has a clear text and yet errs as did the heretic Arius? I trust much more in the dear saints than in my own blunt reason.

. . .

I know not whether Luther had a devil in his box or under his cowl; but no one at Leipsic ever heard me say anything about it. It is true that he had something on a chain, and a silver ring on one finger which caused much talk. If Dr. Luther thinks I am a slanderer and abuser of your Grace, he does me as much wrong in this as in other matters. For I was always desirous of serving your Grace, as much as I could, as an honored and famous German prince, and I offered to do so.

It is certain that the heretics rejoiced in his doctrine, for they publicly prayed for him,[1] and certain of them were secretly at the debate.[2] But now he throws up against me this argument, and I lay it before your Grace to ask if you consider it good: The heretics in Bohemia rejoice in Luther's doctrine and turn it against the Christians, but contrariwise the pious Christians in Bohemia have conceived displeasure against his doctrine, and are wroth with it and against it.

---

[1] Eck learned this from Poduska's letter to Luther, *cf. supra*, no. 161.
[2] This was true; *cf.* Smith, *op. cit.*, p. 67.

Can't anybody see from this that his doctrine is obnoxious to the suspicion of heresy? . . .

196. ULRICH ZAZIUS TO ULRICH ZWINGLI AT ZURICH.
Corpus Reformatorum, xciv. 218.

FREIBURG IN BREISGAU, November 13, 1519.

Ulrich Zwingli, the Reformer (January 1, 1484-October 11, 1531), was born on the Toggenburg, studied at Basle, Berne, Vienna and again at Basle, where he took the degree of M. A. in 1506. Then he became parish priest at Glarus. After some years here, and a short stay at Einsiedeln, he moved to Zurich in 1519, where he remained as leader of the Reformation till his death. He began his reforms at once by an attack on indulgences, as had Luther, though his movement was quite independent at the start. Luther crossed his horizon soon after the posting of the 95 Theses. The present letter is in answer to one from Zwingli, lost, asking for information about Luther. It is doubly interesting for this reason and as showing the cultivated, conservative opinion of Luther at this stage in his career. An excellent life of Zwingli in English has been written by Prof. Samuel M. Jackson. A new edition of his works is being published by Drs. E. Egli, G. Finsler and W. Köhler, in the *Corpus Reformatorum*, vols. lxxxviii.ff.

. . . I should like to say much to you about Martin Luther, if the brevity of a letter could hold it all. Much in him you would praise and defend; but again there are some things which seem a bit too strong. He has rightly taught that all our good works are to be attributed to God and that nothing but evil is to be credited to our own will. He proves this from many authorities, and especially cites the book of Psalms in every possible place. The Church doctors teach the same: Chrysostom in several places in his commentary on Matthew, Gregory most openly in his sermons, and others whom I have consulted and brought together with the purpose of pleading the cause of this most upright man on this point, if the Lord permit.[1] But as to indulgences, I have my opinion, but I have nothing to say. For I have no wish to attack dangerous men.[2] For it is an old complaint, and a doubtful question, as the commentator says.[3] But the subject of peni-

---
[1] Zazius never did so publicly, but other references in his works show that he was really reading the Fathers here mentioned at this time.
[2] Literally "men who have their horns bound in hay," a figure taken from cattle whose horns had to be wrapped up. Horace, *Satires*, i. 4, 34.
[3] *Decretal, Gregor.*, ix. lib. v. tit. xxxviii., *De poenitentiis*.

tence and remission of sins needs the decision of a council, not being of private interpretation. Our Luther has tried to loose the Gordian knot with more boldness than success; yet many think that what that learned man has written is gospel truth. Imagine the rest! What Luther has written on penitence and faith I think quite salutary. For the whole purpose of our life is that it may cast off vices and grow in virtues, and we must strive always to be armed against our immortal enemy, to take up the cross, to buffet our body and thus to improve, for this is the true business of a Christian. Who flees from it flees from salvation; who resists it commits suicide. For[1] this end nothing is more apt than penitence. Who has dared to deny that faith is most potent in the sacraments? But as it is not my profession to discuss these things, I appeal to the theologians, I mean those who love the truth.

In the aforesaid matter I follow and admire Luther, and, as much as my legal studies enable me, I am prepared to defend him on them. But there are blemishes in the Lutheran doctrines which I dislike. His proposition that we sin even when we do good, unless properly understood, is a strange assertion. For in a certain sense we can tolerate this proposition, considering the doer of good not in the particular good act, but in his general character, so that even a righteous man sins, being imperfect and at fault in many things.[2] Thus far I understand Luther; I agree with his opinion and even embrace it, for it takes away pride, cultivates humility, excites love and reverence for God, and is founded in the Holy Scripture. But I see the *Theses*[3] of the Wittenbergers seem to understand the aforesaid proposition in a complicated sense, even of the very good act, as though he who did a good deed sinned even in doing it. I do not see how this can be so, or else I do not understand their meaning. It seems to be mere nonsense with what it implies, as I explain more fully else-

---

[1] Reading "ad" for "at," p. 220, line 6.
[2] This is a complete misunderstanding of Luther's position, which was that any "natural" good act, uninspired by God's grace, is insufficient to merit his favor, and thus cannot be considered above the usual level of our sinful nature. *Cf.* Smith, *op. cit.*, p. 66.
[3] *I. e.*, the *Theses* for the Leipsic debate.

where. It would be better to refrain from such deceptive propositions which lead to sophistical fallacies, and to strive after those doctrines which give wisdom to the simple. Moreover Carlstadt, a learned and upright man, as I think, unless led astray by self-love, asserts in his *Theses*[1] that that cannot by called the literal sense of Scripture which is gathered simply by examining it, nor even that given by the meaning of the words; in short, that that is not expressly stated which appears from the intention of the speaker; and other propositions of that sort. . . .

Finally, in his last book[2] Luther treats some fundamental positions in which he thinks he proves that the Pope is not by divine right the universal bishop. I can hardly say how much this displeases me. In the first place, that is repugnant to the decrees of St. Leo[3] and other Popes, which Luther makes light of and almost spits on, as "vain," although he has no right nor ground for doing so. In short, supposing that what he says were true, which I do not concede (for I intend to confute him on this point, thinking that it is one in which a layman is competent to do so), yet what does he gain by wearing himself out in these arguments, which are fruitless and poisonous as well? We see how wretched is the condition of man, how easily he falls and declines who thinks he stands and can stand easily. Luther's case shows us how much danger lurks in a bitter controversy. How much harm will the determination to win at all costs bring? The Wittenbergers try to refute Eck even where he is right, and thus they have hurt themselves almost as much as him. How safe it is to be humble, not to think loftily, not to strive obstinately, but rather to yield where you can conquer than to try to annihilate your foe! On whom does the spirit of the Lord rest, if not on the lowly and the peaceable? Would

---

[1] Carlstadt's *Theses* on the authority of Scripture, Löscher: *Vollständige Reformations Acta und Documenta.* Leipsic, 1720ff., iii, 81. Barge, *Karlstadt,* i. 117. Zasius seems slightly to have misunderstood Carlstadt, the essence of whose position was that the literal meaning of Scripture was not the important meaning.

[2] *Resolutio Lutheriana super propositione sua tercia decima de potestate papae,* Weimar, ii. 181.

[3] In the work just cited, Luther examines the decrees of Pope Leo I. and others to show "how weakly they prove their point."

that some upright man would urge Luther not to go so far, but to keep the moderation he is always praising, and not to mix dross with his gold! Then we shall name him Elijah,[1] and whatever else is greater than that. . . .

   Yours,
    ULRICH ZASIUS, Litt. D., *Professor at Freiburg.*

197. JOHN HESS TO JOHN LANG AT ERFURT.

Kolde: *Analecta,* 9.   NUREMBERG, November 19, 1519.

I returned to Bologna (for I had been at Rome and would have gone on to Naples had not the robbers prevented it), and there, dear Father, I found your letter, for which, Heaven knows, I was thankful. I showed the account of the Leipsic debate to the lovers of Martin, of which there are a great number in Italy, and they read it with pleasure, their joy being proportionately greater inasmuch as the Roman indulgence sellers, those *evil speakers and spoilers,*[2] as the poor Greeks of our age call them, had previously triumphed, having heard from Eck's letters that he had won. But I will tell you more when I see you, which I hope will be soon. I left Italy a few days ago, for two reasons: first, on account of my health, and, secondly, to hear Martin. For that upright and learned scholar, Crotus Rubeanus, and I, have both recently become theologians. Therefore, I am now going to Wittenberg, though all my patrons believe I am still deep in Italy.
. . .

198. LUTHER TO SPALATIN.

Enders, ii. 263.   (WITTENBERG), November 20, 1519.

Greeting. I am sending you the work for one Sunday,[3] as a sample, dear Spalatin, so that you, who are more skilled in polite letters, may more easily and happily point out places in the others of my collection. I am too busy to do it myself, but I might get Melanchthon to do the work, by which he would at least show his devotion to the elector.

---

[1] Here Zasius employs a term from Zwingli's letter he is answering, for Zwingli uses the phrase in a letter of January 4, 1520. *Corpus Reformatorum,* xciv. 250.
[2] The words in italics are in Greek.
[3] *I. e.,* the *Postilla, cf. supra,* no. 194. Luther wanted Spalatin to correct them all according to the sample he gives in this one.

Dr. Breitenbach[1] and Dr. Henry von Schleinitz[2] honored me by an invitation to dinner. They were very civil to me; I never knew them before. We talked of nothing but of the Leipsic theologians, of whom Breitenbach does not seem to think much. From him I learned one apothegm: "If anyone," said he, "sees theologians of that sort, he sees the seven deadly sins." See what reputation we carnal sophists have given our profession of theology before the people. For, except our belly, our purse and our pomp, is there anything notable in us who are of this sort? For what good is it to count envy, wrath, lust and sour laziness? May God have mercy on us.

Emser pours out his fury,[3] but in such a manner that he confirms my letter. I regret that such coarse, stupid, gross bullies interfere in this business. If respect for my name, or rather the fear of Christ, did not prevent me, I have not found anyone who has given me a better reason for writing. What mockery I could heap on this mole, and perhaps also on the men of Leipsic! Truly I will keep silence and wait for Eck, so that, if necessary, I can answer the lies and curses of both at once.[4]

I send some letters received to-day from high quarters, so that you can see what is being done there. Please return after reading. Farewell, and please attend, as you promised, to my petition for Melanchthon, though I made it against his will. MARTIN LUTHER, *Augustinian.*

199. ISIDORE DE' ISOLANI TO LUTHER.

Enders, ii. 527. CREMONA, November 22 (1519).

In Enders this letter is superscribed "Fr. I. Italus to Luther," the person being unknown to the editor, and the date is given "November 20, 1520," with a question mark. The "November 20" is a simple misprint, for the epistle is dated on the day of St. Cecilia, which is

[1] George von Breitenbach, a Leipsic jurist, in 1525 professor at the university. Later turned against Luther, who called him a "devilish lawyer." In 1539, however, at the accession of the Protestant Henry the Pious (*cf.* Smith, *op. cit.*, p. 302), he made friends with the Reformer again. In 1540 he entered the service of Joachim of Brandenberg. He died soon after.
[2] The Head Marshal of Duke George.
[3] Emser's answer to Luther's *Additio*, entitled *A venatione Aegocerotis assertio.*
[4] Eck's *Pro Hier. Emser*, dedicated to the Bishop of Meissen and dated October 28, 1519.

November 22. The "1520" is found in the first edition of the epistle, entitled "Revocatio Martini Lutheri ad Sanctam Sedem," but it is certainly a misprint here, as shown by allusions Luther and others make to it as early as August, 1520. Luther mentions it in the beginning of his *Babylonian Captivity* (Weimar, vi. 498; *Werke,* ed. Clemen, i. 427).

The author of the work was simultaneously identified by Kalkoff (*Zeitschrift für Kirchengeschichte,* xxxii. 49ff), and by F. Lauchert: *Die Italienischen Gegner Luthers,* 200ff. Isidore Isolani of Milan entered the Dominican cloister in that city, taught theology 1513 at Pavia, 1515 at Verona, 1517 at Milan, 1519 apparently at Cremona, and 1521 again at Pavia. In this year he also took his doctorate at Bologna. He died between April 22 and July 9, 1528, at Milan. He published various things, the first the *Immortality of the Soul* in 1505. He attacked Luther again in his *Disputationes Catholicae,* 1522.

Amiable brother, I am greatly astonished that a man of such excellent parts as you, one who has penetrated the deep mysteries of divine writings, and who has been initiated into the family of the holy mendicant order, should be so obstinate and so bound by the chains of a mind wandering out of the paths of salvation, and that, although publicly anathematized, you should not amend, but should rely on the uncertain protection of a future œcumenical council. Unlearned wise man, endowed with noble mind, do you really do this and worse? Do you try to execute so mad a plan, O man of candid mind and clear eloquence? Alas! alas! why, more savage than any wild beast, do you turn your hand and sword against your own bowels? Why do you hold down the truth of God in unrighteousness?[1] When you know God, why do you not glorify him, instead of using up your powers in your vain thoughts?[2] Your foolish heart is weeping and mourning and quenched in hell. . . .

There is little light in your two letters to the very reverend legate.[3] Walk while you have the light, that the darkness overtake you not.[4] . . .

200. LUTHER TO SPALATIN.

Enders, ii. 265.   (WITTENBERG, before November 29, 1519.)

Greeting. First, if you cared at all for my opinion, you

---
[1]Romans, i. 18.   [2]Romans, i. 21.
[3]The two letters of October 14 and 18, 1518, had been published in the *Acta Augustana,* 1518.   [4]John, xii. 35.

would see that it is beyond the power of one master alone to administer the school.¹ Secondly, if both Quintilian and Aristotle cannot be read on natural history, it is better to omit Aristotle, especially as Pliny will easily supply his place. Quintilian is the only author who will make the best youths, or rather men. But above all I beg that whether Fach² or Hess³ is made teacher of this subject, at least they should have the same method. For myself, I prefer Quintilian to almost all authors, because, while instructing, he also teaches eloquence; that is, he teaches the subject and style most happily. Everything else is all right. Farewell.

BROTHER MARTIN LUTHER, *Augustinian.*

201. LUTHER TO JEROME DUNGERSHEIM AT LEIPSIC.

Enders, i. 437. (WITTENBERG, near December 1, 1519.)

In the years 1519-20, Dungersheim engaged in a long-winded private controversy with Luther, which he himself printed in 1531. The first letter is placed by Enders (i. 355) on January 18, 1519, but should rather be dated October 7, 1519. See Knaake in *Theologische Studien und Kritiken*, 1900, p. 269; Köstlin-Kawerau, i. 258. Luther's reply came soon after this, Enders. i. 365. Dungersheim wrote again, late in November, Enders, i. 373 (placed in January, 1519), and Luther replied with the letter part of which is here translated.

Greeting. Behold, excellent Sir, I have received your second letter, in which you write again about the papacy, and among other things again review the case of Athanasius and the statutes of the Nicene Council. Pray take a brief reply, for I am still waiting for Eck's answer,⁴ which, having again poured forth insane words, he bombastically promises. Pray, what ought I to confess more than I have done? For I allow that the Roman Pontiff is superior to all in dignity, and is to be reverenced, from which it follows that he is consulted in crises, although I do not know how I can defend even this opinion against the Greeks. Nor have you showed

---

¹This doubtless refers to the boys' school connected with the monastery, of which Luther was at one time master.

²Balthasar Fabricius von Fach, matriculated at Wittenberg 1502. Rector of the University 1517 and 1522, Dean 1528. Married in 1530, died July 4, 1541. *Cf.* Enders, xiv. 28ff.

³John Hess, also called Montanus, of Wittenberg, was Rector of the University 1521. He died, in the position of Chancellor of the University of Marburg, in 1558. Enders, ii. 424.

⁴*Supra*, no. 198, note; Luther received it on December 3.

me how to do so. It does not follow that he *must* be consulted, or that no bishop has any power without him in any place, nor that nothing can be done in the Church except by his command. . . .

In this manner, therefore, I desire that the superiority of the Roman see be maintained, if necessary, although, as I said, neither at Leipsic was I able to demonstrate this, nor am I able to-day, nor to show any text of Scripture to those who oppose it. For thus I have no fear, lest, in case a war arises with heretics, we be exposed to mockery for having relied on our commentaries and for having spoken without the authority of Scripture. For the devil does not fear the reed of Egypt, but the sword of the spirit. In this matter you and all others would greatly please me by examining the words of the Fathers in the light of Scripture, as we read in Acts[1] that even Paul's words were received by men who examined the Scriptures to see whether these things were so. You and Eck are accustomed to accommodate the words of the Bible to the words of the Fathers, as though they did not desire to draw us to the Bible, rather than to themselves. But contrariwise it is my custom, following the example of Augustine, but reverently, rather to follow up the streams to the source, as Bernard boasts that he did.

As to the second place, in Philippians, ii.,[2] which you think that I, following Erasmus, have misunderstood, it is really you, who have cited not the text, but the opinions of the Fathers. . . .

It is necessary to defend theologians against Satan by the one simple, sole sense of Scripture. This is my desire and the essence of my controversy with Eck, who defends a multiplicity of senses, which does not please me. Finally, I am glad that out of our debate has arisen the zeal for inquiry, but I am sorry that this inquiry is directed not to the necessary things, but to this one point which is not necessary, in which I give up a good deal more than I am able to justify by argument. But I see quite well what many people seek in this debate. But God lives. Farewell in him, excellent Sir.

[1] Acts, xvii. 11.
[2] Philippians, ii. 5ff. Dungersheim's argument. Enders, i. 392.

202. ADRIAN OF UTRECHT, CARDINAL OF TORTOSA, TO THE DEAN AND FACULTY OF THEOLOGY AT LOUVAIN.

Lutheri opera varii argumenti, iv. 176. P. Fredericq: *Corpus inquisitionis Neerlandicae,* iv. (1900), p. 17.

PAMPELUNA (SPAIN), December 4, 1519.

Adrian of Utrecht (1459-September 14, 1523), matriculated at Louvain 1476, in 1493 became professor of theology. In 1507 he was appointed tutor to Prince Charles. In 1516 he was made Bishop of Tortosa, Cardinal June 1, 1517, and Pope January 9, 1522. As Pope he tried both to reform the Church and suppress Lutheranism. L. Pastor: *History of the Popes,* English translation, vol. ix., 1910. P. S. Allen, *op. cit.,* i. 380.

Famous and learned Professors, and dearest Friends! Your letter of November 7 was delivered to me on the 26th of the same month. In it you show plainly what affection you have for Christ and what zeal for his most holy faith. I saw the errors which you copied from the divers writings and tracts of Luther and sent to me; they are such crude and palpable heresies on their face that not even a pupil in theology of the first grade ought to have been caught by them.

He proves himself a heretic most of all by saying that he is ready to undergo the stake and death for his opinions, and that anyone who thinks the contrary is a heretic. I pass over the reasons which might be adduced to show the heresy of his single articles, so that I may avoid prolixity in matters not ambiguous or requiring it. I am greatly surprised that one who errs so manifestly and obstinately and who scatters his opinions broadcast, is allowed to err with impunity and with impunity to draw others into his pernicious errors.

You certainly deserve praise for having resisted, as much as you could, the pestiferous dogmas of the man, opposing to them a doctrinal condemnation so that his errors should not involve you, and that you should not be held guilty before the Lord of souls, which perish by reason of Luther's perverse doctrine. This would have happened had not you proved the falsity and perniciousness of his doctrine by your censure and by showing the plain truth, as the Saviour said:

Whoso is not with me is against me, and who gathereth not with me scattereth.[1] . . .

203. LUTHER TO SPALATIN.
Enders, ii. 271. (WITTENBERG), December 7, 1519.

Greeting. I see, Spalatin, that the plan which we heard from rumor and hoped was true, namely, that the whole court was coming here, has been changed. But I see that princes must first make and then see their works, for they also are gods.[2] For what is said and expected before it happens usually fails. I had much to talk of [with you and the elector], especially about our curriculum. For I hear that the course on Aristotle is not as successful as we hoped.

Dr. John Hess has brought from Italy a mystic Aristotelian theology,[3] recently, as they write, found in Syria, that is, as I suppose, concocted by some rascal in order to dress up against Christ more speciously this enemy of Christ. Hess also brought letters of learned men.[4]

I know not yet whether to publish my *Tesseradecas*, especially in Latin, as that sort of work, which savors of Christ, is very hateful to the sophists. . . .

BROTHER MARTIN LUTHER.

204. PETER MOSELLANUS TO JULIUS PFLUG.
J. Jortin: *Life of Erasmus*, ii. (1760), 353ff.

MEISSEN, December 7, 1519.

Julius von Pflug (1499-September 3, 1564), pupil of Mosellanus at Leipsic, a moderate Catholic who took a prominent part in the religious controversies of the day. In 1541 he was elected Bishop of Naumburg, but was prevented from taking possession of the see by John Frederic, who installed Amsdorf. After the Schmalkaldic war, in 1547, Amsdorf was removed and Pflug given the position.

I see that you are desirous of learning the history of the cause of Martin the theologian, which has been brought to the point at which it now is by the emulation of the sophists.

---
[1] Matthew, xii. 30; Luke, xi. 23.
[2] Psalm lxxxii. 6, "I said, Ye are gods . . . nevertheless ye shall die like men, and fall like one of the princes." Luther always applied this verse to princes, as terrestrial deities. On "first making, and then seeing their works," cf. Genesis, i. 31.
[3] *Sapientissimi Philosophi Aristotelis Stagiritae Theologia.* Rome, 1519, June 1. It was, of course, as Luther judged, apocryphal.
[4] *I. e.*, of Crotus Rubeanus, *supra*, no. 186, 190.

Although my opinion of it is such as would be unsafe to commit to any letter, no matter how carefully sealed, yet, not to seem to neglect my Julius, I will briefly and in good faith set forth the whole tragedy. But alas, beware how you let anyone see this letter. Also remember that I was present [at the Leipsic debate] by chance.

In the first place, it is too well known to need my repeating it, how much hatred Martin has won from all who do not know the impiety of the Romanists, from those who are seduced by their vices, and from those who spend their whole lives in trumpery sophisms. It is also known how both sides fought by publishing theses throughout Germany, Luther exploding from the theater of the theologians Aristotle's philosophy to which they hold without understanding it, and they defending it like their mistress, with what arms they could, force and fraud, all fair in war. Not only did our Leipsic professors oppose Martin's theses with their own, but Eck also, the Bavarian theologian, *walking on air and like Socrates despising even God from his basket,*[1] moved by the novelty of Luther's propositions, he drew up certain deductions against him and showed them to the Bishop of Eichstädt. When Luther heard of this from his friends, he sent Carlstadt, Archdeacon of Wittenberg, against Eck, thinking to force the man *to retract*. Eck answered once and again, but in my judgment too coldly to win the confidence of any wise reader. For Eck's pen is not as able as his tongue is prompt: *a terrible talker, but a weak speaker*. Wherefore, despairing of victory in a combat of reason, *like a horse let loose in a meadow,*[2] he challenged them to a public debate. The Wittenbergers did not refuse. So they got permission to debate in the *thinking-shop,*[3] rightly so called, of our theologians, beginning on June 27. Both sides arrived promptly. Eck came with only a single personal servant, and with letters of introduction to our duke from the Fuggers.[4] Luther and

---

[1] In this letter all words in italics are Greek in the original. In Aristophanes' *Clouds*, Socrates was drawn up into the air in a basket.
[2] Greek proverb for extreme eagerness.
[3] The comic word applied by Aristophanes in *The Clouds* to Socrates' school.
[4] The great bankers of Augsburg, for whom Eck had debated on the right of taking interest on money.

Carlstadt brought with them the greater part of their university, among their companions being Barnim, Duke of Pomerania, a modest youth loving letters and particularly gracious to me. Men of every estate gathered to see the debate, abbots, counts and knights, learned and unlearned, so that this large university had no hall big enough to accommodate such an audience. The duke showed his foresight in providing a capacious hall in the castle for this event. And as the Bishop of Merseburg, instigated by our theologians, was unwilling to allow this debate, the duke took the whole responsibility on himself. He charged the town council to provide lodgings, and he had an armed force ready lest a tumult should arise. All things were done rightly, especially as your father [Caesar Pflug], at the duke's command, was not only present at all the events, but presided over them.

When the day set dawned, there was at six o'clock at St. Thomas's a magnificent mass for the success of the affair. Then in a splendid procession all hurried to the castle. To prevent a tumult armed guards were stationed at the doors. When all had come in and taken their assigned seats, I, poor man, in a fever, came in through the back door and ascended the platform, to speak, in the name of the duke, to the expectant audience. I confess that at first I was frightened by so great a concourse of prominent men, all expectant, and before so great a prince, whom I feared I would represent unworthily. Yet I spoke, if not with great applause, at least so that the duke and other grandees approved of it. When I came to the peroration, and all were anxiously expecting me to finish (for I spoke almost twice as long as usual),[1] some musicians, prepared at my suggestion, were introduced through the same back door and started the hymn *Veni sancte Spiritus*, which they sang sweetly while the audience reverently kneeled. The time until noon having been consumed with these *preparations,* we went to lunch. A trumpet announced when to come back. All returned expectant.

Carlstadt and Eck, each asking the usual indulgence for himself, descended into the arena. They debated on free will, *i. e.,* what it has to do with the work of salvation. For

[1] Effluxerunt enim duae pene clepsydrae.

Carlstadt sought to prove that whatever was meritorious in the words or deeds of a man was due wholly to God, and that man, of his own accord, could will nothing good, unless he received an influx of divine grace; in short, that God was the smith and our will the hammer with which he forged our salvation. Eck rebutted this opinion, which, if I understand aught in these matters, is by no means absurd. For almost three days he argued that merit was due partly to grace, partly to man's will. It finally came to this, that Eck conceded the whole good work was from God, but not wholly.[1] This fine distinction Carlstadt not only confuted on the spot, but afterwards, in a long public letter, exposed as an invalid fiction.

Luther followed Carlstadt to sustain the thesis that it was only by recent decretals that the Roman Church was proved to be superior to other Churches, against which stood the authority of Scripture and the Nicene Council. Eck left no stone unturned to overthrow this opinion; he summoned all the forces at his command, spending eight days on it and doing his best especially to make his opponent invidious by dragging in some Hussite articles. Luther at once understood the snare, and raged as though inspired by some spirit at being thus insidiously betrayed *on a side issue*. With great indignation he rejected some of the dogmas imputed to him, while embracing some of them as Christian, relying everywhere either on well weighed testimonies of Scripture, or on the decrees of ancient councils. In short, his main effort was to remove far from himself the suspicion of favoring the Bohemian schism. Eck also bent his whole energy on impressing the audience with this opinion of Luther, no matter how much the latter rejected it. In like manner they debated on other things, the state of souls in purgatory, fear as the root of penitence, and indulgences, consuming nearly twenty days in all.

When they had finished each side claimed the victory. Eck triumphs in the opinion of all who like *asses playing the harp* do not understand the subject at all, men who from

---

[1] Totum sed not totaliter. O. Seitz: *Der authentische Text der leipziger Disputation*, p. 54.

boyhood have been brought up on Peter Hispanus,[1] or who have some reason for wishing the Wittenbergers ill. The victory of Luther and Carlstadt is less acclaimed, because learned and judicious men are fewer and less confident in proclaiming their own opinions.

You have the story for which you asked, told briefly and in desultory manner, for I left out much not to the point. What? Don't you applaud? Perhaps I seem clumsy or *artificial* to you, or else you want more. I will fill you to repletion with these banquets, and I will give you portraits of the leaders in this war. Martin is of middle height with slender body worn out both by study and care, so that you can almost count his bones. He is in the vigor of manhood; his voice is sharp and clear. He is so wonderfully learned in the Bible that he has almost all the texts in memory. He has learned enough Greek and Hebrew to form a judgment of the translations. He has no lack of matter in speaking, for an immense stock of ideas and words are at his command. Perhaps you might miss in him judgment and method in using his stores. In daily life and manners he is cultivated and affable, having nothing of the stoic and nothing supercilious about him; rather he plays the man at all seasons. He is a joker in society, vivacious and sure, always with a happy face no matter how hard his enemies press him. You would hardly believe that he was the man to do such great things unless inspired by the gods. But what most men blame in him is that in answering he is more imprudent and cutting than is safe for *a reformer of the Church,* or than is decorous for a theologian. I know not whether this vice is not also common to the *pedants.*

Carlstadt is like Luther, but smaller. He is shorter, his face dark and burned, his voice thick and unpleasant, his memory is weaker and his anger more prompt.

Eck has a tall stature, a solid, square body, a full, German voice, strong lungs as of a tragedian or cryer, but emitting a rough rather than clear sound. So far is he from having that native sweetness of the Latin tongue, praised by Fabius

---

[1] The author of a work called *Summulae.* Long identified, but without certain grounds, with John XXI., Pope 1276-7.

and Cicero! His mouth and eyes, or rather his whole face, would make you think him a butcher or Carian soldier rather than a theologian. He has a fine memory; were his understanding only equal to it he would possess all nature's gifts. The man cannot grasp a thing quickly nor judge it acutely, so that his other talents are vain. This is the reason why in debate he brings together all his arguments and texts of Scripture and quotations from authors without any selection, not considering that many of them are inept and impertinent to the subject, and that some are *apocryphal* or mere sophistry. He only tries to discharge a copious mass of matter, thus deceiving his audience, most of whom are stupid, and from whom he thus wins the opinion that he is victor. Add to this incredible audacity covered by admirable craft. If he thinks he is falling into the snares of his adversary, he turns the debate into another channel, sometimes embracing his opponent's opinion, clothed in other words, as his own, and, with equal guile, imputing his own absurdities to his antagonist. . . .

205. ULRICH ZAZIUS TO CONRAD MUTIAN AT GOTHA.
Krause, 647.   FREIBURG, December 13, 1519.

. . . I should like to know your opinion of Luther, O most candid of all men, for I know that you cannot judge good men amiss. There is among our Germans a marvellous variety of opinions about this man, whom I might well call a hero. All those instructed in the pure doctrine follow Luther without reserve. But the monks and scholastic theologians, except a few good men, condemn him. Two of the best approved and most learned theologians of our university, John of Breisgau and George Wägelin [Achaeus] receive, bless and favor Luther and compare him to the ancient and true theologians. The whole of Switzerland, Constance, Augsburg, and a good part of Italy adhere to Luther. If we disagree with some ecclesiastical lawyers and some litigious slaves of business, we have to fight for the man now in this way, now in that. I accept Luther with reservations. For I do not approve his calling the decretals "vain," by which he intends to overthrow Leo's claims. And it is not necessary for human salvation, for which the good man so constantly labors, to outdo himself in paradoxes and thus give occasion to his enemies to slander him by saying that he is not very different from a wicked Hussite. So, though I consider Luther the best of men, by whose doctrine I have learned to follow Christ more truly, yet I cannot agree with what he says of the primacy of the pope, which can be easily confuted. But I will not write against him, and would consider it a sin to wound him. Yet I pity the condition of humanity, that we are so fragile and so little that even those who are most perfect deviate from the right way when they seem to conquer and become powerful. . . .

206. LUTHER TO SPALATIN.
Enders, ii. 277. WITTENBERG, December 18, 1519.

Greeting. There is a rumor that Charles Miltitz yesterday passed through here. I am surprised at it, but let it pass. I have read what you write of his mocking me by my picture.

I do not know whether I can write sermons on the Gospels and Epistles for Lent, as you urge me, for I have much to do and am very busy. Don't you believe it? My lectures on the psalter require a whole man; my sermons to the people on the gospel and Genesis need another whole man; a third is required by the little prayers and regulations of my order; a fourth might do this work you ask, not to mention my correspondence and my occupation with the affairs of others, including my meetings with my friends, which steals so much of my time that I almost think it wasted. I am one man; certainly I prepare for work, but if what you ask is to be accomplished, all else must be omitted. Would that I could give myself quietly to this alone. I should consider it a great pleasure, so far am I from not wanting to do it.

But there is no reason why you or any man should expect from me any sermon on the other sacraments,[1] until I learn

---

[1] Luther had already preached on baptism, the eucharist and penance, dedicating his sermons to Margaret of Brunswick, *supra*, no. 184, middle of October. The Catholic Church also recognized as sacraments, confirmation, orders, extreme unction and matrimony. Luther's views were expanded in his work, *On the Babylonian Captivity of the Church*. (1520.) *Cf.* Smith, *op. cit.*, 89f.

by what text I can prove that they are sacraments. I esteem none of the others a sacrament, for that is not a sacrament, save what is expressly given by a divine promise exercising our faith. We can have no intercourse with God save by the word of him promising, and by the faith of man receiving the promise. At another time you will hear more about their fables of the seven sacraments. . . .

207. LUTHER TO JOHN LANG AT ERFURT.

Enders, ii. 280. WITTENBERG, December 18, 1519.

Greeting. Reverend Father, the money of Brother Caesar[1] shall be treated as you suggest. Caesar was not at home when your letter came. You shall decide whether to leave him here. Formerly you wrote for him to stay here until he could return to you as lecturer. He gives lectures on theology, and his work is not bad, except that I am sorry I cannot send all the brothers to Melanchthon's lectures on Matthew at six o'clock in the morning. This little Greek beats me even in theology.

I do not know whether you have received both commentaries on the Psalms, mine[2] and Melanchthon's. I expect that my other trifles reach you without my sending them. I have recalled my sermon on usury[3] after sending it to the press, as the pure doctrine of Christ offends many. I send everything else. Please let us have the report of the debate as soon as it is printed.[4]

Eck threatens something dreadful to me and Melanchthon and Carlstadt and our whole university, not to say the elector. He vomited up a chaotic German letter[5] to the elector; you would have thought him God Almighty talking. It is lucky that such a sophist has met such a prince.

Your Erfurt faculty are pleased to delay judgment. For the debate is now vain, and it is vain to expect the judgment of the Parisians, which, by God's favor, will give an opening

---

[1] John Caesar, an Augustinian, who matriculated at Wittenberg in May, 1518.
[2] The *Operationes in Psalmos*.
[3] The little sermon on usury. Weimar, vi. 1.
[4] The notes of the Leipsic debate were submitted to the Erfurt faculty for judgment, and printed there, probably under Lang's care.
[5] *Supra*, no. 195.

for speaking against the Roman Antichrist. A tract by a certain Bohemian, as is thought, is being circulated here. It is written, in both German and Latin, with great theological learning against the tyranny of the Roman curia.

I did not quite understand your meaning when you wrote Greek, that it was due to your efforts that the debate was sent back to Duke George, and why you and your theologians and doctors were so *smitten*.[1]

I shall not answer Emser in a separate book, for the man is so clumsy that he affirms and admits what I charge him with, and he doesn't speak to the point at all, but only reviles. When Eck's promised attack comes out I shall answer him and Emser together.

Charles Miltitz is doing his best, now at Torgau, now at Lochau, to get me to go to Trier with him. My enemies are frightened and while plotting against me rage to think that my destruction is yet unaccomplished. The bishops write to Rome against me. I do not yet know what will happen. Perhaps, under safe-conduct, and if summoned by the archbishop, I shall go to Trier.

Our reverend father Vicar Staupitz is well and honored at Salzburg. He writes that Eck is everywhere courting the favor of prominent men, but that his "moderation" displeases Cardinal Lang.

Lotther of Leipsic is founding a printing establishment, with Greek, Latin and German types, at Wittenberg.

Study goes on apace, especially in theology. Leipsic is Leipsic, according to her custom. I am very busy. Farewell and pray for me. . . .

BROTHER MARTIN LUTHER, *Augustinian*.

208. LUTHER TO THOMAS FUCHS AT RATISBON.
Enders, ii. 283. De Wette, i. 381. German.

WITTENBERG, December 23, 1519.

On December 12, 1519, Fuchs wrote Luther asking his advice, on behalf of the Ratisbon Town Council, as to a strife with the local bishop. Enders, ii. 276. The present letter is his answer.

My poor prayers and good wishes for you. Noble, honor-

[1] Greek.

able, dear Sir and Friend: I have received and carefully read your letter and question. Now I know that I am bound to serve your Honor, as I found you so true to me at Augsburg, and, therefore I should like to answer this letter clearly and rightly. But the gospel prevents me, for in all such matters Christ gives a short judgment, saying: And if any man would go to law with thee, and take away thy coat, let him have thy cloak also.[1] Therefore, it becomes me as a theologian and is on my conscience not to give other advice herein. No party among you will satisfy the gospel unless it lets the other do what it will. The bishop should let the council do what it wishes, and contrariwise. The bishop is not helped by his spiritual right, nor the council by its use and custom, for the gospel supersedes everything. It is, indeed, true that the Pope has decreed that the third part of such an offering should go to the bishop,[2] but I leave it to him to answer for his power to make such a law. It makes no difference to selfishness. For we are obliged to suffer violence and even wrong. Wherefore it would be my advice and prayer, that the bishop and council agree in friendly wise without insistence on their rights; perhaps the bishop may be prevailed upon to give in. But if not, they have no right to reserve the case for the judgment of Rome. Take this opinion kindly and in friendship from me as from a theologian, whom it does not become to advise strife and lawsuits, but peace and patience. I am always ready to serve your Honor.

BROTHER MARTIN LUTHER, *Augustinian at Wittenberg.*

209. DUKE GEORGE OF SAXONY TO THE ELECTOR FREDERIC OF SAXONY.

Gess, i. 110. DRESDEN, December 27, 1519.

Highborn Prince, dear Cousin. On Christmas eve I received a book containing a sermon[3] published by Dr. Luther on the body of our Lord. When I had looked through it I found that it was very Bohemian and had much heresy and scandal in it, especially as it is in German, and seems

[1] Matthew, v. 40.
[2] In the Canon Law, Decret. P. 11, caus. 10, qu. 1, c. 7.
[3] Weimar, ii. 738. On this complaint and Luther's answer, which was more radical than the original sermon, *cf.* Smith, *op. cit.*, 78.

to me likely rather to break down than to build up simple folk. As I know well that your Grace would not willingly have strangers damage our holy faith, so was I sure that you would be still more unwilling for your subjects to do it. Especially as Dr. Luther is a famous man at your university of Wittenberg, he will doubtless bring great notoriety to your Grace and the land of Saxony, and do something contrary to the Christian religion and favorable to the Bohemian heretics. For many already have thought that the Scripture commands that the sacrament be taken in both kinds, and hold many other articles which are unchristian.

210. ELECTOR FREDERIC OF ERNESTINE SAXONY TO DUKE GEORGE OF ALBERTINE SAXONY.

Gess, i. 112.   Lochau, December 29, 1519.

Highborn Prince, dear Cousin. I have received your Grace's letter about a printed pamphlet published by Dr. Martin Luther, which contains a sermon on the venerable sacrament of the true body of our Lord Jesus Christ. I have also received your Grace's notice and opinion of the same, and in friendship to your Grace will not conceal from you that I have never undertaken to defend or champion Dr. Luther's sermons or disputations, and do not do so now, but keep aloof from such matters as I told the papal cardinal legate, and the nuncio Charles von Miltitz both by letters and orally. Although I cannot know how the said book will be esteemed, yet I hear that hitherto Dr. Luther's doctrine has been by many learned and wise men considered Christian. However I leave it to its merits and him to his reckoning, for your Grace knows that Dr. Luther's affair and disputation is awaiting judgment, for which he also offered himself to the papal nuncio, who commanded him to come forth in the proper manner. Now, however this comes out, I will act, God willing, so that no one can rightly blame me, for it would be a heartfelt sorrow to me to have some error in the holy faith appear in the lands of my brother,[1] your Grace and myself, or in any other place, and still more would it wound me to have it protected by me, from which may God guard me. . . .

[1] Duke John.

211. RECTOR, PROFESSORS AND DOCTORS OF THE UNIVERSITY OF ERFURT TO DUKE GEORGE OF SAXONY.
Gess, i. 113. (ERFURT), December 29, 1519.

We have received your Grace's letter recently sent us, concerning certain articles and points which Dr. Eck, Dr. Luther and Dr. Carlstadt publicly debated at your Grace's University of Leipsic, and stating your Grace's desire and the said university's friendly request that we should diligently examine the said disputation and give you our opinion and judgment on the same. In this as in all other matters we desire to serve your Grace with all our power, but, after repeated consultation, we find that in this case it is not fitting for us to decide and judge the contentions which were brought forward between the aforesaid doctors in this debate, inasmuch as the disputants did not agree to ask our opinion, either in letters or otherwise. Moreover we are credibly informed that they are not of one mind and accord on this matter. Furthermore it is not agreeable to us to exclude from the decision the learned doctors of the two orders, Dominicans and Augustinians in our university, as your Grace requests. Wherefore, we humbly pray your Grace to excuse us. . . .

212. ERASMUS TO MARTIN LIPSIUS OF BRUSSELS.
Erasmi opera (1703), iii. 534. LOUVAIN,[1] (Late), 1519.

. . . They are starting a foolish and pernicious tragedy against Luther. They will later know that I favor not Luther, but the peace of Christendom. However Luther may have written, this tumult does not please any wise man. . . .

213. WILLIAM NESEN TO ULRICH ZWINGLI AT BASLE.
Corpus Reformatorum, xciv. 378. (LOUVAIN, end of 1519.)

William Nesen (1493-1524), of Nastätten, matriculated at Basle 1511, M. A. 1515. About this time he became proofreader for Froben and met Erasmus. Early in 1517 he went to Paris as tutor to the sons of Nicholas Stalberger, remaining with them till 1519 when, at Erasmus' invitation, he came to Louvain. His lectures were prohibited by the university, so he undertook to teach a Latin school at Frankfort 1520-3. He then visited Luther at Wittenberg, the Reformer dedicating to him his *Adversus armatum Virum Cochlaeum*,

[1] Ex museo nostro.

February, 1523 (Enders, iv. 82, Weimar, xi. 292). He carried Luther's letter of April 15, 1524 (Enders, iv. 319), to Erasmus, and shortly after his return, July 5-6, was drowned while boating for pleasure on the Elbe. Life by Steitz in *Archiv f. Frankfurts Gesch.* N. F. vi. 1877. Allen, ii. 65.

This letter was written about the end of 1519, after the University of Louvain had condemned Luther (November 7), and before the death of Briard, January 8, 1520. It was expanded to the length of a pamphlet and published about a year later. *Cf.* Kalkoff, in *Corpus Ref., loc. cit.*, 419, no. 5. I translate only the principal passage about Luther, pp. 384-7.

When Luther's works came out he [Egmond] terribly feared for his gains, mindful of how much he had made from papal pardons. He had not yet read one page, and he was so stupid that he would have read in vain, but over his cups he heard from his gossips that there were things in those writings which would injure that trade. So he lept into the pulpit and confounded everything with his insane cries, calling Lutherans heretics, seducers and antichrists, and proclaiming that the world would fall unless he propped it up with his shoulders. I am not the man, my dear Zwingli, to understand the deep points in Luther's books, nor do I mix in his cause, especially as he has no need of patrons like me. Yet I am not so dull as to admire Egmond's stupidity. Here is one example from which you may learn how well that ass understands Luther's dogmas. More than a hundred times he shouted to the people that Luther taught that it was not necessary to confess mortal sins except those which were known.[1] Luther meant, known to us, that is, which we judge to be mortal, which is certainly, in my opinion, not in everyone's power. But this beast thinks that he means known publicly. What would you do with such silly brothers? He constantly bawls against Luther, and only brings it to pass that people all buy Luther's books thinking that there must be some good in them if they so displease this cheese-eater.[2] Then they complain that some buy Luther's books, when they not only stimulate the appetite for them by their vociferations, but also disturb the peace of the Church with a dangerous quarrel. This monk thinks he is very holy if he does not

[1] *Cf. supra*, no. 192.
[2] A common term of contempt for the monks as hunters of delicacies.

eat meat Wednesdays, but fills himself up to the point of vomiting with eggs and fish, and yet he does not think it a sin to attack the reputation of a good man with manifest lies and wicked calumnies, and to infect the minds and ears of his hearers with such sycophancy, Latomus[1] shouts, Egmond shouts, Ruard[2] stammers against Luther as a heretic, and an unlearned and stupid one, and no one admonishes Luther, no one teaches him, no one refutes him, although he himself asks to be taught, and desires to be heard and to hear. I do not know what kind of man Luther is, except that the books which he has hitherto published testify that he is well versed in the writings of theologians, not so much the ancient as the recent; moreover they show that his mind is sane and his heart graced with many and various Christian gifts. But I know these others to be such men that if there were no other Christians beside them, so love me God, I would not want to be one, so much are they given to ambition and avarice. They help none, and wish well to none except themselves; they hurt many and wish to be feared under the pretext of religion. Luther does not offend them by treating the Pope's majesty too severely, of which they themselves do not think very highly, nor because he attacks indulgences, which they themselves do not approve when they are frank with each other. But they call Luther a heretic because he despises Aquinas, whom the Dominicans take as a fifth evangelist, because he rebukes the professors whose authority they want held sacred, because he does not keep before his eyes the scholastic dogmas, to which, putting it mildly, the world owes so many monks' quarrels, so many ceremonies, and, if not the extinction, at least the corruption

[1] *Cf.* De Jongh, p. 173. James Masson (Latomus) of Cambron, b. *circ.*, 1475, studied at the College of Montaigu at Paris, moved to Louvain 1500, where he began to teach about 1510, and received the D. D. in 1519. He died March 29, 1544. He was the ablest of the opponents of Luther and Erasmus in the Netherlands. Luther's answer to his defence of the Condemnation by Cologne and Louvain, 1521, reprinted, Weimar, viii. 36ff. In 1525 Latomus wrote on the power of the pope against Luther, and later attacked W. Tyndale and Melanchthon. *Realencyclopädie.*

[2] *Cf.* De Jongh, p. 180. Ruard Tapper of Holland, B. A. at Louvain 1507, studied under Adrian of Utrecht, D. D. 1519. He took an active part against the Reformers, particularly in their condemnation by his university 1544 (Smith, p. 400), and took part in the Council of Trent. He was also inquisitor for a time. He died March 2, 1559, at the age of seventy.

of the Christian religion. To these also the world owes the existence of unlearned theologians, and the neglect of good authors, and on these dogmas Professor Latomus promised a third book, but when he saw his first two received by all the learned with a loud laugh, he thought it better to suppress it, rather than to disgrace the scholastic doctors by coming on the stage again. . . .

Now hear how mad they are. Listen! They expect Luther's capture. What is this but to thirst for human blood? They are unable to teach him, yet they want to destroy him. Is this the rôle of hangmen or of theologians? How great will be the indignation of posterity if they read that Luther was a good man, of a life miraculously pure, brilliant, learned, candid, a good Christian, and a German patriot, and yet that when he first, in this age of perverse theologians and detestable monkish tyranny, dared to warn them and to vindicate Christ, whose worship had been stained and almost wiped out by human doctrines, he was crushed not by arguments or texts of Holy Scripture, with which he always invincibly defended his own innocence, but by a fraudulent and tyrannical conspiracy of scoundrels? . . .

214. JOHN REUCHLIN TO MICHAEL HUMMELBERG AT RATISBON.

Sitzungsberichte der phil.-hist. Classe der Akamedie der Wissenschaften. Wien., lxxxv. (1887), 175. INGOLSTADT, January 3, 1520.

Hummelberg of Ratisbon (1487-1527), studied at Paris 1504-11, and at Rome 1514-17, his specialty being Greek. Shortly after his return to Ratisbon he became a teacher, and as such enjoyed much reputation with the humanists. Some of his letters published in J. Paquier's edition of Aleander's correspondence. Allen, *op. cit.*, i. 515. *Allgemeine deutsche Biographie.*

. . . I am holding Melanchthon back lest he should be blamed for being such a faithful Achates to his Luther. But youths have no prudence. Perhaps he is sorry for so learned and so upright a theologian and takes it ill that Luther has suffered so much reproach for the love of the orthodox Church.[1] . . .

[1] Reuchlin, Melanchthon's uncle, was trying at this time to get him to Ingolstadt to withdraw him from Luther's influence. Eck also took part in this plan.

215. THOMAS VENATORIUS TO WILIBALD PIRCKHEIMER.
Pirckheimeri opera, ed. Goldast (1610), p. 332.

EPSTETT, January 8, 1520.

Venatorius (Gechauf) b. 1488, at Nuremberg, Dominican in Bavaria, called to Nuremberg through Pirckheimer's influence 1520, 1523 the first Lutheran pastor at the New Hospice church, 1544 for a while at Rothenburg, died at Nuremberg 1551. Enders, vii. 301.

Pirckheimer (1470-1530), born at Eichstädt, studied in Italy 1490-7. After his return to Nuremberg became a councillor, and, having inherited wealth, a patron of the arts (Dürer) and learning, and himself translated a good deal from the Greek. *Allgemeine deutsche Biographie.* He was at first an enthusiastic Lutheran, was accused of writing a satire on Eck (*Der abgehobelte Eck*), and was excommunicated by the bull *Exsurge Domine,* afterwards making submission to the Pope and receiving absolution. See a sketch by F. Roth in *Schriften des Vereins für Reformationsgeschichte,* no. 21.

. . . Do not let what you wrote about that false theologian Eck bother you, for he is impious and seeks occasion to quarrel with all learned men, which is easy for him to do. For Reuchlin and the best part of the University of Ingolstadt disagree with him. Recently, when a bookseller had imported some tracts of Martin Luther, Eck, together with the university, decreed that they should all be burned. But when he did this I cannot say how much laughter he awakened against himself, and how he departed alone covered with blushes. His only triumphs are those of calumny. . . .

216. LUTHER TO SPALATIN AT ZERBST.

Enders, ii. 290. WITTENBERG, January 10, 1520.

Greeting. I send you, Spalatin, a letter[1] with some news, by which you will see how unhappy is the hatred of Leipsic, and how malignantly they abuse the simplicity of Duke George, not fearing to allege that it is a great error and heresy to communicate in both kinds.[2] And yet, although Christ's gospel ordained this, I would not command it to be done except by the authority of a council. By this example alone you can easily learn what they say in other matters. Please

[1] On this, Smith, p. 78, and *supra,* no. 209.
[2] Luther's *Sermon* had on the title-page two monstrances, which Duke George considered a symbol of communion in both kinds.

read the rest about the mysterious meaning of the monstrances, and about my birth, education and family. I hope they will soon pretend that I have a wife and children in Bohemia.[1]

I do not wish to send Eck's slanders published by him in reply to my articles.[2] If you desire you shall see it when you are here. You have read *The Unlearned Canons*,[3] I think, eloquently and loftily attacking the sophist. Farewell in Christ, and may the Lord be propitious in this affair of the princes.[4] Amen.

BROTHER MARTIN LUTHER, *Augustinian.*

217. LUTHER TO SPALATIN.

Enders, ii. 292. (WITTENBERG), January 14, 1520.

Greeting. I am very glad and thank God, dear Spalatin, that my cause has gone so far that, other charges being dismissed, I am now accused of taking the eucharist in both kinds[5] and with my family. I hope by the signal mercy of Christ shown to my unworthy self that I shall not lose on account of any worthy opinion which has real weight, such as my doctrine of free will, of grace or of the keys of the Church. For now my enemies seem to despair of doing anything against them, since they seek out such ridiculous accusations. For just as Christ was crucified for the words "king of the Jews," so am I on account of taking the sacrament in both kinds, which I never either commanded nor forbade, just like the schoolmen who treat of it.

On my family no one can speak more certainly than the Counts of Mansfeld. I believe these heroes at least have so much reputation and authority in the Empire, that they deserve to be credited on this subject. I believe that this fic-

---

[1] Luther means the rumors circulated by his enemies that he was of Bohemian origin, of which, however, there is nothing in Duke George's letter. Spalatin speaks of the first in his *Annales, ap.* Menck, ii. 599. Another rumor is found about 1531 in a writing of Peter Sylvius (Grisar, ii. 675), and in Cochlaeus' *Commentaria,* quoted here by Enders. According to this, Luther was begotten by an incubus.
[2] Eck's often-mentioned *Pro Hier. Emser.*
[3] A satire against Eck by Oecolampadius.
[4] A meeting of the German princes at Zerbst (see superscription of this letter) to stop the war between Brunswick and Lüneburg.
[5] *Cf. supra,* no. 216.

tion was cooked up by the Leipsic theologian Ochsenfart,[1] a man who represented that Eck was crushed, for the sake of spying on us, a man who cannot stand peace either for himself or anyone else, always ready to hurt, wretched and yet impotent.

I was born at Eisleben, and baptized in the church of St. Peter there. I do not remember this, but I believe my parents and compatriots. My parents had migrated thither from Eisenach hard by. Eisenach has almost all my relatives, and there I am to-day recognized and known to most of them, since I studied there four years,[2] nor does any city know me better. I hope they would not be so foolish, that one should call the son of Luther nephew, another uncle, another cousin (of whom I have many there), if they knew that my father and mother were Bohemians and other than natives of their town. The rest of my life I spent at the university and monastery of Erfurt until I came to Wittenberg, except one year, my fourteenth, when I was at Magdeburg.

You have the story of my life and family. I should prefer, as Christ did before Herod and Annas, to keep silence on this matter, so these furious men could imagine anything worthy of themselves about it until they blushed. For it is a generation moved neither by song nor by mourning, in whom we vainly seek a profitable man.

This same hour I have received your letter about Charles von Miltitz, who, you say, swore that he had not seen me. Why then did he confess to Andrew the barber, who accompanied him to Pretzsch[3] (as the latter openly boasts here) that he both saw me and did I know not what terrible things against me? But let them lie, invent and be as wise as they please. Everything is against me, and would that something would happen quickly to free me from the duty of lecturing and teaching. For I desire nothing so much, as far as in me lies. But if I must continue teaching, I do not understand

---

[1] Ochsenfart had just written to Luther again, Enders, i. 451, placed in March, 1519, but should be in January, 1520. *Supra*, no. 201. In this letter, however, there is nothing about Luther's family.

[2] 1497-1501. Smith, *op. cit.*, p. 4ff. These facts about Luther's early life are well known and amply attested, but this account is interesting, being, as far as I know, the earliest extant.

[3] A little village on the Elbe near Wittenberg.

your council, Spalatin, and that of your friends, that I might teach sacred theology without offending the prelates. Scripture is especially hard on the abuse of sacred things, and that is what the prelates cannot bear.

I gave and offered myself in the name of the Lord, whose will be done. Who asked him to make me a doctor? If he has made me one, let him keep me for himself, or else, if he repents, let him destroy me. But my trouble does not so wear me out as fill the sails of my heart with an incredible wind, so that I now feel in myself why devils are in Scripture likened to winds,[1] which empty themselves by their fury, but fill what they blow upon with the intent of hurting it. My only care is that the Lord may be propitious to me in the private affairs between him and me. Pray deign to help me, as you can, in this.

Let us in faithful prayer commit this human cause to God, and let us be at peace. What can they do? Kill? Can they raise up to kill again? Will they brand me as a heretic? Christ was condemned with the wicked, seducers and cursed men; whenever I consider his passion, I burn to think that this trial of mine should not only seem to be something, but should even be considered great by many strong men, when in truth it is nothing, unless we would altogether do away with suffering and evil, that is, with the Christian life.

Let them do as they please; the more powerful they are the more securely I laugh at them. I have determined in this to fear nothing, but to despise all things. Did I not fear to involve the elector, I would publish an apology full of confidence in order to provoke those furies more, and to mock their silly rage against me. . . .

MARTIN LUTHER, Augustinian.

218. ULRICH VON HUTTEN TO PHILIP MELANCHTHON AT WITTENBERG.

Corpus Reformatorum, i. 131.   MAYENCE, January 20, 1520.

Perhaps you have already noticed how Francis von Sickingen[2] by his own power, but at my instigation, has freed

---
[1] Hebrews, i. 7. Luther regarded the devils as evil angels.
[2] Sickingen (1481-May 7, 1523), of the Ebernburg near Kreuznach, a knight

Reuchlin for us from those barbarous scoundrels; to Sickingen they gave him and will be obliged even to pay the costs. Now the same hero bids me write to Luther, that if he suffers any mischance in the present affair and has no better alternative, he should come to him and that *he* will do what he can. Doubtless he can do as much as he did for Reuchlin. I have not done as he asked for many reasons, but I write to you in his name, to tell Luther what a protector he has, who with such kindness offers his assistance, and that he should write to Sickingen. Believe me, there is no better chance of safety anywhere. Would that you had seen what he wrote to the monks. I left him four days ago at Neustall, where he now is. I will also take care of Erasmus' business, for he writes me tragic letters about his rivals. First, we must conciliate Ferdinand,[1] of whom Sickingen deserves well. After that it will be easy to frustrate the wicked. Sickingen loves Luther partly because he seems good to him and to others, and is therefore hateful to those men, and partly because one of the counts of Solms[2] commended him in a letter. Tell him at once where his hope and safety lies, and farewell.

219. MARTIN BUCER TO LUTHER.
Enders, ii. 298.   HEIDELBERG, January 23, 1520.

Hail, reverend Father, sincerest of theologians and strongest of Christians. When, in your debate here a year and a half ago,[3] you illuminated our university with your Christian rather than quaint learning, I, smitten by great love for you, as though wounded by the sharp arrows of your words, or rather of God the Mighty, dared to have a conference with you. If it was impudent to seek it, the result was assuredly happy. For received at dinner by you and your pious superior, John Staupitz, I was wonderfully and bountifully

who succeeded his father in 1505 to large domains. He had a feud in 1513 about Worms, and one with Hesse. On October 25, 1519, he was made Imperial Councillor and Chamberlain. He was interested by Hutten in the cause of Reuchlin and Luther. In 1521 he was made general of the army against France, but failed to accomplish much, chiefly through lack of funds. In 1522 he attacked Trier with the purpose of leading an insurrection, but was defeated and killed at Landstuhl. Life by H. Ulmann, 1872, and in *Allge. Deutsche Biographie.*

[1]The Emperor's brother (1503-64), elected King of the Romans 1531, Emperor, 1558.
[2]Perhaps Philip, count of Solms, a courtier of Albert of Mayence.
[3]On this, *cf. supra,* no. 57.

refreshed, not only by the excellent delicacies of the table, but by the exquisite and sweet meat of the Scriptures, for which, indeed, I came more hungry than for the bodily food. Among the other excellent gifts of your mind, *the genuine humility of our Lord Jesus*[1] manifested itself with special brilliance; your face, words, gesture and whole body testified to it. This is the reason why I now dare to approach you, so great a priest of eternal wisdom, who perpetually sacrifice to wisdom from the field of your genius richer and more fertile than any Arabia, sweet incense, and to write you a letter, not only in poor Latin, but inept and most unseasonable. I am sure that you will condone this sin.

The occasion of my writing now for the first time is my immense desire for your Commentary on the Epistle of Paul to the Galatians. For I only had a chance to see it, when a certain man brought it here from Nuremberg. By various wiles I extorted it from him and sent it to Beautus Rhenanus,[2] so that, if no one gets ahead of us, it can be reprinted by Lazarus Schürer.[3] For each of them is now at Schlettstadt, our common birthplace. And having no little need of the commentary, which seemed to me a treasury full of the dogmas of pure theology, I ordered someone else to procure me your works. Then, by chance, a certain messenger was starting out hence from our prince to yours. But your Peter,[4] secretary of Wolfgang Count Palatine, relieved him of this burden, and transferred it to Spalatin,[5] a man who deserves well on account of his learning and piety.

Peter also urged me to write,[6] although unknown to him and inexperienced in all polite literature. I had previously given myself altogether to him, nor could I return to my former state. Moreover I could not trifle with your dogmas, or rather with the pure doctrine of Christ. I ap-

[1] The words in italics are Greek.
[2] With a letter dated Spires, January 15, 1520. *Briefwechsel des Beatus Rhenanus*, p. 203.
[3] This hope was probably not fulfilled. Weimar, ii. 439. Schürer was a printer of Schlettstadt.
[4] Perhaps Peter Beymann, a client of Wolfgang, matriculated at Wittenberg 1515.
[5] From whom Bucer received a copy by March 19. *Cf. Briefwechsel des Beatus Rhenanus*, p. 216.
[6] Bucer's letter to Spalatin, January 23, printed in Kolde: *Analecta Lutherana*, p. 437, and Stähelin: *Briefe aus der Reformationszeit*, p. 6.

prove all your teachings without exception, but I am especially pleased at what you say about charity, rightly execrating that always present curse of a Christian, the sayings: Charity begins at home, and, Be your own neighbor. . . . [Bucer tells of a debate on this point held under his presidency at Heidelberg.] . . .

You have here not a few disciples, though on account of the Pharisees they have not yet dared to come out openly. I pray your charity, most learned Father, to forgive what I have said amiss in expounding this charity, and please deign to write me to lead me back into the right path. For next to the canonical Scriptures, I hold nothing more sacred than your opinion or that of Erasmus. You know what others think of you, but your opponents need a physician no cleverer than themselves. I hope, or rather I know, that Christ, whose cause you are so strongly advancing, will never desert you.

Tell all who love learning, and first of all your Philip Melanchthon, that Francis von Sickingen, a most noble knight, by declaring war on our order, at length compelled our provincial vicar to make a *treaty* with that Phœnix, our Reuchlin. For, as he promised, the vicar sent to Reuchlin at Ingolstadt two professors,[1] who are most hostile to Hochstratten as far as this quarrel is concerned, to make peace with him. If they do not succeed, the thirteenth of March is set to have the matter decided by arbitration at Worms. Hochstratten's perverse zeal grieves almost everyone, but none of us dared to offend the majesty of the inquisitor. Thanks be to God, who has at length forced better councils to prevail by arms. This is the fifteenth day since the legates departed, and we hope they will soon return, and return with peace made. For we offer to write even to the Pope, to ask that if he will do nothing else the provincial may at least end the quarrel by imposing perpetual silence and keep Hochstratten from reviling. I know that this will please Philip, and not him alone, but all good students.

[1] A fuller account of this business, which happened in December, is given to Bucer's letter to Rhenanus of January 15. The professors were the head of the theological school at Heidelberg and the prior of Esslingen. They left on January 8, arriving at Ingolstadt just ten days later, so Reuchlin wrote Pirckheimer, *Opera Pirckheimeri*, p. 261.

Farewell in Jesus our Lord, and may you always be superior to your enemies. . . .

MARTIN BUCER OF SCHLETTSTADT,
Your Reverence's son in Christ. . . .

220. LUTHER TO JOHN LANG AT ERFURT.

Enders, ii. 304. (WITTENBERG), January 26, 1520.

Greeting. We have no news, reverend Father. For you have seen *The Unlearned Canons*. We shall print the Nuremberg German *Apology*[1] if we have time. I send an explanation of my sermon on the eucharist against the men of Leipsic, who have scattered the rumor that I am a born Bohemian with such confidence that they have persuaded even the courts of princes. They have captured Duke George and made him most hostile to me, for he warned[2] the Dresden brothers of my expulsion, as they call it. . . .

Some people have in their possession a noble epistle[3] of Erasmus to the Cardinal of Mayence. Perhaps it will be printed sometime. Erasmus, who is very anxious about me, nobly defends me, and yet in such a manner that he seems to do nothing less than to defend me, so great is his habitual dexterity.

The Spanish ambassador[4] is with our elector. Philip and I were invited to dinner with him and handsomely entertained. You will soon see Melanchthon's oration delivered yesterday printed. Farewell and pray for me. Greet from me the reverend Father Bartholomew Usingen, and Nathin and all.

BROTHER MARTIN LUTHER.

[1] Lazarus Spengler's *Schutzrede*, cf. *infra*, no. 221.
[2] This letter is quoted by Enders. The Dresden cloister apparently kept favorable to Luther notwithstanding.
[3] This letter, *supra*, no. 192. It had been entrusted for delivery to Ulrich von Hutten, who was doubtless responsible for opening it and showing it around, and also for having it printed, as was done at once. *Bibliotheca Erasmiana*, i. 93. Erasmus naturally took this very ill, blaming Hutten for his "more than punic perfidy" (*Erasmi epistolae*, Londini, 1642, xiii. 42), and especially the liberty taken, as he avows, with the text in changing "Luther" to "our Luther." *Ibid.* xvii. 19. It was reprinted at Wittenberg in 1520 (according to *Corpus Reformatorum*, i. 157), as well as at a number of other places. *Bibliotheca Erasmiana*, loc. cit. Cf. also Smith, *op. cit.*, p. 201.
[4] Jerome Bronner, Secretary and Councillor of the Emperor elect, Charles V.

221. ALBERT DÜRER TO GEORGE SPALATIN.

E. Heidrich: *Albrecht Dürers schriftliche Nachlass.* (Berlin, 1908), p. 180. German. (NUREMBERG, about February, 1520.)

Dürer, the celebrated artist of Nuremberg (1471-1528) had sent Luther some of his engravings early in 1518, from which time till his death he was an enthusiastic Lutheran. His artistic works reproduced in *Klassiker der Kunst,* iv., München, 1908. His literary works edited by Heidrich, *op. cit.* Life by Thausing with English translation by Eaton. *Cf.* also Heidrich: *Albrecht Dürer und die Reformation,* 1910.

Honored and dear Sir:—I have already thanked you in my note for what you sent me, but had then only read the little slip with the address. Your letter, being inside the book, was overlooked, and I have just found it and learn that my gracious Lord Frederic is sending me some of Luther's pamphlets. Wherefore I beg your Honor to express my highest thanks to his Grace, and humbly to commend to him the excellent Dr. Martin Luther, on account of Christian truth which concerns us more than riches and power of this world, for temporal things pass away, but truth lives forever. If God help me I will go to Dr. Martin Luther and make his likeness in copper[1] for a lasting memorial of the Christian man who has helped me out of great anguish. I beg your Honor if Dr. Luther writes anything more in German, please to send it to me at my expense.

You wrote about *Luther's Defence,*[2] but there are no more copies to be had; a second edition is being printed at Augsburg, and when it is ready I will send you one. This pamphlet written here is called heretical in the pulpits, and it is said they will burn it, and they vilify it for being published anonymously. They say Dr. Eck will burn it publicly at Ingolstadt, as happened to Dr. Reuchlin's books.

I am sending my most gracious lord three copies of my engraving of the Cardinal of Mayence. I sent the plate with two hundred copies to the cardinal for which his grace

---

[1]Unfortunately Dürer never carried out this plan.
[2]Lazarus Spengler's *Schutzrede und Christliche Antwort,* mentioned by Luther in a letter to Spalatin, *supra,* no. 220. This probably caused Spalatin to write to Dürer about it, from which we get the approximate date of this letter.

kindly gave me two hundred gulden in gold and twenty ells of damask for a coat. This I receive with pleasure, especially as I am needy at this time. For his Imperial Majesty of excellent memory, who departed this life prematurely, had given me a pension of one hundred gulden[1] which my masters will not pay me now. So I must want in my old days and lose the reward of my work done for his Imperial Majesty. For my eyesight and freedom of hand is going, and I cannot work much longer. This I cannot conceal from you, my trusted and kind friend.

If my gracious lord wishes to have something handsome made out of the stag's antlers I can make a pair of candlesticks out of them. . . . Recommend me to my gracious lord, the elector. Your devoted,

ALBERT DÜRER.

222. LUTHER TO ALBERT, ARCHBISHOP AND ELECTOR OF MAYENCE.

Enders, ii. 307. WITTENBERG, February 4, 1520.

I commend myself in the Lord with all subjection and reverence. Most reverend Father in Christ and most illustrious Prince, I, a man of the lowest condition, would never dare to address your Grandeur, even in a letter, to which more is allowed than modesty permits saying orally, were I not compelled to do so for a great cause, namely, the profession of Christian faith and truth, and our common care for the salvation of all in Christ. If I brought danger on these I would be most impious to keep still. Moreover I have been credibly informed that men who perchance praise and defend me elsewhere, in your presence, most reverend Father in Christ, excite hatred and envy against me. . . .

If the things with which I am accused are right and true, will the grace of my Lord allow me to utter a complaint? Why do they not teach me better? Why do they not show me my error? Why do they condemn me in the presence of

---

[1] A previous letter speaks of two hundred gulden. Probably the hundred gulden had been granted before, and this was raised to two hundred at the Diet of Augsburg, 1518, but the increase was not received by Dürer owing to Maximilian's death in January, 1519.

the great before they convict me, especially as I so often promise to listen to instruction, and as I am prepared to yield on my opinion, or rather I greatly desire to be relieved of the burden of teaching and to hide in a corner?

I am compelled to teach what I have learned and read in Holy Scripture, and I am blamed for teaching what they either will not or cannot blame. Would that my most gracious Lord had leisure to read or hear read my works; your Reverence would doubtless then learn how foreign to me are the charges brought against me. I have not yet heard that my writings have been condemned by any except by those who had not read or heard them, except by a few who are moved by envy to pervert whatever they read, and pretend that I said what I never thought of. Such are those accusations about taking the eucharist in both kinds and about the power of the Pope, in which, if they confess the truth, they really think as I do, though they pretend otherwise, as anyone can easily see who reads my writings.

Wherefore I humbly pray your Reverence by your celebrated loving kindness towards sound learning and men of letters, that your Lordship will deign to hear me more kindly than those spies demand, not so much for my sake as for that of your own salvation and the salvation of many others, and for the sake of Christian truth, which must needs be wounded if I am unjustly either condemned after hearing, or before I am instructed and heard.

Jesus Christ, the judge of all, is witness to my soul that I am conscious of having taught nothing save Christ and the commandments of God, and, again, that I am not so obstinate, but that I desire to be instructed, and when I see my error, to change my opinion. Would that I might owe that favor to your Reverence. For hitherto I have been attacked by many lies, and yet after the truth was revealed shown to be innocent. Therefore I am obliged to suspect that those who attack me in other ways do not act sincerely, especially as they will not teach one ready to be taught, but only criminate him. . . .

Your Reverence's most devoted son,

MARTIN LUTHER.

223. MARCO MINIO TO THE SIGNORY OF VENICE.

Marino Sanuto: *Diarii* (Extracts on Luther, edited by G. M. Thomas under the title: *M. Luther und die Reformationsbewegung. . . . in Auszügen aus Marino Sanuto's Diarien.* Ansbach, 1883), xxviii. 136, Italian. R. Brown: *Calendar of State Papers . . . In Venice.* London, 1869, iii. 11. English. ROME, February 4, 1520.

Minio was Venetian ambassador at Rome 1516-19.

In Germany, an Austin friar, called Friar Matthew [!] Luther, had written works against the Pope and the Church, and had preached publicly at Nuremberg to that effect, which facts having come to the knowledge of the Pope, he had appointed a commission of learned Observant friars, and had appointed two cardinals as their chiefs, namely, the Bishop of Ancona and Cajetan, who were very learned, that they might suppress this opposition in the Church.

224. MARCO MINIO TO THE SIGNORY OF VENICE.

Sanuto, xxviii. 141. Italian. Brown, iii. 12. English.

ROME, February 4, 1520.

Three days ago a commission of all the Generals of the Mendicant orders was held, and such as were not present at Rome were represented by the Procurators of such orders, the chiefs of this commission being the Cardinals of Ancona and Cajetan.

This Commission was appointed in order to condemn certain propositions of Friar Martin Luther, who had preached in Germany against the authority and power of the Pope, and has a considerable party and is much favored by the Elector of Saxony. An attempt is thus being made to deprive Luther of the protection he enjoys, and of his adherents, and the bull is being drawn up; but the course taken by the Commission was injudicious for the said friar's propositions were read and the votes on them demanded without any deliberation.

This friar Martin founds his arguments chiefly on the gospels; he acknowledges the doctors of the Church, such as St. Augustine, but not the other doctors, and he scoffs at St. Thomas Aquinas, Scotus and the like. It is a very scandalous affair.

225. LUTHER TO SPALATIN.

Enders, ii. 315. (WITTENBERG), February 5, 1520.

Greeting. At length I send my letters[1] to the bishops; you find out whether it is best to send them, especially after, in the manner of the Leipsic party, the Bishop of Meissen has posted up an inhibition[2] against my sermon on the sacrament, with whom they hope many others will agree. But I will publish a contradictory notice, and with God's help will show up these silly carnival masks.

Insane Eck foully attacks Carlstadt and me in a new pamphlet.[3] Carlstadt is preparing to answer him, and in such heat that he has given his reply the title: *Against the blockish ass and pretended doctor,* etc. If possible, persuade him either to abstain from cursing back, or not to answer at all; for in his book that wretched sophist has made himself sufficiently contemptible and disgusting, so that no one could make him more so by upbraiding him, and would only make a cover for his baseness, by which it would seem less base. For I have begun to despise the man as I never before despised anyone. Carlstadt will not suffer my advice in this matter, nor would it be safe for you to let him think I had spoken to you about it, for the man is very suspicious. . . .

I remember that I wished that Melanchthon had a wife suited to his character, nor am I sorry for this wish. For I fear the fate which pursues great geniuses will overtake him, especially as he is very careless about domestic matters and his health. But I do not see that he is yet inclined to matrimony. . . .

226. MARCO MINIO TO THE SIGNORY OF VENICE.

Sanuto, xxviii. 143, tergo. Italian. Brown, iii. 16. English.

ROME, February 11, 1520.

The Commission of Franciscan Observants appointed by the Pope against that Friar Martin Luther in Germany, had

[1] Letter to Albert of Mayence, *supra,* no. 222, and one of the same date and similar purport to Adolph, Bishop of Merseburg. Enders, ii. 311. The letters were sent on by Spalatin.

[2] Dated Stolpen, January 24. Printed, Erlangen Edition, *Opera varii argumenti,* iv. 139.

[3] *Contra Martini Ludderi obtusum propugnatorem Andream,* etc. Dedication dated Ingolstadt, December 3, 1519.

intended to draw up a bull against him, but they subsequently made the Pope determine to discuss the matter more fully by making another Commission of other eminent men.

227. LUTHER TO SPALATIN.
Enders, ii. 322. (WITTENBERG), February 12, 1520.

Greeting. Here is the letter[1] of Bucer, a young brother who almost alone in his order gives some promise. At Heidelberg he received me eagerly and simply, and conversed with me showing himself worthy of love and trust, and also of hope.

Your admonitions came late. All that in one lost day, under the auspices of Melanchthon, I conceived, I am now bearing, with the presses as midwives.[2] Suppose there is to be a new and great conflagration, who can resist the plan of God? They are raging so without cause from God or fault from me; and unless God humbles me I will despise them, for you yourself see how easily I can bear their learning and malice. Who knows whether they are predestined to be the cause of revealing the truth, and whether they are not preparing for themselves the punishment of the hatred they have so long nourished against us, namely, the shame which the enemies of the truth ought to win. I have honored the bishop, but if they go on I won't let a bubble like him stop my fighting for Christ's truth.

When his Inhibition was posted up at Oschatz, some brothers of Waldheim who came hither yesterday, told me that someone had written on it: "Behold the bishops of this age post up their ignorance even on Church doors! Alas, Bishop, reread the gospel!" And more. Pray let the matter go its own way; God only is guiding it. We are carried along, as I think, and are passive rather than active. Farewell and pray for me.

MARTIN LUTHER, *Augustinian.*

[1] *Supra*, no. 219.
[2] The Reply to the Bishop of Meissen's Placard, *supra*, no. 225. It was taken at once to the Bishop at Stolpen by the secretary of Mayence, Michael Reysch, and read by him to the bishop and the "Official" (Christopher Beczschicz). They were displeased, but the more the Official cursed the more Reysch laughed.

228. LUTHER TO SPALATIN.

Enders, ii. 327.   WITTENBERG (between February 12 and 18), 1520.

Enders dates this "soon after February 18," but internal evidence seems to me to make it more probable that the letter was written after that of February 12, but before that of February 18. In this dating I follow Hoppe in the St. Louis Walch edition, vol. xxi., no. 263.

Greeting. Good Heavens! Spalatin, how excited you are! More than I or anyone else. I wrote you before not to assume that this affair was begun or is carried on by your judgment or mine or that of any man. If it is of God, it will be completed contrary to, outside of, above and below, your or my understanding.

But let me tell you again that I would not have the least part of this cause decided by your fate or by mine, and that my only fear has always been that I should be left to myself and thus write what would please human wisdom. You must beware of being too wise and I of being too foolish. Too much folly, I confess, displeases men, but too much wisdom still more displeases God, who has chosen the foolish things of the world to confound the wise.[1]

You do not see that my long suffering in not answering five or six wagonloads of Emser's and Eck's curses was the sole cause why those bloated makers of placards[2] dared to revile me with their ridiculous folly.

Secondly, I know that I do not care that at Leipsic my sermon[3] was forbidden and suppressed in a public edict, for I despise their suspicion, reproaches, injuries and malice. Forsooth must we allow these bold men to add to their other furious acts the publication of libels, stuffed not only with lies, but with blasphemy against the gospel truth? Do you forbid us even to bark against these wolves?

The Lord is my witness, how much I have restrained myself for the sake of the bishop's name, not to treat this

---

[1] 1 Corinthians, i. 27. Luther is answering Spalatin's objections to the too great violence of his answer to the Bishop of Meissen. *Cf. supra*, no. 227.

[2] "Schedularii," referring to the "Schedula" of the Bishop of Meissen.

[3] *Sermon on the Sacrament of the Body and Blood.* Weimar, ii. 738.

cursed and impotent edict irreverently. I shall say elsewhere what their brains ought to hear, when they acknowledge that they have published the edict and begin to defend themselves. I consider them unpeaceable and in a future tract shall not abstain from treating them as violators of law, gospel and common sense, so that they may know how much I have hitherto spared their ignorance and malice.

I see that you have not read the edict with sufficient care. If they were not more ignorant than any asses, they would know that nothing was ever written against me, or rather against God's word, more venomous, pestilent, malignant and mendacious. On this account should we exult, or change our manner of writing, or suffer more? You know how I despise that inconvenience.

If you think properly of the gospel, please do not imagine that its cause can be advanced without tumult, offence and sedition. You will not make a pen from a sword, nor peace of war. The Word of God is a sword, it is war and ruin and offence and perdition and poison, and, as Amos says,[1] it met the sons of Ephraim as a bear in the way and as a lioness in the wood. I wrote much more vehemently against Emser, Eck and Tetzel, and you never complained. What if even the official[2] or the bishop himself does not acknowledge publishing the edict?

They write in greater danger than I do, for they have so forgotten all gospel, laws, reason and common sense, that they care for nothing but to condemn me unheard, unwarned and untaught. They do to me what I have never done to them, at least never to the bishop and the official.

Let them go on as they please. If they have forgotten the dignity of the episcopal office, or even that of his subordinate, doubt not that I will soon remind them of it by citing texts of the Bible. God so carries me on that I cannot fear their rash and untaught hatred. Let God see to it, for he acts through me, since I am certain that none of these things have been sought by me, but that they were drawn from me, one and all, by a fury not my own.

[1] Rather Hosea, xiii. 7f. *Cf.* Amos, iii. 8.
[2] *Supra*, no. 227, note 1.

Be of good cheer, and do not brood over the apparent facts. Faith is the proof of things not seen;[1] why, then, do you judge according to what is seen? What is done, Spalatin, and what is seen in this affair are different. I seek nothing; there is one that seeketh.[2] Let it stand or fall, I neither gain nor lose anything. You have my opinion.

Our friends are not as much displeased as are you and as you wrote. The provost[3] thinks that I have treated these brawlers rightly. If everything which comes forth under the name of bishops is to be received, what tyranny will reign! I am sure that the Bishop of Meissen is not the author of this edict, and I firmly hope that he will not recognize it. Even if he does this I assume that my warning will make him act more prudently and wisely in future.

Yet I cannot deny that I have been more vehement than I should; but as they knew that I would be, they should not have irritated the dog. You know yourself how hard it is to moderate an angry pen. This is the reason why I am sorry to be in the public eye; and the more I am involved in such business, contrary to my monastic vow, the more sorry I am. But they act against me and God's Word so criminally and fiercely, that were I not moved to write warmly, even a mind of stone might be moved to war by indignation. Far from having such a mind, however, I am naturally warm, and have a pen which is not at all blunt. So I am carried beyond the bounds of moderation by these monsters.

Moreover I wonder whence this new scrupulousness is born, which calls all that is said against an opponent scurillity. What do you think of Christ? Was he scurrilous when he called the Jews a perverse and adulterous generation, offspring of vipers, hypocrites and children of the devil? Paul speaks of dogs, vain babblers, seducers, unlearned, and in Acts xiii. so rages against a false prophet that he might seem insane, saying: "O full of all guile and all villainy, thou son

[1] Hebrews, xi. 1.
[2] John, viii. 50.
[3] Dr. Henning Göde, professor at Erfurt till 1509, when he went to Wittenberg as professor of canon law and provost of the City Church. In 1516 he returned to Erfurt for two years, when he came back to Wittenberg. He died January, 1521. He was against the Reformation.

of the devil, thou enemy of all truth."[1] Why did not Paul rather flatter him to convert him than thus thunder? The consciousness of truth cannot be patient against the obstinate and unconquered enemies of the truth.

But enough of this trifling now. I see that all demand moderation from me, even my enemies who least practice it. If I am immoderate, at least I am simple and open, in which I think I am better than they who invent stories full of guile. Farewell and fear not. BROTHER MARTIN LUTHER.

P. S.—You write among other things that your advice was scorned, and don't remember that I wrote you that your advice came late when the books were almost printed.

229. LUTHER TO SPALATIN.

Enders, ii. 324. (WITTENBERG), February 18, 1520.

Greeting. Dear George, by God's grace I have courage enough against the conflagration of Meissen,[2] and you will see me obeying your advice to answer as gently as possible. Indeed, I will let you and your friends see a copy of my Latin answer before it is printed, which I should also have done with the German answer, had it not been printed before your letter came. But neither in this latter have I touched the ulcer of this edict on account of my reverence for the bishop, although truly the edict is blasphemous and more furious against Christ's gospel than any heresy. I shall point this out in future, and unless they beware I shall treat them as they deserve in exposing their ignorance. I will not suffer a condemned error to be assumed in God's gospel even by all the angels of heaven, much less by the idols of one terrestrial church.

If it seem good to you, let us do our enemies this favor. Write them, if there are any there who will listen to you, warning and begging them to act against Luther as prudently and cautiously as they can, for he took great care to spare them in this pamphlet. If they begin to shun the frost, perhaps they will be buried in snow. For unless God has de-

---

[1] Acts, xiii. 10.
[2] *I. e.*, the affair of the edict published by the Bishop of Meissen at Stolpen, against which Luther was publishing two answers, Latin and German.

prived me of all sense (which he may do in his excellent will), it will happen that the more they stir up this dung (so to speak), the more it will stink. I would not threaten so great and so many men, save that I grieve for and pity their shame, which they have irrevocably fixed on themselves by this edict, and because I desire to offer them the same terms in this matter that I desire for myself. I would not take all the wealth in the world to be found the author of such an edict. . . .

230. LUTHER TO GEORGE SPALATIN.

Enders, ii. 331. (WITTENBERG), February 24, 1520.

Greeting. . . . I believe the men of Stolpen[1] will not keep quiet; perchance the Lord will do something through them which neither they nor I expect; in the meantime, let them find an interpreter of their pamphlet how they may. I have written the bishops[2] and am expecting an answer.

I do not remember about my *Sermon on Good Works;* as I have printed so much there is danger that I shall weary the buying public at length. I do not know the German *Apology* which you say is a supplement to the one printed at Nuremberg. Send it along if you have it, so that I may see it. Let the *Answer of the Unlearned Canons*[3] follow. . . .

Yesterday Matthew Adrian[4] sent me word by Dr. Conrad König,[5] the son-in-law of Dr. Wolfgang Stehelin,[6] requesting an answer. I think I have answered him, but the letter has been lost. König also asked how much salary Adrian would require to teach Hebrew here. For he thought ninety or one

---

[1] *Supra,* no. 227, note 2.

[2] Of Mayence and Merseburg; Luther wrote them, at the elector's suggestion, in answer to their charges against his *Sermon on the Lord's Supper. Supra,* no. 222.

[3] A work of Oecolampadius to support Luther against Eck.

[4] A baptized Spanish Jew, a physician. He taught Hebrew at Basle, then at Heidelberg, then (1517) at the *Collegium Trilingue* at Louvain, then in Wittenberg, where he remained about a year (to February, 1521). Fuller references, Enders, ii. 223.

[5] Of Stuttgart, doctor of law, Dean of the faculty of arts at Wittenberg 1509, and Rector 1510.

[6] Of Rotheburg, came to Wittenberg from Tübingen in 1502; 1521-5 chancellor of Duke Henry of Saxony at Freiberg. Later against the Reformation. Enders, i. 190.

hundred gulden would suffice, as I had already heard several times from Adrian himself. Please tell us what you think or hope in the matter.

I have at hand, by the kindness of Schleupner,[1] Lorenzo Valla's proof[2] (edited by Hutten), that the Donation of Constantine is a forgery. Good Heavens! what darkness and wickedness is at Rome! You wonder at the judgment of God, that such unauthentic, crass, impudent lies not only lived, but prevailed for so many centuries and were incorporated into the Canon Law, and (that no degree of horror might be wanting), became as articles of faith. I am in such a passion that I hardly doubt that the Pope is the Antichrist, which the world at large expects, so closely do their lives, acts, sayings and laws agree. But more of this when I see you. If you have not seen the book, I shall take care that you read it.

I do not know what to say about the students and the painters. I fear it is a little thing artificially blown up to look big. I spoke of it in a sermon, but did not satisfy all. Some said I favored the students too much, and some the contrary. This affair of the devil is so hard to manage that it would have been better to let it cool off of itself, rather than start putting it down with so much tumult and noise. There are only a few actors in the tragedy, and they poor ones, on account of whom the whole city and university are disturbed. Indeed, it is impossible (as Antiochus said to Herod) that in a great sick body an ulcer or pus or something like it should not occasionally break out, which, if you let it take its course, will die down of itself, but if you keep it in and stop it up will infect and ruin the whole body. I shall do what I can.

Farewell and pray for me. Our prior Helt went to Magdeburg as soon as your letters came.

MARTIN LUTHER, *Augustinian.*

[1] Dominic Schleupner of Breslau, matriculated at Wittenberg 1519 and later became preacher of St. Sebald in Nuremberg. Spoken of by Luther last on December 1, 1530. Enders, viii. 326.

[2] The brilliant Italian humanist Valla (1406-57) had proved that the so-called Donation of Constantine to the Pope was a forgery. Hutten published this, 1519. On the influence of the work on Luther, *cf.* Smith, *op. cit.,* pp. 72ff.

231. ALBERT, ARCHBISHOP AND ELECTOR OF MAYENCE, TO LUTHER.

Enders, ii. 336. CALBE, February 26, 1520.

Greeting in the Lord. Honorable and beloved in Christ, we received your letter[1] in which you try to free us from the danger of crafty suggestion and yourself from the peril of being thought hatefully hypocritical and obstinate. We could not but be pleased that you promised to listen to better doctrine, and, if you are taught, to give up your own opinion. Although, as befitting our office, we profess that all matters of Christian faith and piety are very close to our heart, yet we have not hitherto had leisure given us to read or even to glance at your works which are now in everybody's hands. Wherefore it is not our intention to pass judgment on them, but to leave that to others who are greater than we, whom we reverence, and to whom we rightly yield precedence, and who have already taken up the discussion of these matters.[2]

But we do greatly wish that you as well as all others who have undertaken a spiritual life, should treat sacred things reverently, piously, modestly, without tumult, hatred and contumely, as becoming. For not without serious pain of mind and vehement displeasure we daily learn that distinguished men professing to be Christians fiercely fight, as though for a great, serious matter, for their own frivolous opinions and notions, as, for example, whether the power of the Roman pontiff is divine or human, and of free will, and many other similar trifles, which do not concern true Christianity. Everything is treated as a matter of vital importance, everyone defends his own opinion haughtily not without reproaching and reviling his opponent. Thus, to the great peril of inciting disobedience and sedition, many strange opinions are scattered among the fickle crowd and the unlearned people, and much is rashly suggested to the ears of the laity contrary to the long established customs of the Church of Christ,

---

[1] *Supra*, 222.
[2] Luther resented this refusal of Albert to discuss his books, as he wrote him December 1, 1521: "To my second letter to your Grace, humbly asking for instruction, I got a hard, improper, unepiscopal, unchristian answer, referring me to higher powers for information." Smith, *op. cit.*, p. 128.

forsooth that the venerable sacrament of communion should be indiscriminately distributed in both kinds to all assembled, as well laymen as clergy. Moreover we have heard that some men audaciously belittle the authority of general councils in order to uphold and defend their own opinions.

We do not see why it is expedient for you or others to treat such matters, nor how it can make for the majesty, purity and dignity of Christianity and for the peace and tranquillity of the Church. Perhaps these things could be considered at a more convenient time and place by men skilled in letters and to whom the duty should be assigned. This method of discussion would yield more fruit and less danger, without envy and incitement to disobedience and scandal to the populace, and without insulting anyone. This would be better than to have such matters rashly bandied about by the unlearned and by the prating rabble.

Finally, we cannot disapprove your assumption to teach what you read and have learned in Holy Scripture, provided only that you do it piously, gently, without bitterness and without inciting to disobedience to the public authority of the Church. If your work be of God, it will be praiseworthy and fruitful, and, as we say to you with Gamaliel, Acts v.,[1] strong and invincible; but if your work be of hatred, pride and ill will, it is of men and can easily be overthrown. For everyone is in danger of abusing the benefits of God, and of fighting against the truth and against God. May he grant that we and you and all other Christians may do right. Farewell in Christ.

232. ULRICH VON HUTTEN TO PHILIP MELANCHTHON AT WITTENBERG.

Corpus Reformatorum, i. 147. STECKELBERG, February 28 (1520).

I enclose a letter[2] I wrote long ago, which has been returned to me, having been badly cared for by those to whom I entrusted it. Please tell Luther at once and privately what I wrote about Sickingen, but so that no one shall know that I have had anything to do with the affair. There is a reason

[1] Acts, v. 38f.
[2] *I. e.,* that of January 20, *supra,* no. 218.

not mentioned in the letter. If Luther is in trouble, and can get help nowhere else, here is safety. Here he can mock his detractors in perfect security. Sickingen and I have important reasons, which I would tell you if I saw you. I fear that some evil will happen to the barbarians and to all who support the Roman yoke. My dialogues, the *Roman Triad* and the *Inspicientes* are being printed; they are very free against the Pope and the despoilers of Germany. I believe you will approve, or at least not disapprove of them. Above all things warn Luther. If his business is doubtful, bid him at once without delay betake himself to Sickingen. He could see me on the way, but I do not know if I would then be here. . . .

233. LUTHER TO GEORGE SPALATIN AT ALTENBURG.
Enders, ii. 342.   WITTENBERG, February 29, 1520.

Greeting. At length the Bishop of Merseburg has sent me back my messenger with a letter, after keeping him waiting three days. I am still waiting for the answer of the Cardinal Archbishop of Mayence. I have Merseburg's communication and it does not displease me except that he confesses he was moved against my sermon by the letters and reports of others. Perhaps he never read it himself, but condemned it on vicarious testimony. Then he deprecates the strife about the Pope, and very properly, as though I delighted to be blown around by these whirlwinds and would not prefer to live in peace as he writes that he would. Truly while we are well we scorn the advice of the sick, as Terence says, and yet if you would remain well you must give heed to them.

It was hardly to spite me that the Archbishop of Mayence forbade the monks to beg. Our Prior Held, just returned from Magdeburg, is full of complaints against him. For the cardinal begins to tyrannize and dare all things, even offending the dignitaries of his own church. Who knows for what purpose he has been called to fill such a responsible position? Doubt not that the Lord will use him for some future miracle. As for me, I should much prefer to have this begging done away completely; this is one of the opinions for which Eck makes me a heretic and boasts of so doing. For I hate that shameful way of life and should prefer to learn a trade to-day to support myself rather than live thus, and I shall die in this opinion, Eck notwithstanding.

I am surprised that my former letters have not reached you.

I am glad to read of the conflict of Emser and Schott.[1] Farewell and pray for me.

MARTIN LUTHER, *Augustinian*.

234. LUTHER TO SPALATIN.
Enders, ii. 346. (WITTENBERG), March 2, 1520.

Greeting. I send some things[2] just out against Eck, dear Spalatin, which please return after reading. You see how Leipsic and Eck are going to be another Cologne and Hochstratten. In my judgment the *Dialogue* smells of Pirckheimer, for he is offended with Scheurl, and there are other indications. I am not pleased with this matter of raging against Eck, for it is a libel, and an open attack is better than a bite from under cover. Farewell and pray for me in the Lord.

235. G. COWPER TO HIS FATHER, THOMAS COWPER.
MSS. of the Shrewsbury and Coventry Corporations, 1899, p. 47.
English. (SHREWSBURY or COVENTRY), March 3, 1520.

This fragment is interesting as proving the early spread of Lutheran opinions in England. Thomas Cowper is mentioned quite frequently in the State Papers as a tax-collector and financial agent of the English government.

. . . As for newes, ther ys none but of late ther was herytykes here which did take Luters opinyons. . . .

236. HERMANN HUMPIUS PHRYSO TO LUTHER.
Enders, ii. 350 PARIS, March 14 (1520).

The author of this epistle, identified as Hermann Hajo Frisius (*i. e.*, of Holland), is occasionally mentioned in the letters of Erasmus and his friends. *Cf.* Enthoven: *Briefe on Erasmus,* p. 129, and De

---

[1] John Schott of Oberlindt made a pilgrimage to Palestine 1517; was with Luther at Worms 1521; later an officer at Coburg. Enders, iv. 332. I can find nothing of his quarrel with Emser.

[2] This refers to the *Eccius dedolatus* (a pun on Eck, which in German means "corner," the whole phrase meaning, "The planed-off corner"), a broadside probably by Pirckheimer, though he denied the authorship of it.

Vocht in *Englische Studien*, xl. 376. In 1532 he was a jurist and imperial councillor. Allen, iii. 444.

Inasmuch as I could not explain to you, even at great length and with much art, how much I favor your difficult as well as fair and pious undertaking, I shall certainly not try to do so in this short familiar epistle. How much should I favor Luther, who, I see, is approved by all good men and rightly extolled by the greatest, and who also is hated and reviled by the wicked! I observe both these facts with the greatest, that is, with equal joy, for I consider them equal praise. Recently, when I was living with Erasmus (for although unworthy I did so about eight months) I learned well how high an opinion of Luther that man of most exquisite judgment held, and which he would testify to his *table companions*,[1] among whom, as among faithful friends, he was accustomed to lay bare his mind. William Nesen[2] was of the same opinion with him, for he all but adored Luther. But as much as the deliberate judgment of these two pleased me, so much did that precipitous condemnation[3] of you by the sophists of Cologne and Louvain disturb me. But again, when I learned how unjust and unlearned their condemnation was, I greatly rejoiced, and finally exulted and applauded, for I saw that this would be as a *branding-iron*[1] by which both of those Kakademies[4] would stamp themselves with a mark of lasting infamy. And so a few days ago, when I was preparing to leave Louvain for Paris at the urgent request of the theologians,[5] there came into my hands, I hardly know from where, some marginal notes on that most beautiful book.[6] *By Hermes*[1] they were neither foolish nor unlearned; with the aid of the Muses I will see to it that they are printed at my own expense if necessary, and, if there is anything

[1] Greek.

[2] *Supra*, no. 213.

[3] The University of Cologne condemned Luther's doctrines on August 30, and this was ratified by Louvain on November 7, 1519.

[4] An untranslatable pun, combining the Greek words for "bad" and for "academy."

[5] Hermann was evidently one of the younger scholars, who, like Nesen, was expelled from Louvain about this time.

[6] This book was perhaps the volume of Luther's *Works* issued by Froben which was the one condemned by Cologne and Louvain.

lacking to them, I will supply it with my own pen. If Wolfgang Wilder, who is to carry these letters to you, were not in such a hurry that he cannot conveniently wait three days, your Reverence should have a copy of them; however, you will shortly see copies of them everywhere. Finally, please take my service for the best, and hereafter number this Dutchman, hitherto unknown to you even by name, among your strongest supporters. Farewell, reverend Father in Christ, and continue strongly to assert our faith. I pray that the Holy Spirit may be your continual comforter and *true paraclete*.[1] Hail and farewell a thousand times. . . .

237. GABRIEL DELLA VOLTA TO JOHN VON STAUPITZ.

Zeitschrift für Kirchengeschichte, ii. 478.　　　　March 15, 1520.

We were very anxious to see and speak to you at the general chapter celebrated last year[2] at Venice. For we had need of speaking with you about many things concerning the honor of the Congregation, and particularly concerning Martin Luther's affair, for at that time the volume[3] which he himself published on the virtue of indulgences began to appear, the doctrines of which, though they were a scandal to small and great, would have been susceptible of easy treatment, had we all agreed on one course. He himself confesses in his writings that his respect[4] for you and his love for the monastic profession is so great, that we doubt not that every old disagreement would have been settled and under God's leadership have been extinguished and prevented from growing worse. But as we were deprived of the advantage of seeing you for reasons which, as we believe, were honorable, we thought it necessary to write you this letter, to inform you what enormous evils threaten your Congregation and our whole Order unless Martin ceases from speaking and writing about those matters which are either disagreeable to the Holy Roman Church, or scandalous to her. As to the

[1]Greek.
[2]In June, 1519.
[3]The *Resolutiones disputationum*, which first appeared in September, 1518, are meant.
[4]In the letter to Staupitz of May 30, 1518, printed as a preface to the work mentioned. *Supra*, no. 65.

hurt of the Order, you know that our profession is made odious in the eyes of all, and the habit and name of the Augustinians is so hateful, that we are, as it were, insulted as worthless by the apostolic see. We must appear to the public the more slack, in that having been the only mendicant order never accused nor suspected of heresy, we are now, like heretics, forced to flee the face of men. The thing ought to be the more intolerable to us as it seems to touch our most innocent Pope Leo X., to whom our profession owes as much as it could owe to any mortal. On account of the innumerable benefits he has conferred on us it is our interest not to cross him, but to please him and to be humble and, if necessary, pour out our blood and lay down our lives a hundred times a day. . . .

We have heard that great men are turning their attention to this affair, and that the ax is laid at the root. We have been credibly informed that a bull is being drawn up against a number of the writings of the said Martin, in which, however, our Supreme Lord, out of respect to our profession, has not decreed that either the name of the Order of St. Augustine or that of Martin Luther should be wiped out, from which we can see how kind, gentle and benevolent to the Augustinian family Pope Leo shows himself, who, though he has been provoked for four years, can hardly be induced to defend himself, not to mention taking vengeance. He rather covers up the offence of the man, dreading our common confounding, and only expecting improvement. . . . Wherefore we conjure you by the bond of charity for these reasons to use all your power, care, industry and diligence to make Martin abstain from speaking against the Holy Roman Church and indulgences, that he may not, relying on his own genius, begin to move against her whom the Lord founded upon a firm rock, but that he may cease from publishing books and keep silence when he sees that daily more dangerous offences arise, and that he may remember those words of Christ: "Woe unto that man through whom the offence cometh."[1] . . .

Wherefore we write you praying by your piety and pro-

[1] Matthew, xviii. 7.

fession and love to God, if the zeal, honor, advantage and health of your profession and Congregation mean aught to you, that you should give all your care, study and thought to this one thing, that Martin may help you and at length come to himself, that with him our Order may be saved from great infamy and calamity. Farewell in the Lord.[1]

238. GABRIEL DELLA VOLTA, GENERAL OF TE AUGUSTINIANS, TO LAWRENCE BRAGADIN, A VENETIAN GRANDEE.

Sanuto, xxviii. 215. Italian. Brown, iii. 28. English.

ROME, March 16, 1520.

Bragadin was ambassador to France 1526, to Rome 1535-7.

Nothing has been done about Martin save that all the theologians of Rome have debated together three times, in presence of the Cardinals of Ancona and Cajetan, discussing certain propositions of the said Martin, part of which were considered heretical, part scandalous.

All the generals of the orders have in like manner stated in writing their objections, and the reasons which cause them to remonstrate. It is now said that a decretal will be drawn up, reproving his said false propositions without naming him, but I think he will be admonished by a private breve and invited to retract, and should he not retract, but persevere in his obstinacy, they will proceed against him as a heretic.

239. LUTHER TO SPALATIN.

Enders, ii. 362.   WITTENBERG, March 19, 1520.

... I send you the work of the asses of Louvain and Cologne, which I am now answering in print.[2]

Please read John Huss[3] and return him. He not only pleases me, but both his spirit and learning seem to me mi-

---

[1] This letter may have decided Staupitz to lay down his office of Vicar, as he did in August, 1520. Luther writes on May 5 that Staupitz expects to do so.

[2] The Condemnation of Luther's doctrine by Cologne (August 31, 1519), and Louvain (November 7), was printed in February, 1520, with a dedicatory epistle by Adrian, Cardinal of Tortosa, later Pope Adrian VI. Luther's answer appeared in 1520, Weimar, vi. 170.

[3] Luther now read Huss's *De Ecclesia*, sent him by Rozd'alowsky at the time of the Leipsic debate (*supra*, no. 161). The effect it made on him is best painted in a letter translated, Smith, *op. cit.*, p. 72.

raculous. Two thousand copies are being printed by Thomas Anselm.[1]

It is said that at Vienna you saw visions in the sky,[2] namely flames and conflagrations. I, too, would like to see them; perhaps my tragedy is contained in them, as it was in the former ones. Farewell and pray for me.

MARTIN LUTHER, Augustinian.

240. LUTHER TO JOHN LANG AT ERFURT.

Enders, ii. 364.   WITTENBERG, March 21, 1520.

Greeting. I think, reverend Father, that you received my letter from Brother Martin Benedict. We have no news. My answer to the damning theologs is in press. My friend Eck goes to Rome to arouse the forest of Lebanon.[3] But I believe that even Rome is subject to Christ, the Lord of all, who, if I am worthy, will act for me there also, but if I am unworthy will not act for me even here. Pray the Lord for me that I may sometime become good and plead his cause worthily in this unworthy age.

I commend to you the wife of Dr. Thomas Eschaus,[4] for I think the woman has either already died or will die to-day, as she has no hope of life. Farewell in Christ.

BROTHER MARTIN LUTHER, Augustinian.

241. LUTHER TO MARTIN SELIGMANN AT MANSFELD.

Enders, ii. 367.   WITTENBERG, March 25, 1520.

Greeting. Thanks for your gift,[5] dear Martin. The same monster was sent me before, and I am now answering it, expecting my pamphlet to be published to-morrow. There are many here, and even in the elector's court, who think

---

[1] A publisher who started at Strassburg, 1488, then removed to Pforzheim and Tübingen, and at this time was at Hagenau.

[2] These were described as occurring at Vienna, January 3-7, 1520, in a book by John Virdung of Hassfurt.

[3] Reference to Judges, ix. 15? On Eck's trip to Rome and its effect, Smith, p. 96.

[4] Eschaus or Esch, matriculated at Cologne 1491, came to the University of Wittenberg in 1502, where he acted as notary, and took several degrees, including bachelor of canon law 1504-5, and doctor of medicine September 13, 1518. He continued practising and teaching privately until his death in 1535. He frequently attended Luther, who considered him the best local physician. Smith, p. 94. <i>Archiv fur Reformationsgeschichte,</i> vii. 256.

[5] The <i>Condemnation by Cologne and Louvain.</i>

that this was made up by one of the *Obscure Men,* whom rivals suborned to attack me and seek an occasion. But Dorp's[1] letter will show you that the work is genuine. You will learn all from Melanchthon. Give my regards to your pastor,[2] Jonas, John Reinecke[3] and William;[4] also to my flesh and blood. The men of Leipsic and Meissen keep cawing away without getting anywhere. I hear that my sister Barbara has died. May she rest in peace. Amen. We shall all follow her. Farewell and pray the Lord for me.

MARTIN LUTHER.

242. LUTHER TO SPALATIN.

Enders, ii. 369. (WITTENBERG), March 26, 1520.

Greeting. Dear George, I recently forgot to send you the letter of Dorp, which I received with others from Antwerp. Read it and see whether you can think the thing a fiction[5] which was published there. For Dorp, as I think you know, is the most learned of all the Louvanians, not only by the witness of Erasmus, but by that of this, his letter, and the other which Erasmus has inserted in his *Farrago.*[6]

I thank the Lord who has occupied my mind with other things so that I should not read the Cardinal of Tortosa[7] carefully, for he writes most impiously of all that divine and natural law is in the hand of the man possessed of divine authority. This is such a horrible portent that I could not pass over it, were my mind present. Farewell and pray the Lord for me. MARTIN LUTHER, *Augustinian.*

[1]Martin Bartholomew van Dorp (1485-May 31, 1525), studied at Louvain, where he became professor in 1504. He took his doctorate in theology 1515. From 1514 till his death he was, in spite of temporary disagreements with Erasmus, his warm friend and principal supporter at Louvain. He was also favorable to Luther, though cautiously. This letter is lost. *Cf.* Allen, ii. 11, with references, and de Jongh, 162 (De Jongh wrongly thinks this letter was the *Acta Academiae Lovaniensis,* which, as it was not composed until November, 1520, is impossible).
[2]Kammerer.
[3]Reinecke was an old school friend of Luther, the son of the Mansfeld Bailiff, Peter Reinecke, later iron-master at Mansfeld. Died July 15, 1538. Enders, iii. 402, xii. 1, Smith, 250f.
[4]Reifenstein of a baptized Jewish family, from 1502 till his death, 1538, collector of taxes at Stolberg. Enders, vi. 378.
[5]*Supra,* no. 241.
[6]Dorp to Erasmus, July 14, 1518, in the *Farrago nova epistolarum Des. Erasmi,* Froben, October, 1519.
[7]Adrian, later Adrian VI., no. 202.

243. LUTHER TO JOHN DUKE OF SAXONY.

Enders, ii. 372. De Wette, i. 434. Weimar, vi. 203. German.

WITTENBERG, March 29, 1520.

This is the dedication to the treatise *On Good Works*, Weimar, vi. 196.

John the Steadfast, born 1468, elector from the death of his brother, Frederic, May 5, 1525, till his own death, August 16, 1532. He was a warm supporter of the Reformation from the first. *Cf. Realencyclopädie*, and J. Becker: *Kurfürst Johann von Sachsen und seine Bezeihungen zu Luther.*

Serene, highborn Prince, gracious Lord! Pray accept my humble service and poor prayers. Gracious Prince and Lord, I have long been desirous of showing my humble service and duty to your Grace with some spiritual goods which are at my command, but considering my ability I have always found it too small to undertake to offer something worthy of your Grace. But as my most gracious Lord, Lord Frederic Duke of Saxony, Grand Marshal of the Holy Roman Empire, Elector and Vicegerent, etc., has not disdained, but has graciously accepted my mediocre book[1] dedicated to his Grace, which has now, contrary to my expectations, been printed; I have taken courage from this gracious example, and have presumed to hope that, as the same princely blood runs in your veins, you would have equal clemency and good will, and accordingly that your Grace would not disdain my poor, humble offering, which I think more important than any of my sermons or tracts, in that it treats of good works. For good works contain more poison and deceit than any other creature, and the simple man is easily led astray by them, so that our Lord Christ commanded us to beware of the sheep's clothing under which wolves were hidden. For neither gold, silver, gems nor any precious thing has so much adulteration and dross as have good works, which must all have one simple virtue without which they are mere dissembling, hypocrisy and deceit. I know well and daily hear some who despise my lowliness say that I do nothing but make tracts and German homilies for the unlearned laity; but I do not care for

[1] *The Tesseradecas.*

that charge. Would to God that in my whole life with all my power I had helped one layman to improve; I would be satisfied with that and thank God and willingly after that would let all my books die. I let others judge whether it is a great art, and profitable to Christianity, to make books wholesale. But I think, if I cared to make big books of their sort, I might, by divine help, do it more quickly than they could make a small sermon of my sort. If success were as easy as failure Christ would long since have been cast again from heaven and God's throne itself turned upside down. If we can't all write poetry, at least we all want to judge it. I am heartily willing to leave others the honor of doing great things, and will not be ashamed myself to preach and write German for the unlearned laity. And, though I have little power in this, yet it seems to me that if we had hitherto applied ourselves to this and would apply ourselves to it henceforth, it would be more profit and improvement to Christianity than all the big books and disputations of the learned in the schools.

Moreover I have never compelled or asked anyone to hear me, or to read my sermons. I have freely served the public with that which God has given me and for which I am responsible; let anyone who does not care for it read and hear others. Also I do not care much whether they need me or not, it is enough and too much for me that some laymen, and fine men, too, humble themselves to read my sermons. And if nothing else impelled me, yet it would be more than enough that I have learned that your Grace likes such German books, and is very anxious for instruction on good works and faith. It became me to do my best to serve such men. Wherefore I humbly pray your Grace kindly to receive this testimony of my good intentions until God gives me the time to write a German exposition of faith.[1] Even in the present work I desired to show how we use and need faith in all good works, and consider it the principal work. If God permit, at another

---

[1] *Glaube* is the German for both "faith" and "creed." The treatise *On Good Works* followed the order of the Ten Commandments. It is interesting to see how the exposition of these, with the Creed and the Lord's Prayer, which later became the substance of the *Catechism* (1529, *cf.* Smith, 234f.) were thus early the staple of Luther's preaching.

time I will treat the creed by itself as we daily pray, or speak the same. I humbly commend myself to your Grace.

Your Grace's humble chaplain,

DR MARTIN LUTHER,
Augustinian at Wittenberg.

244. ULRICH ZWINGLI TO OSWALD MYCONIUS AT LUCERNE.

Corpus Reformatorum, xciv. 292.   ZURICH, April 2, 1520.

Myconius (also Geisshüsler and Müller), of Lucerne, matriculated at Basle 1510, B. A. 1514, then became public reader. In 1516 he went to Zurich, where he was instrumental in getting Zwingli. In the autumn of 1519 he returned to Lucerne to open a school, which he had to give up when he joined the Reformation in 1522. After a year at Einsiedeln he came early in 1524 to Zurich, where he taught school until after Zwingli's death (1531), when he went to Basle as successor to Oecolampadius. He died here in 1552.

. . . I would not have you ignorant, that, earnestly as Zasius commended himself to us he recently wrote that he was so minded that he could do no other than write against Luther,[1] because the latter had dared to make light of the majesty of the sacred canons. Here you see the jurist dedicated to his own profession! I not only warned Zasius not to do this, but I even politely admonished him to consider this only: namely, that though, as I must admit, Luther lacked moderation, yet by freely exposing and censuring the crimes of the prelates, if they continued to be bad, he would finally frighten them and put some sense of shame into them. Zasius was pleased with this advice. . . .

245. ERASMUS TO JUSTUS JONAS.

Sitzungsberichte der phil.-hist. Classe der kaiserlichen Akademie der Wissenschaften. Wein, 1880, xcv. 598.   LOUVAIN, April 9, 1520.

. . . I would not like the Dominicans to know what a friend[2] of Luther they have made. The university has conceived incurable madness; Atensis[3] has perished, but Eg-

---

[1] *Supra,* no. 196, and the letter of Zasius to Zwingli, February 16, 1520. *Corpus Reformatorum,* xciv. 265.

[2] Text, "amicum," which I think correct, believing that Erasmus refers to himself. Horawitz, *loc. cit.,* suggests "animum," which, in my opinion, would be less sensible.

[3] John Briard of Ath, thence known as Athensis and Noxus (ἄτη being

mond and Latomus, the one blear-eyed, the other halt, act more odiously than he.¹ . . .   Your Erasmus.

246. MELANCHTHON TO SPALATIN.
Corpus Reformatorum, i. 153.   (Wittenberg, April 13, 1520.)

As Luther has written you about the sentence in John,² there is no need for my writing anything. For why, as Cicero says, should I play the actor before Roscius? . . . It was about this very sentence that a dispute arose with the French mathematician. He said that he would give in something to the desires of the people if he professed Luther's doctrines, but that it was generally thought that even Luther did not believe all his own dogmas. *He meant to say that all that Luther said was not true,*³ but thought that he could more easily entice people with this circumlocution. Then I said that I thought this was an evil purpose, and, what was the last thing an honorable man would consent to, underhanded. A good man ought to say freely and boldly what he thought. Truth does not need to be adulterated with either art or fraud. A suspicion of falsehood was a derogation to Luther's doctrine. He whose life was different from his doctrine would by that very fact raise suspicion, and nothing ought to be so entirely avoided as all suspicion of falsehood. The authority of one teaching by fraud was impaired. For what would the people think of one who taught by lies when they found them out? I added much of the same sort. Then he, to guard against being thought to have made a false or captious criticism, took refuge, as it were, in these words: That by no means was fraud to be used, but that he would consent to be taken for a liar if all that Luther said, everywhere, by chance, seriously or in joke, were true, for every man was said to be a liar.

the Greek for *noxa*), began to teach at Louvain 1492; was made doctor of theology 1500, Rector 1505 and 1510, the leading theologian after the departure of Adrian of Utrecht. He was the most determined opponent of Erasmus, and would have been of Luther, had it not been for his death on January 8, 1520. De Jongh, p. 149ff.

¹On the campaign of Egmond and Latomus against Luther, *supra*, no. 213.
²Enders, ii. 379. The sentence was, "Ye can do nothing without me," John, xv. 5.
³The words in italics are in German.

Now you can see, dear Spalatin, how absurd and clumsy he was. For what on earth have Luther's jokes with his friends to do with his doctrine? Even thus it is my opinion that he never jokes, but that some serious meaning lies behind the jests. O truly ridiculous Parisian! Yet he would defend this opinion with his teeth! Farewell, Spalatin.

YOUR PHILIP.

247. LUTHER TO SPALATIN AT LOCHAU.
Enders, ii. 382. (WITTENBERG), April 16, 1520.

Greeting. Dear Spalatin, we have agreed with Adrian[1] that he should delay a little. He promised to wait eight days in Berlin for letters from us. Now we must try to get an answer from Werner of Bacharach as quickly as possible. He demands a salary of a hundred gulden. In this whole affair we must take great care not to fall between two stools (as they say), by losing one, while the other is called by Mayence or goes of his own accord. Many of our professors strongly urge me to keep Adrian for one year at least, if only, as they think, to prevent the shame of having him called by eclipsed Leipsic;[2] for there is a rumor that they will take him to spite us. If you are not able to write briefly what we should do, at least write to him at Berlin not to mind this delay. I suspect that he will go as professor of Hebrew to Frankfort on the Oder or to Leipsic if we turn him down. Answer quickly.

There is a rumor[3] that the direst bull against me is about to be issued. Thus the provost of Neuwerk[4] warns and advises me, as the saying is. Moreover, certain even of my enemies who pitied me have asked my friends in Halberstadt to warn me that there is a certain doctor of medicine, who can make himself invisible by magic when he wants to

---

[1] This first paragraph refers to the efforts of Wittenberg to secure a Hebrew professor, the candidates being Matthew Adrian and Werner, of whom nothing else is known.

[2] An untranslatable pun borrowed from *Eccius dedolatus,* on the Latin accusative *Lipsim* (Leipsic) and *eclipsin.*

[3] Preparations for drawing up a bull against Luther had been going on at Rome ever since the beginning of the year; they were greatly stimulated by the arrival in that city of Eck towards the end of March. *Cf.* Smith, *op. cit.,* 95ff.

[4] Nicolas Demuth of Neuwerk, near Halle, in the service of Albert of Mayence. Enders, iv. 123f.

kill somebody, and who has a command to kill Luther, and that he is coming hither next Sunday[1] when the relics are shown. This is a persistent rumor. Farewell.

247a. GUY BILD TO LUTHER.

Zeitschrift des historischen Vereins für Schwaben und Neuberg.
1893, xx. 221. AUGSBURG, April 16, 1520.

Greeting in Christ. Some years ago, reverend Father, when I was writing to my intimate friend George Spalatin, I included a note to be given by him to your Reverence, in which among other things I humbly sought to commend myself to your Reverence, so that by his mediation I might deserve to receive a little letter from your Reverence. But as hitherto most merciful God has willed to try your Reverence with various storms, that he might crown you victor with the crown of righteousness, so at present all have not a little hope that your Reverence will soon reach a port of quiet rest; wherefore, relying on your kindness, I was not able to omit giving a letter for your Reverence to our common friend George Spalatin. For I am bound by such love to your Reverence that I do not believe any mortal could break the bond. For neither by chance nor lightly (Spalatin is witness) did I conceive great love for your Reverence, but it was in gratitude for a service. For your Reverence's writings so changed and renovated my mind oppressed as it was by the consciousness of the stuff over which I had formerly sweated, that they instilled into my nostrils not only the sweet savor of doctrine, but the splendor of it. I thank God greatly that by you I desired to learn the words of Christ (which are the words of life) and that I began under your guidance to weigh and keep before my eyes the salvation of my soul. Your friends and supporters, Bernard Adelmann, John Oecolampadius and the Prior of the Carmelites, once your host,[2] know with how much love and praise I follow you. May your Reverence accept the greeting of a poor little monk like me and if possible when you plan writing to our Bernard Adelmann,

[1] April 22. The elector's relics were exhibited every year on this Sunday. Rumors of attempts against Luther's life were common at this time.
[2] While Luther was at Augsburg in October, 1518, he lodged at the convent of the Carmelites, because there was no Augustinian chapter in that city.

as you often do, or to Oecolampadius, be mindful of me and do not disdain to write me a consolatory sheet.[1] For it will be a perpetual memorial both of your friendship and of your kindness. Farewell and be commended to God Almighty. May he deign to keep you long safe and sound for the common utility of his Church. Amen.

BROTHER GUY BILD *of Höchstadt.*

248. GEORGE SPALATIN TO CHRISTIAN BAYER AT WITTENBERG.

T. Kolde: *Friedrich der Weise* (Erlangen, 1881), p. 41.

WITTENBERG CASTLE, April 22, 1520.

Bayer of Langheim matriculated at Wittenberg 1503, B. A. 1504, M. A. 1505, then became professor at the university and burgomaster. About 1528 he became Chancellor of Electoral Saxony, in which capacity he attended the Diet of Augsburg 1530, and there read the famous Confession. He died October 21, 1535. Enders, vii. 135.

Peace. Dear Colleague, you have always been so ready to please me that I have conceived the hope that nothing I ask will ever be refused by you, and especially when it concerns my friend Dr. Luther. Wherefore please draw up and send to me to-day a memorandum as to how you think we should act in case Luther is excommunicated, either singly, or (which God forbid!) with most clement and Christian elector, or with this university and now illustrious city. You can do nothing worthier of yourself or more pleasing to good men. . . .

G. SPALATIN.

249. LUTHER TO JOHN HESS AT BRESLAU.

Enders, ii. 384. WITTENBERG, April 27, 1520.

Greeting. Dear Hess, I will write more elsewhere; at present I am very busy and must write briefly so that you will at least not think that your letter to me was not delivered. Moibanus[2] will tell you more. I thank you for the Emperor Honorius[3] and more for the prayers you promise to offer up for me, which, as I greatly need them, I rely on not a little.

---

[1] Luther did write to Bild (*infra*, no. 254), but neither this letter nor those he wrote to Adelmann have been preserved.

[2] Later a colleague of Hess at Breslau, where he taught Greek. He had spent a short time at Wittenberg.

[3] Probably an old Roman coin, such as Hess collected.

May the Lord have respect for your bishop[1] and keep him long for us. Your colleagues will teach you what is necessary for your ordination as priest,[2] as far as ceremonies go; my German homily[3] has something to say about the spirit of the faith, to which will be added another sermon by me on the use of the mass.[4] For in the mass no distinction ought to be made between priest and layman; there is one bread, one faith, one communion, only the priest is the minister, the layman is not. More of this elsewhere. Now farewell and pray for me as you do.

Yours,

MARTIN LUTHER.

250. MELANCHTHON TO JOHN HESS AT BRESLAU.
Corpus Reformatorum, i. 155. April 27,[5] 1520.

... Luther is too busy at this time to write anything on the prophets, but I hope, when he has finished some of his work, unless God shall tear him from us, that he will be moved to write a commentary on Genesis or Isaiah. Genesis is more difficult than Isaiah, as I, who am now busy with it, know. ...

251. CROTUS RUBEANUS TO LUTHER.
Enders, ii. 386. BAMBERG, April 28, 1520.

Having returned safe from Italy, I have been entertained here by the noble Fuchses,[6] who are great admirers of yours. A little later my friend Hutten came hither, although we had no plan to meet, but, I am firmly persuaded, at the summons of Christ, who, because he rejoices in no sacrifice as much as in mutual love between men, thus unexpectedly brought friends together. When then we celebrated Easter[7] together, and sang: "This is the day which the Lord hath made; we will rejoice and be glad in it,"[8] our services were interrupted

---

[1] John VI. von Thurzo, Bishop 1506 to August 2, 1520.
[2] Hess was about to be ordained priest, as he was, on June 2.
[3] *Sermon vom hochwürdigen Sacrament*, Weimar, ii. 738.
[4] *Sermon von dem neuen Testament, d. i. von der heiligen Messe*. Weimar, vi. 349. August, 1520.
[5] This is dated "April 17," but the 27th is the more likely date. *Cf. Luthers Werke*, ed. O. Clemen, i. 299.
[6] James and Andrew Fuchs, *cf. supra*, no. 186.
[7] April 8.
[8] Psalm cxviii. 24.

by the cursed pronouncement of Louvain and Cologne, sent to Hutten by Erasmus of Rotterdam. It gave us great material both for laughter and for wrath; we mingled the laughter with our festive and pious joy, and we modulated our indignation to the harp of David, so that it should not become so great as to be sin, although we do not read without sin, if everything is sin which proceeds from a mind moved by indignation. For we are not such Stoics that we can free our minds from every malady, especially when we see men audaciously rage to mock Germany, to hurt religion, to destroy innocence, men, too, who ought to be the ornament of Germany, the honor of religion and the last to hurt innocence. In this opinion I always contained myself by a sort of happy assent. If any wish to show the innocence of their life, to hold burning lamps in their hands, to defend the cause of truth with the sword of the Holy Spirit, to lay down their lives for the salvation of their brethren, they ought to be the theologians. But it is far otherwise; hardly any more monstrous tyranny rages among Christians than that of the theologians, especially those who are commonly called monks and inquisitors. Instead of light they show darkness and unhappy envy, instead of the lamp of virtue they breathe from their nostrils fire, as the poet[1] says; the sword of the executioner has taken the place of the sword of Scripture, sophistry the place of God's Word. For from caring for their brother's salvation their mind is not a sweet savor of Christ[2] redolent with the ointment of charity, but one which, clad in a deadly garment of foul hatred, attacks the vitals of one's neighbor.

I still remember how I heard at Cologne[3] a monstrous and more than bloody deed done by Hochstratten in Lower Germany, which I shudder to think of. How much more, therefore, should you beware of false brothers thirsting for blood, unless perchance you have decided to follow the example of Huss and increase the number of Christian martyrs. I would, if I could, dissuade you from this decision, for how can you be a saint unless the Pope, who alone has the power as was

---

[1] Virgil, *Aeneid*, vii. 281.
[2] 2 Corinthians, ii. 15.
[3] Crotus matriculated at Cologne, November 17, 1505.

recently decreed,[1] presents you with the freedom of the city of the saints? And will he, whose authority you have weakened and whose indulgences your disputation has made go hungry, give it to you? It will profit you nothing to wash your robe in the blood of the Lamb.[2] For eternal life what need is there of a bull of the "representative Church"[3] and the agreement of the professors, without which you will certainly be non-suited before the celestial tribunal for deciding the right to be called saint. O wretched Christianity! O primitive faith! Thus must all divine things depend on and be contaminated with human ones? Let anyone who can, now deny that the Church of God is smitten with a terrible persecutor. . . .

In the judgment of all you have been condemned not according to sound doctrine, but according to Louvain. Even so the Pope's thunder smites many not Christianly, but Romanly—for new words must be coined to describe new errors. If, indeed, they have written anything, yet they suppress it expecting the agreement of their allies, so that they can all rush upon you together and so crush you. They labor much to accomplish this plan both in Italy and in Germany; and by delaying their refutation they win hatred for themselves for daring publicly to condemn a Christian without giving their reasons for so doing. For it may come to pass that their allies will change their opinion and not wish to subscribe to the doctrinal condemnation, as it is now rumored of our friends at Erfurt.[4] Dorp, whose authority with the learned is greater than all the rest of the university, has refused to assent to the condemnation of you by Louvain. Would that they would publish something less insane, so that in the strength of Scripture you might break their frivolous folly to shivers like the vessel of the potter,[5] and might slay their foolishness with the sword of the Holy Spirit. You would not have great difficulty in doing this, but would add

[1] In the Lateran Council of 1516.
[2] Revelation, vii. 14.
[3] A quotation from Prierias' *Dialogue*.
[4] This probably refers to the judgment of Erfurt in the Reuchlin case; the desire of the university to withdraw this is spoken of in the *Epistolae Obscurorum Virorum*, ii. 32.
[5] Revelation, ii. 27.

reverence to the most reverend Cardinal of Tortosa[1] whom those old fools have found a worthy assistant, just like themselves, *a babbler, a coward and a good-for-nothing.*[2] When he wished to show the majesty of the "virtual Church,"[3] he spoke thus, with moderation, in something he did not understand: "I wonder much that a man entertaining such obvious and obstinate errors in matters of faith should be permitted to scatter his errors abroad with impunity and bring others into the same pernicious opinions."[4] With like moderation he said previously: "I saw Luther's errors; and they seemed to me such gross, palpable heresies, that not even a student in theology who had passed the first stage ought to make such slips."[5] Who will call this man most reverend in Christ, or who will respect his red embroidered hat and robe trailing on the ground? Who will apply spurs to those who run furiously of themselves? Since in his whole letter he is sordid, dirty, impudent and light, let the professors gather from him flowers worthy of their nostrils, and let them pluck this one from him, unless he took it from them: "In this Luther proves most of all that he is a heretic, in saying that he is ready to die at the stake for his opinions and to be a heretic against all wise men."[6] Martin, you have many companions in that heresy, and if alone you tread the true winepress,[7] I think the number of those prepared to undergo the stake with you depends on the gift of Heaven. Let sharp men dispute and condemn as they please, they will never make me doubt that any mortal justified by faith has access to God.[8] . . .

Martin, most upright of theologians, guard the divine light now deserted by all, and show by the virtue which we cherish in you, what is the difference between a creature of the Pope and a creature of God. The King hath brought thee into his

---

[1] Adrian of Utrecht, later Pope Adrian VI.
[2] Greek, after the Iliad, i. 293.
[3] Quotation from Prierias's *Dialogue*.
[4] Quotation from Adrian's letter of December 4, 1519, prefixed to the *Condemnation of Luther by Cologne and Louvain, supra,* no. 202.
[5] *Ibid.*
[6] *Ibid.*
[7] *Cf.* Isaiah, lxiii. 3.
[8] Romans, v. 1f.

chamber[1] and hath given thee the tongue of them that are taught[2] to know how to refuse the evil and choose the good.[3] You are known to me, but you daily appear greater and greater. After the clouds of passion the sun is risen; we see with what skill and diligence you confute the doctrinal condemnation of the Luther-scourges; we admire your learning; we adore your genius; we are tremendously pleased that you temper serious matters with jokes, bitter with sweet, so that when the wormwood is drunk it is not tasted before it enters the stomach; you draw and paint everyone to the life. I do not well retain the image of my Martin on account of the years since I have conversed with him. You were formerly in our company a musician and a learned philosopher; but lately I saw the boxer Entellus fighting old Dares in the arena;[4] then you came forth as the swift hunter of the wild goat;[5] now you paint in lively colors the judgment of the theologs; what will you be next? In what line will you win the prize? I think that of the sculptor is left. Come then, good Polycletes,[6] make us triumphal arches to commemorate your vanquished enemies, and show us in living marble that Jesus Christ. May he keep you from the mouth of the Lion[7] and the horns of the sophist unicorns forever![8]

Francis von Sickingen, that great leader of the German nobility, requests, as Hutten tells me, that you flee to him, and he will give you peace, a theological home, a servant, food and protection against enemies, with all the necessaries of life in abundance. Hutten has written in full of this to Melanchthon.[9] Such kindness is not to be despised. The holy fathers exercise their wits to no purpose more than to alienate from you the mind of the Elector Frederic, so that destitute of all protection you may finally be forced to flee to the Bohemians, which they think would be the end of your fame and

---

[1] Song of Songs, i. 4.
[2] Isaiah, l. 4.
[3] Isaiah, vii. 15.
[4] The debate with Prierias, so designated by himself, *supra*, no. 68.
[5] The controversy with Emser, commonly called "the wild goat."
[6] A noted ancient sculptor.
[7] Pun: Leo X.
[8] Psalm xxii. 22.
[9] *Supra*, nos. 218, 232.

doctrine. You know with what contempt these people are regarded, and how strong is an age-long opinion. Eck now has his nail in your wound at Rome; wherefore we must beware, and you should let me know your opinion of my advice by letter. The favor of Sickingen should be kept, lest he should think his great kindness to you scorned, he who with one letter for Reuchlin more terrified the Dominicans than did all the breves of Emperor and Pope.[1] John Huss has come to life again at Basle,[2] after having been so long dead through the tyranny of the Thomists. What, pray, will be safe hereafter, when such holy writings deserve such a judgment? But he is not dead; he will live as long as truth lives, but he wasted away and blameworthy hatred passed to his ashes. Your letter[3] found various fortune with me; when I return to Germany, that letter goes to Italy, but has not gone yet. Farewell. CROTUS RUBEANUS.

P. S.—I send a letter to Hess,[4] but not to trouble you. If he is with you, as some say, give it to him; but if the rumor is false tear it up or keep it until he comes, for he will go thither where he may profit by Martin's doctrine. Hutten is leaving, and asks to send his greeting, he is going to Ferdinand,[5] the brother of King Charles, in whose court, we hope, he will find a place which will not be without advantage to you and to good studies. He showed us an epistle[6] of Erasmus of Rotterdam commending you earnestly to the Archbishop of Mayence. A copy will be sent to you; take it and read the learned eulogy of this learned man.

252. LUTHER TO SPALATIN.

Enders, ii. 395. WITTENBERG, May 1, 1520.

Greeting. I send the letters of your dean with those I received from Nuremberg. Matthew Adrian thinks we should

---

[1] *Cf. supra*, no. 219.
[2] *Supra*, no. 239.
[3] Lost, answer to Crotus's letter of October 31, *supra*, no. 190.
[4] This letter to John Hess, April 29, printed in Krafft: *Briefe und Dokumente*, p. 20.
[5] Hutten was disappointed in trying to win him over to the side of German freedom.
[6] *Supra*, November 1, 1519, no. 192. Luther had already seen the letter.

write to Dr. Pascha[1] at Magdeburg for Hebrew books. When you have done it first I will do it and quickly; please see to it. I will look out for my own affairs.

The number of students increases daily, so that the little city cannot receive them all, and many are forced to return. We are not able to provide Adrian with a lodging suitable to him, nor are we pleased that others should be turned out for him, which, however, he has begun to do. If in this affair he has written anything or done anything (for he wished to see you about it personally) you know my opinion and Melanchthon's: we will not second him nor consent to his turning out anyone unwillingly from the house of the bailiff or anyone else; if they kindly wish to go, we shall be pleased and thankful. . . .

I have received a letter from Staupitz at Nuremberg, praising me at last and more hopeful in my cause than he was formerly wont to write. Wenzel Link writes that they have received the "doctrinal asses,"[2] and that he has good hope. Thus my ship is tossed; now hope, now fear is at the helm; but it is nothing to me. MARTIN LUTHER, *Augustinian.*

253. JOHN ECK TO [JOHN FABER AT CONSTANCE].

Lutheri opera varii argumenti, iv. 256.　　　ROME, May 3, 1520.

This letter is addressed simply "To a Vicar"; Professor G. Kawerau kindly identifies him for me with John Heigerlin, called Faber (1478-May 21, 1541), who studied at Tübingen, took orders and matriculated at Freiburg by 1509. In 1516 he was chancellor of the Bishop of Basle, in 1518 he became Vicar of the Bishop of Constance, and in 1521 Suffragan Bishop; 1523 minister to Ferdinand, 1528-38 Coadjutor Bishop of Neustadt, Bishop of Vienna 1530. P. S. Allen, ii. 189.

Greeting. Most worthy Vicar, your John Ulrich came to me on the journey, and we went to Rome happily together. I took our most holy Lord [the Pope] the book on the *Primacy of Peter.* I would rather tell you face to face than write you on a dead paper, how kind the Supreme Pontiff and the very reverend cardinals were and are to me.

The first draft of a bull has been made against Luther, and

---

[1] The identity of this person is not certain; perhaps Alvesleben.
[2] The Condemnation of Luther by Cologne and Louvain.

will be brought before the next consistory of cardinals, if the most holy one follows the advice of Eck; then all the cardinals and bishops will subscribe to it. It has been a good thing that I came to Rome at this time, because the others did not sufficiently know the errors of Luther. At another time you shall hear what I have done in this cause. Recently the Pope, two cardinals,[1] Dr. Hispanus[2] and I deliberated on this matter five hours; each was asked in turn to give his opinion. The form of the bull will please good men, for it is compounded according to the usage of the councils and popes ancient and modern, and forty-one errors are expressly condemned. . . .

Yesterday I was in counsel with our most holy Lord on the Lutheran business, telling him what had been done by the cardinals appointed to consider it; to-morrow, again, I am going to the Pope to ask on what day the consistory will meet, etc. . . .

Farewell. Yours to command,   Eck.

P. S.—The cardinals favorable to me are the Cardinals of the Holy Cross,[3] of Ancona,[4] of Agen,[5] of the Four Saints,[6] Jacobacci,[7] of St. Sixtus,[8] and Campeggio,[9] etc.

---

[1] Cajetan and Accolti. *Cf.* Smith, 96.

[2] The Spanish Augustinian Johannes, whose last name is unknown. *Cf.* Smith, *ibid.*, and *Zeitschrift für Kirchengeschichte*, xxv. 99. Professor Kawerau refers me on the letter as a whole to Uhlhorn: *Urban Rhegius*, which, however, I have not been able to obtain.

[3] Bernardino Carvajal of Placentia, in Spain, Bishop of Carthagena and Ostia, cardinal since 1493. He was an opponent of Julius II. at the Council of Pisa, and as such declared by the Pope unworthy of the red hat which was restored to him by Leo X. He died December 16, 1522. It has been conjectured that he opposed the designation of Luther's appeal to a council as heretical. On him, *infra*, no. 288, and Smith, *Luther*, p. 97.

[4] Peter Accolti of Arezzo, Bishop of Ancona, made cardinal by Julius II. in 1511. He was one of the commission to investigate Luther's heresy, and drafted the bull *Exsurge Domine*, promulgated June 15, 1520. On this Smith's *Luther*, 96.

[5] Leonard Grosso della Rovere, Bishop of Agen, made cardinal by Julius II. in 1505, and later legate, first at Viterbo and then at Perugia.

[6] Lawrence Pucci, a professor of law at Pisa, papal datary under Julius II., given the red hat by Leo X. in 1513. He was at the sack of Rome in 1527, and under Clement VII., Grand Penitentiary.

[7] Dominic Jacobacci of Rome, a learned canonist, Bishop of Nocera dei Pagani, created cardinal July 1, 1517.

[8] Cajetan.

[9] Lawrence Campeggio of Milan (1474-1539), auditor rotae at Rome 1511, bishop 1512, cardinal 1517. He was legate to Germany in 1511, and again at the Diet

254. LUTHER TO SPALATIN.

Enders, ii. 397. WITTENBERG, May 5, 1520.

Greeting. I send a letter to Guy Bild, dear Spalatin, together with one of Peter Aquensis,[1] as he ordered. Both of us have written to Hutten, Capito,[2] Pelican,[3] Erasmus and many others.

At last brother Augustine Alveld[4] has come out with his stuff; truly he is too stupid for me to lose time answering him. His mind, brain, nose, mouth and hair, in short, his whole book, reminds me of that Leipsic ox,[5] for he uses figures and devices here similar to those the other used in his vile book against the Beghards.[6] Others[7] will answer him, and I will give it as an exercise to my *famulus*[8] to make verses and orations against this stolid ox.

Please thank the elector for me. For you know it is not easy for me to get his busy ear with my letters. Good Heavens! how much has come to us and how much more is promised in the letters of many men! Farewell and pray for me.

MARTIN LUTHER.

of Nuremberg 1524. He was legate to England in the affair of Henry VIII.'s divorce from Catharine of Aragon, 1528-9.

[1] Peter Aquensis (*i. e.*, of Aix-la-Chapelle), a canon of St. Martin's at Münster.

[2] By "us" (utroque nostrum) Luther probably meant himself and Melanchthon. None of these letters is in print, but that to Capito is known to exist in MS.

[3] Conrad Pelican (1478|1556) of Ruffach in Alsace, became a Franciscan in 1493, General Vicar of Alsace in 1499, studied Hebrew with Reuchlin and Matthew Adrian; 1502 began to lecture on Hebrew at Basle; 1517 went to Rome, returning to Basle 1519, at which time he became a follower of Luther, and after 1522, a warm friend of Oecolampadius. In 1523 he began to lecture on the Old Testament. In 1527 he was called by Zwingli to Zurich, where he remained till his death. *Cf.* further Förstemann-Günther, p. 402. He wrote Luther, March 15, 1520. Enders, ii. 354.

[4] Augustine of Alveld, a Franciscan, first appears in history as reader of the Bible in the cloister at Leipsic in 1520. At this time he was asked by Bishop Adolph of Merseburg to defend the primacy of the Pope, which he did in the book here mentioned by Luther. The Reformer's friends, Lonicer and Bernhardi answered him, he rejoined and Luther surrejoined. The controversy continued for some years on the sacraments. In 1529 Alveld was elected Provincial Vicar. He died soon after, October, 1532. Life by L. Lemmens 1899.

[5] Ochsenfart.

[6] In 1514 Ochsenfart wrote two books against the Beghards (extreme Hussites), for titles of which *cf.* Enders ii. 165f.

[7] He was answered by Bernhardi of Feldkirchen.

[8] The *famulus* was a student who waited on a professor in return for tutoring. Luther's *famulus* at this time was John Lonicer, a young Augustinian, who studied in Wittenberg till December, 1521, then went as teacher of Hebrew, first to Strassburg then to Freiburg (*cf.* Engentinus to T. Blaurer, December 17, 1521),

P. S.—Please return the letter of Aquensis for me to answer.

255. JOHN MANUEL TO THE EMPEROR CHARLES V.
Calendar of Letters, Despatches and State Papers, relating to the Negotiations between England and Spain, ed. G. A. Bergenroth, London, 1866, ii., p. 305. ROME, May 12, 1520.
(English translation of Spanish original.)

Manuel was a Spanish grandee who had fallen into disfavor and been imprisoned in 1513 for rendering bad services to Ferdinand. Later he became Imperial Ambassador at Rome, an office which he held from 1520-23, when, apparently on account of the hostility of Pope Adrian, he was removed.

If your Majesty go to Germany you ought to show some favor[1] to a certain friar who calls himself Friar Martin, who is staying with the Elector of Saxony. The Pope is exceedingly afraid of him as he preaches openly against the authority of Rome, and is said to be a great scholar. I think he would be a good means of forcing the Pope to conclude an alliance. I am, however, of the opinion that these means ought to be employed only if the Pope refuses to make an alliance, or if he afterwards breaks it.

255a. JOHN FABER TO JOACHIM VADIAN AT ST. GALL.
Vadianische Briefsammlung, hg. von E. Arbenz and H. Wartmann, St. Gallen, 1890ff, ii. 277. CONSTANCE, May 12, 1520.

Joachim von Watt, known as Vadianus (1494-1551), of St. Gall, matriculated at Vienna 1502. After graduation he taught Latin and Greek there. He then took the degree of M. D., and was rector of the University. He was crowned Poet Laureate. In 1518 he returned to St. Gall. He wrote history and geographical studies. In warm sympathy with the Protestant movement, he carried through the Reform of his native town. On his lost correspondence with Luther, *cf.* Appendix II. to this book. His life by his friend, J. Kessler, published in the last edition of the latter's *Sabbata,* 1902, pp. which he was obliged to leave in 1523 either for Esslingen or Strassburg, which he left in 1527. In 1520 he wrote a work against Alveld. Enders, ii. 399, iv. 215.

[1]Strange to say, Dr. Pastor: *History of the Popes,* viii. 17f., has exactly reversed the meaning of this despatch, interpreting it "Your Majesty ought to refrain from showing favor." A more literal translation of the Spanish, kindly furnished me by my friend, Prof. S. L. Galpin, of Amherst College, is: "And your Majesty may come to Germany, at which they will again be greatly afraid, and a little favor may secretly (be done) to a friar who calls himself Friar Martin." Both the language and the context show that Bergenroth's translation is correct.

601ff. Modern life by E. Götzinger in *Schriften des Vereins für Reformationsgeschichte,* no. 50.

Greeting.[1] Dear Joachim, your commendation is to me the best possible commendation. For you always recommend that which approves itself without any recommendation. But were the object in the greatest possible need of praise, yet would your recommendation have so much weight with me, that it could and ought to illumine dark matters, and give grace to things worn out.

You ask for Eck's works. I have none to send you save those of which you already have seen too much. Either nothing of that kind is brought to Constance, or else the author, out of respect to pontifical ears, lets his indefatigable pen rest a while. He brought *The Primacy of Peter* to the feet of Leo X., expecting not a roar, but applause. May God grant that this learned man may spend his time better and turn his by no means effete mind to better studies.

I thank your kindness for sending me the report of Luther's debate.[2] I also will send you anything new that comes to me. That man's writings wonderfully please me, but I regret that he so rashly propagates ideas which are indeed true, but yet too strong for the crude stomach of the populace to digest. Take for example his tract on *Confession*,[3] which every old woman on the street knows. Paul had not a few things which he hid away on account of the times, giving milk to babes until they grew up in Christ, that he might speak wisdom among the perfect. What Luther writes is surely most true, but it is not expedient to lay such hard matters before the whole world. For if Paul passed over part of the doctrine of the gospel, in order to win the frail and fickle multitude, how much more fitting is it nowadays either to connive at that which cannot be changed without a revolution, or else to heal the sick world by some entirely different means, for, as you know, the medicine is strong for the times. It is by no means sufficient to know what drugs to apply to a sick-

---

[1] Greek.
[2] *Schedam disputationis Lutherianae,* probably refers to the minutes of the Leipsic debate published soon after it took place, and reprinted, Weimar, ii. 250. It may, however, refer to the *Resolutions* for debate, Weimar, ii. 153.
[3] *Eine kurze Unterweisung wie man beichten soll,* Weimar, ii. 57.

ness, unless you also know when and how to administer them. An ancient error cannot be thus impetuously rooted out, but must be treated patiently. The axioms which you sent about penitence,[1] may please learned men, but they are a plague to unlearned ears, for they almost extinguish a good part of piety among common people, who have neither the genius nor the judgment to receive at once the rare paradoxes of our most learned Luther. Indeed, they are often a puzzle even to men who are tolerably well educated. Nor are you ignorant that even if the good man wrote in Latin for the sake of eliciting the truth, and not in the language of the Rhine and the Danube, yet the printers, mindful of their own gain, would immediately translate everything into the vernacular and publish thousands of copies, so that no one, no matter how illiterate, should be ignorant of the Lutheran tumult. Such men are like spider-webs, who catch whatever is pernicious in Luther's doctrine. For how many people are there, Vadian, who with true judgment can weigh antecedent and consequent, which, I think, is of special importance in this matter? I write this not with disaffection, for I greatly wish that all men were truly Lutheran, that is, learnedly pious and piously learned. . . .

256. LUTHER TO SPALATIN.

Enders, ii. 401. (WITTENBERG), May 13, 1520.

Greeting. I am very glad that I determined to answer Alveld in the name of my brother.[2] For the man is so far beyond my capacity that I should not be able to answer his folly worthily. I have never seen, heard of, nor read a book so silly and stupid in every syllable; in fact, I lack language with which to describe it. To-day I finished the notes to give my brother for him to put into shape. The work will soon be done. Likewise I hope my sermon on good works will soon be done.

We will pray for the elector; only do not begin to trust in our prayers, but rather in the goodness of God who promises

---

[1] Probably the *Sermo de Penitentia*, Weimar, i. 317. Possibly however, both this and the reference to the *Scheda disputationis* are to the *Ninety-five Theses*.
[2] Lonicerus, *supra*, no. 254.

to hear those who pray. I hope the Lord will preserve him for us, or rather for himself in these matters.

I am not worrying about Miltitz, the Elector of Mayence and the rest. I should like to see all the tyrants at Rome ill at ease that they might know that they are men who have a God.

I know that Lucas Cranach has a cloth, but that he does not know to whom he owes it, nor did I ask. I saw also chamois-hair cloths, nor does he know to whom he owes these, nor were they inquired for, lest perchance there should be some error, if the same thing should be sold to different people. Perhaps they all have come to you to-day.

Day before yesterday I had a message from Sylvester von Schaumburg,[1] a Franconian noble, who has a son[2] here commended to Melanchthon. He promises me sure protection if the elector should be endangered by my cause. While not despising this offer I prefer to rely only on Christ as my protector, who perhaps has given Schaumburg this idea. Farewell in the Lord.   MARTIN LUTHER, *Augustinian*.

257. ERASMUS TO OECOLAMPADIUS.

Erasmi epistolae (Lond.), xxxiii. 21. *Erasmi opera* (1703), iii. 555.

LOUVAIN, May 14, 1520.[3]

. . . The kings of England and France are preparing for a conference at Calais about June 1.[4] The Archbishop of Canterbury[5] invites me to be present. They almost burnt Luther's books in England, but a humble, though seasonably

---

[1] A knight of Münnerstadt in Franconia, born between the years 1466 and 1471. He led a wild life of feud with his neighbors, for which he was thrice outlawed by the Empire. He entered the service of the Count of Henneberg 1502, of the Bishop of Bamberg 1511, later of the Teutonic Order and of the Bishop of Würzburg in 1522. The fall of Sickingen endangered him in 1523, though he was only indirectly concerned with the rising. He died 1534. Life by F. Kipp, 1911.

[2] Ambrose von Schaumburg, the oldest son of Sylvester, at this time probably between 16 and 18 years old. In 1529 he went on a campaign against the Turks in company with his father. He died about 1535. Kipp, *op. cit.*

[3] Wrongly dated in the *Opera* of 1703, as June 14.

[4] On this *cf.* Preserved Smith, in *English Historical Review*, c. 657.

[5] William Warham (1450?-August 22, 1532), won advancement by his legal attainments. He was Master of the Rolls 1494-1502, Bishop of London 1501, Archbishop of Canterbury 1503, Lord Chancellor of England 1504-15; Chancellor of Oxford University 1506 till his death. His attitude to the Reformation is shown by one of his letters published below.

vigilant friend prevented it. Not that I can judge Luther's works, but this tyranny by no means pleased me. . . .

258. ERASMUS TO MELANCHTHON AT WITTENBERG.
Corpus Reformatorum, i. 204.　　　　　LOUVAIN (May, 1520).[1]

. . . There is a variety of news about Luther. I favor the man as much as I can, even though they [my enemies] always join my cause with his. It was decided that his books should be burned in England, but I stopped this by writing letters to Cardinal Wolsey. At my suggestion also, he imposed silence by a public proclamation on those who clamor foolishly before the people, mentioning Standish[2] by name. He favors sound learning, and is offended by nothing in Luther except by the denial that the primacy of the Pope is of divine right. Those who favor Luther (and almost all good men favor him) wish that he had written more civilly and moderately. But it is too late to warn him now. I see that there is going to be trouble, but I pray that it may be for the glory of Christ. Perhaps it is necessary that scandals should come, but I should not like to be the cause of the scandal. The plan of those fellows is truly diabolic, for they desire nothing else than to suppress Christ and to reign in his name. Commend me to Luther and to all your friends. I have written this hastily, while ill and while the messenger was waiting.　　　　　　　　　　　　　　YOUR ERASMUS.

P. S.—Luther's *Answer*[3] *to the Condemnation of Cologne and Louvain* wonderfully pleased me. At length they have begun to be ashamed of their premature pronouncement. I should have preferred that my name had not been mentioned, for it simply compromises me and does not help Luther. Hutten is here, soon to go to the court of Charles, which is now

[1]This letter seems to be about the same time as that to Oecolampadius of May 14, 1520, no. 257.
[2]Henry Standish, D. D., died 1535, a Franciscan, studied at Oxford and Cambridge, preached at court various times between 1511 and 1520, when he became the chief spiritual adviser of Henry VIII. He was made Bishop of St. Asaph, May 28, 1518. He was a stout conservative, bitterly opposed to Colet, Erasmus and the Reformers. *Dic. Nat. Biography.*
[3]March, 1520. Weimar, vi. 183. *Cf.* Smith, *op. cit.,* 201-2.

occupied by the *beggar tyrants*.¹ Farewell again, dearest Philip.

259. CONRAD MUTIAN TO LANG AT ERFURT.
Krause, 649. (GOTHA), May 15, 1520.

. . . Zasius extolls our Luther to the skies. The illustrious Pirckheimer has written of him, what I have just read to my dear friend Adam Crafft,² as follows: "All ages will remember that the Wittenbergers were the first to see the truth, the first to open their eyes after so many centuries, and to begin to separate the degenerate from the Christian philosophy. And who among those wise men is so eminent a preacher of Christ as Luther?" . . .

260. ALVISE GRADENIGO TO THE SIGNORY OF VENICE.
Sanuto, xxxviii. 315, tergo. Italian. Brown, iii. 51. English.

ROME, May 22, 1520.

Gradenigo was Venetian Ambassador at Rome 1520-3.

A consistory has been held on the affair of Martin Luther in Germany and nothing determined. The matter was postponed in order not to render the scandal greater by showing that importance was attached to his errors.

261. SILVESTER DE GIGLI, BISHOP OF WORCESTER, TO WOLSEY.
Letters and Papers of Henry VIII., ed. J. S. Brewer, London, 1867, iii., no. 847. (English condensed translation of Latin original.)

ROME, May 28, 1520.

Gigli (1463-April 18, 1521), of Lucca, succeeded his uncle as Bishop of Worcester and English agent at Rome in 1498. From 1504-12 he was on a mission to England, when he returned as Ambassador to the Pope. *Dictionary of National Biography.*

Some months ago the works of Friar Martin arrived. Much of their contents is disapproved of by great theologians, by reason of the scandals to which they might give rise, and

¹Text πυγωτύραννοι for πτωχοτύραννοι, Erasmus' favorite name for the mendicant orders.
²Kraft or Crato of Fulda (1493-1558), an admirer of Erasmus, later a strong Lutheran, after 1527 professor at Marburg. Enders, vi. 21. This letter of Pirckheimer is not in Goldast.

part is condemned as heretical. After long debates it has been decreed by the cardinals to declare Martin a heretic, and a bull is in preparation on that subject, of which I will send a copy.

262. LUTHER TO HENRY VON BÜNAU, ARCHDEACON AT OSTERWICK.

Enders, ii. 404. WITTENBERG, May 30, 1520.

Bünau later became pastor at Camitz, where we find him married in 1535. In this same year he was obliged to leave on this account, went to Silesia and became pastor at Hayn, where he died in 1536.

Greeting. Dear Sir, I also knew that Thomas Münzer[1] could not be moved from his purpose; yet I am glad that all have become attentive to the work of grace. I will take counsel with my friends and endeavor to procure chaplains for your Excellency. In the meantime let constancy be like itself, that is, constant in the Lord. It is nothing new if the world is now perturbed on account of the Word of God. Herod and the whole of Jerusalem were disturbed only to hear of Christ's birth;[2] why shall the earth not be moved and the sun darkened when they hear of Christ's death?[3] Truly to me it is a sign that our doctrine is sound, that many and great and wise men are offended at it. For thus says Psalm lxxvii.[4] "It slew the fattest of them, and smote down the chosen men of Israel." And, again: "He is set for the falling and rising up of many"[5] not among the Gentiles, but "in Israel," and among the elect. God always chooses the foolish and weak things of the world, and those things which are naught[6], and it is written that the conversation of

---

[1] Münzer (1490-May 27, 1525), matriculated 1506 at Leipsic, 1512 at Frankfort an der Oder, in 1513 went to Halle. Later he became professor at Leipsic, where he probably met Luther at the time of the debate, 1519. Early in 1520 he went to Zwickau to take the place of Egranus, and here began an energetic reform, far more radical than Luther's, which he believed should be carried through by force. Expelled by the authorities in April, 1521, he went to Bohemia, and in 1523 to Alstedt, where he again preached insurrection. After a sharp controversy with Luther he was again expelled, 1524, and went to Mühlhausen. He became a leader in the Peasants' War, was captured at Frankenhausen, May 15, 1525, and after being forced to recant, executed. *Realencyclopädie.*
[2] Matthew, ii. 3.
[3] Matthew, xxvii. 52; Luke, xxiii. 45.
[4] Psalm lxxviii. 31.
[5] Luke, ii. 34.
[6] 1 Corinthians, ii. 27.

wisdom is with those that walk simply.[1] The Lord Jesus keep your Excellency. Amen.

Yours,

MARTIN LUTHER.

263. LUTHER TO SPALATIN.

Enders, ii. 405.   WITTENBERG, May 31, 1520.

Greeting. I am sending letters, Spalatin, to Hutten, Sickingen and our Taubenheim;[2] please let it be your care to forward them. Let Taubenheim, in particular, have his at once, for I have put off answering him longer than I hoped.

Lonicerus will be done to-morrow. The Leipsic professors, anxious to retain their scholars, boast that Erasmus is coming to them. How busy and yet unhappy is hatred! When a year ago they insulted us as vanquished they did not see that this cross was waiting for them. The Lord rules, as we can feel. Ochsenfart is said to be arming against Feldkirchen by whom he is traduced. I have finished something in German against that ass Alveld; it will soon be printed.

Advise me whether I should write to the elector in behalf of our state. Everything is very dear, and enough is not brought in; nor is anything lawfully regulated in this most confused and neglected administration. Something could be done at Wittenberg, if there were any order in the government. There is need here of the counsel and authority of the elector. Answer and farewell.

MARTIN LUTHER, *Augustinian*.

264. LUTHER TO JEROME DUNGERSHEIM AT LEIPSIC.

Enders, ii. 162.   (WITTENBERG, June, 1520.)

This letter, placed by Enders in September, 1519, is in answer to one of May, 1520, placed by Enders, ii. 141, in September, 1519. Dungersheim answered it at once with a short letter and a long

[1]Proverbs, iii. 32. "Cum simplicibus sermocinatio ejus." Vulgate.

[2]John von Taubenheim, mentioned in 1490 as a page of Frederic the Wise, matriculated at Leipsic 1504, B. A. 1505. At latest in 1511 he entered the official service, becoming treasurer and collector of taxes. In 1515-6 he collected moneys and paid salaries (including those of the professors) at Wittenberg. In 1528 he was one of the Church visitors. On his warm relations with Luther cf. Smith, op. cit., 369. He died 1541 or 1542. *Archiv. für Reformationsgeschichte*, viii. 37ff.

Dialogue, both printed by Enders, ii. 166ff. This closed the correspondence. For dates, *cf. supra,* no. 201.

Greeting. Truly, my man, you have excellent major premises, but very poor minors. You keep saying only "The Church, the Church, heretics, heretics!" and will not allow that the text "Prove all things"[1] was said to one man. But when we ask for the Church, you show us one man, the Pope, to whom you attribute everything, though you do not offer the least proof that his faith cannot fail. But we find more heresies in his *Decretals* than in any heretical book. Thus, in what alone is to be proved by you, you perpetually beg the question, as though you were ignorant that the worst fault of argument was *petitio principii.* This, I say, you must prove, that you have the Church of God, and that it is nowhere else in the world. We wish to be judged by Scripture, you wish to judge it. Please stop wearying me with such words, or, as you threaten, publish what you wish. If the Fathers are to be read without selection and judgment, the Scripture is taken away. Of the form of God[2] and of the papacy I think as I thought; nor do I doubt that I will easily answer whatever you publish on these subjects. Don't be impertinent, my man; for a whole year you have tried to do much and have not greatly succeeded. Many words do not move me, but solid arguments; nor do I therefore accuse the saints of falsehood, as you are wont to deduce from my words, if I say that Scripture is sometimes twisted by them. Pray beware, if you do write anything, not to deduce such consequences and corollaries from my words and put your own construction on them. You will need sharp eyes. For a good doctor should not say that one has lied who has barely erred, since Augustine himself confesses that many obscure texts bear a manifold sense, although we must believe that the sense is simple. . . .

If you use such methods against me, you will succeed finely; there will never be an end of writing and disputing. For always when I say one thing you understand another, just

---

[1] 1 Thessalonians, v. 21.
[2] This refers to a debate on the text, Philippians, ii. 6.

as that ass[1] of yours does. I know not whether the nature of Leipsic men is such as to allow you to be such careless readers, such audacious judges, and so slow in understanding others. Believe me, I will have something to say to you. Formerly you wrote against the Beghards;[2] you know with what success! Take a friend's advice and write not so much, but more to the point. I know that victory does not depend on the numbers exposed to slaughter, but on military art. Vainly do you complain that you are betrayed by me. I confess that I let some others read your letters, so as not to be the sole judge in my own cause, which you are always complaining of. If you are aggrieved herein, I allow you to retaliate, and I will not fight with you nor attack you on this ground. If in matter of faith concord were easy between us, no syllable would be written. Do you also consider how much we have suffered and do daily suffer from your friends, which could not be done without your assent? Take care lest God will repay it. This affair is none of your business, and hitherto you have always declined to take part. Now at last you are coming in; take care lest you become involved. I am perfectly well aware, my dear Jerome, how much you tried to do me behind my back, as I wrote you at Leipsic,[3] which I have always ignored and do still. But take care lest my exhausted patience shall burst out. I am a man like you, except that you secretly bite in leisure and quietly; I, very busy, am attacked by the teeth of all, and I am asked to be moderate who alone am surrounded with so many ravenous wolves. The world presses me down and gnaws me piecemeal. Good God, how I am accused, and yet, if we are but a little moved thereby, you cannot bear it. I write this that you may know that I prefer peace and concord; but if that is impossible the Lord's will be done!

You need not write me about the other matters, for I understand you. Take care to understand my propositions, for,

---

[1] Augustine Alveld.
[2] *Supra*, no. 254.
[3] This letter is lost and it is difficult to ascertain when it could have been written. Luther is apparently referring to the slanders about him, which he attributed to Dungersheim, *cf. supra*, no. 217. But it is not known that he was at Leipsic at this time or anywhere near it. The time of the debate would be too early.

as they cannot be overthrown by you, with Christ's aid I will not suffer you to do it. Farewell and pray, not only that we may have the right opinions, but that we may live and be saved.

265. LUTHER TO JOHN HESS AT BRESLAU.

Enders, ii. 411. (WITTENBERG), June 7, 1520.

Greeting. Although you salute me alone, dear Hess, I will return more than you send, but briefly as my business requires. Crotus wrote from Bamberg both to you and to me.[1] I wonder why his letter to you did not come. I think I would have kept it fairly and faithfully, although he wrote me to tear it up if you were not here. My letters went to Italy just as he was leaving it, and he did not know I had written him.

Eck is enjoying his wished-for glory in Rome. Presented to the Pope by the Cardinal of the Four Crowns[2] he kissed the blessed feet. Then, to the astonishment of all, the Pope, sitting in public view on the throne of his majesty, kissed him. Let them lick, lap, spit on and bite each other thus![3] My correspondent writes: "Luther has propitious gods at Rome, but no propitious men." What do you think will come of this? Perhaps the sky will fall and many pots will collide. Sylvester Prierias has vomited up something more,[4] and that so blasphemous that it almost kills me just to read it. We will publish the infernal pamphlet with notes by Luther. Meantime, do what you do, and greet Michael[5] and Crautwald[6] and all my friends. I wish the most reverend bishop[7] the grace of Christ. Farewell in Christ.

MARTIN LUTHER, *Augustinian*.

266. LUTHER TO SPALATIN.

Enders, ii. 413. WITTENBERG (before June 8), 1520.

Greeting. I send letters from Nuremberg, dear Spalatin,

[1] *Cf. supra*, no. 251.
[2] Lorenzo Pucci.
[3] I have slightly changed the punctuation of this to make better sense.
[4] *Epitoma responsionis ad Lutherum*, published by Luther in June, 1520, Weimar, vi. 325.
[5] Wittiger, a canon at Breslau.
[6] Valentine Crautwald, an old friend of Hess and Melanchthon, a Hebrew and Greek scholar, later a Schwenkfeldian, and as such, frequently mentioned with hostility by Luther in 1525-6. Enders, v. 294f, 329, 343.
[7] John von Thurzo.

with Prierias' *Epitome*,[1] which that barbarous Greek and cooker of Latin[2] himself calls "Epithoma." Send it right back; it will be printed[3] soon to the praise and glory of all enemies of the truth, with my notes. *I think that at Rome they have all become mad, silly, raging, insane fools, stocks, stones and devils of hell.*[4] See now what we have to hope from Rome who allows this infernal writing to go out against the Church. These portents overwhelm me with the greatness of the folly.

While inveighing against the ass Alveld I am not forgetful of the Roman Pontiff, though I will please neither of them. I am forced to write thus, for at length the secrets of Antichrist must be revealed. For they press on and will not lie hidden any more.

I have the intention of publishing a broadside[5] to Charles and the whole German nobility against the tyranny and wickedness of the Roman court.

My postilla to the Epistles and Gospels are being prepared for the press.[6]

I am writing to the most illustrious elector in behalf of the commonweal. Pray do what you can to help us. Otherwise we shall soon go hungry, or buy food at too high a price. Farewell and pray for me.

BROTHER MARTIN LUTHER.

267. MELANCHTHON TO JOHN HESS AT BRESLAU.

Corpus Reformatorum, i. 201.   (WITTENBERG), June 8, 1520.

... Wittenberg is not yet under the interdict, and things are said to be peaceful at Rome, except that Sylvester Prierias is publishing an *Index* of his dialogue against Luther,[7] his

---

[1] Greek.
[2] So called because of his title, as written on the heading of his *Epitome*, "*magiri* [instead of *magistri*] *sacri Palacij*." "Magirus" means "cook." This is not a misprint, as Enders thinks, but a regular, though peculiar, form, misunderstood by Luther.
[3] *Cf. supra*, no. 265.
[4] German.
[5] This became the famous *Address to the Nobility*, of which the preface was dated June 23, 1520. It appeared early in August. Smith, *op. cit.*, 79ff.
[6] These first appeared in March, 1521. Weimar, vii. 458.
[7] The *Epitoma responsionis ad Lutherum*, with the subtitle: *Index quidem longissimus sed brevissimum Epitoma*. *Cf. supra*, 266.

purpose being, if I mistake not, to terrify the man by false watch-fires. You will see the book when it is printed here. Francis von Sickingen, the rare glory of German knighthood, of his own accord invites Luther to himself. Hutten is going to Ferdinand, the brother of Charles, to make way, with the help of the greatest princes of the Empire, for German liberty. What may we not hope? . . .

I am sending Luther's tract on *Faith and Good Works,* which, like all his books, you will read with pleasure.

Crotus has written to you here, and also to Luther. Our letters are on the way to Italy, although he is coming to Germany.

Luther is answering your question on Paul, and what is more apt than his answer? No one known to me of all the Greek and Latin writers has gotten nearer Paul's spirit. . . .

268. ALVISE GRADENIGO TO THE SIGNORY OF VENICE.

Sanuto, xxxviii. 360. Italian. Brown, iii. 74.   ROME, June 9, 1520.

Friar Martin Luther in Germany is very much followed by the Elector of Saxony and other lords, who have written in his defence to the Pope, telling him to send anyone he pleases to dispute with Luther, who will show that what he preaches and says is perfectly true and based on the words of Christ.

269. SYLVESTER VON SCHAUMBERG TO LUTHER.

Enders, ii. 415. German.   MÜNNERSTADT, June 11, 1520.

My unknown service and friendship to you, learned, excellent, dear Sir and Friend! Many learned persons have told me that your doctrine and opinions are grounded on the holy, divine Scriptures, and that you are opposed by unfavorable, envious persons, given up to greed, which is serviceable to idolatry. And though you allow your opinion to be passed upon by an œcumenical Christian council, or by other impartial, wise and learned men, yet you suffer for it danger to your life, and are compelled to betake yourself to a foreign nation, probably to the Bohemians, who do not highly esteem spiritual, arbitrary punishment.

I beg and admonish you in God the Lord, in case the elector or any other government should expel you rather than disobediently endure arbitrary spiritual punishment for you, that you should not let such desertion trouble you, nor betake yourself to the Bohemians, from whom in former times certain learned men obtained much contradiction and offence, and thus increased the disfavor in which they were held. For I, and, I believe, a hundred gentlemen whom I can bring together, will keep you safe and protect you against your opponents, until your opinions have been canvassed and examined by a common Christian council or by impartial learned judges, and you yourself better instructed; for you yourself have agreed to submit in such a case. As you are one to whom, though unknown, I am minded to show service and friendship, I did not wish to conceal the above from you, for you to comfort yourself with.

SYLVESTER VON SCHAUMBERG.

270. LUTHER TO GEORGE KUNZELT, PASTOR AT EILENBURG.

Enders, ii. 418. WITTENBERG, June 15, 1520.

Nothing is known of Kunzelt, except that a little later (December 10, 1520, Enders, iii. 19), he requested permission to go away to study for eight years, on the ground that he had been so much ordered about by his superiors that he deserved a little leisure.

Greeting. You inquire, venerable Father, as to my practice in beginning and ending a sermon; my usage is not the common one. Omitting wordy prologues I briefly say: *"Invoke the divine grace, and say an inward Ave Maria or Paternoster, that the word of God may be fruitful to us and God accept us."*[1] Then I read the text, without announcing the topic. Then[2] I explain or propound doctrines from it. At the end I say: *"Enough of this,"* or, *"More another time,"* or, *"Having said this, we will pray God for his grace to enable us to do it,"* or thus: *"God help us do it."* Then most briefly: *"Let us commend to God the spiritual and temporal estates, particularly so and so, for whom and for all, as we ought, we will recite the Lord's prayer in common."* After

[1] The words in italics are German.
[2] Reading "Deinde" for "Davidem."

this as all rise: "The blessing of God the Father, etc. Amen." This is my manner of preaching. Farewell in the Lord.

     BROTHER MARTIN LUTHER, *Augustinian*.

271. LUTHER TO SPALATIN.
Enders, ii. 423.   (WITTENBERG), June 25, 1520.

Greeting. Dear Spalatin, I and many others think Melanchthon should not be burdened with lecturing on Pliny on account of his lectures on the Apostle Paul, which are so fruitful. The hearers ought not to be deprived of this good, since what they would get from Pliny would not be enough to compensate them. It is to be feared that some spirit who is not rashly to be resisted impels him to do this, lest it should turn out a device of Satan to prevent, on this excuse, the cultivation of good fruit. They think that if Pliny is to be given at all it should be by Professor John Hess.[1] I know not what Melanchthon will do about marrying, especially the girl you suggest.[2] I want him to take a wife, but wish neither to dictate nor to advise whom he shall marry, nor do I see that he is particularly anxious to marry.

Although I hope Melanchthon will not go to Bavaria,[3] yet I have always wished that he might have a larger salary, so that they might lose the hope they have conceived of getting him, since they see that he is paid less here than he would be there.[4] If there is any chance, be vigilant. For when opportunity calls, it is not to be neglected, for it is God calling.

I will speak of the Strassburg tragedy[5] in a proper place. To-morrow my Prierias and German Romanist will be finished.[6] Farewell.   MARTIN LUTHER, *Augustinian*.

272. CONRAD MUTIAN TO JOHN LANG AT ERFURT.
Krause, 654.   (GOTHA), July 1, 1520.

. . . Who is that Martin Luder who together with John

---
[1] This was not John Hess of Breslau, but the Wittenberger.
[2] Melanchthon married Catharine Krapp on November 27, 1520.
[3] Ingolstadt and Reuchlin were still trying to get Melanchthon. *Cf. supra*, no. 214.
[4] Melanchthon got the increase on his marriage.
[5] This refers to an incident described in the *Address to the German Nobility*. Bishop William of Strassburg was prevented from reforming his cathedral by the Pope.
[6] Luther means the *Epitome* of Prierias and *Vom Papstthum zu Rom wider den Romanisten zu Leipzig*. Weimar, vi. 277ff.

Fug and Wenzel Link follows John Lang and precedes John Staupitz the head of your order? It is signal carelessness and remarkable ignorance to put him who had the first place in chapter xlii. down among the following numbers. I will not call it malice, for Luder and Luther might be different persons.[1] . . .

Zasius does not think ill of Martin. He knows that he is quite learned in our theology both modern and ancient, he knows that he is a luminary of the Augustinian order, he knows that he sustains the attacks of many, in short, he knows that the innocent man is wrongly bound by the curses of the Pope. He is not ignorant how much hatred is brought by the Hussite name, and how much odium by blessed Bohemia. Perhaps he thinks that it would be more for the peace and concord of the people if Luther would keep within the fold of his gentle and taciturn monasticism, and leave to secular priests the interpretation of the divine law. There are some men neither bad nor unlearned, whose names I refrain from giving, who think that it is wicked and impious for a doubly consecrated priest thus to tear to pieces Leo, the head of the apostolic see. I agree with no authors of dissension, contumely and strife. Let us have fair play. If they stir up sleeping dogs, and revive the dormant folly of the Bohemians, or for the sake of vengeance violate the majesty of the Roman see, rubbing the scar from the old wound, their audacity is nothing to me. I am peaceful, not for fear of outward foes, but for myself; my moderation is due to gentleness rather than to prudence. Finally you ask my opinion of the papal decrees. I esteem the decrees of philosophers more than those of priests. . . .

273. ERASMUS TO SPALATIN.
Erasmi opera, iii. 559. LOUVAIN, July 6, 1520.

. . . I wrote recently to Melanchthon in such a way that the letter[2] was as much for Luther as for him. I pray that Christ Almighty may temper the pen and mind of Luther so

---

[1] This refers to the *Exegesis Germaniae* by Irenicus, which refers to (ii. 42) "Martin Luther, priest of Wittenberg, a learned theologian and captain of the Germans," and later enumerates John Lang, John Fug, Link, *Luder* and Staupitz.
[2] No. 258.

that he may bring forth the greatest fruit to evangelic piety, and that Christ may give a better mind to some who seek their own glory at his expense and their own profit with his loss. In the camp of Luther's opponents I see many who savor more of the world than of Christ, and yet both sides have sinned. Would that Hutten, whose genius I singularly love, had tempered his pen. I should prefer that Luther left these tumults alone for a while, and devoted himself to the gospel alone; perhaps dispassionate action would succeed a little better. Hatred of good learning is fatal to us and barren to him. There is danger lest the public corruption of morals, which everyone admits needs a public remedy, may gradually increase like the plague and become firmly established. Truth is not always to be advanced, and it makes much difference how it is championed. Farewell, excellent man, and commend me to your prince.

274. POPE LEO X. TO FREDERIC, ELECTOR OF SAXONY.
Lutheri opera varii argumenti, v. 10. ROME, July 8, 1520.

Beloved Son, greeting and the apostolic blessing! Grave men have testified to us that your Lordship, according to your surpassing wisdom and piety towards God and his orthodox faith, and according to the nobility of your soul and of your ancestors, who were always ready to serve the Christian state and the holy see, has always been hostile to the attempts of that son of iniquity Martin Luther, and has never either aided or favored him. This pleases us the more in that it greatly increases the opinion which we have of your splendid virtue and our paternal goodwill towards you.

We cannot say whether we think you have acted more wisely or more piously in this affair. For it is singular wisdom to recognize that a furious man, by no means obedient to his vow of humility, moved by ambition to resuscitate the old heresies of the Wyclifites, Hussites and Bohemians, already condemned by the universal Church, one who manifestly seeks the money of the people, one who by his interpretation of Scripture gives occasion of sinning to the simple, one who breaks the bonds of chastity and innocence, and by his profane words also confession and contrition of heart, one who favors the Turks and deplores the punishment of heretics, one, in short, who tries to mix the highest things with the lowest; it is singular wisdom, I say, to recognize that such a one has not been sent by Christ, but by Satan, for the man has been carried to such a height of pride and madness that he has dared openly to say and write that he will have faith neither in the writings of the holy doctors, nor in the decrees of the Roman Pontiffs, but only in himself and his own opinions, which is more than any heretic has hitherto presumed to do.

Therefore your Lordship has wisely spurned the company of this pestilent and venomous man, who, as you can judge, brings some stain on your noble house and much on the German nation. It is also to the credit of your piety that you never consented to any of his great errors, but rather withstood them. By you, at least, no occasion has been given for turning from the old and eternal order of the orthodox faith, preserved for so many ages by the Holy Spirit. . . .

Wherefore, having convoked a council of our venerable brothers, and of others, including all who are expert in the Canon Law and the Holy Scripture, after thorough ventilation and discussion of the affair, at last, under the inspiration of the Holy Ghost, who in such matters is never absent from the holy see, we issued a decree,[1] written in apostolic letters and sealed with the leaden bull, in which, among the almost countless errors of this man, we commanded to be written down in order those which are partly simply heretical and subversive of the right faith, and partly scandalous and impious through their undoing for simple men of the bonds of obedience, continence and humility. For the other numerous errors, which in the gall of unjust hatred he vomited forth against this holy see, are to be judged rather by God than by us.

We send your Lordship a copy of this bull, printed in our fostering city, that when by it you have learned the errors of this minister of Satan, you may, as is prescribed in the bull according to the apostolic mercy, first exhort and warn him

---

[1] The bull *Exsurge Domine*, June 15, 1520. Reprinted by B. J. Kidd: *Documents*, no. 38.

to put away his contumacious and haughty spirit and return to sanity and thus experience God's clemency and ours by publicly revoking and reprobating his opinions. But secondly, if he persists in his insanity, and at the end of the term prescribed in the bull should be a declared heretic, then you should take care and zealously try to capture him and send him bound into our custody. . . .

275. LUTHER TO SPALATIN.

Enders, ii. 428. (WITTENBERG), July 9, 1520.

Greeting. Dear Spalatin, with great and silent grief, I read the letter[1] from Rome, seeing such great dullness and impiety in the heads of the Church. I fear that they are so confounded by the light of conscience and truth that they can have no judgment or sense left. They condemn my books, though they confess that they show genius and learning, and yet they have neither read them, nor asked for them. The Lord have mercy on all of us!

What can I advise the excellent elector to write? Therefore I rather write to you. In the first place you know that I could complain in this matter much more justly than they. My published books bear witness how often I confess and lament that I have been drawn into this affair by no desire, but have been driven by force. Then I often offered peace and silence. Where do I not ask and try to extort instruction? Hitherto I have been of such a mind that I would keep silence if I were allowed, that is, if they also would hold their peace.

Everyone knows that Eck's sole reason for forcing me to debate on the power of the Pope was to make a mock of and trample on me, my name, all my works and our university. Now, when they see that the man was divinely thwarted, they accuse me of insane boasting. Why should a wretch like me seek glory, who only ask to be allowed to live privately and hidden from the public?

Anyone who wishes may have my position; anyone who wishes may burn my books. What more do they want me to do? At the same time I say this: If I am not allowed to lay

---

[1] The letter of Cardinal Riario to the elector, Smith, *op. cit.*, 74.

aside my office of teaching and preaching the Word, at any rate I shall be free in the way I teach it. Loaded with enough sins I will not add this unpardonable one, that, when I am made a minister of the Word, I should fail in my ministry and be found guilty of impious silence, of neglecting the truth, and of thousands of lost souls. Let that cardinal boast that his Church does not need defence; why then, does he defend it?

I am entirely satisfied that the most illustrious elector should keep himself apart from my cause as he has hitherto done, and that he should thrust me out to be taught or convicted. But as he cannot be my instructor, let him not be my judge or executioner until I have been duly sentenced. He sees that he cannot punish anyone, Jew or Turk, without a cause being known, which, in this case, they have not even touched upon. Do the Romans wish that he should obey God rather than man, and oppress one of whose guilt or innocence he is not sure? He could not do so with a safe conscience, nor can his conscience be prompted to such an act by any divine command.

Let them punish Prierias, Eck, Cajetan and others, who for their own glory causelessly started this tragedy for the Roman Church. I am innocent. What I have done and do, I am obliged to do, always ready to keep silence provided only they do not bid the gospel truth to keep silence. They will obtain everything from me, and I will offer everything of my own accord, if they will allow the way of salvation to be free to Christians. This is all I ask from them in return; nothing else. What could be more honest? I do not seek a cardinal's hat, nor gold, nor whatever else Rome now prizes.

If I do not obtain this request, let them deprive me of my cure of souls, and let me live and die in some desert corner. Miserable man that I am, I am forced to teach against my will, and at the same time suffer for doing so, when others teach of their own free will and are honored for it. My mind is simply not able to fear threats nor to prize promises. Do they want me really to be affected by fear and hope, or only to pretend to be?

You have my opinion. I hope the most illustrious elector

will write so that those Roman heads may understand that Germany, by an inscrutable judgment of God, has hitherto been oppressed not by her own stupidity, but by that of Italians. Farewell. I send this letter sealed, as you did yours. MARTIN LUTHER.

276. ELECTOR FREDERIC OF SAXONY TO CARDINAL RAPHAEL RIARIO AT ROME.

Lutheri Opera latina varii argumenti (Erlangen, 1865), ii. 351.

LOCHAU, July 10, 1520.

In the reprint here cited the date is given as "Augsburg, August 5, 1520." On the true date *cf.* Enders, ii. 431.

Rafael Riario (1461-July 9, 1521), of Savona, one of the most powerful men in Rome. He had been created cardinal 1477. *Cf.* Pastor, vols. vii., viii. He had written the elector urging him to make Luther recant (*cf. supra,* no. 275); this is Frederic's answer.

Most reverend Father in Christ, and dear Lord, your kind letter dated Rome, April 3, was delivered to me on July 7. . . . I already knew, my dear Sir, what you write about Dr. Martin Luther. Please understand that with God's help I will never do nor be other, and that I never had the purpose or wish of being other than an obedient son of the Holy Catholic Church.

I have never hitherto undertaken to defend either the writings or the sermons of Dr. Martin Luther, nor do I do so to-day, as I showed to his Holiness's legate Cardinal Cajetan, and to the papal nuncio Charles Miltitz, both by my letters and orally.

Moreover I hear that Dr. Luther has never shown himself unready obediently to appear, armed with a safe-conduct, before just, convenient, disinterested and prudent judges to defend his doctrine in person, and, when he has learned better and more holy doctrine from Scripture, submissively to obey.

To this duty I hear the Archbishop Elector of Trier has been appointed commissioner, a friend of mine, at whose summons I doubt not that Luther, provided with safe-conduct, will appear. So no one can rightly blame me on this account. It is a heartfelt sorrow to me that in my time errors in the Catholic faith should arise, and this would annoy me still more, that such errors should be promoted by me. . . .

277. LUTHER TO SPALATIN.

Enders, ii. 439. (WITTENBERG), July 14, 1520.

Greeting. Dear Spalatin, if you have any influence with the elector, please get him to write a severe and caustic letter to our rector.[1] The man's signal folly yesterday almost involved us in murder and blood. Insanely he stirred up a riot[2] on the part of the students against the town-council and innocent people, he who ought to have quieted them. I was present at the meeting, where they were all mad with drink; nothing was said except what might inflame the fierceness of the youths. This confusion in our university shames me, for it will at length bring us opprobrium. Peter Lupinus spoke well against the tumult, but he was so received by Dr. Thomas Eschaus that I at once arose and left, seeing that Satan was presiding over the meeting. It is said that the youths are allowed to carry arms against the order of the elector.

It is better that a smaller number should study here than that we should have these riots. All the good condemn this madness. To-morrow, with God's help, I shall try to do what I can to quiet this. Nothing was done according to the elector's recent decree. The old men were wilder than the young. I know it is the doing of Satan, for as he cannot hurt the Word of God which is now returning to us, he seeks this way to disparage it. Truly we must strive against him with what power we can lest he should prevail with these men of blood.

I think you have received my letter and this of Schaumburg.[3] Please send them back to our friends when you have read them. Farewell and pray for me.

MARTIN LUTHER, *Augustinian*.

278. LUTHER TO SPALATIN.

Enders, ii. 441. (WITTENBERG), July 17, 1520.

Greeting. Dear Spalatin, we think that Lira's dream[4] meant

[1] Peter Burkhard.
[2] *Cf. supra*, no. 230. The students were for some reason exasperated against Lucas Cranach, who, besides being a painter, drove various trades. Student riots were not uncommon then, and, indeed, are not unknown now on the continent of Europe. I have myself seen riots at the Sorbonne, which, but for the intervention of the police, might have led to bloodshed.
[3] No. 269.
[4] Something of which apparently Spalatin had written, of which nothing else is known.

nothing else than our riot. In almost all prophecies and visions a big man signifies the gross commonalty. Yesterday[1] from the pulpit I preached against the tumult as though I were partial to neither side; I simply described the evil of sedition in the abstract whether it was supported by the citizens or by the students, and I commended the power of magistrates as one instituted by God, so that seditions should not lay everything waste. Good Heavens! How much hatred I won for myself![2] They shouted that I was taking the part of the town council. At length they thus betrayed the thoughts of their hearts, so that we learned who had truly imbibed our theology and who had only pretended to do so. Such a sieve is needed to separate the wheat from the chaff. I see Satan in this affair, who, when he saw that he could do nothing at Rome and abroad against us, found this evil to hurt us badly from within.

This thing was small at first, but behold, the more it is treated, the more bitterly does it seize and corrupt hearts, a strictly diabolic quality, for Satan augments the disease by what you would think would cure it. I do not fear him, but I am afraid that we offend the Lord with our ingratitude and vainglory, who in his anger permits Satan thus to burst forth in the midst of the sons of God. Nor does this so much move me, as fear of what may happen in the future, forsooth that we should become hard and filled with Satan and thus incorrigible. Thus we should fill up the measure of our wickedness, and the wrath of God should come and smite us with some great plague to our confusion, because we did not receive the Word of God when it was offered to us, or did not receive it worthily.

On this account I am much alarmed. Every one of the past three years I have suffered some signal danger, first at Augsburg, then at Leipsic, now at Wittenberg. We need not wisdom and weapons, but humble prayer and strong faith to win Christ for us; otherwise it is up with us, if we confide in our own strength. Wherefore betake yourself with me to prayer,

[1] Rather July 15.
[2] A student who had come from Leipsic was heard to say that if the monk spoke like that they ought to hit him on the tonsure with a stone, and another that they ought to make an end of him.

lest from this spark an evil spirit of the Lord should make a conflagration. Small things are not to be despised, especially when Satan is their author.

I send news from Rome. I learned more from him[1] than I read in this broadside. Agricola[2] noted this down as he spoke and gave it to Melchior Lotther. When he gives it to you please return it to us. Farewell and remember that we must suffer for the Word. Since Sylvester von Schaumburg and Francis von Sickingen made me secure from the fear of men, the fury of the devils must needs take its place. It will be the last, for I shall be severe with myself. Thus is the will of God. MARTIN LUTHER, *Augustinian*.

279. LUTHER TO WENZEL LINK AT NUREMBERG.
Enders, ii. 443. WITTENBERG, July 20, 1520.

Greeting. I am sending my little essay,[3] a stumbling-block to hypocrites. I think *Der abgehobelte Eck* has reached you. They say the wild ass of Leipsic is braying against me again, but we shall see.

Recently we almost experienced a schism and rebellion here,[4] but with Christ's aid Satan has been beaten down.

Sylvester von Schaumburg, a Franconian noble, has written to ask me not to flee to Bohemia or elsewhere, but to him, should the Roman furies wax hot. He promises the splendid protection of a hundred Franconian knights. So the rage of Rome is at length despised even by the Germans. Francis von Sickingen has also written to the same purpose.

My enemies wrote the elector against me from Rome,[5] as did a certain court in Germany. I have in press a book in the vernacular against the Pope: *To the Nobility of Germany*

---

[1] John von Wick of Münster, who had been an attorney in Reuchlin's affair at Rome. In 1528 he became Syndic at Bremen, and took part in the introduction of the Reformation in Münster. In 1533 he was captured by the Bishop of Münster and put to death. The information he brought Luther at this time on his way back from Rome was a chief source for the *Address to the German Nobility*.
[2] John Agricola.
[3] *Of the Papacy at Rome against the Romanist of Leipsic*. The Romanist was "the wild ass," Augustine Alfeld.
[4] The student riots spoken of above, no. 277.
[5] *Supra*, nos. 275, 276. The German court was probably that of Duke George.

on *Reforming the Christian Estate*.[1] It will mightily offend Rome by exposing her impious arts and usurped powers. Farewell and pray for me.

BROTHER MARTIN LUTHER.

280. LUTHER TO MICHAEL WITTIGER, CANON AT BRESLAU.

Enders, ii. 449.   WITTENBERG, July 30, 1520.

Greeting. I was unwilling to write to you, excellent Sir, since our common friend Schleupner could tell you everything better by word of mouth. He knows everything about us, but he desired me to put down at least a line. So I do as he wishes. Various books are written against me in Germany and Italy, but it is well. None write but most asinine asses who betray themselves by their stupidity. I am quite well in body and mind, except that I should prefer to sin less. I sin more every day, for which I complain to you and your prayers. The Dominicans have quieted down, an edict[2] having been published forbidding them to write against me. In their place have succeeded the people of Samaria, the priests of Bethaven,[3] the Franciscan Observants. If they conquer, they will do it by their excessive stupidity. I never remember to have read stupider men, who never know whether they conquer or are conquered. Poor people, to be exposed to these wolves! But the Lord will see to it. Farewell in him.

281. ERASMUS TO [LEWIS PLATZ] RECTOR OF ERFURT.

Erasmi epistolae (London, 1642), xii. 23. *Erasmi opera* (1703), iii. 334.   LOUVAIN, July 31 (1520).

In both reprints of this letter just cited the name of the rector is omitted and the date is given "1518." The name of the addressee and the date of the letter are given by the *Akten der Erfurter Universität*, ed. J. C. H. Weissenborn (Halle, 1884), ii. 314, which show that Platz was rector at this time, and speak of Erasmus' letter to him in the following terms: "The humanities ought not to burst in on a university like ravaging enemies, but to come as guests to cherish culture. . . . Therefore we have elected Lewis Platz, of Melsungen,

---

[1] Luther's greatest work, Weimar, vi. 497. English by Wace and Buchheim: *Luther's Primary Works*. *Cf.* Smith, *op. cit.*, chap. viii.
[2] Nothing is known of this; perhaps a satire is meant.
[3] "The house of vanity," *i. e.*, "of idols." Joshua, vii. 2.

rector ... both because he is devoted to this cause and because he has been exhorted thereto by a letter of the great Erasmus of Rotterdam, written in the midst of his labors, in which letter he shows his extreme good will to the university of this city." Platz matriculated at Erfurt in 1497 (*ibid*, 202) and devoted himself to theology. He became a well-known humanist and the master of Eoban Hess (Krause: *Eoben Hess*, i. 26).

Dear Sir, I am not able to withhold my love for you, since I have learned from Draco,[1] that serious youth, that you are most learned and eagerly favor sound learning, and that you take care that it shall flourish at Erfurt, now under your auspicious presidency. It is the special honor of your prudence that you bring this about without tumult, which we see is excited elsewhere by the imprudence of some men. The classics ought to come to a university not like enemies to spoil it, but like guests to live in peace. I never liked the tumult, and either I am much mistaken or more will be accomplished by moderation than by impotent force. I think it is the part of good men to desire to carry through their reforms with injury to few, or, if possible, to none. Vain, controversial theology has arrived at that point of inanity that she must be recalled to her sources. But I should prefer to have even her corrected rather than hissed off, and that she should be borne until a more potent theological method be developed. Luther has given some splendid warnings, but would that he had done it more civilly. He would then have had more favorers and allies, and would have reaped a richer harvest for Christ. And yet it would be impious to leave him entirely undefended in what he has rightly said, lest hereafter none should dare to tell the truth. This is not the place, nor is mine the ability to pronounce on his doctrine. Hitherto he has certainly profited the world. Some men have been forced by him to

[1] John Drach (Draco, Draconites), born 1494 at Carlstadt on the Main, matriculated at Erfurt in the summer of 1509, following the examples of Hess and Jonas he made a visit to Erasmus in 1520. (Erasmus had been in correspondence with him before; *e. g.*, there is a letter from Erasmus to Draco, October 17, 1518, in the *Hodoeporicon* (January, 1519) of Eoban Hess.) Later Draco went to Wittenberg, where he was inscribed in the summer of 1523, and shortly afterwards took his doctor's degree. In the same year he became evangelic preacher at Miltenberg, but was driven out by Albert of Mayence. Enders, iii. 156-7. From 1534-47 he was professor at Marburg, 1551-60 at Rostock; he then became the Protestant Bishop of Pomeranna. He died 1566. Allen, iii. 406.

turn to the writings of the ancient Fathers, either to defend themselves or to attack Luther. . . .

282. MELANCHTHON TO JOHN HESS.

Corpus Reformatorum, i. 208.   WITTENBERG, August 1 (1520).

Hail, sweetest Hess! You will learn from the letters of Luther and Schleupner how others bear your perpetual silence. . . . I believe you must have received Luther's answer and mine to your last letters which you sent by the priest. . . .

I know no news. Thank God Martin is yet alive; and do you pray that he may live long, for he is the one champion of divinity. A few days ago Cardinal Riario[1] wrote our illustrious Elector Frederic urging him with prayers and threats to bind Luther. The elector answered craftily; you know the Ulysses of persuasion. . . .

283. LUTHER TO SPALATIN.

Enders, ii. 456.   (WITTENBERG), August 5, 1520.

Greeting. I have not written for some time, waiting for the agitation which friends have put you in to die down. I am not pleased with Amsdorf's excessive affection for the other side. The students never suffered what the citizens did, but they don't care for that, thinking only of their own inconveniences. But enough of them. All speak of my abuse, but none of them is right. It is nothing to me if my authority declines. If every scolding is abuse, none has sinned more than the prophets. But in our time we are unaccustomed to hear truth distasteful to us.

Hatred is vexing Leipsic, which in the person of Alveld is acting a tragedy. Even if my trumpet-blast[2] will meet the approval of none, yet it must meet my approval, as a necessary attack on the tyranny of the Roman Antichrist who destroys the souls of the whole world. It is very sharp and vehement, so that I hope it will make even those languid little evil-speakers gasp. I will not answer Alveld,[3] but he will be

---

[1] *Cf.* Smith, 74f.

[2] This name was applied by Lang to Luther's *Address to the German Nobility.* Smith, p. 86.

[3] Who had recently published a *Tract on Communion; cf.* Lemmens, 52.

the occasion of publishing something by which the vipers will be more irritated than ever.

If you are not successful, I will write nothing to the elector about Melanchthon's salary. What I wrote formerly I did so that the man might have no reason for leaving us; but if nothing can come of it, the Lord's will be done. Finally I tried to get him to marry for the profit of the gospel, for I thought he would live longer in this state; but if nothing comes of this, let it pass. I fear he will not long survive his present manner of life. I try to do what I can for the Word; perhaps I am unworthy to accomplish anything. I also should prefer, if God willed, to be freed from teaching and preaching; I am almost disgusted to see how little fruit and gratitude to God comes from it. Perhaps it is all my fault. Farewell and pray for me.   MARTIN LUTHER, *Augustinian*.

284. LUTHER TO SPALATIN.

Enders, ii. 459.   WITTENBERG, August 14, 1520.

Greeting. We by no means believe that Eck is at Meissen;[1] either they are again trying us with their fictions, or else the words sent to you were written at Rome. This can be inferred from the fact that he writes that he hopes the bull will be moderated, which could not be done at Meissen.

You formerly wrote several times for me to recall the parish priest of Lochau, and recommend him to the elector for another position. Now here is Francis Günther of Nordhausen,[2] well fitted for the place, although he once seemed harsher to you than you ought easily to forget. If there is still doubt about the affair you can let me know. He is eloquent and powerful to speak the Word before the court, and altogether such a one as I would wish to have at Lochau

---

[1] The bull *Exsurge Domine* was signed by Leo on June 15 and entrusted to Eck to post in Germany. This was done first at Meissen on September 21.

[2] *Supra*, no. 39. On January 31, 1520 (Enders, ii. 307), Luther had sent a certain James Gropp to fill the place. He is not the same as the Gropp (whose first names were Francis Gottschalk) mentioned later in the letters of 1523, though they are confounded by Seidemann in his index. De Wette-Seidemann, vi. 665. Günther matriculated at Wittenberg 1515, later became parish priest at Jüterbogk, in which place the Franciscans prosecuted him for Lutheranism. He obtained the living of Lochau on Luther's recommendation and died there 1528. Enders, ii. 36, 162.

and near us. Steps are being taken to provide a cure for him out of Saxony. Answer as soon as you can, and farewell.

MARTIN LUTHER, *Augustinian.*

285. ULRICH VON HUTTEN TO ERASMUS AT LOUVAIN.

Böcking, i. 367.　　　　　　　　　STECKELBERG, August 15, 1520.

... I advise you to be perfectly still and to moderate your pen so as to keep yourself safe for us. And listen to what I have to tell you, relying on our friendship. When Reuchlin's affair was all of a glow you seemed to fear those fellows more than was worthy of you. And now in the affair of Luther you are trying as hard as possible to persuade our adversaries that you are as far as may be from defending the cause of Christian truth, although they well know that your sympathies are all the other way. This is not noble. I know the friend to whom I am writing and that you will not take umbrage at my warnings. I heard with sorrow what men said and then I defended the fame of my friend, although some of his acts displeased me. Now that I am in danger, I conceal nothing from you. Therefore I pray you as a friend who loves you and wishes to deserve well of you, not to do more for me than you did for Luther and Reuchlin. You know with what triumph your letters are carried about by those whose hatred you seek to deprecate, though in doing so you win the hatred of others. Thus you have been abusing the *Epistolae Obscurorum Virorum,* which at first you greatly approved, and thus you now damn Luther for stirring up things which ought to be left alone, although you have always treated the same subjects in your books. You will never get them to believe that your sympathies are not with us. You will offend us and not placate them; if, indeed, you do not irritate them further by such open dissimulation.[1] ...

286. MELANCHTHON TO JOHN LANG.

Corpus Reformatorum, i. 210.　　　　　　(August 18?, 1520.)[2]

Greeting, excellent and learned Father. At first I rather

---

[1] This letter marked the beginning of the breach between Hutten and Erasmus, on which *cf.* E. Emerton: *Erasmus* (1900), chap. ix.

[2] The date is inferred from the letter of Luther to Long, Enders, ii. 460.

did not disapprove than approved the plan for writing an epistle to the German nobility.[1] For our friend was urged to do so by some whose opinion we must both respect. Moreover the thing itself, being of God, I would not try to obstruct. I would not rashly hinder Martin's spirit in this cause, to which he seems to have been called by Providence. Besides, the book is now printed and distributed and cannot be recalled. . . .

287. LUTHER TO SPALATIN.
Enders, ii. 464. WITTENBERG, August 23, 1520.

Greeting. . . . I forwarded your letters to Nuremberg. The additions to the book[2] will be put in the second edition, which Lotther is bringing out. The book will also be corrected. I send my statement and letter to be corrected.[3]

The tenor of my letter to Cardinal Carvajal is as follows: As his fame is great in the world, I desire to ask that, with all possible zeal, he should make himself the agent for composing the present affair. I offer all conditions of peace, except that I will not recant, suffer the stigma of heresy or be deprived of the freedom of teaching the Word. I do not fear censures and force, for I can be safe in the midst of Germany. Rather let them beware lest if they crush me they should arouse many. In talent and learning I am, with God's aid, equal to my enemies.

Farewell and pray for me.

MARTIN LUTHER, *Augustinian.*

P. S.—I commend Günther to you. Please give these letters to the elector.

288. THE ELECTOR FREDERIC OF SAXONY TO HIS BROTHER, DUKE JOHN.
C. E. Förstemann: *Neues Urkundenbuch zur Geschichte der evangelischen Kirchen-Reformation.* Hamburg, 1842, i. 2.

LOCHAU, August 25, 1520.

High-born Prince, kind, dear Brother and Kinsman. Here-

[1] Luther's pamphlet of this title is meant.
[2] Several important changes and additions were made in the second impression of the *Address to the German Nobility.*
[3] Luther here means his *Offer and Protestation* and his letter to the Emperor Charles V. Smith, *op. cit.*, 98ff.

with I send you a book[1] written by Dr. Martin Luther, in which you will find many wonderful things. God Almighty grant that it turn out well, for truly things are coming to light which many people conceal; may God Almighty vouchsafe to us poor sinners that we be improved and not made worse thereby. I would not keep this from you as you asked me to send you whatever Dr. Luther wrote, and I am always willing to serve you. In haste. . . .

                        FREDERIC, *with his own hand.*

289. CHARLES VON MILTITZ TO LUTHER.
Enders, ii. 466.   EISLEBEN, August 29, 1520.

Hail, most learned Martin! I attended the chapter of your Order celebrated at Eisleben, chiefly that I might see you as a much loved friend. As I did not have this pleasure, I decided to write you. In the chapter, with the authority of our Most Holy Lord the Pope, I said something to the brothers which will not hurt you, but prove greatly to your advantage. Wherefore I exhort you not to gainsay the brothers who will visit you,[2] but that you should follow and obey their counsel and that of the whole chapter, which I hope you will never repent. I myself would come to you, save that perhaps your friends who think that I am your enemy would lay snares for me. Yet I believe that I shall not leave these parts before conversing with you as with my special friend. Farewell.
    Yours,
           CHARLES VON MILTITZ, *with his own hand.*

290. LUTHER TO SPALATIN.
Enders, ii. 471.   (WITTENBERG), August 31, 1520.

Greeting. We will write again about the changes in the lectures, when the bridegroom[3] gets used to having the bride. I hope the new parish priest, Francis Günther, will turn out well, only try to initiate the man gently into the manners of the court. We did not know the bad reputation of his sister, but she will be separated.

---

[1] Presumably the *Address to the Christian Nobility.*
[2] On this *cf. infra,* no. 295.
[3] Agricola.

I send my *Offer and Protest*[1] printed, and letters to Francis von Sickingen and the Emperor Charles. Very little of my work *On the Captivity of the Church*[2] is printed, but we shall see. Farewell in the Lord.

MARTIN LUTHER, *Augustinian.*

Agricola's wedding day is set for the Tuesday after the Nativity of Mary.[3] Do what you promised.

291. ULRICH VON HUTTEN TO ALL GERMANS.
Böcking, i. 430.   (EBERNBURG, August ?, 1520.)[4]

Behold, men of Germany, the bull of Leo X. by which he tries to suppress the rising truth of Christianity, which he opposes to our liberty, lest, after her long bondage she should again grow strong and revive. Shall we not resist him in this attempt, and take public counsel lest he should go farther and before we know it accomplish something for his insatiable cupidity and impudence? . . . Luther is not touched in this, but all of us; nor is the sword drawn against one only, but we are all threatened. They will never complain of his tyranny, never uncover his fraud, never lay bare his guile nor resist his fury nor impede his robbery. . . . Remember to act like Germans. . . . I have published this bull that when you read it you may learn all from this one.[5] Farewell.

292. FREDERIC, ELECTOR OF SAXONY, TO VALENTINE VON TEUTLEBEN, HIS AGENT AT ROME.
Luther opera varii argumenti, v. 7.   TORGAU, (September 1 ?), 1520.

This letter is dated *loc. cit.,* "Kalend. April," but this must be wrong as the reference to Luther's *Oblatio sive Protestatio* shows. Weimar, vi. 474.

You write, perhaps correctly, that this and other business

[1] *Supra,* no. 237.
[2] *The Babylonian Captivity of the Church,* Weimar, vi. 497. Smith, p. 88ff.
[3] September 8; the wedding day, September 10.
[4] This is Hutten's preface to his edition of the bull *Exsurge Domine,* which he printed thinking it would do more harm to the Church than to Luther. The bull was signed by the Pope, June 15, 1520, and officially published in Germany by Eck and Aleander towards the end of September. Smith, *op. cit.,* p. 98. Hutten's edition is placed by Böcking in November or December, but I believe it to be earlier. The next letter of Erasmus shows that the bull had been published before September 9, and the following epistle by Hutten shows that he knew it before September 11.
[5] Virgil: *Aeneid,* ii. 65-6.

of ours is going very badly with his Holiness the Pope, all of which, in your opinion, is to be attributed to the excesses and rashness of Dr. Martin Luther, who has scattered, as you express it, "I know not what" new dogmas against the Pope's Holiness and the holy see and the Roman Church, and has not submitted himself with due reverence and moderation to the very reverend lord cardinals; and you further write that general rumor affirms that he is supported, favored and shown mercy by us alone.

To this we answer briefly and in good faith: We have never undertaken and do not now undertake to protect and defend by our patronage the doctrine and writings of Dr. Martin Luther, for we do not presume to give judgment as to what he has written rightly and lawfully and what contrariwise, and what he has taught piously and Christianly, and what otherwise.

Yet we do not think we ought to conceal that we have heard that this man's doctrine is considered and approved as pious and Christian by many learned and intelligent men. On this, however, we give no opinion, nor do we prejudge his doctrine, for we leave to him, the author of these dogmas, their whole defence, especially as the whole cause has been referred to the legitimate tribunal, to which he submits. He will offer himself to the examination of the commissioner chosen by the Pope's Holiness on just conditions, that is, with safe-conduct. To him Luther will give the justification of what he has written or taught, offering all submission and obedience, so that, if he is convinced of error by the Word of God and the true testimony of Holy Scripture, he will of his own accord offer to change his opinion and recant, as appears from the form of this *Offer and Protestation*[1] drawn up by himself. . . .

Now that Germany is flourishing in geniuses and in men of learning and wisdom, expert in the tongues and in all sorts of learning, and since even the laity have begun to be educated, and are moved by the zeal of knowing the Holy Scripture; many think that it is greatly to be feared, if the fair terms offered by Luther are neglected and he himself without due process of law simply smitten by ecclesiastical cen-

[1] Weimar, vi. 474. *Cf.* Smith, 98f.

sures, that this controversy and strife should only be exasperated, so that it could hardly ever afterwards be quieted and composed. For Luther's doctrine has now for some years past taken deep root everywhere in Germany, so that, if he is not refuted by reason and Scripture, but is only proceeded against by the terror of the ecclesiastical power, it looks as if much trouble and a horrible and fatal rebellion would take place in Germany, which would be of no advantage either to his Holiness the Pope nor to others. . . .

293. LUTHER TO SPALATIN.

Enders, ii. 472. (WITTENBERG), September 1, 1520.

Greeting. First of all, Spalatin, thank the most illustrious elector in my name for fattening me with game, although I am a monk.

The reverend Father Staupitz will come to-day and with him his new successor, Wenzel Link.[1] Yesterday our brothers returned. Charles von Miltitz wrote me a letter, saying that in the public assembly of the fathers he delivered an oration in his Italian Latin seeking some plan to keep me quiet. For he sees that he brought the golden rose in vain, as he obscurely hinted. The fathers say they answered that they had nothing in common with me, and did not know my plans. Of which we shall hear more to-day. The Counts[2] treated him magnificently.

I send a letter from Antwerp written by the prior[3] of that place, so that you may see what is being done about me. Our friend Lang, I am surprised to say, is made prior of Dresden;[4] Melchior Mirisch of Ghent. I know not whether they are animated by the spirit of power, so much are all things disturbed for the new reign of the new vicar. I think that you have received the letter of Father James Vogt. Farewell.

BROTHER MARTIN LUTHER, *Augustinian*.

[1] At the Eisleben chapter, August, 1520, Staupitz resigned as vicar and Link was elected in his stead.
[2] Of Mansfeld.
[3] James Probst (Propst) of Ypern, 1519 studied at Wittenberg, and again 1521. Returning in 1520 to Antwerp he was very active in the evangelic propaganda, for which he was arrested and forced to recant February 9, 1522. Escaping from the Netherlands he again professed Lutheranism, and in 1524 became pastor at Bremen, a position he held until his death, June 30, 1562. *Realencyclopädie*.
[4] This was a mistaken rumor.

294. ERASMUS TO GERARD NOVIOMAGUS.

Erasmi opera (1703), iii. 577. LOUVAIN, September 9, 1520.

Gerard Geldenhauer, of Nymegen (Noviomagus), (c. 1482-1542), an author and the secretary of Philip and Maximilian of Burgundy. In 1525 he visited Wittenberg and went over to the Reformers, about which time his friendship with Erasmus cooled. Married 1527; after 1532 professor at Marburg. Allen, *op. cit.*, ii. 379.

. . . I fear the worst for poor Luther, so hot is the conspiracy against him, so deeply are the princes and especially Pope Leo offended in him. Would that Luther had followed my advice and had abstained from that of hateful and seditious men. He would have had more fruit and less envy. It would not satisfy his enemies to put one man to death; if they succeed no one could bear their insolence. They won't stop until they have subverted all study of the classics. They are already attacking Reuchlin again only from hatred of Luther, who, against my advice, tried to join his name to that of Reuchlin, and thus hurt *him* while not helping himself. Eck debated; Hochstraten published I know not what axioms to which all had to subscribe. The professors of Louvain disputed and even published. The judgment of the University of Paris was expected, when lo! the whole thing suddenly seems to turn into a bull and into smoke. The terrible bull is published, although the Pope forbade its publication. I fear it will lead to a terrible riot. I do not judge the piety of those who have advised the Pope in this matter, but certainly their counsel is most dangerous. The affair arose from the worst sources and has hitherto been carried on in the worst manner. The whole tragedy began in the hatred of sound learning and the stupidity of the monks. Then it was nourished to madness by reviling and malicious conspiracy. There is no doubt whither the thing is tending; namely, to the extinction of sound learning and to the reign of barbarism. I have nothing to do with this tragedy. I might have a bishopric if I wrote against Luther. I regret that the gospel is thus oppressed, and that we are driven rather than taught, and taught those things which are repugnant to the Bible and common sense. Farewell, dear Gerard, and write when you can.

295. LUTHER TO SPALATIN.

Enders, ii. 477.   WITTENBERG, September 11, 1520.

Greeting. Dear Spalatin, I received your letter from Altenburg yesterday, but the one you wrote later from Buttstädt[1] I received earlier. Nothing was done about me at Eisleben,[2] except that Charles von Miltitz took counsel with the fathers and finally induced them to send the reverend Father Staupitz and the new Vicar Link to me, to beg me to write a private letter[3] to the Roman Pontiff witnessing that I had never tried to do anything against him personally. Miltitz hopes that this plan will turn out well.

Although this plan does not appeal to me, nor to the fathers, yet we will oblige Miltitz, who perhaps in asking it is grinding his own ax. I shall, therefore, write the exact fact that I never had the slightest cause to attack the person of the Pope. What could be easier to write or truer? I must take care in writing not to treat the apostolic see too ferociously, but I will be a bit caustic.

Hutten sent me a letter[4] boiling over with great indignation at the Pope, writing that now he is rushing on the priestly tyranny with pen and sword, because the Pope planned to assassinate him and commanded the Archbishop of Mayence to send him bound to Rome.[5] "Madness," he exclaims, "worthy of a blind[6] Pope." You will see a copy when I get it from Henry Stromer who asked to see it.

The worst of it is that the Archbishop of Mayence had a mandate issued from the pulpit, mentioning Hutten by name and forbidding his books to be read or bought under pain of excommunication, and adding that the same held good of similar books, by which he meant a covert attack on mine. If he only mentions me by name, I will join with Hutten and excuse myself in such a way as will not please the Archbishop of

[1] The elector was starting out to meet the new Emperor in the Netherlands. Smith, p. 98.
[2] *Supra*, no. 289.
[3] This letter became the introduction to Luther's tract *On the Liberty of a Christian Man*, cf. Smith, p. 91.
[4] Lost.
[5] The papal breve of July 12 to Albert of Mayence says nothing of this, but there is other evidence to show that Hutten's story was at worst an exaggeration.
[6] Leo X. was very short-sighted.

Mayence. Perhaps they are hastening the end of their own tyranny by this plan. . . .

Take this in good part and farewell in the Lord. Be careful not to let everyone have access to our elector, lest someone should try to poison him. The Romanists will stop at nothing. Hutten cannot warn me enough against poison.

MARTIN LUTHER.

296. ULRICH VON HUTTEN TO ELECTOR FREDERIC OF SAXONY.

Böcking, i. 383. S. Szamatólski: *Ulrichs von Hutten deutsche Schriften*, 1891, p. 127. German.   EBERNBURG, September 11, 1520.

Now, at last, Prince Frederic, I see that we must rage against the Roman tyranny; now, at last, our Romanist brothers, after so many fraternal warnings and so many convincing arguments, not only do not act more mildly in those things which offend us, but they even act more ferociously than ever before. Have you not heard that they have ordered me sent bound to Rome? You will see how worthy that deed was of them. And now, good Heavens! what a violent and cruel bull they have drawn up against Luther! You would call it the roar of the Lion (Leo), hearing which the miserable sheep of Christ do not recognize the pious voice of a shepherd, but the bloody cry of a wild robber. Is there any vestige of Christian gentleness, or any indication of apostolic moderation therein? He roars, he rages. But his ferocity is all the plainer because often in that bull he pretends that he is other than he is; he craftily simulates benevolence when he smoothly invites Luther to Rome, as though we were ignorant that it made no difference to him how he got us, whether Luther was inveigled by a promise or I haled by force. If Luther listens to me he will never go thither to certain death, and I much wonder who persuaded Leo X. that I should so easily be captured in the midst of Germany and taken through the steep passes of the Alps to Rome. . . .

[The rest of this long letter is a prophecy of the downfall of "Babylon," an account of the ancient liberties of the Germans and the modern iniquity of Rome.] . . .

I see that the Pope thinks you are obedient to him in all but protecting helpless Luther. . . . That you do this bravely I exhort you again and again, partly because you are his natural protector and partly because he has little hopes of any other, or at least any better. For the Saxons were always free, always unconquered. . . .

297. ERASMUS TO POPE LEO X. AT ROME.
Erasmi opera (1703), iii. 578.   LOUVAIN, September 13, 1520.

Although I did not fear, most blessed Father, that your goodness could be induced to hurt an innocent man, or that your prudence would rashly believe the calumnies of the wicked, yet when I see that your Holiness is flooded with so much business from the whole world, and when I consider the unexampled wickedness of some who conspire against sound learning—never ceasing, daring all things and leaving no stone unturned—I have thought it concerned me to fortify your Holiness, remote and busy, with this antidote. I see there are some, who, to strengthen their own faction, seek to confound the cause of sound learning, of Reuchlin and of myself with the cause of Luther, although there is really nothing common to them. I have always said this, both orally and in my published writings. I do not know Luther nor have I read his books except ten or twelve pages, and those hastily. From these, which I glanced at, it seemed to me that he wrote well on the Scriptures, explaining them according to the manner of the ancients, while our age is excessively addicted to clever rather than to necessary questions. I therefore favored what was good in him, not what was bad; or rather I favored Christ's glory in him.

I was almost the first to discover any danger, fearing that a tumult, which I have always abominated more than anyone, would arise. I therefore plead with John Froben, the printer, even using threats, that he should print none of Luther's works. Then I wrote diligently to his friends that they should admonish him to remember Christian gentleness in his writings and to respect the tranquillity of the Church. And when he wrote me himself two years ago, I warned him lovingly to avoid trouble, and I only wish he had taken my advice. I hear that this letter has been reported to your Holiness and used against me, though it really deserves the favor of your Holiness. For what needful advice does it not give? True, I did it civilly, by which I thought to accomplish more than by severity, and I was writing to a stranger. After I had almost taken him to task, lest my freedom offend him, I added: "I write this, not to tell you what to do, but to encourage you in doing as you have always done," thus assuming that he would do of his own accord what I wanted him to. For if his previous manner of writings had pleased me why should I need to advise him to adopt another? I know that this passage has been twisted against me by some, but that the words I added "that he had many adherents," have been interpreted still worse. But what I wrote was true. Many men favored what was good in him just as I did. I wished him to know this, not so that he might be encouraged by their support to write seditiously, but that he might make their support perpetual by following my advice to moderate his pen. I am surprised that the name of the Bishop of Liège was put in by the men of Leipsic,[1] who by some means or other published a secret letter which had not been edited at Basle. It is absolutely true that he never had anything to do with Luther any more than I did. Even if I had mentioned his name it would only have been in this sense. I wrote that letter almost two years ago, before the affair had gotten to its present state of bitterness, or even to be disputed.

If anyone has ever heard me, even in my cups, defending Luther's dogmas, I shall not refuse to be called a Lutheran. But they say I have not attacked him. But in the first place, I could not refute him unless I read his books attentively once and again, for which my assiduous studies did not give me leisure. Secondly, I saw that it was above the mediocrity of my learning and talents. Again I did not wish to deprive the universities which had undertaken the task of their glory in it. Finally, I feared to excite the hatred of powerful men, especially as no one had commanded me to engage on this labor. Wherefore, if the enemies of good letters revile me on this account, I have a certain protection in your wisdom and my

---

[1] *I. e.*, when the letter was printed at Leipsic. *Cf. supra*, no. 155. The Bishop of Liège was Erard de la Marck.

own innocence. I am not so insane as to dare to do aught against the chief vicar of Christ, since I am unwilling to cross even a bishop. I am not so ungrateful that I should not endeavor to respond to your more than paternal indulgence towards me. Thus I shall save whatever little talent I may have for the glory of Christ and the peace of his fold. Whoever is the enemy of this fold will also be my enemy. I did not patronize Luther even when it was free for anyone to do so. Only I disapproved their mode of attack, not for Luther's sake, but for the dignity of the theologians. . . .

I had decided to winter at Rome to consult the library of your Holiness, but the congress of kings[1] has kept me here. I hope to go to Rome next winter. May Christ Almighty guard your Holiness.

298. ERASMUS TO FRANCIS CHIREGATTO.
Erasmi opera (1703), iii. 579.   LOUVAIN, September 13, 1520.

Chiregatto (†December 6, 1539), employed by Leo and Adrian in various ways, was made Bishop of Teramo in the Abruzzi on September 7, 1522. Allen, iii. 61.

If I did not embrace your candid, officious and affable friendship, I should be more inhumane than any Thracian.

Perhaps there are few men who regret this Lutheran tumult as much as I do. Would that I could have kept it off in the beginning, or could compose it now. . . . When the bull came out, commanding them to preach against Luther, two or three of the beggar tyrants[2] agreed over their potations to traduce me along with Luther before the people. . . . There is a man with a white pall, but a black heart, both stupid and furious and so morose that the whole university dislikes him. When he published the bull here he spoke more against me than against Luther. In his public lectures he always joined my name with those of Luther and Lefèvre d'Étaples, and when it was pointed out to him that we all differed, he replied that heretics never agreed. . . . At Bruges there was a certain Franciscan, a suffragan of the Bishop of Tournay, who, full

---
[1] *I. e.*, meeting of Henry VIII. and Francis I. at Calais in July.
[2] πτωχοτύραννοι, *i. e.*, begging monks.

of wine, bellowed whole hours before the people against Luther and Erasmus, calling us beasts, asses, geese and stocks, but not refuting a single word. When he said that there was heresy in my books and was asked by someone, who had been instructed by the magistrate, what it was, this buffoon of a bishop replied: "I have not read Erasmus's books; I tried to read the *Paraphrases,* but the Latin was too deep." . . .

I have no fear for myself. I have never been the teacher of error nor the leader of tumult. And yet you would hardly believe how strongly I am urged to mix in the Lutheran affair, and had I wished to do so it would have been far different from what it is. But hitherto I have preached peace and quiet, hitherto I have labored for Christ. . . .

299. MARTIN BUCER TO GEORGE SPALATIN.

R. Stähelin: *Briefe aus der Reformationszeit.* Basle, 1887, p. 9.

HEIDELBERG, September 19, 1520.

. . . I have read the pamphlet of *the most Christian*[1] Reverend Father Martin to our nobility. Good Heavens! what wise liberty is in it! There is no jot of it to which I can oppose anything from Scripture. But rather, as I previously learned to expect from his other works, I seem to myself to have found a man undoubtedly acting out the spirit of Christ. Capito, that finished theologian, my special patron, was at first horrified by what rumor said of the book, but when he read it, he acted, as he always does, as becomes a sincere theologian, as an interpreter and champion of the truth neither blinded nor timid. When you meet him you will learn his virtues most clearly. May our breasts not hesitate to accept the gifts which, as it were, the Holy Spirit shows the Church in most sacred Luther and other men not a few, whose erudition and piety are both above suspicion. I pray Christ for that. If you can steal time from your other occupations, please write briefly what result I may expect from the present hazard, and if most pious Luther comes to you, commend me warmly to him. . . .

[1] Greek.

300. LUTHER TO GÜNTHER VON BÜNAU, CANON OF MERSEBURG.

Enders, ii. 481.   WITTENBERG, September 28, 1520.

A Günther von Bünau, of Elsterberg, was in 1523 Church visitor in Meissen and Voigtland. He seems to have written Luther about a rumor which circulated about a debate held at Wittenberg.

Greeting. Excellent Sir, I read with joy and wonder the letter testifying your great faith in me. What lies will that poisonous old serpent not vent?[1] The debate was as follows: Carlstadt presided; I argued with others in the usual way. The question was whether Christ in the passion opposed the will of the Father? For he prayed that the cup might be taken from him, which was tantamount to not wanting it and refusing it. Then the argument showed that not wishing was equivalent to hating and rebelling. This was denied and not proved. Nothing was asserted, but only talked over familiarly. What, pray, do we not say in argument, even against orthodox belief? Are we not accustomed to impugn even articles of faith? Why then do those men rave and lie about my assertions, when I only argued for the sake of argument, asserting nothing, and rather openly confessing that I did not understand the mysteries of Christ? I know not whether we treated that saying of the apostle, "he that knew no sin was made to be sin,"[2] and other sayings which attribute to Christ sin, a curse and despair; as do Paul and the prophets. As we do not grasp these things, it is right that we should assert nothing about them. I never debated publicly on this matter of Christ's sorrows, and I know nothing about it except what I said above. If anyone says otherwise you can convict him of falsehood on the testimony of our whole audience. Let these virulent men cease to criminate one who argues, or else let them first condemn their own Aquinas, who upsets all Christian doctrines, arguing pro and contra. Do they wish to forbid us to question articles of faith simply in argument and for the sake of learning? I am ashamed that even you should be moved by these nonsensical fictions. Here you have the facts and my opinion.

[1] Revelation, xii. 9.   [2] 2 Corinthians, v. 21.

I know nothing of Eck,[1] except that he has come with his beard, his bull and his money. The Lord grant that one of the condemned articles be that the bag of the Mendicant is nothing. I also will laugh at this bull or bubble. I send Marforius.[2] The Lord keep you always. Amen. Farewell, dearest Günther.   MARTIN LUTHER, *Augustinian.*

301. LUTHER TO CONRAD SAUM AT BRACKENHEIM.
Enders, ii. 483.   WITTENBERG, October 1, 1520.

Conrad Saum (Sam, Som), (1483-June 20, 1533), at this time priest at Brackenheim in Würtemberg, had already embraced the Reformation, on account of which he was driven out, going to Ulm in 1524, where he introduced a Zwinglian reform. *Realencyclopädie.*

Greeting. Dr. Heilingen[3] has commended you, Conrad, to me, praising your piety and learning. He pleased me not a little in bearing witness that your heart is possessed by that pure and sincere doctrine of Christ, which in all possible ways the sophists strenuously resist by force and guile. Satan aids them, for who cannot see that he is the author of these storms in them? For our wrestling is not against flesh and blood, but against spiritual wickedness, against the authors of this darkness in heavenly places.[4] Let us therefore be constant, and in our turn let us hear the trumpet of our leader who calls to us: "Be strong in war, fight with the old serpent[5] and receive the eternal kingdom." For this fellow Satan does not fight with us, but with Christ who fights in us, and who is greater than he that is in the world.[6] The Lord has chosen new wars, says Deborah, Judges vii.[7] and we also fight not our own battles, but those of the Lord. Be strong therefore and mighty; if God be for us who can be against us?[8]

Why this? you say. Because you will hear that the Pope

---

[1] Eck arrived at Meissen, September 21, where he posted the bull.
[2] The name of the statue of a river-god at Rome, on which satires were posted. The satire Luther sent may have been *Pasquillus Marranus exul* . . . Clemen: *Beiträge zur Reformationsgeschichte,* i. 1.
[3] Probably John Geyling, later a well-known Reformer in South Germany, is meant.
[4] Ephesians, vi. 12.
[5] Revelation, xii. 9.
[6] 1 John, iv. 4.
[7] Rather, Judges, v. 8.
[8] Romans, viii. 31.

through his legate Eck has attacked Luther and his books and all who adhere to and follow him, with a harsh bull. This wretched instrument of Satan is now at Leipsic, trumpeting forth his bull with great pomp and glory. I know not what will happen, nor am I anxious to know, for I am sure that he who sitteth in heaven takes care for all things and has foreseen the rise, progress and end (which I wait for) of this affair from eternity. Whichever way the lot falls it will not move me, for it only falls where it falls by God's excellent will, who cannot err and is thus bound to please someone. Be not therefore anxious, for your Father knows what things you need before you ask him;[1] a leaf of a tree does not fall to the ground without his will;[2] how much more must we fall only there where he wishes us to fall.

I thought best to encourage you thus myself, so that if a powerful spirit come up against you, you will not abandon your post, but hold fast what you have, lest another should receive your crown.[3] It is a small thing for us to die for the Word which was incarnate[4] and died first for us. We who perish with him and who have gone with him where he has gone, will rise with him and attain to the same place that he has attained to and will remain with him forever. See then that you do not hold your holy calling cheap, but that you gratefully persevere in it through all evil. He will come and will not tarry who shall deliver us from all evil.[5] Farewell in the Lord Jesus Christ. May he strengthen and preserve our heart and mind. Amen. MARTIN LUTHER.

302. CHARLES VON MILTITZ TO ELECTOR FREDERIC OF SAXONY.
Walch, xv. 928. German. LEIPSIC, October 2, 1520.

Most serene, high-born Prince, most gracious Lord! My humble service to your Grace. As at my departure from Gotha your Grace gave me a letter to Fabian von Feilitzsch,[6]

[1] Matthew, vi. 8.
[2] *Cf.* Matthew, x. 29.
[3] Revelation, iii. 11.
[4] John, i. 14.
[5] Hebrews, x. 37. 2 Timothy, iv. 18.
[6] A Councillor of Frederic, who died early in December, 1520. He was a warm

at the very hour of my arrival at Erfurt I sent it to him by my own messenger. At Erfurt, however, I was ill, and had to wait there seven days. At that time the new vicar, Dr. Link, came and visited me and asked whether I had received Dr. Staupitz's letter about Dr. Martin. I said no, which horrified his reverence, for he would have been glad to have had me receive said letter while I was with your Grace, that your Grace might thereby have understood Dr. Luther's attitude and the diligence of the fathers who were sent to him; for Link did not neglect to inform me what they had done and decreed, and told me that Luther was perfectly willing to write humbly to his Holiness, and show himself an obedient son, which I heard with great joy, and thereupon arose and rode to Altenburg. There I found Dr. Staupitz's letter and Luther's to Spalatin, of the former of which I send your Grace a copy. Then I rode back to Eisleben to the father vicar to find out whether he were minded to journey with me to a convenient place to meet Luther and come to a final decision in this affair. I found him at home, and thereupon went to Leipsic, where I found Dr. Eck making a great outcry and noise. I did not hesitate to ask him to visit me, to find out what his purpose and will was. He acted hastily and frivolously, and began to speak of his commands and how he would teach Dr. Luther, and with sharp words he said that he had posted up the papal bull at Meissen on September 21, at Merseburg on the 25th and at Brandenburg on the 29th. He gave me an accredited copy of the said bull, which I send your Grace. He carries his bull around in procession with great pomp. His Grace Duke George wrote one of his councillors to give Eck a gold-plated cup full of gulden.

But not minding his commission and bull, good pious children[1] on September 29 posted up a notice in ten places, of which I send your Grace a copy, threatening Eck so hard that he had to flee into the cloister of St. Paul, and dared not show himself.

supporter of Luther (*cf.* Smith, *op. cit.*, pp. 53, 55), and took a considerable part in the negotiations with Miltitz.

[1] *I. e.*, students at the university.

Caesar Pflug complained of this notice, and commanded the rector of the university to issue a mandate against those who thus plagued Eck, which was done. I send your Grace a copy of it; it did no good. They have made a song about him which they sing in the streets. He is much troubled; his self-confidence and boasting are charged against him; people daily write him hostile letters in the cloister and refuse him personal or financial aid. There are more than fifty students from Wittenberg here, who make it their business to annoy him. To-day he published a pamphlet against Luther, of which I send your Grace four copies. The grey monk has also printed something against Luther. Only one quaternion is finished as yet, which I also send to your Grace.

To-day I intend going to Fabian von Feilitzsch to ask him to write Luther to come to Lichtenberg or Eilenberg, where I hope to negotiate with him to get him to fulfill his promise. I will bring him security from this bull, for it has no power for twenty-one days, during which period I shall have ample time to go to him and to write of it. I told Eck that he did wrong to publish the bull while things were being negotiated in a friendly way, and that he should properly have written first to ask me what I had done. He kept silence thereupon and sighed, as if he were sorry. I cannot write your Grace how bitter people are against him. I fear the safe-conduct will not help him, but that he will be smitten. . . .

303. LUTHER TO GEORGE SPALATIN.

Enders, ii. 486. (WITTENBERG), October 3, 1520.

Greeting. I have received many letters from you, dear Spalatin, and am surprised that the one I wrote in answer to yours dated at Buttstädt has not yet reached you. That which I wrote later contained the same request about sending me the writings of the fathers from Eisleben, but I hope my letters have reached you in the meantime. Miltitz has begged me to write privately to the Roman Pontiff saying that I never meant to twit him personally. I have not yet written,[1]

---
[1] Luther later decided to do so, however, and this resulted in his third great pamphlet of 1520, the *Liberty of a Christian Man. Cf.* Smith, *op. cit.*, 88.

and shall not do so now that Eck[1] has dared turn those bulls —and such fierce ones!—loose against me. What he is aiming at is not yet known.

Many think that I should ask the elector to obtain an imperial edict in my favor, declaring that I should not be condemned nor my books prohibited except by warrant of Scripture. Please find out what is intended; I care little either way, because I rather dislike having my books so widely spread, and should prefer to have them all fall into oblivion together, for they are desultory and unpolished, and yet I do want the matters they treat known to all. But not all can separate the gold from the dross in my works, nor is it necessary since better books and Bibles are easily obtainable. I would much rather increase the number of living books, that is, of preachers, and protect them so that they could explain the state of affairs to the public. I am sending what was sent me on this subject from Italy. If the elector acts as this suggests I think it would be most worthy of him. The Italian public could then grasp the condition of affairs and our cause would be stronger. Perhaps God has raised them up and will preserve our elector to us to advance the Word by him. See what you can do for the cause of Christ. The man[2] who wrote me from Venice is a brother of Lazarus Spengler[3] who sent the letter to me from Nuremberg.

My book on the *Captivity of the Church*[4] is coming out next Saturday and will be sent to you.

Carlstadt has cast his die and takes courage against the Pope.

I have just heard that Eck is not safe at Leipsic, but is detested and is caricatured by posters stuck up everywhere and that he has found a far different reception and opinion there than he hoped; for he is not now what he was a year ago.

[1] Eck published the *Exsurge Domine* at Mayence, Merseburg and Brandenburg in the last days of September. Smith, p. 98.

[2] George Spengler, originally of Nuremberg, set up as a merchant in Venice, died March 21, 1529.

[3] Lazarus Spengler (1479-September 7, 1534), studied at Leipsic 1494, became town clerk at Nuremberg 1507. He warmly embraced Luther's cause, publishing a *Defence* of it, 1519, for which he was excommunicated by the bull *Exsurge Domine*. He visited Wittenberg in 1525, and Luther dedicated to him his work on *Schools*, 1530. Weimar, xxx., part ii., 508. *Realencyclopädie*.

[4] *The Babylonian Captivity of the Church*, Weimar, vi. 484. *Cf.* Smith, 88ff.

Indeed, he has changed his lodging and has gone into a Dominican monastery, openly giving out that he can neither escape their snares nor return to Ingolstadt. I should not wish him murdered, although I see his plans will be frustrated. The Lord do what is good in his eyes.

We have no news except the rumor of war with Prussia. The Archbishop of Mayence commands the books of Hutten to be publicly prohibited, calling down a curse on his head. Hutten girds himself with great courage to try his arms and genius against the Pope.

Our Adrian[1] rages against me, carried away by I know not what fury, perhaps seeking an occasion of withdrawing. Though I have done nothing to him he rails at my sermons, ready to teach me the Gospel, though he does not understand his own Old Testament. There are various possible explanations of his madness, but let it pass, time will show what it is. MARTIN LUTHER, *Augustinian*.

304. LUTHER TO SPALATIN.

Enders, ii. 490. WITTENBERG, October (11), 1520.

Greeting. At last that Roman bull brought by Eck has arrived.[2] Our friends are writing to the elector about it. I despise it, and am now attacking it as impious and fraudulent, Eckian to the core. You see that Christ himself is condemned in it. It says nothing to the purpose, but summons me not to be heard, but to recant, so that you may know that they are full of fury, blindness and insanity, seeing and considering nothing. I shall still act without mentioning the Pope's name, as though it were a fictitious and forged bull,[3] although I believe it is their true work. Would that Charles[4] were a man to grapple with these devils for Christ!

I fear nothing for myself. God's will be done. Nor do I know what the elector ought to do, except that I think it

---

[1] The professor of Hebrew.
[2] Eck sent the bull with a note to Burckhart, the Rector of Wittenberg, on October 3. Burckhart refused on technical grounds to post it, but forwarded it to Duke John. Schubert: *Luthers Berufung auf Worms*, p. 18ff.
[3] Cf. Luther's *Von den neuen Eckischen Bullen und Lügen*, Weimar, vi. 576. Erasmus also pretended to doubt the genuineness of the bull, hoping thus to make it possible for the Pope to withdraw it.
[4] The Emperor-elect, now twenty years old.

best for him to dissimulate. For both the bull and Eck are held in utter contempt at Leipsic and everywhere else; whence I suspect that it may acquire authority by excessive care and solicitude on our part, whereas, if left to itself, it will easily quiet down. I send a copy of it, for you to see the Roman monsters. If they rule, it is over with the faith and the Church.

Yet I rejoice with my whole heart that for this best of causes I suffer evil, who am not worthy of being so tried. Now I am much freer; for I am certain at length that the Pope is Antichrist and that the seat of Satan has been openly found. God will keep his own lest they be seduced with his specious impiety. Erasmus writes that the court of the Emperor is possessed by the "beggar-tyrants"[1] so that there can be no hope in Charles. This is no surprise; put not your trust in princes nor in the sons of men in whom there is no help.[2]

This hour I am going to Lichtenberg to offer myself again to Charles von Miltitz as the elector commanded. The preceptor[3] is unwilling that I should go, for he fears something. Farewell and pray for me. I will renew my appeal[4] and will do what our friends think ought to be done. Although I should prefer that the excommunication threatened in the bull should be carried out against me, yet I must consider others.

MARTIN LUTHER, *Augustinian*.

305. LUTHER TO SPALATIN.

Enders, ii. 494. LICHTENBERG (October 12), 1520.

Greeting. Dear Spalatin, Miltitz and I have met at Lichtenberg, and, as I hear from him, have with much hope made the following agreement: that I am to write a letter to the Pope and publish it in Latin and German as a preface to some little work in which I shall narrate my history, showing that

---

[1] *I. e.*, the mendicant friars. *Supra*, no. 258. *Infra*, February 27, 1521, no. 406.
[2] Psalm cxlvi. 3.
[3] Wolfgang Reissenbusch, matriculated at Wittenberg 1502, bachelor of theology 1503, Rector of the University 1511. Then he became teacher of a boys' school at Lichtenberg, where he married, April 26, 1525. He is mentioned by Luther in 1537. *Cf.* Enders, v. 146. Smith, 172ff, 347.
[4] He did it on November 17. Weimar, vii. 74.

I would never have attacked the Pope's person, but throwing the whole blame on Eck.

As this is all true, I will easily do it, and offer silence as humbly as I may, provided only the others keep silence, so that I may seem to omit nothing in my power to make peace. I have always been ready to do this, as you know. I shall, therefore, do this as soon as I can; if it turns out as we hope, it is well done, if otherwise, it will also be good, because it will please the Lord. Farewell.   MARTIN LUTHER.

306. WOLFGANG REISSENBUSCH TO FABIAN VON FEILITZSCH.

Walch, xv. 947. German.   (LICHTENBERG), October 13, 1520.

Kind Sir and Patron! Last night at ten o'clock my curate of Lichtenberg wrote me that Dr. Luther came on Thursday [October 11] at four in the afternoon, bringing with him Philip Melanchthon, a brother of his order, a nobleman and four riders. My assistant also tells me that no fewer than thirty horsemen were also present. At six o'clock Miltitz entered with four horsemen. They were cheerful and happy with one another, for I had left instructions to entertain them well and give them enough. Miltitz relates what they did in his letter, to which I refer you. Yesterday at one o'clock Luther left; Miltitz would have accompanied him but that one of his horses was sick. My assistant tells me that he remained yesterday at Lichtenberg, at which I am well pleased.

Upon my honor, Sir, I would not have taken one hundred gulden to have remained at home. For I fear something would have happened to me. Miltitz would gladly have brought me, poor devil, into the game, so that he could have revenged himself on me for what he could not do to Dr. Luther. . . .

307. CHARLES VON MILTITZ TO FREDERIC, ELECTOR OF SAXONY.

Enders, ii. 495. German.   EILENBURG, October 14, 1520.

. . . Luther has offered to write a humble letter to the Pope's Holiness, in Latin and German, to dedicate a little book to his Holiness, and in the preface to write an epistle, showing his Holiness why he first wrote and how it came about, and who started and strengthened the errors and who preached so diligently to the detriment of the Holy Church. ... The book will appear in twelve days and will have the date September 6,[1] just ten days after the embassy left Eisleben. ... This is so that no one can say that Eck and his followers with the bull caused him to write this book to his Holiness, for the bull was published on September 21, so that this book would have been written fifteen days before anyone knew anything about the bull. Luther will also give a fair account of the Leipsic debate and the diligent attempt of my gracious Lord of Merseburg to hinder the same, and he will also praise the Pope personally. ... Dr. Luther has also written Spalatin a partial account of our negotiation and conclusion, which letter I now send to your Grace. ...

308. CASPAR HEDIO TO ULRICH ZWINGLI AT ZURICH.
Corpus Reformatorum, xciv. 355.   MAYENCE, October 15, 1520.

Hedio, or Heyd, of Baden (1494-1552), matriculated at Freiburg 1513, B. A. 1514, M. A. 1516. In 1519 he was a chaplain at Basle, in 1520 went to Mayence. In 1523 to Strassburg, where he was one of the leading Reformers until his death. *Realencyclopädie*. He had written to Luther from Basle, June 23, 1520. Enders, ii. 421.

Greeting. Although I am long absent from you, dearest Zwingli, yet would I be present with my letters. Capito called me to Mayence, where I shall be preacher until he returns from the coronation of the king,[2] and perhaps afterwards, if Christ will, for Capito is going to give up this office, having been made councillor of the Archbishop of Mayence. You will hardly believe how valuable he is in this position. Luther[3] would long ago have been burnt in this district and Lutherans *excommunicated*,[4] had he not persuaded the archbishop otherwise. ...

---

[1]This disingenuous plan was followed, so that Luther's preface to *The Liberty of a Christian Man*, actually written about this time, bore the false date September 6, or, as Miltitz says, just ten days after the embassy (Staupitz and Link) had gone to Luther from the chapter at Eisleben. *Supra*, no. 293. For the book cf. Smith, 91ff.
[2]*I. e.*, of Charles V. at Aix-la-Chapelle, October 23, 1520.
[3]*I. e.*, his books.
[4]Greek.

The Pope has sent a bull about Luther, a real bull, I hear. He urges the angels of heaven, Sts. Peter and Paul, and every creature to take part against Luther and his adherents; they are to be slaughtered, burned and so forth. If the bull really is what they tell us it has little apostolic spirit and no Christian mercy. O free Germany, where is our freedom? Not even our tongue is free. Hutten is hiding, for the Romanists have prepared poison for him and have hired men to take him bound to Rome or to kill him. He will not remain hidden long, as the monks of this province, who are furious papists, think. The Elector of Saxony is very liberal towards learned men; they say no prince is more upright or greater than he. Luther will burst forth from personal vices[1] and before the next fair we shall have thunder. Cease not, help good men and Christian piety as much as you can. The monks will try everything. . . .

309. WILIBALD PIRCKHEIMER TO HENRY STROMER OF AUERBACH AT LEIPSIC.

Pirckheimeri opera, ed. Goldast, 402.   NEUSTADT, October 18, 1520.

Hail, dear Stromer. I have received Luther's book[2] which you sent, but what good will it do us if we are not allowed to read it, and if we who are innocent are cursed so fiercely? I hear that Eck has posted some bulls or other things at Meissen and has publicly traduced my name.[3] How just it is that I who live at Nuremberg should be accused in Saxony! As I presume he has left a copy of the bull at Leipsic I pray you let me know the contents thereof. . . . Moreover, I hear that a book called *Der abgehobelte Eck* is handed around and that everybody says that I am the author of it, as though no one but I knew how to play the fool. . . . Charles von Miltitz has informed me of the contents of the bull, but he sent me no copy of it, supposing, I know not why, that I already had one.

[1] Allusion to close of Luther's *Address to the German Nobility.* Weimar, vi. 469.
[2] Presumably the *Address to the German Nobility.*
[3] When Eck was given the bull to post in Germany (Smith, 97f.), he was allowed to mention by name those of Luther's followers who he thought should be excommunicated with him. He named Carlstadt, Spengler and Pirckheimer, the latter probably because of the satire spoken of in this letter.

310. THE COUNCILLORS OF THE ELECTOR FREDERIC TO PHILIP MELANCHTHON.

Corpus reformatorum, i. 269. (October),[1] 1520.

Our kind service to you, learned, honorable and good friend. The coadjutor[2] and councillors of our gracious lord the Bishop of Freising and Naumburg have written to us about the Pope's bull and Dr. Eck's doings, and have asked us to give their messenger letters to Wittenberg so that he can get a printed or written copy of the learned Dr. Luther's appeal against this bull, as you will learn further from their letters. But as we have no knowledge, except what rumor has brought us, of Luther's appeal against the papal bull, we have replied to the said coadjutor and councillors that we have sent their letter to you as to one who is well posted on Luther's actions and that they should find out all about it from you. Wherefore in the absence and place of our gracious Elector Frederic we kindly beg you to give the messenger of the said coadjutor and councillors whatever information you can in order that he may announce it to them at Zeitz. Our gracious lord will take this in good part, and so shall we, personally. THE COUNCILLORS.[3]

311. ERASMUS TO GODSCHALK ROSEMUND, RECTOR OF THE UNIVERSITY OF LOUVAIN.

Erasmi opera (1703), iii. 585. LOUVAIN, October 18, 1520.

Letters nos. 311-14 evidently belong close together soon after the burning of Luther's works at Louvain, October 8, and the consequent attack on Erasmus. The only one which can be accurately dated is no. 311. The others must, at any rate, fall between August, 1520, and February, 1521, while Rosemund was rector. I believe that they all come in October, before Erasmus left for Cologne, where we find him in the first days of November.

Rosemund (1483-December 5, 1526) studied at Louvain, where he began teaching arts in 1509 and theology in 1515. In 1518 he became

---

[1]The *Corpus Reformatorum* dates this November 15, but the events alluded to show that it must have been earlier, perhaps "15 Kal. Novemb.," *i. e.,* October 18.

[2]Henry Schmiedberg, on whom and this affair, *cf. infra,* November 13.

[3]Probably Fabian von Feilitzsch, Haugold von Einsiedel and John von Taubenheim, spoken of by Luther in the aforementioned letter of November 13.

dean of the faculty, and rector during the winter-semester, 1520-1. In November, 1524, he was made president of Adrian VI.'s College. *Allgemeine Deutsche Biographie,* and de Jongh, 165-7.

I do not think it necessary to admonish you of your duty, of which a part is not only to keep from hurting others yourself, but to prevent anyone doing an injury to another. The many things which Nicholas Edmond, either at your command or at the Pope's, said against Luther, do not, I think, pertain to me; but what he did beyond all command and contrary to the will of the Pope, who wishes even those who have hitherto followed Luther dealt with gently, and that none others should be involved, this, I say, which he did in attacking me falsely and undeservedly, pertains to your authority and jurisdiction. You should silence this man of peevish tongue, especially as he is a bad example and injurious both to the order of theologians and to this university. . . . On October 9, in the church of St. Peter, while preaching on charity, as I happened to be present, he suddenly and ignobly turned his sermon against me, and said that I favored Luther, although from the beginning I have always said with perfect truth that I had no commerce with Luther except what one Christian might have with another. . . . From the taste of his works which I have had, I liked his gifts, by which I conjectured he might have been a chosen vessel for Christ had he wished to use his gifts for Christ's glory. As there were many fierce sermons against him and many false charges I preferred that, if in error, he should rather be corrected than put to death; if that is to favor Luther, I frankly confess that I favor him, as I think the Pope does, and you all do if only you are true theologians and Christians. . . . Egmond even said that I defended Luther, because in my letter to the Cardinal of Mayence I spoke of the Carmelite who blamed Luther for saying that some mortal sins should not be confessed, although he did not understand Luther's meaning. . . . Surely if it is pious to refute Luther it is necessary to understand him. . . . [Follows a long apology for this and for the letter to Luther.] . . .

I do not think that you approve of those who have hitherto written against Luther, of whom the first was Prierias, the second a certain Franciscan,[1] the third[2] wrote anonymously, though he confessed he was a Dominican and received a salary from the French King. . . .

If I were devoted to your order and most hostile to Luther what other advice could I have given than I did give? Burning Luther's books may remove them from the bookstores; I doubt whether they can thus be removed from the minds of the people. But this might have been done if you had followed my advice. Even if my counsel did not please you, yet it ought not to be thrown in my teeth as a bit of hypocrisy that I gave it honestly to the Cardinal of Mayence who deserved this service from me. I gave him the advice in a sealed letter, thinking nothing less than that it should be published, but I hear that it was published before it was given to the cardinal, and not edited as I wrote them. For when they charge me with saying *"our* Luther" it is certain that I never said it, and would not have said it even if he had been mine.[3] . . .

312. ERASMUS TO GODSCHALK ROSEMUND, RECTOR OF THE UNIVERSITY OF LOUVAIN.

Erasmi opera (1703), iii. 536.   (LOUVAIN, October?, 1520.)

In this letter Erasmus relates the course of his quarrel with Egmond. This letter is dated *loc. cit.*, and in the London 1642 edition, xii. 18, 1519, but the contents show that it should rather be 1520. Moreover, Rosemund was rector only between August, 1520, and February, 1521.

. . . Invoking St. Paul Egmond prayed that as Paul had been changed from a persecutor of the Church into a doctor of the Church, so Luther and Erasmus might be. Why do they do such things? Because they desire nothing so much as to annoy. They take it ill that I am not a Lutheran, as truly I am not, unless it be for Christ's service. I know that I am too free with my tongue, but no one has ever heard me approve Luther's doctrine. I have never cared to read his books except a few pages which I only glanced at. I always favored your debates against Luther, especially the

---

[1] Perhaps Augustine Alveld.
[2] I do not know who is meant.
[3] Erasmus means that in publishing his letter to Albert of Mayence (no. 192) they changed "Luther" into "our Luther." Smith, 201.

writings of John Turenholt,[1] who, as I hear, disputes learnedly and without passion. When Luther's books were burned[2] no one saw me sadder. I have constantly averred that much in him displeased me. I have written much privately and said much to restrain him from his turbulent manner of writing, and lo, I am called a Lutheran. If your university likes these jokes I can stand them, and I prefer to do so than to revenge myself. But in my opinion things should be done differently. Vincent[3] has blamed me for the tumult in Holland, when, after an idiotic sermon, he was almost stoned by the people, but I never wrote to any Hollander either good or bad about Luther. Farewell in Christ, magnificent Rector.

313. ERASMUS TO THOMAS MORE AT CHELSEA.
Erasmi opera, iii. 607.   LOUVAIN (October?), 1520.

[Erasmus has been traduced by Nicholas Egmond, and has therefore appealed to the rector of the university. A public conference is arranged in which Erasmus and Egmond may accuse each other and defend themselves. The conversation between them on that occasion was in part as follows:]

"You publicly lied about me," said I, "in asserting that I favored Luther, whom I never favored in the sense you meant." He replied, not with emotion, but with fury: "Rather you are the author of the whole affair, an old fox switching your tail over everything." He vomited rather than said many similar things, until at last a word—not "raca,"[4] but another word smelling worse than it sounds—burst forth as the prelude to his intemperate speech. . . . After a long altercation he returned to the same subject and said that he would never cease talking against Luther until he had fin-

---

[1] John Nijs of Turnhout, commonly called Driedo, taught philosophy at Louvain 1499, then studied theology with Adrian of Utrecht; tutor of the princes of Croy; D. D., 1512, Dean of the faculty of theology 1515, 1523, 1526, 1528, 1531. Canon of St. Peter's (Louvain), 1520. Died August 4, 1535. De Jongh, 156ff. The book against Luther, spoken of by Erasmus, was refused by the printer, Thierry Martens. Driedo published other works.
[2] At Louvain, October 8, 1520. *Cf.* Smith, 98.
[3] Vincent Diercx (Theodorici) of Beverwyck-lez-Harlem, became a Dominican in this city, studied at Paris, where he began to teach in the convent of St. James in 1514. He published various books, and on returning to Louvain in 1517 was made doctor of theology. He died August 4, 1526, at the age of forty-five. He was one of Erasmus' bitterest enemies, to whom is addressed letter no. 314, published with the address "To his most persistent slanderer." De Jongh, 172f.
[4] Matthew, v. 22.

ished him. I replied that he might shout against Luther until he burst, provided only that he said nothing against me, for by doing the latter he accomplished nothing, but only made himself ridiculous in the eyes of all good men, as I saw that the audience were even then laughing at him. "Ya!" said he, "they are your friends." . . . He charged me with writing an epistle to Luther. "In which," say I, "I warn him what to shun." "Rather," says he, "you teach him what to write." For it seemed that the man took it ill that Luther should write correctly—and *so* ill, that he preferred to have him dead than corrected. But he could not brook it that I wrote Luther: "I do not advise you what to do, but only to do what you do of yourself." When I excused this as a bit of rhetorical civility, according to the rule that we should deny that we are giving advice even when we are, he grew hot again. "You say rightly," says he, "that the rule of rhetoric is to paint, pretend and lie about everything." I smiled and confessed that rhetoricians sometimes lied, but added that so did our professors sometimes. Again, when I said that I was consulting the dignity of the theologians, he replied: "Leave that to us, we'll attend to it." When I said that by burning Luther's books they might be removed from the libraries, but not from men's minds: "Ya," says he, "you could do that if you wished." . . .

After some irrelevant bickering the rector[1] bade us return to Luther who was the chief subject of the conference. "Come," says Egmond, "you have written for Luther, now write against him." Denying that I had written for him, but rather for the theologians against him, I gave many reasons for not writing against him again, as lack of leisure and of skill, fear and the desire not to hit a man already down. "Well, then," says he, "at least write that we knocked him down." I replied that there were not wanting plenty to shout this even if I kept silence, and that it would be more fitting for those who won the victory to celebrate it, and finally that, as their books were not yet published, it was not certain whether they had beaten him or not. Turning in desperation to the rector, "Did I not say," says he, "that we would ac-

[1] Godschalk Rosemund.

complish nothing here? As long as he refuses to write against Luther we shall consider him a Lutheran." "Then you are a Lutheran yourself," say I, "for you have written nothing against him and not only you, but all your friends." Then bowing a farewell to the rector, but not to me, he departed. . . .

314. ERASMUS TO HIS PERSISTENT SLANDERER [VINCENT DIERCX].

Erasmi opera, iii. 620. LOUVAIN, (October?), 1520.

[This long letter of 12,700 words recapitulates most of the charges to which Erasmus had been exposed. Towards the end he returns to the quarrel with Egmond:]

So to make himself, as they say, like a dancing camel, he [Egmond] invoked the epistles of Paul, saying: "Paul, once a persecutor of the Church, from a wolf was made a sheep. Let us pray that the same may happen to Luther and Erasmus." O Attic charms! O slander like to blows! Although he was laughed at and hissed by all he spared me no reproach, even in his sermons. When he published the bull against Luther, he chanced to see me present, and suddenly changing the subject of his discourse, he spoke more against Erasmus than against Luther, nor did he make any end, but repeated his charges over and over. But when the audience began to nod to each other and to laugh, his face witnessed the impotent rage of his mind, and he broke off, rather than ended, his slanderous discourse. When I complained of it to Godschalk Rosemund, the rector of the university, he ran wild against me with the same sort of accusations and lies, so that one might rather think it was a clown talking to a rustic than an old man to an old man, a theologian to a theologian, a priest to a priest, and that in the presence of the rector.

[Erasmus then recites the substance of the colloquy given in the letter to More, *supra,* no. 313.]

His disciple, the prior of Antwerp, a doctor of the violet hood, excused himself before the magistrates for inciting to riot against Luther by saying that he had not read Luther's books, but that he acted at the command of Nicholas Egmond. At the same time the chiefs of the Dominican monastery acted in such a disgraceful way as to alienate the minds of all good men. One of their number said in the hearing of some laymen: "Would that I could fasten my teeth in Luther's throat; I should not fear to go to the Lord's supper with his blood on my mouth." . . .

315. LUTHER TO MICHAEL MÄURER, CISTERCIAN AT ALT-CELLE.

Enders, ii. 497.   WITTENBERG, October 20, 1520.

Mäurer, a friend of Mosellanus, a learned philosopher and theologian and a musician, taught for some time at Alt-Celle before his death in 1523.

Greeting in the Lord. Dear Michael, you would hardly believe how much I am pleased to see enemies rise against me more than formerly. I am never prouder and bolder than when I hear that I displease them. They are doctors, bishops, princes—what then? If the Word of God were not assailed by them it would not be the Word of God as it is written: "The heathen raged and the people imagined a vain thing. The kings of the earth set themselves and the princes took counsel together against the Lord and against his Christ."[1] Lo, here you see the attitude of princes, kings and bishops towards the Word of Christ; what more do you want? I would greatly grieve if they praised me, for what misery is greater than to please them? Let everything pass, Michael; the things of God are hidden and spiritual. . . . See to it that you preserve your soul in this Babylon. The judgment of God hangs over them and works terribly, which the blind men do not see. Let the blind lead the blind, says he.[2] If the Word of God had to be defended with the might and eloquence and genius of man, Christ would not have called fishermen to do it, nor would he have defended it with his own blood. I do what I ought. Having received for nothing, I give for nothing,[3] even with danger to my life, fame and goods, yea even of my soul. I wrote at home, I worked sin-

[1] Psalm ii. 1f.
[2] Matthew, xv. 14.
[3] Matthew, x. 8. I give the true sense of the word translated in our Bible "freely" and sometimes misunderstood.

cerely, wishing to teach all what I myself believed. I am clean from the blood of all,[1] at which I rejoice. In time they will see whom they have repulsed and persecuted.

I care nothing if my work *On the Babylonian Captivity* is prohibited. What does it matter if all my books are prohibited? I will write nothing against those who use force against us. It is enough for me to have taught the truth against those stupid babblers, and to have defended it against the learned who alone are able to hurt. Both the style and the matter of the Italian book of "Thomas Rhadinus" show that it is Emser's.[2] The Lord's will be done. I so despise those devils, that were I not held here I would of my own accord go to Rome in spite of Satan and all the furies. What if they kill me? I am not worthy to suffer aught in so blessed a cause.

It makes no difference if my letters written to you are delivered to someone else. I do not fear to have them public property, for I write under God's sight; if he approves, who shall disapprove? I beg you, learn to despise men strongly, as Christ says: "Beware of men."[3] It is a great thing to have a propitious God and to trust in him. Farewell in Christ, dearest Michael.

I will not write to Duke George. You, too, know what I got from him with my three letters before the Leipsic debate. If he is worthy he will hear the truth; if he is unworthy, the labor will be vain.

Your brother,
MARTIN LUTHER.

316. BONIFACE AMERBACH TO HIS BROTHER BASIL AMERBACH AT BASLE.

Burckhardt-Biedermann, 142. AVIGNON, October 20, 1520.

We have some of Luther's works here. Of him there are various opinions and judgments according to the various thoughts of men. Those who have imbibed sophistry and the

[1] 2 Samuel, iii. 28.
[2] Thomae Rhadini Todeschi Planentini O. P. . . . in Martinum Lutherum . . . Oratio, Rome, August, 1520. Luther was mistaken in ascribing the book to Emser; it was by Rhadinus, a Dominican of noble German family which had settled at Piacenza.
[3] Matthew x. 17.

dregs of learning do not easily learn better, but prefer to be pigs with Gryllus,[1] especially in this papal state, where the Pope's purse is an oracle and where it is impious to deviate a hair's breadth from the constitutions of the canonists. There are some Italians who, having published volumes from these shades, croak to the field and swamp, but they are men of mediocrity whose lucubrations are colder than the water of Monacris.[2] But truth herself, having laid aside her mask, now shows her face in spite of them. However, the good man was not a little injured by a libel of a poor impostor, who, by pretending that Martin had recanted, brought back even those who had entered the way of truth to their former errors.[3] So great is the desire of these rascals to deceive, that, when they see themselves otherwise vanquished, they think up some new way to crush truth for their own gain, traducing the fame and doctrine of excellent Martin as heretical. . . .

317. JOHN KOTTER TO BONIFACE AMERBACH IN AVIGNON.
Burckhardt-Biedermann, 141.

(FREIBURG IM ÜCHTLAND, October 22, 1520.)

Kotter, of Strassburg, was an organist and composer at Freiburg until 1530, when he was banished. He then found an asylum in Bern, and taught music until his death 1541. Cf. O. Clemen: *Beiträge zur Reformationsgeschichte*, iii. 20ff.

. . . Doctor Martin Luther has published a book *To the Christian Nobility of the German Nation on the Improvement of the Christian Estate,* which was printed at Basle, October 13,[4] and was sent me by the agent. I have never read nor heard the like; all men wonder at it; some think the devil speaks out of him, some the Holy Ghost. He shakes the ground in a way that the Holy Father and the Romans won't find to their taste. At the end of his book I find the

---

[1] γρύλλος, "Porker." Cf. Plutarch, *Moralia*, pp. 985-6.
[2] An Arcadian spring, proverbially cold. Pliny, *Hist. nat.*, xxxi. 27.
[3] Luther himself mentions this work in the beginning of his *Babylonian Captivity* (November, 1520): "Scripsit quidam frater Cremonensis Italus 'revocationem Martini Lutheri ad sanctam sedem,' hoc est, qua non ego, ut verba sonant, sed qua ipse me revocat: sic enim Itali hodie incipiunt latinisare." Cf. Weimar, vi. 486. Cf. *supra*, no. 199. Luther spoke of it in August. Enders, ii. 456.
[4] "Sambstag vor galli." It came out first at Wittenberg in August.

words: "I think truly that I have sung highly."[1] . . . This shows all the wickedness that goes on at Rome. It can't stand. There must be a reformation. Charles[2] must begin it. . . .

318. JEROME ALEANDER TO POPE LEO X. AT ROME.
Deutsche Reichstagsakten, ii. 454.

(AIX-LA-CHAPELLE, October 23, 1520.)

Jerome Aleander (1480-1542) met Erasmus at Venice 1508, after which he taught at Paris till 1513. After serving the bishops of Paris and Liège, he returned to Italy in 1516 and was made Papal Librarian in 1519. July, 1520, the Pope sent him as legate to Charles V. to act against Luther, where he conducted himself with conspicuous success. Smith, *op. cit.,* 98-104. In 1538 he was also sent as legate to Germany. His *Journal* published by Omont 1895; several works on him by J. Paquier, including his *Letters,* 1909. *Realencyclopädie* and Allen, i. 502.

I kiss your blessed feet, most holy Lord. May God Almighty keep your Holiness for us long and happily.

That your Holiness may know all things that were done here in order in the Lutheran affair, the Emperor, while we were at Antwerp, signed an edict commanding that all Lutheran and other seditious books, wherever found in his dominions, should be burned publicly with fire. . . .

We have not been able to do anything against Luther's person, nor shall we be able until we can prove to the Emperor and other princes that the bull entrusted to Eck has been published in Germany and the sixty days allowed by the bull have elapsed. I have no doubt that Eck has already done what he was commanded, but I have no certain news of it yet, which I attribute to the long distance.

The Emperor[3] entered this town yesterday.

319. ALEANDER TO POPE LEO X. AT ROME.
Reichtagsakten, ii. 457.   (AIX-LA-CHAPELLE, October 25, 1520.)

. . . The other nuncio[4] and myself were received to-day by the Archbishop of Mayence . . . and I noted that he

---
[1] Long verbal quotation from the book, to the end: "Dear Rome, what I think."
[2] Charles V. *Cf.* Smith, 98ff., 387ff.
[3] Charles was crowned at Aix, October 23.
[4] Marino Caracciolo of Naples (1469-January 28, 1538), had been sent to Rome by Maximilian Sforza to represent him at the Lateran Council, 1515. He was made protonotary by Leo X., and in 1518 was appointed papal nuncio to the

was not only in words but in heart most deeply moved against the Lutheran errors and against Hutten's mendacity, so that he would have burned Luther's books in his dioceses long ago.[1] . . . He expressed surprise that Eck had not visited him, and had done nothing about publishing the bull in Saxony. . . .

320. JOHN LANTSCHAD TO ELECTOR FREDERIC OF SAXONY.

Archiv für Reformationsgeschichte, ii. 394. German.

(STEINACH), October 25, 1520.

Lantschad was a Swabian knight, who wrote in favor of the Reformation in 1522, and in 1525 introduced it in his estates on the Neckar. He died in 1531. *Loc. cit.,* p. 393. The letter is an interesting testimony to the reception won by Luther's *Address to the German Nobility.*

Most Gracious Prince and Lord! I have read a little book, written, doubtless, at the inspiration of the Holy Ghost, by the learned Dr. Martin Luther to his royal Roman Majesty and the electors, princes and other estates of the Holy Empire. In this he thoroughly and clearly shows (what is generally known to the greater part of Christendom) the great faults, crimes and grievances at present existing in the Christian Church, both in her higher and in her lower chiefs, who ought to be maintainers of the faith and of divine righteousness, but who, on the contrary, more and more uphold abuses to the hurt of God's honor and the Christian faith and to the destruction of the Christian commonweal and particularly of the German nation. . . . Wherefore I pray, warn and admonish you as a Christian elector and as a member of the Holy Empire, to help act for the common advantage of Christendom . . . by which you will doubtless win everlasting salvation and in this world praise and honor from pious people.

Your Grace's humble,

JOHN LANTSCHAD OF STEINACH, *Knight.*

321. LUTHER TO JOHN VON GREFFENDORF AT WEIMAR.

Enders, ii. 503. WITTENBERG, October 30, 1520.

Von Greffendorf was a Chamberlain of Duke John of Saxony; in Emperor, a position he held for a number of years. He was finally appointed by Charles, Governor of Milan. *Biographie Générale,* Pastor, vii. 417, note.

[1] The influence of Capito prevented Albert from burning Luther's books for a while. Cf. P. Kalkoff: *W. Capito im Dienste Albrechts von Mainz,* 1907.

1524 his ambassador to King Louis of Hungary, in 1526 interested in the Evangelical Church visitation.

Greeting. Dear John, I rejoice in the spirit you show in the midst of these tumults caused by the bull. Surely Duke George and the Bishop of Merseburg, transported with fury, are doing their best to destroy me and my university. Eck tried to post the bull at the University of Erfurt, but they contemptuously refused to allow him to do so, alleging some points of law. The students also tried to get after him, but could not find him. It is said that he pleaded with tears to induce the authorities to let him post the bull, so that he should not have to leave ingloriously without accomplishing anything. The bull was printed at Erfurt and exposed for sale, but the students seized the copies and threw them into the river, saying, "Let the bull swim."[1] When the bookseller brought an action for damages against them, he was non-suited, as the town council refused to notice the students' act. I expect the bull will turn into a bubble, for it is nothing more. Therefore I greatly despise it, howbeit I have had a suspicion that at the instance of Duke George I may be forced to depart from Wittenberg; this I leave in God's hand. May his will be done. I have read the letter from that see of the apostles, or rather apostates, written to Duke John.[2] Good Heavens! how giddily do these men act! Farewell, and let me commend the cause to you.

MARTIN LUTHER, *Augustinian.*

322. SPALATIN TO ELECTOR FREDERIC OF SAXONY AT COLOGNE.

Zeitschrift für Kirchengeschichte, ii. 119 (1877).   (October, 1520.)

Most gracious Lord. Doctor Martin's books are also to be burned at Merseburg. They would have burned them at Leipsic last week, Monday or Thursday, but they didn't, for some reason unknown to me. A good friend told me that, having learned it from the written order. . . .

---

[1] Pun on the word *bulla,* which also means bubble.
[2] A letter of the Pope to the elector, read in his absence by his brother, Duke John, is meant. Enders, *loc. cit.*

323. ALBERT, ARCHBISHOP OF MAYENCE, TO POPE LEO X.

Böcking, i. 363. (MAYENCE? c. November 1?, 1520.)[1]

Most blessed Father and most clement Lord, I humbly kiss your feet. On October 25 I received with becoming reverence five breves from the reverend Lord Marino Caracciolo and Lord Jerome Aleander, the nuncios of your Holiness. The first signified how your Holiness had made Caracciolo a nuncio to his Imperial Majesty, and at the same time sent me a pleasing gift of the consecrated golden rose. The second and third breves bade me aid with all diligence and zeal the said lords Caracciolo and Aleander in executing the bull against Luther, the fourth instructed me how to proceed to extinguish the Lutheran conflagration, and the fifth was about silencing Hutten. In the first place, I thank your Holiness for seeing fit to give me the golden rose which binds me by a new bond to you, and makes me, who was always most diligent, still more diligent to obey you. For hitherto, although not commanded, I have remembered my duty and done my best not only to keep Hutten's libellous books, which were published before I had any suspicions, from the hands of readers, but also I have studied to suppress the nascent fury of Luther, and at the very first I warned your Holiness of that movement which has now, alas, become a mighty conflagration throughout almost all Germany. I left nothing undone which either theologians or jurists advised me to do. I published an edict against Hutten's works . . . and in the same edict included the works of Luther, although I had also prohibited them the year before. It would be long to narrate all my negotiations with other princes, but I beg your Holiness to believe that I left no stone unturned to oppose the growing evil. For which reason I have been obliged to bear with many unjust men, who have favored the opposing faction, of whom some blandly warned me to correct I know not what corrupted morals, and alleged, I hope not falsely, their desire for peace. Yet I am forward to despise their hatred, considering the benefits which your Holiness has poured out upon me, of which the memory is always fresh

[1] Böcking dates this July, but the reference to the reception of letters from Leo on October 25 proves that the true date is later. *Cf.* no. 319.

and would stimulate me, if I were at all slothful, to satisfy every desire of your Holiness. Wherefore, most blessed Father, considering not so much the words as the intent of the present commands to publish the bull against Luther in the dioceses of Mayence and Magdeburg and in those of my reverend suffragans, I am now doing my best, with the advice of the nuncios, to conciliate the favor of the secular princes without which every effort of ours will be in vain. What success we shall have I know not, but I have good hope. . . .

324. HENRY GLAREAN TO ULRICH ZWINGLI AT ZURICH.
Corpus Reformatorum, xciv. 360.   PARIS, November 1, 1520.

Henry Loriti, of Glarus (1488-1563), matriculated at Cologne 1506, M. A. 1510, matriculated at Basle 1514, where for a time he worked with Froben, and became a devoted friend of Erasmus. From 1517 to 1522 he was at Paris teaching school, he then returned to Basle, but, being unable to follow his friend Zwingli in the Reformation, retired to Freiburg in 1529. He published an original work on music in 1547. Life by O. F. Fritzsche, 1890; Allen, ii. 279. Glarean is particularly interesting to Americans as having made the first map of the New World in which the continent is called America. The MS. of this, dating 1513, was sold by Sotheby in 1912. It was printed under the title *De Geographia,* in 1527 at Basle.

. . . Now hear some news about Luther! When the debate between Geck[1] and Luther was laid before the University of Paris for judgment, although it perhaps would have censured some of the articles, now, after it has heard that Luther is condemned by the Pope, it refrains from giving judgment. No one's books are bought more eagerly. A certain bookseller told me that at the last Frankfort fair,[2] he had sold fourteen hundred copies of Luther's works, which had never before happened with any other author. Everyone speaks well of Luther. Truly the monk's chain is long. . . .

325. OSWALD MYCONIUS TO ULRICH ZWINGLI AT ZURICH.
Corpus Reformatorum, xciv. 365.   LUCERNE, November 2, 1520.

. . . You know, and much more clearly than I do, what that Roman rascal who is with us proposed or rather commanded

[1] *I. e.,* Eck, *cf. supra,* no. 178. Duke George first sent the debate to Paris, *cf. supra,* no. 180.
[2] The great bookmart of Germany held every spring. *Cf.* Smith, 77.

under pain of excommunication at the Swiss congress at Baden, about burning Lutheran books.[1] First, we want to know your opinion, whether we ought to obey or not, after the command shall be published, and then, what your men of Zurich decided to do. Briefly, my own opinion is that the excommunication is to be disregarded, not so much because I favor Luther as that I would unwillingly lose the money I spent for the books, and also because I think the thing is too unjust to be obeyed. When was it ever heard in the Church that anyone should be condemned before he had a chance to state the reasons for his opinions, especially when he particularly wished to do so? It is proclaimed through the whole town here that Luther and the schoolmaster[2] are to be burned, although I never speak of him except to my intimates, and that rarely, nor have I ever brought forward a single opinion from him. Yet I know why they join my name with Luther's; it is because in my classes I speak the gospel truth, and say what the subject demands, though no more. And because this agrees with what he says in several places, they think that that is from Luther which is really from the gospel. I could easily answer this charge if necessary. Yet I would not willingly lose his books, for I have not one or two, but a great many. Wherefore advise us and we will follow your advice. Do quickly and briefly more than we ask. . . .

326. FRANCIS VON SICKINGEN TO LUTHER.

Enders, ii. 506. German.   COLOGNE, November 3, 1520.

Honorable, learned, kind, dear Doctor, and singular, good Friend! My willing service with all my body and estate is heartily yours! I have received your two last letters at Cologne, and have read them together with your *Offer and Protestation*[3] and have heard what George Spalatin has to say, and am glad to learn that you are minded to show forth

---

[1] On October 22, at Baden, the Pope's Nuncio Pucci made this proposition in accordance with instructions he had received from Aleander. His speech cited at length, *loc. cit.*

[2] Myconius means himself. The emphasis upon reliance on the Bible independently of Luther is characteristic of the Swiss Reformation.

[3] *Cf. supra*, no. 287. At Worms, later, Sickingen handed Luther's *Offer and Protestation* and his letter to Charles V. to that monarch, who tore them to pieces without reading them. He had certainly seen them previously at Cologne. Grisar, i. 344f.

the Christian truth and to abide by it, and I am inclined to give you what help and favor may be in my power for this end. I would not conceal this my answer to your letter, for you will find me ready to do you any pleasure I can. God bless you and govern your affair according to his will!

FRANCIS VON SICKINGEN, *with my hand.*

327. LUTHER TO HERMANN MÜHLPFORT, BAILIFF AT ZWICKAU.

Enders, ii. 505.　De Wette, i. 537.　German.

WITTENBERG (circa November 4), 1520.

Hermann (not Jerome, as Luther mistakenly called him) Mühlpfort came of an old Zwickau family. He was later burgomaster of this town, where he died August 25, 1534. In his last years he had an unfortunate altercation with Luther, on which *cf.* Smith, 281. This letter is the dedication to the German translation of *The Liberty of a Christian Man,* on which *cf.* Smith, 91ff. Mühlpfort visited Luther at Wittenberg on November 4. O. Clemen, *Luthers Werke,* ii. 1.

Prudent, wise Sir and kind Friend! The worthy John Egranus, preacher to your excellent town, has often highly extolled to me the love you bear the Holy Scriptures, which you zealously acknowledge and do not neglect to praise before men. Wherefore he desired to make me known to you, of which I am willing and glad. For it is a special pleasure to me to hear of men who love the divine truth, since alas, so many, and chiefly those who bear titles, strive against it with all their might and cunning. Yet it must come to pass that many should stumble, fall and rise again on Christ, who is set for a stumbling-block and a sign to be spoken against.[1] Wherefore, to start our acquaintance and friendship, I desired to dedicate to you this little tract and sermon in German, which in Latin I dedicated to the Pope, so that everyone may see that my doctrine and writing about the papacy has not, as I hope, a reprehensible. Herewith I commend myself to you and to God's grace. Amen.

328. LUTHER TO SPALATIN.

Enders, ii. 508.　　　　　　　WITTENBERG, November 4, 1520.

Greeting. I, too, wonder, Spalatin, what prevents you getting my letters. For I have written twice and I know that

[1] Luke, ii. 34.

you received neither letter. I am glad that at last you see how vain are the hopes of the Germans, since you say not to trust in princes and you cease to regard, as you have hitherto regarded, the judgment of men who either praise or condemn my writings. If the gospel were such that it could be either propagated or preserved by the powers of this world, God would not have confided it to fishermen. Dear Spalatin, it is not the part of the princes and prelates of this world to defend God's Word, nor by his grace do I seek the protection of any of them, as they must rather set themselves against the Lord and against his Christ. What I do, I do rather that they may deserve well of the Word of God by their service to me, and may be saved by the Word. For I pity those who have heard and known. For they cannot, without their own eternal destruction, deny, desert and cover up the Word. It is to be feared that you, together with us and many of our friends, can be found among this class; and we must pray for a courageous spirit.

It is a hard thing to dissent from all prelates and princes, but no other way is left of escaping hell and God's wrath. So take care, lest those who are offended by my bitterness should be such as hold the cause of the Word cheaply and are influenced by I know not what human considerations. It is no wonder that one who estimates the affair at its true worth should cry out and be torn asunder. Even had you not urged me to do so, I should have committed the whole cause to God, and have done nothing more than I have done, since I know that we must act only by his counsel and co-operation.

I have published the Latin Antibull,[1] which I send; it is also being printed in German.[2] Please do not let those move you who take it ill that I speak so sternly against gently expressed commands. Those mandates of the Roman Pontiff are not gentle by which Christ is suppressed and people commanded to deny the faith. I was forced to be brief by the very unworthiness of the cause. That Satanic bull so tortures me that I almost kept silence altogether. For since the

---

[1] *Adversus exsecrabilem Antichristi Bullam*, Weimar, vi. 595.
[2] *Wider die Bullen des Endchrists*, Weimar, vi. 613.

beginning of the world, when did Satan ever speak so impudently against God? What shall I say? The magnitude of the horrible blasphemies of this bull overwhelms me, and yet no one notices them. Many strong arguments have persuaded me that the last day is at hand. The reign of Antichrist is beginning to end.

Duke George rages against me with his sophists and the Bishop of Merseburg. I see that this disordered bull is breeding a rebellion, just as the Roman Curia ought to do. Emser has put forth his fury against me under the name of Thomas Rhadinus Todiscus;[1] now he publishes at Rome and now at Leipsic. They all take credit for the incredible fury of their insanity.

I shall not write privately to the princes, but shall publicly renew my Appeal,[2] thereby summoning all Germans, great and small, to stand by me, and expound the villainy of the affair. Then I shall lay it to the conscience of each man, lest in the hour of his death he should be condemned for having obeyed these impious monsters.

I will do nothing with the Archbishop of Mayence, but I will approach Duke George and the Bishop of Merseburg with letters and with my German Antibull when it is published, not that I hope to soften those hard spirits, but that I may satisfy my conscience in warning them of their danger. For it is impossible for those to be saved who either favor this bull or do not fight against it. The Lord and you will attend to the result.

Egranus told us the same about Matthew Adrian as you did. He has become my enemy, alleging as the cause that I have taught that good works avail nothing, but only faith. He has hardly been prevented from reviling me publicly. Finally, this man, most ignorant of theology, attacked and challenged me. He is useless and must soon be dismissed. Perhaps he will go to Leipsic to make common cause with Eck. The Lord's will be done.

The University of Erfurt, when imperiously summoned by Eck, refused to receive the bull, on the ground that it was

[1] *Supra*, no. 316.
[2] *I. e.*, the Appeal to a General Council, made November 28, 1518. Luther renewed it November 17, 1520, Weimar, vii. 74, 83.

illegally sent. The Bishop of Bamberg[1] refused it on the same ground. The armed youth of Erfurt surrounded Eck and tearing the printed bulls into small bits, threw them into the water, so that it is now a real bubble.[2] The town council connived at this, and the court at Mayence hears nothing of it.[3] I expect you know how gloriously Eck was received at Leipsic, hated as he is by almost all except the duke and the bishop. Do what your spirit tells you, and farewell.

MARTIN LUTHER, *Augustinian.*

329. MELANCHTHON TO GEORGE SPALATIN.

Corpus Reformatorum, i. 267. WITTENBERG, November 4, 1520.

. . . Luther has answered the bull,[4] charging Eck with the responsibility of it, for he certainly was the author of this tragedy. A few days ago he wrote a letter[5] to the Roman Pontiff, which I think you will approve as being sufficiently moderate and pious. I beg you to be watchful and not to neglect any human precautions, although not relying on them, but on divine providence. Martin seems to me to be driven by a certain spirit. We shall bring about his success more by prayers than by schemes. My friendship for Luther is now so firmly established that nothing sadder could happen to me than to be without him. Wherefore, for my sake as well as for the sake of the public, do what you can to prevent this man from being crushed, for I dare to prefer him not only to all living men, but to the Augustines, Jeromes and Gregory Nazianzens of all time. Farewell, dearest Spalatin. . . .

330. ALEANDER TO LEO X. AT ROME.

Reichstagsakten, ii. 460. (COLOGNE, November 6, 1520.)

. . . I know that your Holiness is very anxious to know what we did with the Elector of Saxony, wherefore I will give you a brief account of a long affair. It is his nature to

---

[1] George III., Bishop 1505-22. As Nuremberg was in his diocese, Eck sent him the bull which was also directed against Pirckheimer and Spengler.
[2] Pun on "bulla," meaning both "bull" and "bubble."
[3] Erfurt was an enclave in Saxony under the government of Mayence.
[4] *Von den neuen Eckischen Bullen und Lügen.* Weimar, vi. 579. Luther at first doubted the genuineness of the bull, and so did Erasmus.
[5] The preface to *The Liberty of a Christian Man.*

seem good and religious and a devout frequenter of churches, but all his counsellors are more Lutheran than Luther himself. Moreover, he is extremely hard to see, but we did see him on November 4,[1] and worked on him so that he seemed to be persuaded by us and said that he had never spoken twenty words with Luther.

331. ERASMUS TO JOHN REUCHLIN.
Erasmi opera (1703), iii. 589.   Cologne, November 8, 1520.

... You see what a fatal tragedy is now being enacted, the catastrophe of which is uncertain. Whatever it may be, I pray that it may be for the glory of Christ and the evangelic truth. I prefer to be a spectator rather than an actor in this play, not because I deny the cause of Christ, but because I see it is beyond my littleness. Would that I were able to do what is best, as I wish. ... The silent judgments of the good have perpetual authority and weight even with posterity. It has always been my endeavor to separate the cause of Luther from yours and that of sound learning, which would only bring odium on it and on us without helping Luther in the least. But others have acted otherwise. They hate me so that those conspirators against sound learning and the gospel have almost attacked me. There is no doubt about their actions, although they cloak them with high names and irritate the mild Pope to his own hurt for their advantage. ...

332. BEATUS RHENANUS TO BONIFACE AMERBACH.
Briefwechsel des Beatus Rhenanus, 250.   Basle, November 8, 1520.

... Our Erasmus of Rotterdam is now officiating as councillor to the Emperor; it is an honor to him, but a loss for literature. For some days he has been at Cologne, after the Emperor was crowned at Aix-la-Chapelle, on October 23. The Pope has sent Jerome Aleander with a monstrous bull to the Emperor to induce him to crush Luther. He also sent Caracciolo, Cajetan and Miltitz. It is to be feared that the Emperor will give his consent, as one too young to understand these things. The whole of Germany is for Luther. Hutten has fairly translated the Pope's bull which curses

---

[1] On this interview and its results, *cf.* Smith, *op. cit.*, 100.

Luther, that is, he has explained and mocked it with witty, caustic notes. In the title page of the booklet he has surrounded the Pope's arms with this verse: "At his right hand stood a bull in cloth of gold and many-colored garments." You never read anything more cutting. For as you know the Pope anathematized Hutten and wrote to some of the princes either to kill him or send him bound to Rome. Hence the bitterness of his invective. Pucci, who tried to do much against Luther in Switzerland, is simply despised.[1] You know that hitherto Zasius favored Luther. Now he has somewhat changed his opinion, because Luther wrote it would be better for priests to have wives than harlots. But I am abusing the patience of my Boniface to go on with trifles like these. Farewell, Boniface.

P. S.—The Pope has recently condemned Reuchlin's article to please the monks, whose help he now needs, and to spite Luther.

333. ERASMUS TO CONRAD PEUTINGER, IMPERIAL COUNCILLOR.

Erasmi opera (1703), iii. 590.   COLOGNE, November 9, 1520.

I know that you have no leisure to read all sorts of letters, excellent Sir, nor have I much more time to write, yet I was induced to do so by John Faber,[2] a Dominican theologian, whom I discovered, by careful examination, to be very different from some of that brotherhood, for besides solid learning, integrity and affability, I found in him excellent judgment. We have often consulted on the method of composing this Lutheran tragedy without a cataclysm of the whole globe. For what lover of mankind is not moved by the beginning of this drama, seeing that there is imminent peril, unless something is done, that it shall lead to a catastrophe dangerous to Christianity? The most horrible wars are often started

[1] *Cf. supra*, no. 325.

[2] Of Augsburg (1470-1530), not to be confounded with the man of the same name who was Bishop of Vienna. Studied in Italy and became Dominican Prior at Augsburg. He met Erasmus at Louvain, October, 1520, and with him planned a peaceful solution of the Lutheran schism, composing at this time at Cologne, with Erasmus' help, the *Consilium cujusdam cupientis consultum esse* . . . which he pressed on the Emperor's advisers, and at Worms offering a similar plan of arbitration. He also spoke very freely at the funeral of Chièvres, January, 1521 (*cf. infra*, no. 383). Life in N. Paulus: *Die deutsche Dominicaner* (1903), 292-313.

by trifles. And in my opinion Cicero was right in saying that an unjust peace was better than the justest war. Now this drama has gone farther than I could have wished, but I think the evil is curable; certainly it is more so now that if it goes on increasing. I should also wish it so healed, that it may not merely be suppressed for a time to become worse later, as happens to patients when physicians cool their fever with a potion without bleeding, or to those who scarify a wound which has not been sufficiently cleansed.

Some think that severity had better be used, and Faber would not disagree with them did he not fear that it would hardly succeed. He says that it is not sufficient in this matter to follow your inclination, but that several things must be considered. First, we must consult the dignity of the Roman Pontiff, whom all lovers of Christ must favor as Christ's vicar, lest the gospel truth should suffer. And I doubt not that Leo is of this mind, that he considers his only glory to lie in the flourishing of the doctrine of his Prince. Faber says we should not consider only what Luther deserves, or who favor Luther, but what conduces to the public peace. It makes a great difference who lay hands on this evil and with what medicines it is cured. Some mix in this affair only to exasperate it with their misplaced zeal, and double it, consulting not the authority of the Pope, but their own advantage. Briefly, they so act that they hurt sound learning more than they do Luther. For it is not right that innocent, or rather holy studies should suffer on account of Luther, nor ought other men, without cause, to be involved in his affair. He added that we should consider from what fount the whole thing flowed, namely, from hatred of good learning. . . .

It is not for men like me to judge the Pope's breves. But there were some who missed in the bull brought by the nuncio the gentleness worthy of Christ's vicar and of this peaceful Leo; and they impute the bull not to him, but to his advisers. . . .

But Faber himself will explain his plan more fully to you in person, and if you approve it you can help him at the Diet of Worms to carry through a plan which all will approve. . . .

334. THOMAS GRAMAYE TO THE THEOLOGICAL FACULTY OF PARIS.

Gess, i. 144. Antwerp, November 10, 1520.

Gramaye was at this time secretary, councillor and mint-master of Charles V. For many years he had been Duke George's banker and general representative in the Netherlands. Earlier in this year he had written to the Sorbonne on behalf of Duke George for their opinion; the professors deliberated on the question on July 17, appointing James Barthelemi and Noel Beda to consider the answer. The present letter was apparently received and discussed on November 15. The final condemnation was dated April 15, 1521. See Gess, *loc. cit.,* and Smith, *op. cit.,* p. 453, where for "Frederic" should be read "George" —both names being represented in contemporary documents simply by the words "Dux Saxoniae."

Most learned Fathers and venerable Sirs! Your kindness has again made me bold to write. Recently, in behalf of the most illustrious Duke of Saxony, I asked your worships, for the love of truth, which doubtless occupies your minds, to deign either to approve if true or to reprove if false the writings of Martin Luther, which have taken hold of the minds of many everywhere and are embraced as most true by some. According to your habitual benevolence, you answered that you were busy day and night reading and discussing them and would take no rest until you had discovered the truth which Martin seems to seek, and had pronounced on it. Truly, the aforesaid duke, anxious to know the truth, received this letter with high honor and read it with great pleasure, hoping that your worships would soon do what you promised. But as this is delayed he awaits anxiously, hearing various opinions, some saying that Luther is good, others shouting that he seduces the common people. . . . Now the tumult increases, and no small tragedy is excited here in the sight of the world and with the connivance of our professors at Louvain, while others of sounder mind weep and wail, and all await your judgment. . . .

335. LUTHER TO SPALATIN.

Enders, ii. 523. Eilenburg, November 13, 1520.

Greeting. I have received the "Bull"[1] you sent, Spalatin,

[1] A pseudonymous satire which appeared about this time under the title, *Dialogus Bulla.*

and we daily expect your happy return[1] with many new things to tell us and one old thing, namely, that there is no hope in the court of Charles. I am glad that Hutten has come out; would that he had intercepted[2] Caracciolo or Aleander.

We do not fear the excommunication threatened by the bull, although we hear that those two bishops[3] are about to set forth; I will receive them fairly and give them their proper titles. Duke George, although in a rage, is said to control himself externally. Our Philip Melanchthon, under the name of Faventinus Didymus, is answering[4] Thomas Rhadinus, that is, Emser.

Melanchthon's wedding will be on November 26. The danger of malicious gossip forces us to hurry the day.

Henry Schmiedberg,[5] deceased, left me one hundred gulden, which pleased me particularly, as the dying just man condemns the unjust living, as the wise man says,[6] and those who offered Eck cups full of gold[7] for traducing God's Word may have something to make them angry, but which I never sought for. By this second sign Christ now warns them. For who would not consider Eck's ignominious reception at Leipsic and Erfurt as one of God's wonderful works? Yet hitherto hardened Pharaoh perseveres that there may be many signs. But be of good cheer and despise all that curse. Christ has begun this business and will complete it, whether I die or fly. Called in his name by Schmiedberg, I came to Eilenburg, but, in the meantime, he departed to the Lord. He is said to have died most constant in the faith, and (what is a great cross to my opponents) to have publicly professed and com-

[1] Spalatin and the elector left Cologne on November 7.

[2] "Intercepisset"; the meaning is somewhat doubtful, whether merely "frustrated" or "seized."

[3] Probably the bishops of Merseburg and Brandenburg. The latter passed through Wittenberg on his way to the Diet of Worms and tried to post the bull.

[4] His answer appeared first in February, 1521, *Corpus Reformatorum*, i. 285.

[5] Schmiedberg, of a prominent Leipsic family, Chancellor of Archbishop Philip of Naumburg and Freisingen, and Administrator of Naumburg. When the bull was sent to Naumburg the people stormed Schmiedberg's palace; the latter fell ill with fright and went to Leipsic, where he drew up a will, remembering Luther. Then he went to Eilenburg, and on growing worse had Luther summoned to him, but died on November 5 before the latter arrived. Enders, ii. 526.

[6] Book of Wisdom, iv. 16.

[7] Duke George gave Eck a cup full of gold.

mended my doctrine. See the presence of Christ! The Roman Antichrist presses on, and Satan through him, but he who is in us shows himself greater than he who is in the world.[1]

The bishop of Breslau died[2] in the same faith, the best of all the bishops of this age. The Bishop of Merseburg has lost much in the opinion of the public, and his pigmy holiness does not suffice for the work of impiety, which bids him obey the Pope rather than his God. Others will tell you the rest. Farewell in the Lord. MARTIN LUTHER.

P. S.—Melanchthon, who salutes you, and I are splendidly entertained by these heroes, Fabian von Feilitzsch, Haugold von Einsiedel and John von Taubenheim.

336. ULRICH VON HUTTEN TO ERASMUS AT COLOGNE.

Böcking, i. 423. EBERNBURG, November 13, 1520.

May what I have begun at this time with so much peril turn out badly for me, if, excellent Erasmus, I am not more solicitous for your safety than for my own success. You may see plainly the state of affairs, and I greatly wonder what you are doing there where, as elsewhere, there is so much hostility to us, and where, as I hear, the mandates of Leo X. are cruelly executed. Do you even imagine that you can be safe while Luther's books are burnt, and that his condemnation will not prejudice your cause, or that those who condemn him will spare you? Fly, fly, and keep yourself safe for us! I have sufficient, even infinite peril, but my mind is used to danger and to whatever fortune may bring; with you it is different. Fly, excellent Erasmus, fly while you can, before some disaster falls on you (a thought I detest). Then, when it is no longer safe for you, you will have to say what no wise man has said: "I did not think." All of those fellows cry out that you are the author of this business and that from you, as the fountain head, has flowed whatever now displeases Leo; they say that you went before us, that you

---

[1] 1 John, iv. 4.
[2] John Thurzo, to whom Luther had written on July 30, 1520. Enders, ii. 447. He died on August 2.

taught us, that you first incited the minds of men with the love of liberty, and that we are all your followers. . . . For by so long flattering and praising the Pope you have deserved the mortal hatred of Aleander who will wish to destroy you, especially when he sees his fury resisted by arms. We would have done this before had not Sickingen advised first to try the mind of the Emperor, hoping that he would do something or at least allow us to do it. And we will do it unless that wicked Slav [Aleander] subverts all things and seizes the Emperor's crown, the reward of which deed Luther and I demand. . . .

337. LUTHER TO LAZARUS SPENGLER AT NUREMBERG.
Enders, ii. 527. De Wette, i. 525. German.

WITTENBERG, November 17, 1520.

My service, etc. Honorable, wise, dear Sir and Friend! I have read your letter and learned your great courage for the Christian truth with especial joy; God strengthen you and all of us with his grace! I thank you heartily for your great, friendly care for me and for all Wittenbergers. You must certainly believe that Dr. Carlstadt and Melanchthon are entirely at one; for a while one spoke to his classes in a different way from the other, from which circumstance perhaps this rumor grew. By God's grace Philip is minded to have no quarrel with him. Neither did it ever occur to me to harbor annoyance or dislike of Erasmus. It pleased me well that he desired me not to mention him.[1] I wrote to him about it and promised not to speak of him any more, nor of any other good friends if it displeased them. People have many such false rumors to write about me, but don't let their gossip deceive you. If God will, Erasmus and I will remain at one. It is true that I sometimes privately discuss with Melanchthon how near or far Erasmus is from the way; he and everyone can do the same about me with impunity and in friendship. I will attack no one first; it is sufficient to me to defend myself when attacked.

[1] Erasmus was offended by Luther's reference to him in the *Answer to the Condemnation of Louvain*, and made this request, in a letter to Melanchthon; *cf. supra*, no. 258. Luther's letter is lost. *Cf.* Smith, 201f.

I am having my *Appeal* renewed and printed in Latin and German, although I thought there was no great need of it, so open and shameless is the bull with its Antichristian anathemas. We know not whether the bishops will execute the bull. We hold that they have been legally answered by us. Herewith I commend myself to you before God. Amen.

      Dr. Martin Luther, *Augustinian.*

338. OSWALD MYCONIUS TO RUDOLPH CLIVANUS AT MILAN.

S. Hess: *Erasmus von Roterdam* (Zürich, 1790), ii. 707.

           Lucerne, November 20, 1520.

Rudolph zum Buhl (Clivanus, 1499-1578), teacher of Greek at Zurich and after 1519 a friend of Zwingli. On him, *Corpus Reformatorum,* xciv. 339.

. . . Would you like to hear something about Luther? You have it in the letter of Ammann.[1] Of Erasmus? I will tell you something. He is a scoundrel. Hear what he did. He was summoned by the king of England to a conference.[2] The king patted him on the shoulder and said: "Erasmus, why don't you defend that good Luther?" Erasmus answered: "Because I am not enough of a theologian; now that the professors of Louvain have put me down as a grammarian I don't touch such things." After a long conversation the king said: "You are a good man, Erasmus," and dismissed him with a gift of fifty ducats. Then Erasmus went to Frankfort. When his friends came to see him, he waved them away. "Look out," said he, "don't touch me," and held out his hands as if he feared to be hurt. When they expressed sympathy and asked him what was the matter, he told them he had a wound. When they asked him where, he replied: "In the purse." Thus he tried to turn the bargain into a joke. He was going to Basle, but was prevented by the king of Spain and is now also kept in Germany. . . .

[1] John Jacob Ammann of Zurich (died 1573), student of Myconius, on whom see *Zwinglis Werke,* vii. 198.
[2] At the conference at Calais, July, 1520. It is doubtful how much Myconius knew about it. Erasmus himself only says that he talked with Henry VIII. of his (Erasmus's) writing against Luther, but more of ways of making peace. *Erasmi opera* (1703), iii. no. 650. Cf. *English Historical Review,* c. 657.

339. BASIL AMERBACH TO BONIFACE AMERBACH AT AVIGNON.

Burckhardt-Biedermann, 143.   BASLE, November 22, 1520.

... I have nothing to write of Luther except that Pope Leo is trying to ruin him, and for that reason keeps sending legates to make Charles hostile to him. Charles has not yet determined what to do. A certain virulent and biting lampoon,[1] which I will send by the next messenger when I have a chance, has come out against Aleander, the learned Greek scholar who is the Pope's legate.

340. ULRICH VON HUTTEN TO MARTIN BUCER.

Böcking, i. 427.   EBERNBURG, November 25, 1520.

... Luther[2] is burned at Cologne also. Therefore the holy Muse of truth-speaking Luther will go into the flames and die. ... I hear that all orders of men greatly grieved at the act and only a few priests were pleased with it. I hear that some of the nobles favor Luther so strongly that Sickingen thinks that there would have been an extremely dangerous rebellion at Cologne if only Frederic of Saxony had been there, for he left a short time ago. We are waiting to see what will happen at Mayence, for our adversaries are trying something there. I hear that Luther published something[3] or other to-day excommunicating and anathematizing Leo X. ...

341. WILLIAM DE CROY, SEIGNEUR DE CHIÈVRES, AND HENRY OF NASSAU TO ELECTOR FREDERIC OF SAXONY.

Reichstagsakten, ii. 466, note.   OPPENHEIM, November 27, 1520.

Soon after leaving Cologne Frederic had written to Chièvres and Nassau a letter which has been lost. The following is the answer.

Croy (1485-May 27, 1521), was made Stadtholder of the Nether-

---

[1] Several attacks came out on Aleander at this time, of which perhaps the most likely in this instance is the *Acta Academiae Lovaniensis*, perhaps by the pen of Erasmus, reprinted in *Luthers Werke* (Erlangen), *Opera latina varii argumenti*, iv. 308-14. The proof of the authorship, P. Kalkoff: *Die Vermittlungspolitik des Erasmus*, etc., p. 23ff. The similarity of the style to that of Erasmus was early noticed. *Vadianische Briefsammlung*, ii. 346. Cf. further, P. Kalkoff: *Anfänge der Gegenref. in den Niederländen*, ii. 35ff, and the article by the same scholar in *Zwinglis Werke*, vii. 409.

[2] I. e., his works, Nov. 12.

[3] *Adversus execrabilem Antichristi bullam.* Weimar, vi. 595.

lands 1506; in 1509 took charge of the education of Charles V., to whom he became a chief adviser after 1516. He died at Worms.

Henry of Nassau (1483-September 14, 1538), an officer of Maximilian. In 1516-7 he was in command of the siege of Arnheim; in 1521 fought against France. He was then made Governor of the Netherlands. He visited Spain in 1522 and 1534. He was at the Diet of Augsburg in 1530. *Allgemeine deutsche Biographie.* The following anecdote of him is found in a contemporary publication, reprinted by P. Fredericq: *Corpus Inquisitionis Neerlandicae,* iv. no. 37. "The Count of Nassau said to the preachers at the Hague: 'Go and preach the gospel simply like Luther, offending no one.' . . . Then the professors of Louvain complained to Margaret, sister of Charles V., who said: 'Who is Luther?' 'An unlearned monk,' said they. 'Then,' said she, 'all you learned men write against one unlearned, and the world will rather believe many learned than one unlearned.'"

We have received the letter of your Lordship on the affair of Martin Luther, the contents of which, and especially your Lordship's wishes, we carefully explained to his imperial and Catholic Majesty. Your Lordship will learn more at large from his Majesty's letters what he has decided upon. It seemed to us at all events that your Lordship ought, for the sake of your piety and zeal for the orthodox faith, to bring Luther with you to the imperial Diet, so that the affair might be quieted and extinguished, for which we both promise our good offices with his imperial Majesty, especially as we are sure that your Lordship desires this. . . .

342. THE EMPEROR CHARLES V. TO ELECTOR FREDERIC OF SAXONY.

Reichstagsakten, ii. 466. German.   OPPENHEIM, November 28, 1520.

Highborn, dear Uncle[1] and Elector. We have been frequently and urgently requested by the nuncio of the Pope's Holiness, to guard against farther damage from Dr. Martin Luther's books, as we did in our Lower Burgundian Hereditary Possessions, and we should like to have them burned here and everywhere in the Holy Empire. Now our highborn, dear uncle,[1] William of Chièvres, and our dear and trusty Henry Count of Nassau, our viceroy in the Netherlands, have shown us that you desire that we should not touch Luther, nor do anything more against him before he is heard. And as

---

[1] This title is not to be taken literally.

we should like to put down this movement, from which we fear much disorder and error may arise, we earnestly request you to bring the said Luther with you to the next Diet at Worms, where we will have him sufficiently examined by learned and wise persons, and have no wrong nor anything illegal done to him. We beg you to prevent farther trouble and to command the said Luther in the meantime not to write or publish anything against his Holiness or the Roman see. Thereby you will do us special pleasure which we shall graciously acknowledge.

343. LUTHER TO JOHN LANG AT ERFURT.

Enders, ii. 532.   WITTENBERG, November 28, 1520.

Greeting. Reverend Father, we rejoice that the elector has returned.[1] I pray you to pray for us. Duke George is insane; he is more than furious. We daily expect anathemas and thunderbolts from that quarter. We think to stick to our appeal. I see that the affair is verging to a great tumult; may God turn it to the good! We have read the answer[2] of our elector given to the papal Nuncios Aleander and Caracciolo; it is so learned and acute that we see they got nothing from him. I will send it later. The same Aleander is taxed with many vices in a libellous but clever book.[3] The men of Cologne and Louvain have burnt my books. We know not what will happen. Farewell in the Lord. Our vicar[4] has gone to Sternberg; brother John has turned to follow him.

MARTIN LUTHER.

344. LUTHER TO SPALATIN.

Enders, ii. 534.   WITTENBERG, November 29, 1520.

Greeting. Dear Spalatin, I gave a letter for you to the messenger going to Grimma; now that the reverend Father

---

[1] The elector returned to his own land on November 20.

[2] On November 4, at Cologne, the nuncios had interviewed Frederic and demanded that Luther be punished or delivered up. After consulting Erasmus on November 5, Frederic refused the requests of the legates on November 6. *Cf.* Smith, 100.

[3] Aleander was attacked in many contemporary satires; perhaps the one meant is the *Acta Academiae Lovaniensis*, on which *cf.* Smith, 98.

[4] Wenzel Link.

James[1] is going I will give him another, which perhaps will arrive before the first. I will soon take up and defend one by one all the articles condemned by the bull, as you wrote and as I understand they[2] wish. Unless you translate it into German with more freedom than you have hitherto done,[3] please let me do it. For absolutely no translation except a very free one can reproduce figures of speech and the cogency of the argumentative style. I do not mention the extreme difficulty of giving the author's spirit. I doubt not that you could do it, for you translate with wonderful facility, but I see that you are a little too closely bound and afraid to change a single sentence as is sometimes necessary.

I intend to dedicate this book to Fabian von Feilitzsch, a gentleman who is greatly to my liking. Wherefore please send me his full title as soon as possible in Latin and German. You use the German title, but I desire to know both so as to be able to judge how the Latin title is derived. Thus I will go before and do you follow fast.

My parents and sisters[4] honored the wedding of Melanchthon as did many honorable and learned men.

Please let us have another copy of the elector's answer,[5] for they would not let us read it twice. You will learn the rest from my former letter with my booklet *On Christian Liberty*. Farewell and pray for me.

MARTIN LUTHER, *Augustinian*.

345. ERASMUS TO JOHN NIJS DE TURNHOUT, KNOWN AS DRIEDO.

H. de Jongh: *L'ancienne Faculté de théologie de Louvain*, 1911, p. 158, n. 3. LOUVAIN, November 30, 1520.

... I am sorry that Theodore Martens[6] refuses to print the book of Professor Turnhout. In the first place, he ought not

---

[1]Probably Vogt, the elector's confessor.
[2]Luther probably means the elector.
[3]Spalatin translated Luther's work *On Christian Liberty*. Luther himself translated the work he is speaking of now, the *Assertion of all the Articles wrongly condemned*.
[4]Luther at this time had three sisters, married to men named Kaufmann, Polner and Mackenrodt.
[5]*I. e.*, to the legates, *cf. supra*, no. 343. Who "they" were is uncertain, perhaps some Wittenberg canons with whom Luther was not friendly.
[6]Martens (c. 1450-May 28, 1534), "the Aldus of the Netherlands," studied the

thus to show his animus. Then I should like the work printed for many reasons. The man is one of the most skilful in theology; nor do I doubt that he writes as he has disputed, using solid arguments and not invective. As I do not approve having Luther crushed by mere vociferations and conspiracies, I am all the more desirous of seeing him refuted by the Bible and good reasons. Let us attribute all we possibly can to the Pope's bull, yet such a refutation would be more convincing to the learned and to the intelligent. Do you therefore persuade the man not to refuse, and I will do the same as much as I can. Farewell.

346. ERASMUS TO ———.

Erasmi opera (1703), iii. 1889. (Late in 1520.)

. . . You know what a smoke has been raised at Louvain by the theologians who fathered the bull;[1] the same was done at Liège with the connivance of the bishop who is ambitious of the cardinal's hat; finally it was also done at Cologne in an even more hateful way under the rule of Hochstraten. But though Luther's writings are not approved by all, yet there is none who is not displeased by this way of acting and this savage tyranny. Nor would they have acted with impunity at Cologne had not the presence of the king protected them. Now Luther's works are sold there as before.

Two men, Latomus and Turnhout, have here written against Luther, but neither publishes his books on account of diffidence, I think. Indeed, it is much easier to conquer him with bulls and with smoke than with arguments. I have never mixed in the Lutheran affair, but yet I have not approved the clamors nor the pamphlets of these who have hitherto opposed Luther. They take this ill, for if I stood by Luther the same engines would be directed against me; if I wrote against him these men of evangelic meekness and simplicity would use the hatred of the Germans thus aroused against

---

art of printing at Venice, set up a shop at Alost, and in 1493 moved to Antwerp, in 1498 to Louvain, in 1502 back to Antwerp, in 1512 to Louvain, until 1529 when he retired to Alost. P. S. Allen, i. 514.

[1] Much of the theological material in the bull *Exsurge Domine* was taken from the condemnation of Luther by the University of Louvain. "The smoke" refers to the burning of Luther's books, at Louvain October 8, at Liège October 17, at Cologne November 12.

me for my destruction. They have laid false charges against me before the papal nuncio, as though I alone upheld Luther and prevented his death, which, rather than his correction, is what they alone desire. Francis von Sickingen related that when he expostulated with the Emperor about the mandate against Luther, which is being carried around, the Emperor said that he had never issued such a mandate. When the Elector Frederic of Saxony spoke with him about Luther he received the reply that Luther should not be condemned unheard. The bishops are forced to dissimulate, only when they showed the elector the breve in which he was commanded to throw Luther into prison, he said that he was surprised that the Pope should make such a demand of him, a layman, when he was not convinced that Luther deserved such treatment and when the affair had been referred to the Diet of Worms. The nuncios took this answer very ill. It is clear that the bull was published contrary to the command of the Pope. Aleander, who brought it, had no commission save to confer with the universities. He is a man skilled in the three languages, and if all say that he is a Jew, surely his life lends color to the assertion. What *he* has done in Lower Germany furious Eck does in Upper Germany. The Germans publish seditious tracts, and I wonder that no one is able to quiet the tumult. Luther writes more fiercely every day and seems to be aiming at rebellion against my advice. He writes that he simply despises the Roman bull, but renews his old appeal at the advice of friends. A breve[1] was shown to Matthew Lang, Cardinal of Gurk, at Cologne, commanding him to invite Staupitz, vicar general of the Augustinians, who favors Luther, and force him to abjure all Luther's dogmas, and if he did not do this throw him into prison or punish him some other way.

There are many things in Luther's books which are worthy of being known; some things which had better have been omitted and all things too violently, not to say seditiously, written. For if he had said what was necessary more moderately, even if he had accused the intolerable vices of the Roman Curia, he would have had the support of all.

[1] On this, cf. Smith, *op. cit.*, 107. On Lang, *supra*, no. 80, note.

Yet I know not how it is that all who have written against him have composed nothing worth reading. If he has gone mad in writing, they are madder in their answers. And among those who wish Luther dead I see no good man. The letters of Adrian of Utrecht are full of bitterness; he favors disciples worthy of himself, vain, deceitful, ambitious and revengeful. . . . I have seen Hutten's letter[1] complaining that the Pope has written to have him cast into chains; he was not to be found when I was at Cologne, it was said that with forty companions he lay in ambush for the Romanists on whom he has declared war. . . .

347. LUTHER TO FABIAN VON FEILITZSCH.

Enders, iii. 1.   WITTENBERG, December 1, 1520.

This is Luther's dedication to his *Assertio Omnium Articulorum*, Weimar, vii. 94. Feilitzsch died only a few days later, while the work was in print.

You, Fabian Feilitzsch, or rather Foelix, prove what I have often said, that laymen have a spirit of judgment and zeal, for when my Philip and I were with you at Eilenburg[2] you gave a splendid example of how purely, learnedly, piously and felicitously you could judge and talk of Christian affairs. Nor do I doubt that in this court you have many rivals, so that I simply rejoice to see the admirable plan and judgment of God, who with the froward shows himself froward and with the elect is elect.[3] For we who are the clergy, that is the chosen ones of the Lord,[4] who ought to be the masters of the laity, turned our backs on Christ and his gospel, in so much that he in like manner turns his back on us. And as we provoke him with that which is not God, and with the word which is not the gospel, so again he provokes us with those who are not clergy and with those who are not learned, by giving them pure knowledge of himself, and leaving us our foolish and impious doctrines. Thou art just, O Lord, and thy judgment is right.[5]

[1] *Supra*, no. 296. This was published.
[2] *I. e.*, in November, *supra*, no. 335.
[3] Psalm xviii. 26f.
[4] "Nos enim, qui de clero Domini sumus."
[5] Revelation, xvi. 7; xix. 2.

Since, therefore, I have written and spoken much, not knowing that there was such blindness in the shepherds of Israel,[1] I deserved only that they should revile me instead of loving me, and render evil for good,[2] until they became so senseless to their own salvation that they publicly condemned and burnt my books at Cologne and Louvain. For they have a zeal for God above others, but not according to knowledge.[3] I am so far from being angry at them that I greatly pity their blindness and perdition, or rather their childish folly. For what is easier than to burn books which you cannot refute? The impious king Jehoiakim burned the books of Jeremiah the prophet,[4] but he was not justified thereby. Truly, as I said, this is due to our perversity and to the wicked mind to which God has given us up,[5] that we the clergy should condemn the truth which the laity embrace, so that those become priests who are not priests, and laymen who are not laymen.

Wherefore I thought best to address you laymen, as a new race of priests, and to bring my remarks together felicitously (God grant) under your felicitous name, to assert and strengthen all that those incendiaries have damned with their bull so like themselves. Do you commend me in this work, or rather the Christian doctrine to yourself and all your nobility. Farewell.

348. SPALATIN TO THE ELECTOR FREDERIC OF SAXONY.
Zeitschrift für Kirchengeschichte, ii. 121.

WITTENBERG (December 3, 1520).

Most serene, highborn Prince, most gracious Lord. I will not conceal from your Grace that I arrived here at Wittenberg last evening shortly before four o'clock, and, thank God, found everything right and well. . . .

I found Dr. Martin merry, who thanks your Grace humbly for your greeting. He thinks the pusillanimity of the priests is increasing. It has occurred to him and perhaps to some others that possibly the university annoyed your Grace by

---

[1] Isaiah, lvi. 10.
[2] Psalm cix. 4f.
[3] Romans, x. 2.
[4] Jeremiah, xxxvi. 23.
[5] Romans, i. 24

its last letter. He is entirely undaunted, and has already begun his new book refuting the articles in the bull, and done a sixth of it. He promises according to your Grace's advice to write more courteously henceforth. He has also begun to expound the *Magnificat* and to dedicate it to my young lord. . . .

The provost of Liska near Zerbst, who was charged by the Bishop of Brandenburg to execute the bull, has written Dr. Martin that he will sooner lose his provostship than do it.

Dr. Martin has gathered the canon law and decretals to burn them as soon as he hears that they have undertaken to burn his books at Leipsic. He has also decided to burn the bull publicly in the pulpit unless they mend their abuses. Dr. Martin has so long meditated the papal rule that he says he is now commanded by them to sin and do evil and forbidden to do good and even to act and live honorably and Christianly. On which a new allegorical picture has been painted which I will bring your Grace to-morrow.

I think I will bring you thirty letters to Dr. Luther from princes, lords, and learned, famous people from Swabia, Switzerland, Pomerania, Breisgau, Bodensee, Bohemia and other lands, all comfortable and Christian writings. . . .

349. WOLFGANG CAPITO TO LUTHER.

Enders, iii. 3. MAYENCE, December 4, 1520.

Greeting. I hear from friends that you are often threatened and that the evil increases daily; the tumor will soon burst and the whole power of its evil go elsewhere. The affair is carried on with a strange sort of violence, but it is partly human; no wonder that it has some human frailty about it, for such will always accompany humanity.

Eck has written a triumphant epistle[1] to Cologne in which he boasts of the success of Christ's work at Leipsic, for thus he calls his own sycophancy. I have never seen anything more noxious than the barbarian sophists there, fools, *atheists, uncultured*,[2] without style, the graces or faith, relying abso-

---

[1] A letter to Hochstraten, July 24, 1519, published with the date July 24, 1520.
[2] The words in italics are Greek.

lutely on human intellect. You have often blown the trumpet, and Hutten, who will soon try arms, shouts war for us. I think you will be safe there, nor shall our chief lack an asylum. Our enemies are protected by strong bulwarks, castles and moats, relying on money, arms and numerous dependents. The people stand unanimously for you; not the smallest part is with the Romanists. "Alas!" the latter exclaim, "what is this monstrosity, that a private man should unpunished call into question the ancient decretals!" To which the saner reply: "What impiety it is to extinguish Christ's doctrines with human laws!" Why do I say all this? Only to show that everything is tending towards a tremendous revolution, of which the outcome is uncertain. There are men who fear that such a strife would obliterate all show of religion. For they take your teachings in a sinister way, as it were.

Someone has written a satiric dialogue[1] at Cologne against Hochstraten, taxing Eck and Aleander with burning the books, and even casting some aspersions at me, who certainly did not wish the books burned, but who did conceal my opinion about it. Eck wrote back furiously to Cologne. Aleander digests the insult in silence, making not very witty jokes about it; therefore he has been branded with another sharp letter, and with a by no means bad song, and another more learned one with much gall in it. The man speaks hostilely of me, although, as you know, I study nothing but peace and tranquillity. He burned your books with much bluster at Cologne, but as I was absent the attempt was unfortunate and the issue much more unfortunate. He was hissed by the people as a Jew[2] who under the pretext of religion would labor for the glory of Moses, as though he were not a sincere Christian, having been recently converted. The people are of two minds. The shame of the burning terrified some, but exacerbated the

---

[1] The *Hochstratus ovans*, reprinted Böcking, supplement, i. 462. *Cf. Archiv für Reformationsgeschichte*, i. 58.

[2] Aleander was at this time often charged with being a Jew, even by Erasmus. His skill in Hebrew was at the basis of this untrue allegation, the purpose of which was not solely to excite odium against him, but also to cast doubts on his capacity to discharge the duties of legate from which converted Jews were legally excluded.

hatred of many against the Romanists. Thomas Murnar[1] has published two books on the subject, sticking to the Church,[2] but in a very popular way, that is, with spleen against the Romanists; his reputation is black, but his tongue is skilful. He is wont to run much out of the road, as one who cares not for the ignorant and humble people.

I see that what I always feared will come to pass, that tyranny will be the head of the whole business, and that those who do all things with cunning do not see that what is below the requirement of the law is above the power of man born of Adam. You gather what I hint at; turn your mind back to former times and consider what bloody wars sprang from bloody tyranny. I want Christ to be strong again; you know whether he prospers by doing or by suffering violence. Religion was born, grew and became strong by innocent, unwarlike men; by suffering wrong the unarmed struck arms from furious hands. I have not noticed that any race received pure religion from bloody soldiers; although I know that the ancient Jewish religion (to which we are in many respects similar) was often maintained by force. I know that we have often tried to do the same, though I cannot say with much piety or success, since our religion has rather grown weaker thereby. Wherefore pray deter your followers from relying on arms. I understand the reason for your plan, but with me it is another reason to the contrary. For what is deep rooted is not eradicated all at once; it must be gradually torn down until at last it falls under the hand pushing it. Now that everything is in commotion everyone who knows the nature of the mob can see what a revolution and what passions will result. Wherefore I see no hope of safety, unless with calm mind and free from earthly passions we come together and each yield something to the other. If the evil

---

[1] *Cf. Schriften des Vereins für Reformationsgeschichte*, xxx. and xxxii., studies by W. Kawerau. Murnar (1475-1537), entered the Franciscan order at Strassburg 1491, and became priest 1494. He studied at Paris 1497, and after wandering returned to Strassburg 1502. In this year he had a literary feud with Wimpfeling. In 1506 he became D. D., and in 1515 was crowned Poet Laureate. Of his many satires his *Conspiracy of Fools*, 1512, is the best. He was the most popular writer against Luther, particularly in his *Big Lutheran Fool*, 1522. In 1525 he was banished by the Strassburg Protestants to Oberehenheim.

[2] A little freedom is here necessary in treating the text.

should have been stirred up, now I think it ought to be quieted again. The Lamb[1] is able to make all things new. We can easily stir things up, but it does not seem within our power to settle them again, but to do that we must humbly strive for Christ's divine aid. He sees what we hardly think of. I frankly confess to you, dearest brother, that daily I more and more doubt about this business, nor do I mean this ill. For practical life easily teaches us how small an impulse can turn the people either to good or to evil. I do not say that we should cease doing Christ's work, but that we should pardon much to the coarse people. As you say, some things are necessary to a Christian, and there are some things expressly overlooked which will be readily understood from the former. You have recent experience of this yourself, as one armed in a holy war to fight daily for your positions with enemies. Consider our weakness, that we need milk rather than strong meat;[2] do not extinguish the devotion of the people by asking too much of them, and preach the Word of Christ not from strife, but from charity.[3] All this foolish letter, is, as you know, from Capito who desires the best for Luther, and who wishes for peace and who is striving with all his might for concord. I doubt not that you desire the same, but that hitherto your adversaries have thwarted you. Their end shall be death[4] whether they were born of contention or whether they were begotten by guile, sycophancy and imposture. We must pray for peace in our time through Jesus Christ. Farewell in him, Christian soul, dear to my heart.

Yours,

CAPITO.

350. CROTUS RUBEANUS TO LUTHER.

Enders, iii. 8.   ERFURT, December 5, 1520.

Hearty greeting. I have not time to write much, nor have you leisure to read long letters, especially idle ones. It is enough for me to send a friendly salutation to our Martin, the evangelist given by God's mercy at this time, although so hated by little saints and chaste theologians that they would

[1] Revelation, xxi. 5.   [2] 1 Corinthians, iii. 2.
[3] Cf. Philippians, i. 16f.   [4] Cf. Philippians, iii. 19.

willingly let the Lord's doctrine be destroyed if thereby they could crush you. If that wage is paid to the soldiers of Christ in these earthly tempests, we rightly venerate the saints, who to defend the truth suffered mockings and scourgings, were hewn and sawn asunder, and were slain by the sword.[1] Rumor constantly tells us how little you are frightened by the threats of tyrants, how bravely you despise death, how much you wish to endure a thousand dangers for Christ's sake. We approve your courage and recognize the spirit of the Lord, but we fear that danger will accrue to the world through this holy alacrity of yours. For when Martin is gone another will not soon appear so mighty in the Scriptures. Make haste slowly; when the roots of holy doctrine have been more deeply planted and when success seems assured then say: "I desire to die and be with Christ."[2] Meantime, we want to hear you saying, "If God be for us, who can be against us?"[3] only on condition that you take care of your life. How many perish in war by too great rashness, who, by taking care of themselves might have saved others! For God helps us in such a way that his providence excites our own care; he wants brave but not rash followers, courageous, not audacious men. Who neglects to care for himself seems to me to tempt God. I suppose that I shall seem an importunate adviser; I gladly admit the fault in which I have many associates, for they think that you are incurring great danger by your forwardness, which many consider carelessness.

With my own ears I heard a lusty centaur, a canon, say in public that it would not be hard for anyone who wished, to kidnap Luther and thus deliver him into the hands of the Pope. Look around you; be Argus. You know not how many win wealth, while some are promised the titles of bishop and cardinal with immense rewards. A great multitude is inspired by hatred. If my[4] Colognians did not fear to burn

[1] Hebrews, xi. 36.
[2] Philippians, i. 23.
[3] Romans, viii. 31.
[4] Crotus calls them "my" Colognians either because he studied at Cologne or because he made fun of Gratius and other citizens of Cologne in his *Epistolae Obscurorum Virorum*.

the gospel of Christ or rather Christ himself publicly in your books, what will they not dare to do to ruin you? Much money was spent for burning the books; what then? will not much be spent against their author? The wrath of the stars is heavy against this place, and the men subject to their influence go incurably mad. I remember that old tragedy of reverend Reuchlin, of which I was a spectator for a whole year together. Both my tongue and pen are insufficient to describe the madness of the theologians, whose passions I found more ticklish than the whims of little women. Would that the "Obscure Men" with their art would again come forth to depict these obscurant fathers according to their deserts anew; the fathers desire not to be illuminated by anything but their own light, which they receive from their own sky. But I hope the obscure ones will appear. The Louvainians have not sinned as much, since, whatever may be their insanity in this condemnation, they took it from Cologne and Hochstraten. That man will not rest until his miserable soul shall be tortured in his lost body. The error of Louvain seems to have extenuating circumstances; Cologne sins with intent. Their criminal leader would recently have perished by the sword of Hutten not far from Louvain had not that noble-minded youth thought the death of Hochstraten unworthy of him, so he let him go trembling and bloodless. With great threats he stopped him agitating against you and Reuchlin, but he does not know where his fury will end. The scroundrel after that laid many snares which perhaps it would be tedious to relate; time will show how the rebellious father will take his revenge. Hutten staid with me at Fulda five days after he had met Hochstraten. I wish you could know the wiles of the most holy fathers both in Italy and Germany, since Rome has invaded also the latter country. I cannot write them because there are so many ambushes all around. We wrote a satire on the arm of the Lord versus the secular arm, which they, who invoke all that is impious, summon to their aid. But how I am wandering on, though I want to be brief! I am falling into the contrary vice. Forgive me, most holy Pope Martin; my love for you makes me loquacious and steals away part of my time.

As I wished to communicate with the most learned Melanchthon, his most learned letter, which arrived late, challenged me to reply. For it sought me in Italy, as did yours, and after half a year found me wandering in Germany. That year I was very unsettled, now in Italy, now in Germany; where I most desired to stay I was most obliged to wander. Recently it happened that as I was on the road to Dornheim, I stopped here at Erfurt with old friends. Two days had not passed until, to my great surprise, they made me rector of the university.[1] I declined the honor, but was forced to accept it, so that, contrary to nature, neglecting my own people, I discharge the duties of paterfamilias to strangers, in this republic of students which your Eck is trying to disturb. Greet Melanchthon respectfully from me and ask his pardon if I don't write him soon, or if I write briefly. He has married a wife; may God prosper that most holy union, so that the happy father may see his children round about his table. For some years I have been disputing with Mutian who despises marriage and praises the life of the priests, whereas I prefer marriage. Wherefore let those who follow my guidance take to themselves wives.

351. ERASMUS TO CARDINAL LAWRENCE CAMPEGGIO AT ROME.

Erasmi opera (1703), iii. 594.   LOUVAIN, December 6, 1520.

I have been obliged greatly to compress this letter of nine thousand words. It is an interesting contrast to the one written to Capito on the same day.

[Erasmus defends himself from the charge of supporting Luther with the same arguments and often in the same words as he has used in previous letters. He begins by recounting the trouble he has had with the monks of Louvain, who have used the Lutheran cause, without the shadow of an excuse, to attack him.]

. . . In the first place, one or two prefaces, in fair Latin, to Luther's books, were sufficient argument that Luther had been helped by me to write, although in his pamphlets there is not a jot from my pen. As though Wittenberg, not to speak of the rest of Germany, were lacking in men who could write Latin!

[1] Crotus was elected rector on October 18, 1520.

[Erasmus then speaks of his letters to Luther and Albert of Mayence, complaining of their publication and of their being shown to the Pope, as he has heard from Aleander that they were. He has not read Luther's books. He has heard that his life is approved even by his opponents. He warned him to spare the Pope, the princes and the universities—this, perhaps, in allusion to Luther's plan for reforming the universities set forth in the *Address to the German Nobility*, published August, 1520. This does not show that Erasmus favored Luther, for he would have answered the Sultan as politely. He has not written against Luther because it is above his powers and the judgment of the University of Paris is expected. No one hurts the Pope as much as the monks. Of those who have answered Luther, Prierias pleased Erasmus little, Augustine (Alveld) less; Thomas Rhadinus he cannot judge, and only John Turenholt is to be commended for using arguments rather than abuse. Erasmus closes by expressing the profoundest reverence for the Roman Church.]

352. ERASMUS TO WOLFGANG CAPITO AT MAYENCE.

S. Hess: *Erasmus von Roterdam* (Zürich, 1790), ii. 551.

LOUVAIN, December 6, 1520.

. . . The theologians think Luther cannot be completely vanquished except by my pen, and they tacitly implore me to write against him. Far be this insanity from me! Dorp is not concerned in this hateful scheme, and yet he could not be more hurtful to me than he is. Farewell.

The Italians seem to conspire against us to destroy the whole glory of German erudition. Aleander has this more at heart than the Lutheran affair. If he does this unpunished by the Germans I will become a Frenchman. Again farewell. . . .

353. LUTHER TO SPALATIN.

Enders, iii. 12. WITTENBERG, December 7, 1520.

Greeting. I enclose letters and I am writing to the pastor of Lochau,[1] Spalatin, and do you try to restrain yourself a little in giving me so many commands. A man could not so suddenly start such a conflagration in this little hole if he gave the world nothing. I received the bone image. The book dedicated to Fabian von Feilitzsch had begun to be printed, so that it could not be changed; but what does it matter that it is dedicated to him who now lives more than

[1] Francis Günther.

he did before?¹ All my friends do not think that I ought to dedicate the German book² to Francis von Sickingen, for fear of exciting the jealousy of many, particularly of the Franconian nobility. I am disputing with myself whether to dedicate something to my Counts of Mansfeld,³ as they have long wished and as there are so many of them. We shall see what we shall decide. Farewell and pray for me.

MARTIN LUTHER, *Augustinian.*

354. ULRICH VON HUTTEN TO MARTIN LUTHER.
Enders, iii. 13. Szamatólski, 150.   EBERNBURG, December 9, 1520.

You would pity me if you saw my difficulties; so slippery is man's faith. As fast as I get new help the old fails me. Whoever fears many things doubts many things. In the first place, superstition terrifies men, planting in their minds the idea that opposing the Roman pontiff, even if he is the most unjust and wicked of men, is the inexpiable crime. Yet I strive, nor do I yield to adversity. Francis von Sickingen, the only really constant man, protects us; yet some men have almost caused him to waver by persuading him that some things which you were said to have written, but which, I am sure, you never did write, were monstrous. I have thought it my duty to do whatever I found to do to prevent so great a bulwark for us being occupied by the enemy. I accomplished this by reading your writings, which he had only glanced at hastily before. In the first place, I at once made him as docile as I could; then this affair began to interest and please him. A little later, when he saw what a fort you built and on what a foundation, he said: "Who dares attack this, or if any one dares, who can overthrow it?" Gradually his mind has become more and more inflamed. He is now so entirely devoted to us that he lets no dinner pass without hearing something either of yours or of mine. He is a man of acute judgment; you will find none more learned without the classic

¹*Supra*, December 1. Feilitzsch had just died.
²*I. e.*, the German translation of the *Assertio Omnium Articulorum*, which was eventually dedicated to all pious Christians. On June 1 Luther dedicated to Sickingen a work on *Confession*, Enders, iii. 168.
³Later in this year Luther dedicated to Count Albert of Mansfeld part of his *Postilla*.

education. How eloquent he is to carry out and amplify whatever he conceives! In our affair we could not find a better or more apt champion. For that reason there are many who try hard to turn him against us; but I am sure they will not succeed, for I know how faithful he is. For, a few days ago, when some friends and relatives tried to get him to desert so doubtful a cause, he obstinately resisted them, affirming that what he defended was not doubtful, but was the cause of Christ and the truth and especially that it was due to Germany that our admonitions should be heeded, even for the sake of defending the faith. I would not have you ignorant, Luther, that he is the person who has prevented me doing anything by force. Relying on his advice, I contain myself the longer that more favor may be shown to the cause, and that our enemies may grow the more insolent, thinking it has been overcome and oppressed by bearing my weight. . . .

I send the bull of [Leo] the Tenth flouted by me[1] in some places, as much as I was able to in the short time given me by Christ. They say that you have written something,[2] which I have not seen any more than I have seen other pamphlets said to be hawked around. I am surprised that you do not at once send me your things so that I can show them to Sickingen. . . .

Sickingen sends kind greetings and bids you be safe, sound and of good courage. Farewell, dearest and best brother. . . .

355. LUTHER TO GEORGE SPALATIN.

Enders, iii. 18.   WITTENBERG, December 10, 1520.

Greeting. In the year 1520, December 10, at nine o'clock, at the eastern gate, near the Church of the Holy Cross were burned all the papal books, the *Decretum*, the *Decretals*, *Liber Sextus*, the *Clementines*, the *Extravagantes*,[3] and the last bull of Leo X.;[4] likewise the *Summa Angelica*, with some

[1] *I. e.*, Hutten's edition, with mocking notes, of the bull, under the title *Bulla Decimi Leonis contra errores Martini Lutheri et sequacium*. A copy of the first edition in the Bodleian Library, Quarto B 9 Th. Seld. Reprinted with Hutten's notes in *Lutheri opera varii argumenti*, iv. 261.

[2] Luther's *Adversus exsecrabilem Antichristi Bullam* is meant.

[3] For these parts of the Canon Law, *cf.* note to letter to Spalatin, February 24, 1519, Smith, p. 62.

[4] For the burning of the *Exsurge Domine*, *cf.* Smith, *op. cit.*, 100f.

books of Eck and Emser and others which sundry persons threw on. We did it to show the incendiary papists that it took no great power to burn books they could not refute. This is my news. . . . Farewell.   MARTIN LUTHER.

356. ERASMUS TO CHRISTOPHER HEGENDORFINUS AT LEIPSIC.

Erasmi opera (1703), iii. 601.   LOUVAIN, December 13, 1520.

Hegendorfinus (1500-40), a pupil of Mosellanus at Leipsic, in 1519 wrote a poem on the Leipsic debate. In 1525 he became professor of Greek at Leipsic, 1536 was called to Frankfort, 1537 to Lüneburg, 1539 to Rostock. *Allgemeine deutsche Biographie.*

. . . What Eck is doing at Leipsic others are doing with greater zeal here. But I have determined to be a spectator of this play, so that even if it turns out well I shall ask no praise, and if otherwise I shall have no blame. But it displeases me to hear that Eck is mocked in posters. It is a dangerous example which might be used against anyone. Again, what is more foolish than to provoke those whom you cannot control? Finally, what is less becoming Germans, whose warlike qualities have been especially praised, than to fight by means of anonymous books, by which they hurt some who are innocent and help the cause of their opponents? . . . Now Luther provokes men who, even if they are in the wrong, which I do not determine, cannot be put down. In the meantime, odium is heaped on good learning, against which they send out these hornets, which could hardly be borne as the last resource of the vanquished. What then shall we say of the victors doing this? Either I am blind or else they are aiming at someone other than Luther. They hasten to fight with the Muses. If the event does not confirm my suspicions, I shall not refuse to be taken for a fool.

357. THE ELECTOR FREDERIC OF SAXONY TO CHIÈVRES AND NASSAU.

Reichstagsakten, ii. 467, note.[1]   German.   ALSTET, December 14, 1520.

Frederic received the letter of Chièvres and Nassau at Eilenburg, December 7 (*supra*, no. 341), and answered it as follows:

[1] A different form of this note is given from a German original by H. von Schubert: *Die Vorgeschichte der Berufung Luthers auf den Reichstag zu Worms.* (*Sitzungsber. der Heidelberger Akademie*, vi. 1912), p. 27.

[The announced Imperial letter has not arrived.] ...
Truly we beg you thus to treat the affair of Martin Luther
that he may not be crushed by force, notwithstanding his
frequent protests and offers. For since our departure from
Worms we have been told that his books have been burned
at Cologne, Mayence and elsewhere, for which I was totally
unprepared, partly because Luther has protested and to-day
protests and offers to do whatever he can and ought with
Christian honor, and partly because I myself prayed that
neither Martin be condemned nor his books burned without
trial. If, therefore, moved by the acts of his enemies, Luther
has done anything of the same sort, I hope that his imperial
Majesty will regard it clemently, and I beg that you will
kindly explain it to him and commend Luther and his cause
to him. ...

358. ALEANDER TO THE VICE-CHANCELLOR, CARDINAL JULIUS DE' MEDICI.

P. Kalkoff: *Die Despechen des Nuntius Aleander vom Wormser Reichstage,* 1521. Halle, a. S., 1897, 2d ed., p. 29.[1]

WORMS (December 14), 1520.

Julius de' Medici, born 1478, made Archbishop of Florence and Cardinal 1513, was elected Pope, as Clement VII., in 1523, and died 1534. At this time, as Leo's chief minister, he took an active part against Luther.

I received your Lordship's letter of the third on the eleventh instant, and will answer it after I have sketched the course of my hard undertaking since I wrote last on November 28. I then told you that on account of the brevity of the Emperor's stay[2] at Mayence, and on account of the Archbishop's occupation with other matters, and, to speak frankly, on account of the evil animus of the councillors[3] who were trusted with the Lutheran affair, and on account of the hostility of the citizens (who have always been worthless and

---

[1] Kalkoff gives these despatches in German translation of the mixed Italian and Latin original. The originals are found in the *Reichstagsakten,* also in T. Brieger: *Aleander und Luther,* 1521, Gotha, 1884, and in P. Balan: *Monumenta reformationis Lutheranae,* Regensburg, 1884. I translate from Kalkoff, to whom I refer in future as: "Kalkoff: *Aleander.*"
[2] Charles entered Mayence, on his way from Cologne, on November 23, and left it for Worms via Oppenheim on the 28th.
[3] Specially Capito.

who played me an ugly trick), it was very difficult for me to execute the bull.

Now, however, I must relate that, on the very evening after the despatch of my previous letter, the Cardinal [of Mayence] expressed his extreme displeasure that his subjects had not acted as the citizens of other cities acted, and he promised to make good the fault which was excused by his officers. So, on the following morning, November 29, he had the condemnation of the books announced with blare of trumpets in all the city, and invited the people to the public burning of the same. So it happened, although the cardinal, as he said, was annoyed the whole night by many importunate noblemen, who advised him against the burning and wouldn't let him sleep, that it all turned out happily in the end.

These rascal Lutherans in disguise pretend to act in our interest in advising against burning the books, so that, as they say, we may not thereby arouse more hostility, as if that were possible! Nevertheless, after careful consideration, it seems that this course is useful and wholesome. For in the first place, the condemnation of such writings in Germany and other countries is more surely made known by burning than it would be by communicating the bull to the bishops and their agents, although I have not neglected to do this also in all quarters. Again, such an execution of judgment by papal and imperial power makes on the laity who are already tainted by the sermons and tracts of this heretic a thousand times worse than Arius, so deep an impression that many of them become convinced of the badness of the condemned writings and by a common impulse give them freely to the flames. I have been completely decided for the advisability of these measures by observing that all those who advise us against them are found to be without exception Lutherans, and that avowed Lutherans also do their best to prevent the burning by fraud or force. In short, there is no better method, indeed, no method whatever at all effective, if this scoundrel will not be moved to recantation. . . .

Alas! for some reasons unknown to me, the sky which has hitherto been so clear, seems to have become cloudy at

Worms, and the hitherto so fortunate journey of our little boat has met with a check.

As previously related I obtained from the Emperor a mandate against the writings of Luther and all others who attacked the Pope and the Holy See, for the imperial hereditary dominions and kingdoms. I always carry it with me. At present we request urgently a mandate good for the whole Empire and threatening the ban, for the imperial councillors before the coronation at Aix stated that they could not at that time draw up such an edict, although according to the decree of the Lateran council it is desirable, indeed, indispensable, as a weapon against Luther's person and against his printers. Now, however, the imperialists are sullenly crawling behind the worthless excuse that the condemnation of a German unheard by them would cause grave scandal; wherefore they say it is advisable to hear him and to summon him to the Diet. Yet they say that he shall only come to recant, and therefore they have already in good faith requested the elector to bring him to the Diet.[1] Others again advise him to demand only the recantation of the opinions condemned by general councils and emperors. So it appears that they make absolutely no mention of the present Pope and his predecessors, and leave the question of the papal primacy undiscussed. What rascality! Contrariwise, we represent to them that there can be no question of trial or investigation of that which is only too loudly proclaimed by Luther's writings; that in earlier times many heretics were thus condemned by the Popes, who have sole jurisdiction in such cases, whereas princes were obliged to execute the temporal punishment at the demand of the Pope; that finally, as St. Jerome teaches in his work against the Luciferians, "the safety of the Church depends on the absolute and supreme power of the Pope; for otherwise there would be as many schisms as priests."

Finally, yesterday evening at eleven o'clock, the Bishop of Liège took me to the Emperor, who heard my account of the whole business with great attention and satisfaction, and thereupon assured me that the honor of the Pope and of

[1] *Supra,* no. 342.

the Church would be consulted at every turn, and that he himself would act as a truly Catholic prince. The Nuncio Caracciolo, on account of illness, as I am told, was unable to attend the sitting of the German Council, to which Charles invited me the following morning. This took place under the presidency of Cardinal Matthew Lang, and was attended by the Bishop of Liège as a Prince of the Empire, by the Bishop of Trieste[1] as Imperial Councillor and by many temporal princes. As I had long ago made it my disagreeable duty thoroughly to study all the writings of the basilisk, the old ones as well as the recent, I almost knew them by heart, so I was able to give a general review of the errors repugnant to the Catholic Church and displeasing to my hearers. Then I quoted the texts of the New Testament on which Luther announces that he chiefly relies, and also the sayings of the councils and the ancient Greek and Latin Fathers which make against him, for the dog won't listen to the works of the more recent theologians and canonists, in fact, he mocks them and rejects them all as contemptible.

When I had brought the princes to the right understanding of these texts and had won their favor, I demanded an edict and other suitable measures; they referred this demand to the Emperor, to whom the purport of our interview should be communicated, and they decided to wait for the arrival of the Archbishop of Mayence, who, as Chancellor of the Empire, holds the imperial seals.

Then I betook myself to the Emperor's privy council, and had an interview with the minister of state,[2] who still held to the remarkable idea that it would be a good thing to let Luther come to the Diet. I replied that I, too, should wish it, provided he would recant, which, however, as far as I could see, he was too ambitious and proud ever to do; and if he did not recant, and on account of his safe-conduct could not be punished, the moral judgment of the world would be confused, and everyone led to the opinion that he had justified his godless doctrine. For this reason the Lu-

[1] Peter Bonomo, Bishop of Trieste 1502-46, a humanist and a capable officer.
[2] Mercurino Gattinara, whose career had begun as diplomatist at the League of Cambrai 1509; President of the Parlement of Franche-Comté 1511, Grand Chancellor of the Netherlands 1518-30.

therans passionately desire their Mohammed to come, and preach from all the house-tops that he will come and work miracles. Honored Patron, if agreeable to the Pope's instructions, and if it brings danger to no one but myself, by God I wish nothing so much as to measure myself with this Satan. If for that purpose I do not see him face to face, I hope immediately after discharge of my present mission to write against him, without appeal to the works which he rejects. So much occasion have I found to refute him in his last work[1] on which he and his followers spent all their diligence. However, as already said, it is not permissible to discuss the primacy of the Pope and submit it to the judgment of the laity, of whom many are already tainted with heresy. Moreover, what judges could one have if the supreme authority of the Pope be set aside? In his Protestation[2] Luther rejects as judges all theologians, philosophers and doctors of both laws as insignificant, contemptible men. . . .

359. ALEANDER TO CARDINAL DE' MEDICI AT ROME.

Kalkoff: *Aleander*, p. 37. Worms (Middle of December), 1520.

In my last letter I sketched the state of affairs; in this one I will say something about the persons involved.

The Emperor is a man of the best disposition, such as has hardly appeared for a thousand years; were it not for him our business would be very much complicated by private passions.

The confessor[3] has been taught by the favors shown him by the Pope to think much more favorably of Rome than he previously did, and he gives us good service; thus we see how kindnesses bear fruit.

Chièvres is certainly well intentioned and influential, although he declares that as a layman he must in this affair

[1] *The Babylonian Captivity.*
[2] *Oblatio sive Protestatio*, cf. Smith, 97f.
[3] John Glapion, born in the Province of Maine, France, became a Franciscan at Bruges. At the time of the election of Charles as Emperor he visited that monarch in Catalonia, and in 1519 or 1520 was recommended to the position of his confessor by P. de Croy, Marquis of Arscot. (*Letters and Papers of Henry VIII.*, iii. 1028.) He was then made Bishop of Toledo. He died September 15 or 22, 1522. *Nouvelle Biographie Générale.* Cf. Smith, 110-2.

rely on the advice of councillors. The only thing against him is that he desires by the most peaceful procedure to keep the Emperor in possession of all his crowns; as the Germans promise to escort the Emperor in force to be crowned at Rome, he conducts this matter of Luther as they desire, listens to them and tries to put off deciding, but they will deceive him and not fulfil one of his wishes of their own accord. . . .

The minister of state [Gattinara] is a rising man and conducts himself well, but will not do more than Chièvres wants, and the latter is strongly under the influence of Marlian.[1] . . .

Among the Germans the powerful Archbishop of Mayence shows himself in his words entirely devoted to the Pope, the Church and your Lordship, as it is both his duty and his advantage to be; yet he is so good-natured and timid, and according to ancient custom so considerate of the other princes and knights of Germany, that truly I would have wished him warmer than he has hitherto been, and I hope that he will be so in future. But though we cannot doubt of his good disposition and will, yet his zeal easily cools as he is not superior to the influence of the surrounding company of his old, respected counsellors, who are mostly Lutheran, and, what is worse, declare themselves enemies of Luther but act quite otherwise. . . .

The Saxon [Frederic the Wise] is certainly an able prince, but is led astray by his councillors, who are all disciples of Luther. He is angry at us, I hear, on account of a commendam[2] to which his natural son[3] had been appointed in Rome, notwithstanding which, and although in possession of the certificate of appointment, he was obliged, on his return to Germany, while at Bologna, at the death of the previous occupant, to pay a large sum to a cardinal. The elector, who in general is a close, taciturn man, who does not easily betray his thoughts, cannot get over this, as one of his people

---

[1] Aloisius Marlian of Milan, made Bishop of Tuy 1517. Early in 1521 he published an oration against Luther (Clemen: *Beiträge*, iii. 4). He died in September or October of the same year.

[2] *I. e.*, a benefice to which the Pope appointed.

[3] Frederic was never married, but left by Anna Weller two sons, Sebastian and Frederic von Jessen, and a daughter.

told me. His dislike of the clergy and his hatred of the Archbishop of Mayence arose from a quarrel over the city of Erfurt, which has resulted in a mortal enmity between them. Nevertheless, to my great surprise, they converse with each other like tender brothers; and yet people talk about Roman politeness and hypocrisy! At the coming Diet, with the help of the Emperor, we shall try all means to win this Saxon, and I doubt not that we shall succeed. . . .

Against us are a host of poor German nobles, who have banded under Hutten's leadership, and, thirsting after the blood of priests, would like to fall on us at once.

The German professors of the Roman and Canon laws, and priests such as those who have married, are all our opponents and avowed Lutherans. Although Luther has condemned their teachings and cries out that their writings should be burned from A to Z,[1] yet the blinded scoundrels preach and argue for him. The reason for this is, that although they understand precious little of their subjects, yet, once they have obtained their doctor's degrees, though without thorough study, they are taken into the universities and as leaders give the tone to public opinion. Worse than these is the morose tribe of humanists and poor poets with whom Germany swarms. They think they will pass for learned and particularly for masters of Greek when they declare that their opinions differ from those of the universal Church.

The followers of Reuchlin, Luther and Erasmus have published dialogues against me, and posted up verses on the imperial palace at Cologne, in which they call me a traitor to the liberal arts, a trainbearer to courtiers, a protector of sodomites, a hangman and burner of good books (Hutten's and Luther's!) and give vent to a thousand other calumnies over which, by Heaven, I can only laugh. I am simply outlawed by all Germans, and my former students are still more embittered against me and flee from me as from an outlaw; but it is nothing to me. Others want to dispute with me to defend Luther. It would be easy enough to confute them, but they can't be brought to confess they are wrong.

They refuse to let me have the lodgings engaged for me,

---

[1] In the *Address to the German Nobility*, §25; cf. Smith, p. 85.

although I pay more than anyone. They strike my name off the door, and play me a hundred other rude, bold tricks, which are very extraordinary and would hardly be credible, although I write of them in order to inform your Lordship fully. More anxiety has been caused me by the widespread rumor that Hutten and his friends have sworn to murder me. Not only do my friends advise me of this, but certain imperial secretaries warned me through the Bishop of Liège that I had better be on my guard or I would hardly escape from Germany. I feel less safe in this city than on the Campagna; wherefore, with much trouble and expense, I hired myself a little chamber near the court in the house of a poor man. I suffer unaccustomed hardship. On the icy bank of the Rhine, I, who have been accustomed to a comfortable heated room from September to May, lack a fire. I can hardly keep well. . . .

I cannot express sufficient surprise that so many clergy and monks of other orders than Luther's are devoted to him to the death. . . . Almost all the clergy except the parish priests are deeply tainted with heresy, particularly those who have been appointed from Rome are worse than the others. . . .

The book of the Arius on the *Babylonian Captivity* will soon be known at Rome well enough. Its perfect wickedness and monstrous godlessness help us, and I make the most of them. Otherwise I would have sent the book to you before. Moreover, the scoundrel has published some German writings and other foolish stuff against the bull; I hope to burn it all as soon as I can get it. . . .

360. LUTHER TO SPALATIN.

Enders, iii. 20. (WITTENBERG), December 15, 1520.

Greeting. Dear Spalatin, behold Hutten's book[1] sent to me as you see by Crotus. Please give the elector his copy; I keep mine. Good heavens! what end will there be to these innovating tracts? I begin to think that the papacy, hitherto invincible, will be broken beyond all hope, or else the last

---

[1] Containing his letters to Charles, the Princes of Germany, Albert of Brandenburg and Frederic of Saxony.

day is at hand. I expect that you have long since received copies of the letters you ask for.

Bernard Adelmann writes that the Bishop of Augsburg[1] at Eck's suggestion would have proceeded against him [Adelmann] and others, had not the Dukes of Bavaria intervened. Thus that restless man rages. Adelmann also writes that he has heard from credible authority that the Parisian theologians have decreed that all the articles condemned by the bull are quite Christian except two which they consider disputable.[2] We have heard the same from the Low Countries. God grant that it be so!

The Cardinal of Mayence has publicly forbidden my books at Magdeburg. The citizens of Halberstadt burned them, and so did the Franciscans of Cottbus. The ass Alveld writes against me again,[3] but I despise him and do not care to read him. Farewell and pray the Lord for me.

MARTIN LUTHER, *Augustinian.*

361. THE EMPEROR CHARLES V. TO FREDERIC, ELECTOR OF SAXONY.

Reichstagsakten, ii. 468, German. WORMS, December 17, 1520.

We recently wrote you from Oppenheim. [Here follows the contents of the previous letter of November 28, no. 342.] But in the meantime we have received credible information that the said Luther has come under the Pope's ban, and that all places where he is fall under the papal interdict, and that those who treat with him fall under the said hard papal ban, and we have considered that if the said Luther should come here with you, error might arise therefrom and foreign nations might animadvert on the Holy Empire and the estates, all of which, as you can see for yourself, ought to be prevented. And in order to prevent it we earnestly beg you to request the said Luther to recant all that he has written against the Pope's Holiness and the See of Rome and the

---

[1]Christopher von Stadion, Bishop of Augsburg, in October, 1520, made difficulties about publishing the bull, but did so in December. He was a patron of Erasmus.

[2]This was a false rumor.

[3]This refers (not, as Enders thinks, to the *Sermon on Marriage,* but) to two small *Sermonen über die Beichte* (confession), published by Alverd in 1520 against Luther's *Babylonian Captivity.* L. Lemmens: *Alveld,* 60, no. 3.

decrees of the councils and to submit himself to the judgment of the Pope before he departs from home, and we also beg you to bring him with you, not to Worms, but to Frankfort on the Main or some other place thereabouts, where he shall wait for further orders. But if he will not do this let him remain where he is until we have spoken to you personally on the subject.

362. ALEANDER TO CARDINAL LAWRENCE PUCCI AT ROME.

Kalkoff: *Aleander,* 51.   Worms (December 17), 1520.

... I answered Chièvres that we by no means needed to fear a meeting with Martin Luther, as though we knew that we were wrong and he was right, but that we ought not to allow further discussion of things which the Holy Father as the true judge had condemned; and that as he was the sole competent authority in the world, as history teaches, the princes and estates of the Diet had no right to assume jurisdiction in such affairs. Finally, I said that Luther, in the *Protestation,* in which (as I stated in my letter from Cologne) he demands a debate, refuses as judges all representatives of the Church, all theologians, jurists and philosophers, in short, all whom he suspects, that is, the whole learned world outside of Germany. It seems that the only court he will allow is Hutten and his miserable crowd of German humanists. I added that if Luther agreed to recant, or if the imperialists hoped that he would, his recantation must be in the form prescribed by the bull, before he could appear before the Diet, or elsewhere. In this case the Pope would forgive him as is usual in such cases, and receive him again as a son of the Church, for the Holy Father did not wish Luther's blood, but his salvation, and the good of the Church.

Chièvres answered that they had planned to summon Luther before the Diet only in certain expectation of his recantation, but that, since I had called his attention to the scandal which would result if Luther refused, he would be on his guard. He recommended me further to be present at the session of the German council early next morning. I was there, and under the presidency of Cardinal Matthew Lang and in the presence of many bishops and councillors gave, in an oration of an hour and a half, a summary of the grossest errors of this rascal, taken from all his writings, which, in order to be able to give an answer to them, I have, in spite of their voluminousness, read through and through so often that I remember every part of them. First I touched on the points which would particularly offend the laymen, the married doctors in the council. Then to refute him I cited many sayings of the oecumenical councils, and of the Greek and Latin Fathers, without daring to take a word from the theologians of the last seven centuries, for Luther will have nothing to do with them. So I, poor man, have wasted the good time which otherwise I would have devoted to the study of Peter Lombard or St. Thomas Aquinas or the Nominalists, in testing the doctrines of this wretch. I must consider this time as good as lost. Thus we see how baneful is this assassin to everyone.

As in support of their opinions on the papal power, purgatory and invocation of saints, the Lutherans appeal to the doctrines of the Greek Church, which, in their opinion, often differ from those of the Roman, I laid before them many citations from Greek Fathers and the bull of the Florentine Council in Greek and Latin. This bull, the original of which I discovered in the archives of the church at Worms, testifies the complete union of the Eastern and Western Churches, achieved through the adherence of the Emperor John Palaeologus. The German court was completely dumfounded at sight of it, and felt lively satisfaction at this confutation of that rascal's assertions. Not content with that, I spent every day of rest looking through old libraries in German cities, and thereby I found many histories of the time of Charlemagne and the Ottos, in which the title "Papa Romanae et Universalis Ecclesiae Pontifex" was frequently used. As I held these documents from their own libraries with the title in letters an inch high under their eyes, my opponents became helpless and numb with fright, and my friends were satisfied and strengthened in their opinions. As the whole quarrel is about the authority of the Pope, I made thorough studies on the subject. In his new blasphemous book on the Babylonian captivity, this Mohammed says that there are no distinctions among Christian men; that where the Pope can dispense, every simple layman has full freedom both for himself and for his neighbor, and other monstrosities which I fear to repeat. At the close of my address, all the members of the council were for us. . . .

On the same day the Bishop of Liège gave a dinner to Chièvres and other princes, to which he also invited me. We talked much of Luther's writings. There was present a certain magnate who had Luther's popular works in his head and was deeply tinctured with heresy, but whose name, as long as I am here, I dare not trust to paper, as little as I dare to set down that of another still more powerful and still worse heretic, for by so doing I might, if they found it out while I was still in Germany, bring a storm about my head. This gentleman, after we had risen from table and closed the doors, brought up many points, which I was able to answer in the hearing of all with such skill that he was completely won for us, though I do not know whether he will remain so. Finally, Chièvres and all the others were much edified, and began to hope that the affair was at last getting on the right track.

The whole complicated affair should not be treated in such a way as to arouse the doubts of the court or the displeasure of the Saxon Elector or of his friends, nor even should it be guided by the wish to make them more complaisant to our Lord the Pope in other matters. So I earnestly begged Chièvres and the other ministers not to confound the matter of faith with other special interests on which the Pope and Emperor were negotiating, for the latter would suffer severe losses should the Lutheran doctrine spread wider. For as in his last book Luther sets out to kill all obedience to the spiritual authorities, so he secretly wished to do against the temporal powers. I clearly proved this from his book, and the proof greatly helped our side.

Yesterday morning after the consecration of the Archbishop of Palermo,[1] at which the Emperor, the court and the

---

[1] John de Carondelet, Primate of Sicily, a Burgundian, who attained high

cardinals were present, the Emperor of his own accord asked the meaning of the text: "Whatsoever you loose on earth shall be loosed in heaven."[1] When he had heard the explanation he replied with disdain: "What will this wretch of a Luther reply to that?"

Those two great lords,[2] whose names I dare not mention, always have Luther's German books in their hands and publicly defend them. When recently one of them spoke about them too freely in the Emperor's room, the Emperor said to him, although he was a powerful man who for many reasons had to be treated with consideration, that he did not care for such words, and if the lord insisted on repeating them he had better stay at home. This sounds even ruder in French. When the lord heard it he blushed deeply and held his peace.

363. ALEANDER TO THE VICE-CHANCELLOR, CARDINAL JULIUS DE' MEDICI.

Kalkoff: *Aleander,* 56.   WORMS (December 18, 1520).

. . . That basilisk, the Elector of Saxony, said to-day to three electors that he knew certainly that the Pope would give Luther a rich bishopric and the cardinal's hat to get him to recant. He said he knew this positively. The Archbishop of Trier assured me that he had heard from the Saxon that the Pope had already made Luther such an offer. He asked me the facts, and opined that it would cause general scandal. I told him the truth and said that if any man would know of such an offer I would be the one. Your Lordship must not be surprised that Frederic is conscienceless enough to invent a pack of lies, inasmuch as he does not fear to persecute the Church of God. He thinks every means right to accomplish his devilish end.

These scoundrels so honor Luther that some of them in a public debate with a Spaniard held in the crowded marketplace, said that he was without sin and had never erred, and

---

office under Maximilian and in 1522 was made President of the Privy Council. He died in 1544.

[1] Matthew, xvi. 19.

[2] As a mere conjecture it may be suggested that one of these lords was Francis von Sickingen, with whom the Emperor had some words on this subject at Worms. *Cf.* Grisar, i. 344f.

that he was therefore to be more highly esteemed than St. Augustine, who was a sinner and both could err and had erred. So, recently, they have made likenesses of him with the Dove over his head and with the cross of the Lord, and on another sheet with an aureole. The people buy these pictures, kiss them and carry them even in the palace. Your Lordship can see from this what people we have to deal with. Not the good old Catholic Germany! God grant that worse does not come to pass!

The good Erasmus daily sends messengers with letters here, in which, although no one accuses him, he protests that he has had nothing to do with certain books, of which he writes that Luther has denied having written them. The result of his excuses is that the Emperor and many important men have of their own accord come to believe that he is the author of these books, as I, too, in my letters have stated, although I now deny it. I am much surprised that in Rome people have shown my despatches to others who, it seems, have informed Erasmus about them, so that now he loudly complains of me and urges his friends to attack me, which, however, does not worry me much. I wish he would have some consideration at least for the faith and the Church, and of me as long as I am in this dangerous land. But if he continues to speak evil of others, he will find someone who can tell much worse things about him and with more truth. . . .

364. ELECTOR FREDERIC OF SAXONY TO THE EMPEROR CHARLES AT WORMS.

Reichstagsakten, ii. 470. ALSTET, December 20, 1520.

Most gracious Lord. Your Imperial Majesty's letter from Oppenheim on November 28 has been received becomingly and humbly by me. [Here follows the contents of the letter.] I humbly give your Majesty to know that I have never undertaken to answer for Dr. Martin's writing or preaching, and do not now, but have left him to answer for himself, as I have often written to his Holiness the Pope and to his ambassadors. But I wrote to Chièvres and Nassau humbly to beg your Majesty to do nothing against Luther before he is heard, so that the truth whether he has erred in his writings might be established; for the said Luther has always offered on sufficient guarantee to come out and be heard by fair, honorable and impartial judges, and if he is overcome by the Holy Scriptures to let it be shown him, as he has explained at length in his printed *Offer and Protest*. That and nothing else induced me to make my petition to your Majesty through the said gentlemen. I had hoped that Luther's opponents would give the matter a rest for a while; but now that the Pope's nuncio and others have thought fit to act against me, forcing themselves into my business, it is necessary that I should propose my plan. I am informed that since I departed from your Majesty, Luther's books, without trial or proof from Holy Scripture, have been burned at Cologne, Mayence and elsewhere.[1] This I did not expect, but rather hoped that, if they had no respect for Luther, they at least might for me. But as this happened against my humble prayer and against the promise of the Pope's nuncio, and as I cannot discover from your Majesty's letter that it was done at your command, and as perhaps before this reaches your Majesty, Luther may have done something in revenge, it appears to me hard, as your Majesty may graciously imagine, to bring Luther with me to the Diet. Wherefore I have caused all this to be shown to your Majesty, and humbly beg you graciously to spare me and not to insist that I bring Luther with me to Worms, and not to take it ill that I omit doing so for the said reasons, for otherwise I am ready humbly to obey your Majesty's wishes.

. . .

365. CASPAR HEDIO TO ZWINGLI AT ZURICH.

Corpus Reformatorum, xciv. 376.   (MAYENCE), December 21, 1520.

. . . We burned Luther here in obedience to the Pope's decree, but it was a ridiculous affair. Some swear that it was not Luther who was burned, but Aeneas Silvius; some that it was Eck and some Prierias. But whatever books were burned, it was done to hurt Luther. The people almost threw Aleander into a cesspool. It has been decreed by the council of princes to summon Luther to Worms to give an answer for his writings. Good Heavens! how the Roman legates

[1]The elector left Cologne on November 7; the books seem to have been burned on the 12th. At Mayence they were burned on November 29.

withstand this! They don't want a heretic to be heard. They make many threats, but I think their efforts are vain. We shall soon see what will happen. . . .

366. THOMAS MURNAR TO LUTHER.
Enders, iii. 26, German. (STRASSBURG, before December 24, 1520.)

All Christendom, Martin Luther, would rejoice in you as a particularly learned man, if only you did not use your learning and clear reason to hurt the fatherland and destroy the faith and the laws of the Fathers, and if you did not enjoy writing with a sword as much as anyone. For this cause instead of the honor which we owe your reason, we are, alas! obliged to defend ourselves against you as against a renegade enemy, and we must change our fraternal and patriotic favor to disfavor, against our heart's desire, for we would rather see your praise, honor and glory as a born German and an able man than your shame. But as with unwashed hands you have attacked your and our Christian faith, you force us to summon Emperor, kings, princes and lords to defend the truth against you, although you, too, are not ashamed to summon our pious Emperor and all the serene nobility of Germany to protect your false, seditious, senseless and criminal plans. Truly you might have done them more honor than to ask them to help you establish your unchristian lies, and to accomplish your unreasonable, dishonorable venture. You made yourself their counsellor, against the ancient proverb, and though no one asked your opinion, you advised that pious young scion of Austria, our Emperor, at the beginning of his reign to snatch two crowns from the Pope,[1] who would have enough honor and too much with the third, also to abolish all the cardinals but twelve,[2] to destroy cloisters, to abolish and make a bonfire of the Canon law, throwing away the child with the bath [as the proverb is], and butchering the cow with the calf. This is a warm proposition truly, fresh from the bath-room,[3] advice hot enough to have been given to King

[1] This refers to various attacks on the "triple crown" of the Pope in the *Address to the German Nobility*. Smith, 82f.
[2] All these alleged proposals have some counterparts in the *Address to the Nobility*. Smith, *ibid*.
[3] At that time the best heated room in most German houses.

Rehoboam by the young nobles at the beginning of his reign.[1] These proposals are strong enough to stop the Rhine flowing; stabbing, murdering, hewing and smiting which show nothing but a squinting, near-sighted vision, which no one would follow unless he wanted to destroy land and people. If you had only known the nature of the Austrian princes, you would not have advised our peaceful scion of Austria to such warlike acts, for his race has no love for blood, but detests it. You say you offer this advice as a court fool,[2] and though a clergyman, utter unseemly jests and idle words. You think, when you have poured forth all your delirium, falsehood and reviling that you have fastened fools' bells on everyone, just like Erasmus of Rotterdam, who speaks truth in the person of folly; but you have not succeeded as well as he did. As you are a fool, we must answer you according to your folly, as Solomon says,[3] so that you won't think that you are a wise man. We should willingly have given you your ordinary titles of doctor and reverend, had you not transformed yourself into a fool. Wherefore it befits us to treat you as a fool, for in truth you are such an one that you call Pope Julius a bloodsucker, and the present Pope with his friends thieves, gluttons, rascals and all such opprobrious names. If you think you have anything against him, it would be more honorable, reverend, seemly and pious to speak of him by his customary names, and to present your grievance to him with Christian moderation, in such wise that it might be remedied and you helped. But you want to arouse our young Emperor and liege lord against the princes of hell, as you say, and you call it a game, which, if it is not begun in the fear of God, will drench the whole world with blood. You want to move us to a great rebellion. But I see no one following you with spear or halberd, nor any who wants to be as foolish as you are. For truly they know that everything that you pretend to reform, can be reformed without any tumult, in time and with gentleness, by the prudence of our noble Em-

[1] 1 Kings, xii.
[2] So Luther modestly says in his introduction to the *Address to the German Nobility*, Smith, 80.
[3] Proverbs, xxvi. 5.

peror and of our electors, and everything can thus be set in order.

Wherefore we deeply resent it that you show so little honor to the said princes and lords, and that with many German books you try to arouse and make seditious the commonalty, although you ought to know that as soon as they came together they would of themselves find out what ought to be done without following you. So I desire briefly to warn you not to disobey the Emperor's command by disputing and raising questions about our faith before the unlearned. Then we will all help to get your many misdeeds and libels forgiven, hoping that you will turn to Christian moderation, and quietly with us praise God the Lord. Amen.

367. CHIÈVRES TO ELECTOR FREDERIC OF SAXONY.
Reichstagsakten, ii. 467, note. German.   WORMS, December 24, 1520.
Answer to Frederic's letter of December 14, *supra,* no. 357.

. . . As to Luther's affair, I have no doubt that now your illustrious Lordship has received the letter of his Imperial and Catholic Majesty [November 28, no. 342] and afterwards another from this city [December 17, no. 361] in which his Imperial Majesty says that Luther shall not be brought here except on certain conditions. . . . And as his Imperial Majesty greatly desires your presence here, I beg you again and again to come so that you can confer with his Majesty and all can be settled by prudent counsel.

368. THE ELECTOR FREDERIC OF SAXONY TO THE EMPEROR CHARLES V. AT WORMS.
Reichstagsakten, ii. 473.   SPANENBERG, December 28, 1520.
The letter begins with recapitulating the contents of Charles' letter of December 17.

. . . Your Majesty's letter of December 17 I received on the 27th of the same month with due respect. . . . In my letter I humbly showed your Majesty that it appeared to me hard to bring Luther with me to the Diet . . . and as your Majesty among other things has graciously bidden me to leave Luther at home while you treat of the affair with me orally I have a humble hope that your Majesty has noticed my answer. . . .

28

369. ANDREW ROSSO TO A FRIEND.

Marino Sanuto: *Diarii.* Extracts edited by G. M. Thomas in *Martin Luther und die Reformationsbewegung in Deutschland, 1520-32, in Auszügen aus Marino Sanutos Diarien.* Ansbach, 1883, p. 5. (Italian.) P. Kalkoff: *Briefe, Depeschen und Berichte über Luther vom Wormser Reichstage, 1521.* Halle, 1898, p. 25. (German translation.) R. Brown: *Calendar of State Papers . . . in Venice,* London, 1869, iii. 147. (English translation, wrongly dated December 20.)

WORMS, December 30, 1520.

In future I refer to the books cited above as "Sanuto," "Kalkoff: *Briefe*" and "Brown."

Rosso was secretary of Francis Cornaro, who in 1520 was Venetian ambassador with the Emperor.

Everywhere where the court goes they have not only burned images of Luther and all his books, but they would have done the same with him if they caught him, unless he confessed his errors. This persecution is very recent. Letters to certain persons have been received here, in which there are many monstrous utterances against ecclesiastical ordinances. However, if he only inveighed against the morals of the Roman curia, people would wink at it. But among other things he now declares that as he has learned for certain that his best books have been burned in several places, he will also show the Pope what he can and dares do in the place where he lives, in the land of the Elector of Saxony, and so he now burns books on the canon law. News of this fact has been received in several ways. Truly that is a great event, and the more significant because both in Saxony and the rest of Germany he has a large following. Important and well-informed men have told me that he certainly has twenty thousand comrades of like mind. Even if the Elector of Saxony wanted to drive him out of his present place of residence or otherwise punish him, these Germans would not allow it. Many are also sure that he stands in close relations with Erasmus of Rotterdam and other Dutch savants. Truly Luther is an evil plague and an incurable evil!

The papal Nuncio [Caracciolo] and Aleander de Motta, who is the special commissioner for this affair, do all that they can. Aleander has been advised to be careful of his personal safety, so many threats have come in from different quarters.

We shall see what measures will be adopted by the coming Diet.

370. JAMES LATOMUS TO RUDOLPH VON MONCKEDAMIS, CURATE OF GOUDA.

H. DeJongh, appendix, p. 69ff.   Louvain, December 31, 1520.

This long letter is an apology for the action of the Louvain theologians in condemning Luther. I only reproduce the two most interesting passages, which are apparently directed against Erasmus's defence of Luther.

Although it was not necessary for us to give the reason of our condemnation of Luther, inasmuch as the Apostolic See approved our side and rejected the side of our opponent, yet, as there are still not lacking some who, as though fascinated by the writings of Luther and his friends, think that Luther relies on the authority of the Bible and the ancients, and that we are supported only by the writings of recent authors —although both ancient and modern authorities follow the same path of truth—I have collected reasons and testimonies only from the Scripture and the ancients, and endeavored to show that the Scripture and the ancients were not interpreted by Luther in their natural sense. You will judge of my success.

Let me briefly make you acquainted with the method of the theological faculty. More than two years ago when Luther's book[1] was printed and published everywhere, it came into our hands and on account of the sayings of many men was strongly suspected of false doctrine; it was then diligently and privately read by the various professors, and was examined several times in a general meeting. Thus at length by common counsel some articles were extracted verbatim, enough, as it seemed, for our purpose, for it would have taken long and have been unnecessary to collect them all. But as the faculty did not wish in so great a matter to rely on its own wisdom, as soon as it was rumored, though falsely, as was afterwards found out, that our very reverend Bishop

---

[1] *I. e.*, the collection of Luther's *Works* printed by Froben in October, 1518.

of Liège favored this doctrine,[1] the faculty sent to him three professors, whom he received with much kindness, to whom he declared, on the word of a priest, that he had never seen nor read Luther's book, and that he was so far from favoring a dangerous unknown thing, that, as became a bishop, he promised us his aid. When he remembered the recent success that Reuchlin's cause had won (for it was then awaiting judgment at Rome, although all the universities had agreed to condemn it, an action in which the Apostolic See later concurred) the bishop took care, before our condemnation of Luther was published, to submit it to the examination of the Cardinal of Tortosa, that it might come forth fortified by his wisdom and authority. His letter[2] printed at the head of the condemnation shows what his opinion was. Hence you see how ripely and with how little precipitancy this affair was treated, so that it ought certainly to satisfy a reader little learned or much occupied, and prevent his agreement with Luther's errors.

That he is said to be a good man is nothing against us, who have not said that he was bad; but whatever he is, it is certain that his writings are not good. We have not condemned him, but his errors. . . .

We always deny the allegation that we condemn in Luther what is read as pious in Augustine, Cyprian and other orthodox teachers. . . .

371. BONIFACE AMERBACH TO BEATUS RHENANUS.

Burckhardt-Biedermann, 144.   (AVIGNON, end of 1520.)

I cannot sufficiently wonder at what you write of Luther. Things are so bad, if the report be true, that he dare not show his face in public. *O tempora, O mores!* Where will this tyranny bring us? What the devil is this madness, what plague is it, that their vain-speaking greed should be preferred to Christian purity? Is it thus that the Christian religion will pack up and leave? . . . What is more blameless than Luther, what more honest than Reuchlin, what more constant than Hutten? I am uncommonly sorry that Eras-

---

[1] In Erasmus's letter to Luther, *supra*, no. 155.
[2] *Supra*, 202.

mus has become entangled with these curial toys, since formerly he thought nothing worse than their triumphs.

372. JOHN VON STAUPITZ TO WENZEL LINK.

Zeitschrift für hist. Theologie, vii. (1837), 123. W. Reindell: *W. Linck aus Colditz,* 263.   SALZBURG, January 4, 1521.

Greeting and kind regards. Our land is full of rumors about Martin, and our eyes are in suspense, waiting to see which shall conquer, power or truth. To us also has come the roar of the lion [Leo] seeking whom he may devour. For our very reverend Cardinal [Lang] has been instructed to compel me to assert that Martin's opinions are respectively heretical, erroneous and offensive to pious ears, and to reject them in the presence of a notary and witnesses. But as I am unable to recant and reject opinions which I never asserted and which are not mine, I begged the lord cardinal to have me excused.[1] I know not what will happen. It would be sufficient to have written this concerning me to the Father, and perhaps one other. I thought I was going to enjoy peace at last, and now this perplexing trial comes up. I am not able to fly with wings, as I am not distinguished either for learning or for holy life, and yet I think it the worst impiety to desert the truth. Therefore I shall take the wholesome cup and invoke the name of the Lord. Reverend Father, pray give me your counsel and aid. Martin has begun a hard task and acts with great courage, divinely inspired; I stammer and am a child needing milk. Farewell, reverend Father, and do not desert me under this dark star at the back of the world.[2] My fellow-captives Mayr[3] and Bessler[4] salute you, desiring to see the face of your Reverence and to drink wine together, which is excellent at Salzburg. They promise to bear adversity with you calmly.

[1] Staupitz had now retired to Salzburg to get peace. He signed an equivocal declaration that he submitted to the Pope. For this and Luther's answer, *cf.* Smith, 107ff.

[2] "Nos zum finstern Stern in culo mundi"; an inelegant expression.

[3] One of Staupitz's oldest friends, who had matriculated with him at Tübingen 1497; later Prior at Munich; in 1508-9 went on business of the Order to Italy. Kolde: *Augustiner-Congregation,* 213, 236.

[4] Also an old friend, who had succeeded Staupitz as Prior of Munich. In 1505 he made a trip to Italy, on business of the Order, and was detained there forcibly for four years. Later Prior of Nuremberg, and after accompanying Staupitz to Salzburg, Prior of Cologne, where we last hear of him in 1529. Kolde, index.

373. THOMAS BLAURER TO AMBROSE BLAURER.

Kolde: *Analecta*, 25.   T. Schiess: *Briefwechsel der Blaurer*, 1908, i. 29. (Leipsic, January 4, 1521).

This letter is dated "pridie nonas Decembres, 1521," an evident mistake corrected by Kolde to December 4, 1520, and by Schiess as above.

Ambrose Blaurer (1492-1564) and his younger brother Thomas took a considerable part in the Swiss Reformation, particularly at Constance. Ambrose studied at Tübingen, where he learned to know Melanchthon. Thomas spent part of the years 1520-21 at Wittenberg in study. He was now, apparently, on a visit to Leipsic. The correspondence of the brothers, with a long biographical introduction, is being published by T. Schiess, to be complete in four volumes, of which three have appeared.

I recently confessed to Luther who exhorted me to take the Lord's Supper which I did frequently during this holiday time. Melanchthon has entirely left human learning to devote himself to sacred; and he exhorts us to do the same with such good purpose that there is no one near Wittenberg who does not carry a Bible in his hand. Luther lectures on the Psalms, Melanchthon on Paul, others on other things. But all have conspired against Luther and even against Melanchthon. . . .

The Elector Frederic lately bade Luther prepare himself, for he will be summoned to the Diet at Worms. . . .

374. BEATUS RHENANUS TO BONIFACE AMERBACH AT AVIGNON.

Briefwechsel des Beatus Rhenanus, 266.   Basle, January 7, 1521.

As you are far from us I know that you are anxious to learn what is done here, especially as the whole of Germany is agitated in a way which I think never happened before. Unless the Pope and the princes have the wisdom to deal rightly with this affair, I fear that it will not end peacefully. Luther will not be heard by the princes at Worms because Aleander persuaded the Emperor that this should not be done, first, because heretics are eloquent; second, because no heretic should be listened to; finally, because if Luther should come to Worms, the city would have to be put under an interdict, which would make any action of the princes illegitimate. Clever reasons! But Luther is given permission to come to

Frankfort and there to wait for the edict of the princes. Francis von Sickingen and Ulrich von Hutten, with all the nobles, have undertaken to defend Luther. Aleander burned Luther's books at Mayence. On the first day nothing was done, for when the hangman standing on the platform asked whether he whose books were to be burned had been legitimately condemned, the whole multitude replied that he had not yet been condemned. At this the hangman leapt down, saying that he would execute judgment against no one save against him who had been convicted by due process of law. The whole thing was made a mockery and Aleander was so reviled that he will wish he had never undertaken this duty. He hardly escaped being stoned. They called him a Jew, a traitor, a scoundrel and what not. The next day, when he had made loud complaint and had said that an injury was done to the Pope, whose commands were despised, he by his threats forced the Cardinal of Mayence and the canons to cause some books to be burned in the market-place by a gravedigger, for the hangman refused to officiate. No spectators were present save a few market-women. A bitter song was published against Aleander; they say it was posted at night in many places on the house where he lives. Truly he will buy dearly the miter or red hat he expects as reward for this service.

Now hear what Luther did at Wittenberg in revenge. He burned the Pope's bull, the whole canon law and books of the *Sentences,* and that publicly; so it is announced from the Emperor's court. He has published a book on the *Babylonian Captivity* in which he treats with freedom great matters. They say that what he has hitherto written is nothing compared with this. . .

375. FELIX ULSCENIUS TO WOLFGANG CAPITO.

J. W. Baum: *Capito und Butzer,* 1860, p. 54. (German translation of Latin original.)   WITTENBERG, January 13, 1521.

The man of God, Luther, mightily expounds the Scripture. I often hear him; he preaches very freely. My pupils do not miss a single one of his sermons, by which they direct their life, and they consider themselves superlatively fortunate to live in a time when they can see a man like Luther and hear his evangelic doctrine. There is nothing here at Wittenberg to keep anyone from studying; the place is pleasant, the people well-behaved, board is good, and drunkenness, so hurtful to the Muses, is here unknown. Even if my pupils desired to live a dissipated life, they would, I feel safe in affirming, be withheld by the example of others, both sons of the nobles and of commons, so perfect is the discipline and the love of the sciences at Wittenberg.

376. LUTHER TO STAUPITZ AT SALZBURG.
Enders, iii. 70.   WITTENBERG, January 14, 1521.

Greeting. When we were at Augsburg, most reverend Father, while conversing of my cause you said to me: "Remember, brother, that you have begun this in the name of our Lord Jesus Christ." I received this saying not as yours, but as given me through you, and I have kept it in my mind ever since.

Now I attack you with your own saying; remember that you said it to me. All hitherto has been child's play; now it begins to be serious, and, as you said, unless God accomplishes it, it cannot be accomplished, for everyone can see and no one can deny that it is in the hand of God. Who has planned it? What have men thought? There is such a tremendous commotion that I do not think it can be quieted except by the last day. So great is the determination on each side.

The papacy is not now what it was yesterday and the day before. Even if it excommunicates me and burns my books and if it should kill me, something portentous is at the door. How happy would the Pope have been had he tried by good means to make peace, rather than by force and whirlwind to destroy Luther. I burned the Pope's books and bull, at first trembling and in prayer, but now happier than any other deed of my whole life has made me, for they are more pestilent than I believed.

Emser has written against me in German[1] at the hest of the raging Duke George, who in his court proposes to act

[1] *Wider das unchristliche buch Martini Luthers Augustiners, an den Tewtschen Adel.* . . .

most impiously against me, breathing out threats and slaughter.

I was summoned by a letter of the Emperor to the elector, but now he has reconsidered it and has recalled the first letter by a second. God knows what will happen. Our Vicar Wenzel Link has gone to Nuremberg. Teschius[1] is at Grimma; he is said to have left; God keep him! All flourishes here as hitherto. Hutten has arraigned the bull with witty notes against the Pope, and is planning further steps in this affair.

They burned me thrice, at Louvain, Cologne and Mayence, at the latter place with derision and danger to those who did it. Thomas Murnar has written furiously against me, not to mention that barefoot ass of Leipsic.[2] Farewell, Father; pray for the Word of God and for me. I am carried hither and thither in the floods.

MARTIN LUTHER, *Augustinian.*

377. LUTHER TO WENZEL LINK.

Enders, iii. 72. WITTENBERG, January 14, 1521.

Greeting. Reverend Father, I received your letter from Merseburg. But how could I write when I knew not whither the Spirit of God would snatch you? I was much surprised at your suggestion that I should publish a book saying that I had never written anything against the civil power, for all my writings show that plainly. But how can I stop the mouths of everyone, when many will not read my books solely because they have heard that my books cannot be read without the reader being either reproved by them or believing in them? What can I do to such impudent men?

I was summoned by the Emperor, but now my summons is recalled. Emser writes against me; I will meet that beast, for he acts at the command of his raging Duke George. We have heard evil of Teschius. Everything with us is as formerly.

[1] By Teschius, otherwise unknown, is it possible that Luther meant Wolfgang Zeschau, Augustinian Prior of Grimma, and later Master of the Hospice of St. John at the same place? Luther speaks of him on November 5, 1518 (Enders, i. 276), and on July 26, 1519, mentions him in connection with Staupitz's and Link's visit to Grimma, saying that he fears Zeschau will be dismissed. *Supra*, no. 166.

[2] Alveld: the Franciscans were popularly called "barefoot monks." Alveld had just published a book on marriage. Lemmens, 55.

I received my hundred gulden,[1] and I rejoiced the prior[2] with the money and more strongly with the Lord.

Farewell and pray for the Word, seeing this tumultuous tumult; perhaps this is the flood predicted for the year 1524.[3] Melanchthon greets you.   Yours,

MARTIN LUTHER.

378. LUTHER TO SPALATIN AT WORMS.

Enders, iii. 73.   WITTENBERG, January 16, 1521.

Greeting. Dear Spalatin, I send Hutten's letter to me, with the bull and other works by him, as you see, and also Bucer's letters, of which one, as you see, was injured when it reached me, perhaps having been rubbed by one of the messengers. I sent some pages of my Latin *Assertion* to you before, now I send the whole of it with the supplement. Do not think it bitter; the German translation will be smoother and simpler. I had to put in a little spice for Latin stomachs. Emser has risen against me; the Lord be my counsellor.

You see what Hutten wants. I would not fight for the gospel[4] with force and slaughter. The world is overcome by the Word,[5] the Church is saved, and will even be reformed, by the Word, and Antichrist also will hereafter, as formerly, be restrained without violence by the Word. I send my letter to the elector.[6] I read with grief the last letter of Charles recalling his former one; what hope can there be there, when this is what they think and write? The Lord's will be done.

To-day I saw the Margrave of Brandenburg[7] and other princes[8] for, wishing to see a man,[9] they summoned me.

---

[1] *I. e.*, those left him by Schmiedberg, *cf. supra*, November 13, 1520, no. 335.

[2] Helt.

[3] The signs in the sky had caused someone to prophesy a deluge for the year 1524. References in Enders, *loc. cit.*

[4] At about this time the word "evangelium" in Luther's writings began to take on the meaning "evangelic faith" or "evangelic Church."

[5] 1 John, v. 4f.

[6] Luther, however, did not write this letter until January 25; translated Smith, *op. cit.*, 106.

[7] Luther means the Elector Joachim I., born 1474, reigned 1499-1535, now on his way from Berlin to Worms. He was a strong papist.

[8] Among them was Duke Albert VII. of Mecklenburg (1486-1547), who began to reign in conjunction with his uncle and brothers in 1503. When the land was partitioned on May 7, 1520, he got the Duchy of Güstrow. In 1531 he tried unsuccessfully for the Danish crown.

[9] Or "the man."

I received the hundred gulden left to me through Taubenheim; Schart also gave fifty, so that I begin to fear that God is thus rewarding me. I protested against being thus enriched by them, saying that if they continued I would return it or throw it away. What need have I of so much money? I gave half to the Prior [Helt] thus making him happy.

The younger prince[1] wrote me graciously, telling me what his uncle the elector answered about my cause.

I have sent my *Postilla* on the Epistles and Gospels to the press. I will dedicate them to the elector unless you advise otherwise. . . . MARTIN LUTHER, *Augustinian.*

379. ULRICH VON HUTTEN TO GEORGE SPALATIN AT WORMS.

Böcking, ii. 4.   EBERNBURG, January 16, 1521.

Although I was going to write you anyway, yet I must now do so on behalf of Sickingen. He bids me ask you first of all to use your elector as an intercessor with the Emperor for Reuchlin, as he himself is doing by a letter to the Emperor which I translated into Latin. Then he says to warn Luther to take all possible care of himself in every place, for he knows certainly of ambushes which it will be difficult for Luther to avoid. He fears all the more because Luther seems to be quite calm and to despise danger. I myself add warning in this regard. Now what is the real reason, famous Spalatin, that Luther does not write even a word to me? Please tell me whether you and he received in Saxony the books and letters I sent you, for I sent him two of my pamphlets. Does Luther not think there is any reason for writing to me in such a revolution? Please inform me of everything, especially what we may hope from your elector. I have written to you twice or thrice to sound his mind and find out what he would do if the papists resorted to arms.

---

[1] John Frederic (1503-1554), son of Duke John of Saxony, whom he succeeded as elector in August, 1532. A pupil of Spalatin, he became an even more ardent Lutheran than his father and uncle. The Schmalkaldic war between the Protestants and the Emperor was disastrous to him. Defeated and captured in the battle of Mühlberg April 24, 1547, he was kept a prisoner for five years, his electoral vote was given to Maurice of Albertine Saxony, together with Wittenberg and the surrounding territory. His life in three volumes by G. Mentz, Jena, 1903-9.

If you have found out anything and dare to communicate it to another in good faith, write in confidence. Farewell.

380. ELECTOR FREDERIC OF SAXONY TO HIS BROTHER, DUKE JOHN.

Förstemann: *Neues Urkundenbuch,* i. 5.   German.

WORMS, January 16, 1521.

. . . I am glad that the books I sent pleased you and my son.[1] Please tell the dear boy that I am informed that the cardinals and Romanists with their followers are taking counsel against Dr. Luther to put him under the ban of the Empire and persecute him to the uttermost. But there are many other people who wish him well. God grant graciously that it be for our good. . . .

381. POPE LEO X. TO THE EMPEROR CHARLES V. AT WORMS.

Förstemann: *Neues Urkundenbuch,* i. 27.   ROME, January 18, 1521.

Most famous Son in Christ. Greeting and the apostolic blessing! Elsewhere by our letters and nuncios we have signified to your Highness that many false and heretical errors have been disseminated in your German nation by a certain Martin Luther, and have been published in printed books, and that some persons, seduced by the errors of Martin who seeks cause for rebellion, have added unto his errors others of their own. It is our proper duty to purge the vineyard of the Lord from such brambles, and, as much as in us is, under the divine guidance, to preserve the unity of the Church and to oppose scandals, particularly when they are widespread. Wherefore, after taking diligent counsel with our brothers, we condemned his errors partly as false and heretical, partly as alien to Christian piety and wounding good consciences, and we ordered the books of the said Martin containing these errors or others to be burned with fire, and we commanded Martin himself to abstain from all preaching and disputation and within a given time to burn his own books and retract the errors contained in them, and to inform us of the re-

---

[1] *I. e.,* Frederic's nephew, Duke John Frederick.

traction or else to come to us under our safe-conduct. He contemptuously refused to obey these commands, and is obstinate in his false opinion, when he should have preferred to have followed better advice. Wherefore we have declared that this abuser of our patience and his aiders and abettors are contumacious heretics. . . .

Wherefore we exhort your Highness in the Lord and require you by the bowels of the mercy of Almighty God, according to the custom of your predecessors, who in doubtful and dangerous matters always assisted the Roman Pontiffs, to act as a Catholic prince, and to agree with us, as you ought, in all things which can be done by you for the maintenance of the Catholic faith, and that you will fulfil all that we have spoken of by the issuance of declaratory letters. Thus it will become known to all the faithful by the general edict to be published by your care in all places of Germany, that the said Martin and his heretical aiders and abettors are to be smitten with those punishments which we decreed against them in our letter, unless they recant. . . .

382. LUTHER TO SPALATIN AT WORMS.

Enders, iii. 75. WITTENBERG, January 21, 1521.

Greeting. Dear Spalatin, I expect you have received or soon will receive what I sent you with my *Assertion* by Taubenheim. Meantime, I have read your letter to Stromer. My German translation of the *Assertion* is in press. I send a specimen of it; it is better than in Latin. . . .

They say the Bishops of Meissen and Merseburg have decided to execute the bull; the Lord's will be done. We have no other news; you have new experiences daily. Farewell in *Christ our Lord*.[1] Amen.

MARTIN LUTHER, *Augustinian*.

383. CUTHBERT TUNSTALL TO CARDINAL WOLSEY.

Brewer: *Reign of Henry VIII.* (1884), i. 615, English.

WORMS, January 21, 1521.

Tunstall (1474-1579) studied at Oxford and Cambridge and in Italy. Returned to England by December, 1506, and in 1509 became

---
[1] Greek.

Chancellor to Archbishop Warham of Canterbury. He was Ambassador to Charles in 1515, 1519 and 1520-1. In 1522 made Bishop of London, Bishop of Durham 1530. He remained a Catholic. His writings on mathematics enjoyed some reputation (Rabelais, i. chap. 23). Life in *Dictionary of National Biography*.

The Germans are everywhere so addicted to Luther, that rather than he should be oppressed by the Pope's authority (who hath already condemned his opinions) the people will spend a hundred thousand of their lives. They have informed the Emperor that he is a good and virtuous man, besides his learning. He offereth to make his defence and revoke those opinions which he cannot defend by Scripture.

After he perceived that he should not be permitted to come to the Diet hither, as once it was accorded and safe-conduct granted unto him (which at the insistence of the Pope's orator was revoked) despairing to be heard in his defence, he did openly in the town of Wittenberg gather the people of the University together, and burn the decretals, etc., as books erroneous, as he there declared; which his declaration he put in print in the Dutch [German] tongue and sent it all about the country, which declaration by some idle fellow hath been translated into Latin, which I send your Grace herein enclosed, to the intent ye may see it and burn it when ye have done and also that your Grace may call before you the printers and booksellers, and give them strait charge that they bring none of his books into England nor translate them into English, etc.[1]

The matter is run so far the princes cannot appease it. The original was the great sum of money that goeth yearly to Rome for annates, which the country would be rid of, and the benefices to be given by the Pope to such persons as do serve Rome, unlearned, as cooks and horsekeepers, etc.; so the easiest I can think will be that the Pope shall lose[2] the said annates and benefits.[3]

He hath written a book since his condemnation, *De Captivi-*

---

[1] Wolsey issued a mandate to this effect May 14, 1521. Wilkins: *Concilia Magnae Britanniae*, iii. 690. On the burning of his books, *cf. English Historical Review*, c. 657-8.

[2] *I. e.*, "give up."

[3] *Cf.* Luther's *Address to the Christian Nobility*, l. 2.

tate Babylonica Ecclesiae,¹ wherein he holdeth that four of the sacraments be only *de jure positivo,* by the Pope's ordinance, so called, *viz.: Confirmatio, Ordo, Extrema Unctio* and *Matrimonium;* and that *Baptismus, Eucharistia* and *Penitentia* be *de jure divino et evangelii.* They say there is much more strange opinion in it, near to the opinions of Boheme. I pray God keep that book out of England.

At the exequy of the Cardinal of Croy,² in the presence of the Electors, the Emperor, the Pope's ambassador and the cardinals, a friar preacher³ made a sermon, and in the beginning said the Pope was *Vicarius Christi in spiritualibus,* and the cardinals and bishops were *apostoli,* etc. But how his tongue turned in his head I cannot tell; but after he concluded that the Emperor, when they do amiss, should reform their abuses, *etiam usque ad depositionem;* whereupon the Pope's Nuntius, having commission against Luther, called him, laying the premises to his charge; which the said Nuntius hath been openly threatened by many gentlemen not to meddle with him. In his said sermon he⁴ exhorted the Emperor and all the princes to go into Italy, which is of the Empire, and to reform such abuses as be there; whereunto I understand many of the princes be inclined, because every man thinketh to gain thereby. . . .

Luther offereth, if the Emperor will go to Rome to reform the Church, to bring him 100,000 men, whereunto the Emperor, as a virtuous prince, will not hearken. The said Luther hath many great clerks that hold with him, save in some points, which the said Luther hath put forth more than he can or will justify, to the intent that on the residue he might not be heard, and a council called for reformation, whereof the Pope will not hear, but standeth to his sentence of condemnation.

[1] It is interesting to note that this was the book refuted by Henry VIII. in his *Assertion of the Seven Sacraments. Cf. English Historical Review, loc. cit.*

[2] William de Croy, Archbishop of Toledo, made Cardinal 1517, died January 6, 1521. Kalkoff: *Briefe,* 72f. His funeral was on January 21. Brown, iii. 156.

[3] John Faber, Dominican Prior of Augsburg, on whom *cf. supra,* no. 333. This sermon aroused the ire of Aleander ("the Pope's ambassador"). *Cf.* Paulus: *Deutsche Dominicaner,* 311.

[4] *I. e.,* Faber. These ideas correspond closely to those expressed in the *Address to the Christian Nobility.*

384. BONIFACE AMERBACH TO BASIL AMERBACH AT BASLE.

Burckhardt-Biedermann, 145.　　　　　Avignon, January 25, 1521.

I have seen the bull against Luther printed at Paris. All true Christians must mourn that those whose business it was to nourish truth should have conspired against his life. But what will not the cursed thirst for gold and human ambition bring about? Beatus has written that the bull is published with notes by Hutten. Please send me this and any other new and agreeable German publications when you can. I mean little pamphlets, for it is sufficient to give me the titles of large books. . . .

385. ERASMUS TO A POWERFUL GENTLEMAN.

Erasmi opera, iii. 631.　　　　　Louvain, January 28, 1521.

. . . I am not sorry to hear that Luther's books are, as you write, in your hands, provided only that you read them as I do; gathering the good in them and skipping the bad. . . . I have never had anything to do with Luther, except what common Christian friendship demanded. This is true and I have often asserted it. I am neither the author nor patron nor attorney nor judge for his books. . . . Now the bull has been published, which, terrible as it is, will not be able to alienate the minds of men from him. . . .

You exhort me to join myself to Luther and I would easily do so if I saw him on the side of the Catholic Church. Not that I say that he is not, or that I am able to condemn him. . . .

386. DUKE JOHN OF SAXONY TO THE ELECTOR FREDERIC IN WORMS.

T. Kolde: *Friedrich der Weise*, 42.　　　　Coburg, January 28, 1521.

. . . I am very sorry to hear that Luther is so persecuted, but I shall trust in God, who will not abandon him. There are also many respectable persons who will do their best for Luther, for it always seems to me that he is in the right way. . . .

387. SPALATIN TO THE ELECTOR FREDERIC OF SAXONY.
Zeitschrift für Kirchengeschichte, ii. 120.

(WORMS, c. January 29, 1521.)

This letter is dated by the editor 1520. It might have been written at Cologne, November, 1520, when the Elector Frederic, Duke George, Spalatin and Faber (the Dominican prior of Augsburg) were all together and there was talk of getting a mandate against Luther. It seems preferable, however, to refer this last notice to the Sequestration Mandate of March 10, which was prepared on February 2 (*infra*, no. 393), and of which there was, of course, talk previously. Moreover, in a letter of C. Pflug to Kochel of January 29, 1521 (Gess, under date), there is an allusion to Frederic's answer to Duke George about posting the bull, which seems to fit in well with the first words of this letter.

Most gracious Lord. The book which your Grace received from Duke George of Saxony is nothing more than the archpapal, bare and naked bull, brought hither by Eck. . . . My brother writes me that the whole council and community of my home, which is in the bishopric of Eichstädt, are wonderfully well inclined to Doctor Martin. Indeed, I have no rest from my brother, he keeps so constantly asking for Doctor Martin's books. The prior of the Dominican cloister[1] of Augsburg informed me to-day that some people were going to get up an imperial mandate against Luther. But he doesn't praise them much. God give us his grace.

Your grace's humble servant,
SPALATIN.

388. SPALATIN TO THE ELECTOR FREDERIC OF SAXONY.
Zeitschrift für Kirchengeschichte, ii. 123.

(WORMS, end of January, 1521.)

Most gracious Lord, I have received the following news from Wittenberg. The Elector Joachim of Brandenburg and the princes coming with him spoke to Dr. Martin at Wittenberg, especially Duke Albert of Mecklenburg.

The hundred gulden from the late Dr. Schmiedberg have been paid Dr. Martin by Taubenheim.[2] Schart has also given him fifty gulden. Dr. Martin writes: "I see God is paying

---
[1] John Faber.
[2] This was the legacy spoken of by Luther. *Cf. supra*, nos. 335, 378.

me here. But I have protested I shall not on that account be satisfied, or that I shall throw it away soon. What should I do with so much money? I have given half to my prior, and made him happy with it. . . ."

Dr. Martin informs that he is writing to your Grace, so I hope your Grace has received his letter. He writes that he is horrified that his Imperial Majesty has written against him, and he says: "What hope is there when people think and write like that?"

He will not answer Murnar. He writes that Meissen and Merseburg have decided to publish the bull. When the Bishop of Brandenburg was with the elector at Wittenberg, the cry was raised that he would post the bull there. But note if it had happened thus nothing good would have come from it. But it didn't happen.

Dr. Martin has written to Hutten, that he does not want men to fight for the gospel with force and murder. For the world is overcome by God's Word. By the Word was the Christian Church upheld and sanctified, and will by the same means be renewed and raised up. Yes, even as Antichrist had begun to act without force, he would be overcome by the Word. . . .

389. LUTHER TO HAUGOLD VON EINSIEDEL.

Enders, iii. 79. De Wette, i, 546, German.

(WITTENBERG, end of January or beginning of February, 1521.)

This was the dedication to Luther's answer to Emser, entitled: *Auf des Bocks zu Leipzig Antwort D. M. Luther,* Weimar, vii. 266ff.

Honored Sir and Friend! I have received Emser's pamphlet *Against the Bull of Wittenberg,* together with your letter. And although many people advised me not to answer him as a public liar and libeller, yet I could not omit pointing out his lies to him, lest the sow's belly grow too big. He is thickheaded, for when he writes nothing reasonable, but mere lies, he thinks he has the right and has won. So it did not become me to keep silence while all his lies are directed against my doctrine. This I would not conceal from you. God bless you.

390. LUTHER TO WENZEL LINK AT NUREMBERG.
Enders, iii. 79.   WITTENBERG (February 3?), 1521.

This letter is dated by Enders beginning of February or end of January. A MS. has since been found bearing the date "dominica XX.," probably for "dominica LX.," *i. e.,* Sexagesima Sunday, February 3. *Theologische Studien und Kritiken,* 1913, p. 296.

. . . Emser rages against me at Leipsic. We have no other news, for I think that you have Hutten's works on this affair. We daily expect news from Worms, for the princes do not wish me to come, but desire only to condemn and destroy me.

Spalatin writes that Aleander dared to say: "Even if you Germans, who pay less than any other nation to the Pope, should break the yoke of Rome, yet will we take care that, consumed by mutual slaughter, you should perish in your own blood." This is his news. I always said and wrote that the Romans cherished this monstrous plan against us. Behold how the Pope feeds Christ's sheep. Farewell.

Yours,   MARTIN LUTHER.

391. LUTHER TO SPALATIN AT WORMS.
Enders, iii. 81.   WITTENBERG, February 3, 1521.

Greeting. Wonderful is the boldness of Christ, who dared to kill so great a cardinal[1] in the midst of the Diet, fearing neither his creator[2] nor the creature. Link writes that a similar creature suddenly perished in like manner in Hungary.

The Pope has accused our Staupitz before the Cardinal of Salzburg for holding with me. Staupitz has answered; I know not whether he will be taken away. I am publishing the history of that noble Florentine Council,[3] and my articles for consoling those who are about to confess,[4] although the presses are very busy. I dined with Duke Bogislav[5] of

---

[1] *I. e.,* Croy, *cf. supra,* no. 383. A sudden death was then often regarded as a divine judgment. Croy was thrown from his horse.

[2] *I. e.,* the Pope.

[3] The council of 1439, which tried to heal the schism of the Greeks and Romans. Aleander had cited it against Luther, as he recounts in his letter of December 17, 1520, *supra,* no. 362, which perhaps gave Luther the idea of editing it.

[4] *Unterricht der Beichtkinder über die verbotenen Bücher,* Weimar, vii. 284.

[5] Bogislav X. of Pomerania (1454-October 5, 1523), attended the Diet of Worms. *Allgemeine deutsche Biographie.*

Pomerania, who also heard my sermon at the parish church to-day.

A learned youth from Bohemia has sent me his book,[1] trying to prove that St. Peter was never at Rome. He advances eighteen conjectural reasons for his thesis, but does not prove it. They have also sent my *Sermons on the Ten Commandments and on the Lord's Prayer* translated into Bohemian and printed in their type; they are strongly preaching the Word among their people. . . .

392. MELANCHTHON TO GEORGE SPALATIN.
Corpus Reformatorum, i. 281.   WITTENBERG, February 3, 1521.

Hail, sweetest Spalatin. May Almighty God preserve our elector, the Nestor of the Empire. Day before yesterday I received your letter in which, except the death of the Cardinal of Croy, you announced no news. It seems almost a miracle that such furious enemies can keep quiet, but we doubt not that they are doing all they can in secret. *Is there any hope in Charles?*[2] We doubt not that he will confer with our most illustrious elector about the cause of Martin. Emser here is publishing an oration against Martin in German, which, even if posterity admires it, yet is so impious and inept that our women and boys could write better.[3] O, unexampled insanity of the man to dare to contend with our Hercules, a man full of the divine spirit, not considering what even the impious king of Egypt saw, that what Martin does is done by the finger of God. . . .

393. RAPHAEL DE' MEDICI TO CARDINAL DE' MEDICI.
Kalkoff: *Briefe*, 34.   WORMS, February (6 and) 7, 1521.

Raphael de' Medici, Chamberlain of Leo X., was nuncio to Charles V. 1516-7, and from August, 1519, to April, 1521. He died 1523.

. . . Recently, in Saxony, when a priest held forth on Luther, the latter's followers made as if to stone him, as happened to St. Stephen. Then they went to the dwelling of

---

[1] *In hoc libello . . . probatur Apostolum Petrum Roman non venisse*, November 25, 1520, by Ulrich Velenus. Answered by John Fisher and others.
[2] Greek.
[3] *Wider das unchristliche buch Martini Luthers Augustiners, an den Teutschen Adel aussgangen Verlegung Hieronymi Emser.* Leipsic, January 20, 1521.

John Eck, who had fled from it, and threw out of the windows his servants and others whom they found there, thereby causing the death of one.[1]

The enclosed writings[2] were handed to the King[3] yesterday morning, but his Majesty, without looking at a word of them, publicly and at once tore them up.

Three days ago the Cardinal of Sion[4] spoke with some nobles about this Lutheran affair, and said that he feared after the departure of the Emperor these beasts would renounce obedience to Rome, and that the priests would suffer much. The worthy gentleman has spoken with many of these princes and has found almost all of them embittered against the Roman curia, only on account of things they have seen and heard, especially things done by Arcimboldi,[5] who played a thousand useless tricks, and with the help of the cowl-bearers raked in all the money in sight. They are angry, too, at the grants made by the Roman Curia in disregard of previous privileges, and for many other reasons.

If a bishop seizes a priest to do justice on him, suddenly these monks come to light with their privileges, which they only need to make valid to take the priest from the bishop's hand. There are many other causes which have brought them to endure all these machinations of Martin, even though they see right well that he speaks pure nonsense. The worthy gentleman said that these things greatly displeased him, and in fact, since the preparation of a mandate against Luther has been assigned to him, to the Bishop of Trieste[6] and to

---

[1] This riot happened at Leipsic on September 29, 1520.
[2] Luther's *Offer and Protest* is meant.
[3] *I. e.*, Emperor.
[4] Matthew Schinner, a Swiss, made Bishop of Sitten 1499, made Cardinal May 10, 1511; February, 1512, Bishop of Novara. A strong supporter of the Medicis, he had great influence with Leo X. He was ambassador to Henry VIII. in 1516; in 1521 he was sent to Switzerland to raise troops, with which the Pope was able to drive the French from Lombardy. In March, 1522, he submitted a scheme of reform to Adrian VI. He died October 1, 1522. Pastor-Kerr: *History of the Popes*, vols. vi.-ix. *Cf.* further, P. S. Allen, *op. cit.*, ii. 307.
[5] John Angelo de Arcimboldi was the special commissioner for the indulgence granted by Leo X. in 1514, for the ostensible purpose of building St. Peter's Church. Except the dioceses of Mayence and Magdeburg, which were reserved to Archbishop Albert, he was given the whole of Germany and Burgundy as the territory in which to sell papal pardons. He became Bishop of Novara 1525, Archbishop of Milan 1550, and died 1555. *Cf.* Pastor, *History of the Popes*.
[6] Peter Bonomo, Bishop of Trieste 1502-46.

Bannissius,[1] everything has gone finely. But when the Cardinal of Gurk [Matthew Lang] ordered him not to consider the mandate without consulting two other German councillors, the Cardinal of Sion became angry, for at every session for the last three days they have sent to get the others without being able to find them. The Cardinal of Gurk was responsible for this, desiring, in order to please the Elector of Saxony, to put off the mandate. The Cardinal of Sion was certain that he [Cardinal Lang] had arranged that the councillors should not be found at home. The Count Camillo of Gambara told me that at the table of the Cardinal of Gurk, in his presence, they had spoken evil of his Holiness, but he did not tell me what they said.

Four days ago the King held a council of state four hours long on the preparation of the mandate. The councillors, in giving their opinions on it, generally spoke German. When they had finished the King said: "Do you believe I did not understand you? You said so and so; *this* displeases me for such and such reasons, and *that* for other reasons has my assent." Everyone wondered at that; and thus the mandate was at once drawn up in the best form and translated into German. Jerome Aleander will have it printed and sent everywhere. The King has acted splendidly, but many of these princes say that a council must pronounce on these matters, and the whole people declare that this council will take place and that they will not pay any more annates. . . .

394. ALEANDER TO CARDINAL DE' MEDICI.

Kalkoff: *Aleander,* p. 69.   WORMS (February 8), 1521.

Although heaven and earth, and especially the whole of Germany, seem to have conspired to frighten me from carrying out my mission, or at any rate to cool off my zeal, yet the devil will not bring me to leave my duty unaccomplished, at least, as far as in me lies. I only deplore that the necessary documents,[2] which I asked for, will perhaps come too late to be of use. I see well that the extreme energy and shrewdness with which I succeeded, within three days of my

[1] James Bannissius, an Imperial Councillor.
[2] These were certain bulls granting favors to various influential persons in Germany. They had been despatched from Rome on January 28.

arrival in Flanders, in getting an imperial mandate and forthwith burning Luther's books and other libels, have rather hurt the cause and myself than otherwise, for it has made my lords at Rome think that the Lutheran rebellion has been thereby crushed, and has given them a full sense of security in thinking that the Germans are the best of Christians and the truest sons of the Holy See. For otherwise I cannot understand how they should so long have neglected not only me, but their own honor and advantage and a question of life or death for Christendom and the Papacy.

Your Lordship will be pleased to remember that from the very first by God's grace I worked with such power that, almost before the Emperor and his councillors knew that a mandate had been issued, they saw the books consumed by fire; and that at Cologne, before anyone was aware of it, a similar beautiful execution took place, and that with such skill that the Emperor himself observed to the Bishop of Liège and many other gentlemen, that I really acted with becoming decision. But now the whole of Germany is in full revolt; nine-tenths raise the war-cry, "Luther," while the watchword of the other tenth who are indifferent to Luther, is: "Death to the Roman Curia." All of them have written on their banners a demand for a council to be held in Germany, even those who are favorable to us, or rather to themselves. Some are moved by fear, some by hope, and some by their private interests. Indeed, some sign should be given at Rome to show that the danger is not underestimated. The bull accrediting me, and giving me power to name representatives, should be sent; also the breves to the persons I already mentioned, and numerous letters of introduction to princes and bishops, together with fifty copies of the bull of condemnation to give to bishops and prelates, and money for my expenses and for secretaries and agents. Even if they are all much exasperated against us, yet a handful of gold will make them dance to our pipe, though even thus it is hard to win them, and impossible in any other way. If we delay longer it is to be feared that the Lutherans will gain such strength that the imperialists will fear to pass any edict against them, for they even now hesitate, in order, as they say, not to irritate the people. Yet there is no other means to bridle their spirits, for the Germans have lost all reverence and laugh at excommunications; the monks will not or dare not preach against Luther from the pulpit. A despatch was laid before the Emperor in council of state, saying that at Antwerp a woman came to words with a preacher in the pulpit, showed him a book of Luther's and declared that she would read it to spite him. Innumerable persons have stopped confessing. Recently here at Worms, after the arrival of the Emperor, a wise and respectable canon of St. Martin's church told me of a man in high position who confessed to him a breach of chastity, but would not tell him whether it was with a maid, a matron or a kinswoman, and when absolution was refused him, retorted that according to Luther's holy doctrine he was already absolved by God. I could tell thousands of such horrors, but I won't waste paper and time.

A shower of Lutheran writings in German and Latin comes out daily. There is even a press maintained here, where hitherto this art has been unknown. Nothing else is bought here except Luther's books even in the imperial court, for the people stick together remarkably and have lots of money. Until the edicts shall have been promulgated, we are helpless. The Emperor in council, indeed, commanded that they should be, but their completion has hitherto been delayed by the Elector of Saxony's secret favor to Luther, and by the fierce complaints which all the German princes make against us to the Emperor, by the consultations in which, in spite of all my efforts, I am completely tangled up, and, as I must repeat, by the lack of money for secretaries and for the bailiffs who burn the books. . . .

Another recent annoyance is that those who return from Rome tell everyone that there the Lutheran affair is considered a joke and a matter of no importance. The councillors who have this matter in charge are so exasperated over this that they would be glad to see us depart from the Diet without having accomplished our object, to teach us with our importunity our place. Certainly it will go badly after the departure of the Emperor unless he gets some pronunciamento before the dissolution of the Diet. But if a month ago I had had those breves to the Emperor and others, I could have got out of this business much more easily, and have shown the imperialists that the Pope does not consider this matter such a trifle as those travelers say. I know, indeed, that Rome has held back in order not to make the matter appear too important, lest the imperialists should feel able to set their foot on our neck. But there is a golden mean, to avoid both extremes, especially as the situation is so critical that the Emperor's men do not believe that he will have the power to save it. Nevertheless, we must do all in our power and leave the rest to God's grace. I have positive hope of a good end, if Rome does not fail me, but carries out my plans. . . .

From the warning which the Archbishop[1] of Capua gave my representative at Rome, I learn that Erasmus has complained about me there, for blackening his character to the princes, and that the Pope has expressed his lively displeasure thereat. I am very sorry that the word of Erasmus, who has written worse things against our faith than has Luther, should be more trusted than mine, though I let myself be torn in pieces for this faith. But this Erasmus knows his own advantage, like a faithless wife who gives her husband a sharp scolding before she makes him a cuckold. I have long known that Erasmus is the source of all this evil which he has scattered around Flanders and the Rhine land, but I have refrained from saying so and have instead rather always praised him and have never allowed myself to get into a quarrel or an altercation with him, as the archbishop seems to hint. I shared lodging and bed with him at Venice[2] once for six months, and he considered it not beneath his dignity to hear my daily lectures on Plutarch's *Ethics* according to the Greek text. Later, also, we stood in friendly communion, so that I was greatly surprised when at Antwerp and Louvain Erasmus never let me see him or came to visit me. Everybody tells

---

[1]Nicholas von Schönberg of Meissen, who, while a student in Italy, was so impressed by Savonarola's preaching, that he entered the Dominican order in Florence 1497. As a learned theologian and able diplomatist he rose to favor under Julius II. and Leo X., by whom he was created Archbishop in 1520. He was made a cardinal by Paul III., and died 1537. Aleander's representative was probably his cousin, Peter Aleander.

[2]In 1508. *Cf.* J. Paquier: *L'Humanisme et la Réforme*, 1900, p. 26f.

me that he scatters far and wide doubts as to the genuineness of the bull. I learned from the professors of Louvain that Erasmus had convinced them all that the bull is a forgery. When during the solemn burnings or in conversation, instead of answering them I showed them the original, they were thunderstruck and looked it over doubtfully before and behind as if they were still suspicious.

But at Cologne, where he spent his evenings instilling the worst opinions into the electors,[1] after he heard how well our campaign against Luther was going, he had an interview with me. I said to him the most agreeable and honorable things I could think of and remembered the days gone by. When in the course of the conversation he remarked that he had heard that I was blackening him to the princes, and intended to condemn his and Reuchlin's books, I could answer that I had no such intention, but rather was ready to protect him against every slander, and that I could give no opinion on his books as I had not read his theological works, but that I did not suppose he had written anything repugnant to the institutions of the Church. In short, I dissembled ably and invented some obliging lies, as in the interest of the faith and of my commission I could do no otherwise. But I did tell him that for the sake of our friendship and his honor I was sorry to find him the originator of the opinion that the bull was forged or supposititious. He must give my witnesses credit and recognize the fact. He excused himself by saying that he was not obliged to believe in the genuineness of the bull before he had seen the original. I turned this against him by saying that he ought not then previously to have spoken of the falsity of an unknown document; it was a much worse error to throw away what one did not know; and that wisdom itself should have prompted him to keep silence or to speak rather good than bad. God knows that he then blushed and stammered, and when I saw his embarrassment I turned the matter into a joke and chatted on other things. I took occasion to praise his attitude compared to Luther's, and I exhorted him in his writings to labor rather for the

---

[1] Erasmus had an interview with the Elector Frederic at Cologne on November 5, 1520, in which he thwarted Aleander. *Cf.* Smith, 100.

edification of the Church than, like Luther, for her destruction. As he then expressed the wish to examine some books in the papal library, I invited him to Rome and promised him a hearty welcome from the Pope and your Lordship. After five or six hours in company we separated in the greatest friendship.

When on the two following days he heard of the preparations for burning Luther's books, he requested an interview with me. As I was very busy I sent him word that before our meeting, he must let me discharge a definite business; I knew only too well that he wanted to delay me, so that the short time till the Emperor's departure should be used up, and then we should be frustrated. But when the books had been burned, Erasmus did not let himself be seen again; the court moved to Mayence, and as far as I know nothing more happened. So I pray his Holiness not to trust Erasmus more than me, for his position is just as I have here narrated at length, so that the Pope and your Lordship may know the whole course of events. By this your Lordship may convince yourself of the truth of the remark I made in my last letter, namely, that though Erasmus is the greatest corner-stone of this heresy, yet one must pretend not to notice it. . . .

As you did not believe what I wrote about the libels and insults with which these rascals persecuted me, I send for proof a little pamphlet, more to show your Lordship the course of the rising than to accredit my own afflictions. I could send a thousand such vile buffooneries, but I shall burden the messenger with the most necessary things only, among which are these *Articles* to be laid before the Diet. Although they purport to be a grievance of the whole nation, yet they were probably composed by individuals from private motives of hate or self-interest. For at the Diet all cry for a council, give notice that they will no longer obey Rome, and agitate against the clergy. The most powerful princes favor this agitation and speak of it to the Emperor, who, however, remains indifferent and holds fast to the good cause. I send a letter of Luther to the Emperor, which was recently handed to him by the Lord of Cistein[1] as Luther's representative. In

[1] Sickingen or Nicholas von Ende *zum Stein*, the Marshal of Duke John. The

this he prays the Emperor for a righteous judgment. The Emperor tore it up and threw it on the ground, as you can see by the enclosure. That was a clear indication for the whole Diet of the Emperor's opinion of Luther's cause. If it please your Lordship, I pray you after the Pope has seen it to put it in the secret part of the papal library.

On the same day there appeared two German pamphlets[1] by Luther and an anonymous one[2] against the Pope. There also appeared a right able German pamphlet[3] against Luther's *Address to the German Nobility*.

A little while ago at Augsburg they were selling Luther's picture[4] with a halo; it was offered without the halo for sale here, and all the copies were disposed of in a trice before I could get one. Yesterday I saw on one and the same page,[5] Luther with a book and Hutten with a sword. Over them was printed in fair letters: "To the Champions of Christian Freedom, M. Luther and Ulrich von Hutten." Each was praised in a tetrastich beneath; Hutten was threatening with his sword, according to the poet. A nobleman showed me such a picture, but I have not been able to get another. So far has the world gone that the Germans in blind adoration press around these two scoundrels, and adore even during their lifetime the men who were bold enough to cause a schism, whose words they oppose to the love of neighbor and the command of the gospel in order to tear the seamless coat of Christ. And I am given up to such people!

I enclose also certain reckless articles[6] on Luther's affair, which are in circulation here, composed, as is said, by Erasmus, in order to keep the princes from fulfilling their counsels, and to prevent our success until the Emperor shall have gone away without having given judgment. But we shall find some way to cross their purpose. If I sent all these shameful writings I should have to load a wagon.

piece was Luther's letter to Charles V. of August 31, 1520, translated Smith, p. 99.
[1]One of these was Luther's answer to Emser; the other was probably a reprint.
[2]A work by Paul Phrygio of Schlettstadt (died 1543).
[3]Either Emser's answer to this book, or Murnar's.
[4]See my article in *Scribner's Magazine*, July, 1913, pp. 141ff.
[5]This picture, a woodcut, was discovered by Knaake, who describes it fully in *Theologische Studien und Kritiken*, 1896, pp. 171ff.
[6]Either Erasmus's *Axioms*, which had been printed by this time, or the *Concilium cujusdam*, composed at Erasmus' advice by Faber. Cf. Smith, 100, 103.

I neither can nor will relate all the many and great dangers to which I am hourly exposed. You won't believe me until (may God prevent it!) I am stoned or torn to pieces by these people, who, if they meet me on the street, always put their hands to their swords or grind their teeth, and, with a German curse, threaten me with death. Only yesterday the Bishop of Sion[1] told me that whenever I crossed the square in front of his house his people adopted this attitude. Mindful of what may happen, I now commend my soul to God's mercy, and ask from his Holiness full absolution, and commend my brothers and servants who have to suffer with me, to your Lordship's grace.

Finally, I urgently request your Lordship to answer the questions raised in the enclosed letter,[2] which are of great importance for the pacification of this rebellion. For the danger is so great that if the good Emperor had only shown the least indecision, not to mention the obstacles that he might have put in our way, we should have lost, and the whole of Germany would have fallen away from the Roman See. . . .

395. RUDOLPH AGRICOLA TO VADIAN AT ST. GALL.

Vadianische Briefsammlung, ii. 338. CRACOW, February 8, 1521.

Rudolph Agricola (Baumann, not to be confounded with the elder Rudolph Agricola (Hausmann) of Heidelberg), of Wasserburg, went to Cracow before 1500, where he studied classics and mathematics. From 1515 to 1518 he was at Vienna, then he returned to Cracow, where he died in 1521.

. . . Bovillus[3] writes me from Wittenberg how Luther triumphs, how evangelic he is, how the Pope longs to have Luther taken bound by the legates to Rome and all his books burned, how Frederic protects the man, and how Luther in the presence of a great concourse of people annihilated and burned that great sea of litigious strife, the Canon Law. Until I can be with you, may God grant me my prayer! Write me anything that you desire your friends to know, if I, who am so devoted to you, may call myself one. Philip Melanchthon, that great master of Greek and Latin, Luther's Achates,

[1] Matthew Schinner.
[2] February 6.
[3] Lewis Oechslin of Schaffhausen, mentioned several times in the *Vadianische Briefsammlung*, otherwise unknown to me.

wrote to me excited by the wish to know what I am doing in the North. I answered briefly that I should go to Wittenberg if Vadian would call. . . .

396. ALEANDER TO THE VICE-CHANCELLOR DE' MEDICI AT ROME.

Kalkoff: *Aleander*, 82.   Worms, February 12, 1521.

On the tenth of this month I received your Lordship's letter with the bull[1] against Luther, and some breves, as well as the order for 400 gulden, for which I humbly thank his Holiness and your Lordship. . . . In the preparation of the bull I could mention many errors fatal to our cause, but time presses me, for this morning the Emperor with his own mouth commissioned me to speak[2] of the Lutheran cause and make our demand before his Majesty, the electors and Diet tomorrow. The time is too short to do much, but I shall work all night and pray God to strengthen me to protect his cause. I am of good confidence if only my strength holds out, for almost every night, or at least on many days, I suffer from fever. . . .

397. ALEANDER TO THE VICE-CHANCELLOR DE' MEDICI AT ROME.

Kalkoff: *Aleander*, 85.   Worms (February 14), 1521.

As I learned to-day that the courier who should have left day before yesterday is still here, I had him give back my packet of letters and added this sheet, to inform your Lordship that yesterday, on Ash Wednesday, after dinner, I delivered an oration about three hours long before a very numerous assembly. Present were the Emperor, all the electors save the Saxon—who excused himself on the ground of ill health and was represented by his chancellor[3] and several

---

[1] This was the bull *Decet Pontificem Romanum*, promulgated at Rome, January 3, and sent to Aleander with Medici's letter of January 28. Besides condemning Luther, it mentioned the names of some of his adherents, such as Hutten, which Aleander judged to be unwise. He therefore sent it back for revision, which was accomplished. The bull was thus first posted by him at Worms on May 6.

[2] This speech reprinted in Förstemann: *Neues Urkundenbuch*, p. 30ff. Cf. Smith, 109.

[3] Gregory Brück (1483 or 1486-1557), born near Wittenberg, where he studied 1502-3, then at Frankfort on the Oder, then back to Wittenberg, where he became bachelor of law 1509. In 1520 he entered the elector's service, soon rising to the highest position, that of chancellor. *Allgemeine deutsche Biographie*.

councillors—and also all the princes, spiritual and temporal, as well as the other Estates of the Empire and the imperial councillors. As the emperor's command had been given me only the day before, I had little time for preparation, yet thanks to my continual occupation with the cursed stuff, about which I had often spoken publicly as well as privately, I was, thank God, so well instructed, that, although I said sufficient in three hours, yet I could have talked four hours more. I hear from more than one quarter that my oration is considered able, apt and fortunate; but I, who can never satisfy myself in such things, think it mediocre and only partially successful. Even what was accomplished I do not ascribe to my own talent or eloquence, of which I have little or nothing, but to the grace of God, to the power of the good cause and to the terrible and monstrous opinions of Luther, which I cited from his books only to refute them. I pointed to the disagreeable consequences which might grow from this doctrine, and to the shame which threatened the nation; I reminded them that the Empire was only maintained by the same policy by which it had been won, that the Empire and the College of Electors had only been granted to Charlemagne and Otto on account of their proved attachment to the Roman See; and finally I mentioned, among many other things, the Council of Constance and the Hussites. Among my audience were many princes favorable to Luther, and the secretaries of the Elector of Saxony, who, although from lack of time I spoke very rapidly, took much of my oration down. And now already, as I hear, they spread abroad the lie that I attacked hatefully their prince. They circulated the same slander at Cologne, although when I handed the breve to their lord I took the Bishops of Trieste and Trent as well as Caracciolo as witnesses. The reward for my restraint was that the elector in his answer to my oration as reported by the rascal who wrote it down yesterday complained to us that I had attacked him. These beasts must always invent new lies to give color to their evil speaking and to instigate their prince. His servants, who are all arch-Lutherans, have always done that. However, had he been present, I would moderately and courteously have taunted him a little, for we can no more hope to move him by kind speech, and I should have felt safer in doing this as the Emperor, Chièvres and the Archbishop of Mayence told Caracciolo and me that I should say fearlessly all that seemed to me advisable. By God's help I did it intrepidly, just as though I were lecturing schoolboys, although many Lutheran princes made savage faces and had often previously threatened me. But I think little of death, if I die for the faith and for my patrons.

398. THOMAS BLAURER TO JOHN VON BOTZHEIM.
T. Schiess: *Briefwechsel der Blaurer,* i. 34.

WITTENBERG, February 15, 1521.

John von Botzheim (c. 1480-April, 1535), a noble Alsatian, studied under Wimpfeling, and took the degree of Doctor of Canon Law at Bologna. He returned from Italy to Strassburg in 1504. In 1512 he was appointed Canon of Constance. He wrote several things. A friend of Erasmus, whom he met in 1520, he was at first inclined to the Reformation, and then turned against it. *Allgemeine Deutsche Biographie,* and P. S. Allen, i. 1.

. . . Please change your opinion about Luther writing more bitterly than need be. He does it for the good of the Christian flock, nor can he do it without bitterness. The life of wicked men must be blamed, especially when they are prominent, the people must be called back to other examples and other doctrine from that which they preach. Luther's diligence in the Old and New Testaments, his illumination given by the Holy Spirit, his life and character, the arguments he uses, all prevent us from thinking that he writes wrongly or thoughtlessly. If it seem otherwise to you, it is because of your carnal perception which always opposes human intellect to the spirit. The truth only shines forth when the perception of the flesh has been beaten down. . . .

399. ERASMUS TO NICHOLAS BÉRAULD.
Erasmi opera (1703), iii. 634.   LOUVAIN, February 16, 1521.

Nicholas Bérauld (Beroaldus, 1473-1550) was born at Orleans, where he spent most of his life teaching Greek. Calvin was one of his pupils. He wrote several books, including a commentary on some of the Psalms. *Nouvelle Biographie Universelle.*

. . . Luther is bringing odium on me and on sound learning. Everyone knows that the Church was afflicted with tyranny and with ceremonies and with laws made only for gain. Many either desired or planned a remedy, but ill-considered remedies make things worse, and it comes to pass that when those who wish to break their yoke do not succeed they are drawn into a harder servitude. Would that that man would either abstain altogether from proposing remedies or would do it more gently and circumspectly. I labor not for Luther, but for the glory of Christ; for I see some prepared to do what, if it succeeds, will leave us nothing but to write the dirge of evangelic doctrine. . . .

400. LUTHER TO SPALATIN AT WORMS.
Enders, iii. 86.   WITTENBERG, February 17, 1521.

Greeting. I hope that my letters and books have at last reached you, Spalatin. I wonder what prevented your getting them earlier, as in the meantime I received two letters from you, neither of which mentioned your getting mine. What wind has blown away all that I wrote to Hutten?[1] I know not why I should try so hard to keep writing and sending things. I commanded some pages of my German Assertion to fly to you, snatched wet from the press, but now I see that they limped. I now send the rest, and will continue to send what the press produces.

Emser is vomiting his poison at length to please Duke George. I am obliged to answer the man only on account of his most impure lies. I am not yet able to answer Murnar; who can do all things? Adam Petri has printed my *Commentary on the Psalms* at Basle, which I regret. The Bishop of Merseburg, that holy servant of the Pope, has burned my books.[2]

Matthew Adrian has asked leave to resign, which we immediately gave him. Thus we are freed from that man. Would that Aurogallus[3] deserved to succeed him. . . .

[1] *Supra*, no. 379.
[2] On January 23.
[3] Matthew Aurogallus or Goldhahn (c. 1490-November 10, 1543), of Commotau in Bohemia, is first heard of as school teacher at Schmalkalden. In 1519 he came to Wittenberg, and in 1521 was appointed professor of Hebrew to succeed Adrian. He was a great help to Luther in translating the Old Testament. In 1535 he published a Hebrew grammar. *Allgemeine deutsche Biographie*.

At Madgeburg Emser's book was fastened to a shameful place with the inscription: "The book is worthy of the place." They say that a rod was also fastened up, to indicate his chastisement. But he reigns at Leipsic, able and bold to do much, like a man who will soon meet his end as such men do.

In these days of carnival our youth carried around in ludicrous and lofty pomp a mock Pope; finally in the market-place making as if they would throw him in the fountain, they dispersed him and his cardinals, bishops and chamberlains in the various quarters of the town, all of which was very funny and clever. Christ's enemy, who mocks the greatest kings and Christ himself, deserved to be thus mocked. It will be written up in Latin verses. . . .

401. JEROME ALEANDER TO JOHN ECK AT INGOLSTADT.

Kalkoff: *Briefe*, 40.   WORMS, February 17, 1521.

Honored and learned Friend! The two letters, which, according to your last note[1] you sent to me, I have not received. The fault is presumably with the messengers, and from lack of messengers I have not written you. Moreover, you can hear the rumor of my doings, as my burning of Lutheran books in many places has brought me such hatred from your compatriots that it is with great danger that I stay in Germany. Yet only for the sake of religion I oppose them, and no misfortune, not even death, shall frighten me. . . .

Now, my dear Eck, I will, as you wish, tell you what is going on here. You must know that here there is such a crowd of Lutherans that not only men but stocks and stones shout Luther's name. It is not remarkable that laymen should do so, but in this campaign the priests are the leaders, not so much to favor Luther, that pernicious monster, as to spout forth from his mouth their long accumulated venom against the city of Rome and the priesthood. They do it with such fury that if the Emperor, this best and most pious of all men, did not withstand them, we should soon see a disease in the Church of God, which would bring perdition first of all to the Germans.

[1] One of February 9, *Reichstagsakten*, no. 136.

Recently [December 29] the Emperor decided to put Luther and his books under the ban of the Empire, but before this decree had received the imperial seal, the malicious counsel of certain men brought it about, in spite of my emphatic but vain protest, that the affair should be referred to the German princes and estates at the Diet. For I could easily see that nothing those enemies of the priests meddled with could have a good end. But at all events it happened that in obedience to the Emperor's command, given on some one else's advice, I should discuss the Lutheran affair before him and the princes of the Empire. I spoke on this question about two hours on Ash Wednesday, with close attention from Emperor and princes. The Emperor, as before, defended the faith, and I hear that all the electors save the Saxon who was kept away by a fever, agreed to his decision. The other princes, when asked for their judgment, asked a delay of six days, as, unless I err, Simonides once did when preparing his answer to Hiero. The Emperor has only given them three days. This period expires to-morrow, and we know not exactly what will happen, for the simple, plain affair has been greatly confused by the opposition of opinions.

So we are waiting for the issue, which I will communicate to you in due time. At Cologne I learned from your letter to Hochstraten as well as from your last letter to me, what you have done in this matter, and what you recommend me to do. I esteem you highly, my dear Eck, because you have faithfully, energetically and punctually done all that was committed to you. In like manner I have sent the bull against Luther and all his confederates to all bishops, and have solemnly executed the mandate wherever my path has led me. If I find others among the numerous attendants of this Diet I will do the same, but I already see that all that will help us little unless we get the Emperor's authority. For how is it possible that men who care not a straw for the Pope's excommunication and for the Pope himself, should fear punishment by a bishop? Heretics must be punished with an iron rod and with fire, if they persist in their contumacy, either sinning themselves or leading other unhappy men into their perdition, their bodies must be destroyed that their souls may be saved, as my patron St. Jerome, appropriately advised should be done against Vigilantius.[1]

Indeed I know not what more I could have done or the Pope could have desired at the beginning, as all the enemies of the faith are convinced. First of all, I procured an imperial decree[2] for the execution of the papal judgment, which was published and with the effectual aid of which that which I have just written you was done against Luther's books. It is true that in many places it was done with great difficulty on account of the disturbing violence of the Lutherans, yet it was done everywhere with salutary and holy intentions, not from hatred or revenge, as the Lutherans do, but, so help me God, only to defend our faith. . . . Wherefore I hope, and surely believe, that the little boat of Peter, which has conquered the Syrtes of the Photinian[3] heresy, the Nestorian Charybdis and the Arian Symplegades, in short the assaults of all errors, will also easily overcome the Lutheran floods, and that Luther and all his aiders and abettors will soon suffer the merited punishment. . . .

402. MELANCHTHON TO JOHN HESS AT BRESLAU.

Corpus reformatorum, i. 284. (WITTENBERG), February 20, 1521.

I do not see the cause of your writing so little to us at this time unless you think that you ought not on account of the Pope. If this is true, Hess, where is your Christian courage? Where is your old strength of soul? How can you, who know that Luther stands for piety and truth, yet hesitate? Schleupner has left Leipsic in fear for a safe place; if his example has won you away from us I shall be doubly angry with him. But I hardly know whether other reasons invited him to Leipsic. Martin still lives and flourishes in spite of the rage and roars of Leo, whom people have believed omnipotent hitherto.

No one here approves the bull of Eck except those who

---

[1] On this see Jerome's polemic against Vigilantius, translated in *Nicene and Post-Nicene Fathers*, ed. P. Schaff and H. Wace. Series ii., vol. vi., p. 417ff.

[2] Aleander means the one he got in the Netherlands in September, though this was only good in the hereditary dominions of Charles.

[3] So called from Photinus, Bishop of Sirmium, condemned for his doctrine of Christ's person at Antioch, 345.

have more regard for their bellies than for the gospel. Certainly it has brought us into no danger even if the bishops are promulgating it and thundering. I wish that you knew how frightened the bishops are in carrying out the commands of the Pope, standing, as it were, between the devil and the deep sea, fearing on one side the opinion of the world and on the other the wrath of the Pope. The latter prevails with many who prefer to be openly wicked rather than to seem too little dependent on his pontifical Holiness.

Though I doubt not that you know what is done at the Diet of Worms yet I will briefly relate the plans of our enemies. The Emperor is daily asked to proscribe Luther, and there is a lively altercation over this point. We shall perish if the papists are able to do what their wrath suggests. They regret that the furies of the Pope have accomplished so little and hope that those of the Emperor will be stronger. So they are trying by all legal and all illegal means to wrest such a mandate from the Emperor, but I hope they will act in vain. Martin fears nothing, but would willingly buy the glory and profit of the gospel with his life. Perhaps you have read his *Assertion against the bull of Leo*.[1] It is written in German. . . .

Martin has begun to write commentaries[2] on the gospels and epistles, to be read on holy days according to the custom of the Church. . . .

Luther sends his greeting.   YOUR PHILIP.

403. ULRICH VON HUTTEN TO JOHN REUCHLIN.

L. Geiger: *Johann Reuchlins Briefwechsel*, Tübingen, 1875, p. 327.

EBERNBURG, February 22 (1521).

I have read your letter to the Dukes of Bavaria[3] in which you answer to the accusation of Leo X.[4] Good Heavens! what do I see? You descend to that degree of fear and weakness that you do not abstain from reviling those who have wished to save you and who have even defended your repu-

---

[1] Weimar, vii. 94. It appeared in Latin in January and in German in March.
[2] *The Enarrationes Epistolarum et Evangeliorum.* Weimar, vii.
[3] This letter is not preserved.
[4] Perhaps Reuchlin's condemnation of June 23, 1520. Reuchlin's answer is perhaps his appeal.

tation with great peril. Sickingen was as indignant as possible when I translated your letter to him. For what do you hope to obtain from those from whom you never got any good thing or any justice, by crushing Luther if you can? Even if renouncing Luther could save you from your present danger I cannot think it honorable of you to fight those whose allies you ought to be in every honorable undertaking unless you wish to seem most ungrateful.

It would have been sufficient and more than sufficient for your protection had you written that you had nothing to do with Luther. Erasmus also wrote this, but you add that you have always disapproved of him and that you are sorry that your name is found in his writings and that you have tried to win us, his adherents, away from him. By this base adulation you hope to touch those, whom, if you were a man, you would not even salute with courtesy, so evilly have they deserved of you. . . .

Luther's cause displeases you, you disapprove of him and wish him dead. You do not remember your strong defender Sickingen nor me, who stood by you to the last, even when it was most dangerous to do so. . . . But from this time forth, if you ever oppose Luther, or submit to the Pope, you will have me for an adversary.

404. ANTONY DELLA SASSETA (?) TO FRANCIS DE' PELLEGRINI (?).

Kalkoff: *Briefe*, 45.   WORMS, February 25, 1521.

Sasseta and Pellegrini were both papal chamberlains. On February 15 the former wrote the latter of the opening of the Diet, and the similarity in style of the letter here translated to that leads us to infer the same authorship and addressee.

. . . On the first day of Lent [February 13] the honorable Jerome Aleander at the command of his Imperial Majesty spoke at a session of the council of princes before the Emperor, the electors and the magnates of Germany. He spoke for two hours, although he hurried so as not to tire them. He proved on many grounds that Martin Luther's doctrine was directed against Christ, the apostles, the archangels, the Pope, the Emperor and many other authorities. He earned much praise from these barbarians, and, in fact, acquitted himself excellently. Then the Cardinal of Mayence caused an abbot[1] to read the papal breve to the Emperor, who then requested electors and princes within two days to give him their advice as to what answer to make to the representatives of the Pope in this matter. Then they held a consultation, at which, it is rumored, there was great division of opinion. When the Emperor again requested their advice, he gave them such an exhortation that they sent him a very long written reply, in which, as I understand, they thanked him for asking their advice in this matter, and gave him a touch of the spur by saying that he must never decide any question without their consent. Then they said they thought Martin ought to be heard; if he acknowledged having written all that was printed under his name, then they might proceed as of right, but that many works had appeared which he said he had never written; they also said he must be given safe-conduct.

His Majesty answered them very wisely: "I am astonished that you wish to decide this question, in which I neither will nor can judge, seeing that the Pope has already decided it."

These Germans are acting with the intention of wasting time and procrastinating this affair, so that it will remain unsettled until the departure of the Emperor. Most of them know well enough that it is a very bad matter. They find much occasion to differ about it and are by no means at one; if, nevertheless, they hold together, it is to make common cause against annates, mental reservations[2] and other abuses. In short, it is a bad, a very bad cause. Everyone here, even to the shepherds, speak of nothing else. The evil that is spoken of the Roman Curia, I will leave, reverend Father, to your judgment, but if they go on as they are now doing, soon people will stop talking about the Bohemians, for the Germans will be much worse heretics.

[1]Hartmann von Kirchberg, who is found as doctor of law and priest of the Naumburg diocese in 1494. In 1507 he became coadjutor and the abbot of Fulda, from which position he was expelled in 1517 on account of his prodigal rule. He was favored by Maximilian; in 1521 he received a pension in return for his abbacy, and died at Mayence 1529. Kalkoff: *Aleander*, 47, note 1.

[2]*I. e.*, transfer of an appointment by the Pope, on the ground that when he made it it was with a "mental reservation." On this and annates—payment of half the first year's income of a living to the Pope—*cf.* Luther in the *Address to the German Nobility, apud* Smith, 82.

405. MATTHEW PHILIP TO STEPHAN ROTH AT ZWICKAU.
G. Buchwald: *Stadtschreiber Stephan Roth in Zwickau.* (*Archiv f. Geschichte d. deutschen Buchhandels,* xvi. 6ff.), 1893, p. 30.

WITTENBERG, February 26, 1521.

Matthew is known only as a student at Wittenberg who took his bachelor's degree gratis, March 11, 1521. See Köstlin: *Baccalaurei und Magistri der Wittenberger Facultät,* 1518-37, p. 11.

Roth, b. 1492, studied at Leipsic 1512-17, at Wittenberg 1523, where he became a literary help to Luther. In 1528 he became town clerk of Zwickau. Luther had a quarrel with him in 1531, on which *cf.* Smith, 280. Life of Roth by G. Müller, *Beiträge z. Sächsischen Kirchengeschichte,* i. 437.

I would not have you ignorant that some Lutheran works are in the press which will be very opportune for warding off the enemies of Christian truth. Luther is the man who can keep two printers busy, each working two presses. Can you fancy one man supplying four presses? But Luther does it. . . .

406. LUTHER TO SPALATIN AT WORMS.
Enders, iii. 89.   WITTENBERG, February 27, 1521.

. . . Take care that you also do not believe those who blame my too great bitterness in my writings. They do it to discredit me, which they cannot do in any other way, and I generally find that they are persons who have not themselves read me, but follow the reports of others, and besides they are not accustomed to see vices punished. I myself am not conscious of any such fury as they accuse me of. But enough of them.

My instruction to those about to confess did no good at Merseburg and Meissen, for they burned cartloads of my books.[1] Those little saints are mad. You have not yet persuaded me, Spalatin, that Rhadinus is not Emser, for we have solid arguments to show that he is. It was not my own idea, but the advice of my friends that made me answer him; I would have despised the beast, but they all thought I ought to answer him.

I am busy expounding Mary's canticle[2] for the young

---

[1] In the *Instruction* Luther informs those about to confess that they need not confess having his books nor give them up.
[2] The *Magnificat,* Weimar, vii. 538. *Cf.* Smith, 107.

prince as an answer, though a tardy one, to his recent most gracious letter to me. . . .

We are no less sorry than you that Erasmus's *Axioms*[1] and the reply of our elector have been printed at Leipsic. I know not where they got them, for we were much surprised when they appeared and had no idea where they got their copies, for we have ours. So there is no reason why you should accuse us in this matter, for we are much annoyed at their being printed, which will make people suspect us both of being afraid and of being boastful.

Erasmus wrote long ago that there was no hope in Charles, surrounded as he is by sophists and papists.[2] The Lord himself is the author and the sole protector of his Word; thus we want to meet their fury by the divine plan, for all expect that if their fury breaks loose there will be a rebellion like that of the Hussites, directed against the clergy, even those on our side. I am blameless, for I tried to induce the German nobility to bridle the Romanists not with a sword, but, as they easily could, by wise decrees. For to fight against the ordinary run of peaceful priests is the same as fighting against women and children. But I fear that the fury of the Romanists will not suffer itself to be quieted by edicts, and that this obstinacy in madness will invite some evil on their own heads of itself. Amsdorf is writing you something nice about our helper at the door. Farewell and pray for me. Remember me to the courtiers.

MARTIN LUTHER, *Augustinian.*

407. ALEANDER TO THE VICE-CHANCELLOR CARDINAL DE' MEDICI AT ROME.

Kalkoff: *Aleander,* 91.   WORMS, February 27, 1521.

As I previously reported to your Lordship, notwithstanding our strenuous endeavor to prevent Luther's affair coming before the Diet, the undisguised, senseless partiality for Luther on the part of the princes, or rather the insane, detestable suggestions of Satan, which he has put into the heads of all

---

[1] Some propositions drawn up by Erasmus at his interview with the elector at Cologne, November 5, 1520. *Cf.* Smith, 100.
[2] These words underlined by Luther himself. *Cf. supra*, nos. 258 and 354.

Germans, have won the Emperor for this course. This was even recommended by his Privy Council, who want to please both God and the world, and yet act so as to draw on themselves the displeasure of both. They allege that this conflagration will be more easily dealt with if the edicts of the Emperor are promulgated with the advice and consent of the princes. We pointed out the danger that the princes would have an opinion different from the Emperor's, whose hands would then be bound, and that it would be the safest thing simply to carry out by executive power the judgment given by the Pope in spiritual matters. The Emperor both could and should do that in the Empire, as he had already done in his hereditary lands, Burgundy and Flanders. The majority, almost the whole of the German Council agreed to this, but the Chancellor [Gattinara] replied that the Emperor would guard the freedom of his action; his Majesty would simply, when I made my proposal in the name of the Pope, announce that he had already, on the mature advice of all his peoples, promulgated a decree against Luther and his books, which had already taken effect in his hereditary dominions and kingdoms, and would do so in the Empire when promulgated with the knowledge of the princes, but not by their advice and consent. The chancellor and all the privy councillors declared further that even if the princes raised obstacles the Emperor would none the less proceed in this manner. It has not, however, yet been done. For although on the same day on which I made my demand [February 13] the Emperor announced his pleasure, and the day after at the assembly of the princes again expressed his will by one of his councillors, yet the princes debated a whole week so fiercely that the Electors of Saxony and Brandenburg would almost have come to blows, had not the Archbishop of Salzburg and others thrown themselves between. Such a thing has never happened from the beginning of the electorate till the present day. It conceals the danger of severe complication in itself and all are shocked at it.

The College of Electors in their own chamber were divided, as I am informed, so that the three archbishops and the Margrave of Brandenburg were of one opinion, which, however, did not entirely agree with ours. The Elector of Saxony and the Elector Palatine, who are both extremely obstinate, conducted themselves so senselessly that they left the session under loud protest, although they are bound to abide peaceably by the decision of the majority of their colleagues.

The four electors announced their opinion [on February 19] by the mouth of the Margrave of Brandenburg, who is a master of both German and Latin. Many members of the chamber of princes agreed with them, shortly after which the other two electors announced that they would submit to the majority of their colleagues as they were legally bound to do. Because, however, of the great differences of the original opinions and because of the intrigues of the Saxon, the whole decision, which should have been in our favor, turned so crazily out, that it agreed neither with the views of the Elector of Saxony nor with previous proposals, so favorable to us, of the four electors.

As far as we can learn the four articles on which the whole Diet finally agreed were tendered to the Emperor in German.

First, they thanked him for not promulgating, as he well might have, an edict on his own authority, but that by guarding the rights of the Empire had put himself in touch with them.

Secondly, they warned him by no means to issue the edict we desired, as it would raise a storm of protest and give the people the excuse they wanted to rebel. The Emperor had showed prudence in having requested their opinion, for otherwise they would have seen a great conflagration in Germany. Thus they asserted their right of being consulted in this matter, although the chancellor, God forgive him, had promised that this should not be.

Thirdly, they declared it necessary that before the promulgation of an edict Martin should be summoned under safe-conduct in order to ask him whether he had written these books and to demand an immediate recantation of the articles touching the faith and the sacraments; in case he refused he should be considered a heretic, and proceeded against as such after he had returned home from the Diet as soon as he could be caught. All the princes would stake life and land on that. But these German princes gave the fine advice that he should be heard by imperial judges in a public debate on the articles concerning the power of the Pope and positive laws, only after which the edict could be issued. In this again can be seen the secret plans of the Saxon, who desires to draw the matter out. Many of the other princes may perhaps sincerely have held this bad decision as the best; they do evil not from wickedness, but from shortsightedness. At the same time they keep saying that they leave it all to his Imperial Majesty, and only warn him against the great indignation that the promulgation of an edict contrary to their advice would excite in the Empire.

Finally they prayed the Emperor to free them from the tyranny of Rome; taking this occasion to pour out all their wrath against us in a worse manner than I can say.

After the Emperor had had their decision translated into French, he wisely answered that the grievances against the Roman Curia should not be confounded with Luther's cause, that is, with a question of the faith, and that he would write to the Pope in hopes that his Holiness would remedy the abuses which were really as represented.

The Emperor declared that under no circumstances would he allow a debate on the authority of the Pope and the Canon Law, but that if Luther should come, he should only be asked whether he had written the books, and, if he confessed that, whether he would maintain and defend what he had written contrary to the faith, the laws and the customs "which our fathers have in all points observed unto the present day." If Luther should recant, he, the Emperor, would take upon himself to get papal absolution for him, but if he adhered obstinately to his heresy, as soon as he had returned under safe-conduct to the point from which he had set out, he should be seized and punished as a heretic.

Thereupon he summoned the councillors of all his nations together, and talked with them until ten o'clock in the evening. We awaited the announcement of their decision, but they did not reach one because of the differences of opinion of the councillors of whom some have secret pensions from the Saxon Elector. Finally the Emperor appointed a commission of the Archbishops and Bishops of Salzburg,[1] Sion,[2] Trieste,[3] Palencia,[4] Tuy,[5] the Confessor [Glapion] and three doctors. They were to seek the way to satisfy God and the Pope, to guard the honor and duty of the Emperor, to pacify the princes and quiet the people—if they could! . . .

408. LUTHER TO CONRAD PELICAN AT BASLE.

Enders, iii. 92.   WITTENBERG (end of February), 1521.

I do not understand how it is that you so praise my writings; I fear you are partial. To me, at least, my Psaltery[6] is an object of disgust, not so much on account of the sense, which I believe to be correct, as on account of its verbosity, lack of order and chaotic arrangement. For it is a book which I am forced to conceive, form, nourish and bring forth all at once, on account of my lack of time and leisure. I have long thought of recalling it. For with the living voice, the hearers get much light and grace, such as this chaos of letters neither has nor can receive. If Psalm xi. is not yet printed, please strike out twelve verses at the end of page B, with the three following verses on page C. For you see how sadly I erred about the word סביב. For I was then thinking of other things, as I often am. I am, indeed, very busy, preaching twice a day, treating the Psalter, writing Postilla (as they are called), answering my enemies, attacking the bull in Latin and German and defending myself, not to mention answering my friends' letters and conversing with those of my household and with accidental visitors. One other thing that I forgot, please strike out what I dreamed about the word משביל Psalm xiii., verse 26. I will take care to explain the words of understanding, just as I did of the words of virtue, Psalm xx. There are many other things, but of less moment, for the book is full of typographical errors.

You do well to pray for me; I am overwhelmed with many

[1] Matthew Lang.
[2] Matthew Schinner.
[3] Peter Bonomo.
[4] Peter Ruiz de la Mota, Grand Almoner of Charles V. He died 1522.
[5] Aloisius Marlian.
[6] *I. e.*, his commentary on the Psalms, of which an edition was just coming out at Basle. *Weimar*, v. Luther's criticisms are not without foundation.

evils, am kept from the sacred things and my life is a cross. I am now on the twenty-first Psalm, *"Eli, Eli."* Hoping to finish the Psalter, if Christ please, I am working on it with all my might. But as yet not a fourth part of the Psalter has been treated; I simply have to steal the time I spend on it. You rightly warn me to be moderate, I myself know that I am not master of myself, being carried along by I know not what spirit, though I know that I consciously wish no one evil. They press furiously upon me because I have not paid Satan sufficient respect. So pray the Lord for me that I may learn, speak and write what is worthy of him and of me, not what suits them. Farewell in Christ.

409. LUTHER TO THE ELECTOR FREDERIC OF SAXONY AT WORMS.

Enders, iii. 94.   WITTENBERG, March 3, 1521.

This is the dedication to the Latin *Postilla* for Advent, which appeared at Wittenberg on March 7, 1521. Weimar, x. i. i.

Most illustrious and clement Prince, I know not to what I ought to attribute it, that I have hitherto been unable to reply to your Highness's good wishes, and, as one thing gave rise to another, have been forced to differ it from day to day. It was your excellent advice that I should put aside contentious, sharp and polemic writings, in which I have now lost three years, and devote myself to sacred and peaceable studies. You advised that in addition to my commentary on the Psalter, I should undertake homilies on the Gospels and Epistles (commonly called Postilla) for the ordinary pastor and for the people, for you thought that if I were engaged with such a mountain of work I should have to have peace with my enemies even against their will. Thus your disposition, like your name, is peaceful, so that you often show me plainly how much these contentions about trifles annoy you, for I also can despise those magnificent battles for ecclesiastical lucre, and, with the prophet[1] make Bethaven of Bethel.

I cannot easily express my aversion to being plunged in these whirlpools and taken from my studies. My flesh and blood will not quite allow me to treat the obstinate impudence

[1] Amos, v. 5. Bethaven means "the house of vanity," Bethel "the house of God."

of the wicked with moderation, and less sharply. As I acknowledge my fault in this matter, I hope that pardon will be denied me by no one who once considers what lions of Moab, what Rabshakehs of the Assyrians, how many Shimeis I alone have long been forced to bear with, to my own loss and that of many whom I might have profited in the Word of God. Thus my mind has been tossed by these whirlwinds and yet has never given up hope of getting peace sometime, by which I might please your Highness, through whom, we may not doubt, the mercy of God has brought not a little profit to Christ's gospel.

But as I see that my hope was merely human imagination, and that I am daily more deeply involved in this great sea, in which innumerable reptiles and great and small animals join forces against me, I also see that my hope was a temptation of Satan who only sought to puff me up with the vanity of my own thoughts to divert me at length from my main purpose. He wanted me to go to Babylon before I had fortified and provisioned my Jerusalem. So clever is his wickedness! Considering this I remembered that holy man Nehemiah, and leaving idle musings to Esra, the learned scribe, I began to despair of peace, and arming myself equally for peace or war, I held the sword with one hand to repulse my Arabians, and with the other built the wall,[1] lest, should I give my whole attention to either pursuit I should accomplish neither. Jerome, too, says that one who does not resist enemies of the Church does her as much harm as he does good by building up another part.

The apostle[2] also commands a bishop not only to be powerful in exhortation in sound doctrine, but also to refute those who attack it. Not that I think I am a bishop, for I have not the wealth and insignia of office which to-day are the principal marks of a bishop, but one who ministers to the Word does an episcopal office. Such must needs be an ambidextrous Ehud with his left hand prepared to thrust a dagger into fat Eglon and slay him.[3] So I, in the midst of the papists' sword, bulls, trumpets and horns trying in vain to terrify

[1] Nehemiah, iv. 17. [2] Titus, i. 9.
[3] Judges, iii. 16ff.

me, by God's grace bravely despise them all, and am girt up for a work of peace. Thus I offer your Highness the homilies you asked for. What can I not do in him who strengthens me? If I wanted to rely on my own strength, I should not dare to publish even my book on the Psalter, were I seven times Luther. For that book, not to mention my two sermons daily, requires much genius, learning, diligence and grace. I say nothing of my occupations outside the ministry of the Word.

I fear that the work will fall short of your hopes. For as there is nothing more holy in the heart of everyone than knowledge of the gospel (and rightly, since its majesty is inestimable and adorable), many will expect homilies worthy of the gospel, whereas they will find only a mouse born of the mountain's labor, and that having conceived fire I bring forth straw. I say nothing about my eloquence and elegant Latinity. For I am unskilled in these things, nor do I write for those who are skilled in them, but for the people and for men whose breath is in their nostrils as Isaiah says,[1] and who are considered noble by God. Though they speak artlessly their judgment is what I fear, especially yours, most illustrious Prince, who not only favor sacred studies with incomparable zeal, but who are so formed that you can dispute on these questions with any theologian, no matter how great. This is why the Romanists are unable to impose on you with their silly bulls, and cannot snare you in their impious superstitions, although with this gross nonsense they have to-day sent all the bishops insane.

I shall be satisfied if I lay bare the pure and simple sense of the gospel and thus meet the foolish commentaries of some. Thus the people can hear instead of fables and dreams the pure Word of God purged from human dross. I promise nothing, but this pure and simple gospel truth, meant to capture the lowly and meek. Whether I even do this others must judge, but at least no one shall learn from me to discuss matters which have nothing to do with the subject.

Deign, therefore, most illustrious Prince, in clemency to accept this my gift, and keep yourself, as you do, for the

[1] Isaiah, ii. 22.

gospel of Christ, Frederic, the pious, the great, the Saxon, the duke and the elector. Farewell in Christ.

      MARTIN LUTHER, *Augustinian.*

410. JOHN VON STAUPITZ TO WENZEL LINK.

Zeitschrift für historische Theologie, vii. (1837), p. 124. W. Reindell: *W. Linck,* p. 267.   SALZBURG, March 5, 1521.

For greeting I send you my obedience and reverence. . . . I am answering our Martin,[1] who, like you, blames my pusillanimity. As you are to me another Peter and Paul, I willingly acknowledge my fault, although I could make a verbal defence. May he who is wisdom give us wisdom and he who is the virtue of God give us courage, without whom none are strong or holy. We have no news. We anxiously await what will happen at Worms. The very reverend Lord Cardinal [Lang] has tried nothing against Martin in this diocese of Salzburg, and we hope thus to live in peace until we are stronger in faith and filled with the gospel, when we shall play the man. If news comes from Wittenberg, please communicate it to us. We also will do what will please you.

411. LUTHER TO JOHN LANG AT NUREMBERG.

Enders, iii. 99.   WITTENBERG, March 6, 1521.

Greeting. Although very busy, I write, Father, only to prevent your complaints that I write nothing to you, for I have absolutely nothing else to write. I send my trifles. My answer to Emser is just coming out.

Murnar has written two books against me. Two Italians also are said to have written against me, but I have seen neither of them as yet. The Louvain professors also have an attack on me in press. Thus am I alone assailed by so many hydras, and am forced to overthrow the proverb that Hercules cannot fight with two, for I fight with ten. Preaching twice a day is work enough for one man, lecturing on the Psalter for three, my Postilla for as many, besides which I do not speak of so many enemies, of my occasional works

   [1] Letter of February 9, translated Smith, 108f.

and letters, my conversations and fraternal ministrations. For I am absolved from the rules of the Order and of the Pope and excommunicated by the authority of the bull, of all of which I am glad, although I do not leave my cowl nor my monastery.

Salute Crotus and Jonas kindly, and pray hard for the Word. For Satan slays many thousands of souls by this most satanic bull. The Bishop of Meissen has brought together and burned wagonloads full of my books, as also did the proudly and avariciously humble Bishop of Merseburg. Farewell in Christ. Melanchthon salutes you.

MARTIN LUTHER.

P. S.—Aleander the Apostate[1] Nuncio is striving with all his might to have me smitten with the imperial censure, but hitherto he has accomplished nothing.

412. EMPEROR CHARLES V. TO LUTHER.

Enders, iii. 101. German.   WORMS, March 6, 1521.

Charles, by God's Roman Emperor Elect,[2] at all times Augmentor of the Realm,[3] etc., to the Honorable, our dear and pious Dr. Martin Luther, of the Augustinian Order.

Honorable, dear and pious Sir! As we, and the Estates of the Holy Empire, here assembled, have undertaken and decreed to obtain information about certain doctrines and certain books which formerly originated with you, we have given you and hereby send our and the Empire's free safe-conduct to come hither and to return hence. We desire you to prepare certainly to be here within twenty-one days,[4] rely-

---

[1] Pun, instead of "Apostolic."

[2] Although he had been crowned at Aix, Charles still calls himself "elected" Roman Emperor because he had not yet been crowned by the Pope, which was done at Bologna in February, 1530.

[3] This title was assumed by the emperors to show their zeal for increasing the imperial territory (Mehrer des Reichs). It was recently applied to Francis Joseph on his annexation of Bosnia and Herzogovina. *Cambridge Modern History*, xii. 175. For the same reason the title "Augustus" was assumed by Philip of France, because he thought it came from "augeo" and indicated that he had enlarged the kingdom.

[4] Reckoned from the day on which the herald handed Luther the summons, March 27. On all this *cf*. Smith, 109ff.

ing on our safe-conduct and not fearing any force or wrong. For we will surely maintain you in this our safe-conduct, and will allow you finally on it to come to us, in which you will do our pleasure.

CHARLES. (SEAL)

>Signed by the command of the Emperor: ALBERT Cardinal of Mayence, Arch-Chancellor, with his own hand
>
> NICHOLAS ZIEGLER.[1]

413. SAFE-CONDUCT OF CHARLES V. FOR LUTHER.

Enders, iii. 102. German.   WORMS, March 6, 1521.

We, Charles the Fifth, by God's Grace Roman Emperor Elect, at all times Augmentor of the Realm of Germany, Spain, both Sicilies, Jerusalem, Hungary, Dalmatia, Croatia, etc., King, Archduke of Austria and Duke of Burgundy, Count of Hapsburg, Flanders and Tyrol, etc.

Recognize: As we for good reasons have invited Martin Luther of the Augustinian Order here to Worms, that therefore we have given him our and the Holy Empire's free safe-conduct. We promise him by our imperial power knowingly in virtue of this letter, that within one and twenty days he may come to Worms to answer this our letter and to learn our and the Diet's action on the same, and that he may return hence to his safe place uninjured and unhindered by us and by all men. By this letter we earnestly request all Electors and Princes, spiritual and temporal, Prelates, Counts, Barons, Knights, Captains, Provosts, Bailiffs, Wardens, Lieutenants, Officers, Judges, Burgomasters, Justices, Councillors, Citizens and Commons, and all other our loyal subjects in whatever office, station or condition they may be, to maintain this safe-conduct for the said Martin Luther, to escort and have him escorted on his journey hither and back, and not to injure or vex him, nor let anyone else do it in any way, under pain of

---

[1] Of Nördlingen, secretary under Maximilian, who in 1518 gave him a fief and used him in diplomacy. At this time he was Vice-Chancellor of Germany. He helped Aleander with the Mandate of March 10, and the Edict of Worms. He acted against the Reformation at Nördlingen 1525. He died 1534. P. Kalkoff: *Aleander gegen Luther*, 24ff.

our and the Empire's severe displeasure and punishment. This letter gives notice of our earnest purpose.

CHARLES.

Signed at the command of the Lord Emperor:
ALBERT Cardinal of Mayence, Arch-Chancellor, with his own hand.

NICHOLAS ZIEGLER.

414. LUTHER TO SPALATIN AT WORMS.

Enders, iii. 106.   WITTENBERG, March 7, 1521.

Greeting. Dear Spalatin, this youth of good parts, Michael Creutzer,[1] wishes your support and mine in asking our most clement elector for a living. I owe him nothing, but would not refuse my aid, wherefore, do you try if anything can be done in your name or in mine. For you rightly believe that you have some influence in the court.

We have no other news except that the bull is getting more despised every day. I wrote previously what happened at Leipsic. It is said to have been posted up at Torgau, but secretly and it was soon torn. Posted at Döbeln, it was soon dirtied and torn, and these words written up: *"The nest is here; the birds have flown."*[2]

Duke Henry of Saxony[3] strongly denounced it at Freiberg. I wrote him a letter for they said that he wanted one. The King of Denmark[4] also opposes the papists, having given a

---

[1] A scion of a noble family of Meissen. Spalatin apparently acceded to Luther's request, and was later brought to regret it by the conduct of the youth. Cf. Luther's letter to Spalatin, January 22, 1522; Enders, iii. 287.

[2] German.

[3] Henry the Pious, born 1473, a son of Albert the Brave and younger brother of Duke George of Albertine Saxony. From the first he was inclined to the Reformation, and when he succeeded to the ducal throne, in April, 1539, invited Luther and Melanchthon to Leipsic to institute the evangelic faith. He died on August 18, 1541, to be followed by his son Maurice.

[4] Luther writes "Rex Daciae." He means Christian II. of Denmark, who succeeded to the throne in 1513, but was driven out in April, 1521. In the summer of 1521 he visited the Netherlands to get from Charles V. the dowry for his wife, a sister of that monarch. Brown: *Calendar of Venetian Papers*, iii. 248. Here he met Dürer, Erasmus and others sympathetic to the Reform, which he took up with zeal, visiting Wittenberg in October, 1523. He was reconciled to the Catholic Church in 1529. He spent the rest of his life in exile and prison until his death 1559. *Cambridge Modern History*, ii. 608-14.

command to his University not to condemn my writings. Dr. Martin Reinhard,[1] whom we sent thither, has told us of this, having returned here to take his degree, after which he will go back to Copenhagen.

I wrote formerly what happened to Emser's book at Magdeburg. At length, Ambrose Catharinus[2] has come from Nuremberg. Good Heavens! what an inept, stupid Thomist! He almost kills us first with laughing, then with boredom. I will answer him briefly and thus move the Italian beast's bile.

Two Counts of Stolberg[3] have come to us to study. Farewell and pray for me. Cranach[4] has asked me to sign these portraits[5] and send them to you. Do you take care of them. We are now preparing a comparison[6] of Christ and the Pope, a good book for the laity.

MARTIN LUTHER, *Augustinian*.

[1] A priest of the diocese of Würzburg, later pastor at Jena, from which he was driven out to Nuremberg in 1524. During the winter of 1520-1 he was at Copenhagen assisting the king in introducing the Reformation. *Cf. infra*, April 25, 1521, no. 460, and Kolde, *Zeitschrift für Kirchengeschichte*, viii. 289. Enders, iii. 107.

[2] Lancelot de' Politi of Siena (1484-1553) studied at Siena, where he became Dr. jur. utr. at 17. Later he taught here and in 1514 at Rome. In 1515 he was made by Leo X. Consistorial Advocate at Florence. Under the influence of Savonarola's writings he entered the Dominican cloister here in 1517. He left Florence in 1521, wandering around, until in 1532 he got to Lyons, then to Paris and 1540-3 again at Lyons. He took an important part in the Council of Trent 1546-9, spending the remaining two years of his life at Rome. He wrote a good deal, chiefly against Luther, beginning with an oration to Charles V., published December 20, 1520. Life by J. Schweitzer, 1910, and F. Lauchert in *Die italienischen Gegner Luthers*, 1912, pp. 30-133.

[3] Wolfgang (1501-1552) and Lewis (1505-75), sons of Count Botho. They matriculated in the fall of 1520.

[4] Lucas Müller, of Kronach in Franconia, whence he took his name (1472-1553). Nothing is known of his early life. In 1504 he produced his first and perhaps greatest masterpiece, the "Flight into Egypt" (Berlin). In the same year he became court painter to Frederic the Wise and settled at Wittenberg, where, besides pursuing his artistic profession, he drove the trades of printer, goldsmith, banker and apothecary. His first picture of Luther is dated 1520. *Cf.* Luther's letter to him, Smith, p. 119. The relations of the two were warm for many years, but in 1539 cooled temporarily as Luther suspected Cranach of cornering the wheat and raising prices, and also blamed him for an indecent picture. Life in *Encyclopedia Britannica*, and *cf.* E. Flechsig: *Cranachstudien*, 1900.

[5] I believe these to be Cranach's copper engravings of Luther, reproduced in my *Luther*, opposite, p. 118. This engraving bears the date "1521" and must therefore have been done before Luther left Wittenberg on April 2. Enders did not make this identification, but thought of some of Cranach's illustrations to books, but "effigies" properly means "portrait" and Luther would not sign anyone else's. Spalatin probably gave some of them to his followers at Worms.

[6] The *Passional Christi et Antichristi*, reproduced Weimar, ix., appendix.

415. MICHAEL HUMMELBERG TO VADIAN AT ST. GALL.
Vadianische Briefsammlung, ii. 344.　　　Ratisbon, March 7, 1521.

. . . Your opinion of Luther greatly pleased me. I think him a man of eminent genius and erudition and of singular judgment. His writings for the most part breathe out evangelic and apostolic doctrine and simple truth, that is, Christ himself, and they do it so forcibly that no sophist and impostor, no soft and effeminate man, no Pharisee and self-righteous[1] person, no papist and flatterer either will or can bear it. . . . May God Almighty make Luther and the truth triumph. . . .

416. ALEANDER TO THE VICE-CHANCELLOR CARDINAL DE' MEDICI.
Kalkoff: *Aleander*, 114.　　　Worms (March 8), 1521.

The Emperor, at the advice of his councillors, in order, as they say, to please the princes and quiet the people, has decided to summon Martin, and he has issued a public mandate directing that all his books "be given into the Emperor's hands until his further decision."[2] Under these circumstances I have at least exerted myself to bring the mandate into a form agreeable to the intentions of the Holy See and to the honor and authority of the Pope. In this effort the draftsman of the German Chancery, Nicholas Ziegler, has done me good service, so that, if they do not go behind us and act contrary to the decree of the Diet and the wording of the mandate, I hope that we shall, by it, put a limit to this rascally heresy. Finally, it is much better to have had the Emperor put this out on his own authority, provided that they do not disregard their numerous resolutions to the contrary and act against us. For although I have hitherto doubted that it could be their intention to use Luther as a weapon to put pressure upon the pope in other matters, I have now, alas! been obliged to convince myself of the correctness of this surmise. For yesterday evening when the Emperor betook himself for

---

[1] "Iustitiarius," Luther's word for people who relied for justification on their own works, not on faith.

[2] He issued this mandate on his own responsibility, failing to get the Diet to condemn the books to be burned. Printed by Förstemann: *Neues Urkundenbuch*, p. 61. *Cf.* Smith, p. 110.

recreation to the city fortifications, in order to see a horse given him by the Marquis of Mantua,[1] I determined to urge the preparation of the mandate in a conversation with Chièvres, who, because of his affability and because of our common relations with the Bishop of Liège and his land, has always been accessible to me. We chatted a good while. I exhorted him to give us his help for the decisive suppression of this horrible heresy, by which the position of his Emperor would be considerably improved, and his own fame certainly augmented, for finally all would be ascribed to him. Among other things he answered: "Only take care that the Pope does his duty by us and acts loyally to us, and we will satisfy his Holiness in all things." After further remarks he continued: "If you could only say that your Pope didn't always cross our plans, his Holiness can have all he wants of us; but otherwise we will plunge him into such embarrassments that he will have difficulty in finding his way out." From these and similar confidential expressions I concluded that for some months, or at least since the meeting of the Emperor and Elector of Saxony at Cologne, they had the intention of making a political use of the Lutheran question. Moreover, sometime ago, they wrote to Hutten; since then nothing more has been heard from him; certainly they did not merely command his silence, but also bade him wait for further developments. I have it on good authority that many of them have already thought of taking Hutten into the imperial service and conferring their commissions on him. This was decided in the council of state, in order, as they said, to silence him in that way, for it is hard to punish a German noble and would cause a big disturbance, especially if he has a large following like Hutten, who has conspired with Francis von Sickingen against the Church—that sounds sweeter to German ears than anything else.

Yet it may be possible that they are doing all this with good intentions to keep Germany quiet, and that otherwise his Majesty would only make himself difficulties. So I answered

[1] Frederic (1500-1540), son of Francis de Gonzaga, and his wife, Isabella d'Este, became Marquis at the death of his father 1519. He was educated at Rome, where he was a favorite of Julius II., at Milan and the French court. He received Charles V. at Bologna 1529-30. J. Cartwright: *Isabella d'Este,* 1903.

Chièvres, as seemed to me most judicious, that I did not know exactly what he was alluding to with his generalizations. But I could not refrain from answering boldly to his expression "your Pope," that if they were Christians the Pope was just as much their lord as ours, and that with all their power they had better avoid the wrath of God "who takes princes in their pride,"[1] and that they should not, as though careless of their duty, mix the affair of the faith with private and temporal interests. He replied that they had no intention of destroying the faith, that I only need note carefully what he had said, and he added, smiling, that for himself he did not think the suppression of the Lutheran movement would be so extremely difficult. Then I said to him straight out that if they were not very careful they would soon see such a conflagration throughout the world as all the water in their German Ocean could not put out.

We live in evil times, when men show so little respect for God and his true vicegerent, and everyone turns his conscience according to his need, and if occasion comes up their confessors encourage them not to fear ecclesiastical punishment and to despise that which it is their duty to esteem highly. I know what I say, for I have seen it, without wishing to, for some time, but I can't tell it all in my letters. I only pray his Holiness most earnestly to conduct the Roman policy with the greatest circumspection, at least until we have finished with this Lutheran question, so that no offence be given to these people. I mean the Emperor and his court and the whole German nation.

I notice that the favor for Luther shown by the princes and estates at the Diet has considerably cooled off, and I see clearly that, as many assure me and as I myself would hardly have believed, this is the result of my oration on Ash Wednesday, for these princes and nobles had only read Luther's slanderous attacks on Pope and clergy, but not his expressions about the sacraments and his avowal of all the doctrines of John Huss. Since I pointed that out before a numerous assembly on the ground of his own writings, very many of the princes abhor him, and only the hatred for Rome stands in the way of en-

[1] Psalm lxxvi. 13.

tirely appeasing them. For ten days I have not observed any outbreak of wrath. God grant that we shall get better results every day. I count with certainty on that, if only they do not from some secret reason deceive us, as they would do with passionate eagerness, since they have convinced themselves that they can be good Christians while opposing the Pope, and that the Catholic faith can stand under those conditions. What a serious error! . . .

The German mandate commanding the sequestration of the books and their surrender to the Emperor, will be printed next Monday[1] and sent by couriers of his Majesty to all parts of Germany. I will tell you in time its effect. Your Lordship will be convinced that we have not spared and do not spare doing the utmost in our power. If the result has not entirely come up to our intentions, the reason is that no other road was open to us. With our evident proofs, our good words and flattery, with bold freedom of speech when necessary, we have obtained a thousand good resolutions and promises just such as we wished, but their results have hitherto been no other than those which I have so often veraciously recounted to your Lordship.

417. SPALATIN TO JOHN LANG AT ERFURT.
K. Krause: *Epistolae Aliquot*, 3. WORMS, March 8, 1521.

. . . The cause of the gospel and Luther is much agitated, but it is remarkable what agreement on the man there is among clergy and laity, princes and people, albeit I hear that most of the clergy are passive, not wishing to resist the Pope. Saturday of last week the Emperor had read a document against our Luther and his followers to be published and to say that he will be summoned either here or elsewhere to recant the doctrines which his little professors have told him are heretical; I know not what will happen. God helping us we shall see; meantime, let us pray for the safety of the whole Church. I do not think our elector need be bothered to write letters in Luther's behalf to the town council and people of Erfurt. For Luther will be safe, even though all the enemies of the gospel are unconquered. . . .   G. SPALATIN.

[1] March 11.

418. WILLIAM WARHAM, ARCHBISHOP OF CANTERBURY, TO THOMAS WOLSEY, CARDINAL ARCHBISHOP OF YORK.

Letters and Papers of Henry VIII., iii. no. 1193. English.

KNOLL, March 8, 1521.

I have received letters from Oxford, stating that the university is infected with Lutheranism, and that many books forbidden by you have circulation there. I regret that this should have happened in a place where I was brought up and of which I am now chancellor. The university desires me to be a mean to your Reverence, that such order be taken for the examination of the suspected, as that it incur no infamy. I think it a pity that a small number of incircumspect fools should endanger the whole university with the charge of Lutheranism; a thing pleasant to the Lutherans beyond sea, and a great encouragement, if the two universities, one of which has been void of all heresies [Oxford],[1] and the other boasts it has never been defiled [Cambridge], should embrace these heretical tenets. It would create great slander if all now suspected were brought up to London; I desire, therefore, some commission may sit at Oxford, to examine, not the Heads, but the novices. The university will be glad if you will request the Bishops of Rochester[2] and London[3] to draw up a table[4] of Lutheran writers who are to be avoided, and send it down to Oxford.

419. LUTHER TO JOHN FREDERIC, DUKE OF SAXONY.

Enders, iii. 109. De Wette, i. 571. German. Dedication to the *Magnificat*, Weimar, vii. 538. WITTENBERG, March 10, 1521.

Serene, high-born Prince, gracious Lord! My humble prayer and service to your Grace. I have received your

[1] Oxford had, in fact, been a hotbed of heresy, following both William of Occam and Wicliffe.

[2] Fisher.

[3] Cuthbert Tunstall.

[4] Such a general decree was drawn up by Wolsey on May 14, 1521, reprinted Wilkins: *Concilia Magnae Britanniae*, iii. 690. At Cambridge a commission consisting of Drs. Bullock, Humfry, Watson and Ridley had been sent to London to examine Luther's works in 1520. Later (1521?) his works were burnt at Cambridge. *Cf. Registers of Cambridge*, v. 499.

Grace's kind letter[1] recently written me, and have read all the comfortable contents with joy. As a long time ago I promised your Grace to expound the *Magnificat,* from which work the unhappy quarrels of many opponents have often driven me, I have undertaken to answer your Grace with this little book, thinking that further delay might make me blush, and that I have no more good excuses for hindering your Grace's young mind, which is inclined to love of Holy Writ, and which by exercise in the same might be inflamed and strengthened, for which I wish you God's grace and aid. This is very needful, for many people's salvation depends on so great a prince; if he himself endeavors, he will be ruled graciously by God; and on the other hand many people perish if he lets himself go, and is ungraciously ruled by God.

Although all men's hearts are in the hand of God Almighty, yet it was not vainly said of kings and princes alone: The heart of the king is in God's hand, who can turn it where he will.[2] By this God puts his fear in the great lords, that they may learn not to think that God does not pay particular attention to them. Other men's acts bring either piety or harm only to themselves or to very few; but lords are set up only to be harmful or helpful to other people, the greater number according to the magnitude of their dominions. So too the Bible calls pious, God-fearing princes angels[3] of God, and even gods,[4] and contrariwise it calls noxious princes lions,[5] dragons[6] and wild beasts, which God himself calls one of his four plagues when he enumerates pestilence, famine, war and wild beasts.[7]

And as the human heart is by nature flesh and blood, and easily presumes of its own accord, therefore, when power, wealth and honor are given it, it has another strong cause to presumption and too sure self-confidence, so that it forgets God and does not esteem its subjects, and as it has power to do evil with impunity, it does it and becomes a beast and does what it pleases, and is by name a lord, but in fact a

---
[1]December 20, 1520. Enders, iii. 22.   [2]Proverbs, xxi. 1.
[3]1 Samuel, xxix. 9.   [4]Psalm lxxxii. 6.
[5]Zephaniah, v. 5.   [6]Jeremiah, li. 34.
[7]Ezekiel, xiv. 13-19.

monster, so that also the wise man Bias[1] has well said: *Magistratus virum ostendit,* that is, Rule shows what a man is. For subjects dare not transgress for fear of the government.

Wherefore all rulers, who do not have to fear men, must needs fear God more than do others, and know him and his works well, and act with diligence, as St. Paul[2] says: He that ruleth, let him do it with diligence.

Now I know nothing in the whole Bible which serves his purpose better than this holy canticle of the Blessed Mother of God. All who wish to reign rightly ought to learn it. Truly she here sings sweetly of the fear of God, and what kind of Lord he is, and what his works are to those of high and low estate. Let another listen to his wench singing a worldly song; a prince and lord may well listen to this chaste Virgin singing a spiritual, pure and holy song.

It is no unsuitable custom to have this song sung in all churches daily at vespers, in a special and seemly way, before other songs. May the same tender Mother of God give me the spirit to expound this her song usefully and thoroughly, that your Grace and all of us may get from it wholesome knowledge and a praiseworthy life, by which we may sing this *Magnificat* in the life eternal. God help us to do it. Amen. Herewith I commend myself to your Grace, humbly praying that you will take my small achievement kindly.

Your Grace's humble chaplain,
Dr. Martin Luther.

420. ELECTOR FREDERIC OF SAXONY TO MARTIN LUTHER AT WITTENBERG.

Enders, iii. 110.   Worms, March 11, 1521.

In the name of God! Greeting. Honorable, reverend and learned, dear and pious Sir! We graciously inform you that his Imperial Majesty has requested us also to provide you with a safe-conduct. We send you herewith a written safe-conduct addressed to the officers, cities and other subjects of our brother and ourself, directing them to provide you with

---

[1] Bias of Priene, fl. 570 B. C. Erasmus in his *Adages* gave this saying to Pittacus; Luther was probably quoting from him, but made a slip in memory.
[2] Romans, xii. 8.

sufficient escort through our dominions. His Imperial Majesty also sends you a safe-conduct and writes you as you will have received. We would not conceal this from you, for we are graciously inclined to you.[1]

421. BEATUS RHENANUS TO GEORGE SPALATIN AT WORMS.

Briefwechsel des Beatus Rhenanus, 269. BASLE, March 11, 1521.

I remember that some years ago I received a letter from you requesting me to send the fragment of Velleius Paterculus I had recently found, to Wittenberg to be placed in the library of your elector. I delayed answering your letter only because it was my present intention to publish Velleius and to send, not an empty letter, but the author himself to Wittenberg. . . . Wherefore I have dedicated this author to your elector, because I see that he alone cares for sound learning and true piety. What eternal fame will be his if he does not desert Martin Luther now when the latter most needs protection. Nor will he desert him, if he is inspired by your counsels. Wherefore stretch all the powers of your mind to get him to treat this most happy cause of reviving piety with the mature gravity which religion demands. I know what your elector can do, and how the whole world will then attribute its happiness to him. But why should I urge on one who is eager himself?

. . . Hitherto our nation has suffered itself to be exhausted in buying palls, livings and indulgences to give the Pope the means of waging war. I think that Martin Luther has been summoned by the princes for this reason, that he may help them by his counsel to put a limit to the papal tyranny. Some who fear violence wish he had not been summoned. But I see that his citation is the only way to prevent the imperial edict. He will briefly set forth the essence of Christianity, and will show how much our lives, and especially those of the prelates, have degenerated from it. Moreover, he must begin with the head [of the Church]. I cannot deny

---

[1] Here follows a safe-conduct, dated March 12, in much the same terms as that of Charles given above. There was also one from Duke George, dated March 8. Enders, iii. 108.

that some suspect that if the Emperor seems to favor Luther the Pope will gather an army of French and Swiss to keep him to his duty by threatening the kingdom of Naples. But more than enough of this. Offer your most Christian elector Velleius, and commend me warmly to his highness. Give Luther and Melanchthon my greetings. Please do not publish this letter. Farewell, most distinguished Sir! . . .

422. ERASMUS TO ALEXANDER, SECRETARY OF THE COUNT OF NASSAU.

Erasmi opera (1703), iii. 1695. LOUVAIN, March 13, 1521.

. . . I do not read Luther's books nor have anything in common with him more than with any Christian. Certainly I should prefer him corrected than slain. And if any poison has infected the people, no one can draw it out again as well as he who has put it in. But I do not object if they wish Luther roasted or boiled; the loss of one man is small. And yet we ought to think of the public peace. Would that the crafty rather than wise agents for this affair were as prudent as they seem zealous in the cause of the Pope. Certainly none hurt the Pope's dignity more than those who clamor hatefully against Luther; no one commends him to the people more than they do. So stupidly and tumultuously is the business conducted by certain monks, not one of whom is a good man! The bull commands them to preach against Luther, that is, to rebutt his opinions with proof from Scripture and to teach better ones. But no one takes the pen to refute him, though many desire it; there is none who argues, but all revile and often lie about it. They say that he would abolish confession and purgatory and that he writes blasphemy against God. A certain Jacobin at Antwerp said that he had written that Christ did his miracles by magic. A Carmelite preaching before the king of France said that now the Antichrist had come, and that there were four harbingers: some Franciscan[1] or other in Italy, Lefèvre d'Étaples in France, Reuchlin in Germany, and Erasmus in Brabant. At Bruges a Franciscan, a suffragan of the Bishop of Tournai, preached in the church of St. Donatian a whole hour against Luther and me

---

[1] Savonarola was a Dominican, but perhaps he is meant.

(for the monks have agreed over their cups always to join my name with Luther's, though I have nothing in common with him), but instead of teaching us he only called us geese, asses, beasts, stocks, Antichrists, in short, spoke so that the people all thought him insane. . . .

Whatever Luther may deserve, it is certainly time for Charles to think of the peace of Christendom. This will be done if silence is imposed on both parties, and if Luther ceases to write such books, or rather takes out of those that he has already written all seditious matter. Those who hunt for glory in public misfortunes prefer to end the thing at once by force; would that it were ended for the glory of Christ! But no one would believe how deeply Luther has crept into the minds of many nations, nor how widely his books have been translated into every tongue and scattered everywhere. People are whispering about a terrific mandate of Charles; I pray that whatever the excellent prince does may be fortunate for the Christian world, but I fear that things will not turn out as some think. Do you ask, dear Alexander, why I write this? Only to prevent a pernicious tumult which I see is threatening unless the princes prefer the interests of the state to the desires of some men. I do not plead Luther's cause, nor do I care how he is punished; I only think of the peace of the world. . . .

423. ALVISE GRADENIGO TO THE SIGNORY OF VENICE.

Sanuto, xxx. 17 tergo, f. Brown, iii. 171. (Translation from Italian.)

ROME, March 15, 1521.

A work composed by Friar Martin Luther has been brought to Rome, and the Pope makes great account of it. The Cardinals Lawrence Pucci and Ancona consulted together about this matter, about which the Pope is very anxious. Friar Martin has a numerous sect in Germany.

424. ALEANDER TO CARDINAL JULIUS DE' MEDICI AT ROME.

Kalkoff: *Aleander,* 119.   WORMS (March 15 and 16), 1521.

. . . I now turn to what has happened since my last letter. Your Lordship will know that six days ago a courier of the

Emperor was to have gone to Luther with a safe-conduct drawn up in such a form that many conjecture Luther will not come. I know not how it came about, but four days ago they decided not to send an ordinary courier, but a herald, and they have changed the wording of the safe-conduct. I succeeded in getting them to allow me to glance at the Emperor's letter[1] to Luther, which begins: "Honorable, dear and pious." This title they give to an open heretic against God and reason! When I complained they answered that that was the regular style, and if they had chosen a rough form it would simply happen that he would not come. The further contents of the summons plainly show that the imperialists are very desirous that Luther should come. I know not how it will turn out, but God grant it may be for the best. What makes them want this I do not know certainly, but I guess their reason without daring to write it.

But I will not conceal that on the very day on which the news of Robert de la Marck's invasion[2] arrived, the safe-conduct was suddenly altered. What is the connection between this event and Luther's treatment? The imperialists are accurately informed that the King of France is at the bottom of these disturbances, and they fear that in the impending great war the Pope will give his blessing and his aid to their enemy. I believe, however, that this is a totally wrong surmise, and I have told them so. I got my information from a private conversation which I had with them one day on this movement in our principality of Liège. They do not speak so freely to Caracciolo and Raphael de' Medici. . . .

In any case we will do our duty. I cannot promise myself much good from Luther's coming, although the sequestration mandate has a tone which suggests a result favorable to us. So at least the Emperor and Chièvres promise, though I hardly know what to make of their fine resolutions and regulations in this affair, contrary to which they have so often acted. God alone knows whether Luther will come, which some believe and some deny. That the imperialists

---

[1] *Supra*, no. 412.
[2] *I. e.*, of a French army under this general, Robert II. Comte de la Marck, Prince of Sedan, a brother of Everard, Bishop of Liège, a condottiere general in the service of Francis. He died 1535.

earnestly desire the appearance of this Antichrist is plain from the form of their summons. The Elector of Brandenburg has spoken to me of a splendid plan concerning Luther's affair by himself and his brother, from which he expects great results, but at present he won't say anything more about it. We shall soon see what it is. I hope that God will turn it all to the best. . . .

It is remarkable that some Germans who write against Luther in German and Latin find no printers, and if by money and good words they actually do get their books printed, all the copies are immediately bought by the Lutherans, who, like the Marannos,[1] have common funds, and destroyed. . . .

425. ALEANDER TO THE VICE-CHANCELLOR JULIUS DE' MEDICI.

Kalkoff: *Aleander,* 139.   WORMS (March 19), 1521.

Yesterday morning I set out to press forward the mandate, the printing of which was finished yesterday evening. But those who are entrusted with its preparation exercise pressure on us for its delay for no other reason, as far as I can guess, or rather am almost certain, than that it should not be published before Luther has started to come hither. For the opinion of all these gentlemen is that if he knew of the mandate he would not come, and that would be, as I have already often stated, not according to the wish of the imperial council.

Further I discovered another merchant, who, returning from the Frankfort Fair, brought a great mass of Lutheran books, both the earlier ones and some that have appeared since and are as bad as the others. People are beginning to talk of Martin again. But if these imperialists don't do us an injustice, we will take all these books away within forty-eight hours. . . .

This noon Caracciolo and I dined with a numerous and noble company as guests of the most serene Elector of Brand-

---

[1] The Spanish Jews or Moors who had been converted by force to Christianity. A good many of them were at Antwerp, where they made a very clannish community.

enburg. Present were the Elector of Trier, the Bishops of Bamberg, Strassburg,[1] Hildesheim,[2] Augsburg and Brandenburg. The talk was of Luther's affair and the opinion was that there would be no danger that the Estates would not do what the Emperor commanded. What happens I shall tell your Lordship later.

In Frankfort I hear that many citizens have forbidden their wives and families to confess their secret sins to the priests. The Bishop of Augsburg, an able man, much prized and consulted by the Diet, assures us that in his city many owners of Luther's books refuse to give them up to their confessors, and occasionally make them grant absolution by force.

426. JOHN MANUEL, IMPERIAL AMBASSADOR AT ROME, TO CHARLES V.

Bergenroth, ii. p. 341. (English translation of Spanish original.)

ROME, March 20, 1521.

The Pope urges me to remind your Majesty in every letter I write, that you should not treat the affairs concerning Martin Luther lightly. Some of the cardinals complained in consistory that your Majesty had ordered Martin Luther into your presence, saying that you had thereby arrogated to yourself a jurisdiction belonging to the Holy See. I exculpated you. The Pope said that he had been informed that your Majesty was ill advised when you decided to see Martin Luther, "who would not be well received even in hell." His Holiness begs your Majesty not to forget your obligations towards God, the Church and himself.

427. LUTHER TO NICHOLAS HAUSMANN AT SCHNEEBERG.

Enders, iii. 115.   WITTENBERG, March 22, 1521.

Hausmann (1479-October 17, 1538), born at Freiberg in Saxony, was one of Luther's warmest friends, more than a hundred letters of the Reformer to him having survived. In 1521 he became pastor at Zwickau, from which he was driven by a quarrel with his congre-

---

[1] William III. von Honstein, Bishop of Strassburg 1506-1541.
[2] John IV., Bishop of Hildesheim 1504-1527.

gation in 1531. After spending ten months at Wittenberg, he accepted a call to the court chaplaincy of the Princes of Anhalt at Dessau. In 1538 he went to Freiberg. See E. Kroker: *Katharina von Bora,* 217, and my *Luther,* index.

Greeting. I received your letter, dearest Nicholas, telling me that you had been called to preach at Zwickau, and asking consolation from poor little me. You know how perilous are these times, and that it is simply that time for flight which Christ predicted. For it is a time when sound doctrine is not maintained, when wolves are made shepherds, and there is no consolation for us, save to pray the Lord, by whose aid we may either escape or stand fast in these evil days. I have more experience daily how widely and deeply Satan reigns, so that it is a horror to me to envisage the Church. Daily I am becoming more persuaded that no one can be saved unless he fight against the laws and commands of the Pope and of the bishops with all his might through life and death. Is this surprising or novel to you? But it is so, dearest Nicholas. If you do not grasp it, you are not capable of receiving any consolation from me. We have found that the Pope and his men are simple enemies of Christ, so that no one can preach save he who takes care to subject his sheep to him, and, as it were, to lead them to the wolf. You know how loudly they shout against the crimes of schism and heresy to-day; but what can we do? There is no other way of safety in this time of perdition.

Now, Nicholas, if my advice is evil it is worst of all for him who gives it, and I will let you act on your judgment and at your own risk about following it. If you take the pastorate make yourself the enemy of the Pope and the bishops and fight their decrees; if you do not do this you will be an enemy of Christ. Christ's faith does not stand freely with their snares and fallacies. In all this I judge nothing for you, but as you asked my advice I give it. You should either not ask advice or you should take it kindly when given. I call God to witness that I can give no other. Farewell.

    Yours,

      MARTIN LUTHER, *Augustinian.*

428. GEORGE SPALATIN TO BEATUS RHENANUS AT BASLE.

Briefwechsel des Beatus Rhenanus, 271.   WORMS, March 24, 1521.

Most learned Beatus Rhenanus! If ever a letter pleased me, assuredly yours, recently delivered to me by our friend John Froben, pleased me, the more as it was accompanied by Velleius Paterculus, dedicated by you to our Lord Frederic, most Christian Elector of Saxony. . . .

Luther seems to be summoned to recant, which he so hates that I am sure he will suffer anything rather than do so. But I hope he will come, for he is summoned under the safe-conduct both of the Emperor and of my elector and other princes. Perhaps the wretches will prevent his coming to have a good excuse for treating him as an enemy. Farewell with greeting to all your good friends. In haste,

GEORGE SPALATIN, *Chaplain.*

429. ERASMUS TO ALOISIUS MARLIAN, BISHOP OF TUI, AT WORMS.

Erasmi opera, iii. 543.   LOUVAIN, March 25 (1521).

I have learned from the letters of good friends, though I know not whether they wrote in pure affection, that new rumors and suspicions are spread abroad here by some secret detractors that I favor Luther, and that I know not what evil books are attributed to me of which I hear that some are published here, some elsewhere. I know that these days are the very kingdom of calumny, and that at no time has more unbridled vituperation been allowed, and yet wise, learned and grave men, among whom I consider you one of the first, should not allow any place to such accusations. Your prudence first warned me, though I was, as they say, mindful of it myself, that I should not mix in the Lutheran affair. So far was I from mixing in it that I exerted all my strength to keep the affair from getting to that point where I should least care to see it. Only at the first before I saw where Luther was tending I did not approve turbulent clamors among the people. I advised that the affair be treated in learned books. I preferred to have Luther corrected than crushed, or, if he were to be crushed, I preferred that it should be done without turning the world upside down. Even the Pope would have approved this advice, had he known how things were done, and with what zeal several nations would follow Luther. But the rumors were the fabrications of certain monks, who love me no more than they do sound learning, and who were determined to involve me willy nilly in the Lutheran affair.

On the other hand, those who seemed to favor Luther tried every way to draw me into their party. Those who hated Luther tried also to precipitate me into his faction, frequently in public sermons raging against my name more odiously than they did against Luther himself. But I could be moved by no arts from my own purpose. I recognize Christ, I do not know Luther; I recognize the Roman Church which I think is not different from the Catholic Church. Death shall not make me abandon her, unless she openly is abandoned by Christ. I have always abhorred sedition; would that Luther and all Germans were of the same mind. I see that in many lands this side of the Alps there are men who favor Luther as it were by fatality. Indeed, it is remarkable that as his enemies help him most so he helps them, as if they were in a conspiracy. For no one hurts Luther more than he does himself with his new books, each one more odious than the last. On the other hand, there are some who stir up the people so unlearnedly, so foolishly and so seditiously that they make themselves hateful to all, commend Luther to the affections of men, and compromise the cause of the Pope as bad patrons always compromise their clients. I praise those who favor the Pope, whom every pious man favors. Who would not favor him who is the first imitator of Christ and who spends himself for Christian salvation? But I wish he had wiser defenders. They hunger for nothing but Luther, nor is it anything to me whether they prefer him boiled or roasted. It is certain that they confound me with an affair from which I am totally distinct, and that they thus act both wrongly and foolishly, for they would vanquish Luther sooner if they left me alone. Even in Aleander, a man otherwise kind and learned, I miss the prudence necessary for such an affair; if at least what is written and said about him is true. There was formerly a very close friendship between us;[1] and when he went to France I gave him letters of recommendation and spoke of him very highly even in my writings; I respected the man's learning, liked his character, although it was peculiar, nor did it seem that we got along together badly. He was commanded by all means to win over those who had formerly been of the Lutheran party—so far was it from the Pope's thoughts to alienate those who were innocent. But though not unkind in himself he used force at the instigation of certain men. He would have approached the Lutheran affair better had he joined his advantages to mine. He would have had a helper in a pious work, and one certainly not adverse to the power of the Pope.

They bandy about an impudent lie, that Luther has taken much from my books, but the very first article of the charge refutes it. When have I asserted that all that we do is sin?[2] not to mention innumerable other things, the like of which is not found in any of my writings, even in the sportive ones. And yet of old the heretics have drunk their poison from the gospels and apostolic letters. I speak for the moment as if he had really written something heretical and had taken it from my books. It is said that he does not recognize certain of his books; perhaps he would do well to deny them all; but in any case, by whomsoever the books which pass under his name were written there is not in any of them a syllable of mine; this I do not hesitate to swear solemnly. For many years I have respected your singular prudence and your candid friendship for me, and your authority is known to all. Wherefore I beg you to defend my innocence against such malicious calumnies. Everything is printed, even that which I wrote privately to the bosom of my friends, including some things which were perhaps freer, according to my natural inclination, than was always expedient. Even those things which we are accustomed to say in our cups have

---

[1] In Venice 1508. *Cf.* Allen, i. 502. *Supra,* no. 394.

[2] One of Luther's favorite propositions, condemned by the bull *Exsurge Domine,* article 36. *Cf.* Smith, *op. cit.,* p. 101. The proposition was made in general terms in the *Disputation on Scholastic Philosophy,* and more precisely in the *Heidelberg Disputation* (1518), Weimar, i. 354. *Supra,* p. 82.

been printed, and yet nothing is found except that I said I would prefer Luther corrected than put to death, while there was yet hope that he might devote himself to better things. . . .

[The second half of this letter is an expansion of the same thoughts and a repetition of the letter to Albert of Mayence, November 1, 1519.]

430. ULRICH VON HUTTEN TO EMPEROR CHARLES V. AT WORMS.

Böcking, ii. 38. EBERNBURG, March 27, 1521.

If, O Emperor, you determined to do some great and memorable injury to the common good of Germany, we Germans, on account of the affection we bear you, would do our best to oppose you as though you were taking upon yourself some great danger, for we would take it ill that you treated our interests either to your own peril or to your disadvantage. And should we not do this the more because, deceived by error, you would, to the incomparable loss of Germany, go to your own ruin? For what else is the cause of Luther leading to than the suppression of our liberty, the overturning of the state and the trampling under foot of your dignity? Wherefore I think that we should all strive with our might to recall you from the path you are treading with so much danger both to the state and to yourself, and that we should exhort and pray you to take courage worthy of your race and your fortune. . . . For what unjuster thing could you do than that which these fellows demand, namely, that you should not give Luther when he arrives a chance of explaining his cause, and what could be more calamitous or a worse example to us than that the asserter of the public liberty should be punished? And yet they are striving to get you to do both, and it is said they have extorted from you an edict forbidding his books to be read. . . . They accuse Luther of heresy not considering what crimes that involves; but they accuse him and shout that he should be condemned unheard. . . . For supposing Luther were not the man who with great zeal had brought back the evangelic truth, and had preached it with infinite pains, and had defended your dignity against those who despised it, and had guarded the liberty of

Germany against most violent tyrants, yet no law ever forbade a criminal to defend himself, for even parricides and the worst criminals have this right. . . . Only the slothful clergy would deprive him of this right, and they accuse him solely because he has written and spoken against their habits, their unbridled power, their scandalous luxury and depraved rites, in behalf of Christianity, liberty and morality. [Here follows a long tirade against the wickedness of Rome and of Aleander, and a prophecy that the Emperor will one day wish he had attended to Hutten's exhortation.] . . . Finally as no one doubts that all these things are connected with Luther's cause, you may believe that the whole of Germany is fallen at your feet, and prays you with tears to show mercy and good faith, to preserve her and restore her to herself, to free her from servitude and from tyranny, and that she abjures you by the holy memory of those who, when the Romans conquered the world, refused to be slaves, that you will not suffer us to obey these bad, effeminate weaklings. Farewell and rule us long.

431. LUTHER TO JOHN LANG AT ERFURT.

Enders, iii. 118. (WITTENBERG), March 29, 1521.

Greeting. Next Thursday or Friday[1] I will lodge with you, reverend Father, with the imperial herald[2] who summons me to Worms, unless it is dangerous for me to enter Erfurt or some unknown chance prevents. Then I will speak more fully. Otherwise you will certainly find me at Eisenach on Saturday. Thanks for the gold piece you sent me. You see how I treated my ass Emser.[3] Farewell.

Yours,

MARTIN LUTHER.

[1]April 4 or 5. In fact Luther left Wittenberg April 2 and came to Erfurt April 6.

[2]Caspar Sturm, on whom *cf. Archiv für Reformationsgeschichte*, iv. 117ff. Born at Oppendeim c. 1475, he was educated in the humanities. In 1515 he entered the service of Albert of Mayence, and on October 27, 1520, at Aix, was made imperial herald for Germany. At the same time Dürer made a portrait of him. He took Luther's safe-conduct to him, conducted him to the Diet and back to Eisenach. He wrote an account of the affair friendly to Luther 1521. After that we find him at Mayence 1522, at Nuremberg 1530, at Ratisbon 1532, at Augsburg 1547. He died 1548. He wrote several historical books.

[3]*Auf das überchristliche . . . Buch Bock Emsers*, Weimar, vii. 614ff.

432. ALEANDER TO VICE-CHANCELLOR DE' MEDICI AT ROME.

Kalkoff: *Aleander*, 141.　　　　　　　Worms, March 29, 1521.

. . . Luther has published at Basle a commentary[1] on the first thirteen Psalms of David, with, as preface, a letter of a certain "von Schönberg," who according to his own words is of low estate and not a noble, but who overflows with venomous hatred towards Rome. In his letter he summons the whole of Germany against Rome. I have only been able to read a few pages of the book, as it only came to me yesterday evening from Frankfort. As always, Luther shows himself variable and full of contradictions; in the preface he praises the Pope and in another place pulls down the papacy. Almost in the same breath he praises and blames. If he continues as thoroughly as he begins it will be a monstrous and strange book. . . .

If Luther does not come we shall soon make an end of the business, and if he does, we shall do our duty and take all suitable measures, from which I promise myself good success, if only the imperialists don't give us a shameless box on the ear.

The considerations which your Lordship wrote us in your last letter, which we read with pleasure and due respect, are extremely impressive and have been urged by us, along with other reasons, a hundred times. They are enough to melt stones to pity. But here we preach to deaf ears; they only answer that they act as they must if we expect success and not to have all our trouble in vain. Well, we shall see! Although many doubt that Luther will come, the imperialists think it certain, and, to judge by their citation, they greatly desire his presence. I have heard nothing new as yesterday and to-day[2] I have busied myself a little with God and my conscience and therefore did not go to court. All the princes are now taking thought for their salvation. I have not yet

---

[1] *Martini Lutheri piae et doctae in psalmos operationes,* 1521. (Reprinted, Weimar, v.) With a letter to Germany by Ulrich Hugwald, dated "ex Schonenberga." Published by Adam Petri at Basle. Mutius Hugwald (1496-1571) had already published Luther's *Tesseradecas* at Basle. He came to Wittenberg in July, 1521, and later became an Anabaptist and professor at Basle.
[2] Holy Thursday and Good Friday.

been able to get a copy of the Emperor's letter [to Luther], the flattering style and honorable titles of which I told you about. . . .

433. MICHAEL HUMMELBERG TO JOHN HERKMANN.

Sitzungsberichte der philphist. Klasse der kaiserlichen Akademie der Wissenschaften zu Wien, lxxxv. (1877), 126, note 2. (March, 1521.)

Herkmann was a monk at Salmansweiler, an intimate friend of Hummelberg. Notices of his letters are given by Horawitz, *loc. cit.*

Alas, dear Herkmann, who fooled you by saying that I was a Lutheran? Whoever thought that I should be baptized anew with this name, which I abhor as seditious, was mistaken. For being a Lutheran involves one in as much altercation as being an Eckian in malice. These are the names of heresies and schisms, not of Christian charity. According to the teaching of St. Paul I think not man but Christ is to be regarded, and I wish to bear his name only, and to be called not a Lutheran, but a Christian. . . . But I welcome and cherish whatever I find good in Luther's books, not because it is his, but because it is God's from whom cometh every good gift. Nor does it bother me if he does not please those barbarian theologs, and does not agree with the madness of the sycophants. . . . I shall, therefore, expect the judgment of the universal Church convened by the Holy Spirit in a council. Whatever holy and pious decrees are then made, I also shall follow. . . .

434. GREGORY BRÜCK, CHANCELLOR OF ELECTORAL SAXONY, TO SPALATIN.

Reichstagsakten, ii. 534. German. WORMS (early in April, 1521).

Honored and dear Sir. I hear two opinions from people who are favorable to Dr. Martin. Some warn us that he should by no means come hither simply on his Imperial Majesty's safe-conduct, because his Imperial Majesty's ban is ready for the condemned heretic inasmuch as he approved and sanctioned the Pope's bull. And one is not bound to keep faith with heretics. So if he came hither and would not recant, his opponents and the Romanists might find occasion to persuade the Emperor that he was not bound to observe his safe-conduct, and could not do so with good conscience, but might honorably break it. For his Majesty would have given it to him in the expectation that he would recant, but if he did not, his Majesty ought not to let him leave. For Luther has himself recognized and should know that if he does not recant no safe-conduct or other assurance would avail him. And as he is minded not to recant, as his Majesty hoped in giving him a safe-conduct, he had better remain at home and not put himself in danger, by which his Majesty would be excused. It could not then be said that the safe-conduct was broken, for Luther, as a condemned heretic, has no right to trust a safe-conduct. . . . But as he thinks that all that he has hitherto written has been founded in the Scripture, and that he cannot revoke it, unless he is convinced by sufficient reason, let him consider that his coming hither would be in vain and cause much trouble. . . .

But other friends think that he should by no means stay away for this reason, for as the Emperor recognizes in the recently posted mandate that he invites Martin hither at the advice of the electors and princes, as indeed is the truth, that therefore the electors and princes, especially the temporal ones, would not allow anything contrary to the safe-conduct to be done to him. Secondly, that the Emperor would not break his safe-conduct. . . . On Easter day [March 31] I had an interview with the secretary of Aragon[1] who asked what I thought of Luther's affair and whether he would come hither. I replied that Luther was a reasonable and learned man, and that he undoubtedly would come. That shocked him. . . .

I hardly know therefore what it is advisable for Martin to do, but I fear he will think there is no alternative but to come.

435. JOHN MANUEL, IMPERIAL AMBASSADOR AT ROME TO CHARLES V.

Bergenroth, ii. p. 343. (English translation of Spanish original.)

ROME, April 3, 1521.

The affairs of Luther are very troublesome to the Pope. After having heard what I communicated to him, the Holy

---

[1] The secretary of Aragon was Hugo de Urries, though it is possible that Brück was thinking of someone else.

Father exclaimed: "God be thanked who has sent me in these times an Emperor who takes so much care of the Church!" The Pope is very thankful for all your Majesty has promised, and only begs you to fulfil your promise, and not to permit men who are "hearkening to the counsel of the Devil" to lead you astray, as it is said they will do. These are the very words his Holiness ordered me to write your Majesty.

436. DUKE JOHN OF SAXONY TO ELECTOR FREDERIC AT WORMS.

T. Kolde: *Friedrich der Weise*, p. 44. German.

COBURG, April 4, 1521.

... I have heard that his Imperial Majesty has sent a herald to Dr. Luther, but I know not whether he has reached him yet. I have credible information that during Lent just past a student at Leipsic confessed to a Paulist brother, and prayed him to absolve him, which the brother refused to do, saying that he would not absolve him unless he promised to burn all Luther's books; but the student replied that he had no books written by Luther, and as the brother still refused to absolve him after repeated requests, the student took him by the cowl and threw him out and stamped on him and perhaps hit him, too—so my physician writes from Leipsic, and I do not wish to conceal it from your Grace.

Liutpold von Hermannsgrün was here two days ago and said that bills had been posted at Worms warning people to give up all books in their possession written by Luther to the magistrate. Wherefore a great question has arisen whether such a proclamation could be made agreeably to the safe-conduct. Doubtless your Grace knows the truth in the matter. It is my kind prayer that your Grace will favorably protect the pious man Luther, and also that you will request the other princes from me graciously to keep the said Luther in their protection. ...

437. ALEANDER TO THE VICE-CHANCELLOR DE' MEDICI AT ROME.

Kalkoff: *Aleander*, 145.   WORMS, April 5, 1521.

Since the publication of the imperial mandate which I sent

you on March 29, the tumult of the people seems to me to have quieted down. But to make up for this, chance has revealed the venomous hatred of Luther's princely patrons in its full extent. They care less for the person of Luther, whom they only use as a tool to win the people, than for the confiscation of ecclesiastical property. Such great difficulties are generally anticipated from this side that help and succor can only be expected from God. Indeed, had the mandate ordered the immediate burning and complete destruction of the Lutheran books, I believe that the Lutherans would not stand on ceremony with the defenceless Emperor, but would storm the city and open the battle. . . .

In short, the movement is now quite independent of Luther, for, says Hutten, if Luther were put to death a thousand times a hundred new Luthers would rise up. With a certain jealousy Hutten seems to want to take the leading rôle in the movement; he would do it with pleasure if he could only reckon on as loyal support from the people as Luther gets. He writes that even if he fell the rest of the knights would not desist from the proposed undertaking, which doubtless they have agreed upon for a long time and with a large number of conspirators. All the humanists of the Rhine are coming to Hutten on the Ebernburg, to give him, with great diligence and emulation, what help they can. . . .

Of course, Luther's condemnation, following the expiration of the set period, must be declared in a new bull. It must agree in all points with that[1] already sent, except that it ought to name neither Hutten nor anyone else except Luther. For these people mutter that they do not yet know whether, after the expiration of the term, Martin is really declared [a heretic], and they use that as an excuse to favor him. But this is absolutely not the time to publish the bull previously sent, for Hutten and all the German knights would murder me in the Emperor's arms. Not that he would care much for the excommunication for the sake of his salvation, but he would commit that folly because of the shame done him before the world. Therefore the bull should be sent as soon as possible, so that I can publish it at the Diet and in-

[1]*Supra*, no. 396.

timidate the populace. I am resolved, however, before I leave Germany to publish the excommunication of Hutten, and, when I am once safe, to print it; but God prevent it happening while we are in Worms, for it would not help our cause, but would cost us all our lives.

At Hutten's instigation all men, high and low, are trying to frighten us, but Caracciolo and I are determined to stay till the end, and, if Martin comes, to do our best. If he does not come we shall request a final prohibition of his books and libels and will stick to it without letting ourselves be intimidated by the threats of a thousand deaths.

438. MARTIN BUCER TO BEATUS RHENANUS AT BASLE.
Briefwechsel des Beatus Rhenanus, 272. EBERNBURG, April 6, 1521.

Greeting, most learned Beatus! As all things are uncertain, and the success of the priests against the Lord and against his Christ[1] is doubtful, I preferred to let others write to you about them, myself waiting for a chance to tell you something more certain of the content of the meditations of the wicked, when, that is, the result of the battle of truth and falsehood would be plainer. But when our Valentine came hither I could not omit writing something of the doubtful cause of the gospel. For the wicked are in labor, and with violent throes have brought forth a little mandate. They bear in their womb a great giant, Antichrist himself, who will not only hurl mountain on mountain, but with his[2] own might will thrust from heaven Christ and all the gods. I know nothing of Luther save that he wrote Spalatin that if he were summoned only to recant he would not come, and that he would soon write to Charles that it was just the same as if he had come hither and returned to Wittenberg. For if he wished he could recant there. But if the Emperor were offended at these words and judged that he were an enemy of the Empire, he would offer to come, were he summoned to be punished, for he would by no means flee and leave the Word in the battle. These were his very words. But he writes that he

---

[1] This letter is very poorly printed, due probably to Bucer's bad hand. I change the reading here, for it is evidently an allusion to Psalm ii. 2, so translated in the Vulgate.

[2] Reading "suo" for "tuo." The syntax is as confused as the metaphor.

hopes no hands save those of the papists will be stained with his blood.[1]

Of Sickingen persuade yourself that he alone unites with a spirit and courage truly German, evangelic piety and unspeakable humanity. If he were not ill with the gout, he would doubtless assert the cause of the gospel with his sword, for he desires only to die for Christ. And he is sick of serving the Emperor, although he gets a salary of seven thousand gulden for it, only because the Emperor is obsequious to the Pope. He would be willing to have his stipend reduced to two thousand per annum to get the Emperor to read Luther's works translated into French.[2] I myself think it would be worth a great deal if only the Emperor would read them in the same spirit as Sickingen's, acute and learned, and agreeing perfectly with the gospel. It is known that this hero has met Capito and Erasmus, to whom I think his excellent talents are known. Certainly he loves all learned and studious men, on whom, if possible, he would pour forth his wealth. Valentine is now going. I will write again soon, or else see you at a place where there are no vipers, for there are plenty here as the bull has come from Rome. They are now negotiating to have the affair, which the Pope committed to the Bishop of Spires,[3] transferred to the suffragan of Spires. . . .

439. ALOISIUS MARLIAN, BISHOP OF TUY, TO ERASMUS.
Erasmi opera (1703), iii. 636.   Worms, April 7, 1521.

. . . But when we had returned from Spain and I met you at Brussels, I begged you to have nothing to do with Luther. For there were some men who suspected, though foolishly, that you were not averse to him. But you then promised to do as I asked so that I vouched for you before others as I did for myself. Afterwards this fatal Lutheran calamity grew stronger every day, and possessed the minds of so many that there did not seem to be any number uninfected by it.

[1] On December 21, 1520. Translated, Smith, 105.
[2] Reading "Gallicam" (*sc.* linguam) for "Galliam." Both here and elsewhere in this letter the composition is so bad that I have had to construe with the greatest freedom. French was the only language known to Charles V., who had been brought up at Brussels.
[3] George of the Palatinate, Bishop of Spires 1513-29.

I think the condition of our age, in which evils are so much greater than their remedies, is to be deplored. For we can neither bear the evils nor apply remedies when we see these men rather captured by dreams and madness than moved by sound reasons. From our Aleander, who is, I think, joined to you by the same studies and mutual kindnesses, I have always heard of you what he would wish to be said of himself. . . . In dissuading Luther and the Germans from writing you did a worthy deed. . . . Lest you should think that I had done nothing I have written two orations against Luther, of which one is gentle,[1] the other, composed after his last books, is more severe; not that I wish to condemn so much the man as the cause, that the state and religion may be saved. I am sending them to you. . . .

440. SPALATIN TO THE ELECTOR FREDERIC OF SAXONY.
Zeitschrift für Kirchengeschichte, ii. 125. Böcking, ii. 806.

(Worms, April 7-9, 1521.)

Most gracious Lord. Yesterday a Strassburg printer showed me a letter from Hutten written at Ebernburg, in this tenor:

"Greet Spalatin from me and say that I will write him all that he wants to know. Also that an embassy to Luther has been offered me, or rather pressed on me, and that I have good hope. . . ." The said printer informed me that Hutten would stand like a wall. Also that the Emperor's confessor is entirely won over, but Hutten doesn't trust him much. Yesterday the imperial legation returned from the Ebernburg.
. . .

441. MARTIN BUCER TO —— (SPALATIN?).
Zeitschrift für Kirchengeschichte, ii. 124. Böcking, ii. 806.

(Ebernburg, April 7-9, 1521.)

Salute Peter, to whom I will write to-morrow. To-morrow again we discuss Luther's cause, as we did yesterday with Glapion and Paul von Armstorf.[2] I am not able to send the

[1] This was true. A notice and some extracts from the oration in Clemen: *Beiträge,* iii. 4.
[2] An Austrian noble, once in Maximilian's service, transferred to the Netherlands 1511, at the battle of Guinegate 1513, employed in various diplomatic services. When Charles came to Germany in 1520 Armstorf was made his bodyguard. He met his death probably on December 1, 1521, in battle against the

letters given me, because they are single copies and are being revised by Hutten for the press. I now turn that over to the priests. Hutten was ill on that day when we consulted with Glapion on Luther. He desires only that Luther may be able to defend himself, and in such a way that Luther may bring the reformation of the Church into the consultation without being impeded with the doubts of his enemies. But keep this secret, for we have given our word to be silent. As the case stands we must deceive the Romanists, who are getting out an apparently severe mandate. When you hear the cause you will agree with me. To-morrow I will write by the chamberlain of my illustrious prince Frederic[1] Count Palatine, as much as I honorably may. . . . Pray be careful not to say a word about Luther coming to us, for you would thus brand Hutten, who has written to you, and Francis and myself with levity. . . . And now, if Luther understands his writings as I interpret them, the Emperor has no reason to complain of him, and I think that I am nearly of his opinion. . . .

442. GEORGE STURZ TO JOACHIM CAMERARIUS.
Böcking, ii. 50.   COLOGNE, April 8, 1521.

Sturz (1490-1548) at Erfurt 1505; journeyed to Italy 1519 and 1521; took the degree of M. D. at Wittenberg 1523, then went to Erfurt, which he was forced to leave by the Peasants' War 1525. He then went to Buchholz. In 1537 he ministered to Luther during his illness at Schmalkalden. *Allgemeine deutsche Biographie.*

Camerarius of Bamberg (1500-74) studied at Leipsic, then after 1516 at Erfurt. Attained great proficiency in Greek. M. A. in 1520, 1521 at Wittenberg, where he formed a lasting friendship with Melanchthon. After 1525 he spent most of his life at Nuremberg, where he took an important part in the Reformation. He edited Dürer's works and other things, and wrote some important biographies. *Realencyclopädie.*

. . . Some say that the world is turned upside down by Luther. This is true, but so it was by the teaching of the

---

French. Aleander tried hard to win his support against the Lutherans. *Cf.* P. Kalkoff: *Aleander gegen Luther,* 1908, pp. 54ff.

[1] Frederic II. (1483-1556) spent his early life at the court of Philip the Fair of Burgundy, after which he traveled much, to France, Spain and England, and took part in wars with the Turks and other powers. This part of his life has been charmingly described by Mrs. Henry Cust in *Gentlemen Errant* (1909), 241-396. In 1544 he became Elector Palatine, and in 1545 embraced the Protestant faith. *Allgemeine deutsche Biographie.*

apostles. But if this seems to be the beginning of evil, why do they not nip it in the bud, lest it grow too great for them? It will not be crushed by clamor and threats and cruelty, but it might be appeased by confessing manifest errors and correcting vices and leaving a place for the progress of the gospel. I write what I hear prudent and good men say. But enough of this subject. . . .

443. THE GOVERNORS AND GRANDEES OF SPAIN TO CHARLES V.

Bergenroth, supplement to vols. i. and ii., p. 376ff. (English translation of Spanish.)   TORDESILLAS, April 12, 1521.

The Cardinal of Tortosa [Adrian of Utrecht] and the Admiral of Castile,[1] governors for your Imperial Majesty in these your kingdoms, together with the grandees, prelates, cavaliers, and principal persons who are staying at this court in the service of your Highness, and who here sign their names for themselves and in the name of all other grandees, prelates, cavaliers and other principal persons of your kingdom of Spain, very humbly kiss the royal feet and hands of your Imperial Majesty. We desire you to know that through various channels has been forwarded to these your kingdoms and seignories the intelligence of the discord and schism which the heresiarch Martin Luther has sown in Germany amongst the subjects and vassals of your Majesty, which has caused and still occasions to all of us, as Catholic Christians and supporters of the faith and service and honor of your Majesty, great pain and grief; especially because we have been certified that that seducer, not content with having perverted and deceived Germany, is endeavoring with his malignant and diabolical cunning to pervert and contaminate these your kingdoms and seignories of Spain. And to this end, at the instigation and with the aid of some persons of these parts, who desire to hinder and weaken the holy office of the Inquisition, he has procured means for translating and putting into the Castilian tongue his heresies and blasphemies, and to send them to be spread and published in this Catholic nation.

---

[1] Don Fadrique Henriquez, appointed governor of Spain in conjunction with the Cardinal of Tortosa and the Constable of Castile, in 1520.

From a little spark, most Christian Lord, may spring and burst forth a great fire. If your Majesty does not speedily find a remedy for things which do such dishonor to God our Lord and are so dangerous to the Holy Catholic faith, a great scandal may the more easily be caused, and a still greater flame, and one which afterwards it may not be easy to extinguish, be kindled, since some cities of these kingdoms are in a state of disturbance. Therefore for ourselves and in the name of all who are absent, very humbly and with great urgency, we supplicate your Imperial Majesty, as a most Christian Emperor and Catholic King our Lord, the protector and defender of our holy Catholic faith and of the Roman Church, our mother, that, imitating your glorious progenitors of immortal memory, it would please you to adopt this cause of the faith as your own, which indeed it is, and with the devotion, fervor and zeal which you owe and by which you are bound, to aid, defend and favor it, and to provide in such manner that those damnable and perverse subtilties may cease and be extirpated, so that not only this detestable and corrupt pestilence shall not enter into these your kingdoms and seignories of Spain, but that by the hand of your Majesty it may be extirpated and destroyed throughout all the world, and the said arch-heretic Martin Luther be severely and effectively punished, and that the books which contain his blasphemies and heresies be burnt. . . .

444. ALEANDER TO THE VICE-CHANCELLOR DE' MEDICI.
Kalkoff: *Aleander,* 156.   WORMS (April 15), 1521.

I have received your Lordship's letter and the copies of the bull and the desired breves which will greatly help us. In my last letter I told that the confessor and Armstorf were going to betake themselves to Hutten and Sickingen. This has now happened,[1] and in their opinion with great success, for there in the castle they learned from one of the guides that the resolution had already been taken to hew us and all the prelates and priests at the Diet in pieces within the next ten

---
[1] This was the second attempt made by Glapion, the Emperor's confessor, at reconciliation. The first was an interview with Spalatin, on which *cf.* Smith, *op. cit.,* p. 110, and Förstemann: *Neues Urkundenbuch,* pp. 36-54. On this second interview *cf.* further Smith, p. 111f, and other letters here translated.

days. This could easily happen, for the Emperor has not so much as four crippled soldiers with him, whereas Sickingen is better supplied with troops than any German prince. Moreover, the inhabitants of Worms, who were always enemies of the priests, desire nothing more than the stamping out of the clergy. Hutten said that he had heard from great princes that the Emperor would secretly be quite well pleased with this, even though he might think it necessary to express his public disapproval. In spite of their bad disposition, I do not believe this would be so; at any rate Glapion and Armstorf reported it to the Emperor and us. Moreover, to excuse his plans to violate international law by committing these murders, Hutten said that he regarded it as a worthy and just act, and one pleasing to the Emperor, because he knew only too well that we were sneaking about in the dark to induce the princes to fall away from the Emperor. Either the scoundrel invented that to excuse himself, or he let himself be frivolously persuaded of it by those who work for the ruin of the Church. At that castle Glapion met the Dominican recently mentioned by me, Martin Bucer, who alone does more harm than the others, for while in questions of the faith Hutten was overcome by Glapion and became as gentle as a lamb—although the light wretch immediately returned to his former position—the apostate monk disputed six hours, partly to defend Luther's writings, and partly to give them a good Catholic sense, and said that he would like to have known Luther only to learn his spirit. Finally the confessor proved to him that, as even the doubtful theses were interpreted, the doctrines were heretical and objectionable. Sickingen, a reasonable man whom we must still try to win over, had all Luther's German writings in his memory; he declared that Luther in his books expressed himself differently from what the confessor alleged; and, in fact, he brought out German books in which Luther, according to his custom of contradicting himself, put forward other ideas than those in the Latin works which Glapion had brought and which he showed him. Sickingen was thereby much shaken in his previous opinion; but finally he declared that on his own account he was obliged to favor a universal reformation of the Church, and if Luther spoke of that and of other good and Christian things, he would stake his coat and his own and his children's lives on defending him against all the world, but that if he had spoken evil in articles of faith, he would be the first to throw that into the fire. Hutten also said that in a sense he had never subscribed to Luther's opinions, and did not wish his cause confounded with Luther's; he only desired that the priests should be chastised and forced to renounce their enormous wealth, the source of their vicious life. If the challenge he had sent us had drawn his Majesty's displeasure on him, he would not, against his Majesty's will, go further in the matter, as he had already shown the Emperor in a humble and abject letter, in which, however, he savagely attacked Caracciolo and me. The world has come to such a pass that a miserable wretch and murderer, a vicious ragamuffin and poor parasite like Hutten, puts on the airs of a state reformer, and has the front to say and do such things in the face of the Emperor. We cannot impress the imperialists with the disgrace of letting such things please them, sufficiently clearly to get them to take measures to prevent it. They only shrug their shoulders and regret that in their present position without troops, they can act no otherwise. Even if they had troops, nothing would happen, for our good friend who now rules [Chièvres] abominates war. They are convinced that Hutten, partly by his own person and partly by the support of Sickingen, has the whole knighthood of Germany on his side, and that they desire a general revolution. Indeed, Sickingen alone is king in Germany, for he always has as many followers as he wants at his disposition; the other princes fold their arms on their bosoms, and the prelates tremble and let themselves be swallowed like rabbits. Of the lay princes the Elector of Saxony, the Counts Palatine and the Bavarians are hostile to us; Elector Joachim stands bravely by us, but he does it alone. All the world swears death to the clergy and mutters that the annates, which are contrary to God and reason, should be devoted to the maintenance of the German imperial councillors (as I said before) —not to mention their thousand other villainies.

We have news of Luther, that he is on the way and will

be here in two days, honorably escorted by nobles and by six doctors. We hear that in Erfurt he was respectfully received by the professors of law and the liberal arts and that he preached there. The rumors are so uncertain and various that I can only vouch for one, and that is that the rascally herald who escorts him in his fierce hatred for us acts madly and makes of Martin's journey a triumphal progress. Had we known that he, whose disposition is well known to us, had been selected for this business, we would have done our best to stop it, but the imperialists—who knows for what reason?—kept the person of the herald and the time of his departure secret.

We are busy day and night with the Emperor, the confessor and the members of the privy council, in order to keep the authority of the Holy Father unhurt and to turn Luther's coming to the good of the Church and of God. Indeed, we need all our strength to counteract the secret underhanded efforts of the Saxon Elector and the universal uprising, which has already made the imperialists wish that Luther had never started on his journey and has made them recognize that we always represented the truth and their duty.

The Emperor appears very steadfast, and says that the imperial mandate shall be obeyed. To-day after midday divine service he promised us to do more than he had yet done; at the very worst he will hold to the aforesaid mandate, which, as I previously related, provided that if Martin will not recant the condemned books and others repugnant to the Catholic Church and the present laws and customs, they shall be burned anyway, but that Martin himself, in virtue of his safe-conduct, shall be allowed to return home, after which he will be treated as a heretic, and the princes and people summoned to crush him. If only that happens it will be all the better. . . .

Four days ago the confessor told me that the herald had informed the Emperor, that as he was conducting that monster with him he could not prevent all the world, young and old, boys and girls, from flocking to him. Now we had ten times prayed the Emperor, in as far as practicable, to have

Luther conducted hither with the greatest secrecy, and we got his definite promise, but as the Emperor's servants are only guided by their own selfish interests, they don't bother about the promise. This is the same herald who in the Emperor's hall drew his sword against a retainer[1] of the Bishop of Sion, when the man defended the papal prerogative against the monk John Faber of Augsburg. The last named in his funeral oration for the Cardinal de Croy[2] reviled the Holy See, unmindful of the many favors shown him by the Pope. This herald is an impudent fool and clown, a bitter foe to the clergy, and just the man to invent the story of some miracle done by Martin on this journey, or an appearance of the Holy Ghost over his head, as is already represented in his pictures. And although, as a world-famous liar, the herald deserves no credence, yet the whole populace is possessed of such a passion for Luther, that they would believe the devil himself, who by the way rules them all, if he spoke good of Luther. As the imperialists obstinately concealed from us the name of the herald and the time of his departure, we could not hinder the choice of such a man. They were probably afraid that we should try to bribe the herald to frighten Luther from coming, which they then, as I previously related, greatly desired, but which they now regret. Or else they feared we might waylay Luther; but both their suspicions were absolutely false. The fact is that for a long time we could not by any way learn anything on the two aforementioned points.

Now that the imperialists have certain news of Luther's coming, which they formerly so hotly desired, they appear to be thunderstruck. After the Emperor's gracious letter we never doubted for a moment that Luther would come. On Saturday [April 13] they sent the confessor to confer with the nuncio and me about the measures to be adopted; as we had always declared that reason and propriety, honor and profit alike forbade the appearance of this man, we now insisted, that as they had wished him to come, at least they should do

---

[1] A certain Michael Sander, doctor of law, who had studied at Bologna, and was now secretary of Matthew Schinner, Cardinal of Sion.

[2] The funeral oration was held on January 21st; cf. *supra*, Tunstall to Wolsey, January 21, no. 383.

their duty to God and his vicar and protect the honor of the Emperor. Now that Glapion desired our advice in the name of the Emperor, we declared that it was necessary for the Emperor to have him brought into the city as inconspicuously as possible, that he should assign him lodgings in his palace where no suspected person could talk with him, and, finally, that, as appointed in the imperial mandate, he should simply be asked whether he would recant. If they did not observe this last point, the evil would be made worse than ever. This counsel pleased the confessor; we all then went to the Emperor, gave him our opinion and received his promise that he would act accordingly. On the next day we heard that Luther would dwell in the Augustinian cloister and have a guard, so that no one unapproved by the Emperor could speak with him. I expect, however, that as has always happened before, they will do just the contrary to what they say. . . .

445. SPALATIN TO THE ELECTOR FREDERIC OF SAXONY.

Zeitschrift für Kirchengeschichte, ii. 127.

(WORMS, middle of April, 1521.)

Most gracious Lord. To-day I received secret information that the Emperor's confessor[1] is mortally hostile and averse to Dr. Martin, let him pretend to be as friendly as he likes. He is deeply shocked to hear that Dr. Martin is on the way hither. Yesterday he was with Duke George. . . .

Your obedient chaplain,
SPALATIN.

446. RICHARD PACE TO THOMAS WOLSEY.

Letters and Papers of Henry VIII., iii. no. 1233. (English; partly condensed, partly direct quotation.) GREENWICH, April 16, 1521.

At my arrival I found the King reading a new book of Luther's,[2] the same as that of which you sent a copy written by me. On the King's dispraising the book, I presented the Pope's bull and breve,[3] at which his Majesty was well con-

---

[1] Glapion. *Cf.* Smith, *op. cit.,* 110ff.

[2] This was probably the *Babylonian Captivity* sent by Tunstall, *supra,* no. 383. On Henry's *Defence of the Seven Sacraments* against Luther, *cf. English Historical Review,* c. 656ff.

[3] The *Exsurge Domine,* and Leo's letter to Wolsey, commanding him to burn Luther's books. Rymer: *Foedera* (3d edition 1741), vi. 194.

tented, showing unto me that it was very joyous to have these tidings from the Pope's Holiness, at such time as he had taken upon him the defence of Christ's Church with his pen, afore the receipt of the said tidings; and that he will make an end of his book within these few days; desiring your Grace to provide that within the same space all such as be appointed to examine Luther's books may be congregated together for his Highness's perceiving. He is agreeable to everything desired by you and wishes you to write to the Emperor and to the electors. His book is to be sent not only to Rome, but also into France and other nations as shall appear convenient. So that all the Church is more bound to this good and virtuous prince, for the vehement zeal he beareth unto the same, than I can express.

As touching the said breve his Grace [Henry] is singularly well contented therewith, and read every word of it at his second mass time, and after dinner showed it to my lords of Canterbury and Durham,[1] with great praise and laud thereof. As to the said bull, his Grace showed himself very well contented with the coming of the same; howbeit as touching the publication thereof, he said he would have it well examined and diligently looked to afore it were published.

447. ALEANDER TO THE VICE-CHANCELLOR DE' MEDICI.
Kalkoff: *Aleander*, 166.   WORMS, April 16, 1521.

I had just closed my last letter when I learned from several reports and from the running of the people that the great heresiarch was entering the city.[2] I sent one of my people out, who informed me that about a hundred horsemen, presumably Sickingen's, escorted him to the gate. Sitting in a wagon with three companions[3] he entered the town, surrounded by about eight riders, and took up his dwelling[4] in the neighborhood of the Saxon Elector. As he left the wagon a priest threw his arms around him and touched his gown three times,

---
[1]Warham and Thomas Ruthall, made Bishop of Durham 1509, died February 4, 1523.
[2]About 10 a. m. *Cf.* Smith, 112.
[3]They were his colleague Amsdorf, the Augustinian John Petzensteiner of Nuremberg, and the student Peter von Swaven, a Danish noble, later in the diplomatic service. *Calendars of State Papers.*
[4]At the Hospice of St. John.

and afterwards boasted of it as if he had had a relic of the greatest saint in his hands. I expect they will soon say he works miracles. As this Luther alighted, he looked around with his demoniac eyes and said: "God will be with me." Then he entered a room where many gentlemen visited him, with ten or twelve of whom he dined; after the meal was over the whole world flocked to see him.

What will his Holiness, what will the world now say of the credit and good faith, of the resolutions and promises of the Emperor? God forgive those who have counselled him so ill, or rather who have injured and misguided him. Your Lordship would not be surprised, but amazed by these actions. Yet there is nothing remarkable in the bad result of our efforts; while the imperialists promise miracles they take the very worst measures, so that, if they do not act with evil intent, we must at least consider them not only cowardly, but positively senseless. Already the Elector of Saxony triumphs and demeans himself like an emperor or king, does what he pleases against God and reason, and does so all the more since the Elector of Brandenburg has announced to the Emperor his intention of marrying his first-born to Lady Renée,[1] sister of the Most Christian Queen;[2] on this account the Saxon is treated more respectfully than ever. But they ought to know what I a long time ago told Chièvres privately, that one fine day they would find themselves betrayed by this elector and other German princes. This is the present state of affairs, and it will get worse daily, as it usually does at German Diets. Then as the imperialists have reckoned more with men than with God, the Lord of Heaven will mock them.

448. JEROME DE' MEDICI TO FREDERIC GONZAGA, MARQUIS OF MANTUA.

Kalkoff: *Briefe*, 47.   Worms, April 16, 1521.

Jerome de' Medici of Lucca, doctor of law, count palatine and minister of the Marquis of Mantua, died *circa* 1556. Kalkoff, *loc. cit.*, 92, s. v.

To-day Martin Luther, the heretical monk, came hither. I

---

[1] Renée de France in 1528 married Ercole d'Este, Duke of Ferrara. In 1536 Calvin visited her court and won her sympathy for the Reform.
[2] Claude de France, daughter of Louis XII. and wife of Francis I.

know not whether he has appeared to recant or to prove his obstinacy. As far as I can learn the whole Diet has declared that in case he maintains his evil doctrines he will be struck with the ban of the Empire. But in any case, as he has safe-conduct, he will be allowed to go away, even if he does not recant.

449. GUY WARBECK TO DUKE JOHN OF SAXONY.
Walch, xv. 2182. German. WORMS, April 16, 1521.

To-day arrived in a Saxon cart Dr. Martin Luther in the company of three men, namely, a monk, Amsdorf and a Danish noble named Swaven. Before the cart rode the imperial herald in his costume, with the Eagle Arms, and his squire. Justus Jonas of Nordhausen with his famulus followed the wagon. Many of the nobility met him; of the Saxons, Bernhard von Hirschfeld,[1] John Schott, Albert of Lindenau with six horsemen, and many other courtiers of the elector. At ten in the morning he entered the city, accompanied by more than two thousand people, as far as his lodging, which he has with the Saxon councillors, Frederic Thunau and Philip Feilitzsch, and also with Ulrich Pappenheim[2] the imperial marshal, not far from the Swan Inn, where Lewis, Elector Palatine, lodges. On the journey Luther was very honorably received in Saxon lands; he preached at Erfurt, Gotha and Eisenach. The Erfurters went two [German—four English] miles to meet him and received him honorably. At Leipsic he was given no ovation, but only the usual cup of wine. It is said the papists are not a little frightened at his advent, for they hoped he would not come, which would have given them the better chance to judge him more harshly.

450. ULRICH VON HUTTEN TO LUTHER.
Enders, iii. 123. EBERNBURG, April 17,[3] 1521.

The Lord hear thee in the day of tribulation; the name of

[1]Hirschfeld (1490-May 10, 1545), a feudal retainer of Frederic, visited the Holy Land 1517-8, of which trip he has left a diary, served in various public offices including that of judge at Wittenberg 1528-37. He was in thorough sympathy with Luther. *Archiv für Reformationsgeschichte*, viii. 10ff.

[2]Pappenheim (died 1539) was Hereditary Marshal of the Empire. He lodged with Luther at the Hospice of St. John at Worms and conducted him to and from the Diet.

[3]Enders misprints "April 18."

the God of Jacob protect thee! May he send thee help from his holy place and guard thee from Zion; may he give unto thee according to thy heart, and strengthen all thy council; may he fulfil all thy petitions and hear thee from his holy heaven in the might of his right hand.[1] What else ought I to pray for you, my dearest Luther, my venerable father? Be strong and courageous.[2] You see what is staked on you, what a crisis this is. You must never doubt me as long as you are constant; I will cling to you to my last breath. Many dogs surround you, and the council of the malignant besieges you; they have opened their mouths against you like raging and roaring lions;[3] they exult and rejoice over you, seeking you.[4] But the Lord is careful for you[5] and will repay the proud. He will arise with you against the malignant and stand with you against those who work iniquity; he will repay the impious their iniquity and will destroy them in their evil.[6] Thus it will be, Luther, for God, the just and strong judge, can no longer connive at such wickedness.[7] Fight strenuously for Christ; yield not to evil, but go the more boldly against it.[8] Bear affliction as a good soldier of Jesus Christ,[9] and use zealously the gift[10] of God which is in you, persuaded that he is able to guard that which you have committed unto him against that day. Meanwhile, I, too, will strive for the same thing, but my plans differ from one another, for they are human; you are more perfect and act only from holy motives. Would that I could see with what eyes they look[11] at you; what faces they turn to you; how they knit their eyebrows. I imagine all that is most dreadful, nor do I think that I am wrong, for I expect that the Lord will purge the vineyard of Sabaoth,[12] which the boar of the wood doth ravage and the wild beast feedeth on.[13] This I write briefly in great anxiety for you. May Christ save you!

ULRICH VON HUTTEN.

[1] Cf. Psalm xx. 2-7.
[2] Joshua, i. 7.
[3] Psalm xxii. 17, 14.
[4] Psalm xl. 17.
[5] Psalm xl. 18.
[6] Psalm xciv. 2, 16, 23.
[7] Psalm vii. 12.
[8] Virgil: *Aeneid*, vi. 95.
[9] 2 Timothy, ii. 3.
[10] 2 Timothy, i. 12.
[11] *I. e.*, the men in the Diet before which Luther made his first appearance on this day. Smith, 111ff.
[12] John, xv. 2; Isaiah, v. 7.
[13] Psalm lxxx. 13.

451. ULRICH VON HUTTEN TO JUSTUS JONAS AT WORMS.
Böcking, ii. 56.   EBERNBURG, April 17, 1521.

And so you also have followed the preacher of the gospel to be in his garden![1] O piety worthy of all love! Truly Justus, I loved you before, but on this account I now love you a hundred times more. They say that these fellows, seeing that Martin is protected by the safe-conduct of the Emperor, have turned their attention to you who share his curse. O prudent council, O clever men of the world! This method would empty the Diet, for I doubt not that the greater part of those there agree with you. Would that I might be present and start some commotion or some tumult; but it is better to be quiet. May Christ thus bring it about that no violence may be done to him whom we would rather keep safe alive than avenge dead. Write me what is being done, and what you hope and fear. . . . In haste, as Bucer is departing.

452. ALEANDER TO THE VICE-CHANCELLOR CARDINAL DE' MEDICI AT ROME.
Kalkoff: *Aleander,* 168.   WORMS (April 17), 1521.

This morning early I had a talk with the confessor in order to give the necessary directions for our plan. Then in the palace where they had as yet come to no decision on any question, I arranged that the electors should be summoned before the Emperor at about two o'clock in the afternoon, and the other princes and estates at four, and that then Luther should appear simply to answer the questions put him and not to be heard further. I myself made the necessary arrangements, without however having our names appear, for we have always acted according to the wording of the bull,[2] both because there is no other way for us to act and because this is the best for attaining our end.

An immense crowd greeted the appearance of the archheretic, who was questioned before the Emperor, Princes and Estates, in the name of the Emperor and Realm, as follows.

---
[1] Jonas followed Luther from Erfurt to Worms.

[2] The position of the Curia was, of course, that Luther was already condemned and therefore had no right to be heard. For this reason the nuncios were not present at either of his appearances before the Diet.

Chance entrusted the duty of questioning him to the Official[1] of Trier, a learned and orthodox man, who is very conscientious in carrying out the apostolic and imperial mandates. In Trier he burned the heretical books so thoroughly that not one was left. This truly excellent man, for whom God be praised, lives in the same house with me, in the very next room.

He spoke to Luther as follows: "Martin Luther, the Emperor and Realm have summoned you hither, that you may say and tell them whether you have composed these books," for at the Emperor's orders I had sent in twenty-five or more Lutheran books, "and others which bear your name, and, secondly, that you may let us know whether you propose to defend and stand by these books." Then the titles of the works were read one after another.

Then Luther answered first that all the books were his, and that he recognized them for his own. (This was a lie, for everyone knows that some of the books have other authors, although they go under Martin's name.) To the second question he said, that as it was the most difficult question in the world, concerning the faith, he must pray for time to consider his answer. Then the Emperor with his privy council went apart, as did the electors in their own body, and the other princes and the representatives of the cities.

After due deliberation, the said official again spoke in the name of the Empire and the Realm to this effect: That as Luther had previously been summoned by the Realm, and the reason of his citation communicated to him, they were naturally much surprised that he did not have his answer ready on his arrival. Also that they were under no obligation to grant a respite in questions of faith, as this could only be done with danger and scandal to believers. (Would to God they had acted on this principle five months ago, as they should have.) Nevertheless, he continued, of the pure mercy

---

[1] John Eck, or von Eck or von der Ecken, not to be confounded with the debater, a jurist, of old family of Trier, in which diocese he held various ecclesiastical preferments. In 1515 he was entrusted with a mission to Rome, and was now the leading minister of the archbishop. He was chosen to address Luther before the Diet because the Archbishop of Trier, who had been previously agreed to as an umpire by Luther and Miltitz, had general charge of the affair at Worms. In 1523 he was married, and died in 1524.

and grace of the Emperor a respite was granted him until four o'clock to-morrow. Then[1] the Emperor had the official say to him that he should consider well that he had written against his Holiness and the See of St. Peter, and that he had sown many heresies—for they called things by their right names as was good—from which such scandal had arisen that unless preventive measures were immediately taken, it would kindle a conflagration which neither Luther's recantation nor the imperial power could quench. Therefore they admonished him to change his attitude. Then he was dismissed without speaking further. The fool entered smiling and, before the Emperor, kept his head turning continually hither and thither; but when he left he did not seem so cheerful. Many even of his supporters after they had seen him said that he was foolish; others that he was possessed. But many others thought him a pious man, full of the Holy Ghost. In any case he has lost considerable reputation in the regard of all.

On these two days the Emperor has shown the constancy of his character and of his religious convictions against the efforts of many to confuse the issue. May God keep him thus. After Martin was dismissed to-day he spoke very earnestly to the Elector of Saxony. The Official of Trier communicated to me a saying of his master about the elector, who seems to have somewhat changed his position; for he said: "This reckless monk has ruined everything, and to my annoyance and disgust has gone too far in his ranting opinions." Nevertheless, this prince does all the evil he can, and his people do still more.

This first appearance of Luther has not turned out so ill; if only he is not instigated by his followers to give an answer to-morrow necessitating further delay. We will do our best to meet him. This evening the Emperor commissioned the confessor and the official to come to an understanding with me as to what is now to be done. Delighted at their wish to co-operate with us, I intend first to ascertain their opinions, and then to decide what is best to do.

I pray God that these imperialists, who hitherto from wickedness, cowardice, frivolity or worldly considerations

[1] In Eck's own account this exhortation preceded the first questions.

have in all matters acted against God and the laws, against their own honor and the good of Christendom, now at least may remember God and his vicar and their own sworn duty, and do it. God grant that the appearance of this Antichrist, which we have always deprecated as unreasonable, may contribute to the peace and quiet of Christendom.

453. ALEANDER TO VICE-CHANCELLOR CARDINAL DE' MEDICI AT ROME.

Kalkoff: *Aleander*, 173. Worms (April 18 and 19),[1] 1521.

Your Lordship will already have learned from the oral account of Lord Raphael[2] the result of Luther's first appearance before the Emperor and Estates. From the present imperial courier your Lordship learns that this afternoon [April 18] at four o'clock Martin was summoned to the court, but as the Emperor and princes delayed in an upper room, he had to wait for his hearing more than an hour and a half in a great crowd. When the Emperor, Princes and Estates of the Realm had entered, the Official of Trier, who was spokesman for the Emperor at the first appearance, in a neat, impressive speech, asked this question: "Luther, although in such a matter, the purport of which was known to all the world, you really should not have had any time for consideration allowed you, yet his Imperial Majesty, according to his clemency and mercy, has given you a delay till this hour. Wherefore do you now openly and honestly declare whether you will recant all that you have written against the tradition of our Holy Church, and against the councils, decrees, law and ceremonies which our ancestors and we have held until this day, and whether you will also revoke the opinions condemned by the present Pope. But see to it that your answer be not ambiguous, but clear."

Martin[3] declared that he had written books of three sorts, some against Roman abuses, and here he began venomously

---

[1] Kalkoff dates April 19, but Aleander apparently wrote the first part of the letter April 18.
[2] De' Medici who left Worms the previous day and was in Florence April 26.
[3] A fuller account of the proceedings was written down by Spalatin, who incorporated in it Luther's own notes of his speech. This, with Eck's speeches, is translated in Smith, *op. cit.*, pp. 115ff.

to revile the Holy Father and Rome, which he called the flaying-place of Christendom, and as he continued to expatiate too far, the Emperor told him to drop that subject and continue with others. The second sort of his books he said he had composed against enemies, whose fault it was had he spoken too sharply; under the third class of works, treating the teaching of the gospel, there were some which neither the bull nor his enemies declared offensive. But he would not recant one word of any of these three kinds of books unless he were convinced of error in a debate, and by the authority of the Old or New Testament only. If he recanted on any other ground, to which, however, he would never consent, he would act against his own conscience and divine truth; therefore, he prayed and exhorted his Imperial Majesty not to try to stop the course of his doctrine, by which not only the glorious German nation, but his other dominions and kingdoms might be brought to destruction. Finally he said that in any case he would not deny the Christian truth, for then Christ must deny him before his Heavenly Father.

The official following his instructions replied wisely: "Martin, if your wrong opinions and heresies were new and invented by you, perhaps his Imperial Majesty would request the Holy Father to have them examined by pious and learned men, so that no wrong should be done you. But your errors are those of the ancient heretics, the Waldenses, Beghards, Adamites, Poor Men of Lyons, Wycliffe and Huss, and have all been long ago condemned by holy councils, popes and the usage of the Church, and therefore ought no more to be discussed and brought into question contrary to divine and human law." Then the official added the question, which particularly concerned the German nation, whether he would not recant what he had written against the holy Council of Constance, which had been attended by all nations and was recognized by the whole world. He refused, and would only submit to the decrees of the council in as far as they were founded on the authority of the Bible, for, he said, councils had erred and contradicted one another. The official began to deny that councils did not agree in matters of faith, but then the Emperor declared it was enough, he would hear no more as Luther rejected councils. So Luther left, escorted by all and particularly by many Saxon nobles from the retinue of the elector; and as Martin left the hall he stretched forth his hand as the German landsknechts do when in jousting they exult over a telling blow.

As this morning [April 19] we went to the Emperor, we found that the electors and many other princes had been summoned to him to give their opinions as to what further should be done in Luther's affair. As they desired time for deliberation, the Emperor replied: "Good, I will first let you know my opinion." Then he had read aloud the declaration,[1] a page long, which he had himself composed and written down with his own hand in French, and he also had read a German translation of the same. During this reading in the presence of the Emperor and of the Elector of Saxony many of the princes became as pale as death. The reason for this your Lordship will learn from the declaration of the Emperor, which he handed to his ambassador, in order that he might fittingly announce the good news to his Holiness and the college of cardinals. His declaration will also be printed in Latin, Italian, German, Spanish, French and Dutch, and be sent to all parts of Christendom, to make known the noble and strictly Catholic position of his Majesty in this so dangerous affair. He has publicly expressed his will at a time and under circumstances which made everyone think that he would have to act cautiously with all these princes if he wanted to get their co-operation in his plans. But God strengthened the piety of this most Christian and truly Catholic prince, who has always made us expect that he would act in a manner pleasing to God and the Pope, and has now done so much that we ourselves would have been satisfied with less. He also declared that he had caused the matter to be protracted and had allowed Luther to appear, with the best intentions, so that the German people could not complain that Martin had not been heard, and pretend that wrong had been done him by not having been asked whether he would recant. As this is a fact, the procedure has been much better than

---

[1] *Reichstagsaken*, no. 82. Translated in B. J. Kidd: *Documents of the Continental Reformation*, no. 43. *Cf.* Smith, *op. cit.*, 120.

if an imperial mandate had been promulgated. And although during the protracted negotiations we experienced horrible and almost incredible attacks, cares and dangers, yet now we begin to breathe again and to comfort ourselves for our sufferings with the saying: *et haec meminisse juvabit.*[1]

454. ALEANDER TO VICE-CHANCELLOR CARDINAL DE' MEDICI AT ROME.

Kalkoff: *Aleander,* 178.   WORMS (April 19), 1521.

Greeting. When I returned from the lodging of Caracciolo, where we had composed the other letter[2] together, to my own residence, the Official of Trier communicated to me the oral message from his master that within the hour all six electors[3] had answered the Emperor that they would treat Martin as a heretic, and that they would hold fast to the Catholic faith and the holy councils and decrees which they had always observed, and would altogether walk in the way of their forefathers. Now, when in virtue of the safe-conduct Martin had returned home, his Majesty would promulgate an edict to crush him, and that they would follow him and do his Majesty's will, and in all things conduct themselves as Christian princes should. That is noble news, especially that the Elector of Saxony, who has hitherto favored him, agreed with them. So in agreement with the Emperor they decided to give out an edict that he should return home under safe-conduct and that then they would publish the mandate ordering his seizure and the execution of the bull. If he flees to Bohemia, God will look to it. . . .

455. JEROME DE' MEDICI TO FRANCIS GONZAGA, MARQUIS OF MANTUA.

Kalkoff: *Briefe,* 47.   WORMS, April 19, 1521.

I have no further news except about Luther, who day before

[1] Virgil: *Aeneid,* i. 203.
[2] *Supra,* no. 453.
[3] As a matter of fact, this decision was reached, on the afternoon of April 19, only by the four Electors of Brandenburg, Mayence, Cologne and Trier; the Electors of Saxony and the Palatinate dissenting. (It may here be mentioned that the seventh Elector, the King of Bohemia, took no part in German affairs, except in the election of the Emperor.) This letter was probably never sent by Aleander, who corrected and supplemented it in his despatch of April 29, *infra,* no. 468.

yesterday had a public hearing before the Emperor in the presence of the electors and other princes. He was told in his Majesty's name that his Majesty had summoned him for two reasons, first to ask whether the books published under his name, which were shown him, were composed by him, and, secondly, whether, in that case, he would improve them and make them good again by recanting the errors he had promulgated. He replied that he neither could nor would deny that the works were his, and in regard to the second question, that he had only written what he conscientiously thought true, but as it was so important and hard a thing, he begged his Majesty to give him time for ripe reflection.

After the Emperor had taken counsel, according to custom, with the princes, he had him answered that he had for long known the cause of his summons, and might well have thought out his answer, and, therefore, deserved no respite, especially in so clear a matter; none the less the Emperor in his goodness was satisfied to give him until the same hour the next day, and he exhorted him to repent and recant lest his contumacy should thrust many souls into danger.

Yesterday at the appointed hour he again appeared before the same assembly, and to the question whether he would revoke what he had written against the decisions of the Church, the Canon Law, the power of the Pope and œcumenical councils, he answered in an oration, which, as far as I can find out, was right learned. He said he had only written what he thought true according to the genuine evangelic doctrine; if this had hitherto been corrupted and disfigured he did not desire to follow the errors of others. Then he earnestly begged the Emperor not to let the slanders of enemies frustrate his strenuous endeavors and well-meant works. He also said that he would not recant any part of his writings until he was refuted and overcome by one who understood the gospel better than he did. Then a long reply was made him, in which among other things it was said that it was unthinkable that any living creature could convince an infidel who denied the validity of the Canon Law, the councils, the Church Fathers, and the patron of his own order, St. Augustine. Then he was again asked to answer categorically whether he would recant those errors. But he remained obstinate, so his Majesty allowed him to withdraw.

This morning the Emperor asked the assembled electors and princes whether they had considered what was to be done about Luther's obstinacy. When they answered that they had decided nothing, the Emperor, who was holding a paper in his hand, said: "But I have considered and decided, as stands written here; it is written in the Burgundian [French] language, but I will have it read to you in German." Then he presented a memorandum composed by himself, for one of his secretaries who was present when he wrote it down, told me that it was drawn up by his Majesty without the aid of any person; I have seen the original in the Emperor's hand, and have heard it read by that secretary in Castilian [Spanish], which I do not perfectly understand. He promised me a copy of it, but I could not get it in time to enclose with this letter, but as far as I can remember it the paper had the following tenor:[1] [here follows a fairly accurate report of the contents.] . . .

456. FRANCIS CORNARO TO THE SIGNORY OF VENICE.
Sanuto, xxx. 127. Italian. Brown, iii. 191. English.

WORMS, April 19, 1521.

On a summons from the Emperor, Friar Martin Luther arrived at the court on the 16th, with a herald and safe-conduct, and on the morrow entered the presence of the Emperor, with whom were the electors and princes.

The Emperor inquired whether the books printed in his name were his, and whether he would withdraw them and recant, as they had been condemned by the Pope for heresy. Luther replied the books were his, and requested time for reply, which was conceded with great difficulty until yesterday, when he reappeared before the court. After delivering a long discourse, urging the Emperor and their lordships not to molest him, he endeavored to convince them that what he had written was perfectly true, and said he would persist in this proposition, unless the contrary were shown on the authority of Holy Writ, demanding a disputation to that effect. This was denied

[1] Charles's declaration printed in Kidd: *Documents*, no. 43. *Cf.* Smith, 120.

him, because all the articles had been already condemned by the Church and councils, and therefore he was ordered to declare what he meant to do. He then reasserted his opinion, declaring that it could be demonstrated by true arguments that unjust decrees had been made in the said councils.

On that day, the 18th, the Emperor and the electors and princes dismissed Luther, and caused a writing in the Emperor's hand to be read to him, purporting that as the emperors and princes, his predecessors, had always done their utmost not only to preserve the Catholic faith, but to augment it, and had ever been obedient to the Apostolic See, his Majesty intended to do the like; and, therefore, his firm intention was that all the books of Martin, wheresoever found, should be burnt, and he himself punished as a notorious heretic, and likewise those who favored him in any way. To effect this, the Emperor requested all the electors and princes to unite with him, as they had apparently promised to do when they determined to send for Luther to the court.

457. ULRICH VON HUTTEN TO LUTHER AT WORMS.

Enders, iii. 126.   EBERNBURG, April 20, 1521.

Who will rise with me against the malignant, and who will stand with me against the workers of iniquity?[1] Saviour Christ, Heavenly Father and Holy *Spirit*,[2] what terrible things do I hear? Fury is not fury compared to their rage. I see there is need of swords and bows, of arrows and cannon to resist the madness of these *cacodemons*.[2] But you, excellent Father, be strong of mind and do not let yourself be bent. They clamor, shout and rage, but do you show them your middle finger.[3] More and more I see that all good men favor you. You will never lack defenders nor avengers. We need not give you advice on the secret negotiations[4] of which you write, for we doubt not that you will choose the best course and persist strongly in it. Many have come to me and for their

[1] Psalm xciv. 16.
[2] Greek.
[3] As a sign of supreme contempt; the gesture was considered indecent, something as applying the thumb to the nose and extending the fingers is, to-day. *Cf.* Erasmus: *Adages*, and Latin dictionary.
[4] This letter on the negotiations is lacking, *cf.* Smith, 118.

zeal to you have said to me: "May he not faint; may he answer faithfully; may he not let himself be moved by any terror." I always replied that you would be Luther, nor have I been disappointed, for I know that your answer leaves us nothing to desire. But persevere unto the end. May Christ grant that the wicked may find you what you are to their own great grief! The prudence of my friends, who feared that I would dare too much, has hitherto forced me to keep quiet, otherwise at those walls I would have gotten up some demonstration against that rabble. But I will do it a little later, and whatever happens to me you will see that I, too, am not lacking in that spirit which God has aroused in me. I burn to see you; my love is ardent. Let us know all that you do and farewell.

We have Francis von Sickingen hereabouts, very zealous. I write the rest to Spalatin. Farewell again. Would that you could see Sickingen before you leave. He greatly desires it. I know that they will soon send you away, for a certain imperialist writes me this. Christ preserve you.[1]

ULRICH VON HUTTEN.

458. FREDERIC, ELECTOR OF SAXONY, TO HIS BROTHER DUKE JOHN.

Förstemann: *Neues Urkundenbuch,* i. 15. German.

WORMS, April 24, 1521.

. . . Were it in my power, I should be quite willing to help Martin in as far as he is right. Believe me, they are pressing him hard, even some people of whom you would be astonished to know this. I think they will drive him out. If anyone lets it be known that he wishes well to Dr. Luther, he is considered a heretic. God turn it to the best, for he will doubtless not abandon the right cause. I will inform you later about Luther's departure. . . .

459. GASPAR CONTARINI TO NICHOLAS TIEPOLO AT VENICE.

Sanuto, xxx. 131. Italian. Kalkoff: *Briefe,* 57. (German.) Brown, iii. 197. (English.) . . . WORMS, April 25, 1521.

Gaspar Contarini (1483-1542), of a noble Venetian family, studied at Padua, and then entered the service of his native state, being her

[1]This letter with the one of April 17 was printed almost at once, but the last paragraph in this was left out.

ambassador at the court of Charles V. 1521-5; agent of Venice at the papal court 1528; made cardinal by Paul III. on May 21, 1535, and the next year was a leading member of the commission for reform which drew up the *Consilium delectorum Cardinalium*. In 1541 as papal legate he took part at the Diet and religious conference of Ratisbon. He wrote a good deal against Luther. His biography by F. Dittrich, 1885. *Cf.* also F. Lauchert: *Die italienischen literarischen Gegner Luthers* (1912), 371ff.

N. Tiepolo (died 1551), a Venetian senator, diplomatist and scholar.

I have neither seen nor spoken to Brother Martin, although he remained in this city until yesterday morning. Various considerations compelled me to act thus, for he has very active friends and very powerful patrons, and the whole thing is conducted with incredible passion. But I have heard from many that among other follies he teaches that councils have erred; that every layman, if he is in a state of grace, is able to administer the sacrament of the altar; that marriage is dissolvable and fornication no sin, and that everything happens according to the law of necessity. This last I only learned from the Cardinal of Sion. Besides his errors I learned that he is most imprudent, quite unchaste and ignorant of the doctrine [of the Church]. During the last few days he has been requested to recant by the princes here and in the Emperor's name, but nevertheless he remains obstinate, and so his Majesty with his own hand drew up the declaration against him, of which I enclose a copy for the Signory.

It is hard to express how much support Luther has here. Things are in such a state that I fear after the departure of the Emperor and the dissolution of the Diet something bad will happen, especially against these German prelates. Truly, if this man had been wise enough to confine himself to his first propositions, and had not become entangled in open errors against the faith, he would be, not favored, but adored by the whole of Germany. The Duke of Bavaria[1] and many others told me this at Augsburg, and now I see it myself.

460. MARTIN REINHARD TO KING CHRISTIAN II. of DENMARK.

Zeitschrift für Kirchengeschichte, viii. 289. WORMS, April 25, 1521.

. . . [The main subject of this letter is the proposal to

[1] William.

call Carlstadt to the University of Copenhagen.] . . . Most gracious King and Lord, I can write your Majesty little or no news of the Diet. But the talk is all of Dr. Luther, whom they are threatening and from whom they demand nothing but that he shall recant, and *that* he will not do. . . .

461. PHILIP OF HESSE'S SAFE-CONDUCT FOR LUTHER'S RETURN.

Enders, iii. 127. WORMS, April 26, 1521.

Philip, Landgrave of Hesse, born 1504, became Landgrave 1508, declared of age 1517, died 1567. He met Luther at Worms and wished him God-speed. About 1523 he became a Lutheran and from that time till his death was the leading champion of the Evangelic Church. His state papers are being edited by F. Kück: *Politisches Archiv des Landgraf Philip,* 1904ff. His correspondence with Bucer was edited by M. Lenz in three volumes 1880ff. An interesting and highly laudatory characterization of him is given by the Englishman, Roger Ascham, who saw him in later life. Ascham's Works (1671), p. 370.

We, Philip, by God's grace Landgrave of Hesse, Count of Catzenelnbogen, Dieth, Ziegenheim, Nidda, etc., give all men to know by these presents: That as Dr. Martin Luther is now leaving[1] this Diet at Worms, we give to him and to all who are with him, our free safe-conduct through all our territories and lands and to all our subjects. So with this letter we give him safe-conduct to all places over which we rule, in acknowledgment of which we sealed this letter with our privy seal.

462. JOHN FEIGE TO LUTHER.

Smith: *Life and Letters of Martin Luther,* 473.

(WORMS, April?, 1521.)

John Feige (1482-March 20, 1543) studied at Erfurt about 1503, later taking the doctorate of laws. He entered the service of Philip of Hesse, whose leading minister he soon became, and whom he represented at Augsburg in 1518, and on many later occasions. Life in *Allgemeine deutsche Biographie.* Luther apparently sent him his *Postilla,* just out, for which Feige thanks him in this fragment.

The grace of our Lord Jesus Christ be with all of us. Amen. I received your note, most learned Martin, but truly I did not receive the homilies on the holy evangelists which you say

---

[1] Luther left Worms April 26, arriving at Frankfort on the Main on April 27. From here he wrote Cranach a letter translated in Smith, p. 119.

you sent, and when I asked the messenger he replied that he did not have them. But I am not the less grateful to you, although there was no need of your honoring me with these lucubrations of yours, as my work keeps me too busy to devote much time to sacred studies. . . .

463. GASPAR CONTARINI TO HIS BROTHER-IN-LAW, MATTHEW DANDOLO.

Sanuto, xxx. 128.   Italian and Latin mixed.   Brown, iii. 199.   English.

WORMS, April 26, 1521.

The day before I entered Worms Luther was asked, in the presence of the Emperor and electors, whether the works circulated in his name were issued by him. He replied that he should wish to know what works were attributed to him, as some might not be his. A list of their titles then being read, he admitted their authorship. He was then asked whether he affirmed the truth of their contents. To this question he declined to reply without time for consideration. The Emperor objected to this demand, because Luther did not deserve its grant, and because he had long known why he was summoned, but, as a favor, the matter was deferred until the morrow, and he was desired to return at the same hour.

Luther then departed, and when he came back at the appointed time, he spoke at great length before the Emperor in German, against the Pope and the Court of Rome. He also maintained that the Council of Constance, which condemned John Huss, erred wickedly by passing sentence against him, and that he (Luther) would persist in that opinion until confuted by argument or authority derived from Holy Writ. The Emperor then dismissed him, and very early on the following morning sent a rescript in his own handwriting, stating that he was descended from Catholic Kings and most Christian Emperors, and, therefore, would not degenerate from his forefathers; that with all his might he would oppose the heresies of Luther, and inflict punishment on all his adherents; and for that purpose he (the Emperor) would hazard both his realms and his life.

This rescript being presented to the electors, they requested time to consult and decide on the matter, and went back to the Emperor several times, assenting apparently to the decree, but raising many objections; and as yet nothing is settled. The Emperor, however, seems to be firmly opposed to Luther, and not without reason, for Luther has reached such a pitch of madness and fury that he rejects the decrees of the councils; says that any layman can administer the sacrament of the eucharist; that matrimony can be dissolved; that simple fornication is no sin, and hints at that community of women, treated by Plato in his *Republic*.

During the night after the day on which the Emperor dismissed Luther, a placard was fastened to the doors of the Cathedral, whereby four hundred nobles and persons of inferior rank threatened the opponents of Luther and defied them to battle, especially mentioning the Archbishop of Mayence, whom they vituperated grossly.

Had Luther conducted himself at Worms with greater moderation and prudence, and not meddled so erroneously with sacred matters, but abided by his original propositions, he would have had all Germany on his side, such is the bias towards his ravings of many of the Germans. . . .

Luther's books are sold publicly at Worms, although the Pope and the Emperor, who is on the spot, have prohibited them. At home many of the chief princes encourage Luther. I do not know how the affair will end, but dread the result. I have neither spoken to the man nor even seen him, at which you perhaps will marvel; but the question is treated so acrimoniously that the nature of the times requires reserve. Luther disappointed the expectations of almost everybody at Worms, for he exhibits neither moral purity nor any prudence. Of scholarship he is devoid; in short, he excels only in rashness. . . .

464. MARINO CARACCIOLO AND JEROME ALEANDER TO VICE-CHANCELLOR CARDINAL DE' MEDICI AT ROME.

Kalkoff: *Aleander*, 182.   Worms (April 27), 1521.

On the nineteenth of this month we sent your Lordship an account of the pious and laudable decision of the Emperor, which he wrote down with his own hand and communicated to the princes in the certain expectation of thereby preventing contrary resolutions on their part. It turned out splendidly, for on the same day, as the Archbishop of Trier announced to us by his official, the princes decided in all points to follow the Emperor's will. But an unexpected incident brought everything again into confusion. The following night, the Lutherans, in fierce anger at the Emperor's expression of his will, and as though with the intention of frightening the orthodox from executing it, affixed on the door of the town hall and other public places a notice, the contents of which, as can be seen from the enclosed copy, will be extremely dangerous, if it expresses the real facts. For the three German words[1] with which it is signed, which cannot be translated into Latin, are the token of the peasants and signify their calling out for war against the government and the nobles. Also, on the same night these words were shouted out through the whole city, but as no movement whatever followed, we may surmise that the conspiracy does not rest on very broad foundations. However, a certain prince [Albert of Mayence] who ought to make common cause with us, was put into such a fright by that notice, partly on account of his native discretion or cowardice, partly on account of the advices of his Lutheran retinue, whom we suspect of being the authors of that notice, that before the break of day he sent to the Emperor, to the other princes and to us. The Emperor only laughed and said that he was a bit too timorous, and that as it was incumbent on him to summon the princes to a session, he would do well to get Luther off in a hurry first. Then smiling the Emperor said to us that this conspiracy of four hundred nobles was like that of Mucius Scaevola, who thought he had three hundred companions with him when he stood quite alone. But still that anxious friend could not keep from sending his brother [the Elector Joachim] to the Emperor with a proposal diametrically opposite to that made in writing the day before by the four electors. According to the latter his Im-

---

[1] This placard, posted up on the night of April 20, announced that four hundred knights had sworn enmity to the Romanists and especially to the Archbishop of Mayence. It was signed "Buntschuch, buntschuch, buntschuch," *i. e.*, "tied shoe," the emblem of a large peasant secret society. According to Kalkoff (*Archiv für Reformationsgeschichte*, viii. 341ff, 1911), the author of this notice was Hermann von der Busche. See also: T. M. Lindsay. *History of the Reformation*, i. 296.

perial Majesty should send Luther back in virtue of his safe-conduct, and, as he so obstinately refused to recant, should proceed against his person then, and against his books immediately. But now after the appearance of this notice this same man came to the Emperor, and while he and we together were waiting for an audience, he explained to us that it would be a good thing to question Luther again and have him examined by learned men in the presence of certain princes and in the name of the whole realm. This, he said, was the opinion of all the electors, which I can easily believe, as both our opponents [the Electors of Saxony and of the Palatinate] desire nothing more eagerly than to procrastinate and confuse the whole matter, and the others follow them meekly. Yes, even the most influential man humbles himself from fear of this placard. When we replied that this procedure was unreasonable and highly dangerous, he only remarked that he was charged to inform the Emperor in this sense, and begged us not to cross his intention. Thus he talked to the Emperor in our presence for about half an hour, yet in a yielding tone. But the Emperor, this noble and pious gentleman, who alone in this matter maintains his position unshaken, answered him that he would not change a jot of his resolution, and that he would hear nothing of a further examination of Luther in his presence or in that of his councillors, and that the princes would do well to follow his decision peacefully as they had promised.

The electors received this declaration of his Majesty with great admiration for his courage and constancy, but the influence and cleverness of the Saxon were so great that a petition of the Estates to the Emperor was adopted setting forth that for the good of the cause it seemed advisable to them that Luther should once more be heard and exhorted to recant; if he still refused no one could then any more object to his prosecution, and they would in all points act according to the imperial decision. The Emperor wrote them [April 22] that he would not change his opinion in the least; if they could induce Martin to recant, for which he gave them three days, he would intercede with the Pope for him, but he declined in person or through his councillors to take part in the examination. Meantime, there were so many intrigues against us, and every hour revealed so much deceit and fraud, that we more than once saw our whole work on the point of being shattered, for the Lutherans were universally credited with the purpose of inducing Luther at this examination to recant certain points objectionable to the imperialists, but to maintain all his charges against the Pope. Thereby public opinion would be won back to Luther, for it had been much alienated by his shameless repudiation of the Council of Constance. Obedience to the will of the Emperor was left out of consideration. In these annoying circumstances we were comforted by the dependable stand of the Emperor, and by the fact that his declaration had already been sent to the Pope, so that he would be severely blamed for violating it.

But God lent us his help by another event also. On the twenty-fourth of this month a meeting was held in the residence of the Archbishop of Trier, attended by the Elector of Brandenburg in the name of all the electors, and by the Bishops of Augsburg and Brandenburg in the name of the clergy, and by Duke George of Saxony and the Margrave of Baden in the name of the lay princes, and by some other deputies from the cities. Martin Luther was introduced,[1] and after the Chancellor of Baden[2] in the name of the Empire had exhorted him for more than an hour and had pointed out to him the dangerous results for him of his obstinate refusal, Luther finally declared with great emphasis that he would not recant one tittle of his writings, as he would thereby act against his conscience. According to the report of the Archbishop of Trier the conduct of the princes during this examination was splendid. It is remarkable that even Duke George, who formerly on various occasions had expressed himself recklessly against the clergy and had caused some scandal by an opinion on confession, now did his full duty. The Chancellor, who spoke German, acted like a wise man and a Catholic

---

[1] Between six and seven in the morning, see further Luther's own account, *infra*, May 3, no. 471.

[2] Jerome Vehus, born 1483, studied at Pforzheim, matriculated at Freiburg 1503, where he was a pupil of Wimpfeling and Zasius; professor of law 1510, after 1514 chancellor of Margrave Philip of Baden. He was an Erasmian, opposed to the Reformation. Enders, iii. 134f.

truly devoted to the Holy See; the princes did not admit to this examination the Official of Trier, who in the last few days has come out strongly against us. Immediately after the departure of the princes, the Archbishop of Trier invited Martin to his room accompanied by two doctors,[1] without whom he will take no step and speak no word, as though he were their ward. Present were the Official of Trier and the Dean[2] of the Church of our Lady at Frankfort, who was formerly at Rome and now with the best intentions as a strong Catholic theologian writes against Luther. Then in a Latin oration the official admonished Martin to recant his errors and recognize the councils, decrees, traditions and usages of the Church. Luther answered little (for he is said to have a poor memory) and only refused to subscribe to the decrees of the councils, which he said were full of contradictions and errors, as could be seen by the Council of Constance. The official declared that in matters of faith the councils neither erred nor contradicted each other. Thereupon Martin cited the thesis condemned at Constance, that the Church consisted only of the number of those predestined to salvation, and he cited against the doctrine of the council the words of Christ, in the Gospel of John:[3] "Of those whom thou has given me, I lost not one." "Save the son of perdition,"[4] interrupted the official, and with this weapon, as well he might, he plied Martin so hard that the man knew not what to answer. The same thing happened with two other

[1] They were Jerome Schurff and Nicholas von Amsdorf. Schurff (1481-1554) of St. Gall, studied medicine at Basle, and then, in 1500 or 1501 took up jurisprudence at Tübingen. In 1502 he began to teach and practice law at Wittenberg, where he lived till 1546, after which he was driven by the Schmalkaldic war to Frankfort on the Oder. He was a warm friend of Luther. Present at the Diet of Worms, when Luther was asked if the books there assembled were his, Schurff had cried: "Let the titles be read," which was then done. *Allgemeine deutsche Biographie.*
[2] John Dobneck, always called Cochlaeus (1479-January 10, 1552), born near Nuremberg, studied there and at Cologne 1504, where he took his M. A. in 1507. In 1510 he returned to Nuremberg to teach school, in 1515 went as private tutor to Bologna, and in 1517 took his doctorate in theology at Ferrara. In 1520 he was given ecclesiastical preferment at Frankfort on the Main. He was at the Diets of Worms and Nuremberg 1524. In 1528 he took Emser's place as chaplain to Duke George of Saxony. He wrote much against Luther, including his life, the *Historia de Actis et Scriptis Martini Lutheri*, 1549. *Allgemeine deutsche Biographie.* Life by M. Spahn, 1908 (not seen by me).
[3] John, xviii. 9; cf. John, xvii. 12.
[4] John, xvii. 12.

proof-texts, whereby he was so thoroughly refuted that the archbishop hoped he would give up that position. But the consequence of the informal conversation was that Luther declared he would not recant unless he were better refuted; and as the official brought forward his proof in the form of syllogisms, he declared that he would have nothing to do with logic, which is pure folly on his part, for he must let people treat with him somehow. And yet there are persons so silly that they let the obvious madness of this monster impose on them. Then the archbishop gave him a special exhortation, but he could not be won either by persuasion or by discussion, as he recognizes no judges and unreservedly repudiates the councils, and everything else except the words of the Bible, all of which he expounds in his own manner, mocking differing interpretations of them and rejecting them as insufficient. In this he always has his Lutherans by his side, who shriek applause and swear that he is right. But many of his interlocutors have observed that he is neither a grammarian nor a philosopher nor a theologian, but a mere madman. Everyone is convinced that he did not himself compose the greater part of his questionable books, and he himself has confidentially admitted that these bad books were written by his friends, but that he must keep faith with his confederates, and so only speaks against this one or that when no witnesses are present. Further he said to Cochlaeus that for himself he was accustomed to preach, to lecture on the Psalter and expound it in his writings, but that the books which had raised the whole outcry were composed by his companions, and that if he should recant, more than twenty others would come forth and do worse than he had done. In short, neither instruction nor exhortation nor deceit do any good with him, for he sticks obstinately to the one word, that he will not act against his conscience, and furthermore he said once or twice that he had received a revelation, and then denied it in the same breath. So all our trouble was in vain.

The fact that he did not compose the questionable books seems to me proved by a communication of the Official of Trier, who said that every time he had questioned or warned

Luther, he had heard from his own mouth opinions which directly contradict those contained in his books.

After this third hearing the Archbishop of Trier went to the session of the princes, to relate the progress of affairs; likewise Chièvres, the Chancellor Gattinara and the Bishops of Liège and Palencia appeared to communicate the Emperor's will, to the effect that after such proofs of contumacy it was time to send this dog back and faithfully execute their judgment. Again the princes took council together for a time and then by the said ambassadors sent a petition to the Emperor that his Majesty should allow the Archbishop of Trier to exhort Martin by himself, as the prelate had expressed good confidence of converting Luther. The Emperor agreed to this. Meantime, we exerted ourselves to get the archbishop to discharge this duty quickly, for if delay were allowed it was to be feared that Luther would be induced to recant partially, which would have been fatal. Also we urgently requested the archbishop not to depart from the form of recantation prescribed by us.

On the twenty-fifth of this month after the midday meal Luther went to the court of the archbishop, who in a private conference exhorted him to recant, and in case he refused to do so only from fear of his companions, who, as is said, threaten him with death, the archbishop offered him a rich priory in the neighborhood of one of his castles, and said that he would at once admit him to his table and to his council, under his protection and that of the Emperor and in the high favor of the Pope. He declined all that. Then the prelate made him the four following proposals: 1. That he should submit to the common judgment of the Pope and of the Emperor—an offer of which I cannot approve, as in these matters the Pope is the sole judge and his judgment has been already given. 2. That he should commit his cause to the decision of the Emperor, who would use his good offices with the Pope—a still worse proposition. 3. That he should choose the Emperor and Estates as his judges—which is a horrible and devilish offer. 4. Or, finally, that he should for the moment recant some of his most monstrous errors, and as for the others should submit to a future council. This proposal is also unacceptable and would be most destructive to our cause, which would get no profit thereby.

Your Lordship must not think that we thought out or prepared the way for these four startling propositions; on the contrary, we protested against any recantation other than in the form prescribed by us. Nevertheless, the archbishop said that as he saw that Luther had refused our questions put to him by the official, he had made this offer to Luther, to induce him, in any possible way, to take back even a small part of his errors, which would have turned the whole people against him. But the archbishop remarked that it had never come into his mind that his proposals would be in the least binding, save in so far as the papal authority allowed them, and that he would have previously given us notice of them. But Luther spared him this trouble by positively refusing from the very first to entertain these proposals, all of which he declared suspicious. Nor need we be surprised at this, for the Emperor's confessor told us this morning that ten days ago he had given Luther to understand that if he would recant the already condemned theses and the manifest errors, some means would be found tacitly to allow a discussion of the other points until the decision of a council, but that Luther had sent him word that he would not trust in councils, which perhaps might do something to improve Christian morals, but had always treated the gospel truth evilly.

As to the archbishop, when he saw such obstinacy and when his official warned him that he ran the risk of severe blame if Martin should have closed with one of his offers, he at once hastened to the Emperor, whither we immediately followed him, and laid down the commission he had undertaken. He seemed to thank his Creator that he had come out of it without any scandal. We really believe that he acted with the best intentions, for he has always done his duty and so has his official, and he has shown himself a true servant of the Pope and the Holy See. Then the Emperor commissioned his Secretary Maximilian [des Berghes], the Official of Trier, and the Austrian Chancellor[1] and two wit-

---

[1] Dr. John Schneidpeck, Chancellor of the Lower Austrian government under Maximilian, went to the Netherlands to lay before Charles some complaints of the

nesses, to tell Luther that on the next morning, that is, yesterday, April 26, he must depart, and that on the twentieth day thereafter his safe-conduct would expire. Moreover, they forbade him to do sundry things[1] as you will see by the notary's act sent by the imperialists to the Pope. So the honorable scoundrel left yesterday at nine o'clock with two wagons; just previously in the presence of many persons he toasted many slices of bread and drank many glasses of malmsey, which he extraordinarily loves. At the gate twenty horsemen received him, sent presumably by Sickingen at Hutten's behest. Some think that at the expiration of his term he will go to Bohemia, others that he will go to Denmark. So this morning we prayed the Emperor to inform both kings, and to take the final measures in our cause. He promised to do both, and to unite with the Estates for the completion of the necessary measures. As this scoundrel won't even accept reason, may God at least keep princes and peoples on the right path of the faith. We will do our best, and that with the greatest possible haste, and we will give your Lordship an account of all events.

465. LUTHER TO THE EMPEROR CHARLES V. AT WORMS.
Enders, iii. 129. FRIEDBERG, April 28, 1521.

The original of this letter, formerly in possession of T. G. Keil at Leipsic, was bought for $25,500 in May, 1911, by Mr. J. P. Morgan of New York, and by him presented to the Emperor William II; for this he received the order of the Black Eagle. The original has on it a note in Spalatin's hand: "This letter was never given to the Emperor, because in all this host of nobles there was not one who would give it to him." It was, however, soon printed.

Grace and peace with all subjection in Jesus Christ our Lord. Most serene and unconquered Emperor, most clement Lord! When your Sacred Majesty on the public faith and with free safe-conduct summoned me to Worms to inquire my mind on some books published under my name, and when, obediently and humbly, I had appeared before your Majesty and the whole Imperial Diet, your Majesty com-

---

Austrian Estates, which he printed at Worms in 1520. In 1522 we find him, with the title of Baron von Schönkirchen, in the service of Ferdinand.

[1] Luther was forbidden to preach on the way, but did not obey.

manded that I be asked, first, whether I would recognize the aforesaid books as mine, and secondly, whether I was prepared to revoke them, or whether I would abide by them.

When I had acknowledged that they were mine (provided that nothing was added to them or changed in them by any opponent or wiseacre) I reverently and submissively stated, that as I had fortified my books with clear texts of Scripture, it seemed to me neither right nor just that I should deny the Word of God and thus revoke my books. I humbly begged your Sacred Majesty not to suffer me to be forced to recant, but that either you, or others of any estate, even the least, who should be able, should go through my books and deign to refute the errors said to be in them, by the gospels and prophets. With Christian readiness I offered, were I rebutted or convinced of error, to revoke all my books and to be the first to throw them on the fire and to trample them under foot.

But after I had said all this I was asked and commanded to answer simply and plainly whether I was ready to recant or not. I replied as humbly as I could that as my conscience was bound by the Scripture I was by no means able to recant without better instruction.

Then certain electors, princes and other Estates of the Empire pleaded with me to submit my books to the knowledge and judgment of your Sacred Majesty and of the Imperial Estates. The Chancellor of Baden and Dr. Peutinger also labored with me, and I again offered as formerly, provided only that I were instructed by Scripture or plain reason.

Finally, it was agreed that I should concede and confide some selected articles to the judgment of an oecumenical council. But I, who was always humbly and zealously ready to do and suffer all that in me lay, could not obtain this one concession, this most Christian prayer, that the Word of God should remain free and unbound, and that I should submit my books to your Sacred Majesty and the Estates of the Empire on that condition, nor even that in yielding to the decree of a council I should not submit to anything contrary to the gospel of God, nor should they make any such decree. This was the crux of the whole controversy.

For God the searcher of hearts is my witness that I am most ready to submit to and obey your Majesty either in life or in death, to glory or to shame, for gain or for loss. As I have offered myself, thus I do now, excepting nothing save the Word of God, in which not only (as Christ teaches in Matthew iv.) does man live, but which also the angels of God desire to see (1 Peter, i.). As it is above all things it ought to be held free and unbound in all, as Paul teaches.[1] It ought not to depend on human judgment nor to bend to the opinion of men, no matter how great, how numerous, how learned and how holy they are. Thus does St. Paul in Galatians, i., dare to exclaim with emphasis: "If we or an angel from heaven teach you another gospel, let him be anathema," and David says: "Put not your trust in princes, in the sons of men, in whom is no safety."[2] Nor is anyone able to trust in himself, as Solomon says: "He is a fool who trusts in his own heart,"[3] and Jeremiah, xvii.: "Cursed is he who trusteth in man."

Now in temporal things, which have nothing in common with the Word of God and the eternal values, we trust one another, for submission in them or loss of them does not prejudice our salvation. We shall have to give them all up at length under any circumstances. But in his Word and the eternal values God does not suffer one man to risk trusting another. For he intends that all men and all things shall be subject to him only, for he alone has the glory of the truth, and is the truth itself, "for all men are liars and vain" as St. Paul splendidly argues in the epistle to the Romans, chapter iii. Nor is this wrong, for that trust and submission is true worship and adoration of God, as St. Augustine teaches in his *Enchiridion,* chapter i.[4] But we must not offer this worship to any creature. For St. Paul esteems neither the angels nor himself, and doubtless no saint either in heaven or on earth worthy of this faith, but rather curses them. Nor would they suffer it, still less request it. For to trust to man in matters of salvation is to give to a creature the glory due to the Creator only.

[1] 2 Timothy, ii. 9.
[3] Proverbs, xxviii. 26.
[2] Psalm cxlvi. 3.
[4] Mistaken citation.

Wherefore, as humbly as I can, I pray your Sacred Majesty, not to consider this opinion born of evil suspicion and prejudicial to the Word of God, and not to interpret it unmercifully. For I conceived the opinion from the said Scriptures, to which every creature rightly yields. For, says Augustine, the authority of this Scripture is greater than the capacity of the whole of human reason. Your Sacred Majesty can easily see my loyalty and trust to your Sacred Majesty, in that I appeared most obediently before you under safe-conduct, fearing nothing, although I knew that my books had been burned by my enemies and an edict against me and my books publicly posted in many places under your Majesty's name. These things might well have terrified this poor little monk, had I not expected (as I still do) the best of God Almighty, your Sacred Majesty and the Estates of the Empire.

Although I could not obtain a refutation of my books from Holy Writ, and am forced to leave unconvicted . . . nevertheless I thank your Sacred Majesty humbly for observing the safe-conduct at Worms, and for having promised to keep it until I get to a safe abiding place. Again I beg your Sacred Majesty by Christ, not to allow me to be crushed by my enemies, nor to suffer violence and be condemned, since I have so often offered to do what a Christian and an obedient subject ought. For I am even yet prepared to stand, under your Majesty's protection, before impartial and learned judges, lay as well as ecclesiastical, and to submit my books and doctrines most freely to all, if your Majesty or any of the Estates, councils or doctors or any one else, can and will instruct me on them. I will accept their judgment, provided only that the Word of God, which ought to be the judge of all men, is kept open and free.

In sending this letter back, I plead not my own cause, for I am nothing, but the cause of the whole Church, and I set forth what reason demands. With my whole heart I wish well to your Sacred Majesty, to the whole Empire and to the most noble German nation, and I hope God's grace will keep you all happy. Hitherto I have sought nothing but the glory of God and the salvation of men, not considering my own advantage nor even whether my enemies condemned me or not. Thus Christ my Lord prayed for his enemies on the cross; how much more then should I pray for your Majesty, for the whole Empire, for my illustrious superiors and my native Germany? So I do pray for you with joy and faith in Christ, and, relying on my aforesaid offer, expecting nothing from you but the best.

Under the shadow of your wings I commend myself to your Most Serene Majesty. May our Lord God happily direct and guard you. Amen.

Your Most Serene Majesty's most devoted beadsman,[1]

MARTIN LUTHER.

466. FRANCIS CORNARO AND GASPAR CONTARINI TO THE DOGE OF VENICE.

Kalkoff: *Briefe,* 58. WORMS, April 28, 1521.

A full summary of this letter from the original is given by Brown, iii. 202. My translation is from Kalkoff's German version of the Italian.

In Luther's affair on which I, Francis, sent your Grace an account on the 19th inst., relating all that I had heard till then, what has happened since is as follows: When the Emperor requested the advice of the electors and princes in his declaration against Luther, which we previously mentioned and now enclose, they answered with the assent of all the members of the Diet, that it was a matter of great importance, and, therefore, they desired to negotiate further with Luther to bring him to recant, if his Imperial Majesty wished him to recant what he had taught against the decrees and decision of the Council of Constance and other councils, including his attacks on the papal power, which he called an abuse. It was thought that this was done on purpose to exert pressure upon the Pope to make him yield to the Emperor's wishes. They said the Emperor might send a representative to act in his name at the negotiations in connection with the persons they would depute to this duty. But the Emperor would not agree to this, but only that they should act in their own name, for which he gave them three days. When these had ex-

---

[1] "Orator" in the sense of "one who prays for." In default of a twentieth century equivalent I adopt this word with which letters of the sixteenth century (those of Thomas More, for example), were so often signed.

pired without any result being reached, his Majesty sent a doctor with one of his secretaries to Brother Martin, and made him the final declaration that if he would not recant the known theses he must immediately on the next morning depart to any place he wanted, and that the Emperor would keep the safe-conduct for twenty days to allow him to leave Germany; otherwise, they had decided to seize and punish him as his errors demanded. To which Luther replied that he would not recant, but desired rather to be refuted by the Scriptures. Then he left and no one knows where he will stay. But we are assured that the German princes promised the Emperor to agree to any measure on which he should decide for Luther's punishment. God grant that their resolution remain thus, considering the great love for Luther and the strong support which he has in these parts of Germany.

467. LUTHER TO SPALATIN AT WORMS.

Enders, iii. 143. FRIEDBERG, April 29, 1521.

Greeting. Dear Spalatin, here you have the letters[1] you asked for; do you plan for the rest. We dismissed the herald, and to-day are going to Grünberg. I have nothing else to write. Greet all our friends, especially Joachim[2] and Ulrich von Pappenheim, and others whom we were unable to say good-bye to when we left. Amsdorf also sends greetings. Farewell in the Lord.

MARTIN LUTHER, *Augustinian.*

468. ALEANDER TO THE VICE-CHANCELLOR CARDINAL DE' MEDICI AT ROME.

Kalkoff: *Aleander,* 193. WORMS (April 29), 1521.

. . . Although everything was done that law and mercy, the honor of the Holy See, and the orders of the Pope and your Lordship require, and although nothing else could have been done, as no judges here were competent [to hear Luther], yet

---

[1] *I. e.,* the one to the Emperor last translated, and one of similar tenor to the princes and Estates, Enders, iii. 135. Luther composed them early in the morning and sent them all back with the herald before proceeding to Grünberg in Upper Hesse, eight English miles from Friedberg.

[2] Joachim von Pappenheim (died 1536) was a distant cousin of Ulrich, on whom *cf. supra,* no. 449.

the people esteem him and justify him by the mistaken reflection that he was not allowed to debate. Yet it is certain, if no reasons had prevented this, and if we had not had to fear the endless procrastination desired by the Lutherans, and had therefore allowed him a disputation, that he would never have appeared in the open field. For in one of his private hearings, he was, as those present tell me, convincingly refuted in more than six points by the Official of Trier, and Cochlaeus, I understand, did the same when he invited Luther to his room [April 24] for a debate, which Luther declined in the presence of many nobles. Otherwise his appearance has had the most salutary consequences, for now the Emperor and almost all other persons recognize that he is a foolish, immoral, crazy man. At the very first glance the Emperor said: "He will never make me a heretic," and as the titles of the books were read before the Diet, he said openly and repeated later, that he would not believe they were all composed by Luther. His drunkenness, as well as his many faults in glance, mien and walk, in word and deed, have robbed him of all the glory he enjoyed before the world. . . .

Finally, let me remind you to send the bull against Luther quickly, so that it can be printed and sent all around at once. It should be dated like the first on January 3, and should only name Luther and his followers in general. I will tell you the rest when I leave Germany.

469. MERCURINO GATTINARA TO CARDINAL MATTHEW SCHINNER.

Reichstagsakten, ii. 638.　　　　　　　　　(WORMS, May 1, 1521.)

Very reverend Sir, this morning we held a consultation on Luther's affair, and it seemed best that Aleander should make a draft of the edict,[1] which shall then be read in council and on adoption shall be translated into German and published in order that there may be some execution done before the Diet separates. Please, therefore, have the draft of the said edict made as quickly as possible.

---

[1] *I. e.,* the Edict of Worms, outlawing Luther. Reprinted by B. J. Kidd: *Documents of the Continental Reformation,* no. 45. It was drawn up May 8, but not signed and promulgated until May 26. On it, see further Smith, p. 120.

470. ULRICH VON HUTTEN TO WILLIBALD PIRCKHEIMER AT NUREMBERG.

Böcking, ii. 59. EBERNBURG, May 1, 1521.

I have heard some imperialists say that Luther was summoned to defend his cause. They lied, it was not so, for all they asked him at the Diet was whether he would recant what he had written. He replied most constantly that he would recant whatever they convinced him was erroneous. He was asked again if he would recant, for his writings had been condemned long before. He prayed that they would not force him to an unjust recantation, lest he should condemn against his conscience what he believed was perfectly right. When they urged him a third time to recant, for this is all the Emperor and princes wanted to know, he replied that he neither could nor would deny what was supported by the most convincing texts of Scripture. Was this enough reason utterly to condemn the man of God? Good Heavens, what will be the result of this? Indeed, I think that by this great tempest the princes should learn whether Germany is governed by good laws. The prelates who take counsel against Luther swallow every impiety and every crime. His last letter to me drew tears from my eyes. He told how indignant he was at certain things, among others at the prohibition in the edict that he should preach the Word of God. Detestable iniquity, crime deserving the pitiless wrath of God to bind his Word and to stop the mouth of a teacher of the gospel! Christian princes indeed! What will foreigners say? I have begun to be ashamed of my country.

Their spokesman was that unlearned sophist John Eck of Trier. He spoke against Luther so passionately that there is no doubt he was bribed by the Pope, who, it is said, has thus distributed many thousand gulden. That criminal fool, Eck, dared to revile the pious evangelist. . . . Some of the lawyers asserted that the imperial safe-conduct neither ought to be nor could be kept. . . . The wicked bishops wish to imitate their ancestors who burned John Huss at Constance. . . .

Someone has posted up a notice saying that forty nobles have bound themselves to protect Luther, and has signed the notice with the word "Bundschuh."[1] These men are too rash; they wish to help Luther, but they really hurt him. Indeed, there are some who think that our enemies put up this notice to excite odium against Luther, which seems to me very likely. Rouse the minds of your fellow-citizens, for I have much hope in the cities on account of your especial love of liberty. We have Sickingen on our side, now not only an adherent, but an ardent disciple who has absorbed all that Luther has said and who hears his works read at meals.[2] I have heard him swear that he will not be wanting to the cause of truth no matter at what peril to himself. You may know that this saying is an oracle, for he will be true to his word. You may boast of him to your Nurembergers, saying: "There is no greater soul in Germany." I wish that he had never done anything for me, instead of the great deal that he has done, so that no one would think my opinion of him prejudiced. Indeed, this is the only reason why I do not more loudly praise his heroic virtues and lofty mind. May God sustain the spirit he has excited in him. Thus prays Luther, and thus I pray after him. But I return to him. Borne up by divine inspiration he rejects all human counsel and relies solely on God. He despises death as no man ever did. May Christ preserve his evangelist at least until some true piety has sprung up in the minds of men. My friends write me that an atrocious edict has followed his departure. I greatly fear a large party of Germans will protest against it, for faction is rife. I write briefly about many things. Let me hear from you soon. Farewell.

471. LUTHER TO COUNT ALBERT OF MANSFELD.
Enders, iii. 144. De Wette, i. 601. German.

EISENACH, May 3, 1521.

This letter is dated "die sanctae Crucis," *i. e.*, May 3, as in De Wette, not May 9, as, probably by a misprint, in Enders. Luther traveled from Friedberg to Grünberg on April 29; to Alsfeld April 30; to Hersfeld, where he was entertained by the Benedictine abbot and where he preached on May 1; to Berka and Eisenach May 2; after preaching at Eisenach on the morning of May 3 he went to Möhra to visit his uncle,

[1] *Supra*, p. 540.
[2] Luther dedicated to Sickingen on June 1, 1521, his work on confession.

Henry Luther. On the morning of May 4 he also preached here, setting out in the afternoon towards Schloss Altenstein. On the way, he was captured by friendly retainers of the elector and taken back to the Wartburg, which he reached late at night. *Cf. Festchrift für Philipp von Hessen*, Cassel, 1904, p. 89, n. 2.

This letter was published immediately in several places. I have noted the textual corrections made by Enders on De Wette.

Noble, high-born and gracious Lord! My humble prayers and service to your Grace. Gracious Lord! Lord Rudolph of Watzdorf[1] has bidden me by special messenger while on my journey to write the history (as I may call it) of what happened to me at Worms.

In the first place, they did not wait for me to get to Worms, but they put out a mandate against me, and condemned me in spite of the imperial safe-conduct before I arrived and was heard. Then to make short work of me, they summoned me before his Imperial Majesty, and asked whether I would stand by my books or revoke them. Then I answered as I think has been announced to your Grace. Forthwith his Imperial Majesty, exasperated against me, with his own hand drew up a stern edict[2] and demanded of the Estates what they thought best to do against me, as befitted a Christian Emperor and guardian of the faith against a stiff-necked, contumacious heretic. But he wished to keep the safe-conduct.

Then some personages of the Empire were deputed to give me a gracious and kind warning to submit my books and the whole affair to his Imperial Majesty and the Estates. For this purpose I was summoned before the Bishop of Trier, the Margrave Joachim of Brandenburg, Duke George of Saxony, the Bishop[3] of Augsburg, the Lieutenant Master of the Teutonic Order,[4] the Bishop of Brandenburg,[5] Count George of

---

[1] Since 1484 the Master of Ceremonies at the Mansfeld court, and one of the guardians of the young counts. Vollrad von Watzdorf, another of this old noble family, had been with Luther at Worms, where he had had a warm discussion with Cochlaeus.

[2] Reprinted in Kidd: *Documents of the Continental Reformation*, no. 43. *Cf.* Smith, p. 120.

[3] Christopher von Stadion.

[4] "Deutscher Meister," lieutenant of the Grand Master, had the rank and vote of a prince. The present occupant of the place, which he was the last to hold, was Dietrich von Cleen, 1515-26.

[5] Luther undoubtedly means the old Bishop, Scultetus, although he had been translated to the see of Havelberg, and a new Bishop, Dietrich von Hardenberg, been installed in October, 1520.

Wertheim,[1] and two representatives[2] of the Free Cities. Then the Chancellor[3] of the Margrave of Baden arose, and gave me an able, temperate admonition, so that I must confess the Official of Trier can't hold a candle to him. He said it was not his intention to start a debate with me, but to give me a gracious, loyal and fraternal warning to consider what confusion and sedition would follow and what offence and scandal I would give. He bade me hold in honor the powers that be, and pass over many things for the sake of brotherly love, and put the best construction on everything. Even if the authorities had occasionally erred their power was not lost thereby, but that we were bound to obey them, and so forth.

To which I answered that I was willing to submit my books not only to his Imperial Majesty, but to everyone, no matter how small, provided only that nothing should be recognized or decided contrary to the holy gospel. Also that I had never taught that one should despise those in authority, be they good or bad. Item that I did not attack the Pope nor the council on account of their bad lives and deeds, but on account of their false doctrine. For authority and obedience are abrogated by false doctrine. I pointed to the article condemned at Constance that *"The one holy universal Church was the aggregate of those predestined [to salvation.]"*[4] This article I would not let be condemned, for it is one of the articles of our creed, when we say: "I believe in a holy Christian Church." Therefore scandalous works must be winked at, but faith must remain. For God's Word always scandalizes the great, wise and holy, as Christ himself was made by God for a *sign to be spoken against*[5] and for the falling of many in Israel. Therefore I could yield nothing more to fraternal love, for I would thereby be in so much harmful to the gospel and the faith.

As they accomplished nothing thus, my Lord of Trier took me apart with Dr. Schurff and Amsdorf, and graciously al-

[1] Count George of Wertheim reigned 1509-1530. He became a Lutheran, asking to be supplied with a chaplain on September 4, 1521. Enders, iv. 2.
[2] They were Conrad Peutinger of Augsburg and John Bock of Strassburg.
[3] Jerome Vehus.
[4] Latin.
[5] Latin. Luke, ii. 34.

lowed the official with Dr. Cochlaeus the Dean of Frankfort to examine me. But it was a useless debate, for they tempted me with sharp sarcasm, but did not accomplish their end. I said: The Pope is no judge of matters pertaining to God's Word and the faith, but a Christian man must examine and judge them himself, as he has to live and die by them. For the Word of God and the faith is the property of every man in the whole community. That I founded on St. Paul (I Corinthians, xiv.)[1] *"If a revelation be made to another sitting by, let the first keep silence."* From this saying it is clear that the master should follow the pupil if the latter has the better support in God's Word. And this saying stood and yet stands, as they said nothing against it. Thus we parted.

Afterwards the Chancellor of Baden and Dr. Peutinger were deputed to treat with me to submit my books to his Imperial Majesty without any reservation, saying that I should trust to them, for they would decide as Christians. As they pressed me hard I put it on their consciences whether they would advise me to trust so freely to his Imperial Majesty and others, since they had already condemned me and burned my books, and whether I did not therefore have good reason to take care and make the proviso that they should decide nothing contrary to the gospel, and whether good reason to do so were not found in the prohibition of the Scripture to trust in men, as Jeremiah xvii. says: *"Cursed is he that trusteth in man."*[2] Thus we parted. I agreed to submit on condition that they would decide nothing against God's Word. They were not able to take away that condition.

After that my Lord of Trier gave me an audience alone, in which he showed himself very kind and more than gracious, and tried his best to do the right thing. He made me similar representations, and I answered as before, for I knew not how else to answer; then he left me. Then immediately came the official with a count and the Chancellor[3] of his Imperial Majesty as a notary, and gave me this message from his Majesty: As I would not yield in my undertaking, I should

---

[1] Luther quotes in Latin; the verse is the 30th, which is not given by Luther as the division into verses came after his day.
[2] Latin.
[3] Rather his secretary, Maximilian Transsylvanus von Zevenbergen.

depart and have twenty days' safe-conduct; after that his Imperial Majesty would do against me as befitted him. So I thanked his Majesty and said: *"As it has pleased the Lord, so it has been; blessed be the name of the Lord."*[1] They also charged me not to preach or to write on the way. I said: "I will do all that pleases his Majesty, but I will leave God's Word free, as St. Paul says: *'The Word of God is not bound.'* "[2]

So I departed, and am now at Eisenach, and I imagine they will accuse me of having broken the safe-conduct and of preaching at Hersfeld and at Eisenach. For that is just what they are trying to do. Herewith I commend myself humbly to your Grace. In haste, Your Grace's chaplain,

MARTIN LUTHER.

472. HERMANN BUSCH TO ULRICH VON HUTTEN.

Böcking, ii. 62. WORMS, May 5, 1521.

Busch of Westphalia (1468-April, 1534), educated at Deventer and Heidelberg, 1486-91 traveled to Italy, Paris and Cologne; 1502 at Wittenberg, 1503 at Leipsic, 1507 at Cologne, 1516 to Holland and England. In 1526 he was called to Marburg. He may have had some part in the *Epistolae Obscurorum Virorum*. He was an ardent Lutheran. *Allgemeine Deutsche Biographie*.

I wish that something worse had come of your threats than has been the case. The Romanists who at first greatly feared for themselves now make bold to laugh and joke about you even amongst us. Indeed, their boldness has increased, for they say you only bark and do not bite. "It is easy," they say, "to bear an enemy who hurts only by threats, and never strikes. What on earth did his wild threats mean? When will they end? How long will he thus stultify himself? That impotent cloud spends all its force in thunder. Your Hutten knows how to frighten, not how to wound. . . . We will act more strenuously the more vainly he threatens, nor do we care for the terrors of Hutten or any of the vanquished, but, having damned Luther, we triumphantly and thankfully offer our services to Leo, even if it means the slaughter of those Germans who may be rash enough to resist us." May I die

[1] Latin. *Cf.* Job, i. 21. [2] Latin.

if they do not openly and boldly utter such words. Recently a Spaniard seized a copy of Leo's bull, edited by you, and trampled it in the mud. Day before yesterday a priest of the Emperor's court took from a poor man a bundle of eighty *Babylonian Captivities,* tore up some of them and would have torn up the rest if a neighboring bookseller had not come up and compelled the wretch and his assistants to take refuge in the palace. Aleander has wormed himself into the confidence of the Emperor . . . and the nuncios are of all men the most hostile to liberty, to Luther and to you. If they get out of Germany safe, you will greatly disappoint our expectations, Hutten. . . . I am waiting here for the publication of the imperial edict against Luther and the Lutherans; the Romanists loudly threaten us with it, which they say will be directed not only against the books, but against the persons of Lutherans. Farewell.

473. ALEANDER TO VICE-CHANCELLOR CARDINAL DE' MEDICI AT ROME.

Kalkoff: *Aleander,* 205. WORMS (May 5), 1521.

After the events sketched in my letter of the 29th ultimo, the electors and princes took council together in Luther's affair and resolved to support the Emperor's procedure against Luther and his books. The Saxon said neither yes nor no to this, but maintained an obstinate silence. I am not clear about the position of the Elector Palatine, but I have learned that the majority of the electors are in agreement with the Emperor. After that [probably on May 1] the Emperor and Privy Council charged me with the drafting of the edict, which I was to justify as carefully as possible so as to quiet the people, and that is all the more necessary as Luther has already published in German an account of his hearing before the Emperor, and has thus cleverly vindicated himself, though with lies, in order to strengthen his followers and win back public opinion which was largely estranged by his bad morals and demeanor, his obstinacy and his bestial expressions about councils, all of which made a deep impression on the Germans. But that does not prevent a large number from holding fast to him, not as though they embraced his views, but simply to spite Rome and to get possession of the German ecclesiastical property under the excuses offered by Luther.

Although convinced of my own incapacity, for, poorly as I do other things, I know absolutely nothing of the art of drafting edicts, yet I would not by my refusal give them any excuse against us, fearing, that, as usual in such edicts, sufficient reverence would not be shown the Holy Father. Therefore I worked hard the whole night so that notwithstanding its length the edict could be laid before the Emperor and Privy Council the next morning. Although it met with their full approval, yet they gave it for further examination to the Austrian Council, which did not please me, as some of its members are Lutherans, and others are in the pay of the Saxon, and all of them are bitter against the clergy and especially against Rome. I fear that even if they should act quickly, yet they will not act according to our wishes, especially in executing the ban of the Empire, which would be particularly deplorable. We will do our very best to have it appear in the proper form and none other. This procedure is the more remarkable in that when the imperialists commissioned me as draftsman they urged the greatest expedition, so that I thought they really wanted to have the edict prepared by the Privy Council in the royal cabinet, as they had decreed. This was their duty, for the Estates were reconciled to executing the will of the Emperor. I cannot explain this sudden and unexpected turn in their position . . . for this very morning the Emperor told us that he would have the edict executed, and the Chancellor that we might rest assured that it would be drawn up in Latin, German, Dutch and French. In all their acts they are too procrastinating, to their own disadvantage and that of the whole world; by trying to please all they get the contempt of all. Therefore even the recently published sequestration-mandate, which is observed punctually in other parts of Germany, does not prevent the books of Luther and his infamous comrades being sold here at court and their pictures exposed publicly. With all our complaints we cannot induce the faint-hearted imperialists to order the confiscation of these goods or the punishment of one merchant. And yet that mandate was passed by the unanimous consent of the whole Diet. It is clear that Hutten and his fellow assassins who are near here under Sickingen's protection have a hand in this game. The imperialists, especially during their sojourn here at the Diet, fear to offend them, so I believe that they will not try to execute the edict until after their departure. Yesterday the Emperor with great emotion, laying his hand on his heart, said to Glapion: "I promise you that when the new edict is signed and published, I will have the first man found with a book or picture of Luther pilloried at this window," indicating the one at which he was standing. Certainly he has the best intentions, but his court, on account of some scruples, won't let him act accordingly.

Luther is said to be four days' journey from here at a castle where many nobles are assembled, and he is said to have dismissed the herald who accompanied him, who has now returned to Mayence. But Luther kept the safe-conduct. Rumor here persists in saying that he will go to Denmark. When we told the Emperor this he said that he would certainly get him then, for the king of Denmark had expressed the wish of meeting him,[1] the Emperor, in Flanders, when he returned thither, but he asked us not to say anything more about it. . . .

474. COCHLAEUS TO JEROME ALEANDER.

Zeitschrift für Kirchengeschichte, xviii. 109.

FRANKFORT a. M., May 5, 1521.

Greeting. You were too true a prophet, magnificent Aleander, about the lies of our Lutheran friends. What a long story they have gotten up, which, though I have not yet seen it, they have inscribed *The Acts of Cochlaeus.* In this they circulate the slander that I was suborned by you, under the pretext of a debate, to get Luther to give up his safe-conduct. They add another false statement, that Luther offered to undergo any risk that I would, but that I refused. As witnesses to their fiction I hear that they cite six counts. I will give you my advice on this, not knowing what you will

---

[1] In fact King Christian of Denmark met Charles at Brussels in July. *Cf. Albrecht Dürers Schriftliche Nachlass, in fine.*

find. It is certain that they blushed a good deal to find that when I offered to debate with Luther under judges, *he* refused. Thus they invent the calumny about my being suborned. Why don't you get his Imperial Majesty to force those counts, secretly and quietly, to make depositions before a notary on oath? After their testimony has been taken, if it seem true and favorable to us, it can be published to the great confusion of Luther, but if against us it could be suppressed. I call God to witness how freely I offered to debate with him, which he refused.

I do not remember the names of all the counts, but the Count of Mansfeld sat on my right, and Christopher von Schwartzenberg[1] also. They can tell the others. . . . Let them be asked: 1. Whether they ever heard me refuse to debate on equal terms. 2. Whether they heard me refuse to debate unless Luther renounced his safe-conduct. 3. Whether they did not hear me ask to debate before judges without peril to him, which the Emperor and nobles would have allowed. 4. Whether they did not hear Luther say: "I do not want to debate now." 5. Whether they did not hear Luther say he would like the judge to be a boy of eight or nine years, or one of the pages present whom he pointed out. . . .

Luther said among the nobles at Friedberg that the Emperor had sworn on the blood of Christ that "the monk should pay the penalty." The Lutherans trust only in arms.

475. ALEANDER TO VICE-CHANCELLOR CARDINAL DE' MEDICI AT ROME.

Kalkoff: *Aleander,* 214.   WORMS (May 8), 1521.

After I had written and sealed my last letter, I received your Lordship's letter and the bull[2] in which Luther alone is mentioned by name and his followers in general; this was very welcome to me. If it had reached me somewhat sooner, I would, as the bull requires, have published it here and at

---

[1]Probably Christopher Baron (Freiherr) von Schwartzenberg is meant, a son of John von Schwartzenberg, who died October 21, 1528. The father became a Lutheran, the son remained a Catholic, and a literary controversy between them took place in 1524. On this, Enders, iv. 5f.

[2]The bull *Decet Pontificem Romanum,* published in *Magnum Bullarium Romanum* (Luxemburg, 1727), i. 614f. *Cf.* Smith, 101f.

Mayence, and have mentioned it in the edict. But it is now too late, as the preparation of the latter must no longer be delayed, for some sudden event might come between, and the Emperor threatens to leave soon, and so we fear that the time will be too short for us. . . .

Luther dismissed the imperial herald, saying that he felt safer without him. He had an escort of fifty horsemen. It is surmised that he got rid of the herald to return to this neighborhood, presumably to a castle of Sickingen, from which vantage point he can, especially after the appearance of the edict, raise a rebellion. . . .

476. ALEANDER TO GATTINARA AT WORMS.
Reichstagsakten, ii. 639. (WORMS, May 8, 1521.)

I am sending the edict on the Lutheran affair in Latin and German. May God grant that whatever is best for the peace and preservation of our religion may come to pass. Certainly nothing could be saner, juster or more legal than what is said about Luther in the first part of the edict. For everything has been done, as is stated in the edict, to show that his Imperial Majesty has omitted nothing which might have led to a peaceful solution of the problem, so that in the judgment of all and even of Luther no one can be said to be more clement. The second part of the edict is a prohibition to print bad books, and although it is absolutely advisable and conceded without debate, yet that your illustrious Lordship may be able to show his Majesty that nothing is rashly done, I am sending the decree drawn up by the Bishop of Trieste and adopted after so much discussion, consultation and examination of the German Diet. May your illustrious Lordship consider it and refer it to the Emperor and Diet, showing that we seek nothing in it except what law and equity demand.

477. ERASMUS TO JUSTUS JONAS.
Erasmi opera (1703), iii. 639. LOUVAIN, May 10, 1521.

There has been a persistent rumor here, dear Jonas, that

[1]The Edict of Worms, condemning Luther, was drafted by the Privy Council on May 8, and signed, without changing this date, on May 26. *Cf.* Smith, 120. J. Paquier: *Jérome Aleandre,* p. 268. The edict reprinted in Kidd: *Documents,* no. 45.

you were with Martin Luther at Worms; nor do I doubt that your piety has done what I would have done had I been present, to assuage the tragedy with moderate counsels, so that it would not in future burst forth with greater damage to the world. I am much surprised that such counsels were not followed, since they were pleasing to all good men who desired only the peace of the Church, for without concord the Church loses her proper name. For what else is our religion but peace in the Holy Spirit? Orthodox fathers have borne witness that the net of the Church has taken both good fishes and bad, and that tares have grown up with the wheat, and that vices have grown up, and have deplored that the morals of those who should have been the ensamples of real piety have become corrupt. . . . The study of Holy Scripture had decayed as much as morals, for it was perverted to serve human greed by imposing on the credulity of the people. Pious minds, in which nothing is more deeply rooted than the glory of Christ, groaned at this. This brought it about that at first Luther had such favor from all men as I believe no mortal ever had before for centuries. And as we easily believe what we vehemently desire, men thought that he was a man raised up pure from all the temptations of this world, to bring a remedy for such great evils. Nor did I entirely despair, except that at the first taste of the books published over Luther's name I feared that the affair would bring on a tumult and strife throughout the world. So by letter I warned both Luther and those friends who I thought would have most influence with him; what counsel they gave him I know not, but certainly he acted so that there is danger lest the bad remedies applied should double the evils. I greatly wonder, Jonas, what god inspired Luther, that with so licentious a pen he should attack the Pope, all universities, philosophy and the mendicant orders. For if all his censures were true, and it is said that they are far from true, what other result could he expect by provoking so many than that which we see? I have not yet had time to read Luther's books, but from the little I have glanced at and from what has been told me by others, I have observed that even where his allegations were above my power to judge, his method and argument by no means pleased me. For since truth of herself is a bitter thing, and since it is by nature an odious task to pluck up what has been received by long usage, it would have been wiser to assuage the bitterness by courtesy than to add hatred to hatred. For what did he gain by publishing paradoxes which offended more at first sight than when closely examined? Some things are made disagreeable by the affectation of obscurity. What did he attain by reviling men? If he wished to cure them this must be called imprudent, if he wished to bring a calamity on the whole world, impious. Although a prudent man dispenses truth economically, bringing forth what is sufficient and fit for the occasion, Luther poured forth everything at once in a quantity of hasty books, proclaiming everything to artisans, even that which the learned are wont to treat as *mystic and unspeakable*,[1] and generally with far more zeal to attack them than the facts, in my judgment, warranted. When it would have been sufficient to warn theologians that they attached too much importance to the peripatetic philosophy, or to the sophists, *he* called Aristotle's philosophy the death of the soul. The evangelic spirit of Christ has his prudence and his gentleness. Thus Christ himself tempered his doctrine to the prejudices of the Jews, speaking one thing to the crowds and another to his disciples, and bearing with *them* a long time, leading them gradually to a knowledge of the heavenly philosophy.... [Similar examples of prudent forbearance are taken from Peter, Paul, Augustine, Brutus and Plato.]

I do not even listen to those, Jonas, who say that Luther was unable to practice Christian moderation on account of the intolerable provocation of his antagonists. Whoever undertakes to do what he undertook ought to stand fast no matter how others act. He should have foreseen what would happen when he got into this hole, lest he should have the same fate as the goat in the fable. It is foolish even for pious reasons to try to do what you cannot, especially when if you do not succeed there will be much harm done. We see that things have come to such a pass that there appears to be no happy issue possible unless Christ should turn the rashness of some men into a public good. Some men excuse Luther by

[1] Greek.

saying that he was forced by others to write fiercely and to decline the judgment of merciful Leo and the good faith of the Emperor Charles, the best and gentlest of princes. But why should he have followed the advice of these friends rather than that of others who, being neither unlearned nor unskilful in affairs, advised differently?[1] . . .

[1] This warning had no effect on Jonas, who returned at once to Wittenberg, where he soon became Provost of the Castle Church. From this time on he was one of Luther's most devoted followers.

APPENDIX I.

ADDITIONAL LUTHER LETTERS, TRANSLATED IN PRESERVED SMITH'S LIFE AND LETTERS OF MARTIN LUTHER, 1911.

1. To Andrew Lohr, September 22, 1512, p. 21.
2. To Spalatin, February, 1514, p. 29.
3. To Spalatin, August 5, 1514, p. 29.
4. To John Bercken, May 1, 1516, p. 30.
5. To Spalatin, June 8, 1516, p. 33.
6. To Michael Dressel, June 8, 1516, p. 31.
7. To Lang, October 26, 1516, p. 32.
8. To Lang, February 8, 1517, p. 26.
9. To Albert of Mayence, October 31, 1517, p. 42.
10. To Elector Frederic, November, 1517, p. 34.
11. To C. Scheurl, March 5, 1518, p. 43.
12. To Leo X., May 30?, 1518, p. 44.
13. To Spalatin, August 31, 1518, p. 70.
14. To Spalatin, October 14, 1518, p. 49.
15. To Cajetan, October 17, 1518, p. 52.
16. To Elector Frederic, January 5-6, 1519, p. 54.
17. To Elector Frederic, January 6-7, 1519, p. 56.
18. To John Eck, February 18, 1519, p. 59.
19. To Spalatin, soon after February 24, 1519 (no. 1), p. 60.
20. To Spalatin, soon after February 24, 1519 (no. 2), p. 61.
21. To Erasmus, March 28, 1519, p. 200.
22. To Spalatin, July 20, 1519, p. 64.
23. To Spalatin, February, 1520, p. 72.
24. Ulrich von Hutten to Luther, June 4, 1520, p. 73.
25. To Amsdorf, June 23, 1520, p. 79.
26. To Spalatin, July 10, 1520, p. 74.
27. To Gerard Listrius, July 30, 1520, p. 77.[1]
28. To Lang, August 18, 1518, p. 86.
29. To Link, August 19, 1520, p. 87.
30. To Charles V., August 31, 1520, p. 99.
31. To Leo X., October, 1520, p. 91.
32. To Spalatin, December 21, 1520, p. 105.[2]

[1]This letter is not in Enders. The text is printed in my *Luther*, p. 471.
[2]Knaake in *Theologische Studien und Kritiken*, 1900, p. 273, tries to show that this letter should be dated "Spannenberg, December 29," but Enders is right, as had the letter been written on December 29, Luther, who usually began the new year on Christmas, would have dated it "1521."

33. To Elector Frederic, January 25, 1521, p. 106.
34. To Staupitz, February 9, 1521, p. 108.
35. To Spalatin, March 19, 1521, p. 110.
36. To Spalatin, April 14, 1521, p. 111.
37. To Cuspinian, April 28, 1521, p. 114.[1]
38. To Cranach, April 28, 1521, p. 119.

APPENDIX II.

SOME LOST LUTHER LETTERS

In the correspondence of Luther and his friends we often hear of letters which are not now extant. It would serve no purpose to register all these, but a few of which particularly interesting details are known may be mentioned.

1. DR. JOHN FLECK[2] TO LUTHER.

E. Kroker: *Luthers Tischreden in der Matthesischen Sammlung,* no. 562. (STEINLAUSIG, late in 1517.)

Of this letter Luther tells us in 1542: "I like Fleck. He is a man full of comfort and his words are consolatory. He wrote me a letter, a splendid one, immediately after I had published my Theses. I would give ten gulden to have it now. Its purport was about as follows: 'Venerable Doctor, proceed! Press forward! These papal abuses always displeased me, too, etc.' The monks were also angry at him, for he had said to those at Steinlausig: 'There is a man who will do something.' He never said a mass, which was a good sign."

2. MARTIN LUTHER TO DR. HERMAN.

In the Historical Manuscripts Commission, vol. ix., part ii., p. 413, London, 1884, is the following entry: "Letter of Martin Luther to Dr. Herman, Latin, accompanying one of the writer's principal petitions, in which Herman is enjoined to believe no calumnious report of the writer, but to consider all things done by him as having been done in good faith." There is no date, but it is bound in a volume of manuscripts between July and November, 1519. The original is in the possession of Mrs. Alfred Morrison of London. Efforts to see it while I was there proved unavailing. Among the possible addressees are Antony Hermann, Nicholas Hermann, Hermann Busch, Hermann Mühlpfort and Hermann Tullich. None of these, however, was a doctor, and none is otherwise likely. Until the original can be examined any conjecture must be made with reserve. It is not impossible that the letter is really to Dr. Henning Göde, always referred to as

---

[1] The text of this letter as printed in Enders is poor. The correct form is given in my *Luther,* p. 472.
[2] Fleck was Prior of the Franciscans at Steinlausig. At the opening of Wittenberg (1502) he had preached. On him, Köstlin-Kawerau, i. 80, 163f.

"Dr. Henning," which might easily be misread "Herman." If so, it probably accompanied Luther's "positions" as his Theses were often called. That Luther actually wrote to him may be seen by Enders, i. 57. The date of such a letter as the above must fall between the posting of the Theses, October 31, 1517, and Henning's death, January 23, 1521, probably while Henning was at Erfurt in 1518.

3. LUTHER TO JOHN TETZEL AT LEIPSIC.

De Wette-Seidemann, vi. 18. (Shortly before August 11, 1519.)

Not only the reputation, but also the health of the indulgence-seller, John Tetzel, was broken by the storm started in 1517. When Luther heard that he was mortally ill, he wrote to comfort him, and bade him "not to be troubled, for the matter did not begin on his account, but the child had quite a different father." The letter is lost, but this quotation is preserved in Emser's: *Auff des Stieres zu Wittenberg wiettende replica.*

4. LUTHER TO VADIAN AT ST. GALL.

Vadianische Briefsammlung, ii. no. 249. (1520 or early 1521.)

On March 18, 1521, Lawrence Merus writes to Vadian that a few days ago Salandronius has handed him Luther's letter to him (Vadian). He (Merus) passed it around among his friends until the writing began to grow dim with being kissed, after which he locked it up safely in his desk.

APPENDIX III.

139a. CAPITO TO ERASMUS AT BASLE.

Allen, iii. 526. (Basle), April 8, 1519.

The following letter first came to my knowledge while the present work was in press. It is worth adding for the light it throws on Capito's efforts to act as intermediary between Luther and Erasmus, a rôle he reassumed during the latter part of 1521:

"I pray you not to disparage Luther's course in public. You know how much your opinion counts. I beg this from my heart. It is expedient to let Luther's fame live, for thus notwithstanding his shortcomings courage will be given to the rest of the youth to dare something for Christ's freedom. We shall keep subservient to you Germany and Saxony, where Luther's patron, a powerful prince, the flourishing University of Wittenberg and many illustrious men equally favor Erasmus and Luther. The enemy desires nothing more than to see you angry at him. It is better to have the hostility of all theologians than that of Luther's champions, for there are some princes, cardinals, bishops and famous ecclesiastics who have his cause at heart."

INDEX

Abel, 43.
Accolti, P., 283, 299, 316, 495.
Acta Augustana, 102, 119, 128, 133, 136, 230.
Adamites, 529.
Address to the Christian Nobility of the German Nation, 329, 341f., 344, 347f., 358, 369, 378ff., 412, 422, 431ff., 460, 471, 473.
Adelmann, B., 123, 307, 424.
Adelmann, C., letter, 122ff.
Adrian of Antwerp, 60.
Adrian of Utrecht (later Pope Adrian VI), 6, 209, 301, 312, 403, 436.
    Letters, 256f., 5141
Adrian, M., 290f., 306, 314f., 365, 387, 465.
Aeneas Sylvius (see Pius II).
Agricola, J., 189, 341, 348f.
Agricola, R., letter, 461f.
Agrippa, H. C., 190f.
Aix la-Chapelle, 418.
Aleander, J., 6, 382, 389, 393, 395, 397ff. 402, 406, 411f., 430, 434f., 438f., 446f., 451, 454, 482, 501f., 504, 512, 553, 560, 562f.
    Danger and hardships in Germany, 422f., 430, 459, 461, 466, 509f.
    Letters, 379f., 388f., 416-23, 425-9, 454-64, 466ff., 473-7, 486-9, 495ff., 505f., 508ff., 515-22, 525-31, 539-47, 552., 560ff, 563f.
    Oration at Worms, 463, 467, 470f., 488.
Aleander, P., 457.
Alexander of Hales, 146.
Alexander, secretary of Nassau, 494f.
Alsfeld, 555.
Altenburg, 219, 353, 362.
Altenstein, 556.
Alvarez, J., 242f.
Alveld, A., 317, 320, 325, 327, 329, 341, 344, 372, 412, 424, 441.
Ambrose, 43, 69, 129, 203, 205, 213.
Amerbach, Basil, 377f., 448.
    Letter, 397

Amerbach, Boniface, 378f., 389f., 397, 438f.
    Letters, 221f., 377f., 436f., 448.
Ammann, J. J., 396.
Amsdorf, N. v., 51f., 54, 77, 120, 131, 134, 166, 168, 344, 473, 521, 523, 543, 552, 557, 568.
    Letter, 209ff.
Ancona (see Accolti).
Andrew the barber, 274.
Anhalt, Margaret, Princess of, 244f.
Anna, St., 66f.
Annaberg, 196, 208.
Anselm, T., 300.
Antichrist, 170f., 179, 240, 265, 269, 291, 329, 344, 366, 386f., 394, 442, 450, 494f., 497, 510, 528.
Antiochus, 291.
Antwerp, 301, 351, 379, 456f.
    Jacobin of, 494.
    Prior of, 375f.
Apollonia, St., 67.
Aquensis, P., 317f.
Aquinas, T., 78, 101, 117, 129, 146, 150, 220, 242, 270, 283, 359, 426.
Arcimboldi, J. A. de, 453.
Aristotle, 23, 43, 55, 60, 64f., 77, 81f., 129, 150, 169f, 198, 216, 230, 254, 257f., 566.
Arius, 154, 247, 417, 423.
Armstorf, P. v., 512f., 515f.
Asterisks, 86f., 95.
Athanasius, 129, 154, 254.
Auer, J., 133f.
Augsburg, 76, 102, 142, 156, 204, 233, 262, 280, 460, 536.
    Christopher v. Stadion, Bishop of, 116, 424, 498, 542, 556.
    Diet of (1518), 100f.
    Luther's trial at, 6, 96, 116-24, 130, 136f., 160, 185, 191, 216, 266, 307, 340, 440.
Augustine, St., 41-4, 55, 57f., 68f., 74, 81f., 129, 161, 180f., 203, 205, 213f., 226, 240f., 255, 283, 326, 388, 429, 436, 532, 549f., 566.
Augustinians, 25, 33, 79, 105ff., 222, 233, 268, 297ff., 333.
    Chapter at Eisleben, 348, 351, 353.
Aurogallus, M., 465.

Babylonian Captivity of the Church, 349, 364, 377, 420, 423, 427, 439, 446f., 520, 560.
Baden, 384.
  Philip, Margrave of, 542.
Bader, P., 79.
Bamberg, 230, 382.
  George, Bishop of, 388, 498.
Ban (see Excommunication).
  of the Empire (see Worms, Edict of), 444, 467, 506, 523, 561.
  Sermon on the, 98.
Bannissius, J., 454.
Baptism, 447.
Barbara, St., 67.
Barthélemi, 392.
Bartholomew, St., 37.
Basil, 129.
Basle, 112, 172, 178, 314, 356, 378, 396, 465, 505.
  Christopher v. Uttenheim, Bishop of, 163.
  Council of, 246.
Bavaria, 332.
  Dukes of, 424, 469, 517.
  William, Duke of, 536.
Bayer, C., 308.
Beatus Rhenanus, 80ff., 208f., 277, 436f., 500, 510f.
  Letters, 389f., 438f., 493f.
Beckmann, O., 51, 60, 120, 134, 166, 227f.
Beczschicz, C., 285.
Beda, N., 392.
Begging, 294f.
Beghards (see Hussites), 66, 317, 327, 529.
Benedict, M., 300.
Bérauld, N., 464f.
Bercken, J., 568.
Berghes, M. de, 234, 546, 558.
Berka, 555.
Berlin, 356.
Bernard, 201, 203, 206, 240, 255.
Bernhardi, B., 41, 54, 131, 168, 317, 325.
Beroald, P., 169.
Bessler, N., 437.
Beymann, P., 277.
Bias, 492.
Bible, 6, 75, 77, 81f., 84, 94, 139, 287, 324, 364, 384.
  Free use, 113, 438, 565.
  Interpretation, 43, 203, 247, 250, 435, 558.
  Luther's lectures on, 25f., 31, 41, 49, 54, 61, 156ff., 162, 309, 355, 477.
  Method of study, 68ff.

Supremacy, 78, 89, 149, 153, 155, 159, 214, 230, 255, 326, 529, 548ff., 554.
Tumult results from the study, 376.
Biel, G., 41f., 78.
Bild, G., 137, 317.
  Letters, 114f., 307f.
Black Cloister (Augustinian monastery at Wittenberg), 22, 183f.
Blaurer, A., 438.
Blaurer, T.
  Letter, 438, 464.
Bock, J., 557.
Bodensee, 405.
Bohemia, 273, 313, 330f., 341, 405, 452, 531, 547.
Bohemians (see Beghards and Hussites).
Bologna, 234, 251, 421.
Bonaventura, 146.
Bösschenstein, J., 138.
Bossenstain, J., 124.
Botzheim, J. v., 464.
Brabant, 162, 494.
Bragadin, L., 299.
Brandenburg, 141, 237.
  Jerome Scultetus, Bishop of, 73f., 77, 87ff., 98, 134, 215, 220, 393, 405, 450, 498, 542, 556.
  Joachim I, Elector of, 215, 442, 449, 474f., 497f., 517, 522, 540ff., 556.
Braun, J., 21-4, 38.
Breisgau, 405.
  John of, 262.
Breitenbach, G. v., 252.
Breslau,
  John v. Thurzo, Bishop of, 309, 394.
Briard, 304.
Briselot, 235.
Bronner, J., 279.
Brück, G.,
  Letter, 506f.
Bruges, 357, 494.
Brunswick-Lüneburg, Margaret, Duchess of, 227f.
Brussels, 511, 562.
Brutus, 566.
Bucer, M., 6, 397, 442, 516, 525.
  Letters, 80ff., 208f., 276ff., 358, 510f., 512f.
  Luther's opinion of, 285.
Bünau, G. v., 359f.
Bünau, H. v., 324f.
Burckhardt, F., 195.
Burckhart, P., 204f., 339, 365.
Burgundy, 474.

Busch, H. v., 540, 569.
  Letter, 559f.
Buttstädt, 353, 363.

Cabala, 238.
Caesar, John, 264.
Cajetan, Thomas de Vio, Cardinal,
  100, 131-4, 142, 163, 176, 179,
  209, 242f., 253, 267, 337, 338,
  389, 568.
  On commission to draw up bull
    against Luther, 283, 299, 316.
  Tries Luther at Augsburg, 101-5,
    109, 113, 115ff., 128f., 132, 136,
    156, 172, 186.
Calvin, J., 464, 522.
Calvus, F., 162.
Cambridge, University of, 209, 490.
Camerarius, J., 513f.
Campeggio, L., 316, 411f.
Canon Law, 41, 66, 84, 89, 149, 155,
  157, 170, 175, 262, 291, 326,
  335, 422, 476, 532.
  Burning of, 405, 414f., 431, 434,
    439, 446, 461.
Cantiuncula, C., letter, 190f.
Capito, W. F., 6, 71f., 222, 317, 358,
  368, 412, 416, 511.
  Letters, 110ff., 129, 134, 163f.,
    173, 405ff., 570.
Caracciolo, M., 379, 382, 389, 393,
  399, 419, 434, 463f., 496f., 510,
  517, 519, 531, 560.
  Letter, 539-47.
Carlstadt, A., 41f., 54, 56, 58, 69, 71,
  74f., 90, 112, 118ff., 130f., 134f.,
  138, 140, 143f., 152f., 155ff.,
  160ff., 164f., 167f., 173-6, 181,
  184, 190, 195ff., 199f., 203, 210,
  237, 250, 258-62, 264, 268, 284,
  359, 364, 395, 537.
  Description of, 261.
  Letters, 93, 212ff.
Carmelites, 194, 243, 371, 494.
  Prior at Augsburg, 307.
Carondelet, J. de, 427f.
Carvajal, B., 316, 347.
Catharine, St., 67.
Catharinus, A., 485.
Celibacy, sacerdotal, 390, 411.
Cellarius, J., 188.
Charlemagne, 426, 463.
Charles V, Emperor, 6, 236, 314, 318,
  322f., 329f., 349, 365f., 379f.,
  382, 384, 393, 395-8, 402, 416,
  418f., 421, 427f., 429-33, 438,
  441f., 444-7, 450, 452f., 455ff.,
  459, 461ff., 466f., 469ff., 473-7,
  486, 489, 492, 494f., 498, 503f.,
  506ff., 510f., 513-16, 518ff.,
  521f., 526ff., 531f., 536, 538ff.,
  541, 545ff., 548-52, 554, 556-64,
  567f.
  Character, 420.
  Coronation, 368, 389, 418.
  Letters, 398f., 424f., 482f.
  Mandate against Luther for hered-
    itary dominions, 379, 398, 402,
    418, 455, 468, 474.
  Mandate ordering sequestration of
    Lutheran books, 449, 454, 486,
    489, 496f., 508f., 518, 556, 561.
  Opinion of Luther, 428, 530, 533f.,
    538, 553, 563.
  Safe-conduct for Luther, 482ff.,
    493, 496, 500, 506f., 525, 531,
    541, 547, 550, 552, 556, 559,
    562f.
Chièvres, W., 415, 420f., 425, 427,
  429, 464, 487f., 496, 517, 522,
  545.
  Letters, 397f., 433.
Chiregatto, F., 357f.
Christian II, King of Denmark, 484f.,
  536f., 547, 562.
Christopher, St., 67.
Chrysostom, 129, 203, 206, 213, 248.
Church, 132, 154, 226.
  Abuses in, 29, 50, 63, 141, 165,
    215, 229, 255, 311, 336, 380,
    465, 528f., 565.
  Authority of, 88, 110, 117, 123,
    155, 205, 293, 425, 529.
  Fathers of, 78, 84, 89, 155, 419,
    532.
  Greek, 206, 246, 426.
  Nature of, 146, 201, 326, 543, 557.
  Reform of, 83f., 166, 379, 442, 447,
    465, 513.
  Roman, 102, 107, 118, 153, 156ff.,
    160, 167, 172, 175, 246, 260,
    297f., 412, 501, 516f.
Cicero, 58.
Cistein (see Ende).
Claude, Queen of France, 522.
Cleen, D. v., 556.
Clivanus, R., 396.
Coblenz, 185, 194, 209.
Coburg, 115.
Cochlaeus, J., 543, 553, 556, 558.
  Letter, 562f.
Colet, J., 235.
Cologne, 63, 310, 384, 397, 399,
  401ff., 404, 406, 409f., 416, 422,
  425, 430, 441, 455, 458, 463, 467,
  473.
  Dominicans of, 27ff.
  Hermann v. Wied, Archbishop

Elector of, 474f.
University of, 135, 140, 203, 209, 295f., 299f., 310, 315, 322, 371, 405.
Confession, 240, 242, 269, 319, 451, 456, 472, 494, 498, 508.
Confirmation, 447.
Constance, 262, 319.
Council of, 198f., 201ff., 206, 214, 463, 529, 538, 542f., 551, 554, 557.
Contarini, G., letters, 535f., 538f., 551f.
Copenhagen, 485.
University of, 485, 537.
Cornaro, F.,
Letters, 533f., 551f.
Cotta, Ursula, 22f.
Cottbus, 424.
Council, Œcumenical, authority of, 202, 206, 232, 330f., 426, 447, 506, 529, 532, 534, 536, 539, 544ff., 548, 557.
Luther's appeal to a, 128, 135ff., 141, 145, 366, 370, 387, 396, 402.
Cowper, G., letter, 295.
Cowper, T., 295.
Crafft, A., 323.
Cranach, L., 321, 485, 569.
Crautwald, V., 328.
Creutzer, M., 484.
Crotus Rubeanus, 27, 251, 328, 330, 423, 482.
Letters, 229ff., 236f., 309f., 408ff.
Croy, W. de, Archbishop of Toledo, 447, 451f., 519.
Croy, W. de (see Chièvres).
Cum postquam bull, 148, 154.
Cuspinian, 569.
Cyprian, 43, 58, 129, 201, 203, 206, 239, 436.

Dandolo, M., 538f.
Decet Pontificem Romanum bull, 455, 462, 509, 553, 563f.
Demuth, N., 306.
Denmark, 547, 562.
Devils (see Satan), 275.
Dialogue on the Death of Julius II, 63, 165.
Diercx, V., 373, 375f.
Divorce, 208, 536, 539.
Döbeln, 484.
Dolzig, J. v., 26.
Dominicans, 27, 100, 150, 161, 194, 220, 222, 229, 231, 242f., 268, 270, 278, 304, 314, 342, 372, 376.
Donation of Constantine, 291.
Donatists, 181, 241.

Döring, C., 56, 78.
Dornheim, 411.
Dorp, M., 301, 311, 412.
Draco, J., 343.
Dresden, 207f., 217.
Augustinian Convent at, 37, 279, 351.
Luther visits, 96f., 149ff.
Dressel, M., 39f., 568.
Driedo, J., 373, 400f., 412.
Dungersheim, J., 76f., 175, 254f., 274, 317, 325ff.
Duns Scotus, 42, 78, 81f., 93, 129, 283.
Dürer, A., 6.
Letter, 280f.

Ebernburg, 509, 512.
Ebner, J., 62, 149.
Ecclesiastes, 245.
Eck, John, of Ingolstadt, 62f., 112, 122, 130, 139f., 143f., 146ff., 152f., 155, 160, 162, 164, 167-71, 174f., 182, 184, 186, 188, 190f., 195-207, 210-15, 217, 220, 222, 225, 238, 245, 250, 252, 254f., 258-62, 264f., 268, 272ff., 280, 284, 286f., 294ff., 336f., 352, 361f., 363ff., 366, 383, 387, 393, 405f., 411, 415, 430, 453, 466ff., 506, 568.
At Rome, 236f., 300, 314ff., 319, 328.
Description of, 261f.
Introduction to Luther, 53, 57f., 93ff.
Letters, 90, 135, 165, 195ff., 202ff., 205ff., 246ff., 315f.
Posts bull in Germany, 345, 360ff., 363ff., 366, 368ff., 379ff., 387f., 402, 449, 468f.
Obelisks, 76, 85ff., 90, 95, 135, 140, 160f., 200, 213, 258.
Eck, John, of Trier, 526ff., 529, 531, 540, 543f., 546, 553f., 556, 558.
Egmond, N., 235, 269, 304f., 371ff., 374ff.
Egranus, J. S., 66, 75, 112, 122, 159ff., 196, 385, 387.
Eichstädt, 449.
Gabriel, Bishop of, 135, 140, 258.
Eilenberg, 363, 393f., 403.
Einsiedel, H. v., 370, 394, 450.
Eisleben, 22, 38, 84, 274, 353, 362f.
Eisenach, 22, 34, 38, 274, 504, 523, 555, 559.
Elbe, 186.
Emser, J., 149ff., 176, 197, 218, 252, 265, 286f., 295, 313, 377, 387, 393,

INDEX

415, 440ff., 450ff., 460, 465f., 472, 481, 485, 504, 570.
Enarrationes Epistolarum et Evangeliorum, 469.
Ende zum Stein, N. v., 459f.
England, 162, 164, 193, 295, 321f., 446f.
Eobanus Hessus, H., 121.
Epistolae Obscurorum Virorum, 27, 40, 152, 346, 410.
Erasmus, D., 6, 32f., 37f., 44-7, 82, 112, 141, 159, 173, 177f., 182f., 200, 208, 255, 276, 278f., 301, 310, 314, 317, 325, 346, 366, 394ff., 422, 432, 434, 436f., 511f., 568, 570.
  Adages, 72.
  Aleander's opinion of, 457ff.
  Axioms, 460, 473.
  Dialogues of Lucian, 72.
  Letters, 121, 177ff., 181, 187f, 192ff., 234f., 238ff., 268, 304, 321f., 333f., 342f., 351, 355ff., 357f., 370-6, 389ff., 400ff., 411f., 415, 448, 464f., 494f., 500-3, 564-7.
  Luther's opinion of, 42, 54ff., 63, 68ff., 395.
  Method of Theology, 171f., 177, 191.
  New Testament, edition of Greek, 162, 245.
  Opinion of Luther, 110, 122, 134, 164, 220, 239, 296, 371.
  Against publication of Luther's works, 161, 355.
  Cares not if Luther is roasted or boiled, 494, 501.
  Intercedes for Luther, 179ff., 188f., 390f.
  Nothing to do with Luther, 187f., 355, 371ff., 411, 429, 448, 470, 500.
  Prefers to see Luther corrected than slain, 239f., 371, 401, 403, 494, 500.
  Wishes Luther had avoided tumult, 343f., 352, 403, 411, 565f.
  Querela pacis, 72.
  Suetonis, edition of, 122, 177f., 181f.
Erfurt, 74, 84, 98, 130, 174, 233, 362, 393, 411, 422, 489, 504, 518, 523.
  Augustinian convent at, 24, 30f., 36.
  University of, 21, 24, 30f., 64f., 85, 135, 207, 216f., 220, 229, 237, 264, 267, 274, 311, 342f.,

381, 387f., 411, 518.
Eschaus, T., 339.
  Wife of, 300.
Eucharist, 119, 266f., 272f., 279, 282, 284, 293, 376, 477, 536, 539.
Evangelista, 128.
Excommunication, 118, 120, 308, 366, 384, 393, 424, 440, 456, 509.
  Bull of (see *Decet Pontificem Romanum*).
Exsurge Domine, bull (see Luther, process against), 240, 345, 352, 354, 363, 369, 386ff., 391, 393, 400f., 405, 423, 425, 448, 458, 477, 482, 484, 494, 506f., 515, 520f., 529.
  Burning, 6, 405, 414f., 439f.
  Hutten's edition of, 349, 389f., 414, 441f., 448, 560.
  Preparation of, 6, 298, 306, 315f., 324, 335f.
  Publication in Germany, 357, 360-6. 368ff., 375, 379ff., 383, 387f., 402, 417, 424, 445, 449f., 467ff.
Extreme unction, 447.
Ezekiel, 50.

Faber, J., Dominican Prior of Augsburg, 390f., 447, 449, 460, 519.
Faber, J., Vicar of Constance and later Bishop of Vienna, 315f.
  Letter, 318ff.
Fach, B. F., 254.
Faith (see Justification).
Feige, J., letter, 537f.
Feilitzsch, F. v., 136, 361ff., 367, 370, 394, 400, 403f., 412f.
Feilitzsch, P. v., 523.
Ferdinand, later Emperor, 276, 314, 330.
Fisher, J., 235, 490.
Flanders, 455, 457, 474, 562.
Fleck, J., 569.
Florence, Council of, 426, 451.
Fontinus, P., 221.
France, 161, 164, 196, 220, 494, 502, 521.
Francis, St., 220f.
Francis I, King of France, 236, 321, 357, 372, 494, 496.
Franciscans, 22f., 192, 194, 215, 217, 220f., 342, 424, 494.
Franck, A., 176.
Franconia, 413.
Frankfort on the Main, 142, 396, 425, 439, 498.
  Book Fair at, 72, 161, 164, 383, 497, 505.

Frankfort on the Oder, 73, 90, 136, 306.
Freiberg in Saxony, 484.
Freisingen, Philip, Bishop of, 154, 170ff., 187, 370.
Free Will, 41, 55, 83, 94, 199, 259f., 273, 536.
French mathematician, 305f.
Friedberg, 552, 555, 563.
Froben, J., 161-4, 355, 500.
Frosch, J., 130f., 133.
Fuchs, A. v., 230, 309.
Fuchs, J. v., 230, 309.
Fuchs, T. v., 233, 265f.
Fug, J., 332f.
Fuggers, 258.
Führer, J., 221.
Fulda, 410.

Galatians, Luther's Commentary on, 155ff., 216ff., 219, 222, 277.
Gambara, C. de, 454.
Gattinara, M., 419, 421, 474, 545, 561, 564f.
Letter, 553.
Gera, 196.
German Theology, 41, 48, 55f.
Germany, 196, 233, 283, 310f., 314, 318, 330, 338, 342, 347, 349f., 354, 369, 379f., 382, 389, 396, 410f., 412, 414, 417, 421f., 427, 431, 434, 438, 444, 451, 454f., 461, 471, 473ff., 487f., 493f., 495, 501, 503f., 510, 514, 517, 529, 536, 539, 550ff., 554f., 559f., 561, 570.
Geroldseck, D. v., 163.
Gerson, J., 180.
Geyling, J., 360.
Ghent, Augustinian Convent at, 351.
Ghinucci, J., 102, 105f.
Gigli, S. de, letter, 323.
Glapion, J., 420, 477, 512f., 515f., 518ff., 525, 527, 546, 562.
Glarean, H., 161.
Letter, 383.
Glaser, M., 114, 191.
God, 21, 24, 29, 50, 59, 359.
Göde, H., 288, 569f.
Gonzaga, F. de, 487, 522f., 531f.
Good Works (see Justification by Faith).
Luther's treatise on, 302ff.
Görlitz, 196.
Gotha, 36, 38, 361, 523.
Gradenigo, A., letters, 323, 330, 495.
Gramaye, T., letter, 392.
Gratian, 41.
Greek, 54, 113, 115, 160, 179, 243f., 261.

Greffendorf, J., 380f.
Gregory, Pope, 203, 205f., 213, 248.
Grimma, 207, 399, 441.
Gropp, J., 345.
Grünberg, 552, 555.
Grünenberg, J., 50.
Guldennappen, W. v., 38.
Günther, F., 215, 345, 347f., 412.

Hague, 398.
Halberstadt, 306, 424.
Halle, 75.
Hauen, G., 195.
Hausmann, N., 427f.
Hazius, 84.
Hebrew, 27f., 54, 113, 115, 177, 179, 188ff., 243, 261, 290, 306, 315.
Hecker, G., 106ff.
Hedio, C.,
Letters, 368f., 430f.
Hegendorfinus, C., 415.
Heidelberg, 63.
Castle, 84.
Disputation at, 81-5, 276.
Luther's journey to, 6, 74, 79-85, 98, 100, 276f., 285.
University of, 188, 278.
Heilingen (see Geyling).
Hell, 245.
Helt, C., 192, 291, 294, 442f., 450.
Hennigk, J., 148.
Hennigk, M., 148.
Henriquez, F., 514f.
Henry VIII, King of England, 321, 357, 396, 447, 520f.
Heresy, 28f., 76, 99, 102ff., 106f., 112, 125ff., 179ff., 209, 213, 237, 240, 244, 246ff., 256, 266f., 269f., 295, 312, 326, 335f., 347, 427, 438, 444f., 467f., 471, 475f., 503, 506, 527, 529, 531, 533, 535.
Herholt, J., 189.
Herkmann, J., 506.
Herman, Dr., 569f.
Hermannsgrün, L. v., 508.
Herod, 291, 324.
Hersfeld, 555, 559.
Herzberg, 208.
Hess, John, of Breslau, 229, 232, 257, 308f., 314, 328ff., 344, 468f.
Letter, 251.
Hess, John, of Wittenberg, 254, 332.
Hesse,
Philip, Landgrave of, 537.
Hilary, 43, 58, 129.
Hildesheim, John IV, Bishop of, 498.
Himmel, A., 61.
Hirschfeld, B. v., 523.

INDEX

Hispanus (see Johannes and Peter).
Hochstraten, J., 192, 205ff., 234, 238, 278, 295, 310, 352, 401, 406, 410, 467.
Hugwald, M.
Hugwald, U., 505.
Hummelberg, M., 271.
  Letters, 486, 506.
Hump, H., letter, 295f.
Hungary, 451.
Huss, J., 196, 198f., 201ff., 220, 299f., 310, 314, 488, 529, 538, 554.
Hussites, 76, 93, 196ff., 206, 213, 237, 247, 260, 262, 266f., 333f., 447, 463, 471, 473.
Hutten, U. v., 6, 27, 237, 291, 309f., 313f., 317, 322, 325, 330, 334, 353f., 365, 369, 380, 382, 389f., 393, 410, 422f., 425, 436, 439, 441f., 448, 450f., 460, 465, 487, 509f., 512f., 515ff., 547, 559f., 562, 568.
  Letters, 235f., 275f., 293f., 346, 349, 354f., 394f., 397, 403, 406, 413f., 443f., 469f., 503f., 523ff., 534f., 554f.
Hutter, C., 22.

Indulgences, 38, 63f., 70f., 73f., 79, 88f., 92, 104, 112, 119, 139, 153ff., 161, 172, 175, 209f., 213, 216, 230, 242, 248, 251, 260, 269, 297f., 311, 453, 493.
  Luther's *Sermon on Indulgence and Grace*, 72ff., 110.
Ingolstadt, 237, 280, 365.
  University of, 135, 165, 208, 271f., 332.
Innocent I, Pope, 43.
Interdict, 104, 107, 329, 424, 438.
Irenaeus, 43.
Isolani, I., 252f.
Italians, 378, 412, 481.
Italy, 162, 164, 251, 309, 311, 314, 328, 342, 364, 410f., 447, 494.

Jacobacci, D., 316.
James, an organist, 198.
Jerome, St., 37f., 43f., 46, 55f., 68f., 81f., 129, 201ff., 205, 213, 239, 245f., 388, 418, 468, 479.
Jessen, F. v., 421.
Jessen, S. v., 421.
Jesus Christ, 34, 48, 85, 98, 359, 566.
Jews, 27f., 241, 407, 566.
Joachim of Flora, 117.
Job, 67.

Johannes, a Spanish Augustinian, 316.
John, a German Augustinian, 399.
Jonas, J., 177, 182, 304, 482, 523, 525, 564-7.
Joseph, St., 67.
Judenpach, 79.
Julius II, Pope, 154, 432.
Justification by faith only, 34, 42f., 70, 78, 82, 248ff.
Jüterbogk, friars of, 215, 217.

Kammerer, J., 226, 301.
Kirshberg, H. v., 471.
Kochel, 449.
Kollerburg, provost of, 223.
König, C., 290.
Kotter, J., 378f.
Kunzelt, G., 331f.

Lang, J., 27f., 32, 36, 38, 40f., 54f., 60, 64, 71, 74f., 80, 84, 97, 113, 149, 174f., 193-6, 206ff., 211, 216f., 221, 234, 251, 264f., 279, 300, 323, 332f., 346f., 351, 399, 481f., 489, 504, 568.
  Letter, 33.
Lange, J., 152.
Langenmantel, C., 120, 132f.
Lantschad, J., letter, 380.
Latomus, J., 270f., 305, 401.
  Letter, 435f.
Lawrence, St., 67.
Lefèvre d'Etaples, J., 31, 44, 54, 68ff., 72, 357, 494.
Lehnin, Valentine, Abbot of, 73.
Leiffer, G., 26, 35, 55.
Leipsic, 26, 109, 135, 146, 151, 161, 183, 245, 286, 327, 356, 361, 364, 366, 381, 387, 393, 405, 415, 451, 466, 468, 473, 484, 508, 523.
  Debate at, 6, 90, 130, 135, 143-7, 152f., 155, 160, 162-5, 167, 174f., 182, 184ff., 190f., 194, 207, 209-14, 217, 222, 224f., 234, 236, 245, 247, 251, 255, 258-62, 264f., 268, 319, 340, 352, 368, 377, 383, 405.
  University of, 77, 143f., 146f., 152f., 155, 164f., 167, 174f., 188, 190, 203f., 217, 220, 222, 238, 252, 265, 272, 279, 295, 306, 325, 344, 362f., 405f.
Leitzkau, 50.
Leo I, Pope, 203, 206, 213, 250.
Leo X, Pope, 6, 93, 98ff., 106ff., 112, 117, 124, 129, 132, 142, 148, 166, 181, 186, 225, 232, 236f., 243, 262, 298, 315f., 319, 328,

333, 353f., 355ff., 363f., 366ff., 378-83, 385, 388-91, 394, 397, 402f., 411, 418, 429, 432, 437, 451, 457, 459-62, 468f., 471, 476, 487f., 494, 498, 522, 559, 567f.
Breves, 101ff., 105f., 124ff., 172f., 334ff., 444f.
Opinion of Luther, 318, 495, 498, 507.
Liberty of a Christian Man, 353, 363, 367f., 385, 388, 400.
Liège, 401, 496.
  Erard de la Marck, Bishop of, 192f., 356, 401, 418f., 423, 427, 436, 455, 487, 545.
Lindenau, A. v., 523.
Link, W., 23, 35, 62, 87, 96, 116, 124, 207, 315, 333, 341f., 351, 353, 362, 399, 441f., 451, 481, 568.
Lintz, 142.
Lipsius, M., 234f., 268.
Liska, provost of, 405.
Listrius, S., 568.
Lochau, 219, 265, 345.
Lohr, A., 24ff., 30f., 568.
Lombard, P., 24, 31, 41, 239, 426, 439.
London, 490.
Lonicer, J., 317, 325.
Lotther, M., 217f., 265, 320, 341, 347.
Louvain, University of, 192f., 203, 208f., 234, 256, 268, 296, 299f., 304, 310f., 315, 322, 352, 371, 373, 392, 396, 399, 401, 404, 410f., 435f., 441, 457f., 481.
Lupinus, P., 155ff., 339.
Luther, B., 301.
Luther, H., 555f.
Luther, J., 22. 400.
Luther, Margaret, 22, 400.
Luther, Martin,
  Characterizations of, 6f., 33, 44, 47, 51ff., 81f., 115, 199, 202, 233, 261, 277, 307, 313, 323, 388, 436f., 461, 464, 486, 527, 536, 539, 553, 555.
  Childhood, 21, 274.
  Conversion, 233.
  Courage, 405, 409, 469.
  Danger of assassination, 306f., 354.
  District vicar, 33.
  Doctorate, 25f., 30f., 275.
  Family, 273f., 301, 400.
  First mass, 22.
  Health, 24, 84.
  Latinity, 32, 36, 150, 411.
  Letters, *passim*, 263, 377, 569f.
  Letters to, *passim*, 405.
  Monk, 92, 482.
  Persecution, 97f.
  Political theory, 167, 340, 427, 441, 491f.
  Popularity, 389, 428f., 434, 446, 455f., 460, 466, 473, 488f., 495, 497, 501, 509, 519, 536, 539, 552f., 565, 570.
  Portraits, 460, 485, 519, 561.
  Preaching, 33, 38, 58, 60ff., 137, 141, 151, 153, 170, 189, 207, 227, 244f., 263, 309, 331f., 337, 439, 452, 481, 554, 559.
  Priesthood, 21.
  Process against at Rome (see *Exsurge Domine*), 237, 283ff., 298f., 323.
  Recantation, alleged, 378.
  Student life, 21, 229, 233, 274, 313.
  Teaching at Wittenberg, 23f., 138, 153, 191, 263, 337.
  Temptations, 50, 110, 195.
  Violence of language, 286ff., 464, 472, 478f.
  Works, 129, 161-4, 170, 187f., 191, 239, 364, 383, 427f., 435, 456, 472, 495, 498, 506, 514, 538f., 544, 547f., 553, 561.
    Burned, 368, 372f., 381f., 384, 394, 397, 399, 401, 404ff., 410, 416f., 430, 434, 439ff., 455, 459, 461, 465f., 468, 472, 482, 497, 508f., 511, 515, 526, 534.
Lutherans, 166, 196, 269, 320, 368, 417, 419ff., 455, 466, 502, 506, 509, 540, 542, 544, 553, 560.
Lyons, Poor Men of, 529.
Lyra N. de, 44, 129.

Maccabees, book of, 202, 246.
Magdeburg, 38, 274, 291, 294, 315, 383, 424, 466, 485.
Magnificat, Luther's work on, 405, 472f., 490ff.
Mansfeld, 22.
  Albert, Count of, 96f., 413, 555-9, 563.
  Counts of, 196, 273, 351, 413.
Mantuan, B., 34.
Manuel, J., 6.
  Letters, 318, 498, 507f.
Marck, Robert de la, 496.
Marforius, 360.
Margaret, Regent of the Netherlands, 398.
Marlian, A., 421, 477, 500-3.
  Letter, 511f.

INDEX

Marriage, sacrament of, 447.
Martens, T., 400.
Martin, St., 67.
Martin, a bookseller, 49.
Mary, mother of Jesus, 66f.
Mascov, G., 50f., 59f.
Mass, 22, 309.
Mäurer, M., 376f.
Maximilian, Emperor, 6, 103f., 109, 116, 142, 185, 190, 281.
    Letter, 98ff.
Mayence, 383, 397, 416, 430, 439, 441, 459, 562.
    Albert of Brandenburg, Cardinal Archbishop Elector of, 63, 65f., 71, 140, 196f., 236, 279ff., 284, 290, 294, 314, 321, 353, 365, 368, 371f., 379f., 387f., 412, 416f., 419, 422, 424, 439, 464, 471, 474f., 483f., 539f., 564, 568.
        Character, 421.
        Letters, 292f., 382f.
    University of, 65f., 306.
Mayr, J., 437.
Mecklenburg, Albert of, 442, 449.
Medici, Jerome de', letters, 522f., 531f.
Medici, Julius de', Cardinal Vice-chancellor (later Pope Clement VII), 416-23, 428f., 452-64, 473-7, 486-9, 495ff., 508ff., 515-22, 525-31, 539-47, 552f., 560ff., 563f.
Medici, R. de', 528.
    Letters, 452ff., 496.
Meissen, 345, 472.
    John von Schleinitz, Bishop of, 151, 194, 284ff., 287ff., 445, 450, 482.
    Dean of, 153.
Melanchthon, P., 6, 112, 131, 176f., 181, 206, 234, 236, 251f., 271, 275f., 278, 285, 293, 301, 315, 321, 333, 367, 370, 393ff., 403, 411, 442, 461, 482, 494.
    Letters, 115f., 135, 155, 171, 173, 188f., 200ff., 208, 211, 305, 309, 329, 344, 346f., 388, 452, 468f.
    Luther's opinion of, 113, 118, 139, 220, 264.
    Marriage, 284, 332, 345, 393, 400, 411.
    Opinion of Luther, 144, 388.
    Teaching at Wittenberg, 113, 115, 120, 138, 169, 264, 321, 332, 345, 438.
Merseburg, 245, 381, 387, 441, 472.
    Adolph of Anhalt, Bishop of, 90, 152f., 155, 175, 259, 279, 284, 290, 294, 368, 381, 388, 393f., 445, 450, 465, 482.

    Letter, 147.
Merus, L., 570.
Miltitz, C. v., 125ff., 136, 142f., 145, 153ff., 159f., 168, 172, 185f., 194, 217f., 263, 265, 267, 274, 321, 338, 351, 353, 369, 389.
    Conference with Luther at Altenburg, 142, 148, 160, 166, 168, 185, 223.
    Conference with Luther at Lichtenberg, 363, 366ff.
    Conference with Luther at Liebenwerda, 219, 223f.
    Letters, 348, 361ff., 367f.
Minio, M., letters, 112, 283ff.
Ministry (see Priests' orders).
Miritzsch, M., 149, 351.
Möhra, 22, 555f.
Moibanus, 308.
Monastery at Wittenberg (see Black Cloister).
Monks, 206, 241, 310, 390, 412, 423, 453, 569.
Monckedamis, R. v., 435ff.
More, T., 72, 92, 373ff.
    Utopia, 72.
Mosellanus, P.,
    Letters, 194, 257ff.
Mühlpfort, H., 385, 569.
Munich, 40, 224.
Münzer, T., 75, 324.
Murnar, T., 407, 441, 450, 460, 465, 481.
    Letters, 431ff.
Mutian, C., 33, 36, 262f., 411.
    Letters, 323, 332.
Myconius, O., 304.
    Letters, 383f., 396.

Naples, 251, 494.
Narr, Claus, 143.
Nassau, H. v., 397f., 415f., 429.
Nathin, J., 30, 195, 279.
Nazianzen, G., 43, 200, 388.
Nesen, W., 268ff., 296.
Netherlands, 424.
Neustadt, Augustinian convent at, 38f.
Neustall, 276.
Nicaea, Council of, 254, 260.
Ninety-five Theses, 6, 63ff., 71, 85-9, 98f., 111, 114, 122, 135, 154, 160, 187, 200, 216, 258, 569f.
    Erasmus' opinion of, 110.
Noviomagus, G., 351.
Nuremberg, 25, 62, 101f., 128, 136, 189, 224, 277, 279, 283, 290, 314f., 328, 347, 364, 369, 441, 485.

Ochsenfart (see Dungersheim).

Oechslin, L., 461.
Oecolampadius, J., 6, 173, 200ff., 273, 290, 301f., 321f.
Olympius, 43.
Oppenheim, 424, 429.
Origen, 69.
Oschatz, 285.
Ottos, Emperors, 426, 463.
Oxford, 209, 490.

Pace, R., 72.
  Letter, 520f.
Palaeologus, Emperor John, 426.
Palatinate, Counts of the Rhenish, 517.
  Frederic, Count of, 513.
  Lewis, Elector of, 277, 475, 523, 541, 560.
  Wolfgang, Count of, 83f., 277.
Palencia, P. R. de la Mota, Bishop of, 477, 545.
Paltz, J. v., 30.
Pappenheim, J. v., 552.
Pappenheim, U. v., 523, 552.
Paris, 161, 448.
  University of, 128, 135, 140, 162, 180, 203, 207, 222, 237, 264, 296, 352, 383, 391, 412, 424.
Pascha, Dr., 314.
Paul, St., 42, 50, 58, 67, 78, 82, 92, 111, 129, 156ff., 171, 184, 192, 246, 255, 288f., 319, 330, 332, 359, 369, 372, 375, 479, 492, 506, 549, 566.
Paulist monk, 508.
Pavia, 162.
Pelagians, 42.
Pelican, C., 317, 477f.
Pellegrini, F. de, 470f.
Penance, 91f., 447.
Penitence, 91f.
  Sermon on, 110.
Peter, St., 201, 203, 205, 223, 225f., 369, 452, 566.
Peter Hispanus, 261.
Peter, 512.
Petri, A., 465.
Petzensteiner, J., 521, 523.
Peutinger, C., 116, 121, 390, 548, 557f.
Pfefferkorn, 27.
Pfeffinger, D., 26, 79, 100, 184.
Pflug, C. v., 204, 259, 363, 449.
  Letter, 147.
Pflug, J. v., 257ff.
Pfreind, 196.
Philip, M., letter, 472.
Philosophy, 24, 84.
Phrygio, P., 460.
Pinder, U., 62.

Pirckheimer, W., 272, 295, 323, 554f.
  Letter, 369.
Pius II, Pope, 430.
Plague, whether one may flee from it, 225f.
Plato, 566.
Platz, L., 342f.
Pliny, 254, 332.
Poduska, 197, 219f.
Pomerania, 223, 405.
  Barnim, Duke of, 197, 224, 259.
  Bogislav, Duke of, 451f.
Pope (see Leo X).
  Luther's appeal to, 119, 128.
  Power of the, 66, 76, 95f., 99, 117, 123, 145, 149, 156ff., 163, 166f., 169, 172, 175, 195, 199, 201f., 204, 206, 208, 213ff., 222f., 242, 250, 254f., 282, 292, 311, 336f., 418, 425ff., 447, 476, 489, 502, 532, 551, 557f.
  Tyranny of the, 122, 141, 194, 229ff., 236, 353f., 451, 499.
Possidonius, 226.
Postilla, Luther's, 228, 245f., 251, 263, 329, 443, 477ff., 481, 537f.
Prague, 196, 220.
Pretzsch, 274.
Prierias, S., 95, 148, 152, 162, 168, 232, 242f., 313, 328f., 332, 337, 371, 412, 430.
  Dialogue, 95f., 101, 109, 111, 122, 230.
Priests' orders, 21, 309, 447.
Probst, J., 351.
Prussia, 365.
Psalms, 31f., 58, 248.
  Operationes in Psalmos, 173f., 176, 184, 191, 193, 217, 219, 222, 264, 438, 465, 477f., 480, 481, 505.
  Seven Penitential Psalms, Luther's commentary on, 49, 54, 56, 62, 222.
Pucci, L., 316, 328, 383f., 390, 425ff., 495.
Purgatory, 122, 199, 202, 206, 213, 245, 260, 426, 494.

Quintilian, 254.

Rab, H., 195.
  Letter, 145.
Ratisbon, 265f.
Reformation (see Church, Reform of), 6.
Reifenstein, W., 301.
Reinecke, J., 301.
Reinhard, M., 485.

INDEX

Letter, 536f.
Reissenbusch, W., 366.
　Letter, 367.
Renée de France, Duchess of Ferrara, 522.
Resolutions, 71, 73, 77, 87ff., 91ff., 96f., 109, 146, 230, 287.
Reuchlin, J., 98, 138f., 187, 238, 243, 272, 276, 278, 280, 332, 352, 355, 389, 422, 436, 443, 458, 469f., 494.
　Letter, 271.
　Trial of, 27ff., 32, 46, 99, 173, 314, 346, 390, 410, 436.
Reuter, K., 57.
Reysch, M., 285.
Rhadinus, T., 377, 387, 393, 412, 472.
Rheticius, 43.
Rhine country, 163, 457, 509.
Riario, R., 336ff., 344.
Riccius, P., 188.
Roch, St., 67.
Rome, 73, 75, 195, 223, 251, 283, 341, 357, 456, 459, 461, 521, 529.
　Citation of Luther to, 96, 100, 102, 107, 109, 173, 354, 377.
　Corruption of, 230f., 291, 329, 342, 379, 446, 504.
　Hatred of, in Germany, 466, 488, 505, 561.
　Journey of Luther to, 24.
　University of, 135, 140.
Rose, the Golden, sent by Leo X to Frederic of Saxony, 112, 117, 126f., 133, 142f., 219.
Rosemund, G., 370ff., 374f.
Rosso, A., letter, 434f.
Roth, S., 472.
Rothbart, F., 196.
Rovere, Leonard Grosso della, 316.
Rozdalowsky, W., 219f.
　Letter, 197ff.
Rubeus, J., 224.
Rühel, J., 136.
Ruthall, Thomas, Bishop of Durham, 521.

Sacraments (see Eucharist), 263f., 447, 488.
　Luther's sermons on, 227f.
Sadoleto, J., 104ff., 173.
Saints, Legends of, 37.
　Relics of, 46.
　Worship of, 66ff., 426.
Salandronius, 570.
Salmonius, B., 161.
Salzburg, 101, 265, 437, 481.
　Matthew Lang, Cardinal Archbishop, 116, 154, 160, 265, 402,
419, 426, 437, 451, 454, 474, 477, 481.
Sander, M., 519.
Sangershausen, 36.
Sasseta, A., della, letter, 420f.
Satan (see Devils), 76, 339f., 360, 377, 394, 479, 482, 499.
Saum, C., 360f.
Savonarola, 494.
Saxony (Albertine), 237, 369, 452.
　George, Duke of, 124f., 135, 139f., 143, 147, 152f., 162ff., 182, 184f., 195, 200, 203f., 207f., 258f., 265ff., 272, 279, 341, 362, 377, 381, 387f., 392f., 399, 440f., 449, 465, 520, 542, 556.
　　Letters, 143f., 152f., 155, 166f., 182, 190, 195, 222, 265f.
　Henry, Duke of, 484.
Saxony (Ernestine), 183, 267, 434, 570.
　Frederic, Elector of, 25ff., 45f., 63, 70, 74f., 99, 114f., 117, 120f., 122-7, 130-3, 140-42, 153ff., 163, 167f., 171f., 174, 176ff., 181, 183f., 186, 188f., 194, 196, 200, 202ff., 208, 212ff., 217ff., 223, 225, 228, 235, 238, 246, 251, 257, 264ff., 275, 277, 279ff., 283, 302, 308, 317f., 321, 325, 330, 336, 339, 341, 344f., 347, 354f., 361ff., 365ff., 369f., 381, 397-400, 404f., 423ff., 427, 433, 441ff., 448ff., 452, 454, 458, 467, 473-9, 484, 487, 489, 494, 500, 508, 512, 517, 520, 527, 530f., 541, 560f., 568ff.
　　Care for Luther, 79, 83f., 100, 102, 105f., 108f., 112f., 116, 134, 183f., 198, 235, 313, 330, 334-8, 350, 355, 364, 380, 388f., 400, 402, 416, 418, 428f., 434, 438, 456, 461ff., 492f., 518, 521f., 535, 556.
　　Character, 421f.
　　Letters, 143, 182f., 266f., 338, 347ff., 415f., 429f., 433, 444, 492f., 535.
　　Library, 45, 493.
　　Opinion of Luther, 47, 527.
　　Relics collected by, 46.
　John, Duke of, 267, 302ff., 347f., 381, 444, 492, 523, 535.
　　Letters, 448, 508.
　John Frederic, Duke of, 405, 443f., 427f., 490ff.
Schalbe Foundation, 22f.
Schart, M., 237f., 443, 449.

INDEX

Schaumburg, A. v., 321.
Schaumburg, S. v., 321, 339, 341.
    Letter, 330f.
Schenk, John, 134.
Scheurl, C., 52, 57f., 60ff., 94f., 115, 148, 155, 165f., 295, 568.
    Letters, 51, 53, 55, 62, 124, 142.
Schinner, Matthew, Cardinal of Sion, 163, 453f., 461, 477, 519, 536, 553.
Schleinitz, H. v., 252.
Schlettstadt, 277.
Schleupner, D., 291, 342, 344, 468.
Schleusingen, G., 37.
Schmiedberg, H., 370, 393f., 442f., 449.
Schneidpeck, J., 546.
Scholastica, St., 67.
Schönberg, Nicholas v., 457.
Schönberg, v. (see Hugwald, N.).
Schoolmen, 41, 65, 78, 81f., 89, 119, 129, 180, 220, 426.
Schott, J., 295, 523.
Schürer, L., 277.
Schurff, J., 543, 557.
Schwartzenberg, C. v., 563.
Schwartzenberg, J. v., 563.
Schwertfäger, J., 131.
Sebastian, St., 67.
Seligmann, M., 225f., 300f.
Sentences (see Lombard).
Serralonga, U. de, 116f.
Sickingen, F. v., 275f., 278, 293f., 313f., 325, 330, 341, 349, 395, 397, 402, 413f., 428, 439, 443, 459f., 470, 487, 511, 513, 515ff., 521, 535, 547, 555, 562, 564.
    Letter, 384f.
Sieberger, W., 57.
Sion, Cardinal of (see Schinner).
Solms, P. v., 276.
Spain, 161, 164, 196, 511.
    Letter of the Governors and Grandees of, 514f.
Spalatin, G., 27ff., 31, 33, 37, 40, 42, 48ff., 55ff., 60, 63, 66ff., 72ff., 77, 79f., 84f., 100f., 108f., 112, 114ff., 122ff., 127f., 130, 134ff., 140ff., 149ff., 166f., 169-72, 188ff., 199f., 208-12, 218, 220, 223ff., 228, 237f., 245f., 251ff., 257, 263f., 272ff., 277, 280f., 284-91, 294f., 299f., 301, 305ff., 314f., 317, 320f., 325, 328f., 332ff., 336ff., 339ff., 344ff., 347ff., 351, 353f., 358, 362-8, 384ff., 388, 392ff., 399f., 412f., 414f., 423f., 442ff., 445, 451f., 465, 472f., 484f., 493f., 506f., 510, 535, 547, 552, 568f.
    Letters, 27, 32, 44, 137, 308, 381,
404f., 449f., 489, 500, 512, 520.
Spengler, G., 364.
Spengler, L., 279f., 290, 364, 395f.
Spenlein, G., 33f.
Spires, George, Bishop of, 511.
Standish, H., 322.
Staupitz, J. v., 25f., 34, 37, 40, 46f., 51f., 55, 58, 62f., 78f., 84, 91, 101, 106, 108ff., 117, 119ff., 124, 142, 151, 177, 191, 207f., 214, 219ff., 224, 265, 276, 297ff., 315, 333, 351, 353, 362, 402, 440f., 451, 569.
    Letters, 113, 437, 481.
    Luther's affection for, 220f.
    Opinion of Luther, 437, 440.
Stehelin, W., 290.
Steinlausig, 569.
Sternberg, 399.
Stolberg, L. v., 485.
Stolberg, W. v., 485.
Stolpen, Bishop of, 285, 290.
Strassburg, 110, 332.
    A printer of, 512.
    William III, von Honstein, Bishop of, 332, 498.
Stromer, H., 196, 228, 353, 369, 445.
    Letter, 199.
Sturm, C., 504, 508, 518f., 523, 552, 562, 564.
Sturz, G., letter, 513f.
Supplication against Theologs, 40.
Swabia, 405.
Swaven, P. v., 521, 523.
Switzerland, 163, 224, 262, 384, 390, 405.
Symler, J., 84.

Talmud, 238.
Tapper, R., 270.
Tartaretus, P., 81.
Taubenheim, J. v., 325, 370, 394, 443, 445, 449.
Tauler, J., 41, 48, 56, 78, 146f.
Teschius (see Zeschau).
Tesseradecas, 212, 218, 257.
Tetzel, J., 73, 75, 97, 139, 172, 176, 287, 570.
Teutleben, V. v., 349.
Theology, 24, 84, 129, 222.
    Theses against Scholastic, **60**.
Theophilus, 206.
Theophylact, 129.
Thonamen, 38.
Thunau, F., 523.
Thuringia, 237.
Tiepolo, N., 535f.
Tischer, W., 37.
Torgau, 265, 484.
Tournay, Bishop of, 357f.

Suffragan, 494f.
Transubstantiation, 220.
Trent, Bishop of, 463.
Trier, 265, 526.
   Richard von Greiffenklau, Archbishop Elector, 428, 474f., 498, 540, 542ff., 545f., 536ff.
   Proposed as judge for Luther, 154, 160, 185, 194, 223, 265, 338.
Trieste, Peter Bonomo, Bishop of, 419, 453, 463, 477, 564.
Trutfetter, J., 55, 83ff., 98, 194.
Tucher, J., 124, 149.
Tullich, H., 569.
Tunstall, C., 490.
   Letter, 445ff.
Turks, 335.
   War against, 126, 140f.
Turnhout (see Driedo).

Ulrich, J., 315.
Ulscenius, F.
   Letter, 439f.
Urban, a messenger, 79.
Urries, H. de, 507.
Ursula, St., 47.
Usingen, B. A., 35, 83, 85, 195, 279.

Vadian, J., 318ff., 461f., 486, 570.
Valentine, St., 67.
Valentine, 510f.
Valla, L., 291.
Vehus, J., 542, 548, 557f.
Venatorius, T., letter, 272.
Venice, 297, 364, 457.
   Doge of, 551f.
   Signory of, 112, 283ff., 323, 330, 495, 533f.
Vienna, 234, 300.
Vincent of Beauvais, 246.
Virgil, 32.
Vogt, James, 46, 60, 211, 351, 399f.
Vogt, John, 38.
Volckmar, C., 149.
Volta, Gabriel della, 106ff., 121, 297ff.

Wägelin, G., 262.
Waldenses, 529.
Waldheim, 285.
Walterhausen, 38.
Warbeck, G., 131.
   Letter, 523.
Warham, W., 321, 521.
   Letter, 490.
Wartburg, 556.
Watzdorf, R. v., 556.
Watzdorf, V. v., 556.
Weimar, 141.

Weissestadt, Prof., 150.
Weller, A., 421.
Werner, 306.
Wertheim, S. v., 556f.
Werthern, D. v., 152f.
Wick, J. v., 341.
Wilder, W., 297.
Wimpina, C., 56, 66, 73, 75.
Wimpfeling, J., 81.
Wittenberg, 84, 113, 128, 137, 141, 183, 218f., 251, 265, 274, 308, 325, 329, 381, 404, 438ff., 446, 449f., 461f., 481, 493, 510f., 567.
   University of, 23ff., 30f., 65, 71, 75, 82f., 100, 115, 134, 138, 140, 143, 167, 171, 175, 177, 186, 188f., 202, 221, 257, 264, 267, 306, 308, 315, 336, 363, 370, 404f., 411, 440, 446, 570.
   Letter, 131f.
   Student riot, 291, 339ff., 344.
   Students mock the Pope, 466.
Wittiger, M., 328, 342.
Witzel, G., 22.
Wolsey, T., 187f., 322ff., 445ff., 490, 520f.
Works (see Justification by faith only).
Worms, 142, 278, 416, 418, 425f., 508, 516, 521, 538f., 565.
   Canon of St. Martin's Church at, 456.
   Diet of, 6, 391, 398f., 402, 418f., 422, 425, 430, 433, 435, 438, 446, 451, 456, 459f., 462, 467, 469f., 473ff., 481ff., 486, 498, 504, 509f., 515f., 523ff., 526ff., 529f., 532ff., 536ff., 547f., 551, 553f., 556f., 560ff., 564.
   Edict of, 419, 445, 531, 553, 562, 564.
Würzburg, 79, 84.
   Lawrence von Bibra, Bishop of, 80.
Wycliffe, 529.
Wyclifites, 334.

Zack, 197.
Zasius, U., 188, 221, 304, 323, 333, 390.
   Letters, 248ff., 262f.
Zeitz, 370.
Zerbst, 405.
Zeschau, W., 207, 441.
Ziegler, N., 483f., 486.
Zurich, 384.
Zwickau, 160, 221, 499.
Zwingli, U., 6, 161, 163, 248ff., 268ff., 368f., 383f., 430f.
   Letter, 304.

www.ingramcontent.com/pod-product-compliance
Lightning Source LLC
Chambersburg PA
CBHW071231300426
44116CB00008B/990